# Lecture Notes in Compute

*Commenced Publication in 1973*
Founding and Former Series Editors:
Gerhard Goos, Juris Hartmanis, and Jan van Leeuwen

Doug Lea   Gianluigi Zavattaro (Eds.)

# Coordination Models and Languages

10th International Conference, COORDINATION 2008
Oslo, Norway, June 4-6, 2008
Proceedings

 Springer

Volume Editors

Doug Lea
State University of New York at Oswego
Oswego, NY 13126, USA
E-mail: dl@cs.oswego.edu

Gianluigi Zavattaro
Università di Bologna
Dipartimento di Scienze dell'Informazione
Mura A. Zamboni, 7, 40127 Bologna, Italy
E-mail: zavattar@cs.unibo.it

Library of Congress Control Number: 2008927370

CR Subject Classification (1998): D.2.4, D.2, C.2.4, D.1.3, F.1.2, I.2.11

LNCS Sublibrary: SL 2 – Programming and Software Engineering

ISSN        0302-9743
ISBN-10     3-540-68264-3 Springer Berlin Heidelberg New York
ISBN-13     978-3-540-68264-6 Springer Berlin Heidelberg New York

Springer is a part of Springer Science+Business Media

springer.com

© Springer-Verlag Berlin Heidelberg 2008
Printed in Germany

Typesetting: Camera-ready by author, data conversion by Scientific Publishing Services, Chennai, India
Printed on acid-free paper      SPIN: 12272662      06/3180      5 4 3 2 1 0

# Preface

Modern information systems rely increasingly on combining concurrent, distributed, real-time, reconfigurable and heterogeneous components. New models, architectures, languages, and verification techniques are necessary to cope with the complexity induced by the demands of today's software development. COORDINATION aims to explore the spectrum of languages, middleware, services, and algorithms that separate behavior from interaction, therefore increasing modularity, simplifying reasoning, and ultimately enhancing software development.

This volume contains the proceedings of the 10th International Conference on Coordination Models and Languages, COORDINATION 2008, held in Oslo, Norway in June 2008, as part of the federated DisCoTec conference. COORDINATION itself is part of a series whose proceedings have been published in LNCS volumes 1061, 1282, 1594, 1906, 2315, 2949, 3454, 4038, and 4467. From the 61 submissions received from around the world, the Program Committee selected 21 papers for presentation and publication in this volume on the basis of originality, quality, and relevance to the topics of the conference. Each submission received at least three reviews. As with previous editions, the paper submission and selection processes were managed entirely electronically. This was accomplished using EasyChair, a free Web-based conference management system. In addition to the technical paper presentations, COORDINATION 2008 hosted an invited presentation by Matt Welsh from Harvard University.

We are grateful to all the Program Committee members who devoted much effort and time to read and discuss the papers. Moreover, we acknowledge the help of additional external reviewers who evaluated submissions in their area of expertise.

Finally, we would like to thank the authors of all the submitted papers and the conference attendees, for keeping this research community lively and interactive, and ultimately ensuring the success of this conference series.

June 2008

Doug Lea
Gianluigi Zavattaro

# Organization

Coordination 2008, the 10th International Conference on Coodination Models and Languages, was part of the set of federated conference DisCoTec 2008, also including DAIS 2008, the 8th IFIP International Conference on Distributed Applications and Interoperable Systems, and FMOODS 2008, the 10th IFIP International Conference on Formal Methods for Open Object-Based Distributed Systems.

## Program Committee

### Co-chairs

| | |
|---|---|
| Doug Lea | State University of New York at Oswego, USA |
| Gianluigi Zavattaro | University of Bologna, Italy |

### PC Members

| | |
|---|---|
| Gul Agha | University of Illinois at Urbana Champaign, USA |
| Farhad Arbab | CWI, The Netherlands |
| Roberto Bruni | University of Pisa, Italy |
| William Cook | University of Texas, Austin, USA |
| Rocco De Nicola | University of Florence, Italy |
| John Field | IBM, USA |
| Aniruddha Gokhale | Vanderbilt, USA |
| Mike Hicks | University of Maryland, USA |
| Kohei Honda | Queen Mary, UK |
| Jean-Marie Jacquet | University of Namur, Belgium |
| Amy L. Murphy | ITC-IRST, Italy and University of Lugano, Switzerland |
| Peter O'Hearn | Queen Mary, UK |
| Gruia-Catalin Roman | Washington University in Saint Louis, USA |
| Vijay Saraswat | Penn State/IBM, USA |
| Carolyn Talcott | SRI International, USA |
| Wil van der Aalst | Eindhoven/Queensland, The Netherlands/ Australia |
| Jan Vitek | Purdue University, USA |
| Franco Zambonelli | University of Modena and Reggio Emilia, Italy |

## Additional Referees

| | | |
|---|---|---|
| Lucia Acciai | Michele Boreale | Marco Carbone |
| Paolo Baldan | Carmen Bratosin | Dave Clarke |
| Lorenzo Bettini | Antonio Bucchiarone | Patrick Eugster |

Gianluigi Ferrari
Daniele Gorla
Roberto Guanciale
Philipp Haller
Kevin Hoffman
Tomas Kalibera
Amogh Kavimandan
Christian Koehler
Natallia Kokash
V.A.R. Korthikanti
Ivan Lanese
Alessandro Lapadula
Diego Latella
Isabelle Linden

Alberto Lluch Lafuente
Michele Loreti
Marco Mamei
Ziyan Maraikar
Justin McCann
Hernan Melgratti
L. Gaetano Mezzina
Jayadev Misra
Nataliya Mulyar
Iulian Neamtiu
Olivia Oanea
Gustavo Ospina
Johan Ostlund
Jose Proenca

Rosario Pugliese
Helen Schonenberg
Minseok Song
Saurabh Srivastava
Daniele Strollo
Meng Sun
Nikhil Swamy
Francesco Tiezzi
Eli Tilevich
Eric Verbeek
Marc Voorhoeve
Bin Xin
Francesco Zappa Nardelli
Lukasz Ziarek

## Coordination Steering Committee

Farhad Arbab            CWI, The Netherlands
Paolo Ciancarini        University of Bologna, Italy
Chris Hankin            Imperial College London, UK
Jean-Marie Jacquet      University of Namur, Belgium
Amy L. Murphy           ITC-IRST, Italy and University of Lugano,
                          Switzerland
Gian Pietro Picco       University of Trento, Italy
Gruia-Catalin Roman     Washington University Saint Louis, USA
Carolyn Talcott         SRI International, USA
Jan Vitek               Purdue University, USA
Herbert Wiklicky        Imperial College London, UK

## DisCoTec 2008 General Chairs

Frank Eliassen          University of Oslo, Norway
Einar Broch Johnsen     University of Oslo, Norway

# Table of Contents

A Coordination Model for Service-Oriented Interactions.............. 1
  *João Abreu and José Luiz Fiadeiro*

Implementing Session Centered Calculi ........................... 17
  *Lorenzo Bettini, Rocco De Nicola, and Michele Loreti*

Service Combinators for Farming Virtual Machines.................. 33
  *Karthikeyan Bhargavan, Andrew D. Gordon, and Iman Narasamdya*

Timed Soft Concurrent Constraint Programs ...................... 50
  *Stefano Bistarelli, Maurizio Gabbrielli, Maria Chiara Meo, and
  Francesco Santini*

Multiparty Sessions in SOC ..................................... 67
  *Roberto Bruni, Ivan Lanese, Hernán Melgratti, and Emilio Tuosto*

Formalizing Higher-Order Mobile Embedded Business Processes with
Binding Bigraphs ............................................... 83
  *Mikkel Bundgaard, Arne John Glenstrup, Thomas Hildebrandt,
  Espen Højsgaard, and Henning Niss*

From Flow Logic to Static Type Systems for Coordination
Languages ..................................................... 100
  *Rocco De Nicola, Daniele Gorla, René Rydhof Hansen,
  Flemming Nielson, Hanne Riis Nielson, Christian W. Probst, and
  Rosario Pugliese*

Session Types for Orchestration Charts ........................... 117
  *Alessandro Fantechi and Elie Najm*

Implementing Joins Using Extensible Pattern Matching .............. 135
  *Philipp Haller and Tom Van Cutsem*

Advice for Coordination ......................................... 153
  *Chris Hankin, Flemming Nielson, Hanne Riis Nielson, and Fan Yang*

Modeling and Analysis of Reo Connectors Using Alloy .............. 169
  *Ramtin Khosravi, Marjan Sirjani, Nesa Asoudeh,
  Shaghayegh Sahebi, and Hamed Iravanchi*

Alternating-Time Stream Logic for Multi-agent Systems ............ 184
  *Sascha Klüppelholz and Christel Baier*

A Formal Account of WS-BPEL .................................... 199
  *Alessandro Lapadula, Rosario Pugliese, and Francesco Tiezzi*

How to Infer Finite Session Types in a Calculus of Services and
Sessions ......................................................... 216
   *Leonardo Gaetano Mezzina*

An Event-Based Coordination Model for Context-Aware
Applications...................................................... 232
   *Angel Núñez and Jacques Noyé*

Formal Analysis of BPMN Via a Translation into COWS ............. 249
   *Davide Prandi, Paola Quaglia, and Nicola Zannone*

Encrypted Shared Data Spaces ................................... 264
   *Giovanni Russello, Changyu Dong, Naranker Dulay,*
   *Michel Chaudron, and Maarten Van Steen*

CiAN: A Workflow Engine for MANETs ............................ 280
   *Rohan Sen, Gruia-Catalin Roman, and Christopher Gill*

A Process Calculus for Mobile Ad Hoc Networks .................... 296
   *Anu Singh, C.R. Ramakrishnan, and Scott A. Smolka*

Actors with Multi-headed Message Receive Patterns ................. 315
   *Martin Sulzmann, Edmund S.L. Lam, and Peter Van Weert*

A Compositional Trace Semantics for Orc ......................... 331
   *Dimitrios Vardoulakis and Mitchell Wand*

**Author Index** ................................................. 347

# A Coordination Model for Service-Oriented Interactions*

João Abreu and José Luiz Fiadeiro

Department of Computer Science, University of Leicester
University Road, Leicester LE1 7RH, UK
{jpad2,jose}@mcs.le.ac.uk

**Abstract.** We present a formal model for the coordination of interactions in service-oriented systems. This model provides a declarative
semantics for the language SRML that is being developed under the
FET-GC2 project SENSORIA for modelling and reasoning about complex services at the abstract business level. In SRML, interactions are
conversational in the sense that they involve a number of correlated
events that capture phenomena that are typical of SOC like committing
to a pledge or revoking the effects of a deal. Events are exchanged across
wires that connect the parties involved in the provision of the service.

## 1 Introduction

One of the challenges raised by service-oriented computing (SOC) is to develop
a semantic model that is rich enough for capturing the new kinds of interactions that it introduces but also abstract enough to support the modelling of
systems at the "business level", i.e. independently of the middleware programming model. It is fair to say that the bulk of the research that is being published
in this area is directed to the languages and infrastructures that support Web
Services [2], which is understandable because this is the area where industry
has its most immediate interests. Our research is being developed within a FET
(Future Emerging Technologies) project — SENSORIA [17] — so as to provide
foundations for SOC as a paradigm and not just a technology.

In particular, we have been developing a reference modelling language (SRML)
through which we would like to support building systems with service-oriented
architectures in "technology agnostic" terms. SRML is based on a semantic
model (discussed in this paper) that provides a layer of abstraction above the
languages in which services are programmed and the middleware that supports
the coordination of interactions [2]. In [7] we have shown that SRML is expressive
enough to accommodate orchestrations programmed in languages such as BPEL.
In previous papers we have provided an overview of the SRML language [10] and
of the algebraic semantics of service composition [11]. In this paper, we present

---

* This work was partially sponsored through the IST-2005-16004 Integrated Project
SENSORIA: Software Engineering for Service-Oriented Overlay Computers.

D. Lea and G. Zavattaro (Eds.): COORDINATION 2008, LNCS 5052, pp. 1–16, 2008.

a formal model for the primitives that we are using for the coordination of interactions in service-oriented systems.

SRML supports three different levels of "coordination" in SOC. One concerns the process of discovery of external services that may be required for a certain computation. In SRML, this process is not programmed as part of the computational process performed by services but handled separately; one of the novelties of SOC is precisely in the externalisation of discovery — see [6] for more details about the discovery and binding of new services in SRML. Another level concerns the coordination (orchestration) of the various parties that, together, deliver a complex service. In SRML, we adopt a "classical" architectural approach in which this type of coordination is performed by connectors (in the sense of REO [3]) that link together the different parties involved in the delivery of the service. Other approaches adopt workflow models [16]. We have discussed this level of coordination in [1] and, although briefly discussed in Section 2, it is not the core of our paper.

Our main contribution in this paper is at the third level of coordination: the one that needs to be established between the different events that are involved in interactions. In our model, interactions are conversational in the sense that they involve a number of correlated events between two parties. To the best of our knowledge, this is the first formal model proposed for SOC that adopts a rich ontology of interactions.

In section 2 we give an overview of the SRML approach to the specification of service-oriented architectures and the intuitive semantics that is associated with it; we illustrate it with examples taken from the specification of a travel booking service. In section 3 we formalize the notions presented in section 2 by defining our model of service-oriented architectures and computation, over which SRML specifications should be interpreted. Finally, section 4 concludes and outlines further work already being carried out.

## 2   Modelling Complex Services in SRML

### 2.1   The Compositional Model

Our approach to service-oriented specification follows recent proposals by the Service Component Architecture (SCA) initiative — for a deeper discussion on the relation between SRML and SCA refer to [10]. Like in SCA, the architectural unit for specifying a complex service in SRML is the module. Modules specify how a set of independent parties are interconnected and interact to provide the behaviour of the service. A module consists of an architecture, i.e. the definition of which pairs of parties are connected through wires, and a specification for each of the parties and each of the wires. Figure 1 shows the structure of the module *TravelBooking*, which models a service that manages the booking of a flight and a hotel.

The service is assembled by connecting an internal component *BookingAgent* to the external services *PayAgent*, *HotelAgent* and *FlightAgent* and the persistent component (a database of users) *UsrDB*. The difference between the three

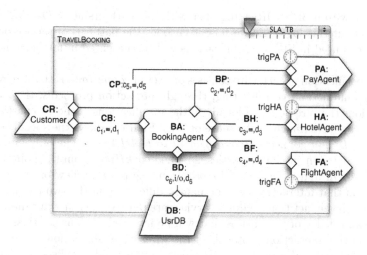

**Fig. 1.** The structure of the module *TravelBooking*

kinds of entities is intrinsic to SOC: internal components are created each time
the service is invoked and killed when the service terminates; external services
are procured and bound to the other parties at run time; persistent components
are part of the business environment in which the service operates — they are not
created nor destroyed by the service, and they are not discovered but directly invoked as in component-based systems. *Customer* is the interface through which
service requesters interact with the *TravelBooking* service. In SRML, interactions are peer-to-peer between pairs of entities connected through wires — *CB*,
*CP*, *BP*, *BH*, *BF* and *BD* are the wires in *TravelBooking*. Complex services
like *TravelBooking* establish multi-party collaborations by orchestrating their
interactions.

The specification of each of the parties contains a declaration of the interactions the party can be involved in and a specification of the properties that
can be observed of these interactions during a session. If the party is an internal
component of the service, this specification is an orchestration given in terms
of state transitions — the language of business roles. If the party is the interface of an external service or persistent component, the specification consists
of a set of temporal properties expressed in temporal logic — the language of
business protocols. Figure 2 shows part of the specification of the component
*BookingAgent* - the orchestration resorts to a set of locally declared variables
in order to define the state transitions the component is involved in. Figure 3
shows the specification of the business protocol that the hotel agent service is
expected to engage in — the language involves abbreviations of temporal logic
formulae. The use of temporal logic has also been adopted by workflow-based
approaches to SOC; in [16] constraint templates based on linear temporal logic
are used to capture common specification patterns for service flows. In order
to capture patterns of service-oriented interactions we use abbreviations of an
action/state branching time logic based on UCTL [12]. This new logic is being

developed within SENSORIA together with our partners at *ISTI-CNR (Pisa)*. Details about this logic and on how it encodes the patterns of service-oriented interactions used in SRML specifications will be presented in forthcoming publications.

The specification of each wire consists of a set of *connectors* [1] that are responsible for binding and coordinating, through interaction protocols, the complex interactions that are declared locally in the specifications of the two parties that the wire connects (much in the sense of [14]). Figure 4 shows the specification of the wire *BH* that connects *BookingAgent* to *HotelAgent*. The only interaction that exist between these two parties is named *bookHotel* from the point of view *BookingAgent* and is named *lockHotel* from the point of view of *HotelAgent*. The reason that interactions can be named differently in the two parties is precisely due to the fact that complex services are put together at run time without a-priori knowledge of the parties that will be involved. Because of this, we need to rely on the interaction protocols of the wires to establish how these interactions are related and coordinated. In this paper, we will not discuss interaction protocols in any great length; see [1] instead. This is because such connector-based coordination is by now well understood. The contribution of this paper is in the coordination model that we propose for the different events that occur as part of the interactions. The following sections will clarify the examples shown in figures 2, 3 and 4 — in particular, the meaning of the icons and symbols that are used will be explained.

## 2.2   Service-Oriented Interactions and Events

In service-oriented systems, typical interactions are of a conversational type and cannot be modelled as simple state transitions because they involve a durative asynchronous exchange of correlated events. In SRML, two-way interactions capture a pattern of dialogue that is prevalent in service-oriented systems: a party sends a request to a co-party that replies either positively by making a pledge to deliver a set of properties (i.e. it gives some kind of guarantee) or negatively, in which case the interaction ends; if the answer is positive the party that made the request can commit by accepting the pledge or refuse the pledge and cancel the interaction. If and after the requester commits, a revoke may be available that compensates for the effects of the pledge. One-way interactions are also supported in SRML: they capture situations in which a party sends a single event and does not expect a reply from the co-party. This type of interaction has only this one event associated with it. The set of events associated with an interaction $a$ is shown in the following table:

| | |
|---|---|
| $a$♦ | The initiation-event of $a$. |
| $a$✉ | The reply-event of $a$. |
| $a$✓ | The commit-event of $a$. |
| $a$✗ | The cancel-event of $a$. |
| $a$⇑ | The revoke-event of $a$. |

```
BUSINESS ROLE BookingAgent is
─────────────────────────────────────────────────

  INTERACTIONS
    r&s bookTrip
        ⌂ from,to:airport; out,in:date
        ⊠ fconf:fcode; hconf:hcode; amount:moneyvalue
    s&r bookFlight
        ⌂ from,to:airport; out,in:date; traveller:usrdata
        ⊠ fconf:fcode; amount:moneyvalue;
          beneficiary:accountn; payService:serviceId
    s&r payment
        ⌂ amount:moneyvalue; beneficiary:accountn
          originator:usrdata; cardNo:paydata
        ⊠ proof:pcode
    s&r bookHotel
        ⌂ checkin,checkout:date,
          traveller:usrdata
        ⊠ hconf:hcode
        ...

  ORCHESTRATION
    local
        s:[START, LOGGED, QUERIED, FLIGHT_OK, HOTEL_OK,
           CONFIRMED, END_PAYED, END_UNBOOKED, COMPENSATING,
           END_COMPENSATED]; login:Boolean;
           traveller:usrdata; travcard:paydata
    transition Request
      │ triggeredBy bookTrip⌂?
      │ guardedBy s=LOGGED
      │ effects bookTrip⌂.out>today ⊃ s'=QUERIED
      │     ∧ bookTrip⌂.out≤today ⊃ s'=END_UNBOOKED
      │ sends bookTrip⌂.out>today ⊃ bookFlight⌂!
      │          ∧ bookFlight⌂.from=bookTrip⌂.from
      │          ∧ bookFlight⌂.to=bookTrip⌂.to
      │          ∧ bookFlight⌂.out=bookTrip⌂.out
      │          ∧ bookFlight⌂.in=bookTrip⌂.in
      │          ∧ bookFlight⌂.traveller=traveller
      │     ∧ bookTrip⌂.out≤today ⊃ bookTrip⊠!
      │          ∧ bookTrip⊠.Reply=False
    transition TripCommit
      │ triggeredBy bookTrip✓?
      │ guardedBy s=HOTEL_OK
      │ effects s'=CONFIRMED
      │ sends bookFlight✓! ∧ bookHotel✓!∧ payment⌂!
      │          ∧ payment⌂.amount=bookFlight⊠.amount
      │          ∧ payment⌂.beneficiary=
      │               bookFlight⊠.beneficiary
      │          ∧ payment⌂.originator=traveller
      │          ∧ payment⌂.cardNo=travcard
```

**Fig. 2.** An extract from the specification of the component *BookingAgent* written in the language of business roles. Some of the interactions in which *BookingAgent* is involved in — *bookTrip*, *bookFlight*, *payment* and *bookHotel* — are declared. A set of local state variables is also declared and the specifications of transitions *Request* and *TripCommit* are shown.

Associated with every positive reply there is a deadline, $a.useBy$, for the party to reply within which the co-party offers a pledge. After the deadline is over there is no guarantee that the co-party will interact with the party any longer. Figure 5 represents the intuitive semantics of a two-way interaction when the co-party

<u>**BUSINESS PROTOCOL** HotelAgent **is**</u>

**INTERACTIONS**
   **r&s** lockHotel
      🔔 checkin,checkout:date; name:usrdata
      ✉ hconf:hcode
**BEHAVIOUR**
   **initiallyEnabled** lockHotel🔔?
   lockHotel✓? **enables** lockHotel⇪? **until**
      today < lockHotel🔔.checkin

**Fig. 3.** The specification of the external interface *HotelAgent* written in the language of business protocols. *HotelAgent* is involved in one interaction named *lockHotel* that models the booking of a room in a hotel. Some properties of this interaction are specified: a room booking can be initiated once the service is instantiated and a room reservation can be canceled up until the check-in date.

| | BA BookingAgent | $c_3$ | BH | $d_3$ | HA HotelAgent |
|---|---|---|---|---|---|
| **s&r** bookHotel | | S | | R | **r&s** lockHotel |
| 🔔 checkin | | $i_1$ | | $i_1$ | 🔔 checkin |
| checkout | | $i_2$ | ≡ | $i_2$ | checkout |
| traveller | | $i_3$ | | $i_3$ | name |
| ✉ hconf | | $o_1$ | | $o_1$ | ✉ hconf |

**Fig. 4.** The specification of the wire *BH* that connects *BookingAgent* to *HotelAgent*. ≡ denotes a straight interaction protocol [1] that binds interaction *bookHotel* (declared in the specifications of *BookingAgent*) to interaction *lockHotel* (declared in the specification of *HotelAgent*).

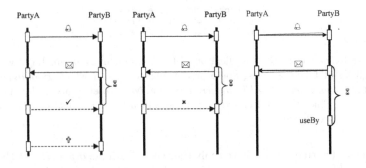

**Fig. 5.** The intuitive semantics of two-way interactions

replies positively. In the case on the left, the initiator commits to the pledge; a revoke may occur later on, compensating the effects of the commit-event. In the middle, there is a cancellation; in this situation, a revoke is not available. In the case on the right, the deadline occurs without a commit or cancel having occurred.

In specifications one-way interactions are typed by either *snd* or *rcv* to distinguish between the points of view of the sending party and the receiving co-party, respectively. The equivalent types for two-way interactions are *s&r* (send and receive) and *r&s* (receive and send). For instance, the specification of HotelAgent, shown in figure 3, declares a two-way interaction lockHotel typed with *r&s* to mean that the co-party that engages with hotel agent in this interaction is responsible for initiating it by requesting a hotel booking.

## 2.3   Asynchronous Coordination

Parties engage in interactions independently of their co-parties, i.e. the workflow that determines when a party interacts, by publishing an event or processing it, is independent of the way these events are transmited [1]. Wires are responsible for establishing and coordinating interactions between parties; events are carried from one party to the other by the wire that connects them. Associated with each wire there is a delay that represents the maximum time that the wire takes to deliver each event to the receiving party after it is sent. The delay of each wire is set at run time as part of the service level agreement that is negotiated when external services need to be procured [6].

We use $e!$ to refer to the publishing of event $e$ and $e?$ to refer to its processing. In the specification of component *BookingAgent*, shown in figure 2, there is a transition named *TripCommit* that is triggered by the processing of event $bookTrip\checkmark$. The effect of this transition is that of publishing events $bookFlight\checkmark$, $bookHotel\checkmark$ and $payment\blacktriangle$.

It is also important to distinguish between the notion of processing an event and that of executing it. Parties are not always in a state in which they are ready to engage in a given interaction. For instance, in order for the processing of event $bookTrip\checkmark$ to have the effect described in transition *TripCommit*, shown in figure 2, the *BookingAgent* needs to be in a state in which the local variable $s$ is set to $HOTEL\_OK$; we say that $bookTrip\checkmark$ is enabled in such states. If the event is processed in a state in which *BookingAgent* is not ready to execute it, then the event is discarded. In the case of interaction *lockHotel* in *HotelAgent*, shown in figure 3, the revoke-event $lockHotel\circlearrowleft$ becomes enabled by the execution of the commit event $lockHotel\checkmark$ that confirms a reservation, but it is enabled only before the check-in - this is specified through the second property of *HotelAgent*.

## 3   The Semantic Model Underlying SRML

In this section we formalize the notions that were given informally in section 2. Throughout the rest of the paper we assume a fixed data signature $\Sigma =$

$\langle D, F \rangle$, where $D$ is a set of sorts and $F$ is a $D^* \times D$-indexed family of sets of operations. We further assume that $time, boolean \in D$ are sorts that represent the usual concepts of time and truth values. We also assume a fixed algebra $\mathcal{U}$ for interpreting $\Sigma$.

## 3.1  Signatures

We use the notion of signature to characterize a service-oriented architecture and as the basis for defining the models of behavior that are valid for that architecture.

**Definition 1 (SRML Interaction Signature)**
*A SRML interaction signature (signature for short) is a tuple $\langle COMP, WIRE, 2WAY, 1WAY \rangle$ where:*

- *$\langle COMP, WIRE \rangle$ is a simple graph (undirected, without self-loops or multiple edges) where $COMP$ is the set of nodes (the parties that form the service) and $WIRE$ is the set of edges (the wires that connect the parties).*
- *$2WAY$ and $1WAY$ are $COMP \times COMP$-indexed families of mutually disjoint sets of names of asynchronous two-way and one-way interactions, respectively, each taking place between a pair of parties; we use $INT$ to refer to $2WAY \cup 1WAY$.*
- *For every $c, c' \in COMP$, $INT_{\langle c,c' \rangle} = \emptyset$ if $\langle c, c' \rangle \notin WIRE$, i.e. there are no interactions between components that are not connected by a wire.*

The graph $\langle COMP, WIRE \rangle$ defines the set of parties that compose the service and how they are interconnected by wires. The graph does not have multiple edges, meaning that for every two parties there is either a single wire connecting them or they are not directly connected. Also the graph does not have loops, meaning that a party cannot be connected to itself. The graph is undirected because wires do not have a direction associated with them; wires are able to transmit events both ways. Interactions are directed: if interaction $i$ belongs to $INT_{\langle c,c' \rangle}$ this means that the interaction is initiated by party $c$. Obviously, in this case, there needs to be a wire between parties $c$ and $c'$ for the interaction to take place; this is captured by the last condition of the definition.

Throughout the rest of the paper we will consider a fixed signature $S = \langle COMP, WIRE, 2WAY, 1WAY \rangle$ over which all definitions will be given.

## 3.2  Events and Pledges

A signature defines which interactions are established between the parties of the system. This information allows us to formalize the notion of event that was introduced in 2.2. We do this by defining which events can be sent and received by each of the parties.

**Definition 2 (Events)**
*For every $a \in INT$ and $x \in COMP$, the set $E_x(a)$ of events associated with interaction $a$ that are received by a party $x$ is defined as follows:*

*If $a \in 2WAY_{\langle c,c' \rangle}$ then*

$$E_c(a) = \{a\boxtimes\}$$
$$E_{c'}(a) = \{a\spadesuit, a\checkmark, a\bm{X}, a\Upsilon\}$$
$$E_{c''}(a) = \emptyset \text{ for any other } c'' \in COMP$$

*If $a \in 1WAY_{\langle c,c' \rangle}$ then*

$$E_c(a) = \emptyset$$
$$E_{c'}(a) = \{a\spadesuit\}$$
$$E_{c''}(a) = \emptyset \text{ for any other } c'' \in COMP$$

*We also define the following sets:*

- *$E_c = \bigcup\{E_c(a) : a \in INT\}$ is the set of all events that can be received by party $c$.*
- *$E(a) = E_c(a) \cup E_{c'}(a)$ where $a \in INT_{\langle c,c' \rangle}$ is the set of events associated with interaction $a$.*
- *$E_{\langle c,c' \rangle} = \bigcup\{E(a) : a \in INT_{\langle c,c' \rangle} \vee a \in INT_{\langle c',c \rangle}\}$ is the set of all events that are carried by wire $\langle c, c' \rangle$.*
- *$E = \bigcup\{E(a) : a \in INT\}$ is the set of all events that can happen in the system.*

*We see $E$ as a WIRE-indexed or a COMP-indexed family of sets when convenient. Given $EV \subseteq E$ we use $EV_w \subseteq E_w$ with $w \in WIRE$ or $EV_c \subseteq E_c$ with $c \in COMP$ to refer to the members of those families.*

Associated with every one-way interaction $a$ there is one and only one event, $a\spadesuit$. Each two-way interaction $a$ has associated with it the set of five events $\{a\spadesuit, a\boxtimes, a\checkmark, a\bm{X}, a\Upsilon\}$. Each event has a direction associated with it; an event is sent from one party to a co-party that receives it. For every two-way interaction $a$ between party $c$ and party $c'$, the events $a\spadesuit, a\checkmark, a\bm{X}$ and $a\Upsilon$ are sent by party $c$ and received by party $c'$, while the event $a\boxtimes$ is sent by $c'$ and received by $c$. As it also described in 2.2, the events associated with a two-way interaction have specific roles and are correlated to each other. This correlation will be formalized further ahead. Also associated with the reply of two-way interactions there is a pledge that is guaranteed to hold within the deadline.

**Definition 3 (Pledges).** *The set $PP$ of pledges is $\{a.pledge : a \in 2WAY\}$.*

The reply of a two-way interaction can be either negative or positive. In the last case there is a deadline before which the party that initiated the interaction can commit or cancel. We capture this through the notion of reply interpretation.

**Definition 4 (Reply interpretation).** *A reply interpretation $RI$ assigns to every interaction $a \in 2WAY$*

- *a parameter $a.reply^{RI} \in boolean_\mathcal{U}$, indicating if the reply is positive.*
- *a deadline $a.useBy^{RI} \in time_\mathcal{U}$ for committing or cancelling.*

## 3.3   Computation States and Steps

As mentioned in 2.3, every wire has a time delay that defines the maximum time that an event takes to be delivered.

**Definition 5 (Wire interpretation).** *A wire interpretation $\Psi$ assigns to every $w \in WIRE$ an element $w.delay^{\Psi} \in time_{\mathcal{U}}$.*

We will adopt a discrete state based model in which for every state of the system there are several possible activities each leading to a different state.

**Definition 6 (Computation state)**
*A computation state for $S$ is a tuple*
$\langle PND, INV, ENB, TIME, PLG, RI \rangle$ *where:*

- *$PND \subseteq E$ is the set of events pending in that state, i.e. the events that are waiting to be delivered by the corresponding wire.*
- *$INV \subseteq E$ is the set of events invoked in that state, i.e the events that have been delivered and are waiting to be processed.*
- *$ENB \subseteq E$ is the set of events that are enabled in that state, i.e. the events that will be executed if they are processed.*
- *$TIME \in time_{\mathcal{U}}$ is the time at that state.*
- *$PLG \subseteq PP$ the set of pledges that hold in that state.*
- *$RI$ is a reply interpretation.*

In any state of the system there is a set of events that are pending in the wires, i.e. events that have been published, but haven't yet been delivered by the wires to the corresponding parties; this is represented by the set $PND$. $INV$ is the set of events that were delivered by the wires and stored locally by each party where they are waiting to be processed. In any given state there is a set $ENB$ of events that each party is ready to execute. Associated with each state there is also a time instant $TIME$, the set of pledges that are true in that state $PLG$ and a reply interpretation for two-way events. The way the system changes from one state to another is given by the notion of computation step.

**Definition 7 (Computation step)**
*A computation step for $S$ is a tuple $\langle SRC, TRG, DLV, PRC \rangle^S$ where:*

- *$SRC$ and $TRG$ are computation states*
- *$DLV \subseteq PND^{SRC}$ is the set of events that are selected for delivery during that step.*
- *$PRC$ is a partial function that selects for each party $c$ such that $INV_c^{SRC} \neq \emptyset$ an element of this set, i.e. it's the function that selects the event that will be processed.*
- *There is a set of actually-delivered events $ADLV \subseteq DLV$ such that for every $c \in COMP$:*
    - *If $PRC(c)$ is defined then $INV_c^{TRG} = (INV_c^{SRC} \setminus \{PRC(c)\}) \cup ADLV_c$*
    - *If $PRC(c)$ is undefined then $INV_c^{TRG} = INV_c^{SRC} \cup ADLV_c$*

- $PND^{TRG} = (PND^{SRC} \setminus DLV) \uplus PUB$ where $PUB \subseteq E$, *i.e. the events that were selected for delivery will no longer be pending in the target state; the new events that become pending in the target state are those that are published during the step*

For each step $\langle SRC, TRG, DLV, PRC \rangle$ *we also define the following set:*

- $EXC = \{PRC(c) : PRC(c) \in ENB_c^{SRC}\}$ *are the events that are executed during that step; those that are selected for processing and are enabled in the source state.*

The set of events that are pending in wires is updated during each computation step by removing the events that the wire delivers during that step — $DLV$ — and adding the events that each party publishes — $PUB$. At each step, parties may choose to process one of the events waiting to be processed; this is captured by the function $PRC$. The fact each party can only process one event at a time is justified by the assumption that the internal state of the parties is not necessarily distributed and therefore no concurrent changes can be made to their states. We assume that not all of the events that are delivered are actually delivered to the receiving party; each wire may not be reliable, i.e. it may loose some of these events. The subset of delivered events that are actually delivered is given by $ADLV$. The set of events that are waiting to be processed in each party is updated in each step by removing the event that is processed and adding the events that are actually delivered to that party. The events that are executed on a computation step — $EXC$ — are those that are processed during that step and are enabled in the source state.

Figure 6 is a graphical representation of the event flow during a computation step from the point of view of parties A and B connected by a wire W. Events $e \in INV_A$ and $e' \in INV_B$ that are waiting to be processed in the source state are selected for processing during the step ($PRC(A) = e$ and $PRC(B) = e'$) and therefore removed from these sets in the target state. The subset of pending events that is selected for delivery during the step is shown in light grey; some of these events are delivered to party $A$ and enter the set $INV_A$ while the rest are delivered to party $B$ and enter $INV_B$. The set of events that are published by each party during the step is given by $PUB_A$ and $PUB_B$; these events become pending in the wire in the target state. The notion of reliability for wires is given by the following definition:

### Definition 8 (Reliable wire)

*A wire $w$ is said to be reliable for a computation step if $DLV_w = ADLV_w$. The following property will necessarily hold for that step:*

- $DLV_w = ADLV_w = INV_w^{TRG} \setminus INV_w^{SRC}$.

That is, a wire is said to be reliable for a computation step if no event is lost by the wire on that step; each event in a reliable wire is either actually delivered to the destination party or it remains pending in the wire.

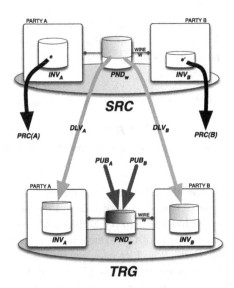

**Fig. 6.** A graphical representation of the event flow during a computation step from the point of view of a wire $w$ between a pair of parties $A$ and $B$. The system changes from state $SRC$ to state $TRG$ during the step.

### 3.4   Computation Trees

The different possible evolutions of a service-oriented system are given by a computation tree. In this paper we will consider only computations for which all wires are reliable for all steps.

### Definition 9 (SRML tree)

*A SRML tree for a signature $S$ is of the form $\langle N, R, q_0, G \rangle$ where $N$ is the set of nodes, $R \subseteq N \times N$ is the set of edges, $q_0 \in N$ is the root node and $G$ is a labelling function that assigns a computation state to every node and a computation step to every edge. We use $n \longrightarrow n'$ to refer to an edge $(n, n') \in R$. Also, we use the following notation to refer to the elements of the labels:*

- *If $n$ is a node we use the names $PND^n, INV^n, ENB^n, TIME^n$, $PLG^n, RI^n$ to refer to the elements of the computation state $G(n)$ (in accordance with the names used in definition 6)*
- *If $r$ is an edge we use the names $SRC^r, TRG^r, DLV^r, PRC^r, EXC^r$, $PUB^r$ to refer to the elements of the computation step $G(r)$ (in accordance with the names used in definition 7)*

*Also, for every node $n \in N$ we define the set $UNPUB(n) = \{e \in E : \text{there is}$ no $r \in R$ such that $r < n$ and $e \in PUB^r\}$, i.e. the events unpublished between the root and node $n$. We use $<$ as a partial order relation on the sets of nodes and steps, $N \cup R$, based on the distance to the root node (e.g. $n < n'$ means that there is a path from the root node to $n'$ that passes through $n$).*

Not all trees represent valid evolutions. Many of the properties of service-oriented systems, described intuitively in section 2, like the sequence of events in a two-way interaction, concern the evolution of the system across several states. The definition of computation tree captures what are considered to be the valid models of service-oriented computation in SRML.

**Definition 10 (Computation tree)**

*A computation tree for a signature $S$ and a wire interpretation $\Psi$ is a SRML tree $\langle N, R, q_0, G \rangle$ that satisfies the following rules:*

**Time elapsion.** *For every edge $n \longrightarrow n'$, $TIME^n < TIME^{n'}$ (time moves forward)*

**Single session.** *For every event $e \in E$ if there is an edge $r \in R$ such that $e \in PUB^r$, i.e. $e$ is published in $r$, then there is no edge $r' < r$ such that $e \in PUB^{r'}$ (events cannot be published more than once during a session — a computation tree models the evolution of a session).*

**Wire delay.** *For every event $e \in E_w$ and edge $r \in R$, if $e \in PUB^r$, i.e. if $e$ is published in $r$, then for every subsequent node $n \in N$ such that $r < n$ and $TIME^{SRC^r} + w.delay^{\Psi} < TIME^n$, $e \notin PND^n$, i.e. $e$ is not pending anymore in nodes where the time delay of the wire has elapsed (If an event is published then it will be delivered with a maximum delay)*

**Event correlation.** *For every two-way interaction $a \in 2WAY$, every node $n \in N$ and every edge $r \in R$ the following properties hold:*

1. *$a\boxtimes \in ENB^n$ if there is $r \in R$ such that $r < n$ and $a\spadesuit \in PUB^r$ and there is no $r' \in R$ such that $r' < n$ and $a\boxtimes \in EXC^r$ (the publication of the initiation-event enables the execution of the reply-event)*

2. *$a\spadesuit \in EXC^r$ iff for all $r < r'$ there is $r''$ such that either:*
   - *$r'' < r'$ and $a\boxtimes \in PUB^{r''}$ or*
   - *$r' < r''$ and $a\boxtimes \in PUB^{r''}$*
   
   *(the reply-event of any interaction will be published after and only after the initiation-event was executed)*

3. *If $a\boxtimes \in PUB^r$ then for every node $n, n', n'' \in N$ such that $r = n \longrightarrow n'$ and $n' < n''$, $RI^{n'} = RI^{n''}$ (The value of the reply, either positive or negative, and the associated deadline become fixed once the reply-event is published)*

4. *$a\checkmark$ and $a\boldsymbol{X} \in ENB^n$ if:*
   - *there is an edge $r' \in R$ such that $r' < n$, $a\boxtimes \in PUB^{r'}$*
   - *$a.reply^{RI^n} = true$*
   - *there is no $r'' \in R$ such that $r'' < n$ and $a\checkmark \in EXC^{r''}$ or $a\boldsymbol{X} \in EXC^{r''}$*
   - *$TIME^n < a.useBy^{RI^n}$*
   
   *(the publication of a positive reply-event guarantees that the execution of the commit-event and the cancel-event becomes enabled until either one of them is executed or the deadline expires)*

5. *$a.pledge \in PLG^n$ if the following conditions hold:*
   - *there is an edge $r' \in R$ such that $r' < n$ and $a\boxtimes \in PUB^{r'}$*
   - *$a.reply^{RI^n} = true$*

- there is no $r'' \in R$ such that $r'' < n$ and $a\checkmark \in EXC^{r''}$ or $a\times \in EXC^{r''}$
- $TIME^n < a.useBy^{RI^n}$

(*The pledge must be true from the moment a positive reply is published until either the commit or the cancel are executed or the deadline expires*)

6. If $a\checkmark \in PUB^r$ where $r = n \longrightarrow n'$ then:
   - there is $r' < r$ such that $a\boxtimes \in EXC^{r'}$
   - $a.reply^{RI^n} = true$
   - there is no $r'' < r$ such that $a\times \in PUB^{r''}$

   (*The commit-event can only be published if the reply-event was executed, the reply was positive and the cancel-event was not published*)

7. If $a\times \in PUB^r$ where $r = n \longrightarrow n'$ then:
   - $a.reply^{RI^n} = true$
   - there is $r' < r$ such that $a\boxtimes \in EXC^{r'}$
   - there is no $r'' < r$ such that $a\checkmark \in PUB^{r''}$

   (*The cancel-event can only be published if the reply-event was executed, the reply was positive and the commit-event was not published*)

8. If $a\mathring{\textit{r}} \in ENB^n$ then there is $r \in R$ such that $r < n$ and $a\checkmark \in EXC^r$ and there is no $r' \in R$ such that $r' < n$ and $a\mathring{\textit{r}} \in EXC^r$ (*the revoke-event can only be enabled after the execution of the commit-event*)

9. If $a\mathring{\textit{r}} \in PUB^r$ then there is $r' < r$ such that $a\checkmark \in PUB^{r'}$ (*The revoke-event can only be published after the commit-event was published*)

## 4   Concluding Remarks and Further Work

The primitives that we are proposing take into account proposals that have been made for Web-Service Conversation [5], in other modelling languages such as ORC [15], and in calculi such as Sagas [8]; they take into account that interactions are stateful and provide first-class notions such as reply, commit, compensation and pledge. The richness of the conversational model that we propose is reflected in the computational model. On the one hand, we need to account for the correlation that needs to be enforced among the different events involved in an interaction. On the other hand, we need to reflect the fact that events are transmitted through "wires" that enforce the interaction protocols that coordinate the joint behaviour of the parties involved in the delivery of the service.

The computational model we have defined captures the properties that are common to all SRML service-oriented systems independently of their specifications and any other interpretation constraints. SRML specifications have the role of defining the properties that are particular to a specific service-oriented system, i.e. restricting the set of trees that represent valid computations for that system. Further work is being carried out to give a complete formalization of the syntax and semantics of the SRML specification languages: the language of business roles, the language of business protocols and the language of interaction protocols. In this paper we have presented the work we have done so far towards formalising the semantic domain of these languages.

In connection with the previous we are working on applying the UCTL branching time temporal logic to the SRML framework. UCTL is an action/state based logic that was originally introduced to express the properties of UML statecharts [12]. The formal power that is attained with an action/state logic is crucial in order to reason about SRML models that, as we have seen in section 3, possess information related to the state of the system and the behaviour that changes the state. UCTL is also being used in other approaches to service-oriented computing: in [4] UCTL is used to reason about an asynchronous protocol for service-oriented applications; in [9] the UCTL framework is adapted in order to reason about a calculus for the orchestration of web services.

By defining the formal grounds over which UCTL can be applied to our models of service-oriented computation we accomplish several objectives. First we can validate the soundness of our computational model by defining the tools that allow us to reason about the model itself and axiomatize it. Second, these same tools will allow reasoning about service-oriented architectures both using proof strategies and automatic model-checking [12]. Finally, we lay the basis for defining the language of business protocols that is used to specify the behaviour of interfaces and that consists essentially of abbreviations of the UCTL temporal logic.

We have introduced time as a property of states, but gave no further insight into what kind of time model we will be using. We are currently investigating the best way to integrate time in our service-oriented model of computation taking into account the expressiveness, verifiability and model-checking requirements of the SRML framework [13].

## Acknowledgements

Thanks are due to Antónia Lopes, Laura Bocchi, Stefania Gnesi and Franco Mazzanti for fruitful discussions.

## References

1. Abreu, J., Bocchi, L., Fiadeiro, J.L., Lopes, A.: Specifying and Composing Interaction Protocols for Service-Oriented System Modelling. In: Derrick, J., Vain, J. (eds.) FORTE 2007. LNCS, vol. 4574, pp. 358–373. Springer, Heidelberg (2007)
2. Alonso, G., Casati, F., Kuno, H.A., Machiraju, V.: Web Services - Concepts, Architectures and Applications. Data-Centric Systems and Applications. Springer, Heidelberg (2004)
3. Arbab, F.: Reo: a channel-based coordination model for component composition. Mathematical Structures in Computer Science 14(3), 329–366 (2004)
4. Beek, M., Fantechi, A., Gnesi, S., Mazzanti, F.: An action/state-based model-checking approach for the analysis of communication protocols for Service-Oriented Applications. In: FMICS 2007. LNCS, vol. 4916. Springer, Heidelberg (2008)
5. Benatallah, B., Casati, F., Toumani, F.: Web service conversation modeling: A cornerstone for e-business automation. IEEE Internet Computing 8(1), 46–54 (2004)

6. Bocchi, L., Fiadeiro, J.L., Lopes, A.: The SENSORIA Reference Modelling Language: Primitives for configuration management (2006), www.sensoria-ist.eu
7. Bocchi, L., Hong, Y., Lopes, A., Fiadeiro, J.: From BPEL to SRML: A Formal Transformational Approach. In: Procedings of the 4th International Workshop on Web Services and Formal Methods (WSFM 2007). LNCS. Springer, Heidelberg (to appear)
8. Bruni, R., Melgratti, H., Montanari, U.: Theoretical foundations for compensations in flow composition languages. SIGPLAN Not. 40(1), 209–220 (2005)
9. Fantechi, A., Gnesi, S., Lapadula, A., Mazzanti, F., Pugliese, R., Tiezzi, F.: A model checking approach for verifying COWS specifications. In: FASE 2008. LNCS, vol. 4961. Springer, Heidelberg (2008)
10. Fiadeiro, J.L., Lopes, A., Bocchi, L.: A Formal Approach to Service Component Architecture. In: Bravetti, M., Núñez, M., Zavattaro, G. (eds.) WS-FM 2006. LNCS, vol. 4184, pp. 193–213. Springer, Heidelberg (2006)
11. Fiadeiro, J.L., Lopes, A., Bocchi, L.: Algebraic Semantics of Service Component Modules. In: Fiadeiro, J.L., Schobbens, P.-Y. (eds.) WADT 2006. LNCS, vol. 4409, pp. 37–55. Springer, Heidelberg (2007)
12. Gnesi, S., Mazzanti, F.: A model checking verification environment for UML statecharts. In: Proceedings of XLIII Congresso Annuale AICA (2005)
13. Henzinger, T.A.: It's About Time: Real-Time Logics Reviewed. In: Sangiorgi, D., de Simone, R. (eds.) CONCUR 1998. LNCS, vol. 1466, pp. 439–454. Springer, Heidelberg (1998)
14. Lazovik, A., Arbab, F.: Using Reo for Service Coordination. In: Krämer, B.J., Lin, K.-J., Narasimhan, P. (eds.) ICSOC 2007. LNCS, vol. 4749, pp. 398–403. Springer, Heidelberg (2007)
15. Misra, J., Cook, W.: Computation orchestration: A basis for wide-area computing. Journal of Software and Systems Modeling (May 2006)
16. van der Aalst, W., Pesic, M.: DecSerFlow: Towards a truly declarative service flow language. In: Bravetti, M., Núñez, M., Zavattaro, G. (eds.) WS-FM 2006. LNCS, vol. 4184, pp. 1–23. Springer, Heidelberg (2006)
17. Wirsing, M., Carizzoni, G., Gilmore, S., Gonczy, L., Koch, N., Mayer, P., Palasciano, C.: SENSORIA: A systematic approach to developing service-oriented systems — white paper (2007)

# Implementing Session Centered Calculi[*]

Lorenzo Bettini[1], Rocco De Nicola[2], and Michele Loreti[2]

[1] Dipartimento di Informatica, Università di Torino
[2] Dipartimento di Sistemi e Informatica, Università di Firenze
{bettini,denicola,loreti}@dsi.unifi.it

**Abstract.** Recently, specific attention has been devoted to the development of service oriented process calculi. Besides the foundational aspects, it is also interesting to have prototype implementations for them in order to assess usability and to minimize the gap between theory and practice. Typically, these implementations are done in Java taking advantage of its mechanisms supporting network applications. However, most of the recurrent features of service oriented applications are re-implemented from scratch. In this paper we show how to implement a service oriented calculus, CaSPiS (Calculus of Services with Pipelines and Sessions) using the Java framework IMC, where recurrent mechanisms for network applications are already provided. By using the session oriented and pattern matching communication mechanisms provided by IMC, it is relatively simple to implement in Java all CaSPiS abstractions and thus to easily write the implementation in Java of a CaSPiS process.

## 1 Introduction

Service-oriented computing is calling for novel computational models and languages and recently specific attention has been devoted to the development of service oriented process calculi that can lay the basis for analyzing and experimenting with components interactions, safe service composition, and for formalizing and reasoning about aspects of service level agreements. Recently, many calculi have been proposed and most of them are based on process algebras enhanced with mechanisms for describing safe client-service interactions and with operators for composing services. Besides the foundational aspects, it is also interesting to have prototype implementations of these calculi, in order to assess their practical usability and to minimize the gap between theory and practice.

In this paper we show how to implement a service oriented calculus, CaSPiS (Calculus of Services with Pipelines and Sessions) [3] using a generic Java framework called IMC (*Implementing Mobile Calculi*) where recurrent mechanisms for network applications are already provided. CaSPiS is the evolution of SCC (Serviced Centered Calculus) [2], a calculus for services, that stemmed from a coordinated effort within the

---

[*] The work presented in this report has been partially supported by EU Project Software Engineering for Service-Oriented Overlay Computers (SENSORIA, contract IST-3-016004-IP-09) by the MIUR project EOS DUE.

D. Lea and G. Zavattaro (Eds.): COORDINATION 2008, LNCS 5052, pp. 17–32, 2008.

EU funded project SENSORIA [12] that aims at developing a novel, comprehensive approach to the engineering of software systems for service-oriented computing.

IMC was prompted by the growing number of experiments on process calculi and by the need of easing the implementation phase and was used as a kind of middleware for different distributed calculi [1]; it provides the necessary tools for implementing the run-time system of new languages directly based on distributed calculi (possibly with code mobility). The aim of IMC was to enable the implementer of a new language to concentrate on the parts that are really specific of the considered system, and to rely on the framework for standard mechanisms for distribution and mobility.

IMC provides means for transparent code mobility, for building communication protocols by composing sub-components dynamically and for managing node topology. All these mechanisms are rendered as abstract as possible to ease, e.g., switching from a specific communication protocol to another, without modifying the other parts of an application. IMC can be straightforwardly used if no specific advanced feature is needed; but a user can customize parts of the framework by providing its own implementations for the interfaces used in the package. Customizations can take advantage of design patterns such as *factory method*, *abstract factory*, *template method* and *strategy* [7] that are used throughout the packages.

CaSPiS [3] is a formalism useful for experimenting with service oriented calculi implementations, with advanced features and a clear theoretical foundation. It is *dataflow* oriented and makes use of a pipelining operator to model the exchange of information between sessions (sequences of structured communications between two peers). Services are seen as passive objects that can be invoked by clients and service definitions can be seen as specific instances of input prefixed processes. The two endpoints of a session can communicate by exchanging messages. A fresh shared name is used to guarantee that messages are exchanged only between partners of the same session, so that two instances of the same persistent service (that was invoked from two different sessions) run separately and cannot interfere. The central role assigned to sessions and the direct use of operators for modeling session interaction renders the logical structure of programs clearer and leads to a well disciplined service specification language that guarantees proper handling of session closures and in general simplifies reasoning on the specified services. The idea of session is not new. Indeed, in [10,8] identifies a simple type-regulated interactions in $\pi$-like languages. The calculus makes use also of a new policy for handling (unexpected or programmed) session closures that in the original SCC calculus was somehow "rudimental". Indeed, in SCC closed session as well as nested subsessions are simply *terminated* and no information is sent to the counterpart. In CaSPiS new primitives are introduced for handling session closure and for reacting to an unexpected session closures.

The rest of the paper is organized as follows. Section 2 provides a brief overview of CaSPiS, Section 3 presents IMC while in Section 4 the actual implementation of CaSPiS is presented. Section 5 shows how the proposed implementation can be used for developing simple services. The final section contains an example of a CaSPiS program and some concluding remarks.

$$P, Q ::= \textstyle\sum_{i \in I} \pi_i P_i \quad \text{Guarded Sum} \qquad\qquad | \; \dagger(k) \qquad\qquad \text{Signal}$$

| | | | |
|---|---|---|---|
| $\mid s_k.P$ | Service Definition | $\mid r \rhd_k P$ | Session |
| $\mid \bar{s}_k.P$ | Service Invocation | $\mid \blacktriangleright P$ | Terminated Session |
| $\mid P > Q$ | Pipeline | $\mid P \mid Q$ | Parallel Composition |
| $\mid$ close | Close | $\mid (\nu n)P$ | Restriction |
| $\mid k.P$ | Listener | $\mid !P$ | Replication |

$$\pi ::= \quad (F) \qquad \text{Abstraction} \qquad F ::= u \mid ?x \mid f(\tilde{F})$$
$$\mid \langle V \rangle \qquad \text{Concretion} \qquad V ::= u \mid f(\tilde{V})$$
$$\mid \langle V \rangle^{\uparrow} \qquad \text{Return}$$

**Fig. 1.** Syntax of full CaSPiS

## 2   CaSPiS

CaSPiS (*Calculus of Services with Pipelines and Sessions*) [3] is a core calculus equipped with linguistic constructs for handling sessions and that relies on three main concepts:

1. service definition/invocation
2. bi-directional sessioning as a means for structuring client-service interaction
3. pipelining as a means of composing services.

The syntax of CaSPiS is in Figure 1. In the following we will comment the main constructs of CaSPiS, skipping the standard process algebras operators (such as, e.g., non deterministic choice $\sum_{i \in I} \pi_i P_i$, restriction $(\nu n)P$, parallel composition $P \mid Q$ and replication $!P$). Interested readers are referred to [3] for further details.

Within CaSPiS, service definitions and service invocations are rendered respectively as $s_{k_1}.P$ and $\bar{s}_{k_2}.Q$ where $s$ is a service name, $k$ is the *handler* used for managing session closures while $P$ and $Q$ implement the service and the client *protocols* respectively.

A service definition $s_{k_1}.P$ and a service invocation $\bar{s}_{k_2}.Q$ running in parallel can synchronize with each other. As a result, a new, private, session $r$ will be created. The session has two ends, one at the client's side where protocol $Q$ is running and one at the service's side where protocol $P$ is running. A value produced by a *concretion* at one side can be consumed by an *abstraction* at the other side.

A concretion $\langle V \rangle P$ can evolve to $P$ emitting value $V$. Dually, an abstraction $(F)P$ is a form of guarded command that relies on pattern-matching: $(F)P$ can evolve to $P\sigma$ retrieving value $V$, provided pattern $F$ matches value $V$. Here, the pattern-matching function *match* is defined as expected: $match(F, V) = \sigma$, if $\sigma$ is the (uniquely determined) substitution that permits identifying pattern $F$ and values $V$.

The return primitive $\langle V \rangle^{\uparrow} P$ can be used to return a value *outside* of the current session, if the enclosing environment is capable of consuming it. Sessions, service definitions and service invocations can of course be nested at arbitrary depth. No activity can take place under the scope of a dynamic operator (service definition or invocation, guarded sum, right-hand side term of a pipeline and replication). On the contrary, when considering non dynamic contexts, including sessions, concurrent activities can take place at any level of session nesting. Sessions do not constrain in any way actions that are not value production, consumption or return, that is, service invocation and silent steps.

CaSPiS is equipped with primitives for handling session closure. These primitives are useful to garbage-collect terminated sessions and, most importantly, to explicitly program session termination in order to manage abnormal events or timeouts.

Upon creation of a session, one associates with the session a pair of names, $(k_1, k_2)$, identifying a pair of *termination handlers* services, one for each side. Then:

1. a session side is terminated when its protocol executes the command close;
2. right after execution of close a signal $\dagger(k)$ is sent to the *listener* on $k$ (such a listener will have the syntactic form $k.R$) running at the *opposite* side of the session.
3. at the same time, the session side that has executed close will enter a special closing state denoted by $\blacktriangleright P$, where all subsessions of $P$ will be gradually and automatically closed.

Information about termination handlers to be used is exchanged by the two sides at invocation time. Operational rules governing service synchronizations are the following:

$$s_{k_1}.P \xrightarrow{\; s(r)^{k_2}_{k_1} \;} r \rhd_{k_2} P \qquad\qquad \bar{s}_{k_2}.P \xrightarrow{\; \bar{s}(r)^{k_1}_{k_2} \;} r \rhd_{k_1} P$$

$$\frac{P \xrightarrow{\; s(r)^{k_2}_{k_1} \;} P' \quad Q \xrightarrow{\; \bar{s}(r)^{k_1}_{k_2} \;} Q'}{P|Q \xrightarrow{\;\tau\;} (vr)(P'|Q')}$$

Hence, process $\bar{s}_{k_1}.Q|s_{k_2}.P$ evolves to $(vr)(r \rhd_{k_2} Q|r \rhd_{k_1} P)$. There, if $Q$ terminates with close, the termination handler $k_2$ of the callee will be activated. Vice versa, if $P$ terminates with close the termination handler $k_1$ of the caller will be activated:

$$\frac{P \xrightarrow{\;close\;} P'}{r \rhd_k P \xrightarrow{\;\tau\;} \blacktriangleright P'|\dagger(k)} \qquad\qquad \blacktriangleright r \rhd_k P \xrightarrow{\;\tau\;} \blacktriangleright P|\dagger(k)$$

A typical behavior for a listener is that of closing the current session as soon as a signal $\dagger(k)$ is received. This listener can be rendered as: $k.$close.

Processes can be composed by using the *pipeline* operator $P > Q$. Whenever $P$ produces a value $V$ that $Q$ can consume, a reduction will trigger a new instantiation $Q'$ of $Q$. After this reduction, $Q$ is again ready to consume the next value produced by $P$, if any:

$$\frac{P \xrightarrow{\;\langle V \rangle\;} P' \quad Q \xrightarrow{\;(V)\;} Q'}{P > Q \xrightarrow{\;\tau\;} (P' > Q) \,|\, Q'}$$

## 2.1   A Small Example

In this section we will show how CaSPiS can be used for modeling a simple system used for computing the basic arithmetic operations. In the example, and in the rest of this paper, we will sometime use standard programming language operators like selection (**if** – **then** – **else**) or iteration (**while** – **do**) that can be implemented as macros in CaSPiS. Service calculator can be implemented in CaSPiS as follows:

$$!(vk)\texttt{calculator}_k.\ !("\texttt{sum}", ?x, ?y)\langle"\texttt{result}", x+y\rangle$$
$$|\ !("\texttt{sub}", ?x, ?y)\langle"\texttt{result}", x-y\rangle$$
$$|\ !("\texttt{mul}", ?x, ?y)\langle"\texttt{result}", x*y\rangle$$
$$|\ !("\texttt{div}", ?x, ?y)\ \textbf{if}\ y = 0\ \textbf{then}\ \langle"\texttt{fail}"\rangle\ \textbf{else}\ \langle"\texttt{result}", x/y\rangle$$
$$|\ ("\texttt{off}")\texttt{close}$$
$$|\ k.\texttt{close}$$

after service calculator is invoked, processes for managing basic arithmetic operations and those for controlling session termination are installed in the established session. The processes for arithmetic operations wait for tuples containing the operation to be computed ("sum", "sub", "mul" and "div") and the two operands ($x$ and $y$) and then send to the callee the result. In case of a division operation, message "fail" is sent to the callee when $y$ is 0. Moreover, when message "off" is received the established session is closed. Finally, listener $k$.close is used for managing unexpected session closing by the client. To avoid interferences, name $k$ is private. Since this service is replicated, it is always available for the invocation.

Service calculator can be used, for instance, for computing *Greatest Common Divisor* between two integers using Euclid's algorithm. Service gcd is defined as follows:

$$!\texttt{gcd}.(?x, ?y)$$
$$\textbf{if}\ (y = 0)\ \textbf{then}\ \langle x\rangle$$
$$\textbf{else}$$
$$\textbf{if}\ (x < y)\ \textbf{then}\ \overline{\texttt{gcd}}.\langle y, x\rangle(?z)\langle z\rangle^\uparrow$$
$$\textbf{else}\ P > (?u, ?w)\overline{\texttt{gcd}}.\langle u, w\rangle(?z)\langle z\rangle^\uparrow$$

where process $P$ is defined as follows:

$$P \stackrel{\triangle}{=} (vk')\overline{\texttt{calculator}}_{k'}.\langle"\texttt{sub}", x, y\rangle("\texttt{result}", ?z)\langle z, y\rangle^\uparrow\langle"\texttt{off}"\rangle|k'.\texttt{close}$$

## 3   The IMC Framework

We now sketch the main functionalities and classes of the framework, for further details we refer to the IMC web page http://imc-fi.sf.net). IMC consists of three main subpackages: protocols, mobility and topology that deal with communication protocols, code mobility and network topology, respectively. Since mobility is not employed in CaSPiS, we will ignore this subpackage in the following description.

IMC provides tools to define customized protocol stacks, which are viewed as a flexible composition of micro-protocols, and permits achieving adaptable forms of communication transparency, which are needed when implementing an infrastructure for global computing. In IMC, a *network protocol* is viewed as an aggregation of *protocol states*: a high-level communication protocol can indeed be described as a state automaton. Thus, the programmer must simply provide the implementation of each state, put them in a protocol instance, and then start the protocol. The protocol states abstract away from the specific communication layers. This permits re-using protocol implementations independently from the underlying communication means: the same protocol can then be executed on a TCP socket, on UDP packets or even on streams attached to a file (e.g., to simulate a protocol execution). This abstraction is implemented by specialized streams: `Marshaler` (for writing) and `UnMarshaler` (for reading). These streams provide high-level and encoding-independent representations of information to be sent or received.

The data in these streams can be "pre-processed" by some customized *protocol layers* that remove some information from the input and add some information to the output: typically this information is a header removed from the input and added to the output. The base class `ProtocolLayer` deals with these functionalities, and can be specialized by the programmer to provide his own protocol layer. These layers are then composed into a `ProtocolStack` object that ensures the order of preprocessing passing through all the layers in the stack. Each layer is independent and the composition of layers in a protocol stack takes place at run-time. For instance, the programmer can add a layer that removes a sequence number from an incoming packet and adds the incremented sequence number into an outgoing packet.

In IMC a participant in a network is an instance of the class `Node` of the package `topology`. A node is also a container of running processes that can be thought of as the computational units. The framework provides all the means for a process to access the resources contained in a node and to migrate to other nodes. A process is an instance of a subclass of the class `NodeProcess`, and can be added to a node for execution with the method `addProcess` of the class `Node`. A node keeps track of all the processes that are currently in execution and handles their termination when the node itself is terminated. The entry point of a `NodeProcess` is the abstract method `execute` that must be implemented in subclasses of `NodeProcess`. Actually, a process can interact with the node it is running on only through a `NodeProxy`, which ensures security by restricting the node interface visibility to a subset.

The framework provides classes and protocols to deal with *sessions*, a base concept of service calculi. The concept of session is logical, since it can then rely on a physical connection (e.g., TCP sockets) or on a connectionless communication layer (e.g., UDP packets). A `SessionManager` instance will keep track of all the sessions. This can be used to implement several network topology structures. A `Session` instance is identified by two `SessionId` objects, one indicating the local end and the other one indicating the remote end. A `SessionId` contains information about the "location" or "address" of a node; this concept depends on the specific communication medium: for instance, for an IP communication it will be a string of the shape IP:port. Moreover, it contains information about the specific low level communication protocol. For instance, `"udp-myhost.com:9999"` represents a UDP communication with the host `"myhost.com"` on port 9999. Upon establishing a session, the `SessionId` is used to determine the low level communication layer. Thus, switching from a communication layer to another is only a matter of changing the `SessionId`, while all the other classes in IMC are independent from this, and do not need to be changed. A `Session` can be established by using the method `connect`, of class `Node`, specifying the `SessionId` of the remote end; a session request can be accepted by using the method `accept`, by specifying the local `SessionId`. These methods return a `ProtocolStack` object (where the lowest layer is already set as explained above); this can then be customized by adding specific `ProtocolLayer` objects. Finally it can be passed to a `Protocol` instance that will run upon it.

IMC provides an implementation of *tuples*, *tuple spaces* and the associated *pattern matching* retrieval mechanism, thus, the programmer can use the *generative* and asynchronous communication mechanisms typical of *Linda* [9]. Notice that the implementation of tuple spaces in IMC also provides extended operations such as non-blocking retrieval operations, and retrieval operations that permit reading/removing any tuple (without specifying its template). Furthermore, there is also a blocking version of the **out** operation: this permits implementing a synchronous communication mechanism still relying on pattern matching (this will be the case of the communication in CaSPiS, Section 4).

Inside IMC inter-objects communication takes place via the *event* based functionalities provided by IMC. In particular, most classes of the framework are endowed with event generation capabilities (e.g., `ProtocolState`, `ProtocolLayer`, `Node`, etc.). This permits keeping the classes loosely coupled and communications among objects in the framework highly flexible. It is then easy to intercept, e.g., new connection requests, connection failures and session closures. With this respect, the framework notifies the processes involved in a session about the closure of the session so that they can perform finalization operations.

## 4   JCASPiS: CaSPiS Implementation in IMC

In this section we present JCASPiS: a Java framework that permits implementing service oriented applications based on CaSPiS paradigm. Notice that, CaSPiS operators like parallel composition and restrictions, can be directly implemented in Java. Indeed, the former is implemented by using *threads*, while the latter is obtained by considering the creation of *new objects* like, for instance, the instantiation of *new services*. Other operators, like *non deterministic choice* and *replication* are implemented in JCASPiS in a restricted way. Indeed, in JCASPiS we will consider only the *choice* between *input* actions while *replication* will be available only on service definitions.

The implementation of other JCASPiS primitives requires more attention. Indeed, to allow JCASPiS programs to interact with existing services, implementation of *service definitions*, *service invocations* and *sessions* has to take into account existing protocols and technologies for services. IMC provides the Java classes that can be easily used for handling connections and disconnections among nodes over a network. JCASPiS specializes these classes in order to handle Service Oriented Protocols. Two kinds of connection protocols are considered: TCP and HTTP. The former is already provided by IMC framework, while the latter has been implemented by using Simple Web Server [13], a Java library, released under the GNU LGPL, providing an extensible HTTP engine.

Three protocols for services interactions have been developed: BYTE_CODE, XML and SOAP. The first one, is used when service interaction is implemented by serializing Java objects. XML and SOAP protocols are used when service interaction is based on XML and SOAP messages respectively. Thanks to the modularity of IMC, new service interaction protocols, as well as new implementations of the one already available, can be easily integrated within JCASPIS.

Provided protocols are implemented as new layers that permit marshaling/unmarshaling data as Java objects or within XML and SOAP messages respectively. BYTE_CODE protocol is directly developed over the existing Java serialization mechanisms while XML and SOAP implementations are based on two standard J2EE [5] libraries, *Java API for XML Binding* (JAXB) [6] and *SOAP with Attachments API for Java* (SAAJ) [14].

*Java API for XML Binding* is a Java library that permits mapping Java classes to XML representations. Indeed, by using JAXB Java objects can be marshaled into XML and vice-versa. In other words, JAXB permits sending and receiving Java objects in XML format, without the need to implement a specific set of XML loading and saving routines for the program's class structure. JAXB is one of the APIs in the Java EE platform, and is part of the Java Web Services Development Pack (JWSDP). It is also one of the foundations for WSIT. JAXB is part of SE version 1.6.

*SOAP with Attachments API for Java* (SAAJ) provides primitives for producing and consuming messages conforming to the SOAP specification and with attachments. Indeed, SAAJ automates many of the required steps for creating/analyzing SOAP messages.

In the following we will describe how key notions of CaSPiS are implemented within IMC.

*Services.* Services are referenced by means of a `Service` object that contains *service name*, the `SessionId`, which is used for identifying the connection protocol and the address of the service, and the protocol used for service interaction. For instance, service `pair` running at host `test.unifi.it:8080` based on XML messages is referenced as:

```
s = new Service(new IpSessionId("test.unifi.it", 8080), "pair", "xml");
```

When a service is invoked, a connection to the remote host providing the requested service is established. Moreover, the protocol `ProtocolStack` implementing the required conversation protocol (i.e., IMC, XML or SOAP) is instantiated and stored within an object instance of class `Connection`. This object, which abstracts from a specific interaction protocol, is used for implementing service interactions.

*Processes.* CaSPiS processes are implemented by classes inherited by the abstract class `Process`. The classes derived from `Process` must provide the implementation of the entry point method `execute`, and can use all the methods for exchanging data through a session and outside the session environment, and for publishing or invoking a service. For instance, CaSPiS process $(?x)(?y)\langle x,y \rangle$, that emits a pair containing two read values, will be rendered in JCASPIS as follows:

```
public class PairServiceProcess extends SessionProcess {
    public void execute() throws IMCException {
        Object first = inAction(); // accept any template
        Object second = inAction(); // accept any template
        send(new Tuple(first, second));
    }
}
```

Similarly, the process $(\langle"a"\rangle|\langle"b"\rangle|(?x)\langle x\rangle^{\uparrow})$, that sends two values, retrieves a pair and emits it in the enclosing context, can be implemented as follows:

```
public static class PairClient extends ParallelProcess {
    public void execute() throws IMCException {
        outAction(new Tuple("a"));
        outAction(new Tuple("b"));
        Tuple t = (Tuple) inAction();
        returnAction(t);
    }
}
```

Each process can execute method `runProcess(Process p)` for activating the execution of process p.

*Contexts.* `Process` instances are executed within a `Context`. Abstract class `Context` provides the following methods for:

- publishing services that will be invoked by remote partners (`publish`);
- invoking remote services and instantiating local processes implementing service interactions (`call`);
- executing basic CaSPiS actions (`inAction`, `outAction` and `returnAction`), for verifying whether an action can be executed (methods `checkIn`, `checkOut` and `checkReturn`) and for closing the enclosing session (`close`).

`Contexts` can be nested. For this reason `Context` also keeps track of all its nested components. By using the IMC mechanisms to react upon session closing, it automatically forwards the session closing operation to all its nested `Contexts`.

*Service Publication and Invocation.* A service is published by invoking one of the following methods on a context:

- `publish(Service s, Process p)`
- `publish(Service s, Class<? extends Process> c)`
- `publish(Service s, Class<? extends Process> c, boolean per)`

These methods publish a service within the current node. When a request for the published service is received, process p (or an instance of class c) is activated. Boolean parameter per is used for determining if the service is persistent, namely if the service is still available after the first invocation.

The following code permits publishing the service s defined above:

*publish*(s, PairServiceProcess.**class**, **true**)

A service can be invoked by executing one the following methods:

```
- call(Service s, Process p)
- call(Service s, Class<? extends Process> c)
```

when one of these methods is invoked, a connection to the remote host is opened and a `Session` (described in the following) is installed within the actual context. Process p (or an instance of class c) is executed within the new session.

To invoke service s, the following code is executed:

*call*(s, **new** *PairClient*(), **true**)

The implementation of publish and call methods in `Context` rely on abstract methods:

```
- Connection publish(ServiceName s)
- Connection call(ServiceName s)
```

The former waits for a request for service s, the latter establishes a connection with the remote host providing service s. Both methods return an instance of `Connection` used for interacting with the caller/callee. Hence, a new session is created and the obtained object is used for interacting with the remote participant.

JCASPiS provides three implementations of abstract class `Context`: `Execution-Environment`, `Session` and `PipeLine`. They define a top level context, a session and a pipeline, respectively.

Class `ExecutionEnvironment` is also devoted to wait for incoming connections. Indeed, its constructor is parametrized with respect to the Internet addresses used for handling incoming TCP and HTTP connections. Moreover, `ExecutionEnvironment` keeps track of the published services. These are stored within a `ServiceRegistry`. When a connection request is received, this object is used for determining the process that has to handle the received service request. Since the same service can be published with different implementations, `ServiceRegistry` can be specialized for implementing different service selection policies. At the moment, implementations of a service are collected in a list, and the first available is selected.

Classes `Session` and `PipeLine` provide an implementation for CaSPiS sessions and pipelines respectively. `Sessions` are installed within a context when a service is invoked. Interactions with the remote participants are performed via an instance of `Connection` that contains a reference to the `ProtocolStack` that is created once the connection is established.

CaSPiS pipelines are implemented by means of `PipeLine`. This class contains a list of `Abstractions`. These are processes parametrized with respect to a `Template`, i.e., an object that permits selecting received messages. Output actions executed by running processes are intercepted in order to activate the processes corresponding to a matching template.

In Figure 2 we report the class diagrams of JCASPiS classes described in this section. Notice that `Process`, `PipeLine` and `Session` implement interface `Activity`. This is the interface that characterize objects that can be executed within a `Context`.

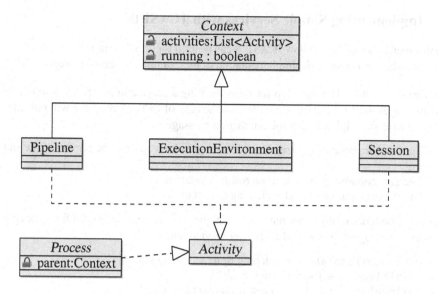

**Fig. 2.** JCASPIS: Class Diagram

*Session Interactions.* The communication mechanism in CaSPiS is based on structured values and pattern matching, thus, we will use the tuple space based communication provided by IMC. The retrieve operation can be performed using the method inAction, that can also accept as a parameter a template, which extends abstract class Template, specifying the data we are willing to receive; the write operation can be performed using the method outAction, that takes as a parameter the message we want to send. Finally, the method returnAction is used for sending a value just outside the current session. This method is implemented by invoking method outAction of the enclosing context.

Classes Session and PipeLine provide different implementations for inAction and for outAction methods. Session sends and receives messages over the corresponding service connection. PipeLine delegates input to the enclosing context while catches output for activating a process that will handle the sent message.

A session is closed when method close is invoked. Afterwards, remote connection and all the nested sessions are closed. Notice that, each action performed within a session that is terminating, or within one of its subsessions, leads to an exception. Moreover, to handle unexpected connection closures, each session is equipped with a *termination handler*. This is a process that is executed for handling proper session closure. Termination handler is associated to a session when service is invoked/published. Indeed, there are methods call/publish described above that take as an extra parameter the process or the process class to use as termination handler.

Methods for session interactions cannot be invoked on a top level context or when a session is closing. For this reason, Context also provides methods that can be used for verifying whether an action can be executed: methods checkIn, checkOut and checkReturn.

## 5  Implementing Simple Services with JCASPIS

In this section we will show how JCASPIS can be used for implementing simple services. In particular, we consider the implementation of the example presented in Section 2.1.

*Service calculator.* The first step for implementing a service in JCASPIS is to define the messages used for interacting with it. In the case of `calculator`, we will consider three classes for implementing the interaction messages:

- `Operation`, containing a reference to an operation (`op`) and the arguments (`x` and `y`);
- `Result`, containing the operation result (`result`);
- `Failure`, containing a text indicating the occurred error;

in correspondence of these, we have also to implement the templates used for retrieving expected messages[1]. The actual calculator service relies on:

- `OperationTemplate`, for matching `Operation` messages;
- `ResultTemplate`, for retrieving results;
- `FailureTemplate`, for intercepting computational failure.

The body of the service `calculator` can be rendered in JCASPIS as follows:

```
runProcess(new DivProcess());
runProcess(new SubProcess());
runProcess(new SumProcess());
runProcess(new MulProcess());
inAction(new StringTemplate("off"));
close();
```

This process first activates sub-processes for computing the arithmetic operations (Java code for `SumProcess` and `DivProcess` is reported in Listing 1) and then waits for a termination string (`"off"`) for closing the actual session. This message is retrieved using a `StringTemplate`. This is a template that matches only strings that are equal to the one passed to the constructor.

Notice that in this case we do not install any handler for intercepting unexpected session closure. Indeed, default termination handler is used. This is a process that automatically closes current session as soon as the remote participant terminates.

Since service calculator is based on a persistent session (many messages can be exchanged over the established connection), service calculator is published by using TCP as connection protocol and BYTE_CODE as interaction protocol:

```
ExecutionEnvironment env = new ExecutionEnvironment(8080, 9000);
Service calc = new Service();
calc.setName("calculator");
calc.setSessionId(new IpSessionId("localhost", 8080));
calc.setLanguage("BYTE_CODE");
env.publish(calc, CalculatorProcess.class, true);
```

[1] Classes for implementing values exchanged after a service invocation and templates to be used in the established session could be generated automatically from a standard XML textual representation like, for instance, WSDL.

```
public class SumProcess extends Process {
  public void execute() throws InterruptedException {
    while (true) {
      Operation op = inAction(new OperationTemplate(Operation.Type.SUM));
      outAction(new Result(op.getX()+op.getY()));
    }
  }
}

public class DivProcess extends Process {
  public void execute() throws InterruptedException {
    while (true) {
      Operation op = inAction(new OperationTemplate(Operation.Type.DIV));
      if (op.getY()==0) {
        outAction(new Failure("Division by 0!"));
      } else {
        outAction(new Result(op.getX()/op.getY()));
      }
    }
  }
}
```

**Listing 1.** Processes for handling sum and div operations

*Greatest Common Divisor.* Service calculator can be used for computing the *Greatest Common Divisor* between two integers. This service, named gcd, operates on two kinds of messages:

- Pair, which contains the values for which we want to compute GCD;
- Result, which contains the computed GCD.

Protocol of service gcd is implemented in JCASPIS as follows:

```
Pair p = inAction(new PairTemplate());
int x = p.getX();
int y = p.getY();
if (y==0) {
  outAction(new Result(x));
}
if (x < y) {
  call(gcd, new RequestResponseProcess(new Pair(y,x)));
} else {
  Match m = new Match();
  m.add(new IntegerTemplate(), GcdAbstraction.class);
  pipeline(new CalculatorClient(new Operation(Operation.SUB, x, y)), m);
}
```

where RequestResponseProcess, which implements the standard request-response service interaction pattern, is defined as follows:

```
public class RequestResponseProcess extends Process {
  Object request;
  public RequestResponseProcess(Object message) {
    this.request = message;
  }
  public void execute() throws InterruptedException {
    outAction(request);
    Object response = inAction();
    returnAction(response);
  }
}
```

while abstraction `GcdAbstraction` is defined as follows:

```
public class GcdAbstraction extends Abstraction {
  public void execute() throws InterruptedException {
    runProcess(new RequestResponseProcess(getActivationMessage()));
  }
}
```

To guarantee interactions with existing web services, service gcd is developed over HTTP and SOAP:

```
ExecutionEnvironment env = new ExecutionEnvironment(8080, 9000);
Service gcd = new Service();
gcd.setName("gcd");
gcd.setSessionId(new HttpSessionId("localhost", 8080));
gcd.setLanguage("SOAP");
gcd.setServicePackage("org.cmg.caspis.ex.gcdulator:org.cmg.caspis.ex.gcd");
env.publish(gcd, GcdProcess.class, true);
```

## 6   Conclusions

The implementation of a language based on a process calculus typically consists of a run-time system (a sort of abstract machine) implemented in a high level language like Java, and of a compiler that, given a program written in the programming language based on the calculus, produces code that uses the run-time system above. In this paper we have illustrated, by means of a case study, a possible methodology to accelerate the development of prototype implementation of such a run-time system, by relying on the IMC framework. In particular, we have described JCASPIS: the implementation of CaSPiS, a calculus that has recently been proposed within the EU project SENSORIA. The use of IMC has permitted accelerating the development of prototype implementations while concentrating only on the features that are specific of CaSPiS. Indeed, JCASPIS composed only by 43 classes and about 1700 lines of code. These classes provide 289 methods, and the average number of lines per method is 2.5.

*Implementing other session based calculi.* JCASPIS can be easily extended to implement two other session based calculi that, like CaSPiS, have directly stemmed from SCC [2], namely SSCC [11] and Conversation Calculus [4]. Notice that, implementation of SSCC and CC would completely reuse large part of the JCASPIS framework.

SSCC is *stream* oriented with primitives for inserting/retrieving data in/from streams. Streams have been easily implemented in IMC by using classes for handling tuple spaces. The interface of Process and Context can be extended in order to consider method feed that is used for inserting a value inside a stream. The new context Stream has been introduced for collecting the values produced by the inner activities.

The Conversation Calculus (CC) has explicit and distinct message passing primitives to model inter and intra session communication. These primitives are based on *communication directions* (see [4]). To implement these primitives, Process as well as Context have been extended to consider communication directions.

As a future work, we plan to develop a high level programming language that, inspired by CaSPiS, could be used for programming services and to orchestrate existing ones. Given a program written in the programming language based on the calculus it will be translated in a Java program that uses JCASPIS classes. One of the advantages of this approach is that programs could be verified by using formal tools that are being developed for CaSPiS.

# References

1. Bettini, L., De Nicola, R., Falassi, D., Lacoste, M., Loreti, M.: A Flexible and Modular Framework for Implementing Infrastructures for Global Computing. In: Kutvonen, L., Alonistioti, N. (eds.) DAIS 2005. LNCS, vol. 3543, pp. 181–193. Springer, Heidelberg (2005)
2. Boreale, M., Bruni, R., Caires, L., De Nicola, R., Lanese, I., Loreti, M., Martins, F., Montanari, U., Ravara, A., Sangiorgi, D., Vasconcelos, V., Zavattaro, G.: SCC: A Service Centered Calculus. In: Bravetti, M., Núñez, M., Zavattaro, G. (eds.) WS-FM 2006. LNCS, vol. 4184, pp. 38–57. Springer, Heidelberg (2006)
3. Bruni, R., Boreale, M., De Nicola, R., Loreti, M.: Sessions and pipelines for structured services programming. In: FMOODS 2008. LNCS, vol. 5051. Springer, Heidelberg (2008)
4. Caires, L., Viera, H.: A note on a model for service oriented computation. In: ESOP 2008. LNCS, vol. 4960. Springer, Heidelberg (2008)
5. J.E. Edition, http://java.sun.com/javaee/
6. J. A.: for XML Binding, https://jaxb.dev.java.net/
7. Gamma, E., Helm, R., Johnson, R., Vlissides, J.: Design Patterns: Elements of Reusable Object-Oriented Software. Addison-Wesley, Reading (1995)
8. Gay, S.J., Hole, M.J.: Types and Subtypes for Client-Server Interactions. In: Swierstra, S.D. (ed.) ESOP 1999. LNCS, vol. 1576, pp. 74–90. Springer, Heidelberg (1999)
9. Gelernter, D.: Generative Communication in Linda. ACM Transactions on Programming Languages and Systems 7(1), 80–112 (1985)
10. Honda, K., Vasconcelos, V.T., Kubo, M.: Language Primitives and Type Discipline for Structured Communication-Based Programming. In: Hankin, C. (ed.) ESOP 1998. LNCS, vol. 1381, pp. 122–138. Springer, Heidelberg (1998)

11. Lanese, I., Martins, F., Ravara, A., Vasconcelos, V.: Disciplining orchestration and conversation in service-oriented computing. In: SEFM 2007, pp. 305–314. IEEE Computer Society Press, Los Alamitos (2007)
12. Sensoria Project. Public web site, http://sensoria.fast.de/
13. Simple Web Server, http://simpleweb.sourceforge.net/
14. S. with Attachments API for Java, https://saaj.dev.java.net/

# Service Combinators for Farming Virtual Machines

Karthikeyan Bhargavan[1], Andrew D. Gordon[1], and Iman Narasamdya[2]

[1] Microsoft Research
[2] University of Manchester

**Abstract.** Management is one of the main expenses of running the server farms that implement enterprise services, and operator errors can be costly. Our goal is to develop type-safe programming mechanisms for combining and managing enterprise services, and we achieve this goal in the particular setting of farms of virtual machines. We assume each server is service-oriented, in the sense that the services it provides, and the external services it depends upon, are explicitly described in metadata. We describe the design, implementation, and formal semantics of a library of combinators whose types record and respect server metadata. We describe a series of programming examples run on our implementation, based on existing server code for a typical web application.

## 1   Introduction

**Farms and Roles.** Abstractly, a *server farm* is a collection of servers that runs one or more (parallel) programs, such as hosting a website or running compute jobs. Servers in a farm may have both local and remote dependencies. They may receive requests from remote clients, such as a web browser. They may also send requests to remote servers, to perform a credit card transaction, for example.

We assume each server boots off a *disk image*, such as the contents of a local hard drive, or an image fetched over the network. Typically, each server plays a particular *role*, such as web server, mail server, application server, and so on. The functionality embodied in disk images is often referred to as *business logic*, as it codifies the steps needed to enact various business processes—how to auction a wardrobe, for example.

**Managing Server Farms in Software.** Conventionally, operations staff manage server farms using a mixture of command prompts, scripts, various graphical tools, and actual physical configuration. Management includes provision and interconnection of servers, as well as responding to events such as peaks and troughs in load, or failures of individual servers. Operator errors are a leading cause of service failures and there is a need for increased automation and static validation of operator actions [Oppenheimer et al., 2003; Nagaraja et al., 2004].

Technologies such as network booting [Intel 1999] and virtualization [Meyer and Seawright, 1970] of commodity hardware [Barham et al., 2003; Wolf and Halter, 2005] allow hardware resources to be dynamically allocated to server roles. Moreover, to eliminate physical configuration completely, virtual machines can even be rented on demand over the web [Bavier et al., 2004; Hoykhet et al., 2004; Ama, 2006; Garfinkel, 2007]. These technologies reduce the need for human intervention and transform server farm

D. Lea and G. Zavattaro (Eds.): COORDINATION 2008, LNCS 5052, pp. 33–49, 2008.

management into a programming problem. The programming problem is to write *operations logic*: programs that codify the management actions of operators—to provision and interconnect servers, for example.

**Service Orientation.** Let a *procedure* be some functionality exposed on a communication port via a protocol such as RPC-style request/response, and let a *service* be a set of procedures. Server roles are increasingly *service-oriented*, in the sense that each role is described as importing and exporting services. A role implements its exports, and has dependencies on its imports. These imports and exports have explicit types that describe message contents and message patterns.

For example, an enterprise order processing application (drawn from published server code [Pallmann, 2005]) has an order entry role implementing a service (its export) consisting of a single procedure SubmitOrder, and conforming to the IOrderEntry interface. We give this and related interfaces below.

**public interface** IOrderEntry { string SubmitOrder(Order order); }
**public interface** IPayment { string AuthorizePayment(Payment payment); }
**public interface** IOrderProcessing { void SubmitOrder(Order order); }

The code for SubmitOrder needs to consult a remote site to make an authorization decision. Hence, the order entry role has a dependency on the IPayment interface (its import). After authorization, SubmitOrder fulfills the order by calling an order processing procedure in the IOrderProcessing interface (its second import).

Service-oriented designs often use SOAP [Box et al., 2000] messages for requests and responses, while service metadata, such as request and response types, is often described using the Web Services Description Language (WSDL) [Christensen et al., 2001]. SOAP and WSDL are platform-independent XML formats. There are many development tools and software platforms for producing service-oriented disk images, where the imports and exports are described with WSDL. In our example, the order processing code is in C#. It relies on .NET communication libraries and tools to exchange SOAP messages and to map between C# interfaces and WSDL metadata.

**Service Combinators for Farming Virtual Machines.** If the server farm is the computer, what is the program? Our proposal is that an application running on a server farm consists of (1) a set of pre-existing disk images, (2) a set of URIs for the services exported and imported by the program, and (3) a script for assembling the roles, interconnecting them (sometimes via intermediaries for tasks such as load balancing), and managing the resulting system. The disk images implement the business logic of the program, while the script implements the operations logic.

Application for a Server Farm = Disk Images + External URIs + Script

Our main goals are (1) to develop a typed combinator-based API for scripting operations logic, and (2) to develop a formal semantics to support reasoning about reachable configurations. We treat service-oriented disk images as components to be interconnected using standard networking protocols.

On the other hand, the tasks of writing business logic and of building disk images are outside our scope—there are many existing tools for these purposes.

In this paper, we describe the design and implementation of *Baltic*, a type-safe API for expressing operations logic. Our API consists of a set of combinators for starting and stopping server roles implemented as virtual machines (VMs), for importing and exporting SOAP web services described by WSDL metadata, and for managing the resulting system. Concretely, the combinators are functions in the F# dialect of ML [Syme et al., 2007]. These combinators allow an ML program to control a small-scale server farm, which consists of a set of SOAP intermediaries interconnecting a set of VMs managed by a Virtual Machine Monitor (VMM) on a single physical server. By *intermediary*, we mean a service situated on the physical server, that performs simple tasks such as forwarding SOAP messages between VMs and the external world, or acting as a load-balancer in front of multiple servers. Our particular VMM is Virtual Server [Armstrong, 2007], running on dual processor hardware suitable for test automation or (modest) production workloads.

The intended scope of this paper is relatively small farms of servers, such as those that could be supported by a small number of VMMs. Our implementation is a research prototype, but if engineered for production, we believe it would usefully support small websites or test environments. We have not attempted to design a comprehensive set of intermediaries, although we can easily add more. Further research on scalability would be needed for our approach to apply to large-scale server farms used for parallel data processing (see Dean and Ghemawat [2004], for example). Still, even if our practical implementation is on a small scale, we demonstrate for the first time scripts that both (1) manipulate VMs and interconnect them with standard TCP/IP protocols, and (2) have a formal semantics suitable for typechecking and static analysis.

**Contributions.** We propose a *resource metadata* format that describes the resources—disk images, and imported and exported services—available in a server farm. We advocate that operations logic for managing a server farm be scripted with respect to such metadata. The main technical contributions of this work are the following.

- The idea that disk images should be seen as functions, with type signatures generated from service-oriented metadata, such as WSDL.
- The design and implementation of a library of service combinators for compositional description of server farms and their operations logic.
- A formal semantics of these combinators by an encoding in a concurrent $\lambda$-calculus. Via a type preservation result for our $\lambda$-calculus, we obtain type soundness for programs running against our API.

The main benefits of our approach, compared to the alternative, low-level scripting languages [Wolf and Halter, 2005], are the following.

- Our method abstracts from networking details and automatically links together the procedures imported and exported by machines and intermediaries.
- Our method catches construction errors by typechecking, rather than at some time during execution. For example, if server metadata stipulates a dependency on a service type, such as IPayment, we never supply a procedure with another type.

**Contents of the Paper.** Section 2 describes our software architecture. Section 3 introduces service combinators by example. Section 4 reviews WSDL service descriptions, and describes our resource metadata format. Section 5 describes the implementation. Section 6 describes the message safety property guaranteed by Baltic, and outlines the underlying theory. Section 7 discusses related work and Section 8 concludes.

For the sake of brevity, this paper omits most formal definitions; a technical report [Bhargavan et al., 2007] includes additional examples, all formal definitions and proofs.

## 2   Architecture

The figure below depicts the Baltic architecture for managing a single physical server. A *remote client* is a consumer of a service located at an address on the physical server, while *remote service* is a service called by computations running on the physical server. The *Baltic server* implements the services exported by the physical server, as well as SOAP intermediaries that are used to interconnect other services. The VMM also runs on the physical server, under control of the Baltic server. (Our VMM is Virtual Server; other VMMs implement management APIs similar to that of Virtual Server, and hence could also support the Baltic API.) Files used by the VMM, such as disk images, are held on disks mounted on the physical server. The Baltic server mediates all access between VMs and the external world, and exports functions for managing the VMM and the intermediaries.

The *Baltic script* is an executable, S.exe, compiled from an ML program; it manages the Baltic server (and hence the VMM) using remote procedure calls, and hence may run either on the physical server, or elsewhere. The Baltic script is linked agains the libraries B.dll and E*m*.dll that implement the Baltic API described in the next section.

The VMM hosts a virtual network to which each VM is attached. The virtual network is isolated from the external network. Hence, VMs can use TCP/IP over the virtual network to call services on other VMs directly. VMs may also use TCP/IP to call

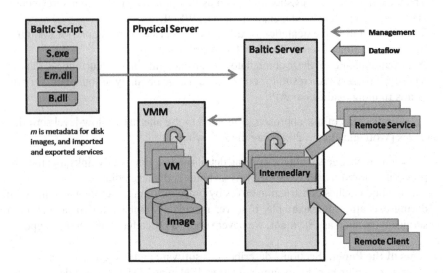

intermediaries hosted by the Baltic Server, but cannot directly call remote services. Remote clients can also call externally accessible intermediaries hosted by the Baltic server, but not those hosted in VMs. Intermediaries hosted by the Baltic server can call all three kinds of procedure: other intermediaries, remote services, or services exported by a VM. As the diagram illustrates, Baltic scripts create and interconnect VMs and intermediaries, but are not (generally) involved in the actual SOAP message flow.

## 3   Service Combinators by Example

We implement several variations of the enterprise order processing application introduced in Section 1. First, we describe the resources available to the application and the typed Baltic API. Then we present a series of examples that manage the application by creating a different configuration of VMs and SOAP intermediaries.

**Generating a Typed Interface to Resources.** The resources available to an application consist of the following: (1) disk images for each server role; (2) addresses of external procedures that the application can use; and (3) addresses of procedures published by the application. We propose a metadata format to describe these resources, with service types being expressed in WSDL. The format is described in more detail in Section 4. (To the best of our knowledge, there is no prior service-oriented metadata format for disk images.) We show below an excerpt from the metadata $m$ for our example application—our implementation uses an XML format, but for the sake of readability we use an equivalent ML syntax.

```
[VM {name = "OrderEntry"; disk = "OrderW2K3.vhd";
        inputs = [payment_ty; orderProc_ty]; outputs = [orderEntry_ty]};
  Import {name = "Payment1"; binding = payment_ty;
        url = "http://creditagency1.com/CA/service.svc"};
  Export {name = "OrderEntry"; binding = orderEntry_ty;
        url = "http://localhost:8080/OE/service.svc"};
  ...]
```

The first record specifies that the OrderEntry role is defined by the disk image in the file OrderW2K3.vhd. The role takes two services as input, described by payment_ty and orderProc_ty, which are the WSDL descriptions (or *bindings*) corresponding to the C# interfaces IPayment and IOrderProcessing, given in Section 1. The role exports a single service described by the binding orderEntry_ty (corresponding to IOrderEntry).

The second and third records describe services imported and exported by the application; the records include the actual URIs as well as their WSDL bindings. The full metadata $m$ for our example contains also records for the other roles and imported services.

The table below lists the Baltic API for this example application. The Baltic API consists of a *basic interface*, B.mli, which is general and fixed, plus an *environment interface*, E$m$.mli, which depends on the resources described by $m$. (The notation E$m$.mli denotes an interface that is a function of the metadata $m$.) The types in E$m$.mli are ML representations of the request and response types in the WSDL bindings in $m$. The functions provide typed access to the various resources. Given $m$ we have a tool that compiles $m$ to the interface E$m$.mli, and also to a module E$m$−c.ml implements the interface. For compilation to succeed, the metadata must be *well-formed* in the sense that it satisfies certain syntactic constraints.

The functions in the Baltic API manipulate procedures; a value of type $(\alpha,\beta)$ proc represents a SOAP procedure that takes a requests of type $\alpha$ and returns responses of type $\beta$. Section 5 describes the implementation and informal semantics of the API in more detail. In the rest of this section, we illustrate its use by example.

| Basic Interface: B.mli | Environment Interface: E$m$.mli |
|---|---|
| type vm <br> type vm_snapshot <br> type event = VM_Crash \| VM_Shutdown \| <br> VM_Overload \| VM_Underload <br> type $(\alpha,\beta)$ proc <br> type $(\alpha,\beta)$ procref <br> val call : $(\alpha,\beta)$ proc $\rightarrow \alpha \rightarrow \beta$ <br> val eOr : $(\alpha,\beta)$ proc $\rightarrow (\alpha,\beta)$ proc $\rightarrow (\alpha,\beta)$ proc <br> val ePar : $(\alpha,\beta)$ proc $\rightarrow (\alpha,\beta)$ proc $\rightarrow (\alpha,\beta)$ proc <br> val eRef : $(\alpha,\beta)$ proc $\rightarrow ((\alpha,\beta)$ proc $\times (\alpha,\beta)$ procref$)$ <br> val eRefUpdate : $(\alpha,\beta)$ procref $\rightarrow (\alpha,\beta)$ proc $\rightarrow$ unit <br> val eVM : vm $\rightarrow$ (event $\rightarrow$ unit) $\rightarrow$ unit <br> val eDelete: $(\alpha,\beta)$ proc $\rightarrow$ unit <br> val shutdownVM: vm $\rightarrow$ unit <br> val snapshotVM : vm $\rightarrow$ vm_snapshot <br> val restoreVM : vm_snapshot $\rightarrow$ unit | type Payment <br> type Order <br> type tPayment=(Payment,string) proc <br> type tOrderEntry=(Order,string) proc <br> type tOrderProcessing= <br> (Order,unit) proc <br> val createOrderEntryRole: <br> tPayment $\rightarrow$ tOrderProcessing $\rightarrow$ <br> (vm $\times$ tOrderEntry) <br> val createOrderProcessingRole : <br> unit $\rightarrow$ (vm $\times$ tOrderProcessing) <br> val createPaymentRole : <br> unit $\rightarrow$ (vm $\times$ tPayment) <br> val importPayment1: unit $\rightarrow$ tPayment <br> val importPayment2: unit $\rightarrow$ tPayment <br> val exportOrderEntry: <br> tOrderEntry $\rightarrow$ tOrderEntry |

**Example 1: Creating an Isolated VM Farm.** Our first example creates a simple instance of the enterprise order processing application. The three server roles are implemented by VMs that are isolated from the external environment, a configuration useful during development and testing.

The script below calls createPaymentRole and createOrderProcessingRole to boot VMs from the disk images of the payment and order processing roles. The disk image is stored as an ordinary file, and a VMM can boot a VM off such a file. These calls return the procedures ePay and eProc exported by these roles. Since these roles import no procedures, the corresponding functions take no parameters. Finally, the third line boots a VM for the order entry role, using ePay and eProc as inputs.

```
let (vm1,ePay) = createPaymentRole ()
let (vm2,eProc) = createOrderProcessingRole ()
let (vm3,eEntry) = createOrderEntryRole ePay eProc
```

A distinctive feature of our approach is that instead of presenting disk images as untyped files, we generate code, like createOrderEntryRole, that presents disk images as functions manipulating typed procedures. Hence, typechecking catches interconnection errors that would otherwise cause failures at run time, either during initial configuration or later during reconfigurations.

The following function, from B.mli, makes a call to a procedure. Given an $(\alpha,\beta)$ proc and a request of type $\alpha$, it serializes the request into a SOAP message, sends it to the procedure, awaits and then deserializes the response, and returns the result.

**val** call: $(\alpha,\beta)$ proc $\rightarrow \alpha \rightarrow \beta$

This function is useful for testing; for example, to test eEntry, we invoke it as follows: (The function makeOrder generates a default Order for user Alice.)

```
let o:Order = makeOrder "Alice"
let result = call eEntry o
```

(The call function allows the Baltic script to send and receive SOAP messages; it is the only exception to the general rule that the Baltic script only sends control messages.)

**Example 2: Importing and Exporting Services.** In our next example, rather than use a local payment service (such as ePay above) to authorize orders, we rely on a remote service. In addition, we export the internal eEntry procedure as a public service on the Baltic server. The external addresses of the payment service and the exported service are specified in the metadata $m$, and are named Payment1 and OrderEntry. These addresses are embedded within the functions importPayment1 and exportOrderEntry in E$m$.mli.

The script below calls the function importPayment1 to create a SOAP *forwarding intermediary* (or forwarder) on the Baltic server, returning the internal procedure ePay. Any request sent to ePay is forwarded to the external URI Payment1. The call to the function exportOrderEntry with parameter eEntry creates another forwarder on the Baltic server, listening at the URI OrderEntry located on the physical server. Any request sent to this URI is forwarded to the internal procedure eEntry.

```
let ePay = importPayment1 ()
let (vm1,eProc) = createOrderProcessingRole ()
let (vm2,eEntry) = createOrderEntryRole ePay eProc
let eo = exportOrderEntry eEntry
```

**Example 3: Load Balancing between Server Instances.** If a server role becomes a bottleneck, we can avoid overloading it by running multiple instances in parallel, together with an intermediary that balances requests between them. The next example runs two instances of the front-end order entry role, to better utilize the multi-processor hardware on our server.

The script below calls createOrderEntryRole twice to create two VMs vm2 and vm2' that export the procedures eEntry and eEntry', respectively. The function call eOr eEntry eEntry' then returns a procedure exported by a freshly created *Or intermediary*, which acts as a load balancer. Any request sent to this intermediary is forwarded to either eEntry or eEntry', chosen according to some strategy. (For now, we use a random strategy, but a more expressive API could allow multiple strategies.) The new procedure eor is then published at the external OrderEntry address as before.

```
let (vm2,eEntry) = createOrderEntryRole ePay eProc
let (vm2',eEntry') = createOrderEntryRole ePay eProc
let eor = eOr eEntry eEntry'
let eo = exportOrderEntry eor
```

The Or intermediary switches between two procedures. More generally, we can program derived combinators in ML; for example, orList creates a series of intermediaries to switch between a list of procedures by using the fold operator to compose a list of binary intermediaries.

```
let orList : (α,β) proc list → (α,β) proc = List.fold1_left eOr
```

**Example 4: References, Updating References, and Events.** In our previous examples, the communication topologies were fixed. Our next example introduces the idea of changing the topology in response to an event.

The combinator eRef e returns a procedure exported by a freshly created *Ref intermediary*, together with an identifier r for the intermediary. Any request sent to this intermediary is forwarded to e. Moreover, the intermediary r is mutable; a call to the combinator eRefUpdate r e' updates r to forward subsequent requests to e'.

A VMM, such as Virtual Server, can detect various events during the execution of a VM, such as changes of VM state, the absence of a "heartbeat" (likely indicating a crash), and so on. Baltic provides a simple event handling mechanism, to allow a script to take action when an event is detected by the underlying VMM. The Baltic function eVM vm h associates the handler function h with the machine named vm. The handler function is of type event → unit where event is a datatype describing the event. (Our present implementation only handles a few kinds of events, but is extensible.)

To illustrate these operators, consider the two VM instances of the order entry role, vm2 and vm2', in the previous example. If one of these VMs crashes, we should reconfigure our application to avoid sending messages to the crashed VM. The code in the following script creates a Ref intermediary that initially forwards messages to the eor procedure. If either VM crashes, an event handler updates the Ref intermediary to forward messages to the procedure exported by the other VM.

```
let (eref,r) = eRef eor
let h other ev = match ev with VM_Crash → eRefUpdate r other | _ → ()
let _ = eVM vm2 (h eEntry')
let _ = eVM vm2' (h eEntry)
let eo = exportOrderEntry eref
```

**Example 5: Snapshots of VMs.** The current state of a running VM consists of its memory image plus the current contents of its virtual disk. Some VMMs, including Virtual Server, allow this state to be saved to disk; typically, the memory image is directly stored in one file, while the contents of the virtual disk are efficiently represented by a *differencing disk*, which records the blocks that have changed since the machine started. We refer to this file system representation of a VM state as a *snapshot*. A snapshot can be saved, perhaps multiple times, and subsequently restored.

Baltic includes a simple facility for saving and restoring snapshots. If vm is the name of a running VM, snapshotVM vm creates a snapshot, and returns a value ss of type vm_snapshot that points to the saved files. Conversely, the call restoreVM ss discards the current state of vm, and replaces it by restoring the snapshot. (These combinators do not allow two snapshots of the same VM to run at once, a restriction imposed by the underlying VMM. However, the create*n*Role functions in E*m*.mli can be called repeatedly to create multiple instances of any one role.)

As a variation of the previous example, we record a snapshot of vm2 and vm2' just after booting and modify the event handler to restore the snapshot if the machine subsequently crashes. Snapshots allow faster recovery then rebooting.

```
let svm1 = snapshotVM vm2
let svm1' = snapshotVM vm2'
let h ss ev = match ev with VM_Crash → restoreVM ss | _ → ()
let _ = eVM vm2 (h svm2)
let _ = eVM vm2' (h svm2')
```

The technical report [Bhargavan et al., 2007] has additional examples to illustrate how to program an array of replicated VMs, where the number of replicas varies depending on the load.

## 4  Metadata for Services and Resources

What we call *resource metadata* is a typed description of the disk images, imported services, and exported services of an application. We gave an example of metadata at the start of Section 3. The purpose of this section is to describe the general format. We begin with metadata for services, and use this to define metadata for resources.

**Service Metadata (WSDL).** We assume that imported and exported services are described in the WSDL metadata format [Christensen et al., 2001]. These WSDL files are generated automatically when the interface for the service is compiled, and are typically used to auto-generate proxy code for accessing the service.

A WSDL document describes a set of operations (procedures), and their input and output types. Types are typically expressed in XML Schema, though other formats are possible. We assume that the named types used within a WSDL document are captured as a set of abstract type declarations in an ML interface $I_{ty}$, and that these abstract types have some concrete implementation $S_{ty}$ corresponding to the XML Schema definition. There are several tools that map XML Schema descriptions to programming language types. In our example, $I_{ty}$ consists of two abstract types Payment and Order.

The following grammar is an abstraction of the WSDL syntax.

**WSDL Metadata for Services:**

| | |
|---|---|
| $T_{req}, T_{res}$ | type |
| $n, a, d, u$ | strings |
| $O ::= \{\text{name} = n, \text{action} = a,$ | operation |
| $\quad \text{request\_type} = T_{req}, \text{response\_type} = T_{res}\}$ | |
| $Bd ::= \{\text{name} = n, \text{ops} = [O_1; \ldots; O_m]\}$ | binding |
| $P ::= \{\text{name} = n, \text{url} = u, \text{binding} = Bd\}$ | port |

We are using ML-style labelled records to represent the XML elements in a WSDL document. For example, our operations, bindings, and ports represent the WSDL elements named <operation>, <binding>, and <port>, respectively. For brevity, we sometimes elide the record labels when they are clear from context.

An *operation* $\{n, a, T_{req}, T_{res}\}$ describes a procedure, referred to as $n$; a SOAP request to this procedure should have a header with SOAP action $a$ and a body encoding a value of type $T_{req}$, while a SOAP response from this procedure should have a body encoding a value of type $T_{res}$.

A *binding* $\{n, [O_1; \ldots; O_m]\}$ describes a service, referred to as $n$, with $m$ procedures described by $O_1, \ldots, O_m$. For example, the payment_ty binding used in our examples is defined as follows:

```
let payment_ty:binding =
  {name = "Payment";
   ops = [({name = "AuthorizePayment";
            action = "http://EOP/IPayment/AuthorizePayment";
            request_type = "Payment";
            response_type = "string"}:operation)]}
```

The payment_ty binding describes a service, called Payment, that exposes a procedure AuthorizePayment, with a SOAP action http://EOP/IPayment/AuthorizePayment; the procedure takes as input an argument of type Payment and returns a string result.

A *port* $\{n, u, Bd\}$ describes a service, referred to as $n$; it is located at URI $u$ and implements the procedures described in $Bd$. For example, the following port describes an external service Payment1 that implements the payment_ty binding and is located at the URI http://creditagency1.com/CA/service.svc.

```
{name = "Payment1";
 url = "http://creditagency1.com/CA/service.svc";
 binding = payment_ty};
```

**Resource Metadata.** Having defined the WSDL format for services, we define a metadata formal for a complete server farm.

**Metadata for Resources:**

| | |
|---|---|
| $r ::=$ | resource |
| $\quad$ VM$\{$name $= n,$ disk $= d,$ | virtual machine |
| $\qquad$ inputs $= [Bd_{in}^1; \ldots; Bd_{in}^n],$ | |
| $\qquad$ outputs $= [Bd_{out}^1; \ldots; Bd_{out}^m]\}$ | |
| $\quad$ Import $P$ | imported service |
| $\quad$ Export $P$ | exported service |
| $m ::= (I_{ty}, S_{ty}, [r_1; \ldots; r_n])$ | metadata |

Let rs be the record list at the start of Section 3; it is an example of a resource list.

Each VM record defines a role in terms of a VM name, a disk image file accessible from the VMM, a list of imported bindings, and a list of exported bindings. In our example, the OrderEntry, OrderProcessing, and Payment roles are defined by such records.

Each Import record defines an external service port that we wish to use from within the Baltic server. In our example, the Payment1 port is imported by such a record.

Each Export record defines an internal service port that we wish to make available externally. In our example, the OrderEntry port is published at the public URI http://localhost:8080/OE/service.svc by such a record.

Recall that $I_{ty}$ consists of the abstract types Payment and Order in our example. Let $S_{ty}$ be an implementation of these two abstract types, for example, a couple of record types. Then $m = (I_{ty}, S_{ty}, \text{rs})$ is the metadata for our examples. In general, the ML interface $I_{ty}$ and corresponding ML implementation module $S_{ty}$ are present simply to define types used in the resource list rs.

## 5   Implementation and Informal Semantics of the Baltic API

An implementation of the Baltic API consists of a module B−c.ml implementing the basic interface B.mli and a module E$m$−c.ml implementing the metadata-specific environment interface E$m$.mli. These modules are compiled to generate the libraries B.dll and E$m$.dll respectively; ML programs linked with these libraries are compiled to assemble Baltic scripts that manage the Baltic server.

In addition to this *concrete* implementation, we also describe a *symbolic* implementation of the Baltic API, consisting of the modules B.ml and E$m$.ml. These symbolic modules simulate the behaviour of the Baltic server in terms of local processes and channel-based communications; as such, they constitute our executable semantics of the API. An ML program compiled with these modules generates a symbolic executable that can be used to trace and debug a Baltic script before deployment.

**Basic Module: B−c.ml.** The module B−c.ml implements the basic interface B.mli by managing intermediaries and VMs on the Baltic server. To manage SOAP intemediaries, we use the web services functionality provided by the Microsoft .NET Framework API; to manage VMs we rely on functions in the Virtual Server API. We outline our implementation of the types and functions in the B.mli below. The technical report [Bhargavan et al., 2007] contains further details.

- A value of type vm is a VM identifier, as defined by the VMM.
- A value of type vm_snapshot is the name of a directory containing a group of files implementing a VM snapshot, together with a VM identifier.
- A value of type event is one of four events detected by the VMM: either a VM has crashed, or shut down, or its processor is overloaded (running close to full capacity), or its processor is underloaded.
- A value of type $(\alpha, \beta)$ proc is a SOAP address, consisting of a URI and a SOAP action, and located either on a VM or the physical server. The API generates a value of this type only when there is a web service of the appropriate type listening at the address.
- A value of type $(\alpha, \beta)$ procref is a mutable variable on the physical server storing the SOAP address of a procedure of type $(\alpha, \beta)$ proc.
- The function call call e a implements a remote procedure call: it takes a procedure e of type $(\alpha, \beta)$ proc and an argument a of type $\alpha$; it sends a as a request to e and returns the response.
- The function call eOr e1 e2 takes two procedures e1 and e2 and creates and returns a fresh address e on the physical server; it starts an intermediary on the Baltic server that listens for requests on e and forwards them either to e1 or to e2 (based on a coin-toss); the intermediary waits for the corresponding response and returns it.

- The function call ePar e1 e2 also takes two procedures e1 and e2 and creates and returns a fresh address e on the physical server; it starts an intermediary on the Baltic server that listens for requests on e and forwards them to both e1 and e2; the intermediary waits for the first response and returns it.
- The function call eRef ei takes a procedure ei and creates and returns a fresh address e on the physical server plus a new mutable variable r on the Baltic server that stores the address of the procedure ei; it starts an intermediary on the Baltic server that listens for requests on e and forwards them to the address currently stored in r.
- The function call eRefUpdate r e modifies the variable r on the Baltic server to point to the procedure e.
- The function call eVM vm h takes a VM identifier vm and an event handler h; it registers this handler at the Baltic server so that whenever the VMM detects an event ev for the VM vm the handler h ev is executed.
- The function call shutdownVM vm shuts down the VM with identifier vm.
- The function call snapshotVM vm saves a snapshot of the current state of the running VM vm in a new directory d and returns a value of type vm_snapshot containing d and vm.
- The function call restoreVM ss checks that ss contains a directory d containing a valid snapshot of VM vm; it shuts down any running VM with identifier vm and starts up a VM from the running state stored in d.

**Environment Module: E$m$−c.ml.** The module E$m$−c.ml which enables access to the resources described in the metadata $m$. The technical report [Bhargavan et al., 2007] describes a tool that compiles $m$ to the interface E$m$.mli and to the module E$m$−c.ml. Given metadata $m = (I_{ty}, S_{ty}, rs)$, E$m$−c.ml is implemented as follows:

- It contains the type definitions $S_{ty}$.
- For every VM record in rs with name $N$, disk image $d$, inputs of type $s_1, \ldots, s_n$ and outputs of type $t_1, \ldots, t_m$, the function call create$N$Role i$_1$...i$_n$ takes $n$ services i$_1$...i$_n$ (of type $s_1, \ldots, s_n$) as arguments, boots a new VM vm from the disk image $d$, configures vm with the SOAP addresses of its inputs i$_1$...i$_n$, and returns vm plus its exported services o$_1$...o$_m$ (of type $t_1, \ldots, t_m$).
  For example, the function call createOrderEntryRole ePay eProc takes two procedures ePay and eProc as arguments; it then boots a new VM vm from the disk image file "OrderW2K3.vhd", configures vm with the addresses of Ise$Pay$ and eProc, and returns vm and the address of the new order entry procedure exported by it.
- For every Import record in rs with name $N$ and url $U$, the function call import$N$ () creates and returns a fresh address e on the physical server; it starts an intermediary on the Baltic server that listens for requests on e and forwards them to the external url $U$, waits for the corresponding response, and returns it.
- For every Export record in rs with name $N$ and url $U$, where $U$ is an externally accessible address on the physical server, the function call export$N$ e starts an intermediary on the Baltic server that listens for requests at $U$ and forwards them to the procedure $e$, waits for the corresponding response, and returns it.

**Symbolic Modules: B.ml and E$m$.ml.** The modules B.ml and E$m$.ml simulate the behaviour of the implementaion modules B−c.ml and E$m$−c.ml, but without contacting the Baltic server or the VMM and without sending any messages on the network. Instead, they model VMs and intermediaries as local processes spawned by the script, and implement SOAP requests and responses as local channel-based communications between processes.

A value of type $(\alpha,\beta)$ proc is modelled as a function that takes values of type $\alpha$ and returns values of type $\beta$; a value of type $(\alpha,\beta)$ procref is a mutable reference to such a function. Hence, in B.ml, the function call eOr e1 e2 creates and returns a new function f; when f is called with an argument $v$, it calls either e1 or e2 with $v$ (based on a coin-toss) and returns the result. The functions call, ePar, eRef, and eRefUpdate are implemented similarly.

A VM is modelled as a *partition*: a named collection of processes sharing state in the form of local communication channels. A value of type vm is a name of a partition plus a channel on which events for the VM are triggered. Hence, in E$m$.ml, the function call create$N$Role $i_1...i_n$ creates a new VM consisting of a partition a and a fresh channel ev; a contains newly spawned processes that use the procedures in $i_1...i_n$ to implement the exported procedures $o_1...o_m$; the processes in a may also send events on ev. For example, the function call createOrderEntryRole ePay eProc creates a partition a with a single process that listens for order requests on a fresh local channel c, then calls the payment procedure ePay and the order processing procedure eProc before returning a response; createOrderEntryRole returns the partition name a and a fresh event channel ev; it also returns an output procedure f that when given an argument $v$, sends $v$ on the channel $c$ within a and returns the response. The function call eVM vm h spawns a process that listens for events e on the event channel corresponding to vm and executes h e. A VM snapshot contains the state of a partition; hence snapshotVM vm saves the current values of all the channels and processes of the partition corresponding to vm; restoreVM ss restores a saved partition.

Each imported service $N$ in $m$ is modelled as a process listening on a global channel $N$chan. For example, the external payment service Payment1 is modelled as a process listening for requests on the channel Payment1Chan. In E$m$.ml, the function call import$N$ () returns a procedure that takes an argument $v$, forwards it on to $N$chan, and returns the response. Conversely, for each exported service $N$ in $m$, the function call export$N$ e listens for requests on a global channel $N$chan and forwards them to the procedure e.

## 6  Message Safety

Since the APIs available to a Baltic script are strongly typed, any system of VMs and intermediaries assembled by a Baltic script is well-typed by construction. In this section, we give an informal description of message safety and its proof by typing. The formal details are in a technical report [Bhargavan et al., 2007].

Let an *entity* be any source of a SOAP message; entities include remote clients and servers, intermediaries on the Baltic server, VMs, and the Baltic script itself.

Let an entity *respect a procedure of type* $(\alpha,\beta)$ proc if and only if

(1) each SOAP message sent by the entity to the procedure has type $\alpha$; and
(2) each SOAP message sent by the entity in response to a message to the procedure has type $\beta$.

The desired property of a system generated by a Baltic script is the following.

**Message Safety Property.** For any metadata $m$, if
  (1) the Baltic script is well-typed against E$m$.mli and B.mli
  (2) all remote entities respect the procedures in $m$, and
  (3) disk images respect the procedures they import and export
then all entities arising during a run respect all procedures.

Many interconnection errors, where servers or intermediaries are connected to the wrong addresses, lead to entities not respecting procedures. Our safety property guarantees, by static type-checking, that such errors cannot arise.

Assuming points (1), (2), and (3) of the Message Safety Property, we can construct a well-typed ML expression that represents the message-passing behaviour of a complete Baltic system. To do so, we generate an ML interface X$m$.mli consisting of typed ML channels to represent each of the procedures exported and imported by $m$. In the case of our running example, this interface is as follows:

```
val Payment1: (Payment × string chan) chan
val Payment2: (Payment × string chan) chan
val OrderEntry: (Order × string chan) chan
```

Our ML expression for the whole system is the composition B.ml E$m$.ml S.ml O.ml of the following modules.

(1) B.ml is the symbolic implementation of the B.mli interface. It has no dependencies.
(2) E$m$.ml is the symbolic implementation of the E$m$.mli and X$m$.mli interfaces. It depends on the interface B.mli provided by B.ml.
(3) S.ml is the Baltic script. It depends on the interfaces B.mli and E$m$.mli provided by B.ml and E$m$.ml.
(4) O.ml represents the remote entities, that is, the external clients and services. It depends on the interface X$m$.mli provided by E$m$.ml.

Since the dependencies of each of the modules in B.ml E$m$.ml S.ml O.ml are provided by preceding members, the whole composition is well-typed. The message safety property can then be obtained from type safety for ML.

We formalize this argument in the technical report [Bhargavan et al., 2007]. In fact, to model VMs with snapshots we need to develop a concurrent $\lambda$-calculus, called the *partitioned $\lambda$-calculus*. We prove type safety theorems for the *partitioned $\lambda$-calculus*. By appeal to these theorems, we formalize the composition B.ml E$m$.ml S.ml O.ml as a $\lambda$-calculus expression, and hence prove the Message Safety Property as a theorem about the partitioned $\lambda$-calculus.

# 7   Related Work

*Related Systems.* Edinburgh LCFG [Anderson, 1994] is a well-developed system for managing the configuration of large numbers of Unix-like machines. LCFG can configure software within disk images, a task not addressed by the Baltic operators. On the other hand, LCFG does not support intermediaries, and uses an untyped scripting language, while Baltic introduces the idea of representing server roles as typed functions.

HP SmartFrog [Goldsack et al., 2003] is a domain-specific language for describing server components, together with an implementation for activating and managing them. The original version worked with JVM-based components, but a more recent version uses operating system virtualization. Like LCFG, SmartFrog can describe the structure of server roles. SmartFrog has a type system, but is not service-oriented, in the sense of treating a server role as importing and exporting typed procedures.

The AppLogic grid operating system [3TERA 2006] allows VM server farms to be constructed and managed with a graphical editor. AppLogic grids are configurable using conventional scripting languages.

HPorter [Huang et al., 2007] is another combinator library written in a functional language for combining and reconfiguring software components written in lower-level languages. HPorter is aimed at robotics applications, and manages pre-existing components written in C and C++, that communicate over TCP/IP sockets. HPorter is written in the pure functional language Haskell, and relies on Haskell's higher-order type theory to encapsulate imperative behaviour.

Like Baltic, PiDuce [Carpineti et al., 2006] is a language and implementation for building SOAP web services, with a formal semantics. Unlike Baltic, PiDuce expresses the behaviour of individual services directly, whereas Baltic relies on pre-existing disk images to implement individual services, and concentrates on management.

*Related Formalisms.* We build both our actual implementation and our formal semantics using the technique of dual concrete and abstract implementations of interfaces; this technique was introduced by Bhargavan et al. [2006].

Our use of the $\lambda$-calculus with partitions as a semantics for combinations of virtual machines is a refinement of an earlier proposal, by Gordon [2005], that operating system virtualization can usefully be formalized using process calculi. There are other process calculi with operators to snapshot, restore, and duplicate running locations, including the Kell Calculus [Schmitt and Stefani, 2005; Lienhardt et al., 2007] and the Seal Calculus [Castagna et al., 2005]. A great many formalisms—see Lapadula et al. [2007], for example, and its bibliography—have been developed to represent orchestration, choreography, and dynamic discovery of web services. We do not address these advanced topics, and instead focus on management of pre-existing systems using simple request/response patterns of SOAP messaging; such systems are the common case in server farms today.

# 8   Conclusions and Future Work

We have described a set of combinators for assembling networks of virtual machines that export SOAP services. A combination of typechecking together with automated allocation of addresses prevents the troublesome configuration errors that may arise with alternatives, such as untyped scripts. There is a semantics based on a typed concurrent $\lambda$-calculus with partitions, and an implementation using Virtual Server with scripts in ML. Our test scripts manage pre-existing components from a sample multi-tier web application.

In future work, we intend to address some of the limitations in our present implementation. Our implementation does not consider security (we are essentially trusting the code on disk images), or the control of multiple VMMs (for performance and fault tolerance), or persistent state (any transient changes to disk images are discarded). A lightweight mechanism to customize each instance of the same disk image would be useful. Intermediaries are limited to SOAP request/responses and do not maintain SOAP-level sessions. We support SOAP services but neither arbitrary webpages nor database connections. On the basis of our formal semantics, we intend to develop techniques for reasoning about operations logic expressed using our combinators.

*Acknowledgments.* Conversations with Úlfar Erlingsson, Philippa Gardner, Galen Hunt, Dave Langworthy, Alan Schmitt, Clemens Syzperski, and Paul Watson were useful. Questions raised during a presentation of a preliminary version of Baltic at the Semantics Lunch at the University of Cambridge Computer Laboratory were extremely useful; thanks are due in particular to Andy Pitts, Peter Sewell, and Viktor Vafeiadis. Galen Hunt suggested the term "operations logic".

# Bibliography

AppLogic: Grid Operating System for Utility Computing. 3TERA (September 2006), http://0301.netclime.net/1_5/8/A/8/3teraAppLogic0906.pdf

Amazon Elastic Compute Cloud (Amazon EC2) - Limited Beta. Amazon Web Services LLC (August 2006), http://aws.amazon.com/ec2

Anderson, P.: Towards a High-Level Machine Configuration System. In: Proceedings of the 8th Large Installations Systems Administration (LISA) Conference, Berkeley, CA, pp. 19–26 (1994)

Armstrong, B.: Professional Microsoft Virtual Server 2005. Wiley, Chichester (2007)

Barham, P., Dragovic, B., Fraser, K., Hand, S., Harris, T., Ho, A., Neugebauer, R., Pratt, I., Warfield, A.: Xen and the art of virtualization. In: Symposium on Operating Systems Principles (SOSP 2003), pp. 164–177 (2003)

Bavier, A., Chun, B., Culler, D., Karlin, S., Muir, S., Peterson, L., Roscoe, T., Spalink, T., Wawrzoniak, M.: Operating system support for planetary-scale network services. In: NSDI 2004 (2004)

Bhargavan, K., Fournet, C., Gordon, A.D., Tse, S.: Verified interoperable implementations of security protocols. In: 19th IEEE Computer Security Foundations Workshop (CSFW 2006), pp. 139–152 (2006)

Bhargavan, K., Gordon, A.D., Narasamdya, I.: Service combinators for farming virtual machines. Technical Report MSR–TR–2007–165, Microsoft Research (2007)

Box, D., Ehnebuske, D., Kakivaya, G., Layman, A., Mendelsohn, N., Nielsen, H., Thatte, S., Winer, D.: Simple Object Access Protocol (SOAP) 1.1 (2000)

Carpineti, S., Laneve, C., Padovani, L.: Piduce—a project for experimenting web services technologies (2006), http://www.cs.unibo.it/PiDuce/

Castagna, G., Vitek, J., Zappa Nardelli, F.: The seal calculus. Information and Computation 201(1), 1–54 (2005)

Christensen, E., Curbera, F., Meredith, G., Weerawarana, S.: Web Services Description Language (WSDL) 1.1 (2001)

Dean, J., Ghemawat, S.: MapReduce: simplified data processing on large clusters. In: Sixth Symposium on Operating System Design and Implementation (OSDI 2004), pp. 137–150 (2004)

Garfinkel, S.: Commodity grid computing with Amazon's S3 and EC2. login, 7–13 (February 2007)

Goldsack, P., Guijarro, J., Lain, A., Mecheneau, G., Murray, P., Toft, P.: SmartFrog: Configuration and automatic ignition of distributed applications, 2003. In: Presented at 2003 HP Openview University Association conference (2003), http://www.hpl.hp.com/research/smartfrog/

Gordon, A.D.: V for Virtual. In: Algebraic Process Calculi: The First Twenty Five Years and Beyond, pp. 114–117 (2005) (Available as BRICS Note NS–05–3, University of Aarhus)

Hoykhet, A., Lange, J., Dinda, P.: Virtuoso: A system for virtual machine marketplaces. Technical Report NWU-CS-04-39, Northwestern University, URL (2004), http://virtuoso.cs.northwestern.edu/NWU-CS-04-39.pdf

Huang, L., Hudak, P., Peterson, J.: HPorter: Using Arrows to Compose Parallel Processes. In: Hanus, M. (ed.) PADL 2007. LNCS, vol. 4354, pp. 275–289. Springer, Heidelberg (2006)

Preboot Execution Environment (PXE) Specification. Intel Corporation and SystemSoft (1999), available at http://www.pix.net/software/pxeboot/archive/ pxespec.pdf

Lapadula, A., Pugliese, R., Tiezzi, F.: A Calculus for Orchestration of Web Services. In: De Nicola, R. (ed.) ESOP 2007. LNCS, vol. 4421, pp. 33–47. Springer, Heidelberg (2007)

Lienhardt, M., Schmitt, A., Stefani, J.-B.: OZ/K: A kernel language for component-based open programming. In: Generative Programming and Component Engineering (GPCE 2007) (2007)

Meyer, R.A., Seawright, L.H.: A virtual machine time-sharing system. IBM Systems Journal 9(3), 199–218 (1970)

Nagaraja, K., Oliveira, F., Bianchini, R., Martin, R.P., Nguyen, T.D.: Understanding and dealing with operator mistakes in internet services. In: OSDI 2004: Proceedings of the 6th Symposium on Operating Systems Design & Implementation, Berkeley, CA, USA, pp. 61–76, USENIX Association (2004)

Oppenheimer, D., Ganapathi, A., Patterson, D.A.: Why do Internet services fail, and what can be done about it? In: 4th Usenix Symposium on Internet Technologies and Systems (USITS 2003) (2003)

Pallmann, D.: Programming Indigo: The Code Name for the Unified Framework for Building Service-Oriented Applications on the Microsoft Windows Platform. Microsoft Press (2005)

Schmitt, A., Stefani, J.-B.: The Kell calculus: A family of higher-order distributed process calculi. In: Priami, C., Quaglia, P. (eds.) GC 2004. LNCS, vol. 3267, pp. 146–178. Springer, Heidelberg (2005)

Syme, D., Granicz, A., Cisternino, A.: Expert F#. Apress (2007)

Wolf, C., Halter, E.M.: Virtualization: from the desktop to the enterprise. Apress (2005)

# Timed Soft Concurrent Constraint Programs[*]

Stefano Bistarelli[1,2], Maurizio Gabbrielli[3], Maria Chiara Meo[1],
and Francesco Santini[2,4]

[1] Dipartimento di Scienze, Università "G. D'Annunzio" di Chieti-Pescara, Italy
`bista@sci.unich.it,cmeo@unich.it`
[2] Istituto di Informatica e Telematica (CNR), Pisa, Italy
`stefano.bistarelli@iit.cnr.it, francesco.santini@iit.cnr.it`
[3] Dipartimento di Scienze dell'Informazione, Università di Bologna, Italy
`gabbri@cs.unibo.it`
[4] IMT - Institute for Advanced Studies, Lucca, Italy
`f.santini@imtlucca.it`

**Abstract.** We propose a timed and soft extension of Concurrent Constraint Programming. The time extension is based on the hypothesis of *bounded asynchrony*: the computation takes a bounded period of time and is measured by a discrete global clock. Action prefixing is then considered as the syntactic marker which distinguishes a time instant from the next one. Supported by soft constraints instead of crisp ones, *tell* and *ask* agents are now equipped with a preference (or consistency) threshold which is used to determine their success or suspension. In the paper we provide a language to describe the agents behavior, together with its operational and denotational semantics, for which we also prove the compositionality and correctness properties. Agents negotiating *Quality of Service* can benefit from this new language, by coordinating among themselves and mediating their preferences.

## 1  Introduction

Time is a particularly important aspect of cooperative environments. In many "real-life" computer applications, the activities have a temporal duration (that can be even interrupted) and the coordination of such activities has to take into consideration this timeliness property. The interacting actors are mutually influenced by their actions, meaning that $A$ reacts accordingly to the timeliness and "quality" of $B$'s behavior and vice versa. In fact, these interactions can be often related to quantities to be measured or minimized/maximized, in order to take actions depending from this result: consider, for example, some generic communicating-agents that need to negotiate a desired *Quality of Service* (*QoS*). In this case, they both need to coordinate through time-dependent decisions and to quantify and publish their respective requirements. These agents can be instantiated to concrete instances, such as web services, internet QoS architectures and mechanisms that provide QoS, workflows and, in general, software agents.

---

[*] The first and fourth authors are supported by the MIUR PRIN 2005-015491.

D. Lea and G. Zavattaro (Eds.): COORDINATION 2008, LNCS 5052, pp. 50–66, 2008.

In [8] *Timed Concurrent Constraint Programming* (*tccp*), a timed extension of the pure formalism of *Concurrent Constraint Programming* (*ccp*) [19], is introduced. This extension is based on the hypothesis of *bounded asynchrony* (as introduced in [20]): computation takes a bounded period of time rather than being instantaneous as in the concurrent synchronous languages ESTEREL [1], LUSTRE [12], SIGNAL [15] and Statecharts [13]. Time itself is measured by a discrete global clock, i.e, the internal clock of the *tccp* process. In [8] they also introduced *timed reactive sequences* which describe at each moment in time the reaction of a *tccp* process to the input of the external environment. Formally, such a reaction is a pair of constraints $\langle c, d \rangle$, where $c$ is the input given by the environment and $d$ is the constraint produced by the process in response to $c$ (due to the monotonicity of *ccp* computations, $c$ includes always the input).

Soft constraints [2,3] extend classical constraints to represent multiple consistency levels, and thus provide a way to express preferences, fuzziness, and uncertainty. The *ccp* framework has been extended to work with soft constraints [4], and the resulting framework is named *Soft Concurrent Constraint Programming* (*sccp*). With respect to *ccp*, in *sccp* the *tell* and *ask* agents are equipped with a preference (or consistency) threshold which is used to determine their success, failure, or suspension, as well as to prune the search; these preferences should preferably be satisfied but not necessarily (i.e. over-constrained problems).

In this paper we introduce a timed and soft extension of *ccp* that we call *Timed Soft Concurrent Constraint Programming* (*tsccp*), inheriting from both *tccp* and *sccp* at the same time. In *tccp*, action-prefixing is interpreted as the next-time operator and the parallel execution of agents follows the scheduling policy of maximal parallelism. Additionally, *tccp* includes a simple new primitive which allows to specify timing constraints. We adopt soft constraints (and the related *sccp*) instead of crisp ones, since we are sure that classic constraints can show evident limitations if applied to entities interactions, mainly because they do not appear to be very flexible when trying to represent real-life scenarios, where the knowledge is not completely available nor crisp. The introduced *Timed Soft Concurrent Constraint* (*tscc*) language, together with its semantics, results in a formal framework where it is possible to solve QoS related problems.

The agents use the centralized constraint store in order to ensure their community acts in a coherent manner, where "coherence" refers to how well a system of agents behaves as a unit. With *tccp*, the agent coordination is enriched with both timed and quantitative/qualitative aspects at the same time; this represents the most important expressivity improvement w.r.t. related works (see Sec. 8). One of the most straightforward applications is represented by the modelling of negotiation and management of resources, since both time and preference are naturally part of the problem. In Sec. 7 we show an example where we model an auction process, which can be seen as a particular instance of negotiation.

In Sec. 2 we sum up the most important background notions and frameworks from which *tsccp* derives, i.e. *tccp* and *sccp*. In Sec. 3 the *tscc* language is presented for the first time. Then, Sec. 4 and Sec. 5 respectively describe the operational and denotational semantics of the *tscc* agents. Section 6 outlines the proof of the denotational model correctness with the aid of *connected reactive sequences*. At last, Sec. 7 shows an application example of the language and Sec. 8 concludes by discussing related work and indicating future research.

## 2   Background

### 2.1   Soft Concurrent Constraint System

A semiring is a tuple $\langle A, +, \times, \mathbf{0}, \mathbf{1} \rangle$ such that: *i)* $A$ is a set and $\mathbf{0}, \mathbf{1} \in A$; *ii)* $+$ is commutative, associative and $\mathbf{0}$ is its unit element; *iii)* $\times$ is associative, distributes over $+$, $\mathbf{1}$ is its unit element and $\mathbf{0}$ is its absorbing element. A c-semiring is a semiring $\langle A, +, \times, \mathbf{0}, \mathbf{1} \rangle$ such that: $+$ is idempotent, $\mathbf{1}$ is its absorbing element and $\times$ is commutative. Let us consider the relation $\leq_S$ over $A$ such that $a \leq_S b$ iff $a + b = b$. Then it is possible to prove that (see [3]): *i)* $\leq_S$ is a partial order; *ii)* $+$ and $\times$ are monotone on $\leq_S$; *iii)* $\mathbf{0}$ is its minimum and $\mathbf{1}$ its maximum; *iv)* $\langle A, \leq_S \rangle$ is a complete lattice and, for all $a, b \in A$, $a + b = lub(a, b)$ (where *lub* is the *least upper bound*). $\langle A, \leq_S \rangle$ is a complete distributive lattice and $\times$ its *glb* (*greatest lower bound*). Informally, the relation $\leq_S$ gives us a way to compare semiring values and constraints: when we have $a \leq_S b$, we will say that $b$ *is better than* $a$. In the following, when the semiring will be clear from the context, $a \leq_S b$ will be often indicated by $a \leq b$.

A *soft constraint* [2,3] may be seen as a constraint where each instantiation of its variables has an associated preference. Given a semiring $S = \langle A, +, \times, \mathbf{0}, \mathbf{1} \rangle$ and a set of variables $V$ over a finite domain $D$, a soft constraint is a function which, given an assignment $\eta : V \to D$ of the variables, returns a value of the semiring. Using this notation $\mathcal{C} = \eta \to A$ is the set of all possible constraints that can be built starting from $S$, $D$ and $V$.

Any function in $\mathcal{C}$ involves all the variables in $V$, but we impose that it depends on the assignment of only a finite subset of them. So, for instance, a binary constraint $c_{x,y}$ over variables $x$ and $y$, is a function $c_{x,y} : V \to D \to A$, but it depends only on the assignment of variables $\{x, y\} \subseteq V$ (the *support* of the constraint, or *scope*). Note that $c\eta[v := d_1]$ means $c\eta'$ where $\eta'$ is $\eta$ modified with the assignment $v := d_1$. The partial order $\leq$ over $A$ can be easily extended among constraints by defining $c_1 \sqsubseteq c_2 \iff c_1\eta \leq c_2\eta$.

Given the set $\mathcal{C}$, the combination function $\otimes : \mathcal{C} \times \mathcal{C} \to \mathcal{C}$ is defined as $(c_1 \otimes c_2)\eta = c_1\eta \times c_2\eta$ (see also [2,3,4]). Informally, performing the $\otimes$ between two constraints means building a new constraint whose support involves all the variables of the original ones, and which associates with each tuple of domain values for such variables a semiring element which is obtained by multiplying the elements associated by the original constraints to the appropriate sub-tuples.

Given a constraint $c \in \mathcal{C}$ and a variable $v \in V$, the *projection* [2,3,4] of $c$ over $V - \{v\}$, written $c \Downarrow_{(V - \{v\})}$ is the constraint $c'$ s.t. $c'\eta = \sum_{d \in D} c\eta[v := d]$. Informally, projecting means eliminating some variables from the support. This is done by associating with each tuple over the remaining variables a semiring element which is the sum of the elements associated by the original constraint to all the extensions of this tuple over the eliminated variables.

To treat the hiding operator of the language, a general notion of existential quantifier is introduced by using notions similar to those used in cylindric algebras. Consider a set of variables $V$ with domain $D$ and the corresponding soft constraint system $C$. For each $x \in V$ the hiding function [2,4] is the function $(\exists_x c)\eta = \sum_{d_i \in D} c\eta[x := d_i]$.

To model parameter passing, for each $x, y \in V$ a diagonal constraint [2,4] is defined as $d_{xy} \in C$ s.t., $d_{xy}\eta[x := a, y := b] = 1$ if $a = b$ and $d_{xy}\eta[x := a, y := b] = 0$ if $a \neq b$. Now it is possible to define a constraint systems "a la Saraswat" [4]. Consider the set $C$ and the partial order $\sqsubseteq$. Then an entailment relation $\vdash \subseteq \wp(C) \times C$ is defined s.t. for each $C \in \wp(C)$ and $c \in C$, we have $C \vdash c \iff \bigotimes C \sqsubseteq c$ (see also [2,4]). Notice that in $sccp$, algebricity is not required, since the algebraic nature of the structure $C$ strictly depends on the properties of the semiring [4].

If we consider a semiring $S = \langle A, +, \times, 0, 1 \rangle$, a domain of the variables $D$, a set of variables $V$, the corresponding structure $C$, then $S_C = \langle C, \otimes, \bar{0}, \bar{1}, \exists_x, d_{xy} \rangle^1$ is a cylindric constraint system [4].

## 2.2 Timed Concurrent Constraint Programming

When querying the store for some information which is not present (yet), a $(s)ccp$ agent will simply suspend until the required information has arrived. In timed applications however often one cannot wait indefinitely for an event. Consider for example the case of a connection to a web service providing some on-line banking facility. In case the connection cannot be established, after a reasonable amount of time an appropriate time-out message has to be communicated to the user. A timed language should then allow us to specify that, in case a given time bound is exceeded (i.e. a *time-out* occurs), the wait is interrupted and an alternative action is taken.

In order to be able to specify this kind of timing constraints, in [20] and [8] the authors introduced a different timed extension of $ccp$ (the differences between these two languages are explained in [8]). In particular, the timed ccp ($tccp$) language defined in [8] introduces a discrete global clock and assumes that *ask* and *tell* actions take one time-unit. Computation evolves in steps of one time-unit, so called clock-cycles, which are syntactically separated by action prefixing. Moreover *maximal parallelism* is assumed, that is at each moment every enabled agent of the system is activated (this implies that parallel processes are executed on different processors). Finally in $tccp$ it is introduced a primitive construct of the form **now** $c$ **then** $A$ **else** $B$ which can be interpreted as follows: if the constraint $c$ is entailed by the store at the current time $t$ then the above agent behaves as $A$ at time $t$, otherwise it behaves as $B$ at time $t$. By using the **now** construct one can express time-out, preemption and other timed programming idioms. For example, the agent **now** $c$ **then** $A$ **else** $ask(true) \to$ (**now** $c$ **then** $A$ **else** $B$) waits at most two time unit for the satisfaction of the guard $c$: If the

---

[1] $\bar{0}$ and $\bar{1}$ that represent respectively the constraints associating $0$ and $1$ to all the assignment of domain values.

guard is satisfied (in two time units) then the agent behaves as A, otherwise as B. By using an inductive definition it is easy to define in terms of the **now** the more general time-out agent $(\Sigma_{i=1}^{n}\textbf{ask}(c_i) \longrightarrow A_i)$ **timeout**$(m)B$ which allows to wait at most $m$ time units for the satisfaction of one of the guards (see [8]).

# 3   Timed Soft Concurrent Constraint Programming

In this section we present the *tscc* language, which originates from both *tccp* and *sccp*. To obtain *tscc* we extend the *cc* language by introducing constructs to handle the cut level and constructs to handle temporal aspects. More precisely, we inherit from *sccp* the **tell** and **ask** constructs enriched by a threshold, which allows to specify when the agents have to succeed or to suspend. Moreover we derive from *tccp* the timing construct **now** $c$ **then** $A$ **else** $B$ previously mentioned. However, differently from the case of *tccp*, the **now** operator here is modified by using thresholds, analogously to the case of **tell** and **ask**.

**Definition 1 (*tscc* Language).** *Given a soft constraint system* $\langle S, D, V \rangle$*, the corresponding structure* $\mathcal{C}$*, any semiring value* $a$ *and any constraint* $\phi \in \mathcal{C}$*, the syntax of the tscc language is given by the following grammar:*

$$P ::= F.A$$
$$F ::= p(x) :: A$$
$$A ::= \textbf{success} \mid \textbf{tell}(c) \rightarrow_\phi A \mid \textbf{tell}(c) \rightarrow^a A \mid E \mid A \parallel A \mid \exists x A \mid p(x) \mid$$
$$\quad \Sigma_{i=1}^{n} E_i \mid \textbf{now}_\phi \ c \ \textbf{then} \ A \ \textbf{else} \ B \mid \textbf{now}^a \ c \ \textbf{then} \ A \ \textbf{else} \ B$$
$$E ::= \textbf{ask}(c) \rightarrow_\phi A \mid \textbf{ask}(c) \rightarrow^a A$$

*where, as usual,* $P$ *is the class of processes,* $F$ *is the class of sequences of procedure declarations (or clauses),* $A$ *is the class of agents. The* $c$ *is supposed to be a soft constraint in* $\mathcal{C}$*. A tsccp process* $P$ *is then an object of the form F.A, where* $F$ *is a set of procedure declarations of the form* $p(x) :: A$ *and* $A$ *is an agent.*

In the following, given an agent $A$, we denote by $Fv(A)$ the set of the free variables of $A$ (namely, the variables which do not appear in the scope of the $\exists$ quantifier). As previously mentioned, differently from the original *cc* syntax in *tsccp* we have a semiring element $a$ and constraint $\phi$ to be checked whenever an *ask* or *tell* operation is performed. Intuitively the level $a$ (resp., $\phi$) will be used as a cut level to prune computations that are not good enough. These levels, with an analogous meaning, are present also in the **now** $c$ **then** $A$ **else** $B$ construct, differently from all the previous cc like languages. The remaining of the syntax is standard: Action prefixing is denoted by $\rightarrow$, $\Sigma$ denotes guarded choice, $\parallel$ indicates parallel composition and a notion of locality is introduced by the agent $\exists x A$ which behaves like $A$ with $x$ considered local to $A$, thus hiding the information on $x$ provided by the external environment. In the following we also assume guarded recursion, that is we assume that each procedure call is in the scope of either an **ask** or a **tell** construct.

# 4   An Operational Semantics for *tsccp* Agents

The operational model of *tscc* agents can be formally described by a transition system $T = (Conf, \longrightarrow)$ where we assume that each transition step takes exactly one time-unit. Configurations (in) *Conf* are pairs consisting of a process and a constraint in $\mathcal{C}$ representing the common *store*. The transition relation $\longrightarrow \subseteq Conf \times Conf$ is the least relation satisfying the rules **R1-R17** in Fig. 1 and characterizes the (temporal) evolution of the system. So, $\langle A, \gamma \rangle \longrightarrow \langle B, \delta \rangle$ means that if at time $t$ we have the process $A$ and the store $\gamma$ then at time $t+1$ we have the process $B$ and the store $\delta$. Let us now briefly discuss the rules in Fig. 1.

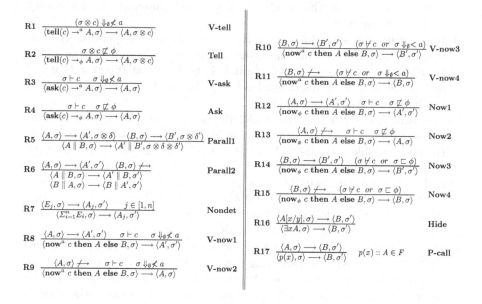

**Fig. 1.** The transition system for *tsccp*

**Valued-tell.** The valued-tell rule checks for the $a$-consistency of the *Soft Constraint Satisfaction Problem* [2] (SCSP) defined by the store $\sigma \otimes c$. A SCSP $P$ is $a$-consistent if $blevel(P) = a$, where $blevel(P) = Sol(P) \Downarrow_\emptyset$, i.e. the *best level of consistency* of the problem $P$ is a semiring value representing the least upper bound among the values yielded by the solutions. Rule **R1** can be applied only if the store $\sigma \otimes c$ is $b$-consistent with $b \not< a^2$. In this case the agent evolves to the new agent $A$ over the store $\sigma \otimes c$. Note that different choices of the *cut level* $a$ could possibly lead to different computations. Finally note that the updated store $\sigma \otimes c$ will be visible only starting from the next time instant since each transition step involves exactly one time-unit.

---

[2] Notice that we use $b \not< a$ instead of $b \geq a$ because we can possibly deal with partial orders. The same happens also in other transition rules with $\not\sqsupseteq$ instead of $\sqsupseteq$.

**Tell.** The tell action is a finer check of the store. In this case, a pointwise comparison between the store $\sigma \otimes c$ and the constraint $\phi$ is performed. The idea is to perform an overall check of the store and to continue the computation only if there is the possibility to compute a solution not worse than $\phi$. As for the valued tell, the updated store will be visible from the next time instant.

**Valued-ask.** The semantics of the valued-ask is extended in a way similar to what we have done for the valued-tell action. This means that, to apply the rule, we need to check if the store $\sigma$ entails the constraint $c$ and also if the store is "consistent enough" w.r.t. the threshold $a$ set by the programmer.

**Ask.** Similar to the *tell* rule, here a finer (pointwise) threshold $\phi$ is compared to the store $\sigma$. Notice that we need to check $\sigma \not\sqsubseteq \phi$ because previous tells could have a different threshold $\phi'$ and could not guarantee the consistency of the resulting store.

**Nondeterminism.** According to rule **R7** the guarded choice operator gives rise to global non-determinism: the external environment can affect the choice since $\mathbf{ask}(c_j)$ is enabled at time $t$ (and $A_j$ is started at time $t + 1$) if and only if the store $\sigma$ entails $c_j$ (and is compatible with the threshold), and $\sigma$ can be modified by other agents.

**Parallelism.** Rules **R5** and **R6** model the parallel composition operator in terms of *maximal parallelism*: the agent $A \parallel B$ executes in one time-unit all the initial enabled actions of $A$ and $B$. Considering rule **R5**, notice that the ordering of the operands in $\sigma \otimes \delta \otimes \delta'$ is not relevant, since $\otimes$ is commutative and associative. Moreover, for the same two properties, if $\sigma \otimes \delta = \sigma \otimes \gamma$ and $\sigma \otimes \delta' = \sigma \otimes \gamma'$, we have that $\sigma \otimes \delta \otimes \delta' = \sigma \otimes \gamma \otimes \gamma'$. Therefore the resulting store $\sigma \otimes \delta \otimes \delta'$ is independent from the choice of the constraint $\delta$ such that $\langle A, \sigma \rangle \longrightarrow \langle A', \sigma' \rangle$ and $\sigma' = \sigma \otimes \delta$ (analogously for $\delta'$).

**Hidden variables.** The agent $\exists x A$ behaves like $A$, with $x$ considered *local* to $A$. This is obtained by substituting the variable $x$ for a variable $y$ which we assume to be new and not used by any other process (standard renaming techniques can be used to ensure this); here $A[x/y]$ denotes the process obtained from $A$ by replacing the variable $x$ for the variable $y$.

**Procedure calls.** Rule **R17** treats the case of a procedure call when the actual parameter equals the formal parameter. We do not need more rules since, for the sake of simplicity, here and in the following we assume that the set $F$ of procedure declarations is closed w.r.t. parameter names: that is, for every procedure call $p(y)$ appearing in a process $F.A$ we assume that if the original declaration for $p$ in $F$ is $p(x) :: A$ then $F$ contains also the declaration $p(y) :: \exists x(\mathbf{tell}(d_{xy}) \parallel A)$[3]. Moreover, we assume that if $p(x) :: A \in F$ then $Fv(A) \subseteq x$.

**Valued-Now.** The rules **R8-R11** show that the agent $\mathbf{now}^a\ c\ \mathbf{then}\ A\ \mathbf{else}\ B$ behaves as $A$ if $c$ is entailed by the store and the store is "consistent enough" w.r.t. the threshold $a$, and behaves as $B$ otherwise. Note that, differently from the case of the ask here the evaluation of the guard is instantaneous:

---

[3] Here the (original) formal parameter is identified as a local alias of the actual parameter.

if $\langle A, \sigma \rangle$ $(\langle B, \sigma \rangle)$ can make a transition at time $t$ and the condition on the store and the cut level are satisfied then the agent **now** $c$ **then** $A$ **else** $B$ can make the same transition at time $t$ (and analogously for B). Moreover observe that, due to rules **R9** and **R11**, in any case the control is passed either to $A$ (if the conditions are satisfied) or to $B$ (if not), also if $A$ and $B$ cannot make any transition at the current time instant.

**Now.** The rules **R12-R15** are similar to rules **R8-R11** described before, with the exception that here a finer (pointwise) threshold $\phi$ is compared to the store $\sigma$, analogously to what happens with the Tell and Ask agents.

Using the transition system described by (the rules in) Fig. 1 we can now define our notion of observables, which considers for each *tsccp* process $P = F.A$, the results of successful terminating computations that the agent $A$ can perform.

**Definition 2 (Observables).** *Let $P = F.A$ be a* tsccp *process. We define*

$$\mathcal{O}_{io}(P) = \{\gamma \downarrow_{Fv(A)} | \langle A, \bar{1} \rangle \longrightarrow^* \langle \textbf{Success}, \gamma \rangle\},$$

where **Success** is any agent which contains only occurrences of the agent **success** and of the operator $\|$.

## 5   The Denotational Model

In this section we define a denotational characterization of the operational semantics obtained by following the construction in [8] and using *timed reactive sequences* to represent *tsccp* computations. These sequences are similar to those used in the semantics of dataflow languages [14], imperative languages [7] and (timed) *ccp* [10,8].

The denotational model associates with a process a set of timed reactive sequences of the form $\langle \sigma_1, \gamma_1 \rangle \cdots \langle \sigma_n, \gamma_n \rangle \langle \sigma, \sigma \rangle$ where a pair of constraints $\langle \sigma_i, \gamma_i \rangle$ represents a reaction of the given process at time i: intuitively, the process transforms the global store from $\sigma_i$ to $\gamma_i$ or, in other words, $\sigma_i$ is the assumption on the external environment while $\gamma_i$ is the contribution of the process itself (which entails always the assumption). The last pair denotes a "stuttering step" in which the agent **Success** has been reached. Since the basic actions of *tsccp* are monotonic and we can also model a new input of the external environment by a corresponding tell operation, it is natural to assume that reactive sequences are monotonic. So in the following we will assume that each timed reactive sequence $\langle \sigma_1, \gamma_1 \rangle \cdots \langle \sigma_{n-1}, \gamma_{n-1} \rangle \langle \sigma_n, \sigma_n \rangle$ satisfies the following condition: $\gamma_i \vdash \sigma_i$ and $\sigma_j \vdash \gamma_{j-1}$, for any $i \in [1, n-1]$ and $j \in [2, n]$.

The set of all reactive sequences is denoted by $\mathcal{S}$ and its typical elements by $s, s_1 \ldots$, while sets of reactive sequences are denoted by $S, S_1 \ldots$ and $\varepsilon$ indicates the empty reactive sequence. Furthermore, $\cdot$ denotes the operator that concatenates sequences. In the following, *Process* denotes the set of *tsccp* processes.

Formally the definition of the semantics is as follows.

**Definition 3 (Processes Semantics).** *The semantics* $R \in Process \to \mathcal{P}(\mathcal{S})$ *is defined as the least fixed-point of the operator* $\Phi \in (Process \to \mathcal{P}(\mathcal{S})) \to Process \to \mathcal{P}(\mathcal{S})$ *defined by*

$$\Phi(I)(F.A) = \{\langle \sigma, \delta \rangle \cdot w \in \mathcal{S} \mid \langle A, \sigma \rangle \to \langle B, \delta \rangle \; and \; w \in I(F.B)\}$$
$$\cup$$
$$\{\langle \sigma, \sigma \rangle \cdot w \in \mathcal{S} \mid \; \langle A, \sigma \rangle \not\to \; and \; either \; A \neq \mathbf{Success} \; and \; w \in I(F.A)$$
$$or \; A = \mathbf{Success} \; and \; w \in I(F.A) \cup \{\varepsilon\}\}.$$

The ordering on $Process \to \mathcal{P}(\mathcal{S})$ is that of (point-wise extended) set-inclusion and since it is straightforward to check that $\Phi$ is continuous, standard results ensure that the least fixpoint exists (and it is equal to $\sqcup_{n \geq 0} \Phi^n(\bot)$).

Note that $R(F.A)$ is the union of the set of all successful reactive sequences which start with a reaction of $P$ and the set of all successful reactive sequences which start with a stuttering step of $P$. In fact, when an agent is blocked, i.e. it cannot react to the input of the environment, a stuttering step is generated. After such a stuttering step the computation can either continue with the further evaluation of $A$ (possibly generating more stuttering steps) or it can terminate, if $A$ is the **Success** agent. Note also that, since the **Success** agent used in the transition system cannot make any move, an arbitrary (finite) sequence of stuttering steps is always appended to each reactive sequence.

### 5.1 Compositionality of the Denotational Semantics for *tsccp* Processes

In order to prove the compositionality of the denotational semantics we now introduce a semantics $[\![F.A]\!](e)$ which is compositional by definition and where, for technical reasons, we represent explicitly the environment $e$ which associates a denotation to each procedure identifier. More precisely, assuming that $Pvar$ denotes the set of procedure identifier, $Env = Pvar \to \mathcal{P}(\mathcal{S})$, with typical element $e$, is the set of *environments*. Given $e \in Env$, $p \in Pvar$ and $f \in \mathcal{P}(\mathcal{S})$, we denote by $e' = e\{f/p\}$ the new environment such that $e'(p) = f$ and $e'(p') = e(p')$ for each procedure identifier $p' \neq p$.

Given a process $F.A$, the denotational semantics $[\![F.A]\!] : Env \to \mathcal{P}(\mathcal{S})$ is defined by the equations in Fig. 2, where $\mu$ denotes the least fixpoint w.r.t. subset inclusion of elements of $\mathcal{P}(\mathcal{S})$. The semantic operators appearing in Fig. 2 are formally defined as follows. Intuitively they reflect, in terms of reactive sequences, the operational behavior of their syntactic counterparts[4].

We first need the following definition. Let $\sigma, \phi$ and $c$ be constraints in $\mathcal{C}$ and let $a \in \mathcal{A}$. We say that

$$- \sigma \tilde{\to}^a c, \; if \; (\sigma \vdash c \; and \; \sigma \Downarrow_\emptyset \not< a) \quad while \quad \sigma \tilde{\to}_\phi c, \; if \; (\sigma \vdash c \; and \; \sigma \not\sqsubseteq \phi).$$

**Definition 4 (Semantic operators).** *Let* $S, S_i$ *be sets of reactive sequences,* $c, c_i$ *be constraints and let* $\tilde{\to}_i$ *be either of the form* $\tilde{\to}^{a_i}$ *or* $\tilde{\to}_{\phi_i}$. *Then we define the operators* $\tilde{tell}, \tilde{\sum}, \tilde{\|}, \tilde{now}$ *and* $\tilde{\exists}x$ *as follows:*

---

[4] In Fig. 2 the syntactic operator $\to_i$ is either of the form $\to^{a_i}$ or $\to_{\phi_i}$.

**The (valued) tell operator**

$$\tilde{tell}^a(c, S) = \{s \in \mathcal{S} \mid s = \langle \sigma, \sigma \otimes c \rangle \cdot s', \ \sigma \otimes c \Downarrow_\emptyset \not< a \ and \ s' \in S \ \}.$$

$$\tilde{tell}_\phi(c, S) = \{s \in \mathcal{S} \mid s = \langle \sigma, \sigma \otimes c \rangle \cdot s', \ \sigma \otimes c \not\sqsubseteq \phi \ and \ s' \in S \ \}.$$

**The guarded choice**

$$\tilde{\sum}_{i=1}^{n} c_i \tilde{\to}_i S_i = \{ s \cdot s' \in \mathcal{S} \mid s = \langle \sigma_1, \sigma_1 \rangle \cdots \langle \sigma_m, \sigma_m \rangle, \sigma_j \tilde{\not\to}_i c_i$$
$$for \ each \ j \in [1, m\text{-}1], i \in [1, n],$$
$$\sigma_m \tilde{\to}_h c_h \ and \ s' \in S_h \ for \ an \ h \in [1, n] \ \}$$

**The parallel composition.** *Let* $\tilde{\parallel} \in \mathcal{S} \times \mathcal{S} \to \mathcal{S}$ *be the (commutative and associative) partial operator defined as follows:*

$$\langle \sigma_1, \sigma_1 \otimes \gamma_1 \rangle \cdots \langle \sigma_n, \sigma_n \otimes \gamma_n \rangle \langle \sigma, \sigma \rangle \ \tilde{\parallel} \ \langle \sigma_1, \sigma_1 \otimes \delta_1 \rangle \cdots \langle \sigma_n, \sigma_n \otimes \delta_n \rangle \langle \sigma, \sigma \rangle =$$
$$\langle \sigma_1, \sigma_1 \otimes \gamma_1 \otimes \delta_1 \rangle \cdots \langle \sigma_n, \sigma_n \otimes \gamma_n \otimes \delta_n \rangle \langle \sigma, \sigma \rangle.$$

*We define* $S_1 \tilde{\parallel} S_2$ *as the point-wise extension of the above operator to sets.*
**The (valued) now operator**

$$\tilde{now}^a(c, S_1, S_2) = \{s \in \mathcal{S} \mid s = \langle \sigma, \sigma' \rangle \cdot s' \ and \ either \ \sigma \tilde{\to}^a c \ and \ s \in S_1$$
$$or \ \sigma \tilde{\to}^a c \ does \ not \ hold \ and \ s \in S_2 \ \}.$$

$$\tilde{now}_\phi(c, S_1, S_2) = \{s \in \mathcal{S} \mid s = \langle \sigma, \sigma' \rangle \cdot s' \ and \ either \ \sigma \tilde{\to}_\phi c \ and \ s \in S_1$$
$$or \ \sigma \tilde{\to}_\phi c \ does \ not \ hold \ and \ s \in S_2 \ \}.$$

**The hiding operator.** *The semantic hiding operator can be defined as follows:*

$$\tilde{\exists} x S = \{s \in \mathcal{S} \mid there \ exists \ s' \in S \ such \ that \ s = s'[x/y] \ with \ y \ new \ \}$$

*where* $s'[x/y]$ *denotes the sequence obtained from* $s'$ *by replacing the variable* $x$ *for the variable* $y$ *that we assume to be new[5].*

A few explanations are in order here. The semantic (valued) tell operator reflects in the obvious way the operational behavior of the syntactic (valued) tell. Concerning the semantic choice operator, a sequence in $\tilde{\sum}_{i=1}^{n} c_i \tilde{\to}_i S_i$ consists of an initial period of waiting for a store which satisfies one of the guards. During this waiting period only the environment is active by producing the constraints $\sigma_j$ while the process itself generates the stuttering steps $\langle \sigma_j, \sigma_j \rangle$. When the store is strong enough to satisfy a guard, that is to entail a $c_h$ and to satisfy the condition on the cut level the resulting sequence is obtained by adding $s' \in S_h$ to the initial waiting period. In the semantic parallel operator defined on sequences we require that the two arguments of the operator agree at each point of time with

---

[5] To be more precise, we assume that each time that we consider a new applications of the operator $\tilde{\exists}$ we use a new, different $y$. As in the case of the operational semantics, this can be ensured by a suitable renaming mechanism.

**E1** $[\![F.\text{success}]\!](e) = \{\langle\sigma_1,\sigma_1\rangle\langle\sigma_2,\sigma_2\rangle\cdots\langle\sigma_n,\sigma_n\rangle \in \mathcal{S} \mid n \geq 1\}$

**E2** $[\![F.\text{tell}(c) \rightarrow^a A]\!](e) = \tilde{tell}^a(c, [\![F.A]\!](e))$

**E3** $[\![F.\text{tell}(c) \rightarrow_\phi A]\!](e) = \tilde{tell}_\phi(c, [\![F.A]\!](e))$

**E4** $[\![F.\sum_{i=1}^n \text{ask}(c_i) \rightarrow_i A_i]\!](e) = \tilde{\sum}_{i=1}^n c_i \tilde{\rightarrow}_i [\![F.A_i]\!](e)$

**E5** $[\![F.\text{now}^a \ c \ \textbf{then} \ A \ \textbf{else} \ B]\!](e) = \tilde{now}^a(c, [\![F.A]\!](e), [\![F.B]\!](e))$

**E6** $[\![F.\text{now}_\phi \ c \ \textbf{then} \ A \ \textbf{else} \ B]\!](e) = \tilde{now}_\phi(c, [\![F.A]\!](e), [\![F.B]\!](e))$

**E7** $[\![F.A \parallel B]\!](e) = [\![F.A]\!](e) \tilde{\parallel} [\![G.B]\!](e)$

**E8** $[\![F.\exists x A]\!](e) = \tilde{\exists} x [\![F.A]\!](e)$

**E9** $[\![F.p(x)]\!](e) = \mu\Psi$     where $\Psi(f) = [\![F \setminus \{p\}.A]\!](e\{f/p\}), \quad p(x) :: A \in F$

**Fig. 2.** The semantics $[\![F.A]\!](e)$

respect to the contribution of the environment (the $\sigma_i$'s) and that they have the same length (in all other cases the parallel composition is assumed being undefined).

If $F.A$ is a closed process, that is if all the procedure names occurring in $A$ are defined in $F$, then $[\![F.A]\!](e)$ does not depend on $e$ and will be indicated as $[\![F.A]\!]$. Environments in general allow us to define the semantics also of processes which are not closed. The following result shows the correspondence between the two semantics we have introduced and therefore the compositionality of $R(F.A)$.

**Theorem 1 (Compositionality).** *If $F.A$ is closed then $R(F.A) = [\![F.A]\!]$ holds.*

The proof of Theo. 1 is similar to the one proposed in [8] for the compositionality property of the *tccp* denotational semantics.

## 6   Correctness

The observables $\mathcal{O}_{io}(P)$ describing the input/output pairs of successful computations can be obtained from $R(P)$ by considering suitable sequences, namely those sequences which do not perform assumptions on the store. In fact, notice that some reactive sequences do not correspond to real computations: Clearly, when considering a real computation no further contribution from the environment is possible. This means that, at each step, the assumption on the current store must be equal to the store produced by the previous step. In other words, for any two consecutive steps $\langle\sigma_i,\sigma_i'\rangle\langle\sigma_{i+1},\sigma_{i+1}'\rangle$ we must have $\sigma_i' = \sigma_{i+1}$. So we are led to the following.

**Definition 5 (Connected Sequences).** *Let $s = \langle\sigma_1,\sigma_1'\rangle\langle\sigma_2,\sigma_2'\rangle\cdots\langle\sigma_n,\sigma_n\rangle$ be a reactive sequence. We say that $s$ is connected if $\sigma_1 = \bar{1}$ and $\sigma_i = \sigma_{i-1}'$ for each $i, 2 \leq i \leq n$.*

According to the previous definition, a sequence is connected if all the information assumed on the store is produced by the process itself, apart from the initial input. To be defined as connected, a sequence must also have $\bar{1}$ as the initial constraint. A connected sequence represents a *tsccp* computation, as it will be proved by the following theorem.

**Theorem 2 (Correctness).** *For any process $P = F.A$ we have*

$$\mathcal{O}_{io}(P) = \{\sigma_n \downarrow_{Fv(A)} | \text{ there exists a connected sequence } s \in R(P) \text{ such that}$$
$$s = \langle \sigma_1, \sigma_2 \rangle \langle \sigma_2, \sigma_3 \rangle \cdots \langle \sigma_n, \sigma_n \rangle \}.$$

The proof of Theo. 2 is similar to the one proposed in [8] for the correctness property of the *tccp* language.

## 7    Programming Idioms and an Auction Example

We can consider the primitives in Fig. 1 to derive the soft version of the programming idioms in [8], which are typical of reactive programming.

*Delay.* The delay constructs $\mathbf{tell}(c) \xrightarrow{t}_\phi A$ or $\mathbf{ask}(c) \xrightarrow{t}_\phi A$ are used to delay the execution of agent $A$ after the execution of $\mathbf{tell}(c)$ or $\mathbf{ask}(c)$; $t$ is the number of the time-units of delay. Therefore, in addiction to a constraint $\phi$, in *tsccp* the transition arrow can have also a number of delay slots. This idiom can be defined by induction: the base case is $\xrightarrow{0}_\phi A \equiv \longrightarrow_\phi A$ and the inductive step is $\xrightarrow{n+1}_\phi A \equiv \longrightarrow_\phi \mathbf{tell}(\bar{1}) \xrightarrow{n}_\phi A$. The valued version can be defined in an analogous way.

*Timeout.* The timed guarded choice agent $(\Sigma_{i=1}^n \mathbf{ask}(c_i) \longrightarrow_i A_i) \mathbf{timeout}(m) B$ waits at most $m$ time-units ($m \geq 0$) for the satisfaction of one of the guards; notice that all the ask actions have a "soft" transition arrow, i.e. $\longrightarrow_i$ is either of the form $\longrightarrow_{\phi_i}$ or $\longrightarrow^{a_i}$, as in Fig. 1. Before this time-out, the process behaves just like the guarded choice: as soon as there exist enabled guards, one of them (and the corresponding branch) is nondeterministically selected. After waiting for $m$ time-units, if no guard is enabled, the timed choice agent behaves as B.

*Watchdog.* Watchdogs are used to interrupt the activity of a process on a signal from a specific event. The idiom $\mathbf{do}\ (A)\ \mathbf{watching}(c)\ \mathbf{else}\ (B)$ behaves as $A$, as long as $c$ is not entailed by the store; when $c$ is entailed, the process $A$ is immediately aborted. The reaction is instantaneous, in the sense that $A$ is aborted at the same time instant of the detection of the entailment of $c$.

Both *Timeout* and *Watchdogs* constructs can be assembled through the composition of several $\mathbf{now}_\phi\ c\ \mathbf{then}\ A\ \mathbf{else}\ B$ or $\mathbf{now}^a\ c\ \mathbf{then}\ A\ \mathbf{else}\ B$ primitives, exactly as sketched in Section 2.2 and explained in detail in [8] (in the soft version of the timeout, the $\mathbf{else}\ \mathbf{ask}(true)$ in Sec. 2.2 must be replaced with $\mathbf{else}\ \mathbf{ask}(\bar{1})$). For example, $\mathbf{do}\ (\mathbf{tell}(c_1))\ \mathbf{watching}(c_2)\ \mathbf{else}\ B \equiv \mathbf{now}\ c_2\ \mathbf{then}\ B\ \mathbf{else}\ \mathbf{tell}(c_1)$, where the $\mathbf{now}$ can be valued or not. Clearly, in *tsccp* all the constraints (e.g. $c_1$ and $c_2$) are soft. With this small set of idioms, we have now enough expressiveness to describe complex interactions.

In Fig. 3 we model the negotiation and the management of a generic service offered with a sort of auction: auctions, as other forms of negotiation, naturally need both timed and qualitative/quantitative means to describe the interactions among agents. The auctioneer (i.e. $AUCTIONEER$ in Fig. 3) begins by offering a service described with the soft constraint $c_{A_1}$. We suppose that the cost associated to the soft constraint is expressed in terms of computational capabilities needed to support the execution: $c_1 \sqsubseteq c_2$ means that the service described by $c_1$ needs more computational resources than $c_2$. By choosing the proper semiring, this load can be expressed as a percentage of the CPU use, or in terms of money, for example. We suppose that a constraint can be defined over three domains of QoS features: availability, reliability and execution time. For instance, $c_{A_1}$ could be *availability* $> 95\% \wedge$ *reliability* $> 99\% \wedge$ *execution time* $< 3sec$. Clearly, providing a higher availability or reliability, and a lower execution time implies raising the computational resources, thus worsening the preference of the store.

$\underline{AUCTIONEER} ::$
$INIT\_A \longrightarrow$
  **tell**$(c_{A_1}) \xrightarrow{t_{sell}} (\Sigma_{i=1}^n$**ask**$(bidder_i = i) \longrightarrow^{a_A}$ **tell**$(winner = i) \longrightarrow CHECK)$ **timeout**$(wait_{auct})$
    **tell**$(c_{A_2}) \xrightarrow{t_{sell}} (\Sigma_{i=1}^n$**ask**$(bidder_i = i) \longrightarrow^{a_A}$ **tell**$(winner = i) \longrightarrow CHECK)$ **timeout**$(wait_{auct})$
      **tell**$(c_{A_3}) \xrightarrow{t_{sell}} (\Sigma_{i=1}^n$**ask**$(bidder_i = i) \longrightarrow^{a_A}$ **tell**$(winner = i) \longrightarrow CHECK)$ **timeout**$(wait_{auct})$
        $\longrightarrow$ **success**

$\underline{CHECK} ::$
  **do** ( (**ask**$(service = end) \longrightarrow$ **success**) **timeout**$(wait_{check})$ **tell**$(service = interrupt)$ )
    **watching**$(c_{check})$ **else** (**tell**$(service = interrupt) \longrightarrow STOP_c)$

$\underline{BIDDER_i} ::$
$INIT\_B_i \longrightarrow$
  **do** ( $TASK_i$ ) **watching**$(c_{B_i})$ **else** **ask**$(\bar{1}) \xrightarrow{t_{buy_i}}$ **tell**$(bidder_i = i) \longrightarrow$
    ( (**ask**$(winner = i) \longrightarrow USE_i) + ($**ask**$(winner \neq i) \longrightarrow$ **success**) )

$\underline{USE_i} ::$
  **do** ( $USE\_SERVICE_i \longrightarrow$ **tell**$(service = end) \longrightarrow$ **success** )
    **watching**$(service = interrupt)$ **else** $(STOP_i)$

$\underline{AUCTION\&SUPERVISE} :: AUCTIONEER \parallel BIDER_1 \parallel BIDDER_2 \parallel \ldots \parallel BIDDER_n$

**Fig. 3.** An "auction and management" example for a generic service

After the offer, the auctioneer gives time to the bidders (each of them described with a possibly different $BIDDER_i$ agent in Fig. 3) to make their offer, since the choice of the winner is delayed by $t_{sell}$ time-units (as in many real-world auction schemes). A level $a_A$ is used to effectively check that the global consistency of the store is enough good, i.e. the computational power would not be already consumed under the given threshold. After the winner is nondeterministically chosen among all the bidders asking for the service, the auctioneer becomes a supervisor of the used resource by executing the $CHECK$ agent. Otherwise, if no offer is received within $wait_{auct}$ time-units, a timeout interrupts the wait and the auctioneer improves the offered service by adding a new constraint: for example, in $\mathbf{tell}(c_{A_2})$, $c_{A_2}$ could be equivalent to $execution\ time < 1sec$, thus reducing the latency of the service (from 3 to 1 seconds) and consequently raising, at the same time, its computational cost (i.e. $c_{A_2} \otimes \sigma \sqsubseteq \sigma$, we worsen the consistency level of the store). The same offer/wait process is repeated three times in Fig. 3. Each of the bidders in Fig. 3 is executing its own task (i.e. $TASK_i$), but as soon as the offered resource meets its demand of computational power (i.e. $c_{B_i}$ is satisfied by the store: $\sigma \sqsubseteq c_{B_i}$), the bidder is interrupted and then asks to use the service. The time needed to react and make an offer is modeled with $t_{buy_i}$: fast bidders will have more chances to win the auction, if their request arrives before the choice of the auctioneer. If one bidder wins, then it becomes a user of the resource, by executing $USE_i$.

The $USE_i$ agent uses the service (with the $USE\_SERVICE_i$ agent, left generic in Fig. 3), but it stops ($STOP_i$ agent, left generic in Fig. 3) as soon as the service is interrupted, i.e. as the store satisfies $service = interrupt$. On the other side, the $CHECK$ agent waits for the use termination, but it interrupts the user if the computation takes too long (more than $wait_{check}$ time-units), or if the user absorbs the computational capabilities beyond a given threshold, i.e. as soon as the $c_{check}$ becomes implied by the store (i.e. $\sigma \sqsubseteq c_{check}$): in fact, $USE\_SERVICE_i$ could be allowed to ask for more power by "telling" some more constraints to the store. To interrupt the service use, the $CHECK$ agent performs a $\mathbf{tell}(service = interrupt)$. All the $INIT$ agents, left generic in Fig. 3, can be used to initialize the computation.

In order to avoid a heavy notation in Fig. 3, we do not show the preference associated to constraints and the consistency check label on the transition arrows, when they are not significant for the example description.

Many other real-life automated tasks can be modeled with the $tscc$ language, for example a quality-driven composition of web services: the agents that represent different web services can add to the store their functionalities (represented by soft constraints) with $\mathbf{tell}$ actions; the final store models their composition. The consistency level of the store sums up to a value the (for example) total cost of the single obtained service, or a value representing the consistency of the integrated functionalities: the reason is that when we compose the services offered by different providers, we could not be sure how much they are compatible. Then, a client wishing to use the composed service can perform an $\mathbf{ask}$ with threshold that prevents it from paying a high price or having an unreliable service. Softness is useful also to model incomplete service specifications that may evolve incrementally and, in general, non-functional aspects. Time sensitiveness is clearly needed too: all the most important orchestration/choreography languages of today (e.g. $BPEL4WS$ and $WSCI$) support timeouts, the raising of events and delay activities [18].

# 8   Related and Future Work

We have introduced the *tscc* language in order to join together the expressive capabilities of soft constraints and timing mechanisms in a new programming framework. The agents modeled with this language are now able to deal with time and preference dependent decisions that can often be found during complex interactions: an example can be represented by entities that need to negotiate a satisfying QoS and manage generic resources. Mechanisms as timeout and interrupt can be very useful when waiting for pending conditions or when triggering some new necessary actions. All the *tsccp* rules have been formally described by a transition system and then also with a denotational characterization of the operational semantics obtained with the use of *timed reactive sequences*. The resulting semantics has been proved to be compositional and correct.

Other timed extension of concurrent constraint programming have been proposed in [16,17,20], however these languages, differently from *tsccp*, do not take into account quantitative aspects; therefore, this achievement represents a very important expressivity improvement w.r.t. related works. These have been considered by Di Pierro and Wiklicky who have extensively studied probabilistic *ccp* (see for example [11]). This language provides a construct for probabilistic choice which allows one to express randomness in a program, without assuming any additional structure on the underlying constraint system. This approach is therefore deeply different from ours. Recently stochastic *ccp* has been introduced in [6] to model biological systems. This language is obtained by adding a stochastic duration to the ask and tell primitives, thus differs from ours.

A first improvement of *tsccp* can be the inclusion of a *fail* agent in the syntax given in Definition 1. The transition system we have defined considers only successful computations. If this could be a reasonable choice in a don't know interpretation of the language it will lead to an insufficient analysis of the behavior in a pessimistic interpretation of the indeterminism. A second extension for this framework could be represented by considering *interleaving* (as in the classical *ccp*) instead of *maximal parallelism*, which is the scheduling policy followed in this paper when observing the parallel execution of agents. According to this policy, at each moment every enabled agent of the system is activated, while in the first paradigm an agent could not be assigned to a "free" processor.

Clearly, since we have dynamic process creation, a maximal parallelism approach has the disadvantage that in general it implies the existence of an unbound number of processes. On the other hand a naif interleaving semantic could be problematic form the time viewpoint, as in principle the time does not pass for enabled agent which are not scheduled. A possible solution, analogous to that one adopted in [9], could be to assume that the parallel operator is interpreted in terms of interleaving, as usual, however we must assume maximal parallelism for actions depending on time. In other words, time passes for all the parallel processes involved in a computation. To summarize, we could adopt maximal parallelism for time elapsing (i.e. for evaluating a (valued) **now** agent) and an interleaving model for basic computation steps (i.e. (valued) **ask** and (valued) **tell** actions).

At last, we would like to consider other time management strategies (as the one proposed in [21]) and to study how timing and non-monotonic constructs [5] can be integrated together.

# References

1. Berry, G., Gonthier, G.: The esterel synchronous programming language: design, semantics, implementation. Sci. Comput. Program. 19(2), 87–152 (1992)
2. Bistarelli, S. (ed.): Semirings for Soft Constraint Solving and Programming. LNCS, vol. 2962. Springer, Heidelberg (2004)
3. Bistarelli, S., Montanari, U., Rossi, F.: Semiring-based constraint satisfaction and optimization. J. ACM 44(2), 201–236 (1997)
4. Bistarelli, S., Montanari, U., Rossi, F.: Soft concurrent constraint programming. ACM Trans. Comput. Logic 7(3), 563–589 (2006)
5. Bistarelli, S., Santini, F.: A nonmonotonic soft constraint based language to model QoS negotiation. In: Doctoral Consortium of AAAI 2008, AAAI Press, Menlo Park (2008) (to appear)
6. Bortolussi, L.: Stochastic concurrent constraint programming. Electr. Notes Theor. Comput. Sci. 164(3), 65–80 (2006)
7. Brookes, S.D.: Full abstraction for a shared variable parallel language. In: LICS, pp. 98–109. IEEE Computer Society, Los Alamitos (1993)
8. de Boer, F.S., Gabbrielli, M., Meo, M.C.: A timed concurrent constraint language. Inf. Comput. 161(1), 45–83 (2000)
9. de Boer, F.S., Gabbrielli, M., Meo, M.C.: A timed linda language and its denotational semantics. Fundam. Inf. 63(4), 309–330 (2004)
10. de Boer, F.S., Palamidessi, C.: A fully abstract model for concurrent constraint programming. In: Abramsky, S. (ed.) TAPSOFT 1991, CCPSD 1991, and ADC-Talks 1991. LNCS, vol. 494, pp. 296–319. Springer, Heidelberg (1991)
11. Di Pierro, A., Wiklicky, H.: Probabilistic Concurrent Constraint Programming: Towards a Fully Abstract Model. In: Brim, L., Gruska, J., Zlatuška, J. (eds.) MFCS 1998. LNCS, vol. 1450, pp. 446–455. Springer, Heidelberg (1998)
12. Halbwachs, N., Caspi, P., Raymond, P., Pilaud, D.: The synchronous data-flow programming language LUSTRE. Proceedings of the IEEE 79(9), 1305–1320 (1991)
13. Harel, D.: Statecharts: A visual formalism for complex systems. Sci. Comput. Program. 8(3), 231–274 (1987)
14. Jonsson, B.: A model and proof system for asynchronous networks. In: PODC 1985: Proceedings ACM symposium on Principles of distributed computing, New York, USA, pp. 49–58. ACM Press, New York (1985)
15. le Guernic, P., le Borgne, M., Gautier, T., le Maire, C.: Programming real-time applications with signal. Proceedings of the IEEE 79(9), 1321–1336 (1991)
16. Nielsen, M., Valencia, F.D.: Temporal concurrent constraint programming: Applications and behavior. In: Brauer, W., Ehrig, H., Karhumäki, J., Salomaa, A. (eds.) Formal and Natural Computing. LNCS, vol. 2300, pp. 298–324. Springer, Heidelberg (2002)
17. Palamidessi, C., Valencia, F.D.: A Temporal Concurrent Constraint Programming Calculus. In: Walsh, T. (ed.) CP 2001. LNCS, vol. 2239, pp. 302–316. Springer, Heidelberg (2001)
18. Peltz, C.: Web services orchestration and choreography. Computer 36(10), 46–52 (2003)

19. Saraswat, V.: Concurrent constraint programming languages, PhD thesis (January 1989)
20. Saraswat, V., Jagadeesan, R., Gupta, V.: Timed default concurrent constraint programming. J. Symb. Comput. 22(5-6), 475–520 (1996)
21. Valencia, F.D.: Timed Concurrent Constraint Programming: Decidability Results and Their Application to LTL. In: Palamidessi, C. (ed.) ICLP 2003. LNCS, vol. 2916, pp. 422–437. Springer, Heidelberg (2003)

# Multiparty Sessions in SOC[*]

Roberto Bruni[1], Ivan Lanese[2], Hernán Melgratti[3], and Emilio Tuosto[4]

[1] Dipartimento di Informatica, Università di Pisa, Italy
bruni@di.unipi.it
[2] Dipartimento di Scienze dell'Informazione, Università di Bologna, Italy
lanese@cs.unibo.it
[3] Departamento de Computación, Universidad de Buenos Aires, Argentina
hmelgra@dc.uba.ar
[4] Department of Computer Science, University of Leicester, UK
et52@mcs.le.ac.uk

**Abstract.** Service oriented applications feature interactions among several participants over the network. Mechanisms such as correlation sets and two-party sessions have been proposed in the literature to separate messages sent to different instances of the same service. This paper presents a process calculus featuring dynamically evolving multiparty sessions to model interactions that spread over several participants. The calculus also provides primitives for service definition/invocation and for structured communication in order to highlight the interactions among the different concepts. Several examples from the SOC area show the suitability of our approach.

## 1 Introduction

Service Oriented Computing (SOC, for short) envisages systems as a combination of *services*, possibly provided by different organizations. Typically, a service can be concurrently requested by many invokers (e.g., users or other services) so that many service instances can be carried on at the same time (e.g., several customers booking flights from the same airline). Hence, it is important to guarantee that the interactions taking place in different instances do not interfere, and messages are routed to the intended recipients.

Emerging standards like WS-BPEL [23] and WS-CDL [25] exploit the idea of *correlation sets*, which allow messages to be routed to specific instances of services depending on a pre-defined subset of the invocation parameters (e.g., requests are routed according to usernames). Though correlation sets guarantee a good expressiveness, we argue that they make analysis harder because the emerging patterns of interaction rely on data values. Also, unrelated sessions can interfere with each other if they know (or use by chance) the "right" values.

Some formal methods [3,19,2,16,4,12] advocate the concept of *session* as an abstraction mechanism for enclosing an arbitrarily complex interaction between

---

[*] Research supported by the EU Project FET-GC II IST-2005-16004 SENSORIA by the UK project HIDEA4SOC and by the Italian FIRB project TOCAI.

D. Lea and G. Zavattaro (Eds.): COORDINATION 2008, LNCS 5052, pp. 67–82, 2008.
© Springer-Verlag Berlin Heidelberg 2008

two partners in order to guarantee e.g., that, during a conversation, messages are routed as desired. As observed e.g. in [2], since modern distributed systems rely on the TCP/IP stack, it is usually accepted that sessions involve only two participants (usually according to the client/server architecture). Consider a scenario where a customer $c$ of a bank $b$ wants to withdraw some money from an ATM $a$; this can be modeled as $c$ invoking the service $a$ that in turn invokes $b$, which closes the protocol by e.g., sending a text message on $c$'s mobile phone. Usually, two different sessions, say $s$ and $s'$, are used during the computation (see, e.g., [2]): $s$ is a session between $c$ and $a$ while $s'$ between $a$ and $b$. Typically, this forces the programmer to explicitly handle communication of $s$ and $s'$ in order to relate events occurring in the two sessions.

In this paper we propose $\mu$se (read "muse", after "MUltiparty SEssion"), a process calculus whose primitives are designed for easing the programming of SOC systems using *multiparty sessions*, namely sessions to which more than two actors can take part, as a high-level abstraction mechanism to coordinate interactions among several participants. We also intend to highlight the relations between sessions and the other main features of SOC: services, communication protocols, sites, etc.

One of $\mu$se main design principles is that programmers should be relieved from the explicit handling of session identifiers. The rationale being that, in our opinion, SOC systems should be programmed by abstracting from the error-prone activity of session handling. Rather, the language should support the implicit creation and exchange of session identifiers. For instance, the previous ATM scenario can be more easily programmed in $\mu$se by merging $s$ and $s'$ into a session delimiting exactly $c$, $a$ and $b$; $\mu$se semantics then guarantees that interactions among $c$, $a$ and $b$ are not disturbed by external processes (cf. Example 3). Another example can be an online game where a server provides the playing platform and users can log into different games. While logged in, users "in the same room" can interact according to a game-specific protocol without interference from users in other rooms. This can be naturally modeled using a multiparty session for each room that would avoid the complication of maintaining the association room/players required if two-party sessions (each containing player and server) were used.

Another important design choice concerns $\mu$se communications, which can be *intra-* or *extra-session*. More precisely, $\mu$se requires that participants on different sites always use intra-session communications, namely they must be endpoints of the same session. Instead, processes at the same site are allowed to communicate also across sessions. Intuitively, co-located processes can exploit local resources (e.g., databases, file systems, etc.) to interact, while remote processes must rely on underlying middlewares (like TCP/IP, SOAP, ... ).

To this end, $\mu$se systems consist of sites where services, sessions and processes live. Services can be dynamically published, sessions are dynamically created, new participants can join them at runtime and concurrent ongoing sessions can be merged. We equip $\mu$se with a (weak) bisimilarity-based equivalence whose appropriateness is illustrated by means of a small proxy scenario.

*Structure of the paper:* The $\mu$se calculus is introduced in Section 2: Section 2.1 provides an informal description of the main elements of the calculus, while Section 2.2 and Section 2.3 formally define the language. The coding of several interaction patterns is given in Section 3. Section 4 proposes an observational semantics for $\mu$se based on the standard notion of weak bisimulation. Related work and final remarks are presented in Section 5.

## 2    The $\mu$se Calculus

This section introduces the $\mu$se calculus and its main features: $(i)$ nested multi-party and dynamically joinable sessions, $(ii)$ intra-session and intra-site communications, $(iii)$ dynamic service publication.

### 2.1    A $\mu$se Walkthrough

$\mu$se has been designed so to keep a clear conceptual distinction, even at the syntax level, between different concerns distilled from the SOC paradigm. This allows for an incremental presentation of the calculus that can serve to emphasize also the interplay between the various features considered.

*Services and multiparty sessions.* The kernel syntax of $\mu$se includes ordinary operators such as the nil process $\mathbf{0}$, parallel composition $P|Q$ and name restriction $(\nu n)P$, together with primitives for service definition, for service invocation, for enclosing a process in a session and for dynamically installing new services.

Available services are written $a \Rightarrow P$, where $a$ is the service name and $P$ is its body. Notably, services are one-shot and not persistent by default: an invocation to $a$ consumes its service definition. New services are dynamically deployed using the prefix $\mathsf{install}[a \Rightarrow P]$, that, combined with recursion, permits to program persistent services (see Example 2 in Section 3), for which we use the syntactic sugar

$$* a \Rightarrow P \tag{1}$$

A session is a logical unit of work composed by different endpoints possibly distributed across sites. Each endpoint is written $r \triangleright Q$, where $r$ is the session name and $Q$ is one of the participants to session $r$. When the endpoint $r \triangleright Q$ invokes $a$ (executing prefix $\mathsf{invoke}\ a$), a new instance $r \triangleright P$ of service $a$ in (1) is activated on the service site as a new partner of session $r$. In fact, $r \triangleright P$ is a service endpoint of session $r$.

Sessions can be nested at an arbitrary level of depth. Services are always installed at the top level and can be invoked from any level of nesting; the instance of the invoked service is opened, in the server context, as an endpoint of the innermost session containing the invoker.

Different endpoints $r \triangleright P_1, ..., r \triangleright P_n$ within the same session can interact by means of *intra-session* input and output prefixes (respectively written $x(y)$ and $\overline{x}w$, reminiscent of $\pi$-calculus prefixes). The shared name $r$ is used to guarantee that messages are exchanged only between partners of the same session. Hence, two instances $r_1 \triangleright P$ and $r_2 \triangleright P$ of (1), invoked from two endpoints of two different sessions $r_1$ and $r_2$, run separately and cannot interfere (unless $r_1$ and $r_2$ are merged).

*Sites.* We envisage services as somehow analogous to methods of a class; therefore, a pool of services (and all their instances) may share some information (e.g., the instances of an airline reservation service must query and update a flights database). In $\mu$se this feature is realized by giving the possibility to group processes into sites and by adding primitives for intra-site communication. We write $l :: P$ where $l$ is the site name (also called location) and $P$ is the process located at $l$. Likewise sessions, sites are logical containers, not necessarily physical (machine-related) ones.

Intra-site input and output prefix are respectively written $x?(y)$ and $x!w$ and, as service invocation, they are executed regardless of the session hierarchy. We could have also used local variables for intra-site communications, but we preferred message passing to follow the style of intra-session communications.

*Merging sessions.* The most advanced feature of $\mu$se is the possibility of merging two distinct running sessions. This is possible only when two endpoints expose the same *entry point* $e$ via prefix $\mathsf{merge}^p\ e$, requiring to merge the respective sessions. Merge prefixes $\mathsf{merge}^p\ e$ are polarized with $p \in \{+, -\}$, with the obvious meaning that complementary merge actions on the same entry point $e$ (i.e., $\mathsf{merge}^+\ e$ and $\mathsf{merge}^-\ e$) can synchronize.

Merging of sessions is guided by entry points $e$ which yield a control flow mechanism for programming when processes can join sessions; for instance, using different entry points it is possible to let processes enter a session at different stages of the computation.

Technically, the merging of sessions is realized by explicit fusion of session names: after their fusion, two names can be used interchangeably wherever needed.

## 2.2  $\mu$se Syntax

We assume that countable pairwise disjoint sets of names are available for

- communication channels (ranged by $x, y, \dots$),
- services (ranged by $a, b, \dots$),
- entry points (ranged by $e, f, \dots$),
- sessions (ranged by $r, s, \dots$) and
- sites or locations (ranged by $l, \dots$).

Channels, services and entry points are *communicable values* (which are ranged over by $v, w, \dots$) while sessions and locations cannot be communicated. We let $n, m, \dots$ range over all names but locations.

The syntax of $\mu$se is defined in Figure 1, where the last two productions for processes account for recursion ($X, Y, \dots$ stand for process variables; we assume variables guarded by prefixes in the body of recursive definitions).

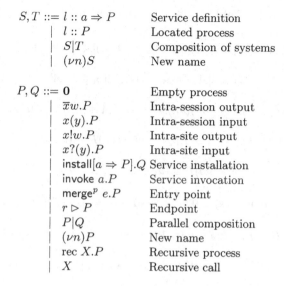

$$
\begin{aligned}
S, T ::= \;& l :: a \Rightarrow P && \text{Service definition} \\
| \;& l :: P && \text{Located process} \\
| \;& S | T && \text{Composition of systems} \\
| \;& (\nu n)S && \text{New name}
\end{aligned}
$$

$$
\begin{aligned}
P, Q ::= \;& \mathbf{0} && \text{Empty process} \\
| \;& \overline{x}w.P && \text{Intra-session output} \\
| \;& x(y).P && \text{Intra-session input} \\
| \;& x!w.P && \text{Intra-site output} \\
| \;& x?(y).P && \text{Intra-site input} \\
| \;& \mathsf{install}[a \Rightarrow P].Q && \text{Service installation} \\
| \;& \mathsf{invoke}\; a.P && \text{Service invocation} \\
| \;& \mathsf{merge}^p\; e.P && \text{Entry point} \\
| \;& r \triangleright P && \text{Endpoint} \\
| \;& P | Q && \text{Parallel composition} \\
| \;& (\nu n)P && \text{New name} \\
| \;& \mathsf{rec}\; X.P && \text{Recursive process} \\
| \;& X && \text{Recursive call}
\end{aligned}
$$

**Fig. 1.** Syntax of systems and processes

Systems (ranged over by $S, T, \ldots$) are parallel compositions of a finite number of *locations* where services are published and processes executed. A location where a service $a$ is defined is meant to be the domain into which all instances of $a$ are executed upon invocation.

A $\mu$se process can be the empty process (we will drop trailing $\mathbf{0}$s), a process prefixed by an action (discussed in the following), a process running in a session (endpoint), the parallel composition of processes, a process under a name restriction, a recursive process or a recursive invocation.

Processes (ranged over by $P, Q, \ldots$) communicate via channels very much like e.g., $\pi$-calculus processes, according to two featured modalities: *intra-session* and *intra-site* communication.

As outlined before, intra-session communications are used to let different endpoints of the same session to interact regardless their running sites. Hence, processes located at different sites but sharing the same session can interact via intra-session input and output. Conversely, intra-site communications allow different endpoints to communicate, provided that they are running in the same site. This is used to model local communications and eases the programming of activities that are independent of the specific session. For instance, a program that counts the invocations to services defined at a given location can be programmed simply as a located process that increments a given variable when it receives a service name via intra-site input on a given channel $x$; on invocation, each service sends its name to the counter with an intra-site output on $x$.

Processes can install new service definitions in their running locations. Service invocations enable processes to activate new endpoints on the service location. Note that service invocation requires only the service name, not its location, thus

**Table 1.** $\mu$se structural congruence

$$\mathcal{A}|\mathcal{A}' \equiv \mathcal{A}'|\mathcal{A} \qquad \mathcal{A}|\mathbf{0} \equiv \mathcal{A} \qquad (\mathcal{A}|\mathcal{A}')|\mathcal{A}'' \equiv \mathcal{A}|(\mathcal{A}'|\mathcal{A}'')$$

$$(\nu n)(\mathcal{A}|\mathcal{A}'') \equiv \mathcal{A}|(\nu n)\mathcal{A}'', \text{ if } n \notin \text{fn}(\mathcal{A})$$

$$(\nu n)(\nu m)\mathcal{A} \equiv (\nu m)(\nu n)\mathcal{A} \qquad (\nu n)\mathcal{A} \equiv \mathcal{A}, \text{ if } n \notin \text{fn}(\mathcal{A})$$

$$l :: P|l :: Q \equiv l :: (P|Q) \qquad l :: (\nu n)P \equiv (\nu n)(l :: P)$$

$$r \triangleright (\nu n)P \equiv (\nu n)(r \triangleright P), \text{ if } n \neq r$$

$$r \doteq r \equiv \mathbf{0} \qquad (\nu r)(r \doteq s) \equiv \mathbf{0} \qquad r \doteq s|P \equiv r \doteq s|P\{r/s\} \qquad r \doteq s \equiv s \doteq r$$

$$r \triangleright (s \doteq t|P) \equiv s \doteq t|r \triangleright P \qquad l :: (r \doteq s|P) \equiv r \doteq s|l :: P$$

$$\text{rec } X.P \equiv P\{\text{rec } X.P/X\}$$

if many services with the same name are available one of them is chosen nondeterministically. Finally, a mechanism for letting processes join existing sessions is given by the prefix merge$^p$ $e$.

Prefixes can be divided into two classes: *session-dependent* and *session-independent*. Intuitively, the former are those whose execution is dependent of and can be executed only within a session; while session independent prefixes do not depend on sessions and can be executed also outside them. The distinction will be clearer when the operational semantics is given, for the moment it suffices to say that intra-session input/output, session merge and service invocation are session-dependent, while intra-site input/output are session-independent.

Finally, usual process algebraic operators like parallel composition and name restriction are introduced, the latter is one of the binders of $\mu$se. In fact, the occurrences of $y$ and $n$ are bound in $x(y).P$, $x?(y).P$, $(\nu n)P$ and $(\nu n)S$ and the typical definitions of set of free, bound and all names, respectively written as fn(_), bn(_) and n(_), are assumed for systems and processes. As usual, bound names can be safely alpha renamed.

### 2.3 $\mu$se Operational Semantics

The semantics of $\mu$se requires a structural congruence relation and an extended syntax, namely *explicit substitutions* $r \doteq s$ of sessions. Note that explicit substitutions are session-independent. Let $\mathcal{A}, \mathcal{B}$ range over systems (including explicit substitutions) and processes.

**Definition 1 ($\mu$se structural congruence).** *The structural congruence over $\mu$se systems (and processes) is the smallest equivalence relation satisfying the axioms in Table 1 (where* fn($\mathcal{A}$) *is defined as expected).*

**Table 2.** Operational semantics

$$\bar{x}v.P \xrightarrow{\bar{x}v} P \qquad x!v.P \xrightarrow{x!v} P$$

$$x(y).P \xrightarrow{xv} P\{v/y\} \qquad x?(y).P \xrightarrow{x?v} P\{v/y\}$$

$$l :: a \Rightarrow P \xrightarrow{r\top a} l :: r \triangleright P \qquad \text{invoke } a.P \xrightarrow{\perp a} P \qquad \text{install}[a \Rightarrow R].P \xrightarrow{a[R]} P$$

$$\text{merge}^p \, e.P \xrightarrow{e^p} P$$

$$\frac{P \xrightarrow{\alpha} Q \quad \alpha \in \{\perp a, xv, \bar{x}v, e^p\}}{r \triangleright P \xrightarrow{r \, \alpha} r \triangleright Q} \qquad \frac{P \xrightarrow{\alpha} Q \quad \alpha \notin \{\perp a, xv, \bar{x}v, e^p\}}{r \triangleright P \xrightarrow{\alpha} r \triangleright Q}$$

$$\frac{P \xrightarrow{a[R]} Q}{l :: P \xrightarrow{\tau} l :: Q \mid l :: a \Rightarrow R} \qquad \frac{P \xrightarrow{\alpha} Q \quad \alpha \notin \{a[R], x?(v), x!v\}}{l :: P \xrightarrow{\alpha} l :: Q}$$

$$\frac{P \xrightarrow{x!v} P' \quad Q \xrightarrow{x?v} Q'}{P|Q \xrightarrow{\tau} P'|Q'} \qquad \frac{A \xrightarrow{\alpha} A' \quad \text{bn}(\alpha) \cap \text{fn}(\mathcal{B}) = \emptyset}{A|\mathcal{B} \xrightarrow{\alpha} A'|\mathcal{B}} \qquad \frac{A \xrightarrow{r \, \bar{x}v} A' \quad B \xrightarrow{r \, xv} \mathcal{B}'}{A|\mathcal{B} \xrightarrow{\tau} A'|\mathcal{B}'}$$

$$\frac{A \xrightarrow{re^+} A' \quad B \xrightarrow{se^-} \mathcal{B}'}{A|\mathcal{B} \xrightarrow{\tau} A'|\mathcal{B}'|s \doteq r} \qquad \frac{S \xrightarrow{r\top a} S' \quad T \xrightarrow{r\perp a} T'}{S|T \xrightarrow{\tau} S'|T'}$$

$$\frac{A \xrightarrow{\alpha} A' \quad n \notin \text{n}(\alpha)}{(\nu n)A \xrightarrow{\alpha} (\nu n)A'} \qquad \frac{A \xrightarrow{\alpha} A' \quad \alpha \in \{\bar{x}w, x!w, r \, \bar{x}w, r \, x!w\}}{(\nu w)A \xrightarrow{(w)\alpha} A'}$$

Structural congruence $\equiv$ includes associativity, commutativity and identity over **0** for parallel composition and rules for scope extrusion. Also, $\equiv$ gives the semantics of recursion and $r \doteq s$ in terms of substitutions. Notice that any explicit substitution $r \doteq s$ is persistent and can freely "float" in the term structure, unless a restriction on $r$ or $s$ forbids its movements.

The operational semantics of $\mu$se is specified through a labeled transition system (lts). We use $\alpha$ to range over labels. Bound variables occurring in labels are in round parentheses, and functions fn(_), bn(_) and n(_) are extended in the natural way to labels.

**Definition 2 ($\mu$se semantics).** *The $\mu$se semantics is the least lts generated by the inference rules in Table 2, closed under structural congruence.*

The rules for prefixes simply execute them, moving the information to the transition label. As usual for early semantics, input prefixes guess the actual value and immediately substitute it for the formal variable. Sessions are transparent to most of the actions, while a session name is added to the label in case of session-dependent actions (intra-session communications, invoke and merge). Notice that only the name of the innermost session is added. Service definitions can produce sessions, and the session name is guessed in the early style. Install requests are executed when the outermost level of the site is reached. Observe that sites are transparent to all actions but install and intra-site communications. Also, most of the synchronization rules can be applied both at the process and at the system level. The only exceptions are $(i)$ intra-site communication, which is meaningful only at the process level, and $(ii)$ service invocation, which can be stated only at the system level since definitions are always at the top level. Finally, restriction is dealt with by moving restrictions to the outermost level using structural congruence, but the rule for extrusions is necessary for interactions with the environment (and notably for bisimulation).

## 3    Programming in $\mu$se

This section illustrates the main features of $\mu$se by showing how it can be used to program simple SOC applications. Example 1 introduces a trivial client-server application, while Example 2 shows how persistent services can be programmed. To illustrate how multiparty sessions can be easily used, more complex scenarios are presented: Example 3 shows how a multiparty session can control interactions among three participants; Example 4 models a multi-player game; and Example 5 gives the definition of a proxy, which is transparent to clients.

*Example 1.* Consider the simple system below

$$l_c :: r \triangleright \mathsf{invoke}\ inc.P_c \quad | \quad l_s :: inc \Rightarrow P_s \tag{2}$$

where the client running at $l_c$ in a session $r$ invokes a service for incrementing integers on another location; client and service adopt a request-response protocol according to $P_c = \overline{data}\ v.ret(v').P$ and $P_s = data(w).\overline{ret}\ w{+}1$. Namely, $P_c$ sends the value $v$ to the service, waits a result, and then continues executing as $P$; accordingly, $P_s$ receives a value $w$ and returns the successor of $w$ (arithmetical operators are assumed and they have precedence over other operators.)

The system (2) evolves as follows:

$$
\begin{array}{llll}
l_c :: r \triangleright \mathsf{invoke}\ inc.P_c & | & l_s :: inc \Rightarrow P_s & \xrightarrow{\tau} \\
l_c :: r \triangleright P_c & | & l_s :: r \triangleright P_s & \xrightarrow{\tau} \\
l_c :: r \triangleright ret(v').P & | & l_s :: r \triangleright \overline{ret}\ v + 1 & \xrightarrow{\tau} \\
l_c :: r \triangleright P\{v + 1/v'\} & | & l_s :: r \triangleright \mathbf{0} &
\end{array}
$$

In words, upon service invocation, $P_s$ is executed as a new endpoint of session $r$ where intra-session communications let parameters to be passed around. ☐

Observe that neither the client nor the service of Example 1 deal with session identifiers. Also, the definition of $inc$ is consumed as soon as it is invoked. Nevertheless, persistent service definitions can be programmed by using recursion, as shown in the following example.

*Example 2.* A persistent $inc$ service can be defined as follows

$$l_s :: inc \Rightarrow \mathsf{rec}\ X.(P_s\ |\ \mathsf{install}[inc \Rightarrow X])$$

(which, by using the notation in (1), can be written as $l_s :: *inc \Rightarrow P_s$).

We consider now the case of two clients running in separate sessions (and in separate sites) but executing analogous protocols:

$$l_0 :: r_0 \rhd \text{invoke } inc.P_c \quad | \quad l_1 :: r_1 \rhd \text{invoke } inc.P_c \quad | \quad l_s :: *inc \Rightarrow P_s$$

The complete system may reduce (in several steps) to

$$l_0 :: r_0 \rhd P_c \quad | \quad l_1 :: r_1 \rhd P_c \quad | \quad l_s :: *inc \Rightarrow P_s \quad | \quad l_s :: (r_1 \rhd P_s | r_0 \rhd P_s)$$

where two instances of the service protocol $P_s$ run on $l_s$, but under different sessions $r_0$ and $r_1$, while two instances of the client run on different sessions at different sites. We remark that the session mechanism of $\mu$se will distinguish the instances of channels *data* and *ret* used by sessions $r_0$ and $r_1$, and will allow synchronizations only over channels belonging to the same session.    □

*Example 3.* The ATM scenario described in Section 1 is shown. Consider

$$hiw :: r \rhd C \mid (\nu \ check, abort)(hiw :: *atm \Rightarrow A \mid branch :: *bank \Rightarrow B) \quad (3)$$

where $C$, $A$ and $B$ are respectively the customer, ATM and bank code (defined below); *check* and *abort* are private channels shared between $A$ and $B$. For simplicity, we assume to have basic types (as numerals or strings), tuples (in angle brackets), nondeterministic choice, **if** statement and polyadic inputs (though channels are not typed). We enclose output tuples in angle brackets. The definition of $C$, $A$ and $B$ is as follows:

$$C \ = \ \text{invoke } atm.\overline{req}\langle c, m \rangle.(cash(x)|sms(y).display!y)$$

$$A \ = \ req(x,y).\text{invoke } bank.\overline{check}\langle x, y \rangle.(\ checked().\overline{cash}\ y + abort().\overline{cash}\ 0\ )$$

$$B \ = \ check(x,y).\textbf{if } ok(x,y) \textbf{ then } \overline{checked}.\overline{sms} \text{ ok } \textbf{else } \overline{abort}.\overline{sms} \text{ ko}$$

After invoking the ATM, $C$ requests to withdraw an amount of money m offering some credentials c and waits for money and for an SMS confirmation. After invoking $B$, $A$ forwards the request to $B$ and waits for $B$'s response either to confirm or abort the transaction (in which case no money is dispensed).

If the customer's credentials are valid, $B$ confirms to $A$ to proceed and notifies $C$ by sending the ok SMS, which is diplayed on $C$'s site. Observe that $B$ enters the session between $A$ and $C$ after the latter invokes the bank service, hence the further interactions with $C$ and $A$ will not be messed up with possible concurrent sessions of the bank service. If the customer's credentials are invalid the bank let the ATM abort and sends a failure notification to the customer.    □

An interesting aspect to highlight in Example 3 is the fact that the interactions between $C$ and $A$ or $C$ and $B$ are mediated by public channels and communications are hiddenly driven by sessions. More precisely, *req*, *cash* and *sms* can be thought of as the known ports through which participants communicate, and sessions avoid interferences among possible concurrent invocations of the ATM and bank services. Also, notice that exactly the same definition of the bank service can be installed on other locations so modeling the existence of different branches without affecting the customer.

In the next example we illustrate how entry points can be used for modeling a distributed game scenario where the number of participants is unbounded.

*Example 4.* Let $s$ be a service that waits for the connection of *at least two* players. Whenever two players connect to the service, they share a session and a match starts. New participants may later join. For simplicity, we let $P_p = start().P$ be the protocol that any player follows after invoking $s$. When $s$ signals the beginning of the match on the channel $start$, the players run as $P$, which codes the (unspecified) logic of the game.

The service has two different states that respectively generate an instance of the following protocols

$$G_1 = \mathsf{merge}^-\ e.\overline{start}.\mathsf{rec}\ X.\mathsf{merge}^-\ e.X, \qquad G_2 = \mathsf{merge}^+\ e.\overline{start}$$

Intuitively, $G_1$ stands for the protocol followed by $s$ for handling the first connection. Note that $G_1$ will run in a session, say $r$, and it will wait a player to join $r$ over the entry point $e$. After the second player arrives, it sends to the player the message $start$ and will repeatedly wait for new arrivals. By contrast, $G_2$ manages all subsequent invocations. In particular, $G_2$ joins an existing session over the entry point $e$ and then it sends the message $start$ to the player.

The game service is $s \Rightarrow G$ where

$$G = G_1\ |\ \mathsf{install}[*s \Rightarrow G_2]$$

Notice that the changes of the state of the service are modeled by using the primitive $\mathsf{install}[\ldots]$ for installing a new definition of the service.

Let us consider the following system

$$l_0 :: r_0 \rhd \mathsf{invoke}\ s.P_p\quad |\quad l_1 :: r_1 \rhd \mathsf{invoke}\ s.P_p\quad |\quad l_g :: s \Rightarrow G \qquad (4)$$

composed by two players and a game service. After several steps, system (4) may evolve to

$$l_0 :: r_0 \rhd P_p\quad |\quad l_1 :: r_1 \rhd P_p\quad |\quad l_g :: *s \Rightarrow G_2\quad |\quad l_g :: (r_0 \rhd G_1\ |\ r_1 \rhd G_2)$$

and $G_1$ and $G_2$ can finally synchronize (over the entry point $e$) so that, after their sessions are coalesced, they signal to the two players that the game starts.

$$r_0 \doteq r_1\quad |\quad l_0 :: r_0 \rhd P_p\quad |\quad l_1 :: r_0 \rhd P_p\quad |$$
$$l_g :: *s \Rightarrow G_2\quad |\quad l_g :: (r_0 \rhd \overline{start}.\mathsf{rec}\ X.\mathsf{merge}^-\ e.X\ |\ r_0 \rhd \overline{start})$$

Note that new invocations of $s$ will create service sessions of the form $r \rhd G_2$. These sessions will join the first created session $r_0$, by merging over the entry point $e$.                                                                                     □

The gaming example serves to show a nice feature of $\mu$se: players protocol need not to be aware of the order in which connections are established, i.e. any player can invoke the gaming service regardless of the fact that a session has been already started or not. Clearly, more complex game services may be written; for instance, a service that allows only a bounded number of participants and creates a new instance of the game when the bound is reached can be simply implemented using freshly created entry points. Remarkably, the programming of the counting mechanism can be straightforwardly achieved by using a local shared counter and intra-site communications.

Our last example shows how proxies can be easily programmed and exploits the intra-site communication of $\mu$se.

*Example 5.* Consider a set of different services $s_0, \ldots, s_n$ providing the same functionality $P$, any of them running on a different site. Let us assume the services to be persistent and defined as

$$S_i = l_i :: *s_i \Rightarrow P$$

Moreover, we assume that each client wants to access the services in a transparent way, i.e., by invoking a service $s$ that acts as a proxy, and forwards the invocation to one of the actual services.

As a first solution, we can model the proxy as a service that nondeterministically selects one of the available providers, as below

$$Ps = \prod_i Av_i \quad | \quad * s \Rightarrow av?(x).\text{invoke } x$$

Any process $Av_i = \text{rec } X.av!s_i.X$ gives a persistent witness of the fact that the service $s_i$ is one of the available providers (in more complex situations, the description of available services may take load balancing into account, exploiting e.g. a sequential list of invocations). The actual definition of the proxy $*s \Rightarrow av?(x).\text{invoke } x$ states that once the proxy is invoked it uses intra-site communication to select one of the available services, and then invokes it. If we consider a client that invokes $s$ and then continues like Q, the whole system behaves as follows.

$$\prod_i S_i \quad | \quad l_p :: Ps \quad | \quad l_c :: r \triangleright \text{invoke } s.Q \xrightarrow{\tau}$$

$$\prod_i S_i \quad | \quad l_p :: Ps \,|\, r \triangleright av?(x).\text{invoke } x \quad | \quad l_c :: r \triangleright Q \xrightarrow{\tau}$$

$$\prod_i S_i \quad | \quad l_p :: Ps \,|\, r \triangleright \text{invoke } s_k \quad | \quad l_c :: r \triangleright Q \xrightarrow{\tau}$$

$$\prod_{i \neq k} S_i \,|\, l_k :: r \triangleright P \,|\, * s_k \Rightarrow P \quad | \quad l_p :: Ps \,|\, r \triangleright \mathbf{0} \quad | \quad l_c :: r \triangleright Q$$

Note that, from this moment on, the client at site $l_c$ and the activated instance of the selected service at site $l_k$ share the same session $r$.    $\square$

## 4   Observational Semantics of $\mu$se

This section proposes an observational semantics of $\mu$se relying on the well-known notion of bisimulation. We prefer to use weak bisimulation as it is more suitable for reasoning on $\mu$se systems and, more generally, for giving coarser equivalence relations amongst systems.

Let $\Rightarrow$ be the reflexive and transitive closure of $\xrightarrow{\tau}$. Let us denote relation composition as juxtaposition (e.g., $\Rightarrow\xrightarrow{\alpha}$ is the composition of relations $\Rightarrow$ and $\xrightarrow{\alpha}$). Let $\overset{\alpha}{\Rightarrow}$ be $\Rightarrow\xrightarrow{\alpha}\Rightarrow$ if $\alpha \neq \tau$ and $\Rightarrow$ if $\alpha = \tau$.

**Definition 3 (Bisimilarity).** *A binary relation $\mathcal{B}$ on systems is a* (weak) $\mu$se *bisimulation if it is symmetric and for any $(S,T) \in \mathcal{B}$*

- *for each $S \xrightarrow{\alpha} S'$ such that $\mathrm{bn}(\alpha) \cap \mathrm{fn}(T) = \emptyset$, $T \overset{\alpha}{\Rightarrow} T'$ with $(S',T') \in \mathcal{B}$.*

*Bisimilarity is the largest bisimulation.*

Definition 3 instantiates the standard notion of weak bisimilarity for $\mu$se.

We will show here that bisimilarity can be used to analyze properties of services, in particular to prove that an implementation of a service is compliant (i.e., bisimilar) to a more abstract specification.

Let us consider a simple service $a$ that computes some mathematical function *fun* (such as the increment in Example 1, or even better some computationally expensive function). We can write the specification as:

$$ l :: *a \Rightarrow P \qquad \text{with } P = data(x).\overline{ret}\ fun(x) \tag{5} $$

The only possible transitions for this service are acceptance of invocations at $a$, followed by a protocol in the created session composed by an input on *data* and an output on *ret*.

Following the ideas in Example 5, a first implementation could ask another service $a_i$ non-deterministically chosen from a pool $a_1, \ldots, a_n$ to do the job:

$$ l :: (\nu a_1 \ldots a_n)\big((\nu av)(\prod_{i=1}^{n} \mathrm{rec}\ X.\overline{av}!a_i.X \mid *a \Rightarrow av?(u).\text{invoke } u) \mid \prod_{i=1}^{n} *a_i \Rightarrow P\big) $$

where, instead of directly computing *fun*, upon invocation the service receives (through an intra-site communication on the private channel $av$) the name of the "private" local service $a_i$ that actually computes *fun*. Notice that these two last transitions are just (non-observable) $\tau$ steps and such system is weak bisimilar to system (5). Also, replacing the definitions of $a_i$ with $a_i \Rightarrow P_i$ still yields a system weak bisimilar to the system (5) provided that each $P_i$ is bisimilar to $P$. On the contrary, removing e.g., the restriction on $av$ breaks the bisimilarity, since the implementation of $a$ could then interact with another channel $av$ in the environment, while the specification does not allow this interaction.

In another possible implementation, $a$ can merge with another session that does the job. For simplicity, we consider just one such session (the case of a nondeterministic choice among many equivalent sessions is analogous):

$$ (\nu e)l :: a \Rightarrow \mathrm{rec}\ Y.(\text{merge}^+\ e.\text{install}[a \Rightarrow Y]) \mid \mathrm{rec}\ X.(\nu r)r \triangleright \text{merge}^-\ e.(P|X). $$

In this case, the invocation in the specification is simulated by the invocation in the implementation plus the merge. Notice that $e$ should be bound to avoid other sessions to come into play instead of the wanted one, and that the merge has to be completed before $a$ can be made available again. Similarly, $r$ is restricted to avoid different recursive calls to interfere. Notice that other instances create further nested sessions, but session nesting is immaterial since only the most internal one matters, e.g., $r \rhd r' \rhd P$ is bisimilar to $r' \rhd P$.

# 5   Related Work and Concluding Remarks

Multiparty sessions are increasingly attracting the attention of researchers in distributed computing. We have introduced $\mu$se, a process calculus tailored to handle multiparty sessions in service oriented scenarios. The presentation includes the full formalization of the operational semantics in the SOS style and the definition of a bisimilarity-based abstract semantics.

$\mu$se builds on ideas emerged in recent works, but adds to them several original elements. From a technical point of view, $\mu$se communication model is inspired by $\pi$-calculus [22] and SOC features are based on the SCC [3,19,7,4] family of calculi developed inside the SENSORIA project [24]. Multiparty sessions are the main novelty of $\mu$se with respect to SCC and they have a strong impact also on other features. For instance, in binary sessions the intended recipient is always understood (the other endpoint of the session), while in multiparty sessions many recipients are possible, and an additional coordination mechanism, such as $\mu$se channels, is needed. Also, $\mu$se and SCC differ on many design choices. For example, the invocation of a service always opens a new session in SCC both on the client and on the service side. In $\mu$se instead only the server session is freshly generated. Another difference is that SCC offers more constrained forms of local communication: pipelining [3,4] and data streaming [19]. In this respect $\mu$se is more similar to [7], but its communication primitives exploit the site structure instead of the session structure as the primitives in [7]. We think that this is an important separation of concerns aspect.

In [2] multiparty sessions are considered, but they are required to include one master endpoint and one or more slave endpoints, and direct communication is allowed only between the master and any slave. Our setting is more general since sessions have no predefined structure. The simpler setting of [2] allows a type system based on session types to be defined [15,16,8,10,13]: developing a similar type system for our generalized setting is more challenging, and is part of our plans for future work. In this respect, also [17,19,1,20,6] offer a good starting point. Also, [2] uses asynchronous communications, while we use synchronous ones.

The global calculus [8] allows for multiparty sessions, but, roughly speaking, session identifiers are modeled just as pi-calculus channel names (freshly created and distributed to participants during the initialization phase of the service protocol). In $\mu$se instead sessions offer a logical context for driving communication on top of intra-session channel names. Moreover, entry points allow to dynamically merge running sessions, an operation not possible in the global calculus.

Recently, *global types* have been introduced in [17] in order to describe conversations among several participants; provided that some conditions (e.g., linearity) hold, global types can be projected on and checked against each participant. Several results on disciplined use of global types show how processes reflecting well designed multiparty choreographies enjoy *progress properties* (i.e., well typed processes either terminate or can interact) and *session fidelity* (i.e., well typed processes interactions mimic those specified in their global types). We consider [17] a very inspiring work and we are currently trying to extend the progress and fidelity results to the dynamic setting of $\mu$se. In fact, dynamic multiparty sessions yield a main difference between $\mu$se and the behavioural model adopted in [17] (where the number of participants in a multiparty session is fixed). Actually, safety and liveness properties of dynamic multiparty sessions pose many challenging and interesting research questions. For instance, progress properties should be revisited so that well typed processes should either terminate, interact or eventually allow session merging that do not spoil further interactions.

The intra-session communication model of $\mu$se resembles the dyadic synchronisation mechanism of the polyadic pi of [9]. Roughly, the $\mu$se process $r \triangleright P$ can be seen as the polyadic pi process obtained from $P$ by substituting any occurence of $x(w)$ and $\bar{y}v$ respectively by $r \cdot x(w)$ and $\overline{r \cdot y}\langle v \rangle$. In this respect, the intra-session communication model of $\mu$se can be thought as a disciplined use of dyadic synchronisations. An important difference is that $\mu$se sessions can be merged via entry points, a feature that would require some form of name fusion on top of [9]. We leave for future work the formal comparison of the two models.

A calculus with coordination mechanism based on event/notification, called XSC, has been introduced in [12] and can model multiparty sessions through a type system. In XSC, components can react to events according to their types that provide a mechanism to associate sessions to events. Though sessions cannot be merged in XSC, its type system permits to correlate events from different sessions. We argue that XSC can be a valid candidate for translating $\mu$se in a framework with mechanisms reminiscent of correlation sets.

We conclude by discussing some of the possible extensions of $\mu$se.

*Closing sessions.* We plan to extend $\mu$se with primitives for explicit session closure, for which nesting of sessions plays a prominent role. In fact, sessions can confine the effect of closure mechanisms so that the part of a running session that must be terminated can be straightforwardly determined.

In the current version of $\mu$se, session nesting is only exploited as a mechanism for controlling intra-session communication within the same party. For example, $P$ and $Q$ can carry an intra-session interaction neither in $r \triangleright (P|Q)$ nor in $r \triangleright (P|r \triangleright Q)$.

*Sophisticated interactions.* Communication mechanisms are somehow orthogonal to sessions. In fact, while CCS-like communication [21] is the obvious choice when only two-party sessions are considered, in the presence of multiparty sessions a more natural and more sophisticated alternative would be some variant of multicast (like broadcast [11] or CSP-like interaction [14], or even some combination of different policies [5]). We contend that multiparty sessions as introduced in $\mu$se provide a reasonable linguistic background for easily extending the calculus with several sophisticated interaction mechanisms (similarly to what has already been done for graphical languages [18]).

**Acknowledgements.** Authors thank Nobuko Yoshida for her valuable comments and suggestions, particularly for highlighting some relationships among $\mu$se and other proposals.

# References

1. Acciai, L., Boreale, M.: A type system for client progress in a service-oriented calculus. In: Festschrift in Honour of Ugo Montanari, on the Occasion of His 65th Birthday. LNCS, vol. 5065, Springer Verlag, Heidelberg (to appear, 2008)
2. Bonelli, E., Compagnoni, A.: Multipoint session types for a distributed calculus. In: TGC 2007. LNCS, vol. 4912, pp. 240–256. Springer Verlag, Heidelberg (2008)
3. Boreale, M., Bruni, R., Caires, L., De Nicola, R., Lanese, I., Loreti, M., Martins, F., Montanari, U., Ravara, A., Sangiorgi, D., Vasconcelos, V., Zavattaro, G.: SCC: A Service Centered Calculus. In: Bravetti, M., Núñez, M., Zavattaro, G. (eds.) WS-FM 2006. LNCS, vol. 4184, pp. 38–57. Springer, Heidelberg (2006)
4. Boreale, M., Bruni, R., De Nicola, R., Loreti, M.: Sessions and pipelines for structured service programming. In: FMOODS 2008. LNCS, vol. 5051, Springer, Heidelberg (to appear, 2008)
5. Bruni, R., Lanese, I.: PRISMA: A mobile calculus with parametric synchronization. In: Montanari, U., Sannella, D., Bruni, R. (eds.) TGC 2006. LNCS, vol. 4661, pp. 132–149. Springer, Heidelberg (2007)
6. Bruni, R., Mezzina, L.: Types and deadlock freedom in a calculus of services, sessions and pipelines (submitted, 2008)
7. Caires, L., Vieira, H.T., Seco, J.C.: The conversation calculus: A model of service oriented computation. In: ESOP 2008. LNCS, vol. 4960, Springer, Heidelberg (2008)
8. Carbone, M., Honda, K., Yoshida, N.: Structured communication-centred programming for web services. In: De Nicola, R. (ed.) ESOP 2007. LNCS, vol. 4421, pp. 2–17. Springer, Heidelberg (2007)
9. Carbone, M., Maffeis, S.: On the expressive power of polyadic synchronisation in pi-calculus. Nord. J. Comput. 10(2), 70–98 (2003)
10. Dezani-Ciancaglini, M., Yoshida, N., Ahern, A., Drossopoulou, S.: A distributed object-oriented language with session types. In: De Nicola, R., Sangiorgi, D. (eds.) TGC 2005. LNCS, vol. 3705, pp. 299–318. Springer, Heidelberg (2005)
11. Ene, C., Muntean, T.: A broadcast-based calculus for communicating systems. In: IPDPS 2001, IEEE Computer Society Press, Los Alamitos (2001)
12. Ferrari, G., Guanciale, R., Strollo, D., Tuosto, E.: Coordination Via Types in an Event-Based Framework. In: Derrick, J., Vain, J. (eds.) FORTE 2007. LNCS, vol. 4574, pp. 66–80. Springer, Heidelberg (2007)
13. Gay, S., Hole, M.: Types and Subtypes for Client-Server Interactions. In: Swierstra, S.D. (ed.) ESOP 1999. LNCS, vol. 1576, pp. 74–90. Springer, Heidelberg (1999)
14. Hoare, C.: A model for communicating sequential processes. In: On the Construction of Programs, Cambridge University Press, Cambridge (1980)

15. Honda, K.: Types for dyadic interaction. In: Best, E. (ed.) CONCUR 1993. LNCS, vol. 715, pp. 509–523. Springer, Heidelberg (1993)
16. Honda, K., Vasconcelos, V., Kubo, M.: Language primitives and type disciplines for structured communication-based programming. In: Hankin, C. (ed.) ESOP 1998. LNCS, vol. 1381, pp. 22–138. Springer, Heidelberg (1998)
17. Honda, K., Yoshida, N., Carbone, M.: Multiparty asynchronous session types. In: POPL 2008, pp. 273–284. ACM, New York (2008)
18. Lanese, I., Tuosto, E.: Synchronized Hyperedge Replacement for heterogeneous systems. In: Jacquet, J.-M., Picco, G.P. (eds.) COORDINATION 2005. LNCS, vol. 3454, pp. 220–235. Springer, Heidelberg (2005)
19. Lanese, I., Vasconcelos, V., Martins, F., Ravara, A.: Disciplining orchestration and conversation in service-oriented computing. In: SEFM 2007, pp. 305–314. IEEE Computer Society Press, Los Alamitos (2007)
20. Mezzina, L.G.: How to infer finite session types in a calculus of services and sessions. In: COORDINATION 2008. LNCS, vol. 5052. Springer, Heidelberg (2008)
21. Milner, R.: A Calculus of Communication Systems. LNCS, vol. 92. Springer, Heidelberg (1980)
22. Milner, R., Parrow, J., Walker, J.: A calculus of mobile processes, I and II. Inform. and Comput. 100(1), 1–40, 41–77 (1992)
23. OASIS. Web Services Business Process Execution Language Version 2.0, Working Draft, http://docs.oasis-open.org/wsbpel/2.0/wsbpel-specification-draft.pdf
24. Sensoria Project. Software Engineering for Service-Oriented Overlay Computers. Public Web Site, http://sensoria.fast.de/
25. World Wide Web Consortium. Web Services Choreography Description Language Version 1.0. Working draft (17 December 2004), http://www.w3.org/TR/2005/CR-ws-cdl-10-20051109/

# Formalizing Higher-Order Mobile Embedded Business Processes with Binding Bigraphs[*]

Mikkel Bundgaard, Arne John Glenstrup, Thomas Hildebrandt,
Espen Højsgaard, and Henning Niss

IT University of Copenhagen, Denmark
{mikkelbu,panic,hilde,espen,hniss}@itu.dk

**Abstract.** We propose and formalize HomeBPEL, a higher-order WS-
BPEL-like business process execution language where processes are *first-
class values* that can be stored in variables, passed as messages, and
activated as embedded *sub-instances*. A sub-instance is similar to a WS-
BPEL scope, except that it can be dynamically *frozen* and stored as a
process in a variable, and then subsequently be *thawed* when reactivated
as a sub-instance. We motivate HomeBPEL by an example of pervasive
health care where treatment guidelines are dynamically deployed as sub
processes that may be delegated dynamically to other workflow engines
and in particular stay available for disconnected operation on mobile
devices. We provide a formal semantics based on binding bigraphical
reactive systems implemented in the BPL Tool as part of the Bigraphical
Programming Languages project at ITU. The semantics is an extension
of a semantics given previously for a simplified subset of WS-BPEL and
exploits the close correspondence between bigraphs and XML to provide
a formalized run-time format very close to standard WS-BPEL syntax,
which also constitutes the representation of frozen sub-instances.

## 1 Introduction

Services implemented and orchestrated by processes written in languages such
as WS-BPEL are being put forward as a means to achieve loosely coupled and
highly flexible computer supported business and work processes. In the current
architectures, services are deployed and managed on web servers by meta-level
tools and cannot be replaced or moved during the life-time of a session with
an instance of the service. In the present paper we propose and formalize a
higher-order WS-BPEL-like language where processes are values that can be
stored in variables and dynamically instantiated as embedded sub-instances. A
sub-instance is similar to a WS-BPEL scope, except that it can be dynamically
frozen during a session and stored as a process in a variable. When frozen in a
variable, the process instance can be sent to remote services as any other content
of variables and dynamically re-instantiated as a local sub-instance continuing
its execution.

[*] This work was funded in part by the Danish Research Agency (grant no.: 2106-07-
0019, no.: 274-06-0415 and no.: 2059-03-0031) and the IT University of Copenhagen
(the TrustCare, CosmoBiz and BPL projects).

D. Lea and G. Zavattaro (Eds.): COORDINATION 2008, LNCS 5052, pp. 83–99, 2008.
© Springer-Verlag Berlin Heidelberg 2008

We envisage a use of HomeBPEL where the necessary services or even active instances can be dynamically moved to a local process engine running on a mobile device and thereby allow for disconnected operation. We exemplify this use by an example of pervasive health care, where treatment workflows are moved between and executed locally on mobile devices belonging to either the doctor or the patient, depending on whether the guideline requires actions by the doctor or it prescribes actions carried out as self-treatment by the patient.

The investigation is part of the Computer Supported Mobile Adaptive Business Processes (CosmoBiz) project [11], which aims to provide a fully formalized runtime engine for a WS-BPEL-like business process language extended to allow for mobile and adaptive processes. Our primary goals of the formalization is 1) to be able to guarantee that the implemented engine actually conforms to the semantics and 2) to form a basis for the development of type systems that can be used to statically guarantee safe and reliable behavior. To achieve the first goal a main concern is to limit the gap between the source language, its formalization, and the implementation. A key element to achieve the second goal is to strive for a *compositional* formalization supporting subsequent formalization of type rules for the individual parts. We want to stress that it is *not* a main concern at this point to provide techniques or principles for verification of processes, which has been the main concern of most WS-BPEL formalizations so far. However, we do hope that future reasoning techniques developed for bigraphs can be employed also to support formal verification.

We build on and extend our previous work described in [12, 2] which exploits the close correspondence between bigraphs and XML to provide a small step rewrite semantics of non-trivial subsets of WS-BPEL using a representation of the state of active process instances which is very close to the XML syntax of WS-BPEL processes. We define the semantics in the BPL Tool[1] developed in the Bigraphical Programming Languages project which supports visualization and simulation of the execution. The extensibility of bigraphical reactive systems enables us to formalize HomeBPEL as an extension of a formalization of a WS-BPEL subset, simply adding formalization of the syntax and semantics for the new primitives for mobile, embedded sub-processes. The syntax and semantics is inspired and guided by our work on the Homer process calculus of Higher-order mobile embedded resources [10, 4, 3]. Not surprisingly, the new features add to the complexity of the language and its formalization. Yet, the formal approach ensures that they are completely unambiguously specified. Also, the close relationship to semantics of process calculi such as Homer and the Mobile Ambients gives a very succinct formalization of sub-process mobility. Indeed, the serialized representation of a mobile process is just a process description. In particular, this means that a future implementation could use the standard XML format for serialized process instances.

The structure of the paper is as follows. In Sec. 2 we motivate HomeBPEL by an example of pervasive health care. Sec. 3 briefly reviews the definition of binding bigraphs and the BPL tool term language for such, and in Sec. 4 we

---

[1] See ⟨http://tiger.itu.dk:8080/bplweb/⟩

provide the formalization of higher-order mobile embedded sub-processes as it is defined in the BPL tool. Finally, in Sec. 5 we conclude and propose future work.

**Related Work.** *Sub-processes* have been proposed by IBM and SAP in [15] as an extension to WS-BPEL (called BPEL-SPE) to allow for modularization and reuse of process fragments to ease the burden of designing large business processes. As argued in [15] one could simulate some of the behavior of sub-processes by invoking another process instead of invoking a sub-process. However, this makes it impossible to establish any coupling between the life-cycles of the two process instance, e.g. enforcing that a sub-process exits if the super process exists prematurely. The sub-processes we propose in this paper extends the proposal in [15] in several aspects. First and foremost, BPEL-SPE requires that the *sole* interaction of a sub-process is an initial receive activity, and a last reply activity, basically making the sub-process act as a method or function call. We allow that the sub-process can communicate unrestricted with the parent process (and vice versa) using invoke-receive. Furthermore, we add facilities for "freezing" and "thawing" sub-processes as well as (sub-)process mobility.

Higher order workflow models applied to health care processes have been considered in the context of Higher-Order (Petri) Nets [13], allowing sub-processes (nets) as values (tokens), which may be dynamically composed. The approach in [13] differs from ours in several ways: Firstly, the approach in [13] is based on Petri Nets as opposed to process calculi, and has no direct relationship to WS-BPEL nor service orchestration. Another central difference is that we execute sub-processes as sub-threads and they can themselves contain sub-processes, whereas in [13] a sub-process is executed step-by-step by the super process and cannot contain sub-processes itself. Finally, the model in [13] allows for dynamic modification and composition of sub-processes, which is not yet supported in our setting.

Our formalization of the core WS-BPEL subset relates to the WS-BPEL process calculus given in [16]. An advantage to our approach is that we can reuse the general theory developed for bigraphical reactive systems, instead of redeveloping an entire theory of a new process calculus. As in [16], we hope to be able to equip our formalization with WSDL-like (or even richer) type systems. As described above, our proposal of higher order mobile sub-processes relates to our work on the higher-order process calculus Homer. The Homer calculus is related to the process calculus of Mobile Ambients [5], the Seal calculus [6] and the higher-order $\pi$-calculus (HO$\pi$) [20]. Indeed, HomeBPEL shares with Seal and HO$\pi$ the combination of name (link) and process passing.

## 2   Motivating HomeBPEL

In this section we motivate the use of HomeBPEL with a simplified example of workflow management for pervasive health care. Each doctor is assumed to run a workflow process, which is initiated when he/she is hired. Every new treatment of a patient causes a new workflow process to be initiated, describing the clinical guideline to be followed for the particular treatment of the patient.

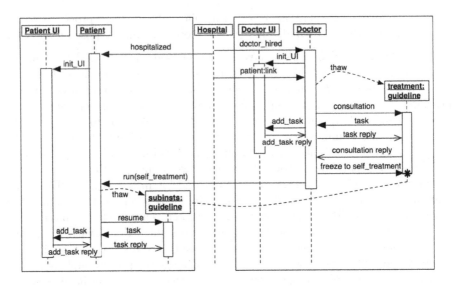

**Fig. 1.** Sequence diagram for the pervasive health care scenario

In a centralized solution, this process would be running as a separate workflow on the workflow server and only be available when connected to the network. In HomeBPEL business processes can be manipulated as first class values, so we can let the doctor's workflow process execute the treatment process as a *sub-process*. By assuming that the doctor carries a mobile device running its own HomeBPEL engine the treatment process can be executed independently of the network. Moreover, if each patient is equipped with a mobile device running a self-treatment workflow process, the doctor may *delegate* the treatment process (or parts of it) by sending a sub-process to the patient's workflow process.

A sequence diagram illustrating a simple example of this scenario is shown in Fig. 1. The two large boxes represent the patient's and the doctor's PDA respectively. The dotted continuation of the "life-line" of the sub-process `guideline` indicates that it is the same process continuing its execution at the patient's PDA. The BPMN diagram in Fig. 2 gives a more detailed view of the patient process, with a group of guideline sub-processes indicated in the dashed box in the middle. Fig. 3 shows the corresponding HomeBPEL process for the patient. We have left out details related to the data-flow which are not relevant for this example. The initial `receive` on the `hospitalized` operation is used to invoke the patient process, as indicated by the `createInstance` attribute. We have only formalized synchronous communication, so most receive operations are immediately followed by a "dummy" reply. As also shown in the sequence and BPMN diagrams, the following invoke instantiates a local user interface process running on the patient's PDA which we assume takes care of handling the task list of the patient. It is followed by a WS-BPEL `flow`, which contains two while-loops executing in parallel. The first while-loop (corresponding to the right-hand loop in the BPMN diagram) allows for arbitrarily many self-treatment sub-processes

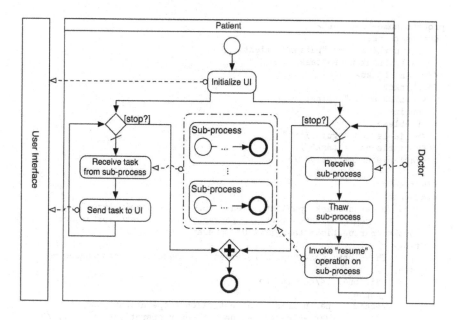

**Fig. 2.** BPMN diagram of the patient workflow process

to be received and instantiated: The `receive` on the `run` operation waits for a message containing a process and stores it in the input variable `guideline`. The following activity `thaw` is part of the new features introduced in HomeBPEL and it is used to create an instance of a process stored in a variable and execute it as a sub-instance within the scope of the corresponding `subLink` (in the example named `subinsts`) of the current running instance. The second while-loop forwards messages received from the guideline sub-processes by the HomeBPEL `receiveSub` activity to the user interface, and in turn forwards the answer back to the sub-process by the HomeBPEL `replySub` activity.

The doctor's workflow process shown in Fig. 4 also invokes a user interface process, and contains an identical loop for forwarding messages from treatment workflows to the user interface process (which we have omitted from the example code to save space). However, different from the patient workflow, the first step of the main loop of the doctor workflow is to receive a link (on the `patient` operation) which is then dynamically assigned to the `patient` partner link by the `copy` operation. Thereby the doctor workflow process can be dynamically linked to different patient workflow processes during its lifetime. The following `thaw` activity instantiates a treatment guideline as a sub-process from the variable named `guideline`. Fig. 5 shows an outline of the treatment process consisting of two phases: A *consultation phase* invoked explicitly by the doctor and carried out within the doctor's workflow, and a *self-treatment* phase carried out within the patient's workflow. To initiate the first part of the treatment, the operation `consultation` is invoked from the doctor workflow by the action `invokeSub`. The reply of this operation signals that the consultation is finished, and the

```
<process name="patient">
  <partnerLinks>
    <partnerLink name="patient_client" />
    <partnerLink name="task_list_UI" />
  </partnerLinks>
  <subLinks>
    <subLink name="subinsts" />
  </subLinks>
  <variables>
    <variable name="guideline" />
    <variable name="task" />
    <variable name="reply" />
    ...
  </variables>
  <sequence>
    <receive partnerLink="patient_client" operation="hospitalized"
             createInstance="yes" ... /><reply operation="hospitalized" ... />
    <invoke  partnerLink="task_list_UI" operation="init_UI" ... />
    <flow>
      <!-- Thaw-loop: Continually receives and executes sub-instances -->
      <while>
        <condition>...</condition>
        <sequence>
          <receive    partnerLink="patient_client" operation="run"
                      variable="guideline" /><reply operation="run" ... />
          <thaw       subLink="subinsts" variable="guideline" />
          <invokeSub subLink="subinsts" operation="resume" ... />
        </sequence>
      </while>
      <!-- UI-loop: Continually receives tasks from sub-instances and
           pass them on to the UI service -->
      <while>
        <condition>...</condition>
        <sequence>
          <receiveSub subLink="subinsts" operation="task" variable="task" />
          <invoke     partnerLink="task_list_UI" operation="add_task"
                      inputVariable="task" outputVariable="reply" />
          <replySub   subLink="subinsts" operation="task" variable="reply" />
        </sequence>
      </while>
    </flow>
  </sequence>
</process>
```

**Fig. 3.** Patient workflow process

treatment process is ready to be frozen (by the **freeze** action) and sent to the patient's workflow process.

Note that we have not specified the specific tasks for each phase in the treatment, which in general could be part of an arbitrarily complex workflow. However, we have illustrated how tasks in each phase can be scheduled at the user interface of the *current* super workflow by invoking the **task** operation by the **invokeSup** action. This shows how *context-dependent communication* is elegantly facilitated in HomeBPEL. One could easily imagine that the treatment processes

```
<process name="doctor">
  <partnerLinks>
    <partnerLink name="hospital" />
    <partnerLink name="patient" />
    <partnerLink name="task_list_UI" />
  </partnerLinks>
  <subLinks><subLink name="treatment" /></subLinks>
  <variables>
    <variable name="guideline"><process name="guideline">...</process></variable>
    <variable name="link" /><variable name="self_treatment" /> ...
  </variables>
  <sequence>
    <receive partnerLink="hospital" operation="doctor_hired"
             createInstance="yes" ... /><reply operation="doctor_hired" ... />
    <invoke  partnerLink="task_list_UI" operation="init_UI" ... />
    <flow>
      <while>
        <condition>...</condition>
        <sequence>
          <receive  partnerLink="hospital" operation="patient"
                    variable="link" /><reply operation="patient" ... />
          <assign><copy>
              <from variable="link" /><to partnerLink="patient" />
          </copy></assign>
          <thaw     subLink="treatment" variable="guideline" />
          <invokeSub subLink="treatment" operation="consultation" ... />
          <freeze   subLink="treatment" variable="self_treatment" />
          <invoke   partnerLink="patient" operation="run"
                    inputVariable="self_treatment" ... />
        </sequence>
      </while>
      <!-- while-loop forwarding tasks to the local user interface -->
    </flow>
  </sequence>
</process>
```

**Fig. 4.** Doctor workflow process

```
<process name="guideline">
  ...
  <sequence>
    <!-- Doctor initializes treatment -->
    <receiveSup operation="consultation" ... />
    <!-- Instruct doctor on how to perform consultation -->
    <invokeSup  operation="task" ... />
    <replySup   operation="consultation" ... />
    <!-- Ready to be moved to patient -->
    <receiveSup operation="resume" ... /><replySup operation="resume" ... />
    <!-- Instruct patient how to perform self-treatment -->
    <invokeSup  operation="task" ... />
  </sequence>
</process>
```

**Fig. 5.** Treatment guideline process

could also access local information, e.g. special expertise of the doctor or relevant characteristics of the patient.

The above example is of course still highly simplified. One would most likely want more control over the behavior of sub-processes, i.e. to disallow malicious processes from entering ones mobile device, to only allow processes from known, trusted sources, etc. We expect to address these questions in future work. A necessary first step is a formal semantics of the execution which will be provided in the following sections.

## 3   Binding Bigraphs

In this section we briefly review the binding bigraphs of Milner and Jensen [14] and introduce the syntactical representation of binding bigraphs as implemented in the BPL Tool. For a complete introduction to bigraphs we refer to [14].

**Binding Bigraphs.** A binding bigraph is a pair of graphs: a *place graph* and a *link graph*. The place graph is an $n$-tuple of finite, unordered trees. Except for roots, every node is labelled by a *control* and has two finite ordered sets of respectively *free* and *binding* ports. The link graph is essentially a hypergraph connecting every free port of the nodes in the place graph to either a closed link, a binding port, or a name in a finite set $X$ of names. Jointly with a collection of pairwise disjoint sets $X_i \subseteq X$ of local names, one for each root in the bigraph, the set $X$ defines the (outer) *interface* of the link graph. The so-called *scope condition* enforces that any binding port and any name in a set $X_i$ is only connected to ports nested strictly inside the node of the binding port and root $i$ respectively.

What we just described above is known as *ground* binding bigraphs. Intuitively, one may think of a ground binding bigraph as an ordered tuple of terms of a process calculus up to structural congruence: Sibling nodes in the place graph represent processes combined by an associative and commutative parallel operator. Each node is a prefix, and each control denotes a distinct prefix operation (e.g. send or receive in the $\pi$-calculus) with free and binding ports representing names and name binders of the particular operation (e.g. for the $\pi$-calculus, any node labelled by a send control would have 2 free ports, while nodes labelled by a receive control would have one free and one binding port). The link graph then maps each name in a prefix to either a local name (closed link), a binder (i.e. a binding port) or a name in the interface.

A ground bigraph with a single root is also similar to the data model for XML, with controls playing the role of the names of XML elements, ports playing the role of attributes and the linking of ports playing the role of attribute values. As we will see below, we exploit this similarity to give a bigraphical semantics to HomeBPEL resembling closely the XML syntax.

A central ingredient of the theory of bigraphs is that bigraphs in general are (multi-hole) *contexts* that can be composed: The place graph has a finite ordered set of *holes* (referred to as *sites* in the usual bigraph terminology), each associated as a child of a node. The link graph has a set of *local names* $Y_i$ for each hole. As for the outer interface, the sets $Y_i$ are pairwise disjoint and contained in a finite set of names $Y$ which jointly with the sets $Y_i$ forms the *inner* interface. As the free ports, the names in $Y$ are connected to either a closed link, a binding port or a name in the outer interface.

Outer (resp. inner) interfaces of binding bigraphs are thus triples $\langle n, \vec{X}, X \rangle$, where the *width* $n$ is a finite ordinal representing the number of roots (resp. sites), $X$ is a finite set of names, and $\vec{X}$ is an $n$-tuple of pairwise disjoint subsets of $X$ which declares some of the names in $X$ as *local* to specific roots (resp. sites). If $x \notin \vec{X}$ then $x$ is said to be *global*, else it is *local*; if an interface $I$ has no global names $x$, it is a *local* interface. We write $G : I \to J$ for the bigraph $G$ with inner interface $I$ and outer interface $J$. The composition $H \circ G : I \to J$ of bigraphs $G : I \to I'$ and $H : I' \to J$ with compatible interfaces is obtained by making the children of the $i$th root of G children of the (parent) node of the $i$th site of $H$, discarding the roots of $G$ and sites of $H$, and by coalescing links as prescribed by the correspondence of $H$'s inner and $G$'s outer names.

A binding bigraphical reactive system is defined with respect to a *signature*, which declare the set of possible controls labelling nodes of the bigraph and for each control $K$ the number of binding and free ports of nodes in the bigraph labelled with $K$. The signature also declares each control as either atomic, active or passive. Only nodes with non-atomic controls can have children, and reactions (as defined below) can only occur in sub-bigraphs nested solely within active controls.

**BPL Tool Term Language.** Binding bigraphs are often visualized graphically. However, binding bigraphs also admit a representation via a term language based on the axiomatization of binding bigraphs [7]. This representation is exploited in the BPL Tool to allow compact and compositional textual descriptions of binding bigraphs and their reaction rules[2].

In the present paper we will use the syntax of the term language as used in the BPL Tool. The language consists of Standard ML constructs which allows the user to write the terms directly in SML, at the cost of introducing a few additional back quotes. (Future versions of the BPL Tool will also support a clean input language stripped of SML artifacts.) The employed subset of the language can be defined by the following grammar.

$$P ::= P \circ P \mid P \parallel P \mid P \text{ `|` } P \mid C$$
$$C ::= c \mid c[N^?] \mid c[N^?][NS^?] \mid -//[N^?] \mid n//[N^?] \mid \text{ `}[N^?]\text{` } \mid \text{ <-> }$$
$$N^? ::= \epsilon \mid N \quad N ::= n \mid n, N \quad NS^? ::= \epsilon \mid NS \quad NS ::= [N^?] \mid [N^?], NS$$

where $n$ ranges over strings representing names and $c$ over strings representing controls. $C$ describes so-called *ions* which are bigraphs consisting of a single root with a single node as child, having a control as defined in the signature. If the control is non-atomic the ion has a single hole inside. For instance, an ion with name

---

[2] The representation is also exploited in the underlying formalization and implementation of matching used for the execution of reaction rules as described in [9].

$c$ and $i$ free ports and $j$ binding ports is written $c[n_1, \ldots, n_i][NS_1, \ldots, NS_j]$ where the $NS_k$ is the set of names bound to the $k$th binding port.

We use the double bars || to separate roots in the place graph and the single bar ' | ' as a separator between sibling nodes. The symbol o denotes composition as defined above (the tool checks that the interfaces of the bigraphs match). The terms $-//[N^?]$ and $n//[N^?]$ denote a bigraph with an empty place graph (i.e. no roots) and a link graph mapping the names in the list $N^?$ to respectively each their closed link and to the name $n$. The term ' [] ' denotes a hole and the term ' $[n_1, \ldots, n_k]$ ' denotes a hole with local names $n_1, \ldots, n_k$. Finally, the term <-> denotes a bigraph just consisting of a single empty root. As an example, we may define two binding bigraphs as follows.

```
val R = If[id] o (Condition o False '|' Then o '[]' '|' Else o '[]')
     || Running[id]
val R' = '[]' || Running[id]
```

The bigraphs R and R' both have two roots. The first root of R has a single node as child with the control If and a single free port linked to the name id. The node has three nodes as children, labelled respectively with the controls Condition, Then and Else. The first node has a single node as child labelled with the atomic control False. The two latter nodes both have a hole as a child. The holes in a bigraph term are ordered from left to right, i.e. the hole below the Then is indexed 0 and the hole below the Else is indexed 1. The second root of R has a single node as child labelled with the atomic control Running and a single free port linked to the name id. The bigraph R' has simply a hole below its first root and the atomic Running control below its second root. The two bigraphs in fact form respectively the redex and reactum of a reaction rule, as defined below, defining the meaning of an if-then-else construct in the case where the condition has been evaluated to false.

**Reactions.** The dynamics of bigraphical reactive systems is defined in terms of a reaction relation generated from a set of reaction rules $\mathcal{R}$. Such rules are generally parametric, and may discard and also duplicate their parameters.

A rule, written "rule name" :::: R --$\bar{\varrho}$--|> R', consists of two bigraphs: the *redex* $R : I \to J$ and the *reactum* $R' : I' \to J$, where both $I$ and $I'$ are local interfaces, and a parameter mapping $\bar{\varrho}$. The mapping $\bar{\varrho}$ indicates for each site in the reactum from which site in the redex the parameter is copied.

The expression "if false" :::: R --[0 |-> 1]--|> R' is a reaction rule for executing an If activity with a false condition. During a reaction, the first tree of R (the if-then-else construct) is replaced by the first tree the reactum R'. Since the second tree of R and R' are identical it simply means that a node with the Running control (and the correct id link) must be present in the context—this is used to ensure that rewrites are only performed on running instances which are ready to execute a step. The mapping [0 |-> 1] specifies that the hole in the reactum (site 0) should contain the contents of the hole in the Else-branch (site 1), while the contents of the hole in the Then-branch is discarded as it is not mentioned in the mapping.

In general parameters may have local names, thus the mapping $\bar{\varrho}$ must also define how the local names of a parameter is mapped to local names in the hole of the reactum. For instance, [0&[x1] |--> 0&[x] , 1&[x2] |--> 0&[x]] is a mapping which (a) maps site 0 of the reactum and its local name x1 to site 0 of the redex and its local name x, and (b) also maps site 1 of the reactum and its local name x2 to site 0 of the redex and its local name x.

A rule matches an agent a if $a = C \circ (id_Z \,||\, R) \circ d$ for some identity linking $id_Z$ and active context C (i.e., no site of C is nested within a passive node); the linking $id_Z$ connects all non-local names in the outerface of d to C. In this case reaction produces a new agent $a' = C \circ (id_Z \,||\, R') \circ d'$, where d' is computed from d as prescribed by $\bar{\varrho}$. When duplicating parts of the agent (by letting $\bar{\varrho}$ map several reactum sites to a single redex site), *local* links in d are *copied* to each copy in d', while *free* links are *shared* between the copies. Binding ports thus enforce a notion of scope and locality on a bigraph's links, resembling the usual notion of binders in the $\lambda$- and the $\pi$-calculus. This feature of binding bigraphs is crucial in our formalization of WS-BPEL to create *fresh* id and scope links when new instances or scopes are created.

## 4   Formalizing HomeBPEL

The formalization of HomeBPEL as a binding bigraphical reactive system in the BPL Tool is given by a signature, determining the allowed controls and the ports for each type of control, and a set of reaction rules, determining the run-time semantics. As described in the introduction, we utilize the extensibility of bigraphs to extend and adapt the previous formalization of WS-BPEL given in [1]. For brevity we do not provide the signature. Instead we present the controls via a grammar in Table 1 which shows the valid nesting of controls in bigraphs representing HomeBPEL processes in our formalization. In the grammar each terminal (written in Typewriter typeface) represents a control in the signature, so for instance **Process** and **PartnerLinks** are two of the controls in the signature. (The grammar does not show ports of controls, i.e. the linking). We let $i$ range over the set $\{0, 1\}$ which we use to index some of the productions to keep the presentation succinct. We write *prod?* for indicating that the terminal or nonterminal is optional and we write Link* to denote that there can be 0 or more Link terminals.

Currently the formalization only supports the constants **True** and **False** and variable references as expressions. But one can easily extend the semantics to more expression types (e.g. XPath expressions), simply by adding rules describing how to evaluate them — without having to alter the current rules. Similarly, values (i.e. *value*) are currently restricted to be either the constants **True** and **False**, processes (higher-order values), or the content of a **PartnerLink** (akin to name passing in the $\pi$-calculus). One could exploit the correspondence between XML and bigraphs to represent any kind of XML-data.

As mentioned in the introduction, the key idea of the formalization is that a process is represented by a bigraph very similar to the XML syntax for

**Table 1.** Grammar for HomeBPEL

| | | |
|---|---|---|
| *system* | ::= | *procs* \| *state* |
| *procs* | ::= | *proc* \| ... \| *proc* |
| *state* | ::= | *topinst* \| ... \| *topinst* |
| *proc* | ::= | Process($scopecontent_0$) |
| *partnerlinks* | ::= | PartnerLinks(*partnerlink* \| ... \| *partnerlink*) |
| *partnerlink* | ::= | PartnerLink(*partnerlinkcontent*) |
| *partnerlinkcontent* | ::= | CreateInstance? \| *link*? |
| *link* | ::= | Link \| *message*? |
| *message* | ::= | Message(*value*) |
| *sublinks* | ::= | SubLinks(SubLink(Link*) \| ... \| SubLink(Link*)) |
| *vars* | ::= | Variables(Variable(*value*) \| ... \| Variable(*value*)) |
| *topinst* | ::= | TopInstance(*inst* \| (TopRunning \| SubTransition)) |
| *insts* | ::= | Instances(*inst* \| ... \| *inst*) |
| *inst* | ::= | Instance(*status* \| $scopecontent_1$) |
| *status* | ::= | Invoked \| Running \| Freezing \| Stopped |
| $act_i$ | ::= | $scope_i$ \| $seq_i$ \| $flow_i$ \| $while_i$ \| $if_i$ \| *assign* \| Invoke |
| | | \| Receive \| Reply \| GetReply \| Exit \| InvokeSub \| InvokeSup |
| | | \| ReceiveSub \| ReceiveSup \| ReplySub \| ReplySup \| Thaw |
| | | \| GetReplySub \| GetReplySup \| Freeze \| FreezingSub |
| $scope_0$ | ::= | Scope($scopecontent_0$) |
| $scope_1$ | ::= | ActiveScope($scopecontent_1$) \| Scope($scopecontent_0$) |
| $scopecontent_i$ | ::= | *partnerlinks* \| *sublinks* \| *insts* \| *vars* \| $act_i$? |
| $seq_i$ | ::= | Sequence($act_i$? \| Next($act_i$?)) |
| $flow_i$ | ::= | Flow($act_i$? \| ... \| $act_i$?) |
| $while_i$ | ::= | While(Condition(*expr*) \| $act_i$?) |
| $if_i$ | ::= | If(Condition(*expr*) \| Then($act_i$?) \| Else($act_i$?)) |
| *assign* | ::= | Assign(Copy((From \| FromPLink) \|(To \| ToPLink))) |
| *value* | ::= | True \| False \| *proc* \| *partnerlinkcontent* |
| *expr* | ::= | True \| False \| VariableRef |

WS-BPEL processes. Also, an active *instance* is represented almost exactly as the process, except it has an outermost node labelled by an Instance control and has an additional status node representing its current run-time status (e.g. the node labelled by the Running control mentioned in the previous section). Instances keep the current content of variables inside the variable node, and are executed as in process calculi by rewriting the bigraph according to the set of reaction rules to be described in the following section.

As an example, the process guideline from Sec. 2 is represented as a binding bigraph in the BPL Tool as shown in Fig. 6. Looking at the representation, it should be clear that the place graph corresponds closely to the nesting of elements in the XML syntax, the ports of controls correspond to attributes, and the link graph corresponds to shared values of attributes. However, already for the formalization of the subset of WS-BPEL given in [1] we needed to introduce some additional structure. For instance, a Next control is embedded in Sequence controls to cope with the fact that children nodes in bigraph place graphs are unordered while children nodes in XML are ordered (which is exploited in the sequence construct of WS-BPEL). To facilitate the definition of reaction rules in the semantics we also needed to add links representing instance and scope

```
val guideline =
Process[guideline][[guideline_id]] o (
    PartnerLinks o <-> '|' SubLinks o <-> '|' Instances o <->
'|' Variables o (    Variable[x, guideline_id] o <->
                     '|' Variable[y, guideline_id] o <->)
'|' Sequence[guideline_id] o (
    ReceiveSup[consultation, x, guideline_id, guideline_id]
'|' Next o Sequence[guideline_id] o (
    InvokeSup[task, x, guideline_id, y, guideline_id, guideline_id]
'|' Next o Sequence[guideline_id] o (
    ReplySup[consultation, x, guideline_id, guideline_id]
'|' Next o Sequence[guideline_id] o (
    ReceiveSup[resume, x, guideline_id, guideline_id]
'|' Next o Sequence[guideline_id] o (
    ReplySup[resume, x, guideline_id, guideline_id]
'|' Next o (
    InvokeSup[task, x, guideline_id, y, guideline_id, guideline_id]
    )))))));
```

**Fig. 6.** BPL tool representation of the guideline process

identities. As mentioned above, an active instance is represented almost as the process, except for a additonal node with a *status* control being either Invoked, Running, Stopped or Freezing. The status node was introduced already in the formalization of WS-BPEL given previously, because the semantics of Invoke and Exit activities requires two consecutive reactions. The extension with mobile sub-instances made it necessary to add the additional status control, Freezing, since freezing an instance into a process in a variable cannot be done atomically either. Also, we needed at top-level to introduce a status control indicating if the top-instance or any of its (arbitrarily nested) sub-instances are allowed to perform normal activities (by the control TopRunning) or if one of them are performing a sub-transition (control SubTransition) as part of a non-atomic activity. These aspects could most likely have been dealt with more elegantly if bigraphical reactive systems had a notion of priority on the reaction rules. We leave it for future work to study this.

### 4.1 Reaction Rules

In this section we present some of the new reaction rules used in the formalization of HomeBPEL, namely the thaw sub rule used for thawing a sub-process, and two of the rules responsible freezing an instance: freeze sub and freeze complete. The full set of reaction rules (in BPL Tool syntax) is available in the full paper [2] and via the online tool[3]. Also, [1] gives a detailed description of some of the reaction rules covering the WS-BPEL subset.

The thaw sub rule is presented below. The Thaw activity in the redex refers via its third port to the process inside the variable var. In the reactum the

---
[3] See ⟨http://tiger.itu.dk:8080/bplweb/index/20⟩.

Thaw activity has been removed (indicating it has been executed) and a new running sub-instance has been inserted within the Instances control. The last part (4&[inst_id_sub] |--> 0&[sub_scope]]) of the instantiation map ensures that the process body (contained in hole 0 in the redex) is copied and used as body of the new sub-instance (hole 4 in the reactum). It also ensures that the local bound link sub_scope of the process body is renamed to inst_id_sub in the new copy. Note also that we insert the status node Running in the new sub-instance. Finally, the rule also insert a Link control within the SubLinks control. The Link control points to the new sub-instance via its link inst_id_sub.

```
    Thaw[sub_link, sub_link_scope, var, var_scope, inst_id_sup]
|| Variable[var, var_scope]
    o Process[sub_name][[sub_scope]] o '[sub_scope (* hole 0 *) ]'
|| (     SubLinks o (SubLink[sub_link, sub_link_scope] o '[(* hole 1 *)]'
                            '|' '[(* hole 2 *)]')
    '|' Instances o '[(* hole 3 *)]')
|| Running[inst_id_sup, active_scopes_sup, inst_id_top]
|| TopRunning[inst_id_top]

    --[0 |-> 0, 1 |-> 1, 2 |-> 2, 3 |-> 3,
        4&[inst_id_sub] |--> 0&[sub_scope]]--|>

    <->
|| Variable[var, var_scope]
    o Process[sub_name][[sub_scope]] o '[sub_scope (* hole 0 *)]'
|| -//[inst_id_sub]
    o (     SubLinks o (     SubLink[sub_link, sub_link_scope]
                            o (Link[inst_id_sub] '|' '[(* hole 1 *)]')
                     '|' '[(* hole 2 *)]')
    '|' Instances
        o (     '[(* hole 3 *)]'
            '|' Instance[sub_name, inst_id_sub, active_scopes_sup]
                o (     -//[active_scopes_sub]
                        o Running[inst_id_sub, active_scopes_sub, inst_id_top]
                '|' '[inst_id_sub (* hole 4 *)]')))
|| Running[inst_id_sup, active_scopes_sup, inst_id_top]
|| TopRunning[inst_id_top]
```

In general, when we thaw a process it may itself contain frozen sub-instances frozen "in place", i.e. within the Instances control. An additional reaction rule (thaw sub instance), which can be seen in the full paper [2], is thus included for thawing frozen sub-instances.

Freezing a sub-instance requires several transitions, initiated by a Freeze activity. The Freeze activity references a running sub-instance through its SubLink and changes the status of the instance from Running to Freezing (thus ensuring that the sub-instance will not execute anymore), at the same time the Freeze activity is replaced by a FreezingSub activity, and the top-level status is changed from TopRunning to SubTransition to indicate that we have started a multistep reaction.

```
    Freeze[sub_link, sub_link_scope, var, var_scope, inst_id_sup]
|| (     SubLinks o (     SubLink[sub_link, sub_link_scope]
                         o (Link[inst_id_sub] '|' '[(* hole 0 *)]')
                    '|' '[(* hole 1 *)]')
    '|' Instances
         o (     Instance[sub_name, inst_id_sub, active_scopes_sup]
                 o (Running[inst_id_sub, active_scopes_sub, inst_id_top] '|'
                   '[(* hole 2 *)]') '|' '[(* hole 3 *)]'))
|| Running[inst_id_sup, active_scopes_sup, inst_id_top]
|| TopRunning[inst_id_top]

 --[0 |-> 0, 1 |-> 1, 2 |-> 2, 3 |-> 3]--|>

    FreezingSub[sub_link, sub_link_scope, var, var_scope, inst_id_sup]
|| (     SubLinks o (     SubLink[sub_link, sub_link_scope]
                         o (Link[inst_id_sub] '|' '[(* hole 0 *)]')
                    '|' '[(* hole 1 *)]')
    '|' Instances
         o (     Instance[sub_name, inst_id_sub, active_scopes_sup]
                 o (Freezing[inst_id_sub, active_scopes_sub, inst_id_top] '|'
                   '[(* hole 2 *)]') '|' '[(* hole 3 *)]'))
|| Running[inst_id_sup, active_scopes_sup, inst_id_top]
|| SubTransition[inst_id_top]
```

A freezing sub-instance cannot be frozen until all its active scopes and nested sub-instances have been frozen. In the same manner an active scope can first be frozen when all its nested scopes and sub-instances have been frozen. To this end we need two additional rules which are described in [2]. When no more sub-instances and scopes are connected to the "active_scopes" link of the sub-instance being frozen, meaning that all the sub-instances and scopes themselves have been frozen, the sub-instance itself can be frozen and placed into the proper variable denoted by var. To indicate that the multistep reaction is completed we change the top-level status from SubTransition and back to TopRunning.

```
-//[inst_id_sub]
o (     FreezingSub[sub_link, sub_link_scope, var, var_scope, inst_id_sup]
    || Variable[var, var_scope] o '[(* hole 0 *)]'
    || SubLink[sub_link, sub_link_scope] o (Link[inst_id_sub] '|' '[(* hole 1 *)]')
    || Running[inst_id_sup, active_scopes_sup, inst_id_top]
    || SubTransition[inst_id_top]
    || Instance[sub_name, inst_id_sub, active_scopes_sup]
         o (    -//[active_scopes_sub]
                o Freezing[inst_id_sub, active_scopes_sub, inst_id_top]
           '|' '[inst_id_sub (* hole 2 *)]'))

 --[0 |-> 2, 1 |-> 1]--|>

    <->
    || Variable[var, var_scope]
         o Process[sub_name][[inst_id_sub]] o '[inst_id_sub (* hole 0 *)]'
    || SubLink[sub_link, sub_link_scope] o '[(* hole 1 *)]'
    || Running[inst_id_sup, active_scopes_sup, inst_id_top]
    || TopRunning[inst_id_top]
    || <->
```

## 5   Conclusion and Future Work

We have proposed the language HomeBPEL extending a WS-BPEL-like language to allow processes as first-class values that can be stored in variables, passed as messages, and activated as embedded sub-instances. We have formalized HomeBPEL using binding bigraphical reactive systems implemented in the BPL Tool developed at the IT University of Copenhagen. The formalization utilizes the extensibility of bigraphs to extend and adapt a previous formalization of WS-BPEL given in [1]. We exemplified the use of HomeBPEL by an example of pervasive health care where treatment guidelines are dynamically deployed as sub processes of personal workflow processes, may be delegated to patients, and stay available for disconnected operation of mobile devices.

**Future Work.** In the CosmoBiz research project we are exploring the use of HomeBPEL primitives for mobile disconnected operation of business applications as developed by Microsoft Development Center Copenhagen [17]. Another interesting path for future research will be to examine different primitives for management and manipulation of processes, such as sub-process reflection and general manipulation, e.g. editing or joining of frozen sub-processes. This relates to the work on Higher-Order (Petri) Nets and applications to workflow studied in [13]. The addition of mobile embedded sub-instances also opens for a study of type systems that can guarantee safe process mobility and manipulation. We plan to examine the approaches done for Boxed Ambients [8] and for the higher-order $\pi$-calculus [18] on the safe integration of higher-order mobility and sessions. Hereto comes a detailed study of the expressiveness of HomeBPEL, e.g. in relation to workflow patterns (e.g. [19]) and in relation to process calculi for mobility such as Ambients, Seal and Homer. Finally, we would like to investigate the possibility of using HomeBPEL as a basis for a standardization of a higher-order process extension of WS-BPEL.

**Acknowledgements.** We would like to thank the anonymous referees for their numerous constructive comments.

## References

[1] Bundgaard, M., Glenstrup, A.J., Hildebrandt, T., Højsgaard, E.: An extensible formalization of WS-BPEL in binding bigraphs (submitted for publication, 2008)

[2] Bundgaard, M., Glenstrup, A.J., Hildebrandt, T., Højsgaard, E., Niss, H.: Formalizing WS-BPEL and higher order mobile embedded business processes in the bigraphical programming languages (BPL) tool. Technical Report TR-2008-103, IT University of Copenhagen (2008)

[3] Bundgaard, M., Hildebrandt, T.: Bigraphical semantics of higher-order mobile embedded resources with local names. In: Proceedings of GT-VC 2005. ENTCS, vol. 154, pp. 7–29. Elsevier, Amsterdam (2006)

[4] Bundgaard, M., Hildebrandt, T., Godskesen, J.C.: Modelling the security of smart cards by hard and soft types for higher-order mobile embedded resources. In: Proceedings of SecCo 2007. ENTCS, vol. 194, pp. 23–38. Elsevier, Amsterdam (2007)

[5] Cardelli, L., Gordon, A.D.: Mobile ambients. Theoretical Computer Science 240(1), 177–213 (2000)

[6] Castagna, G., Vitek, J., Zappa Nardelli, F.: The Seal calculus. Journal of Information and Computation 201(1), 1–54 (2005)

[7] Damgaard, T.C., Birkedal, L.: Axiomatizing binding bigraphs. Nordic Journal of Computing 13(1–2), 58–77 (2006)

[8] Garralda, P., Compagnoni, A.B., Dezani-Ciancaglini, M.: BASS: Boxed ambients with safe sessions. In: Proceedings of PPDP 2006, pp. 61–72. ACM Press, New York (2006)

[9] Glenstrup, A.J., Damgaard, T.C., Birkedal, L., Højsgaard, E.: An implementation of bigraph matching (submitted, 2008)

[10] Godskesen, J.C., Hildebrandt, T.: Extending Howe's method to early bisimulations for typed mobile embedded resources with local names. In: Ramanujam, R., Sen, S. (eds.) FSTTCS 2005. LNCS, vol. 3821, pp. 140–151. Springer, Heidelberg (2005)

[11] Hildebrandt, T.: Computer supported mobile adaptive business processes (CosmoBiz) research project. Webpage (2007), ⟨http://www.cosmobiz.org/⟩

[12] Hildebrandt, T., Niss, H., Olsen, M.: Formalising business process execution with bigraphs and Reactive XML. In: Ciancarini, P., Wiklicky, H. (eds.) COORDINATION 2006. LNCS, vol. 4038, pp. 113–129. Springer, Heidelberg (2006)

[13] Hoffmann, K., Mossakowski, T.: Algebraic higher-order nets: Graphs and petri nets as tokens. In: Wirsing, M., Pattinson, D., Hennicker, R. (eds.) WADT 2003. LNCS, vol. 2755, pp. 253–267. Springer, Heidelberg (2003)

[14] Jensen, O.H., Milner, R.: Bigraphs and mobile processes (revised). Technical Report UCAM-CL-TR-580, University of Cambridge – Computer Laboratory (2004)

[15] Kloppmann, M., Koenig, D., Leymann, F., Pfau, G., Rickayzen, A., von Reigen, C., Schmidt, P., Trickovic, I.: WS-BPEL extension for sub-processes: BPEL-SPE. White paper, IBM and SAP (2005)

[16] Lapadula, A., Pugliese, R., Tiezzi, F.: A WSDL-based type system for WS-BPEL. In: Ciancarini, P., Wiklicky, H. (eds.) COORDINATION 2006. LNCS, vol. 4038, pp. 145–163. Springer, Heidelberg (2006)

[17] Microsoft. Microsoft dynamics mobile development tools white paper - extending business solutions to the mobile workforce. Webpage (June 2007), ⟨http://dynamicsuser.net/files/folders/94158/download.aspx⟩

[18] Mostrous, D., Yoshida, N.: Two session typing systems for higher-order mobile processes. In: Della Rocca, S.R. (ed.) TLCA 2007. LNCS, vol. 4583, pp. 321–335. Springer, Heidelberg (2007)

[19] Russell, N., ter Hofstede, A.H., van der Aalst, W.M., Mulyar, N.: Workflow control-flow patterns: A revised view. BPM Center Report BPM-06-22, BPM-center.org (2006)

[20] Sangiorgi, D.: From pi-calculus to higher-order pi-calculus - and back. In: CAAP 1993, FASE 1993, and TAPSOFT 1993. LNCS, vol. 668, pp. 151–166. Springer Verlag, Heidelberg (1993)

# From Flow Logic to Static Type Systems for Coordination Languages*

Rocco De Nicola[1], Daniele Gorla[2], René Rydhof Hansen[3], Flemming Nielson[4],
Hanne Riis Nielson[4], Christian W. Probst[4], and Rosario Pugliese[1]

[1] Dip. Sistemi e Informatica, Univ. di Firenze
[2] Dip. Informatica, Univ. di Roma "La Sapienza"
[3] Department of Computer Science, Aalborg University
[4] Informatics and Mathematical Modelling, Technical University of Denmark

**Abstract.** Coordination languages are often used to describe open ended systems. This makes it challenging to develop tools for guaranteeing security of the coordinated systems and correctness of their interaction. Successful approaches to this problem have been based on type systems with dynamic checks; therefore, the correctness properties cannot be statically enforced. By contrast, static analysis approaches based on Flow Logic usually guarantee properties statically. In this paper we show how to combine these two approaches to obtain a static type system for describing secure access to tuple spaces and safe process migration for a dialect of the language KLAIM.

## 1   Introduction

Coordination languages allow two or more components of an application to communicate, by reading/removing/adding data to a shared communication medium, in order to accomplish shared goals. These languages are often being used to program applications in open ended systems, namely systems whose overall structure can change dynamically in unpredictable ways because the entities involved can join and leave at any time. This open nature exposes applications/systems to malicious accesses to their data/resources. Also, when process mobility is permitted, one can easily conceive trojan horses or viruses spawned at remote localities by malicious entities.

This scenario makes it challenging to develop tools for guaranteeing security of co-ordinated components and correctness of their interaction. Discretionary *access control* mechanisms have been then designed based either on specifying the permitted operations associated to the objects, or on specifying the *capabilities* that the different subjects have on the objects. The capability-based approach appears to be more appropriate than the access-control one for open distributed systems (see e.g. [12]), because capabilities can be distributed to the subjects, rather than being attached to the objects, and can be passed on. Moreover, their different categories need not to be statically fixed.

---

* This work has been supported by the EU project SENSORIA, IST-2005-016004.

D. Lea and G. Zavattaro (Eds.): COORDINATION 2008, LNCS 5052, pp. 100–116, 2008.

Different techniques have also been devised to enforce access control (see e.g. [11]). The most traditional one is based on a *reference monitor* that dynamically intercepts each attempted access to a (critical) resource and determines whether the intended operations should be allowed or denied. The main disadvantage of this approach is that security properties can only be checked dynamically, thus lowering the performance of systems. In order to limit these drawbacks, many *static analysis* techniques [8] have been devised. These techniques originate from the work on compilers [1] where it is imperative that all relevant behaviour of systems be determined statically. The result of analysing a program is an analysis estimate that gives a *global summary* of the properties of interest. However, these approaches require a knowledge of the full system and make the analysis more difficult.

To overcome all these limitations, hybrid approaches have been investigated that take advantage of both static and dynamic checks. This is, e.g., the case of the capability-based type systems for KLAIM (*Kernel Language for Agents Interaction and Mobility*, [2]), an experimental language specifically designed to program distributed systems made up of several mobile components. KLAIM has proved to be suitable for programming a wide range of distributed applications with agents and code mobility. Its primitives allow programmers to distribute/retrieve data and processes to/from the nodes of a net and extend Linda's notion of *generative communication* [4] through multiple shared tuple spaces.

In the capability-based type systems for KLAIM (see e.g. [3,5]), capabilities are used to specify the access control policies stating which operations (**in**, **out**, **eval**, ...) processes are allowed to perform while running at a given node; type checking then determines if processes comply with the policy of their hosting node. Access requests are mostly checked statically, but some dynamic type check is used to deal with data communication and process migration. In the former case, the dynamic checks are needed because no constraint is put on the kind of data inserted in tuple spaces; hence, withdrawal of data must be type controlled to establish matching with the input pattern. In the latter case, the type check has to be deferred to run-time because the target node of a process migration, and, hence, its policy, could be statically unknown.

In this paper we show how to use ideas from the Flow Logic approach [10] to static analysis to enhance KLAIM's type systems with means for giving a global account of the behaviour of the system. Indeed, this seems necessary in order to deal with the distributed nature of tuple spaces; furthermore, it allows us to develop a fully static type system. On the other hand, the Flow Logic approach borrows from the type-based approach in being compositional in axiomatising when analysis estimates are valid for a given system (although the actual computation of the best, i.e. least, analysis estimate requires global solution of a system of constraints [9]).

The rest of the paper is structured as follows. In Section 2 we introduce the syntax and semantics of the dialect of KLAIM considered; we dispense with an operation for creating new localities but instead use a primitive for accepting processes from the environment. A Flow Logic for the language is developed in Section 3 and used as inspiration to design the fully static type system presented in Section 4. Our major results, stated in Sections 3 and 4, prove that the two analysis techniques are in accordance. We conclude in Section 5.

## 2  A Dialect of Klaim

*Syntax.* The process calculus used here, like other members of the Klaim family, consists of three layers: nets, processes, and actions. Nets specify the overall structure of a system, including where processes and tuple spaces are located. Processes are the actors in this system and execute by performing actions. The syntax for all these components is presented in the upper part of Figure 1, whereas in the lower part it is reported the syntax of the capability-based types.

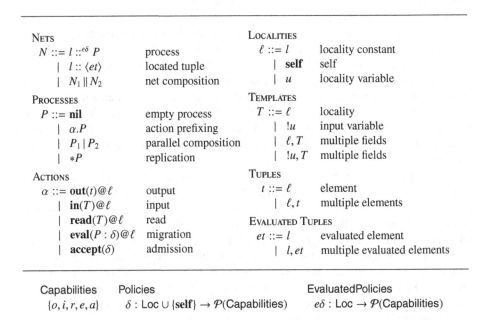

**Fig. 1.** Syntax of Klaim

A net consists of processes or tuples located at a locality *l*, or a composition of two nets. Processes are built up from the special process **nil**, that does not perform any action (and is often omitted), and from the basic actions by means of prefixing, parallel composition and replication. hence, the actual building blocks of processes are actions: **out** and **in** actions permit to produce/withdraw tuples to/from a possibly remote tuple space; **read** is a non-destructive variant of **in**; **eval** models mobility by spawning processes from a locality to another one, where it will be evaluated; **accept** allows processes coming from the environment to get into the system. In fact, **accept**, first introduced in [6], makes the language more suitable to model *open* systems.

As regards the tuples used for communication, we distinguish between *tuples* and *evaluated tuples*. An evaluated tuple is a sequence of values, that in our case are element of the set Loc of localities, and can be stored in tuple spaces. In contrast, tuples are

$$match(l, l) = \epsilon \qquad match(!u, l) = [u \mapsto l] \qquad \frac{match(T_1, et_1) = \sigma_1 \quad match(T_2, et_2) = \sigma_2}{match((T_1, T_2), (et_1, et_2)) = \sigma_1 \circ \sigma_2}$$

**Fig. 2.** Matching function

allowed to contain variables and self-references denoted by **self**. Tuples are used in processes to compose data to be communicated. When inputting tuples from tuple spaces, processes need to be able to select which tuple should be read or input. This filtering is performed by means of *templates*, that are similar to tuples, but can also contain *input variables* denoted as $!u$. In the latter case, $u$ is *bound* in the continuation process and will be used to retrieve information dynamically ($u$ will be replaced with some locality in the continuation process upon successful matching of the template against a tuple – see function *match* in Figure 2). A variable that is not bound is called *free*.

Network nodes are equipped with a *policy* that expresses the discretionary access control policy that should be enforced upon the system. As usual, a discretionary access control policy states which *subjects* can access which *objects* using what *capabilities*. Here we take *subjects* to be the localities where the action is executed, *objects* to be the localities accessed (for example, placing a new evaluated tuple there, inputting or reading an evaluated tuple, or spawning a new process), and *capabilities* to be indicators of the access operation, i.e., elements of the set Capabilities representing the out-, in-, read-, eval-, and accept-capability respectively. Policies are represented as *capability lists*. Thus, a policy, placed at some locality $l_s$, maps an object locality $l_o$ to the set of capabilities with which the subject $l_s$ can access $l_o$. Formally, we distinguish between Policies and EvaluatedPolicies. They both are functions from localities to sets of capabilities and differ only in whether they allow **self** to be used as a locality. Policies $\delta$ embedded in the syntax can use **self**, whereas (evaluated) policies $e\delta$ placed at some locality, written $l ::^{e\delta} \ldots$, may not.

*Semantics.* The semantics is an operational semantics in the form of a reduction semantics. It makes use of the function *match*, defined in Figure 2, for performing the variable bindings when reading or inputting. The matching proceeds by comparing a template $T$ componentwise with an evaluated tuple $et$. There are two possibilities for the match to succeed. Either both the template and the tuple begin with the same locality, or the template begins with an input variable. The result of a successful match is a substitution[1] that replaces the template's input variables with the values that occurred at corresponding positions in the evaluated tuple. In the sequel, we shall assume that templates $T$ are well-formed in the sense that they do not contain both $u$ and $!u$, and do not contain multiple occurrences of $!u$ for the same locality variable $u$.

The reduction semantics operates on closed processes, i.e. processes without free variables, but it still needs to take care of the occurrences of **self**. This is achieved by two auxiliary functions that map tuples (without free locality variables) to evaluated

---

[1] As usual, '$\epsilon$' denotes the empty substitution and '$\circ$' denotes composition of substitutions with disjoint domains.

$$N_1 \| N_2 \equiv N_2 \| N_1 \qquad (N_1 \| N_2) \| N_3 \equiv N_1 \| (N_2 \| N_3)$$

$$l ::^{e\delta} P \equiv l ::^{e\delta} (P \,|\, \mathbf{nil}) \qquad l ::^{e\delta} (P_1 \,|\, P_2) \equiv l ::^{e\delta} P_1 \| l ::^{e\delta} P_2 \qquad l ::^{e\delta} *P \equiv l ::^{e\delta} P \,|\, *P$$

**Fig. 3.** Structural Congruence

tuples, and policies to evaluated policies, respectively. They are both indexed with the locality to be used instead of **self** and we shall allow to use the same syntax for both.

$$(\!|\cdot|\!)_l : (\mathsf{Loc} \cup \{\mathbf{self}\}) \to \mathsf{Loc} \text{ given by } (\!|\ell|\!)_l = \begin{cases} l & \text{if } \ell = \mathbf{self} \\ l' & \text{if } \ell = l' \in \mathsf{Loc} \end{cases}$$

$$(\!|\cdot|\!)_l : \mathsf{Policy} \to \mathsf{EvaluatedPolicy} \text{ given by } (\!|\delta|\!)_l(l') = \bigcap\{\delta(\ell) \,|\, (\!|\ell|\!)_l = l'\}$$

The first function simply replaces any occurrence of **self** with the subscript, which is supposed to denote the intended meaning of **self**. We trivially extend it from working on single localities to working on sequences in a componentwise manner. We also trivially extend it to work on templates (without free locality variables) by defining it to act as the identity on input variables. The second function gives $(\!|\delta|\!)_l(l') = \delta(l')$ except when $l' = l$ in which case it gives $(\!|\delta|\!)_l(l) = \delta(l) \cap \delta(\mathbf{self})$ meaning that both the policies of $l$ and **self** are imposed.

Figure 4 shows the semantics for our calculus. In the reduction rules, we use $L$ to keep track of used localities and test if a given locality exists. The formulae of the form $\mathsf{RM}[\cdots]$ correspond to the checks that the (eventually superfluous) reference monitor must perform and make the intentions of the security policy clear. As an example, for the output action the formula $\mathsf{RM}[e\delta(l') \ni o]$ is intended to ensure that the local policy, $e\delta$, does indeed allow output to the locality $l'$. As usual, reductions are given compositionally and up-to a (quite standard) structural congruence, defined in Figure 3.

The **out** action takes an evaluated tuple and outputs it at the tuple space identified by $\ell$. Note that, as for all other actions, execution of the current subprocess is stuck if the tuple is not fully evaluated, that is if it still contains variables. The **in** action takes a template $T$ and a locality $\ell$, and uses the judgement for *match* previously defined to select a tuple from the tuple space at $\ell$ by matching all tuples against $T$. As an effect of the **in** action, the matched tuple is removed from the tuple space and the substitution $\sigma$ computed by *match* is applied to the rest of the process, thereby substituting input variables in $T$ by the values bound to them. The **eval** action sends its argument $Q$ for evaluation to the locality identified by $\ell$; the policy used is the evaluated version of the one specified and our static analysis techniques will ensure that such a policy conforms to the policy specified for the target node. The **accept** action admits into a system new processes coming from the environment. In case of dynamic enforcement, i.e. using reference monitors, this rule is as straightforward as the rest, since the behaviour of incoming processes is checked dynamically during their execution. In case of static enforcement, as is the focus of the present paper, we need to ensure that a new process, $Q$, is only admitted if it satisfies sufficiently strong guarantees that have been used in validating the known part of the system. We use the formula $\overline{\mathsf{RM}}[\phi_{acc}]$ to

$$\frac{(\![\ell]\!)_l = l' \in L \qquad (\![t]\!)_l = et \qquad \mathsf{RM}[e\delta(l') \ni o]}{L \triangleright l ::^{e\delta} \mathbf{out}(t)@\ell.P \longrightarrow l ::^{e\delta} P \,\|\, l' :: \langle et \rangle}$$

$$\frac{(\![\ell]\!)_l = l' \qquad match((\![T]\!)_l, et) = \sigma \qquad \mathsf{RM}[e\delta(l') \ni i]}{L \triangleright l ::^{e\delta} \mathbf{in}(T)@\ell.P \,\|\, l' :: \langle et \rangle \longrightarrow l ::^{e\delta} P\sigma}$$

$$\frac{(\![\ell]\!)_l = l' \qquad match((\![T]\!)_l, et) = \sigma \qquad \mathsf{RM}[e\delta(l') \ni r]}{L \triangleright l ::^{e\delta} \mathbf{read}(T)@\ell.P \,\|\, l' :: \langle et \rangle \longrightarrow l ::^{e\delta} P\sigma \,\|\, l' :: \langle et \rangle}$$

$$\frac{(\![\ell]\!)_l = l' \in L \qquad (\![\delta']\!)_l = e\delta' \qquad \mathsf{RM}[e\delta(l') \ni e]}{L \triangleright l ::^{e\delta} \mathbf{eval}(Q : \delta')@\ell.P \longrightarrow l ::^{e\delta} P \,\|\, l' ::^{e\delta'} Q}$$

$$\frac{(\![\delta']\!)_l = e\delta' \qquad \mathsf{RM}[e\delta(l) \ni a] \qquad \overline{\mathsf{RM}}[\phi_{acc}]}{L \triangleright l ::^{e\delta} \mathbf{accept}(\delta').P \longrightarrow l ::^{e\delta} P \,\|\, l ::^{e\delta'} Q}$$

$$\frac{L \triangleright N_1 \longrightarrow N_1'}{L \triangleright N_1 \,\|\, N_2 \longrightarrow N_1' \,\|\, N_2} \qquad\qquad \frac{N \equiv N_1 \qquad L \triangleright N_1 \longrightarrow N_2 \qquad N_2 \equiv N'}{L \triangleright N \longrightarrow N'}$$

**Fig. 4.** Operational Semantics of KLAIM

express this. We will need to postpone the explanation of the formula $\phi_{acc}$ used until after the two static analysis techniques have been developed. Intuitively, it will ensure that the incoming process (viz., $Q$) respects the specified policy $\delta'$ that, in turn, respects the policy $e\delta$ of the node where the action is performed (viz., $l$).

As we stated in the Introduction, there are two main approaches to enforce a given access control policy on a system: one is to check it dynamically by means of a reference monitor; the other is to develop a static analysis technique. Subsequently, we shall refer to the reference monitor semantics by writing $L \triangleright N \longrightarrow_{on} N'$. It is specified as in Figure 4 by letting $\mathsf{RM}[\phi]$ mean $\phi$ and $\overline{\mathsf{RM}}[\phi]$ mean *true* (and so can be removed). Similarly, we shall refer to the semantics without reference monitors by writing $L \triangleright N \longrightarrow_{off} N'$. It is specified as in Figure 4 by letting $\mathsf{RM}[\phi]$ mean *true* (and so can be removed) and $\overline{\mathsf{RM}}[\phi]$ mean $\phi$.

*Running Example.* As a running example, throughout the paper we will consider a scenario where a user wants to collect and elaborate some pieces of information, e.g., electronic books, scattered on network nodes. The user can exploit both remote operations and process migration, e.g., to deal with possible network failures. The KLAIM net modelling the scenario includes the user process (located at $l_U$), a directory service process (located at $l_D$), and some data containers; for simplicity sake, we consider only two data containers, located at $l_{C1}$ and $l_{C2}$. Moreover, in the example we assume that some sort of primitive data, like e.g. strings, are available and can be used as fields of data tuples. This is only for convenience, since all of the primitive data can be encoded in terms of localities.

$$l_U ::^{e\delta_U} P_U \,\|\, l_D ::^{e\delta_D} P_D \,\|\, l_{C1} ::^{e\delta_{C1}} \mathbf{nil} \,\|\, l_{C2} ::^{e\delta_{C2}} \mathbf{nil}$$
$$\|\, l_D :: \langle library, l_{C1} \rangle \,|\, \langle library, l_{C2} \rangle \,\|\, l_{C1} :: \langle J.R.R. \text{ Tolkien, The Hobbit} \rangle$$

Each node hosts running processes that must obey a given access policy and/or contains data tuples. The processes are defined as

$$P_U = \textbf{eval}(P_1 : \delta)@l_D. * \textbf{in}(!source, !data)@l_U. < \textit{elaborate data} >$$
$$P_1 = *\textbf{read}(\text{library}, !u)@l_D.\textbf{eval}(P_2 : \delta)@u$$
$$P_2 = \textbf{read}(\text{J.R.R. Tolkien}, !title)@\textbf{self}.\textbf{out}(\textbf{self}, title)@l_U$$
$$P_D = \textbf{accept}(\delta_a)$$

and use the policies

$$\delta = [l_U \mapsto \{o\}, l_D \mapsto \{r\}, l_{C1} \mapsto \{e, r\}, l_{C2} \mapsto \{e, r\}]$$
$$\delta_a = [l_D \mapsto \{r\}, l_{C1} \mapsto \{e, r\}, l_{C2} \mapsto \{e, r\}]$$

while the access policies of nodes are the following ones:

$$e\delta_U = [l_U \mapsto \{i\}, l_D \mapsto \{e\}]$$
$$e\delta_D = [l_D \mapsto \{r, a\}, l_{C1} \mapsto \{e\}, l_{C2} \mapsto \{e\}]$$
$$e\delta_{C1} = [l_{C1} \mapsto \{r\}, l_U \mapsto \{o\}]$$
$$e\delta_{C2} = [l_{C2} \mapsto \{r\}, l_U \mapsto \{o\}]$$

For completeness sake, we note that the example is intended to illustrate how the calculus and, in later sections, the analysis and the type system work. It is not meant to be a complete specification of a distributed system and therefore it does not include modelling of, e.g., scheduling and similar concepts.

## 3   Flow Logic

We shall now develop an analysis that captures the behaviour of nets. The analysis computes an *over-approximation* of the actual behaviour of a KLAIM net. We first present the abstract domains underlying the analysis and next define the judgements for nets, processes, actions and matchings. We conclude this section by analysing our running example and presenting the theoretical properties of our approach.

*Analysis Domains.* We shall use the following analysis domains:

- $\hat{T} \in \text{Loc} \to \mathcal{P}(\text{Loc}^*)$ is an *abstract tuple space*; it is an over-approximation of the set of all tuples (of locality constants) that may at some point reside in the tuple space of a given locality constant.
- $\hat{\sigma} \in \text{LocVar} \to \mathcal{P}(\text{Loc})$ is an *abstract environment*; it keeps a record of all locality constants that a given locality variable might at some point be bound to. (This functionality suffices because the structural congruence does not contain $\alpha$-renaming of bound variables.)
- $\partial \in \text{AbstractPolicy} = \text{Loc} \to \mathcal{P}(\text{Capabilities})$ is an *abstract policy* somewhat like the concrete policy $\delta \in \text{Policy}$; however, it takes the *union* of possibilities rather than the intersection because it is descriptive rather than prescriptive. Abstract policies form a lattice based on the natural ordering on partial functions, written $\sqsubseteq$, i.e. $\partial \sqsubseteq \partial'$ if and only if $\text{dom}(\partial) \subseteq \text{dom}(\partial')$ and $\partial(l) \subseteq \partial'(l)$, for every $l \in \text{dom}(\partial)$.

$$(\hat{T}, \Delta, \hat{\sigma}) \models_P^{\{l\}} P : \partial', \varrho' \qquad \partial' \setminus_{\{l\}} e\delta \sqsubseteq \varrho \qquad \Delta(l) \setminus_{\{l\}} e\delta \sqsubseteq \varrho \qquad \varrho' \sqsubseteq \varrho$$
$$\overline{(\hat{T}, \Delta, \hat{\sigma}) \models_N l ::^{e\delta} P : \varrho}$$

$$\frac{\{et\} \subseteq \hat{T}(l)}{(\hat{T}, \Delta, \hat{\sigma}) \models_N l :: \langle et \rangle : \varrho} \qquad \frac{(\hat{T}, \Delta, \hat{\sigma}) \models_N N_1 : \varrho \qquad (\hat{T}, \Delta, \hat{\sigma}) \models_N N_2 : \varrho}{(\hat{T}, \Delta, \hat{\sigma}) \models_N N_1 \| N_2 : \varrho}$$

**Fig. 5.** Static Analysis of Nets

- $\Delta \in \mathsf{Loc} \to \mathsf{AbstractPolicy}$ is a record of policies for remotely evaluated processes.
- $\varrho \in \mathsf{Loc} \to \mathsf{AbstractPolicy}$ is a *record of violations of policies*. It records all the actions that may have been performed during the evolution of the net and that were *not* permitted by the local policy; the first argument is the subject locality where the action was initiated, and the second argument is the object locality where the action had effect, and the resulting set of capabilities are the offending ones. Hence a program will only be acceptable if it can be analysed with $\varrho = \bot$.
- $\Lambda \in \mathcal{P}(\mathsf{Loc})$ is a set of localities of interest at a given point. In general, we shall analyse processes at sets of localities (rather than a single locality) in order to obtain a context insensitive analysis. A context sensitive analysis, i.e., a more precise analysis, can be obtained by analysing processes at single localities.

*Analysis of Nets.* The judgement for the analysis of a net $N$ has the form

$$(\hat{T}, \Delta, \hat{\sigma}) \models_N N : \varrho$$

and is defined by the inference system of Figure 5. As is usual in Flow Logic, we provide a componentwise definition.

To determine the potential violations of the policy for a located process, we use the following auxiliary notation for "subtracting" two policies:

$$\partial_1 \setminus_\Lambda \partial_2 \qquad : \mathsf{Loc} \to \mathsf{AbstractPolicy}$$
$$(\partial_1 \setminus_\Lambda \partial_2)(\lambda_s)(\lambda_o) = \begin{cases} \partial_1(\lambda_o) \setminus \partial_2(\lambda_o) & \text{if } \lambda_s \in \Lambda \\ \emptyset & \text{otherwise} \end{cases}$$

*Analysis of Processes.* The judgement for the analysis of a process $P$ has the form

$$(\hat{T}, \Delta, \hat{\sigma}) \models_P^\Lambda P : \partial, \varrho$$

and is defined by the inference system of Figure 6. The intention is that when true, the components $\hat{T}$, $\Delta$, $\hat{\sigma}$, $\partial$ and $\varrho$ correctly capture not only the behaviour of the process $P$ (when located at one of the localities $\lambda \in \Lambda$) but also the behaviour of all the processes it may evolve into. Any violation encountered during analysis of the process is recorded in $\varrho$, whereas $\partial$ approximates the actual policy employed by the process. The definition is fairly straightforward in that it inspects the components of a process in a structural way making use of the judgement for actions to be introduced next.

$$(\hat{T}, \Delta, \hat{\sigma}) \models_{\mathrm{P}}^{\Lambda} \mathbf{nil} : \partial, \varrho$$

$$\frac{(\hat{T}, \Delta, \hat{\sigma}) \models_{\mathrm{P}}^{\Lambda} P_1 : \partial, \varrho \qquad (\hat{T}, \Delta, \hat{\sigma}) \models_{\mathrm{P}}^{\Lambda} P_2 : \partial, \varrho}{(\hat{T}, \Delta, \hat{\sigma}) \models_{\mathrm{P}}^{\Lambda} P_1 \mid P_2 : \partial, \varrho}$$

$$\frac{(\hat{T}, \Delta, \hat{\sigma}) \models_{\mathrm{P}}^{\Lambda} P : \partial, \varrho}{(\hat{T}, \Delta, \hat{\sigma}) \models_{\mathrm{P}}^{\Lambda} *P : \partial, \varrho}$$

$$\frac{(\hat{T}, \Delta, \hat{\sigma}) \models_{\mathrm{P}}^{\Lambda} P : \partial, \varrho \qquad (\hat{T}, \Delta, \hat{\sigma}) \models_{\mathrm{A}}^{\Lambda} \alpha : \partial, \varrho}{(\hat{T}, \Delta, \hat{\sigma}) \models_{\mathrm{P}}^{\Lambda} \alpha.P : \partial, \varrho}$$

**Fig. 6.** Static Analysis of Processes

$$\frac{(\!(t)\!)_{\hat{\sigma}}^{\Lambda} \subseteq \hat{T}\langle(\!(\ell)\!)_{\hat{\sigma}}^{\Lambda}\rangle \qquad [(\!(\ell)\!)_{\hat{\sigma}}^{\Lambda} \to \{o\}] \sqsubseteq \partial}{(\hat{T}, \Delta, \hat{\sigma}) \models_{\mathrm{A}}^{\Lambda} \mathbf{out}(t)@\ell : \partial, \varrho}$$

$$\frac{\hat{\sigma} \models_{1}^{(\!(\ell)\!)_{\hat{\sigma}}^{\Lambda}} T : \hat{T}[(\!(\ell)\!)_{\hat{\sigma}}^{\Lambda}] \triangleright \hat{W} \qquad [(\!(\ell)\!)_{\hat{\sigma}}^{\Lambda} \to \{i\}] \sqsubseteq \partial}{(\hat{T}, \Delta, \hat{\sigma}) \models_{\mathrm{A}}^{\Lambda} \mathbf{in}(T)@\ell : \partial, \varrho}$$

$$\frac{(\!(\delta)\!)^{\Lambda} \sqsubseteq \partial \qquad [\Lambda \to \{a\}] \sqsubseteq \partial}{(\hat{T}, \Delta, \hat{\sigma}) \models_{\mathrm{A}}^{\Lambda} \mathbf{accept}(\delta) : \partial, \varrho}$$

$$\frac{\hat{\sigma} \models_{1}^{(\!(\ell)\!)_{\hat{\sigma}}^{\Lambda}} T : \hat{T}[(\!(\ell)\!)_{\hat{\sigma}}^{\Lambda}] \triangleright \hat{W} \qquad [(\!(\ell)\!)_{\hat{\sigma}}^{\Lambda} \to \{i\}] \sqsubseteq \partial}{(\hat{T}, \Delta, \hat{\sigma}) \models_{\mathrm{A}}^{\Lambda} \mathbf{read}(T)@\ell : \partial, \varrho}$$

$$\frac{(\hat{T}, \Delta, \hat{\sigma}) \models_{\mathrm{P}}^{(\!(\ell)\!)_{\hat{\sigma}}^{\Lambda}} P : \partial', \varrho \quad \forall \lambda \in (\!(\ell)\!)_{\hat{\sigma}}^{\Lambda} : (\!(\delta)\!)^{\Lambda} \sqsubseteq \Delta(\lambda) \quad \partial' \backslash_{(\!(\ell)\!)_{\hat{\sigma}}^{\Lambda}} (\!(\delta)\!)^{\Lambda} \sqsubseteq \varrho \quad [(\!(\ell)\!)_{\hat{\sigma}}^{\Lambda} \to \{e\}] \sqsubseteq \partial}{(\hat{T}, \Delta, \hat{\sigma}) \models_{\mathrm{A}}^{\Lambda} \mathbf{eval}(P : \delta)@\ell : \partial, \varrho}$$

**Fig. 7.** Static Analysis of Actions

*Analysis of Actions.* The judgement for the analysis of an action $\alpha$ has the form

$$(\hat{T}, \Delta, \hat{\sigma}) \models_{\mathrm{A}}^{\Lambda} \alpha : \partial, \varrho$$

and is defined by the inference system of Figure 7.

To transform localities $\ell \in \mathsf{Loc} \cup \{\mathbf{self}\} \cup \mathsf{LocVar}$ into the set of localities that they denote, we make use of the auxiliary function

$$(\!(\cdot)\!)_{\hat{\sigma}}^{\Lambda} : \mathsf{Loc} \cup \{\mathbf{self}\} \cup \mathsf{LocVar} \to \mathcal{P}(\mathsf{Loc})$$

$$(\!(\ell)\!)_{\hat{\sigma}}^{\Lambda} = \begin{cases} \{\ell\} & \text{if } \ell \in \mathsf{Loc} \\ \Lambda & \text{if } \ell = \mathbf{self} \\ \hat{\sigma}(\ell) & \text{if } \ell \in \mathsf{LocVar} \end{cases}$$

This transformation is straightforward for locality constants, while it exploits the set $\Lambda$ of locality constants that **self** might stand for, in the case of **self**, and the abstract environment $\hat{\sigma}$, in the case of locality variables. This operation is extended to tuples $t$ by taking the cartesian product of all components. For evaluated tuples $et$, we have $(\!(et)\!)_{\hat{\sigma}}^{\Lambda} = \{et\}$.

To transform concrete policies into abstract policies, we make use of the auxiliary function

$$(\!|\delta|\!)^\Lambda \quad : \text{AbstractPolicy}$$
$$(\!|\delta|\!)^\Lambda(\lambda) = \bigcap\{\delta(\ell)|\, \lambda \in (\!|\ell|\!)^\Lambda_\bot, \ell \in \text{Loc} \cup \{\textbf{self}\}\}$$

This operation is somewhat reminiscent of the way tuples were transformed into evaluated tuples. Since (concrete) policies are not defined on locality variables, it suffices using the empty abstract environment $\bot$ in the conversion of localities. For evaluated policies, we have $(\!|e\delta|\!)^\Lambda(l) = e\delta(l)$.

To more easily express that the appropriate record of actions is captured by the policy component $\partial$, we use the notation

$$[X \to Y] \quad : \text{Loc} \to \mathcal{P}(\text{Capability})$$
$$[X \to Y](\lambda) = \begin{cases} Y \text{ if } \lambda \in X \\ \emptyset \text{ otherwise} \end{cases}$$

where $\lambda$ denotes the locality constant where the action might have effect and $Y$ usually is a singleton set. In the case of **out**, **in**, **read** and **eval**, we take $X$ to be the set $(\!|\ell|\!)^\Lambda_{\hat\sigma}$; in the case of **accept**, we take $X$ to be the set $\Lambda$ of current localities.

Since most of the rules need to take effect for any element in some set $X$ of locality constants, it is frequently necessary to write logical formulae using universal and existential quantifiers. The resulting formulae tend to clutter the understanding of the more subtle features of the Flow Logic specification and we have therefore decided to introduce two notational shorthands so as to reduce the explicit use of quantifiers. The notations are formally defined by:

$$\Psi[X] = \bigcup_{x \in X} \Psi(x) = \{z \mid \exists x \in X : z \in \Psi(x)\}$$
$$\Psi\langle X\rangle = \bigcap_{x \in X} \Psi(x) = \{z \mid \forall x \in X : z \in \Psi(x)\}$$

It is worth pointing out that this permits to use them in inclusions and that they can be expanded away using the following tautologies:

$$\Psi[X] \subseteq Z \iff \forall x \in X : \Psi(x) \subseteq Z$$
$$Z \subseteq \Psi\langle X\rangle \iff \forall x \in X : Z \subseteq \Psi(x)$$

As an example, in the rule for **out**$(t)@\ell$ the premise $(\!|t|\!)^\Lambda_{\hat\sigma} \subseteq \hat{T}\langle(\!|\ell|\!)^\Lambda_{\hat\sigma}\rangle$ expresses that *all* the values that $t$ may evaluate to are included in *all* the tuple spaces that could be associated with the locality $\ell$.

*Analysis of Matching.* The auxiliary judgement

$$\hat\sigma \models^\Lambda_i T : \hat{U} \triangleright \hat{W}$$

defined by the inference system of Figure 8 is used in the rules for **in**$(T)@\ell$ and **read**$(T)@\ell$ in Figure 7 to ensure that the matching may succeed. The set of tuples of interest are those of the tuple space of $\ell$, that is, $\hat{T}[(\!|\ell|\!)^\Lambda_{\hat\sigma}]$. The judgement expresses that matching should start at position $i$ in the template $T$, $\hat{U}$ contains the set of tuples that we are matching against, $\hat{W}$ contains the tuples from $\hat{U}$ that successfully match $T$ from position $i$ and onwards, and $\hat\sigma$ records the appropriate bindings that need to be performed. In the rules of Figure 7, $\pi_i(et)$ denotes the $i$'th component of the tuple $et$ and $\pi_i(\hat{V})$ is the componentwise extension of the operation to sets of tuples.

$$\dfrac{\{et \in \hat{U} \mid \pi_i(et) \in (\!|\ell|\!)_{\hat{\sigma}}^{\Lambda} \wedge |et| = i\} \subseteq \hat{W}}{\hat{\sigma} \models_i^{\Lambda} \ell : \hat{U} \triangleright \hat{W}} \qquad \dfrac{\{et \in \hat{U} \mid |et| = i\} \subseteq \hat{W} \qquad \pi_i(\hat{W}) \subseteq \hat{\sigma}(u)}{\hat{\sigma} \models_i^{\Lambda} !u : \hat{U} \triangleright \hat{W}}$$

$$\dfrac{\{et \in \hat{U} \mid \pi_i(et) \in (\!|\ell|\!)_{\hat{\sigma}}^{\Lambda} \wedge |et| \geq i\} \subseteq \hat{V} \qquad \hat{\sigma} \models_{i+1}^{\Lambda} T : \hat{V} \triangleright \hat{W}}{\hat{\sigma} \models_i^{\Lambda} \ell, T : \hat{U} \triangleright \hat{W}}$$

$$\dfrac{\{et \in \hat{U} \mid |et| \geq i\} \subseteq \hat{V} \qquad \hat{\sigma} \models_{i+1}^{\Lambda} T : \hat{V} \triangleright \hat{W} \qquad \pi_i(\hat{W}) \subseteq \hat{\sigma}(u)}{\hat{\sigma} \models_i^{\Lambda} !u, T : \hat{U} \triangleright \hat{W}}$$

**Fig. 8.** Static Analysis of Matching

*Acceptable Programs.* Before an external program can be accepted into a given net it has to be analysed with respect to an access policy defined by the accepting process. This ensures that the accepting process can control what access privileges it is willing to pass onto programs that may be unknown *a priori*. For an accepting process, $l ::^{e\delta}$ **accept**$(\delta').P$, willing to admit external programs, $Q$, that comply with policy $\delta'$ this check amounts to the following requirement on $Q$:

$$(\hat{T}, \Delta, \hat{\sigma}) \models_{\mathsf{P}}^{\{l\}} Q : (\!|\delta'|\!)^{\{l\}}, \perp$$

The check guarantees that a process $Q$, when evaluated at locality $l$, will only perform actions that do not violate the accepting policy, $\delta'$, as indicated by $(\!|\delta'|\!)^{\{l\}}, \perp$ on the right hand side of the colon. Here $\hat{T}$, $\Delta$ and $\hat{\sigma}$ should be considered "global constants" to be used for an entire execution of a net; this will be clarified in Theorem 1 below. Thus we may complete the semantics in Figure 4 by letting $\phi_{acc} = (\hat{T}, \Delta, \hat{\sigma}) \models_{\mathsf{P}}^{\{l\}} Q : (\!|\delta'|\!)^{\{l\}}, \perp$.

*Analysis of the Running Example.* For the running example, we have $(\hat{T}, \Delta, \hat{\sigma}) \models_{\mathsf{N}} N : \perp$ for the following choice of $\hat{T}$, $\Delta$ and $\hat{\sigma}$:

$$
\begin{array}{lll}
\hat{T} : l_U \mapsto \{\langle l_{C1}, \text{"The Hobbit"}\rangle\} & \hat{\sigma} : u \mapsto \{l_{C1}, l_{C2}\} & \Delta : l_U \mapsto \perp \\
\quad l_D \mapsto \{\langle library, l_{C1}\rangle, \langle library, l_{C2}\rangle\} & \quad title \mapsto \{\text{The Hobbit}\} & \quad l_D \mapsto \delta \\
\quad l_{C1} \mapsto \{\langle J.R.R.Tolkien, The Hobbit\rangle\} & \quad source \mapsto \{l_{C1}\} & \quad l_{C1} \mapsto \delta \\
\quad l_{C2} \mapsto \emptyset & \quad data \mapsto \{\text{The Hobbit}\} & \quad l_{C2} \mapsto \delta
\end{array}
$$

*Properties of the Analysis.* Consistency of the analysis is formalised as a subject-reduction theorem.

**Theorem 1 (Subject Reduction).** *If $L \triangleright N \longrightarrow_{\text{off}} N'$ and $(\hat{T}, \Delta, \hat{\sigma}) \models_{\mathsf{N}} N : \perp$, then $(\hat{T}, \Delta, \hat{\sigma}) \models_{\mathsf{N}} N' : \perp$.*

*Proof.* The proof is by induction on $L \triangleright N \longrightarrow_{\text{off}} N'$, using a few auxiliary results:

- The analysis result is invariant under the structural congruence; that is, if $N \equiv N'$ then $(\hat{T}, \Delta, \hat{\sigma}) \models_{\mathsf{N}} N : \varrho$ if and only if $(\hat{T}, \Delta, \hat{\sigma}) \models_{\mathsf{N}} N' : \varrho$.
- The analysis of matching is correct; that is, if $match((\!|T|\!)_l, et) = \sigma$, $l \in \Lambda$, $et \in \hat{U}$, and $\hat{\sigma} \models_1^{\Lambda} T : \hat{U} \triangleright \hat{W}$, then $et \in \hat{W}$ and $\forall u \in \text{dom}(\sigma) : \sigma(u) \in \hat{\sigma}(u)$. ∎

Note that this result also holds with $\varrho$ in place of $\bot$, but it is more instructive to consider executions where no security policy is violated; the result clearly does not hold if $\longrightarrow_{\text{on}}$ is used (as any accepted process may violate the analysis and the security policy). Overall correctness of the analysis is formalised as an adequacy result.

**Theorem 2 (Adequacy).** *If* $L \triangleright N \longrightarrow_{\text{off}} N'$ *and* $(\hat{T}, \Delta, \hat{\sigma}) \models_N N : \bot$*, then* $L \triangleright N \longrightarrow_{\text{on}} N'$.

*Proof.* The proof is by induction on $L \triangleright N \longrightarrow_{\text{off}} N'$, by inspecting Figures 5, 6, 7, and 8. ∎

More informally, we can show that if $L \triangleright N \longrightarrow_{\text{off}} N'$ and $(\hat{T}, \Delta, \hat{\sigma}) \models_N N : \varrho$, then all offending actions performed are listed in $\varrho$. Finally, existence of best analysis estimates is formalised as a Moore-family result:

**Theorem 3 (Moore Family).** *For all nets $N$, the set $\mathcal{Y}$ of analysis estimates* $\{(\hat{T}, \Delta, \hat{\sigma}, \varrho) \mid (\hat{T}, \Delta, \hat{\sigma}) \models_N N : \varrho\}$ *is a* Moore Family*; i.e.,* $\forall Y \subseteq \mathcal{Y} : \sqcap Y \in \mathcal{Y}$.

*Proof.* The proof is by structural induction on $N$ using that all constraints on $(\hat{T}, \Delta, \hat{\sigma}, \varrho)$ occur in positive positions only. ∎

*Comparison with previous analyses of* KLAIM. The analysis presented in this paper is an extension of a reworked version of the analysis specified in [6]. The main extension being an added $\Delta$ component to give a record of the policies imposed by the local **eval**'s. We have also reworked and rationalised the notation and introduced a number of auxiliary functions (most notably, $\langle \rangle$ and [ ]) to increase readability of the analysis. Finally, we have added the $\Lambda$ component (essentially allowing remotely evaluated processes to be analysed only once rather than at each receiving locality as in [6]). Among other things, this makes implementation easier.

# 4   A Static Type System

Typing approaches to KLAIM usually exploit dynamic checks; we now present a totally static type system whose design has been inspired by the Flow Logic developed in the previous section. We conclude this section by presenting the theoretical properties of the type system and the analysis of our running example.

*Types and Auxiliary Functions.* We can get rid of dynamic checks by following the philosophy underlying the Flow Logic approach. Indeed, it suffices to associate to every locality an upper bound of the tuples it can contain and a lower bound on its policy (like functions $\hat{T}$ and $\Delta$ did in Section 3); moreover, we should also provide an upper bound to the set of localities that can instantiate every variable. Thus, types for localities are pairs $\langle \mathcal{T}; \partial \rangle$, where $\mathcal{T} \subseteq_{\text{fin}} \mathsf{Loc}^*$. Intuitively, if $\langle \mathcal{T}; \partial \rangle$ is the type of $l$, $\mathcal{T}$ is an upper bound on the tuples that $l$ can contain and $\partial$ is a lower bound on $l$'s policy. Types for input variables are, instead, just sets of localities; we can assign to $u$ the type $\mathcal{T} \subseteq_{\text{fin}} \mathsf{Loc}$, meaning that $\mathcal{T}$ are the localities that $u$ can assume. A *typing environment* $\Gamma$ assigns types to localities and variables.

Given a typing environment $\Gamma$, we now define some functions that will be used in the type system. First, we need to specify the values an identifier can assume. Thus, $\mathbf{val}_\Gamma(l) = \{l\}$ and $\mathbf{val}_\Gamma(u) = \Gamma(u)$; the definition of function $\mathbf{val}_\Gamma$ is extended to tuples component-wise. In the type system, we shall frequently look at the possible tuples a node can contain, at its policy or at the privileges it owns over the other nodes of the net. These pieces of information are easily accessible when the node is specified by a locality constant, thanks to the typing environment given. However, it can also happen in the typing phase to have nodes specified by variables (take, e.g., process $\mathbf{in}(!u)@l.\mathbf{eval}(Q : \delta)@u.P$, where $Q$ must be typed at $u$). In this case, the information must be extracted from $\Gamma$ as follows.

The tuples that can appear at a node identified by a variable are obtained by considering the tuples that can appear at every node whose locality is associated to the variable. However, from case to case, we need to know the tuples shared by all such nodes or all the possible tuples; accordingly, we combine the tuples contained at the different nodes by intersection or union. The following functions perform these tasks:

$$\Gamma\langle\ell\rangle = \bigcap\nolimits_{l \in \mathbf{val}_\Gamma(\ell)} \pi_1(\Gamma(l)) \qquad \Gamma[\ell] = \bigcup\nolimits_{l \in \mathbf{val}_\Gamma(\ell)} \pi_1(\Gamma(l))$$

To know the rights a policy grants over a node identified by a variable, we consider the intersection of all the privileges over the localities that the variable can assume:

$$\mathbf{Priv}_\Gamma(\partial, \ell) = \bigcap\nolimits_{l \in \mathbf{val}_\Gamma(\ell)} \partial(l)$$

Similarly, the policy of a node identified by a variable is the greatest subset of access rights present in the policy of every locality that the variable can assume:

$$\mathbf{Pol}_\Gamma(\ell) = \bigsqcap\nolimits_{l \in \mathbf{val}_\Gamma(\ell)} \pi_2(\Gamma(l))$$

where $\sqcap$ denotes the greatest lower bound.

In the typing rules, we shall need to evaluate localities and policies to replace occurrences of **self**. In both cases, we extend the evaluation function for localities and policies introduced when presenting the operational semantics to allow the subscript to also be a variable (in the case in which the node where the evaluation takes place is identified by a variable). This leads to notations $(\!|\ell'|\!)_\ell$ and $(\!|\delta|\!)_\ell^\Gamma$; for the latter, we have that $(\!|\delta|\!)_\ell^\Gamma(l)$ is $\delta(l)$, if $l \notin \mathbf{val}_\Gamma(\ell)$, and is $\delta(l) \cap \delta(\mathbf{self})$, otherwise.

Finally, given a typing environment $\Gamma$ and a template $T$ used by a process running at locality $\ell$, we need to check that $\Gamma$ provides the right information on the variables bound in $T$. Thus, we define the check of $\Gamma$ with $T$ at $\ell$, written $check_\ell(\Gamma, T)$, as the judgement:

$$\forall i. \pi_i(T) = !u \Rightarrow$$
$$\pi_i(\{et \in \Gamma[\ell] : |et| = |T| \wedge \forall j \in \{1..|T|\}. \pi_j(T) = \ell' \Rightarrow \pi_j(et) \in \mathbf{val}_\Gamma(\ell')\}) \subseteq \Gamma(u)$$

In particular, every variable bound in $T$ will be associated to all the possible localities that, at runtime, can be used to instantiate such a variable. The latters are obtained by taking all the possible tuples (of the same length as $T$ and that can match against it) that can appear at $\ell$ and consider their $i$-th projection, for every $i$ such that the $i$-th field of $T$ is a variable.

$$\frac{\Gamma \vdash N_1 \quad \Gamma \vdash N_2}{\Gamma \vdash N_1 \parallel N_2} \qquad \frac{et \in \pi_1(\Gamma(l))}{\Gamma \vdash l :: \langle et \rangle} \qquad \frac{\pi_2(\Gamma(l)) \sqsubseteq e\delta \quad \Gamma; e\delta \vdash_l P}{\Gamma \vdash l ::^{e\delta} P}$$

**Fig. 9.** Typing Nets

$$\frac{(\!\ell'\!)_\ell = \ell'' \quad o \in \mathrm{Priv}_\Gamma(\partial, \ell'') \quad \mathrm{val}_\Gamma((\!t\!)_\ell) \subseteq \Gamma\langle\ell''\rangle \quad \Gamma; \partial \vdash_\ell P}{\Gamma; \partial \vdash_\ell \mathbf{out}(t)@\ell'.P}$$

$$\frac{(\!\ell'\!)_\ell = \ell'' \quad e \in \mathrm{Priv}_\Gamma(\partial, \ell'') \quad (\!\delta\!)_\ell^\Gamma = \partial' \sqsubseteq \mathrm{Pol}_\Gamma(\ell'') \quad \Gamma; \partial' \vdash_{\ell''} Q \quad \Gamma; \partial \vdash_\ell P}{\Gamma; \partial \vdash_\ell \mathbf{eval}(Q : \delta)@\ell'.P}$$

$$\frac{(\!\ell'\!)_\ell = \ell'' \quad i \in \mathrm{Priv}_\Gamma(\partial, \ell'') \quad \mathrm{check}_{\ell''}(\Gamma, (\!T\!)_\ell) \quad \Gamma; \partial \vdash_\ell P}{\Gamma; \partial \vdash_\ell \mathbf{in}(T)@\ell'.P}$$

$$\frac{(\!\ell'\!)_\ell = \ell'' \quad r \in \mathrm{Priv}_\Gamma(\partial, \ell'') \quad \mathrm{check}_{\ell''}(\Gamma, (\!T\!)_\ell) \quad \Gamma; \partial \vdash_\ell P}{\Gamma; \partial \vdash_\ell \mathbf{read}(T)@\ell'.P}$$

$$\frac{a \in \mathrm{Priv}_\Gamma(\partial, \ell) \quad (\!\delta\!)_\ell^\Gamma \sqsubseteq \partial \quad \Gamma; \partial \vdash_\ell P}{\Gamma; \partial \vdash_\ell \mathbf{accept}(\delta).P} \qquad \frac{\Gamma; \partial \vdash_\ell P_1 \quad \Gamma; \partial \vdash_\ell P_2}{\Gamma; \partial \vdash_\ell P_1 \mid P_2} \qquad \frac{\Gamma; \partial \vdash_\ell P}{\Gamma; \partial \vdash_\ell *P}$$

**Fig. 10.** Typing Processes

*Typing Rules.* We are now ready to present the typing system. The typing rules for nets are in Figure 9; they define judgements of the form $\Gamma \vdash N$ that should be read as: "net $N$ respects the constraints specified on its nodes by $\Gamma$". The rules are simple: to type a compound net we should type the components isolately; to type a located tuple, we must ensure that the tuple is allowed by $\Gamma$; to type a located process, we must ensure that the policy $e\delta$ conforms to the policy specified by $\Gamma$ and that the process respects $e\delta$.

The typing rules for processes are in Figure 10 and define judgements of the form $\Gamma; \partial \vdash_\ell P$. Intuitively, such a judgement is needed to type under $\Gamma$ a process $P$ running at $\ell$ (where, by construction of the typing system, $\ell$ cannot be **self**) associated with policy $\partial$. The key rules are for action prefixes. In all cases, it is verified that the policy associated to the process provides a proper access right; moreover, to this aim, if the action can take place remotely, a preliminary evaluation of the locality target of the action is needed. For action **out**, the main thing to check is that the tuples that the action can produce can appear at every possible target locality (thus, we need here the intersection of all the possible tuple spaces, as calculated by $\Gamma\langle\rangle$); of course, we also have to check that the continuation is well-typed. For action **eval**, apart from checking that the continuation is well-typed, we have to check that the specified policy conforms to the policy associated to the target and, in this case, that the spawned process can run under the specified policy at the target locality. For actions **in** and **read**, we have to type the continuation in a typing environment obtained by extending the current environment with the possible values that variables bound in the template can assume. Finally, for action **accept**, we only need to verify that the specified policy conforms to the policy of the hosting node and that the continuation is well-typed.

We can now complete the semantics in Figure 4 by using as $\phi$ in the rule for the **accept** action the judgement $\Gamma; \partial' \vdash_l Q$, where $\Gamma$ is the typing environment used to type the net containing $l ::^{e\delta}$ **accept**$(\delta').P$ and $\partial' = (\!|\delta'|\!)_l$.

*Soundness Results.* A net $N$ is *typeable* if there exists a $\Gamma$ such that $\Gamma \vdash N$. We now prove that typeable nets are exactly the ones that can be accepted by the Flow Logic without errors; as a corollary of Theorems 1 and 2, this result trivially entails that also the type system enjoys subject reduction and adequacy.

**Theorem 4.** *$N$ is typeable if and only if $(\hat{T}, \Delta, \hat{\sigma}) \models_N N : \perp$.*

*Proof.* (*If*) We first sketch how to prove that acceptable nets are typeable. To this aim, given a triple $(\hat{T}, \Delta, \hat{\sigma})$ and a net $N$ such that $(\hat{T}, \Delta, \hat{\sigma}) \models_N N : \perp$, we define the typing environment $\Gamma$ as follows:

$$\Gamma(u) = \hat{\sigma}(u) \qquad \text{for every } u \in \mathsf{LocVar}$$
$$\Gamma(l) = \langle \hat{T}(l); \partial_l \rangle \quad \text{for every } l \in \mathsf{Loc}, \text{ where } \partial_l = \prod_{l::^{e\delta}P \, in \, N} e\delta$$

where "$l ::^{e\delta}P$ in $N$" means that $N \equiv l ::^{e\delta} P \parallel N'$, for some $N'$. Then, the proof works by induction on the length of the inference for $(\hat{T}, \Delta, \hat{\sigma}) \models_N N : \perp$, by exploiting two lemmata:

1. If $(\hat{T}, \Delta, \hat{\sigma}) \models_P^\Lambda P : \partial_1, \perp$ then $\Gamma; \partial_2 \vdash_\ell P$, whenever $\Lambda = \mathsf{val}_\Gamma(\ell)$ and $\partial_1 \sqsubseteq \partial_2$.
2. If $match((\!|T|\!)_l, et) = \sigma, l \in \Lambda, et \in \hat{U}$ and $\hat{\sigma} \models_1^\Lambda T : \hat{U} \triangleright \hat{W}$, then $et \in \hat{W}$ and $\sigma \sqsubseteq \hat{\sigma}$.

(*Only if*) We now sketch how to prove that typeable nets are acceptale. To this aim, given a typing environment $\Gamma$ and a net $N$ such that $\Gamma \vdash N$, we define the triple $(\hat{T}, \Delta, \hat{\sigma})$ as follows:

$$\hat{\sigma}(u) = \Gamma(u) \qquad \text{for every } u \in \mathsf{LocVar}$$
$$\hat{T}(l) = \pi_1(\Gamma(l)) \quad \text{for every } l \in \mathsf{Loc}$$

To define $\Delta$, we first need to remove every occurrence of **self** occurring as target of actions in $N$ as follows (we only give the non-homomorphic cases):

$$(\!|l ::^{e\delta} P|\!) = l ::^{e\delta} (\!|P|\!)_l \qquad\qquad (\!|\alpha.P|\!)_\ell = (\!|\alpha|\!)_\ell.(\!|P|\!)_\ell$$

$$(\!|\mathbf{out}(t)@\ell'|\!)_\ell = \mathbf{out}(t)@(\!|\ell'|\!)_\ell \qquad (\!|\mathbf{eval}(Q : \delta)@\ell'|\!)_\ell = \mathbf{eval}((\!|Q|\!)_{(\!|\ell'|\!)_\ell} : \delta)@(\!|\ell'|\!)_\ell$$

$$(\!|\mathbf{in}(T)@\ell'|\!)_\ell = \mathbf{in}(T)@(\!|\ell'|\!)_\ell \qquad (\!|\mathbf{read}(T)@\ell'|\!)_\ell = \mathbf{read}(T)@(\!|\ell'|\!)_\ell$$

Then, for every $l \in \mathsf{Loc}$, we let

$$\Delta(l) = \bigsqcup_{\mathbf{eval}(P:\delta)@\ell \, in \, (\!|N|\!) \, : \, l \in \mathsf{val}_\Gamma(\ell)} (\!|\delta|\!)_l^\Gamma$$

The proof then works by induction on the length of the inference for $\Gamma \vdash N$, by exploiting two auxiliary lemmata:

1. If $\Gamma; \partial \vdash_\ell P$ and $\Lambda = \mathbf{val}_\Gamma(\ell)$, then $(\hat{T}, \Delta, \hat{\sigma}) \models_P^\Lambda P : \partial, \bot$ and, for every $\mathbf{eval}(Q : \delta)@\ell'$ in $P$, it holds that $(\!(\delta)\!)_l^\Gamma \sqsubseteq \pi_2(\Gamma(l))$, for every $l \in \mathbf{val}_\Gamma(\ell')$.

2. Let $l \in \Lambda$ and assume that, for every $et \in \hat{U} \cap \hat{W}$, it holds that $match(\langle\!\langle T \rangle\!\rangle_l, et) = \sigma \sqsubseteq \hat{\sigma}$; then $\hat{\sigma} \models_1^\Lambda T : \hat{U} \triangleright \hat{W}$. ∎

*Analysis of the Running Example.* Thanks to the previous theorem, we know that the running example can be typed; by looking at the proof of Theorem 4 (that shows how to define a proper $\Gamma$ out of $\hat{T}$, $\hat{\sigma}$ and the typed net $N$), we have that the following typing environment makes the running example typeable:

$$\Gamma(l_K) = \langle \hat{T}(l_K); e\delta_K \rangle \qquad \Gamma(x) = \hat{\sigma}(x)$$

for every $K \in \{U, D, C1, C2\}$ and $x \in \{u, title, source, data\}$.

*Final Remarks.* Notice that $\pi_2(\Gamma(l))$ and $\Delta(l)$ are both used to statically analyze migrations at $l$ of a process labeled with a policy $\delta$, but are defined and used in different ways. The former is a lower bound on the policy of the receiving node and, hence, $\delta$ (properly evaluated) must be lower than $\pi_2(\Gamma(l))$. The latter is an upper bound to the policy specified for the migrating process and, hence, $\Delta(l)$ must be greater than $\delta$ (properly evaluated). For this reason, $\pi_2(\Gamma(l))$ is defined as the greatest lower bound of the policies specified for nodes with address $l$; instead, $\Delta(l)$ is defined as the lowest upper bound of the policies specified for migrations at $l$. In this way, if we have two migrations at $l$ (say, with policies $\delta_1$ and $\delta_2$) and the nodes $l ::^{e\delta_1} \cdots$ and $l ::^{e\delta_2} \cdots$, the type system checks that $\delta_i \sqsubseteq e\delta_1 \sqcap e\delta_2 = \pi_2(\Gamma(l))$, whereas the Flow Logic checks that $\Delta(l) = \delta_1 \sqcup \delta_2 \sqsubseteq e\delta_j$. These two checks are equivalent, in that they are both equivalent to $\delta_i \sqsubseteq e\delta_j$.

# 5  Conclusions and Further Work

We have considered a dialect of KLAIM, an experimental language designed for modeling and programming distributed systems with mobile components, and have presented an operational semantics for it that, by taking advantage of a reference monitor, permits controlling the kind of operations processes can perform at the different localities. We have then considered an alternative approach to access control based on Flow Logic that permits statically checking absence of access violations. Finally, we have reconsidered one of the type systems for access control previously developed that contained some dynamic checks, and, by exploiting concepts already used in the Flow Logic section, we have designed a fully static type system. To the best of our knowledge, this is the first completely static type system for controlling accesses in the context of a tuple space-based coordination language. We have also shown that both static approaches are sound with respect to the dynamic one based on reference monitor and provide the same analysis results.

We see this work just as an initial step towards understanding the relationships between static and dynamic approaches to access control and studying the relative merit of type systems and Flow Logic specifications (expanding on [7]). In future work, we want to investigate the impact of extending the analysis to a language with a primitive for dynamically creating new nodes with assigned policies (this is usually called **newloc** in the KLAIM setting). Indeed, the semantics treatment of such a primitive would require the policies of nodes to change dynamically. Clearly, making policies on nodes much more dynamic, would entail a number of differences in the static analysis, that was never conceived to cater for this possibility. We also want to study the relationships between the global approach of type systems and Flow Logic and the more local one of the more traditional type systems that may contain dynamic components. Finally, we find it challenging to understand the relative expressive power of reference monitors and the static analysis approaches also in light of the considerations of [11], where it is claimed that the two approaches can capture different properties and are somehow incomparable. It would be interesting to understand what assumptions on the models are necessary to guarantee relative soundness.

**Acknowledgements.** We thank the anonymous referees for their useful comments.

# References

1. Aho, A.V., Lam, M.S., Sethi, R., Ullman, J.D.: Compilers: Principles, Techniques, and Tools, 2nd edn., Addison-Wesley, Reading (August 2006)
2. De Nicola, R., Ferrari, G., Pugliese, R.: KLAIM: a Kernel Language for Agents Interaction and Mobility. IEEE Transactions on Software Engineering 24(5), 315–330 (1998)
3. De Nicola, R., Ferrari, G., Pugliese, R., Venneri, B.: Types for Access Control. Theoretical Computer Science 240(1), 215–254 (2000)
4. Gelernter, D.: Generative communication in Linda. ACM Transactions on Programming Languages and Systems 7(1), 80–112 (1985)
5. Gorla, D., Pugliese, R.: Resource access and mobility control with dynamic privileges acquisition. In: Baeten, J.C.M., Lenstra, J.K., Parrow, J., Woeginger, G.J. (eds.) ICALP 2003. LNCS, vol. 2719, pp. 119–132. Springer, Heidelberg (2003)
6. Hansen, R.R., Probst, C.W., Nielson, F.: Sandboxing in myKlaim. In: The First International Conference on Availability, Reliability and Security, ARES 2006, Vienna, Austria, April 2006, IEEE Computer Society Press, Los Alamitos (2006)
7. Nielson, F., Riis Nielson, H.: Types from Control Flow Analysis. In: Reps, T., Sagiv, M., Bauer, J. (eds.) Wilhelm Festschrift. LNCS, vol. 4444, pp. 293–310. Springer, Heidelberg (2007)
8. Nielson, F., Riis Nielson, H., Hankin, C.: Principles of Program Analysis, 2nd edn. Springer, Berlin (2005)
9. Nielson, F., Seidl, H., Riis Nielson, H.: A succinct solver for alfp. Nord. J. Comput. 9(4), 335–372 (2002)
10. Riis Nielson, H., Nielson, F.: Flow Logic: A Multi-paradigmatic Approach to Static Analysis. In: Mogensen, T.Æ., Schmidt, D.A., Sudborough, I.H. (eds.) The Essence of Computation. LNCS, vol. 2566, pp. 223–244. Springer, Heidelberg (2002)
11. Schneider, F.B., Morrisett, G., Harper, R.: A Language-Based Approach to Security. In: Wilhelm, R. (ed.) Informatics: 10 Years Back, 10 Years Ahead. LNCS, vol. 2000. Springer, Heidelberg (2001)
12. Izura Udzir, N., Wood, A.M., Jacob, J.L.: Coordination with multicapabilities. Sci. Comput. Program. 64(2), 205–222 (2007)

# Session Types for Orchestration Charts

Alessandro Fantechi[1] and Elie Najm[2]

[1] Dipartimento di Sistemi e Informatica
Università degli Studi di Firenze, Firenze, Italy
fantechi@dsi.unifi.it
[2] Telecom ParisTech (ENST)
46 rue Barrault, F-75013 Paris, France
elie.najm@telecom-paristech.fr

**Abstract.** We present a novel approach for the sound orchestration of services. It is based on Orcharts and Typecharts: a service orchestration language and an associated behavioural typing language. Sessions play a pivotal role in this approach. Orcharts (orchestration charts) define session based services and Typecharts provide for session types with complex interaction patterns that generalise the request/response interaction paradigm. We provide an algorithm for deciding behavioural well typedeness. We claim that well typed service configurations have the soundness property, i.e., any session that can be initiated in a well typed configuration has its requestor and provider behave in mutual conformance and potentially reach service completion.

## 1 Introduction

Behavioural type systems have been defined in recent years with the aim to be able to check the compatibility of communicating components, not only regarding data exchanged, but also regarding the matching of their respective behaviour [14,8,13]. Recently, the focus moved from components to service-oriented architectures, and several calculi for *service orchestration* have been defined. Of them, Orc [7] uses few simple orchestration mechanisms but shows a very interesting expressive power. In this language, an invoked service provides a simple reply which can be piped to trigger other invocations. Thus, interface compatibility looses its interest because invocations which are not replied or replies which are not listened at are simply lost, with no possible identification of error states.

Although Orc is able to encode most common workflow patterns [5], the simplicity of the language is felt unsatisfactory for dealing with complex services in which different invocations of a service can trigger complex interaction patterns among several services. Often an interaction pattern constitute a *session* which clearly identifies which are the message exchanges belonging to the session. Session types, that is, behavioural types associated to sessions, have been studied for protocols [6] and software components [15]. Service orchestration calculi including the notion of session have also been defined [3,9].

A different approach can be chosen for relating messages of a complex interaction pattern: message exchanges that are logically related among them are identified as sharing the same *correlation data* [10], as it occurs, for example, when a

D. Lea and G. Zavattaro (Eds.): COORDINATION 2008, LNCS 5052, pp. 117–134, 2008.
© Springer-Verlag Berlin Heidelberg 2008

unique id related to a client is passed in any message referring to that client. In both session-based and correlation based approaches, defining behavioural types has often proved difficult: while sessions make simpler, with respect to correlation approaches, to identify the interaction patterns that are to be typed, session based calculi with higher order session communication, defined in a $\pi$-calculus style, make typing non-trivial and not able to support automatic verification [4].

The aim of this paper is to investigate how we can maintain simple session typing, and therefore automatic verification, by defining an ad hoc session based service language which allows for an easy verification of the compatibility of interactions between services. The designed language, orcharts, expressing graphically data and control flows, allows for an easy traceabilty of sessions. This allows a finite-state behaviour type to be associated to a session, so that standard verification tools can be used to check compatibility between the client and the service. Indeed, our approach has been aimed at a language powerful enough to express common orchestration examples, but also simple enough to meet the typability requirement. The typing algorithm is briefly presented and the properties that can be verified over well typed services are discussed.

## 2  Informal Introduction to Typecharts and Orcharts

### 2.1  Sessions

A service oriented architecture is constituted by a collection of interacting services or *sites* (actually, in the following, we tend to use the word site to indicate a named entity that provides a service, and the word service when we refer to its behavioural aspects). Each site provides a service which may use services provided by other sites. Interactions between services occur by message exchange and in the context of shared *sessions*. Before invoking a service, the requestor creates a (unique) session name and attaches it to the name of the invoked service (example - the creation of a new session s bound to service ServiceFoo is written s@ServiceFoo). The session name is then used by the requestor in all subsequent interactions with the server pertaining to the same session (at a given point in time, a requestor may have many ongoing sessions with the same service). For instance, s.m() denotes the sending of message m() in the context of session s and hence s.m() is sent to ServiceFoo since s is bound to ServiceFoo. On the server side, at the reception of a first invocation message pertaining to a new session, a new session is started and a dialogue is initiated with the requestor in the context of this session. This dialogue takes place in both directions and on two new FIFO queues allocated for this purpose. In the present version of our approach we consider that different sessions that are being concurrently executed on the same server do not share information on that server. Sessions that are created on the server side (in order to provide services to requestors) are referred to as root sessions (root sessions are denoted by $\rho$).

## 2.2   Defining Services

The template for service definition is given in figure 1, where one can distinguish four main parts: Service name, Provides, Requires, and the defining Orchart. In figure 2 we present two definitions of services, namely, QuickNews and Collect-News, which revisit examples of News Services presented in [7]. Both services require the services of two News Agencies, CNN and BBC, and provide each a specific type of news service. The QuickNews service provides only one news item based on the first reply from the news agencies. The CollectNews service provides the news items collected from the two news agencies. The constructs used in QuickNews and CollectNews are commented in more detail section 2.4. Note that both required services, CNN and BBC, have the same required type-chart, namely, NewsAgency-T. As can be seen in figure 3(a), NewsAgency-T is a typechart with a single request/response interaction scheme.

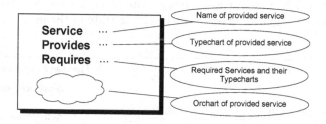

**Fig. 1.** Template of a site service definition

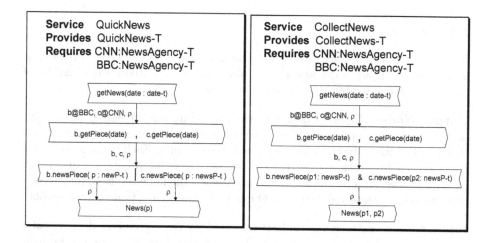

**Fig. 2.** The two versions of News service, with comments

## 2.3   Typecharts

Typecharts are a special kind of deterministic finite labelled transition systems where labels represent messages with parameter types. Parameter types can be data types (characterised by the -t suffix), or names of typecharts (characterised by the -T suffix). The transition system of a typechart has an initial state and one or more final states. States of a typechart are also partitioned in two subsets: sending states and receiving states (initial and final states can only be receiving states). Note that the typechart declared for a required service (e.g. CNN:NewsAgency-T) can be different from the one declared as provided in the service definition of this required service. For instance, 3(b) represents a possible provided typechart for the CNN and BBC services. This typechart allows for repeatable request/response interactions with the requestor. QuickNews and CollectNews do not exploit the possibility of reissuing a request in the same session but still can soundly interact with the CNN and BBC services. The relations between provided and required typecharts will be discussed in section 4.1. Note: we adopt a convention for typechart represntation which is to always adopt server's view. Hence, e.g, a sending state of a typechart has to be matched by a sending state in the server and a receiving state in the invoker.

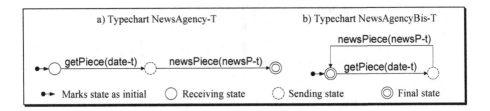

**Fig. 3.** Two typecharts of News Agency services

## 2.4   Orcharts

An Orchart is a finite directed acyclic graph where nodes can be of three types: input nodes, output nodes and instantiation nodes, and where edges can be of two types: data carrying edges and control edges.

**Output Nodes.** Figure 4 describes the input and output nodes. An output node may contain one or more message emissions. Messages may carry values that can be either simple data values or service names. Each message emission refers also to its emission context, i.e., a session name. Informally, one may think of output nodes as immediately executable: when the node receives control each of its messages is inserted in the FIFO queue corresponding to its named session.

**Input Nodes.** have an Internal Structure: They Are Subduivided in capsules (symbol | is used as a capsule separator). A capsule represents a possible branching from the output node. A capsule may contain one or more message receptions.

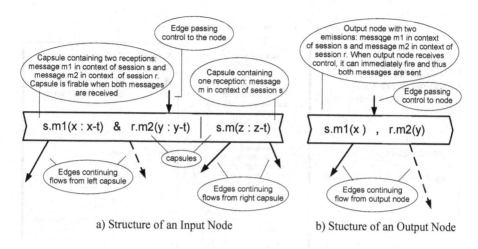

a) Structure of an Input Node          b) Stucture of an Output Node

**Fig. 4.** Structure of Input and Output Nodes

In capsules with multiple receptions, all messages should pertain to different sessions. This constraint can be syntactically enforced. Capsules with multiple receptions are in fact a shorthand that can be rewritten in single message capsules. For lack of space, the details of this rewriting will not be addressed in this paper and in the sequel we conisder capsules to contain a single message. As an informal interpretation one may think of an input node to behave like a guarded command. When an input node receives control, its capsules can consume messages that are awaiting in the FIFO queues. When one message in a capsule is consumed this capsule is fired and the flow continues on all edges having their sources at this capsule. When a capsule is fired, all other capsules of the same input node (and their continuation flows) are discarded.

**Data and Control Flow Edges.** Nodes of an orchart can be joined with either control edges (represented by dotted arrows) or data flow edges (represented by solid line edges). Data flow edges in fact convey both control and data flow. Data flow edges are the means for binding variables with values: a use occurence of a variable can be bound with a binding occurence of this variable only if there is a directed path made of data flow edges starting at the binding occurence and ending at the use occurence. Moreover, variables are write-once, hence, in the semantics, we will use the replacement of variables by their values. Flow edges (control or data) can carry labels. These labels indicate the set of sessions that are continued on the flow and/or the set of sessions created on the flow. Examples of labelled flow edges are provided in the following sections.

## 2.5   Revisiting the QuickNews and CollectNews Examples

In figure 5 we describe the different constructs of the orcharts used in service definitions of QuickNews and CollectNews introduced in section 2.2. For better

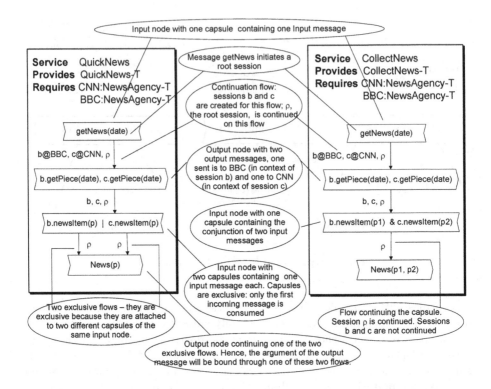

**Fig. 5.** The two versions of News service with comments

readability, we chose not to represent the types of the used data. The comments in the picture follow the flow of the behaviour of the orcharts, explaining the meaning of the various types of nodes and of the flow of session names and variables along the edges. Before being used for an interaction, session names must be bound to a service name. Variables are given a value in an input message (occuring in a capsule), which value is then used in ouput nodes. See for instance how variable date acquires a value in the getNews message which is used downstream in the getPiece output message.

## 2.6   Definition and Instantiation of Named Orcharts

In order to provide for recursion, orcharts use the classical approach of naming and instantiating behaviours. In figure 6 we give the definition of a GetBestPrice service which illustrates the use of a named orchart instantiation. Briefly, the GetBest-Price service returns, for a given product item requested by the user, the name of the shop that sells this item at the best price. The GetBestPrice service requires the services of ShopsFinder which provides all shops selling a given item; and of MinEval which provides the minimum of a set of values. The behaviour of this service is as follows. A (root) service session is started with the input of getBestPrice message, then a session named sf (with ShopsFinder) is created then used to invoke ShopsFinder. Then a session m bound to MinEval is created and the HARVEST or-chart is instantiated with session parameters sf, m and $\rho$ and value item. HARVEST collects shops proposals coming from ShopsFinder and, for each response, invokes the shop to get the price of the item and then sends the price to MinEval. When HARVEST terminates, i.e., when its orchart reaches the exit node (exit nodes are described in the sequel), a flow is continued in which MinEval is invoked to get the shop having the best price. Finally, this information is returned to the user. It is worth noting in this example how orcharts are named and instantiated. Named Orcharts are defined within dotted rounded boxes and instantiated using solid line rounded boxes. The name of the orchart is placed inside the box and is followed by the session parameters (in square brackets) and value parameters (in parenthesis). The definition of a named orchart starts with an initial input node and may have exit nodes (zero or more) represented with small circles placed at the boundary of the definition box (on the dotted line). At exit nodes, the sessions that are contin-ued are given in square brackets whereas the values that are returned are given in parenthesis (the HARVEST example only shows continued sessions). A syntactical constraint is enforced that the sessions continued at an exit node must be a subset of the session parameters. For instance, HARVEST has session parameters [sf, m, $\rho$] but only [m, $\rho$] are continued from the exit node. In order to simplify the pre-sentation, but without a loss of generality, we consider in the present paper that named orcharts may have at most one exit node. To this exit node correspond an exit point in the instantiation diagram of the named orchart (exit points are also represented with a small circle). The dynamic semantics of instantiation is defined through unfolding. When control reaches an instantiation, the instantia-tion node is replaced by the definition of the named orchart. In this replacement,

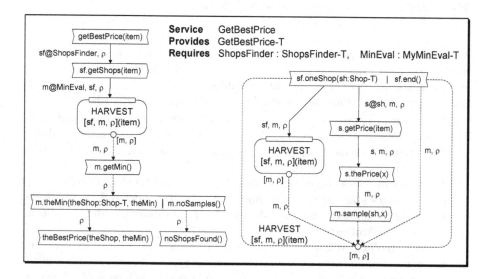

**Fig. 6.** The Get Best Price Service Definition

the edges in the definition orchart whose targets are at the exit node have their target redirected to the successor node of the exit point in the instantiation.

## 2.7  Parallel Flows

The orchart defining HARVEST involves the use of parallel flows. For instance, when message oneShop carrying a shop name sh is consumed, behaviour continues in two flows, the left flow is (re−)instantiation of HARVEST and the right flow proceeds with invoking the shop sh and storing the obtained price in MinEval. Note how sessions m and $\rho$ are present in these two parallel flows whereas session sf is only present in the left flow. Note the use, in the definition of this named orchart, of flow control edges. The parallel flows feature allows for the creation of an unbounded number of sessions. The fact that any definition of a named orchart starts with an input node enforces that the creation of sessions and flows is always guarded.

# 3  Formal Syntax and Semantics

In this section we give a formal definition of the Orchart language. To remain within page limits, we simplify the syntax w.r.t. the one used in the examples, e.g. by considering only one message emitted by an output node, and no conjunction of messages inside a capsule. Indeed, both these constructs can be defined as shorthands for orcharts employing the basic constructs considered in this section.

## 3.1  Syntax of Orchestration Charts (Orcharts)

The syntax of the language assumes the following:

$r, r', s, s', \ldots$ range over session names,    $\rho, \sigma, \sigma' \ldots$ over session values
$w, w' \ldots$ over service names,    $a, a' \ldots$ over orchart names
$m, m' \ldots$ over message names,    $G, G' \ldots$ over orcharts
$n, n' \ldots$ over nodes,    $v, v' \ldots$ over values of any type
$x, x', y, y', z, z' \ldots$ over (any type of) variables

An orchart can be defined as a sestuple $(N, C, E, \mathcal{L}_N, \mathcal{L}_E, Exp)$ where:

- $N$ is a set of nodes: $N = IN \uplus ON \uplus InstN$, where $IN$ is the set of input nodes, $ON$ the set of output nodes, $InstN$ the set of instantiation nodes;
- $IN$ is defined as a partition of a set of capsules $C$: $\forall n \in IN, n \subseteq C$ and $\forall n, n' \in IN, n \neq n' \implies n \cap n' = \emptyset$.
- $E$ is a set of edges connecting nodes: $E \subseteq (C \times N \cup (ON \cup InstN) \times N)$, that is, edges starting an input node are actually associated to a capsule. Moreover, $E$ is partitioned in $DE$, the set of data carrying edges, and $CE$, the set of control carrying edges: $E = DE \uplus CE$;
- $\mathcal{L}_N$ is a labelling function that associates to each node a set of expressions, whose number and syntax is depending on the type of node: $\mathcal{L}_N : N \to 2^{Exp}$; in particular, this function is defined on input nodes by means of a function $\mathcal{L}_C$ that labels capsules: $\mathcal{L}_C : C \to Exp$ ;

- $\mathcal{L}_E$ is a labelling function that associates to each edge two sets of expressions, namely the set of passed data (only for edges in $DE$) and the set of passed sessions: $\mathcal{L}_E : DE \rightarrow 2^{Exp} \times 2^{Exp} \uplus CE \rightarrow 2^{Exp}$;
- $Exp$ is a domain of expression that are used to label nodes and edges: the syntax of the expressions and their association to the various kinds of nodes and edges is reported below.

$$Exp ::= CExp \mid OExp \mid SExp \mid DExp \mid SSExp \qquad CExp ::= s.m() \mid s.m(Xlist)$$
$$Xlist ::= x \mid Xlist, Xlist \qquad OExp ::= s.m() \mid s.m(DExp)$$
$$SExp ::= \sigma \mid s \mid SExp, SExp \qquad DExp ::= x \mid w \mid DExp, DExp$$
$$SSExp ::= \sigma \mid s \mid s@w \mid s@x \mid SSExp, SSExp$$

In this section, for brevity, we ignore the syntax of types of expressions. Indeed, as shown in session 2, it is sufficient to consider typing expressions with the standard notation $x : T$. Expressions are used to label edges and nodes:

- each capsule in an Input node is labelled with an expression in $CExp$;
- each Ouput node is labelled with an expression in $OExp$;
- each Control edge is labelled with an expression in $SSExp$;
- each Data edge is labelled with an expression in $SSExp$;
- each Instantiation node is labelled with an orchart name, followed by an expression in $SExp$ and an expression in $DExp$ (respectively, actual session and data parameters);

The following use the additional notations:
$e, e', \ldots$ range over edges        $c, c' \ldots$ range over capsules

Given an orchart $G = (N, C, E, \mathcal{L}_N, \mathcal{L}_E, Exp)$, with $N = IN \uplus ON \uplus InstN$, we also define:
$Init(G) = \{n \in N \mid \not\exists e \in E, \not\exists n' \in N : e = (n', n)\}$
Given $n \in N :$   $OutE(n) = \{e \in E \mid \exists n' \in N : e = (n, n')\}$;
given $c \in C :$   $OutE(c) = \{e \in E \mid \exists n' \in N : e = (c, n')\}$
In particular, if $n \in InstN, \mid OutE(n) \mid \leq 1 :$ this means that only one edge can go from the exit point of an instantiation node.

A Named orchart $DG$ is a quadruple: $(a, FParms, FRParms, G)$ where $a$ is a name, $FParms \subseteq 2^{SExp} \times 2^{DExp}, FRParms \subseteq 2^{SExp} \times 2^{DExp}$ are respectively a set of formal parameters and a set of formal return parameters, $G$ is an orchart having a single initial node $n$ ($Init(G) = \{n\}$), and a set of Nodes augmented with an Exit Node $r$. That is, for such $G : N = IN \uplus ON \uplus InstN \uplus \{r\}$, $\mathcal{L}_N(r) = FRParms; OutE(r) = \emptyset$ .

## 3.2   Static Constraints

Session names that label an edge departing from a node should be a subset of the union of the session names that label its incoming edges.

A node can refer to a session (for input/ouput messages) only if it is in the union of the session names that label its incoming edges.

As usual, actual parameters of an instantiation node should correspond in number, position and type to the formal parameters of the called definition. To be more precise, session actual parameters should correspond to session formal parameters, while data actual parameters should have the same type of the corresponding actual parameter variables. The same should hold for the return parameters. Session names used as actual parameters in an instantiation node should be a subset of the union of the session names that label its incoming edges. The union of the session names labelling the outcoming edges of an instantiation node should be a subset of the session names used as actual return parameters. The session names used as actual return parameters should be a subset of the session names used as actual parameters (this enforces that sessions created inside a named orchart are forgotten before reaching the exit node).

Any variable declaration in a capsule binds all use occurences of the same variable that can be reached from the capsule using a path made of contiguous data flow edges and not containing other binding occurence of the same variable (i.e., the closest occurence is the binding occurence). In well defined orcharts all use occurences must be bound. Furthermore, for a given use occurence of a variable there may be more than one binding occurence. A static rule (not detailed here) enforces that only one path from a binding to a bound occurence can be executed, i.e., if a path leading to the use occurence is executed then all the others have been discarded, and there is always one such path (there is no execution that discards all the paths linking all binding occurences with a use occurence). The same rules hold for binding sessions, with the particularity that binding occurences are session creations (all other occurences are use occurences) and the binding paths are made of any type of edges (control or data).

## 3.3   Informal Semantics of Orcharts and of Configurations of Services

We recall that a service is constituted by:

- a service name, $w$,
- a provided typechart,
- a set of required service names with their typecharts,
- an orchart, $G_w$, with a single initial node, which is an input node. This orchart can contain instantiation nodes that refer to named orcharts
- a set of definitions of named orcharts which are referred by the "main" orchart and which can refer each other, also in a recursive fashion.

Note: In the sequel, we consider that in definition orcharts, session name $\rho$ is explicitely added as a prefix to the appropriate input and output messages, i.e, those with no session name prefix. Hence, occurence $m(v)$ becomes $\rho.m(v)$.

The dynamic semantics of orcharts is defined based on graph transformations along with the execution of input and output interactions. Depending on the type of the executed interaction, an orchart undergoes a series of transformation steps. These are explicited hereafter.

**Message Output.** This is the case where the orchart has one output node in its set of initial nodes:

- the message contained in the output node is deposited in the appropriate queue,
- the output node is removed, but its set of departing edges are kept (the edges remain pending inward, i.e, with their sources unattached),
- for each session creation label $(s@w)$ occurring on a pending edge:
    - a unique session id, $\sigma$, is generated,
    - an instance of the requested service $(\sigma, G_w)$ is spawned and inserted at the server site hence $w(... \mid ...)$ becomes $w(... \mid (\sigma, G_w) \mid ...)$ ,
    - two empty FIFO queues (one for each direction) are added thus linking the present orchart and the spawned service instance,
    - all use occurences of $s$ in the orchart that are bound to $(s@w)$ are substituted with the created session id $\sigma$.
- when all the session creation labels of pending edges have been treated, all pending edges are removed,
- all instantiations that appear as initial nodes in the resulting orchart are replaced by their corresponding definition,
- the orchart is ready for considering another execution step.

**Message Input.** This is the case where the orchart has no output nodes and at least one input node in its set of initial nodes (all output nodes must be executed before considering the execution of input nodes). If the input node has one of its capsules containing a reception that matches the frontmost message of the corresponding queue:

- the message is removed from the queue,
- the variables declared in the reception are replaced with the corresponding values in the received message,
- the substitution of the variables by their values is carried over all the bound occurences in the orchart,
- the edges originating in the capsules other than the one that received the message are discarded,
- the parts of the graph that are no more reachable from the initial nodes are removed,
- the input node is removed, but its set of departing edges are kept (the edges remain pending inward, i.e, with their sources unattached),
- session creations that label pending edges are treated in a way similar to the message output case,
- when all the session creation labels of pending edges have been treated, all pending edges are removed,
- all instantiations that appear as initial nodes in the resulting orchart are replaced by their corresponding definitions,
- the orchart is ready for considering another execution step.

In the sequel, we proceed with the formalisation of the above steps. We need to revisit the syntax of orcharts in order to include those elements that apppear during execution steps. Thus an *execution orchart* is an extension of orcharts that includes the possibility for nodes to have inward pending edges. The set of such edges for a node $n$ is named $InE(n)$.

## 3.4   Structure of Running Configurations of Services

We first define the structure of a running configuration of services then we provide the rules that govern its global behaviour based on the behaviour of its service instances. A running configuration involves a set $\Sigma$ of active session ids ranged over by $\sigma$. $\Sigma$ is endowed with two functions $Req$ and $Serv$. $Req(\sigma)$ allows to retrieve the session id of the service instance that created $\sigma$ and $Serv(\sigma)$ yields the name of the service that is responding to the request issued in the context of $\sigma$. Hence, if $(\sigma', G)$ executes session creation $s@w$ with session id being $\sigma$ assigned to $s$, we will have $Req(\sigma) = \sigma'$ and $Serv(\sigma) = w$. Furthermore, the execution of $s@w$ creates also service instance $(\sigma, G_w)$ which is dedicated to the execution of service requests from $(\sigma', G)$ in the context of $\sigma$. A running configuration is given by:

$$Conf = Q_{RS} \mid Q_{SR} \mid w_1(S_1) \mid \cdots \mid w_n(S_n) \qquad where:$$

- $S_i$ is a (possibly empty) set of instances of service $w_i$. An element of $S_i$ is a pair $(\sigma, G)$ where $G$ is the current execution orchart of the service instance that is serving session $\sigma$,
- $Q_{RS}$ and $Q_{RS}$ are a pair of functions on session ids. $Q_{RS}(\sigma)$ is the Queue from $Req(\sigma)$ to its provider and $Q_{SR}(\sigma)$ is the dual queue.

The operational semantics of a running configuration of services is given by reduction rules (section 3.5) that define possible execution steps. Configurations can evolve either by an output move by a service instance which puts a message in the proper queue (rules OUT-S and OUT-R define such a move for the two cases, server to requestor and requestor to server, respectively); or an input move of a service instance which removes a message from a queue (rules IN-S and IN-R define such a move for the two cases, requestor to server and server to requestor, respectively); or a creation of a new session by a requestor instance, which adds a new (server) service instance to the configuration, and adds a pair of empty queues to the set of queues, both bound to the requestor and server service instances (this move is mirrored in rule CREATE). As can be seen from the rules, there are many sources of non determinism in the execution of an orchart that the user should be aware of: (i) in case of two parallel flows starting each with the reception of the same message, (ii) in case of the same message present in two different capsules of the same input node, (iii) in case where two FIFO queues have their head messages ready to be received in different capsules of the same node. Initially, a configuration which is made of an empty set of queues and of no service instances cannot proceed. In fact, we need to designate a "main" client (not considered here for lack of space) in order to trigger the behaviour and to animate the configuration.

## 3.5   Operational Semantics Rules

The operational semantics of a running configuration of services is given by reduction rules that define possible execution steps:

$$\text{OUT-S} \ \frac{\begin{array}{c} nocreate(S_1,\dots,S_n),\ (\sigma,G)\in S_i,\ n\in OutN(G)\cap Init(G) \\ \mathcal{L}_N(n)=\rho.m(v),\ G'=rmnode(n,G) \end{array}}{\begin{array}{c} Q_{RS}\mid Q_{SR}\mid w_1(S_1)\mid \dots w_i(S_i)\mid \dots w_n(S_n) \to \\ Q_{RS}\mid Q'_{SR}\mid w_1(S_1)\mid \dots w_i(S'_i)\mid \dots w_n(S_n) \end{array}}$$

where: $S'_i = S_i\backslash(\sigma,G)\uplus(\sigma,G')$, $Q'_{SR}=Q_{SR}\backslash(\sigma,Q_{SR}(\sigma))\uplus(\sigma,add(m(v),Q_{SR}(\sigma))$

$$\text{OUT-R} \ \frac{\begin{array}{c} nocreate(S_1,\dots,S_n),\ (\sigma',G)\in S_i,\ n\in OutN(G)\cap Init(G) \\ \mathcal{L}_N(n)=\sigma.m(v),\ G'=rmnode(n,G) \end{array}}{\begin{array}{c} Q_{RS}\mid Q_{SR}\mid w_1(S_1)\mid \dots w_i(S_i)\mid \dots w_n(S_n) \to \\ Q'_{RS}\mid Q_{SR}\mid w_1(S_1)\mid \dots w_i(S'_i)\mid \dots w_n(S_n) \end{array}}$$

where: $S'_i = S_i\backslash(\sigma',G)\uplus(\sigma',G')$, $Q'_{RS}=Q_{RS}\backslash(\sigma,Q_{RS}(\sigma))\uplus(\sigma,add(m(v),Q_{RS}(\sigma))$

$$\text{IN-S} \ \frac{\begin{array}{c} onlyin(S_1,\dots,S_n),\ (\sigma,G)\in S_i,\ n\in IN\cap Init(G),\ c\in n \\ \mathcal{L}_C(c)=\rho.m(x),\ m(v)=head(Q_{RS}(\sigma)),\ G'=rmcaps(n,c,G)[x/v] \end{array}}{\begin{array}{c} Q_{RS}\mid Q_{SR}\mid w_1(S_1)\mid \dots w_i(S_i)\mid \dots w_n(S_n) \to \\ Q'_{RS}\mid Q_{SR}\mid w_1(S_1)\mid \dots w_i(S'_i)\mid \dots w_n(S_n) \end{array}}$$

where: $S'_i = S_i\backslash(\sigma,G)\uplus(\sigma,G')$, $Q'_{RS}=Q_{RS}\backslash(\sigma,Q_{RS}(\sigma))\uplus(\sigma,tail(Q_{RS}(\sigma)))$

$$\text{IN-R} \ \frac{\begin{array}{c} onlyin(S_1,\dots,S_n),\ (\sigma',G)\in S_i,\ n\in IN\cap Init(G),\ c\in n \\ \mathcal{L}_C(c)=\sigma.m(x),\ m(v)=head(Q_{SR}(\sigma)),\ G'=rmcaps(n,c,G)[x/v] \end{array}}{\begin{array}{c} Q_{RS}\mid Q_{SR}\mid w_1(S_1)\mid \dots w_i(S_i)\mid \dots w_n(S_n) \to \\ Q_{RS}\mid Q'_{SR}\mid w_1(S_1)\mid \dots w_i(S'_i)\mid \dots w_n(S_n) \end{array}}$$

where: $S'_i = S_i\backslash(\sigma',G)\uplus(\sigma',G')$, $Q'_{SR}=Q_{SR}\backslash(\sigma,Q_{SR}(\sigma))\uplus(\sigma,tail(Q_{SR}(\sigma)))$

$$\text{CREATE} \ \frac{\begin{array}{c} (\sigma,G)\in S_i,\ n\in Init(G),\ s@w_j\in InE(n) \\ G'=rmlabel(s@w_j,n,G)[s/\sigma'],\sigma'\ fresh \end{array}}{\begin{array}{c} Q_{RS}\mid Q_{SR}\mid w_1(S_1)\mid \cdots \mid w_i(S_i)\mid \cdots \mid w_j(S_j)\mid \cdots \mid w_n(S_n) \to \\ Q'_{RS}\mid Q'_{SR}\mid w_1(S_1)\mid \cdots \mid w_i(S'_i)\cdots \mid w_j(S'_j)\mid \cdots \mid w_n:S_n \end{array}}$$

where: $S'_j = S_j\uplus(\sigma',G_{w_j})$, $S'_i = S_i\backslash(\sigma,G)\uplus(\sigma,G')$, $Q'_{SR}=Q_{SR}\uplus(\sigma',\emptyset)$, $Q'_{RS}=Q_{RS}\uplus(\sigma',\emptyset)$

The above rules are based on the use of some auxiliary functions, that allow to work on the queues associated to sessions and on the execution graph itself, or to give a priority to the application of the above rules. We present them here informally for sake of brevity:

- $add(m,queue), tail(queue), head(queue)$ - usual functions over a FIFO queue;
- $rmnode(n,G)$ - removes the node $n$ from $G$, with the following steps:
  - cancel n from G, but retaining its outcoming edges from it
  - if any retained edge hits an instantiation node, substitute it with its definition
  - if any retained edge is not labelled with a session creation ($s@w$), it is cancelled
- $rmcaps(n,c,G)$ - (here $c$ is a capsule of $n$) removes the node $n$ from $G$, with the following steps:
  - Given that $OutE(n)=OutE(c)\cup Excluded$, if $Excluded\neq\emptyset$: cancel from $G$ all the edges in $Excluded$, then cancel all the nodes which are

no more reachable from nodes in $Init(G)$, together with their outcoming edges.
  - apply $rmnode(n, G)$
- $rmlabel(s@w, n, G)$ - removes label $s@w$ from the edge pointing at $n$ in $G$, then proceeds with removing all edges in $G$ having no session creation labels.
- $nocreate(S_1, \ldots, S_n)$ is a predicate defined as: $\forall i, \sigma, G : (\sigma, G) \in S_i, n \in Init(G) : InE(n) = \emptyset$
- $onlyin(S_1, \ldots, S_n)$ is a predicate defined as: $nocreate(S_1, \ldots, S_n)$ and $\forall i, \sigma, G : (\sigma, G) \in S_i, n \in Init(G) : n \in IN$.

# 4    Type Verification and Properties

## 4.1    Behavioural Types

A typechart is a quintuple $(S, s_0, S_F, Act, \rightarrow)$ where:

- $S$ is a finite set of states, defined as $RS \uplus SS$, that is, a state is either a *receiving state* or a *sending state*.
- $s_0 \in RS$ is the initial state
- $S_F \subseteq RS$ is the set of *final* states
- $Act$ is a set of actions, which are in the form $?m(Type)$ (input message) or $!m(Type)$ (output message), where m is a message name and $Type$ is either a basic type or a reference to another typechart. Since in general messages can carry more data values, we assume for simplicity that structured types are included in basic types to cover such cases.
- $\rightarrow: S \times Act \times S$ is the labelled transition relation, such that: $s \xrightarrow{?m(T)} s' \implies s \in RS$, $s \xrightarrow{!m(T)} s' \implies s \in SS$.

A session has two ends: the end of the client and the end of the service. Session types differ for a session if seen from the two ends, in the fact that what is an input on one side is an output on the other side. This is called *type duality* in [15]. The type T as seen from the other end of the session is written $Dual(T)$. In particular, subtyping of [15] can be expressed in a way resembling the classical simulation relation typical of a process algebraic framework, by distinguishing sending and receiving states (we abstract here from the exchanged messages, to which a classical notion of subtyping could be applied as well):

$$T_1 \text{ is a subtype of } T_2 \ (T_1 \preceq T_2) \ \textit{iff} \ \begin{cases} T_2 \xrightarrow{?m} T_2' \text{ implies } \exists T_1' : T_1 \xrightarrow{?m} T_1' \text{ and } T_1' \preceq T_2' \\ T_1 \xrightarrow{!m} T_1' \text{ implies } \exists T_2' : T_2 \xrightarrow{!m} T_2' \text{ and } T_1' \preceq T_2' \end{cases}$$

which is read: $T_1$ is a subtype of $T_2$ if in any receiving state, $T_1$ is able to receive all the messages that $T_2$ is able to receive, and in any sending state $T_2$ is able to send all the messages that $T_1$ is able to send. Consequently, substitutability and compatibility are defined, as in [15]:

- a session type $T$ can *safely substitute* $T'$ if $T \preceq T'$;
- a session type $T$ is *compatible* with $T'$ if $T \preceq Dual(T')$.

That is, two type sessions are said compatible if any sending of one is matched by a reception of the other one: hence, a session having at its two ends compatible types does not internally deadlock. The typecharts NewsAgency-T and NewsAgencyBis-T shown in section 2.3 are defined so that NewsAgencyBis-T *can safely substitute* NewsAgency-T.

## 4.2   A Well Typedness Algorithm

Herefater we present a well typedness algorithm, i.e., which verifies that an orchart defining a site conforms to its provided and required typecharts. For the sake of brevity, we limit its description to a brief sketch, sufficient in our opinion to show that well-typedness of orcharts can be computed.

First, the provided and required typecharts need to be transformed. The provided typechart is transformed into its dual. Then its sending transitions are prefixed with $\tau$, i.e., every transition $T \xrightarrow{!m} T'$ becomes $T \xrightarrow{\tau} \bullet \xrightarrow{!m} T'$ where $\bullet$ is a new state with only one sending transition $\xrightarrow{!m}$. On the other hand, the typecharts of the required services only undergo the $\tau$ prefixing transformation. The introduction of $\tau$ transitions is meant to mimic the fact that the decision of sending a message is taken autonomously by the sender.

The algorithm proceeds by discharging proof obligations. Discharging a proof obligation either fails, in which case the whole algorithm immediately terminates concluding a typing error, or produces a set of new proof obligations to be discharged. When no more proof obligations are left to be discharged, the algorithm terminates, establishing conformance. A trivial proof obligation, (e.g. the one in which an empty orchart is compared against a terminal state of a typechart) is immediately discharged producing no new proof obligations.

The initial proof obligation is $(G_{serv}, \ s_0 : T_{prov})$ where $G_{serv}$ is the orchart of the service and $T_{prov}$ the provided typechart (in this algorithm, we chose to rename $\rho$ by $s_0$, which simplifies the presentation). From this initial proof obligation we proceed with symbolic co-execution steps, where the orchart and the associated typecharts are executed in a synchronised fashion. The format of a running proof obligation is given by $(G, \ s_0 : T_0, \ s_1 : T_1, \ldots, s_n : T_n)$ where $G$ is the current state of the orchart, $T_0$ its current provided typechart and $s_1 : T_1, \ldots, s_n : T_n$ the set of active sessions and their associated typecharts. To discharge a proof obligation $(G, \ s_0 : T_0, \ s_1 : T_1, \ldots, s_n : T_n)$, which we assume for the moment having no instantiation nodes, we perform the following steps:

– If some typechart has a $\tau$ transition:
  • For each typechart $T_i$ with a $\tau$ transition $T_i \xrightarrow{\tau} T'$ : create a new proof obligation obtained by replacing $T_i$ with $T'$;
  • Discharge proof obligation $(G, \ s_0 : T_0, \ s_1 : T_1, \ldots, s_n : T_n)$;
– If no typechart has a $\tau$ transition and $G$'s initial nodes are only input:
  • If $G$ has no initial input capsule $s_i.m$ that matches a transition $T_i \xrightarrow{!m} T'$ of its corresponding typechart $T_i$ then the proof fails;
  • For each initial capsule $s_i.m$ matching one transition $T_i \xrightarrow{!m} T'$ of its associated typechart $T_i$: a new proof obligation is produced, applying the

execution step involving the capsule $s_i.m$, so obtaining an execution or-chart $G'$, and advancing to $T'$ the typechart of $s_i$. In this step the set of active sessions is obtained by collecting the labels of the edges outcoming from the capsule. This may involve the creation of new active sessions produced from the labels having the $s@serv$ format;

- When all initial capsules with matching typecharts are treated the cur-rent proof obligation is discharged;
- If no typechart has a $\tau$ transition and $G$ has initial output nodes:
  - for each output node emitting $s_i.m()$, if $T_i \xrightarrow{?s_i.m} T'$, a new proof obliga-tion is produced applying the execution step on that node, so obtaining an execution Orchart $G'$, and advancing $T_i$ to $T'$ ;
  - if for some output node there is no matching typechart, the proof fails;
- If no typechart has a $\tau$ transition and $G$ is empty: if $T_0$ is a terminal state then the proof is discharged, otherwise the proof fails

Since an orchart is acyclic, the algorithm is guaranteed to terminate, since its number of steps depends on static metrics (number of nodes and capsules, of sessions, of alternative sendings in typecharts).

On top of this basic algorithm, orchart instantiation is addressed as follows. If an instantiation of a named orchart is encountered for the first time, it is replaced by its definition and the algorithm continues with the creation of a proof obligation for the definition of this named orchart (parametrized with the states of the active sessions). The created proof obligation is discharged when the algorithm has explored, in the current orchart, the part that comes from the definition orchart. Another condition has also to be checked which ensures that in case of parallel flows, if a session is present in the instantiated part and also in another parallel flow, the behaviour of its associated typechart is uniform (i.e., roughly, the state of the typechart does not change) along all parallel flows where the session is present.

### 4.3 Properties of Well Typed Configurations of Services

A configuration of services is well typed iff (i) each service is well typed (its defining orchart conforms to its required and provided types as given in the algorithm of section 4.2), and (ii) if a service in this configution requires a type $T_1$ and the partner service provides a type $T_2$, then $(T_2 \preceq T_1)$. If we assume that defining orcharts have a stubborn terminal output node (a node with no outgoing edges and which is always reachable - this can be statically checked), if we assume also that there is no invocation cycles (a typical cycle is when service $w_1$ invokes $w_2$ and vice versa - this also can be statically checked) then we claim that well typed configurations have the soundness property: any service invocation potentially reaches a termination state. More precisely, let us consider a sound configuration $Conf = (\ w_0(G_0), w_1(), \ldots, w_n()\ )$ where $w_0$ is a client (with behaviour given by orchart $G_0$) ready to invoke service $w_1$ with some session $\sigma$, then for any run $Conf \xrightarrow{*} Conf'$, there exists a configuration, $Conf''$, reachable from $Conf'$ and such that $Conf'' = (\ w_0(G_0'), w_1(\sigma, G'), \ldots, w_n(\ldots)\ )$ and where $G_0'$ and $G'$ are empty.

# 5   Future Work and Conclusions

We have presented an approach for verifying service composition based on behavioural typing, in which sessions play a pivotal role. In this work we sought for a language powerful enough to express common service orchestration examples, but which is also simple enough to associate finite state behavioural types to sessions. The first results about typing are encouraging: we can cite the fact that the language, admitting parallel flows and recursion, allows infinite state behaviours to be defined while also being typable, that is, to which finite state session types can be associated. It is worth noting that the properties that are claimed for in well typed orchart configurations are similar to those obtained for object configurations in [12] with, however, two major improvements: (i) orcharts are more expressive as they provide for parallel flows; and (ii) orcharts are less constraining as they do not impose that services are always ready for all input messages that are expected for by their current behavioural types. The precise tradeoff between expressive power of orcharts and their finite typability has still to be assessed. Moreover, several improvements to the language are planned, for example in the treatment of abandoned sessions, with the introduction of explicit and implicit abort of sessions.

**Acknowledgments.** This work has been partially supported by the ACI project FIACRE and by the EU project FET-GC II IST-2005-16004 Sensoria.

# References

1. van der Aalst, W.M.P., ter Hofstede, A.H.M., Kiepuszewski, B., Barros, A.P.: Workflow patterns. Distributed Parallel Databases 14(1), 5–51 (2003)
2. de Alfaro, L., Da Silva, L.D., Faella, M., Legay, A., Roy, P., Sorea, M.: Sociable Interfaces. In: Gramlich, B. (ed.) FroCos 2005. LNCS (LNAI), vol. 3717, pp. 81–105. Springer, Heidelberg (2005)
3. Boreale, M., Bruni, R., Caires, L., De Nicola, R., Lanese, I., Loreti, M., Martins, F., Montanari, U., Ravara, A., Sangiorgi, D., Vasconcelos, V., Zavattaro, G.: SCC: A Service Centered Calculus. In: Bravetti, M., Núñez, M., Zavattaro, G. (eds.) WS-FM 2006. LNCS, vol. 4184, pp. 38–57. Springer, Heidelberg (2006)
4. Caires, L., Ferrari, G., Pugliese, R., Ravara, A.: Behavioural Types for Service Composition. Deliverable D2.3.a, Sensoria project (September 2006)
5. Cook, W.R., Patwardhan, S., Misra, J.: Workflow Patterns in Orc. In: Ciancarini, P., Wiklicky, H. (eds.) COORDINATION 2006. LNCS, vol. 4038, pp. 82–96. Springer, Heidelberg (2006)
6. Honda, K., Vasconcelos, V.T., Kubo, M.: Language Primitives and Type Discipline for Structured Communication-Based Programming. In: Hankin, C. (ed.) ESOP 1998. LNCS, vol. 1381, pp. 122–138. Springer, Heidelberg (1998)
7. Kitchin, D., Cook, W.R., Misra, J.: A Language for Task Orchestration and Its Semantic Properties. In: Baier, C., Hermanns, H. (eds.) CONCUR 2006. LNCS, vol. 4137, pp. 477–491. Springer, Heidelberg (2006)
8. Kobayashi, N., Pierce, B.C., Turner, D.N.: Linearity and the Pi-Calculus. ACM TOPLAS 21(5), 914–947 (1999)

9. Lanese, I., Vasconcelos, V.T., Martins, F., Ravara, A.: Disciplining Orchestration and Conversation in Service-Oriented Computing (2007)
10. Lapadula, A., Pugliese, R., Tiezzi, F.: A Calculus for Orchestration of Web Services. In: De Nicola, R. (ed.) ESOP 2007. LNCS, vol. 4421, pp. 33–47. Springer, Heidelberg (2007)
11. Larsen, K.G., Nyman, U., Wasowski, A.: An Interface Theory for Input/Output Automata. In: Misra, J., Nipkow, T., Sekerinski, E. (eds.) FM 2006. LNCS, vol. 4085, pp. 82–97. Springer, Heidelberg (2006)
12. Najm, E., Nimour, A., Stefani, J.B.: Guaranteeing liveness in an object calculus through behavioral typing. In: Proceedings of FORTE/PSTV 1999, Beijing, China, October 1999, Kluwer, Dordrecht (1999)
13. Najm, E., Nimour, A.: Explicit Behavioral Typing for Object Interface. In: Semantics of Objects as Processes, ECOOP 1999 Workshop, Lisbon, Portugal (June 1999)
14. Nierstrasz, O.: Regular types for active objects. In: Nierstrasz, O., Tsichritzis, D. (eds.) Object-Oriented Software Composition, pp. 99–121. Prentice-Hall, Englewood Cliffs (1995)
15. Vallecillo, A., Vasconcelos, V.T., Ravara, A.: Typing the Behavior of Objects and Components using Session Types. Fundamenta Informaticae 73(4) (2006)

# Implementing Joins Using Extensible Pattern Matching

Philipp Haller[1] and Tom Van Cutsem[2],[*]

[1] EPFL
1015 Lausanne, Switzerland
`firstname.lastname@epfl.ch`
[2] Vrije Universiteit Brussel, Belgium

**Abstract.** Join patterns are an attractive declarative way to synchronize both threads and asynchronous distributed computations. We explore joins in the context of extensible pattern matching that recently appeared in languages such as F# and Scala. Our implementation supports join patterns with multiple synchronous events, and guards. Furthermore, we integrated joins into an existing actor-based concurrency framework. It enables join patterns to be used in the context of more advanced synchronization modes, such as future-type message sending and token-passing continuations.

**Keywords:** Concurrent Programming, Join Patterns, Chords, Actors.

## 1 Introduction

Recently, the pattern matching facilities of languages such as Scala and F# have been generalized to allow representation independence for objects used in pattern matching [6,20]. Extensible patterns open up new possibilities for implementing abstractions in libraries which were previously only accessible as language features. More specifically, we claim that extensible pattern matching eases the construction of declarative approaches to synchronization in libraries rather than languages. To support this claim, we show how a concrete declarative synchronization construct, join patterns, can be implemented in Scala, a language with extensible pattern matching.

Join patterns [8,9] offer a declarative way of synchronizing both threads and asynchronous distributed computations that is simple and powerful at the same time. They form part of languages such as JoCaml [7] and Funnel [14]. Join patterns have also been implemented as extensions to existing languages [3,23]. Recently, Russo [17] and Singh [18] have shown that advanced programming language features, such as generics or software transactional memory, make it feasible to provide join patterns as libraries rather than language extensions.

We motivate that our implementation based on extensible pattern matching is an interesting third way to provide join patterns in a library since it has a number of desirable properties. More concretely, we make the following contributions:

---

[*] Supported by a Ph.D. fellowship of the Research Foundation Flanders (FWO).

D. Lea and G. Zavattaro (Eds.): COORDINATION 2008, LNCS 5052, pp. 135–152, 2008.

- We present a novel implementation technique for joins based on extensible pattern matching. We show that it allows programmers to avoid certain kinds of boilerplate code that are inevitable when using existing approaches.
- We discuss a concrete implementation of our approach in Scala. A complete implementation that supports join patterns with multiple synchronous events and a restricted form of guards is available on the web.[1]
- We integrate our library into an existing actor-based concurrency framework. This enables expressive join patterns to be used in the context of more advanced synchronization modes, such as future-type message sending and token-passing continuations.

The rest of this paper is structured as follows. In the following section we briefly highlight join patterns as a declarative synchronization abstraction, how they have been integrated in other languages before, and how combining them with pattern matching can improve this integration. Section 3 shows how to synchronize both threads and actors using our new Scala Joins framework. In section 4 we discuss a concrete implementation of expressive join patterns in Scala. Section 5 discusses related work, and section 6 concludes.

## 2   Motivation

**Background: Join Patterns.** A join pattern consists of a body guarded by a linear set of events. The body is executed only when *all* of the events in the set have been signaled to an object. Threads may signal synchronous or asynchronous events to objects. By signaling a synchronous event to an object, threads may implicitly suspend. The simplest illustrative example of a join pattern is that of an unbounded FIFO buffer. In C$\omega$ [3], it is expressed as follows:

```
public class Buffer {
  public async Put(int x);
  public int Get() & Put(int x) { return x; }
}
```

A detailed explanation of join patterns is outside the scope of this paper. For the purposes of this paper, it suffices to understand the operational effect of a join pattern. Threads may put values into a buffer b by invoking b.Put(v). They may also read values from the buffer by invoking b.Get(). The join pattern Get() & Put(int x) (called a *chord* in C$\omega$) specifies that a call to Get may only proceed if a Put event has previously been signaled. Hence, if there are no pending Put events, a thread invoking Get is automatically suspended until such an event is signaled.

The advantage of join patterns is that they allow a *declarative* specification of the synchronization between different threads. Often, the join patterns correspond closely to a finite state machine that specifies the valid states of an object [3]. In the following, we explain the benefits of our new implementation by means of an example.

---

[1] See http://lamp.epfl.ch/~phaller/joins/.

**Example.** Consider the traditional problem of synchronizing multiple concurrent readers with one or more writers who need exclusive access to a resource. In C$\omega$, join patterns are supported as a language extension through a dedicated compiler. With the introduction of generics in C# 2.0, Russo has made join patterns available in a C# library called Joins [17]. In that library, a multiple reader/one writer lock can be implemented as follows:

```
public class ReaderWriter {
  public Synchronous.Channel Exclusive, ReleaseExclusive;
  public Synchronous.Channel Shared, ReleaseShared;
  private Asynchronous.Channel Idle;
  private Asynchronous.Channel<int> Sharing;
  public ReaderWriter() {
    Join j = Join.Create(); ... // Boilerplate omitted
    j.When(Exclusive).And(Idle).Do(delegate {});
    j.When(ReleaseExclusive).Do(delegate{ Idle(); });
    j.When(Shared).And(Idle).Do(delegate{ Sharing(1); });
    j.When(Shared).And(Sharing).Do(delegate(int n) {
      Sharing(n+1); });
    j.When(ReleaseShared).And(Sharing).Do(delegate(int n) {
      if (n==1) Idle(); else Sharing(n-1); });
    Idle(); } }
```

In C# Joins, join patterns consist of linear combinations of channels and a delegate (a function object) which encapsulates the join body. Join patterns are triggered by invoking channels which are special delegates.

In the example, channels are declared as fields of the **ReaderWriter** class. Channel types are either synchronous or asynchronous. Asynchronous channels correspond to asynchronous methods in C$\omega$ (e.g. Put in the previous example). Channels may take arguments which are specified using type parameters. For example, the **Sharing** channel is asynchronous and takes a single int argument. Channels are often used to model (parts of) the internal state of an object. For example, the **Idle** and **Sharing** channels keep track of concurrent readers (if any), and are therefore declared as **private**. To declare a set of join patterns, one first has to create an instance of the Join class. Individual join patterns are then created by chaining a number of method calls invoked on that Join instance. For example, the first join pattern is created by combining the **Exclusive** and Idle channels with an empty delegate; this means that invoking the synchronous Exclusive channel (a request to acquire the lock in exclusive mode) will not block the caller if the **Idle** channel has been invoked (the lock has not been acquired).

Even though the verbosity of programs written using C# Joins is slightly higher compared to C$\omega$, basically all the advantages of join patterns are preserved. However, this code still has a number of drawbacks: first, the encoding of the internal state is *redundant*. Logically, a lock in idle state can be represented either by the non-empty `Idle` channel or the `Sharing` channel invoked with 0.[2]

Note that it is impossible in C# (and in Cω) to use only `Sharing`. Consider the first join pattern. Implementing it using `Sharing` instead of `Idle` requires a delegate that takes an integer argument (the number of concurrent readers):

```
j.When(Exclusive).And(Sharing).Do(delegate(int n) {...}
```

Inside the body we have to test whether $n > 0$ in which case the thread invoking `Exclusive` has to block. Blocking without reverting to lower-level mechanisms such as locks is only possible by invoking a synchronous channel; however, that channel has to be different from `Exclusive` (since invoking `Exclusive` does not block when `Sharing` has been invoked) which re-introduces the redundancy.

Another drawback of the above code is the fact that arguments are passed *implicitly* between channels and join bodies: in the third case, the argument n passed to the delegate is the argument of the `Sharing` channel. Contrast this with the Cω buffer example in which the `Put` event explicitly binds its argument x. Not only are arguments passed implicitly, the order in which they are passed is merely *conventional* and not checked by the compiler. For example, the delegate of a (hypothetical) join pattern with two channels of type `Asynchronous.Channel<int>` would have two `int` arguments. Accidentally swapping the arguments in the body delegate would go unnoticed and result in errors.

In Scala Joins the join patterns of the above example are expressed as follows:

```
join {
  case Exclusive() & Sharing(0) => Exclusive.reply()
  case ReleaseExclusive() => Sharing(0); ReleaseExclusive.reply()
  case Shared() & Sharing(n) => Sharing(n+1); Shared.reply()
  case ReleaseShared() & Sharing(n) if n > 0 =>
    Sharing(n-1); ReleaseShared.reply()
}
```

The internal state of the lock is now represented uniformly using only `Sharing`. Moreover, two formerly separate patterns are unified (patterns 3 and 4 in the C# example) and the `if-else` statement is gone. (Inside join bodies, synchronous events are replied to via their **reply** method; this is necessary since, contrary to C# and Cω, Scala Joins supports multiple synchronous events per pattern, cf. section 3.) The gain in expressivity is due to *nested pattern matching*. In the first pattern, pattern matching constrains the argument of `Sharing` to 0, ensuring that this pattern only triggers when no other thread is sharing the lock. Therefore, an additional `Idle` event is no longer necessary, which decreases the number of patterns. In the last pattern, a *guard* (`if n > 0`) prevents invalid states (i.e. invoking `Sharing(n)` where $n < 0$).

---

[2] The above implementation actually ensures that an idle lock is always represented as `Idle` and never as `Sharing(0)`. However, this close relationship between `Idle` and `Sharing` is not explicit and has to be inferred from all the join patterns.

**Joins for Actors.** While join patterns have been successfully used to synchronize threads, to the best of our knowledge, join patterns have not yet been applied in the context of an actor-based concurrency model [1]. In Scala, actor-based concurrency is supported by means of a library extension [11]. Because we provide join patterns as a library as well, we have created the opportunity to combine join patterns with the concurrency model offered by actors. We give a more detailed explanation of this combination in section 3. However, in order to understand this integration, we first briefly highlight how to write concurrent programs using Scala's actor framework.

Scala's actors are largely inspired by Erlang's model of concurrent processes communicating by message passing [2]. New actors are defined as classes extending the `Actor` class. An actor's life cycle is defined by its `act` method. The following code shows how to implement the unbounded buffer as an actor:

```
class Buffer extends Actor {
  def act() { loop(List()) }
  def loop(buf: List[Int]) {
    receive {
      case Put(x) => loop(buf ::: List(x)) // append x to buf
      case Get() if !buf.isEmpty =>
        reply(buf.head); loop(buf.tail) }
} }
```

The `receive` method allows an actor to selectively wait for certain messages to arrive in its mailbox. The actor processes at most one message at a time. Messages that are sent concurrently to the actor are queued in its mailbox. Interacting with a buffer actor occurs as follows:

```
val buffer = new Buffer; buffer.start()
buffer ! Put(42) // asynchronous send, returns nothing
println(buffer !? Get()) // synchronous send, waits for reply
```

Synchronous message sends make the sending process wait for the actor to reply to the message (by means of `reply(value)`). Scala actors also offer more advanced synchronization patterns such as futures [12,25]. `actor !! msg` denotes an asynchronous send that immediately returns a future object. In Scala, a future is a nullary function that, when applied, returns the future's computed result value. If the future is applied before the value is computed, the caller is blocked.

In the above example, the required synchronization between `Put` and `Get` is achieved by means of a *guard*. The guard in the `Get` case disallows the processing of any `Get` message while the `buf` queue is empty. In the implementation, all cases are sequentially checked against the incoming message. If no case matches, or all of the guards for matching cases evaluate to false, the actor keeps the message stored in its mailbox and awaits other messages.

Even though the above example remains simple enough to implement, the synchronization between `Put` and `Get` remains very implicit. The actual *intention* of the programmer, i.e. the fact that an item can only be produced when the actor received both a `Get` *and* a `Put` message, remains implicit in the code. Therefore, even actors can benefit from the added declarative synchronization of join patterns, as we illustrate in section 3.

## 3    A Scala Joins Library

We discuss a Scala library (called Scala Joins) providing join patterns implemented via extensible pattern matching. First, we explain how Scala Joins enables declarative thread synchronization, postponing joins for actors until the next section.

**Joining Threads.** Join patterns in Scala Joins are composed of synchronous and asynchronous *events*. Events are strongly typed and can be invoked using standard method invocation syntax. The FIFO buffer example is written in Scala Joins as follows:

```scala
class Buffer extends Joins {
  val Put = new AsyncEvent[Int]
  val Get = new SyncEvent[Int]
  join { case Get() & Put(x) => Get reply x }
}
```

To enable join patterns, a class inherits from the `Joins` class.[3] Events are declared as regular fields. They are distinguished based on their (a)synchrony and the number and types of arguments they take. For example, `Put` is an asynchronous event that takes a single argument of type `Int`. Since it is asynchronous, no return type is specified (it immediately returns `unit` when invoked). In the case of a synchronous event such as `Get`, the first type parameter specifies the return type. Therefore, `Get` is a synchronous event that takes no arguments and returns values of type `Int`.

Joins are declared using the `join { ... }` construct.[4] This construct enables pattern matching via a list of `case` declarations that each consist of a left-hand side and a right-hand side, separated by `=>`. The left-hand side defines a join pattern through the juxtaposition of a linear combination of asynchronous and synchronous events. As is common in the joins literature, we use `&` as the juxtaposition operator. Arguments of events are usually specified as variable patterns. For example, the variable pattern `x` in the `Put` event can bind to any value (of type `Int`). This means that on the right-hand side, `x` is bound to the argument of the `Put` event when the join pattern matches. Standard pattern matching can be used to constrain the match even further (see section 2).

The right-hand side of a join pattern defines the join body (an ordinary block of code) that is executed when the join pattern matches. Like JoCaml, but

---

[3] Actually, `Joins` is a *trait* that can be mixed into any class.

[4] As explained in section 4, `join` is a method of the `Joins` class. In Scala, the body of a class definition serves as the primary constructor of the class which allows this freestanding call to `join`.

unlike C$\omega$ and C# Joins, Scala Joins allows any number of synchronous events to appear in a join pattern. Because of this, it is impossible to use the return value of the body to implicitly reply to the single synchronous event in the join pattern. Instead, the body of a join pattern explicitly replies to all synchronous events that are part of the join pattern on the left-hand side. This is done by invoking those events' `reply` method, which wakes up the thread that originally signaled that event.

**Joining Actors.** We now describe an integration of our joins library with Scala's actor framework. The following example shows how to re-implement the unbounded buffer example using joins:

```
val Put = new Join1[Int]
val Get = new Join
class Buffer extends JoinActor {
  def act() {
    receive { case Get() & Put(x) => Get reply x }
} }
```

It differs from the thread-based bounded buffer using joins in the following ways:

- The `Buffer` class inherits from the `JoinActor` class to declare itself to be an actor capable of processing join patterns.
- Rather than defining `Put` and `Get` as synchronous or asynchronous *events*, they are all defined as *join messages* which may support both kinds of synchrony (this is explained in more detail below).
- The `Buffer` actor defines `act` and awaits incoming messages by means of `receive`. It is still possible for the actor to serve regular messages within the `receive` block. Logically, regular messages can be regarded as unary join patterns. However, they don't have to be declared as joinable messages.

We illustrate below how the buffer actor can be used as a coordinator between a consumer and a producer actor. The producer sends an asynchronous `Put` message while the consumer awaits the reply to a `Get` message by invoking it synchronously (using `!?`).

```
val buffer = new Buffer; buffer.start()
val prod = actor { buffer ! Put(42) }
val cons = actor { process(buffer !? Get()) }
```

By applying joins to actors, the synchronization dependencies between `Get` and `Put` can be specified declaratively by the buffer actor. The actor receives `Get` and `Put` messages by queuing them in its mailbox. Only when all of the messages specified in the join pattern have been received is the body executed by the actor. Before processing the body, the actor atomically removes all of the participating messages from its mailbox. Replies may be sent to any or all of the messages participating in the join pattern. This is similar to the way replies are sent to events in the thread-based joins library described previously.

Contrary to the way events are defined in the thread-based joins library, an actor does not explicitly define a join message to be synchronous or asynchronous. We say that join messages are "synchronization-agnostic" because they can be used in different synchronization modes between the sender and receiver actors. However, when they are used in a particular join pattern, the sender and receiver actors have to agree upon a valid synchronization mode. In the previous example, the `Put` join message was sent asynchronously, while the `Get` join message was sent synchronously. In the body of a join pattern, the receiver actor replied to `Get`, but not to `Put`.

The disadvantage of making join messages synchronization-agnostic is that it introduces the possibility for errors. For example, if a receiver does not reply to a synchronously sent message, the sender remains blocked. However, the advantage is that join messages may be used in many different synchronization modes, including future-type message sending [25] or Salsa's token-passing continuations [22]. Every join message has an associated *reply destination* which is an output channel on which processes may listen for replies to the message. How the reply to a message is processed is determined by the way the message was sent. For example, if the message was sent purely asynchronously, the reply is discarded; if it was sent synchronously, the reply awakes the sender. If it was sent using a future-type message send, the reply resolves the future.

## 4    Integrating Joins and Extensible Pattern Matching

In this section we present a novel implementation that integrates joins into general language-based pattern matching. We explain our technique using a concrete implementation in Scala. However, we expect that implementations based on, e.g., the active patterns of F# [20] would not be much different.

In the following we first look at pattern matching in Scala; this provides some terminology and background used in subsequent sections. After that we review the essentials of Scala's extensible patterns; the small set of necessary concepts suggests that our approach is readily transferable to languages with similar features. In section 4.1 we outline the core of an implementation of joins that builds on extensible pattern matching. In section 4.2 we highlight how joins have been integrated into Scala's actor framework.

**Partial Functions.** In the previous section we used the `join { ... }` construct to declare a set of join patterns. It has the following form:

```
join {
  case pat₁ => body₁
  ...
  case patₙ => bodyₙ
}
```

The patterns $pat_i$ consist of a linear combination of events $evt_1 \& \ldots \& evt_m$. Threads synchronize over a join pattern by invoking one or several of the events listed in a pattern $pat_i$. When all events occurring in $pat_i$ have been invoked, the join pattern matches, and its corresponding join $body_i$ is executed.

In Scala, the pattern matching expression inside braces is treated as a first-class value that is passed as an argument to the `join` function. The argument's type is an instance of `PartialFunction`, which is a subclass of `Function1`, the class of unary functions. The two classes are defined as follows.

```
abstract class Function1[A, B] {
  def apply(x: A): B }
abstract class PartialFunction[A, B] extends Function1[A, B] {
  def isDefinedAt(x: A): Boolean }
```

Functions are objects which have an `apply` method. Partial functions are objects which have in addition a method `isDefinedAt` which tests whether a function is defined for a given argument. Both classes are parametrized; the first type parameter A indicates the function's argument type and the second type parameter B indicates its result type.

In Scala, each pattern matching expression

{ case $p_1$ => $e_1$; ...; case $p_n$ => $e_n$ }

is compiled into a partial function whose methods are defined as follows.

- The `isDefinedAt` method returns `true` if one of the patterns $p_i$ matches the argument, `false` otherwise.
- The `apply` method returns the value $e_i$ for the first pattern $p_i$ that matches its argument. If none of the patterns match, a `MatchError` exception is thrown.

Note that partial functions are not crucial for our implementation of joins. In fact, Scala's partial functions can be encoded using only higher-order functions as follows. The idea is to define a partial function as a regular function that returns an option;[5] either the partial function is defined at the given value, in which case it returns its body *as a thunk* (i.e. a function with an empty parameter list) wrapped in `Some`. If the partial function is not defined, it returns `None`. Operations for testing whether a partial function is defined at a given value, and for applying it are defined accordingly:

```
type PartFun[A, R] = A => Option[() => R]
def isDefAt[A, R](fun: PartFun[A, R], arg: A) = fun(arg) match {
  case Some(_) => true
  case None    => false }
def apply[A, R](fun: PartFun[A, R], arg: A) = fun(arg) match {
  case Some(res) => res()
  case None      => error("PartFun not defined") }
```

---

[5] The optional value is of parameterized type `Option[T]` that has the two subclasses `Some[T](x: T)` and `None`.

Using this encoding, the native Scala partial function

```
{ case x :: xs => println("head: "+x) }
```

can then be represented as follows:

```
(l: List[Int]) => l match {
  case x :: xs => Some(() => println("head: "+x))
  case _       => None }
```

*Join Patterns as Partial Functions.* Whenever a thread invokes an event, each join pattern in which e occurs has to be checked for a potential match. Therefore, events have to be associated with the set of join patterns in which they participate. As shown before, this set of join patterns is represented as a partial function. Invoking join(pats) associates each event occurring in the set of join patterns with pats.

When a thread invokes an event, the isDefinedAt method of pats is used to check whether any of the associated join patterns match. If yes, the corresponding join body is executed by invoking the apply method of pats. A question remains: what argument is passed to isDefinedAt and apply, respectively? To answer this question, consider the simple buffer example from the previous section. It declares the following join pattern:

```
join { case Get() & Put(x) => Get reply x }
```

Assume that no events have been invoked before, and a thread $t$ invokes the Get event to remove an element from the buffer. Clearly, the join pattern does not match, which causes $t$ to block since Get is a synchronous event (more on synchronous events later). Assume that after thread $t$ has gone to sleep, another thread $s$ adds an element to the buffer by invoking the Put event. Now, we want the join pattern to match since both events have been invoked. However, the result of the matching does not only depend on the event that was last invoked but also on the fact that *other events* have been invoked previously. Therefore, it is *not* sufficient to simply pass a Put message to the isDefinedAt method of the partial function the represents the join patterns. Instead, when the Put event is invoked, the Get event has to somehow "pretend" to also match, even though it has nothing to do with the current event. While previous invocations can simply be buffered inside the events, it is non-trivial to make the pattern matcher actually consult this information during the matching, and "customize" the matching results based on this information. To achieve this customization we use extensible pattern matching.

**Extensible Pattern Matching.** Emir et al. [6] recently introduced *extractors* for Scala that provide representation independence for objects used in patterns. Extractors play a role similar to *views* in functional programming languages [24,15] in that they allow conversions from one data type to another to be applied implicitly during pattern matching. As a simple example, consider the following object that can be used to match even numbers:

```
object Twice {
  def apply(x: Int) = x*2
  def unapply(z: Int) = if (z%2 == 0) Some(z/2) else None }
```

Objects with `apply` methods are uniformly treated as functions in Scala. When the function invocation syntax `Twice(x)` is used, Scala implicitly calls `Twice.apply(x)`. The `unapply` method in `Twice` reverses the construction in a pattern match. It tests its integer argument `z`. If `z` is even, it returns `Some(z/2)`. If it is odd, it returns `None`. The `Twice` object can be used in a pattern match as follows:

```
val x = Twice(21)
x match {
  case Twice(y) => println(x+" is two times "+y)
  case _ => println("x is odd") }
```

To see where the `unapply` method comes into play, consider the match against `Twice(y)`. First, the value to be matched (`x` in the above example) is passed as argument to the `unapply` method of `Twice`. This results in an optional value which is matched subsequently. The preceding example is expanded as follows:

```
val x = Twice.apply(21)
Twice.unapply(x) match {
  case Some(y) => println(x+" is two times "+y)
  case None => println("x is odd") }
```

Extractor patterns with more than one argument correspond to `unapply` methods returning an optional tuple. Nullary extractor patterns correspond to `unapply` methods returning a Boolean.

In the following we show how extractors can be used to implement the matching semantics of join patterns. In essence, we define appropriate `unapply` methods for events which get implicitly called during the matching.

## 4.1  Matching Join Patterns

As shown previously, a set of join patterns is represented as a partial function. Its `isDefinedAt` method is used to find out whether one of the join patterns matches. In the following we are going to explain the code that the Scala compiler produces for the body of this method. Let us revisit the join pattern that we have seen in the previous section:

```
Get() & Put(x)
```

In our library, the `&` operator is an extractor that defines an `unapply` method; therefore, the Scala compiler produces the following matching code:

```
&.unapply(m) match {
  case Some((Get(), Put(x))) => true
  case None => false }
```

We defer a discussion of the argument $m$ that is passed to the & operator. For now, it is important to understand the general scheme of the matching process. Basically, calling the unapply method of the & operator produces a pair of intermediate results wrapped in Some. Nested pattern matching matches the two components of the pair against the Get and Put events. Only if both of them match, the overall pattern matches. Since the & operator is left-associative, matching more than two events proceeds by first calling the unapply methods of all the & operators from right to left, and then matching the intermediate results with the corresponding events from left to right.

Since events are objects that have an unapply method, we can expand the code further:

```
&.unapply(m) match {
  case Some((u, v)) =>
    Get.unapply(u) match {
      case true => Put.unapply(v) match {
        case Some(x) => true
        case None => false }
      case false => false }
    case None => false }
```

As we can see, the intermediate results produced by the unapply method of the & operator are passed as arguments to the unapply methods of the corresponding events. Since the Get event is parameter-less, its unapply method returns a Boolean, telling whether it matches or not. The Put event, on the other hand, takes a parameter; when the pattern matches, this parameter gets bound to a concrete value that is produced by the unapply method.

The unapply method of a parameter-less event such as Get essentially checks whether it has been invoked previously. The unapply method of an event that takes parameters such as Put returns the argument of a previous invocation (wrapped in Some), or signals failure if there is no previous invocation. In both cases, previous invocations have to be buffered inside the event.

*Firing join patterns.* As mentioned before, executing the right-hand side of a pattern that is part of a partial function amounts to invoking the apply method of that partial function. Basically, this repeats the matching process, thereby binding any pattern variables to concrete values in the pattern body. When firing a join pattern, the events' unapply methods have to dequeue the corresponding invocations from their buffers. In contrast, invoking isDefinedAt does not have any effect on the state of the invocation buffers. To signal to the events in which context their unapply methods are invoked, we therefore need some way to propagate out-of-band information through the matching. For this, we use the argument $m$ that is passed to the isDefinedAt and apply methods of the partial function. The & operator propagates this information verbatim to its two children (its unapply method receives $m$ as argument and produces a pair with two copies of $m$ wrapped in Some). Eventually, this information is passed to the events' unapply methods.

**Implementation Details.** Events are represented as classes that contain queues to buffer invocations. The Event class is the super class of all synchronous and asynchronous events:[6]

```
abstract class Event[R, Arg](owner: Joins) {
  val tag = owner.freshTag()
  val argQ = new Queue[Arg]
  def apply(arg: Arg): R = synchronized {argQ += arg; invoke()}
  def invoke(): R
  def unapply(isDryRun: Boolean): Option[Arg] =
    if (isDryRun && !argQ.isEmpty)
      Some(argQ.front)
    else if (!isDryRun)
      Some(argQ.dequeue())
    else None }
```

The Event class takes two type arguments R and Arg that indicate the result type and parameter type of event invocations, respectively. Events have a unique owner which is passed as argument of the primary constructor of the Event class.[7] An event can appear in several join patterns declared by its owner. The tag field holds an identifier which is unique with respect to a given owner instance; it is used to check the linearity of patterns (i.e. ensuring that an event occurs at most once in a pattern).

Whenever the event is invoked via its apply method, we append the provided argument to the argQ. The abstract invoke method is used to run synchronization-specific code; synchronous and asynchronous events differ mainly in their implementation of the invoke method (we show a concrete implementation for synchronous events below). In the unapply method we test whether matching occurs during a dry run. If it does not we dequeue an event invocation.

Synchronous events are implemented as follows:

```
abstract class SyncEvent[R, Arg] extends Event[R, Arg] {
  val waitQ = new Queue[SyncVar[R]]
  def invoke(): R = { val res = new SyncVar[R]
    waitQ += res; owner.matchAndRun(); res.get }
  def reply(res: R) = waitQ.dequeue().set(res) }
```

Synchronous events contain a logical queue of waiting threads, waitQ, which is implemented using the implicit wait set of synchronous variables.[8] The invoke

---

[6] In our actual implementation the fact whether an event is parameter-less is factored out for efficiency. Due to lack of space, we show a simplified class hierarchy.

[7] To allow the short syntax for declaring events that we have seen before, the owner is passed *implicitly* in the actual implementation. It is defined to be the current object this of the pattern-declaring class that inherits from Joins. A detailed account of implicit parameters in Scala is out of scope of this paper; the interested reader is referred to the Scala language specification.

[8] A SyncVar is an atomically updatable reference cell; it blocks threads trying to access an uninitialized cell.

method is run whenever the event is invoked. It creates a new `SyncVar` and appends it to the `waitQ`. Then, the `owner`'s `matchAndRun` method is invoked to check whether the event invocation triggers a complete join pattern. After that, the current thread waits for the `SyncVar` to become initialized by accessing it. If the owner detects (during `owner.matchAndRun()`) that a join pattern triggers, it will apply the join, thereby re-executing the pattern match (binding variables etc.) and running the join body. Inside the body, synchronous events are replied to by invoking their `reply` method. Replying means dequeuing a `SyncVar` and setting its value to the supplied argument. If none of the join patterns matches, the thread that invoked the synchronous event is blocked (upon calling `res.get`) until another thread triggers a join pattern that contains the same synchronous event.

*Thread-safety.* Our implementation avoids races when multiple threads try to match a join pattern at the same time; checking whether a join pattern matches (and, if so, running its body) is an atomic operation. Notably, the `isDefinedAt`/`apply` methods of the join set are only called from within the synchronized `matchAndRun` method of the `Joins` class. The `unapply` methods of events, in turn, are only called from within the matching code inside the partial function, and are thus guarded by the same lock. The internal state of individual events is updated consistently: the `apply` method is atomic, and the `reply` method is called only from within join bodies which are guarded by the `owner`'s lock. We don't assume any concurrency properties of the `argQ` and `waitQ` queues.

**Optimization.** Efficient join implementations represent patterns using bit sets [3,17]. An event with tag $n$ forms part of a pattern iff bit $n$ is set in the corresponding bit set. This representation allows one to efficiently check whether an event invocation triggers a join pattern.

The above implementation cannot use such an optimization as is, since the abstract `PartialFunction` class is the only way to interact with the set of join patterns; for instance the number of patterns is not known *a priori*. However, it is possible to *gradually construct* an efficient bit set representation during the matching process. The idea is to keep track of event invocations while matching a pattern. When a pattern matches, the tags of matched events give rise to a bit set that uniquely represents the pattern. At the point where each pattern has matched at least once, the bit sets are used to efficiently check for a match. If the set of events with queued invocations is represented as a bit set $ib$, then invoking an event with tag $n$ triggers a pattern represented as $pb$ iff $pb \subseteq ib \cup \{n\}$.

To test the effectiveness of the above optimization, we compared the performance of a bounded buffer implementation using our library without the optimization with a second one using the optimized library. Concurrently reading/writing $10^6$ items from/to a bounded buffer of size 100 is about 28% faster using the optimized library. However, this is only a first step towards an efficient implementation. Further optimizations are a worthwhile topic for future work.

## 4.2   Implementation of Actor-Based Joins

Actor-based joins integrate with Scala's pattern matching in essentially the same way as the thread-based joins, making both implementations very similar. We highlight how joins are integrated into the actor library, and how reply destinations are supported.

In the Scala actors library, `receive`   is a method that takes a `PartialFunction` as a sole argument, similar to the `join` method defined previously. To make `receive` aware of join patterns, the abstract `JoinActor` class overrides these methods by wrapping the partial function into a specialized partial function that understands join messages. `JoinActor` also overrides `send` to set the reply destination of a join message. When an actor executes a!msg, it invokes the `!` method of a. This method invokes a.`send`, implicitly passing the reply channel of the sender actor as a second argument.

```
abstract class JoinActor extends Actor {
  override def receive[R](f: PartialFunction[Any, R]): R =
    super.receive(new JoinPatterns(f))
  override def send(msg: Any, replyTo: OutputChannel[Any]) {
    setReplyDest(msg, replyTo)
    super.send(msg, replyTo) }
  def setReplyDest(msg: Any, replyTo: OutputChannel[Any]) {...}}
```

`JoinPatterns` is a special partial function that detects whether its argument message is a join message. If it is, then the argument message is transformed to include out-of-band information that will be passed to the pattern matcher, as is the case for events in the thread-based joins library. The boolean argument passed to the `asJoinMessage` method indicates to the pattern matcher whether or not join message arguments should be dequeued upon successful pattern matching. If the `msg` argument is not a join message, `asJoinMessage` passes the original message to the pattern matcher unchanged, enabling regular actor messages to be processed as normal.

```
class JoinPatterns[R](f: PartialFunction[Any, R])
    extends PartialFunction[Any, R] {
  def asJoinMessage(msg: Any, isDryRun: Boolean): Any =
    ...
  override def isDefinedAt(msg: Any) =
    f.isDefinedAt(asJoinMessage(msg, true))
  override def apply(msg: Any) =
    f(asJoinMessage(msg, false))
}
```

Recall from the implementation of synchronous events that thread-based joins used constructs such as `SyncVars` to synchronize the sender of an event with the receiver. Actor-based joins do not use such constructs. In order to synchronize sender and receiver, every join message has a reply destination (which is an `OutputChannel`, set when the message is sent in the actor's `send` method) on which a sender may listen for replies. The `reply` method of a `JoinMessage` simply forwards its argument value to this encapsulated reply destination. This wakes up an actor that performed a synchronous send (`a!?msg`) or that was waiting on a future (`a!!msg`).

## 5  Discussion and Related Work

Benton et al. [3] note that supporting general guards in join patterns is difficult to implement efficiently as it requires testing all possible combinations of queued messages to find a match. Side effects pose another problem. Benton et al. suggest a restricted language for guards to overcome these issues. However, to the best of our knowledge, there is currently no joins framework that supports a sufficiently restrictive yet expressive guard language to implement efficient guarded joins. Our current implementation handles (side-effect free) guards that only depend on arguments of events that queue at most one invocation at a time.

$C\omega$ [3] is a language extension of C# supporting *chords*, linear combinations of methods. In contrast to Scala Joins, $C\omega$ allows at most one synchronous method in a chord. The thread invoking this method is the thread that eventually executes the chord's body. The benefits of $C\omega$ as a language extension over Scala Joins are that chords can be enforced to be well-formed and that their matching code can be optimized ahead of time. In Scala Joins, the joins are only analyzed at pattern-matching time. The benefit of Scala Joins as a library extension is that it provides more flexibility, such as multiple synchronous events. Russo's C# Joins library [17] exploits the expressiveness of C# 2.0's generics to implement $C\omega$'s synchronization constructs. Piggy-backing on an existing variable binding mechanism allows us to avoid problems with C# Joins' delegates where the order in which arguments are passed is merely conventional. Scala Joins extends both $C\omega$ and C# Joins with *nested patterns* that can avoid certain redundancies by generalizing events and patterns.

CCR [4] is a C# library for asynchronous concurrency that supports join patterns without synchronous components. Join bodies are scheduled for execution in a thread pool. Our library integrates with JVM threads using synchronous variables, and supports event-based programming through its integration with Scala Actors. Singh [18] shows how a small set of higher-order combinators based on Haskell's software transactional memory (STM) can encode expressive join patterns. CML [16] allows threads to synchronize on first-class composable events; because all events have a single commit point, certain protocols may not be specified in a modular way (for example when an event occurs in several join patterns). By combining CML's events with all-or-nothing transactions, transactional events [5] overcome this restriction but may have a higher overhead than join patterns.

Synchronization in actor-based languages is a well-studied domain. Salsa [22] is a Java language extension with support for actors. It introduces the notion of a *join continuation*. However, join continuations are not to be mistaken with join patterns: the former only allow an actor to synchronize on multiple replies to previously sent messages. Activation based on message sets [10] is more general than joins since events/channels have a fixed owner, which enables important optimizations. Other actor-based languages allow for a synchronization style similar to that supported by join patterns. For example, *behavior sets* in Act++ [13] or *enabled sets* in Rosette [21] allow an actor to restrict the set of messages which it may process. They do so by partitioning messages into different sets representing different actor states. Joins do not make these states explicit, but rather allow state transitions to be encoded in terms of sending messages. The novelty of Scala Joins for actors is that such synchronization is integrated with the actor's standard message reception operation using extensible pattern matching. Recent work by Sulzmann et al. [19] extends Erlang-style actors with receive patterns consisting of multiple messages, which is very similar to our join-based actors. The two approaches are complementary: their work focuses on providing a formal matching semantics in form of Constraint Handling Rules whereas the emphasis of our work lies on the integration of joins with extensible pattern matching; Scala Joins additionally permits joins for standard (non-actor) threads that do not have a mailbox.

## 6   Conclusion

We presented a novel implementation of join patterns based on extensible pattern matching constructs of languages such as Scala and F#. The embedding into general pattern matching provides expressive features such as nested patterns and guards. The resulting programs are often as concise as if written in more specialized language extensions. We implemented our approach as a Scala library that supports join patterns with multiple synchronous events and guards and furthermore integrated it with the Scala Actors concurrency framework without changing the syntax and semantics of existing programs.

## References

1. Agha, G.A.: ACTORS: A Model of Concurrent Computation in Distributed Systems. MIT Press, Cambridge (1986)
2. Armstrong, J., Virding, R., Wikström, C., Williams, M.: Concurrent Programming in Erlang, 2nd edn. Prentice-Hall, Englewood Cliffs (1996)
3. Benton, N., Cardelli, L., Fournet, C.: Modern concurrency abstractions for C#. ACM Trans. Program. Lang. Syst 26(5), 769–804 (2004)
4. Chrysanthakopoulos, G., Singh, S.: An asynchronous messaging library for C#. In: Proc. SCOOL Workshop, OOPSLA (2005)
5. Donnelly, K., Fluet, M.: Transactional events. In: Proc. ICFP, pp. 124–135. ACM, New York (2006)
6. Emir, B., Odersky, M., Williams, J.: Matching Objects with Patterns. In: Ernst, E. (ed.) ECOOP 2007. LNCS, vol. 4609, pp. 273–298. Springer, Heidelberg (2007)
7. Fournet, C., Le Fessant, F., Maranget, L., Schmitt, A.: JoCaml: A language for concurrent distributed and mobile programming. In: Jeuring, J., Jones, S.L.P. (eds.) AFP 2002. LNCS, vol. 2638, pp. 129–158. Springer, Heidelberg (2003)

8. Fournet, C., Gonthier, G.: The reflexive chemical abstract machine and the join-calculus. In: Proc. POPL, January 1996, pp. 372–385. ACM, New York (1996)
9. Fournet, C., Gonthier, G., Lévy, J.-J., Maranget, L., Rémy, D.: A Calculus of Mobile Agents. In: Montanari, U., Sassone, V. (eds.) CONCUR 1996. LNCS, vol. 1119, pp. 406–421. Springer, Heidelberg (1996)
10. Frølund, S., Agha, G.: Abstracting interactions based on message sets. In: Ciancarini, P., Nierstrasz, O., Yonezawa, A. (eds.) ECOOP-WS 1994. LNCS, vol. 924, pp. 107–124. Springer, Heidelberg (1995)
11. Haller, P., Odersky, M.: Actors that unify threads and events. In: Murphy, A.L., Vitek, J. (eds.) COORDINATION 2007. LNCS, vol. 4467, pp. 171–190. Springer, Heidelberg (2007)
12. Halstead Jr., R.H.: Multilisp: a language for concurrent symbolic computation. ACM Trans. Program. Lang. Syst. 7(4), 501–538 (1985)
13. Kafura, D., Mukherji, M., Lavender, G.: ACT++: A Class Library for Concurrent Programming in C++ using Actors. J. of Object-Oriented Programming 6(6) (1993)
14. Odersky, M.: Functional Nets. In: Smolka, G. (ed.) ESOP 2000. LNCS, vol. 1782, pp. 1–25. Springer, Heidelberg (2000)
15. Okasaki, C.: Views for Standard ML. In: Proc. SIGPLAN Workshop on ML (1998)
16. Reppy, J.H.: CML: A higher-order concurrent language. In: Proc. PLDI, pp. 293–305. ACM Press, New York (1991)
17. Russo, C.V.: The Joins concurrency library. In: Proc. PADL, pp. 260–274 (2007)
18. Singh, S.: Higher-order combinators for join patterns using STM. In: Proc. TRANSACT Workshop, OOPSLA (2006)
19. Sulzmann, M., Lam, E.S.L., Van Weert, P.: Actors with multi-headed message receive patterns. In: COORDINATION 2008. LNCS, vol. 5052. Springer, Heidelberg (2008)
20. Syme, D., Neverov, G., Margetson, J.: Extensible pattern matching via a lightweight language extension. In: Proc. ICFP, pp. 29–40. ACM Press, New York (2007)
21. Tomlinson, C., Singh, V.: Inheritance and synchronization with enabled-sets. ACM SIGPLAN Notices 24(10), 103–112 (1989)
22. Varela, C., Agha, G.: Programming dynamically reconfigurable open systems with SALSA. ACM SIGPLAN Notices 36(12), 20–34 (2001)
23. von Itzstein, G.S., Kearney, D.: Join Java: An alternative concurrency semantic for Java. Technical report, University of South Australia (2001)
24. Wadler, P.: Views: A way for pattern matching to cohabit with data abstraction. In: Proc. POPL, pp. 307–313 (1987)
25. Yonezawa, A., Briot, J.-P., Shibayama, E.: Object-oriented concurrent programming in ABCL/1. In: Proc. OOPSLA, pp. 258–268 (1986)

# Advice for Coordination

Chris Hankin[1], Flemming Nielson[2],
Hanne Riis Nielson[2], and Fan Yang[2]

[1] Department of Computing, Imperial College London
clh@imperial.ac.uk
[2] Department of Informatics, Technical University of Denmark
{nielson,riis,fy}@imm.dtu.dk

**Abstract.** We show how to extend a coordination language with support for aspect oriented programming. The main challenge is how to properly deal with the trapping of actions *before* the actual data have been bound to the formal parameters. This necessitates dealing with *open* joinpoints – which is more demanding than the closed joinpoints in more traditional aspect oriented languages like AspectJ. The usefulness of our approach is demonstrated by mechanisms for discretionary and mandatory access control policies, as usually expressed by reference monitors, as well as mechanisms for logging actions.

## 1 Introduction

*Motivation.* Software development faces the challenge of guaranteeing the compliance of software to security policies even when the software has been developed without adequate considerations of security. This situation might arise due to lack of skills of the application programmers, due to lack of trust in the application programmers or even due to modifications of the security properties after the original development of the sofware (e.g. to cater for new needs of the users).

Taking access control as an example, a number of schemes for discretionary access control (e.g. based on capability lists or access control lists) and mandatory access control (e.g. the Bell LaPadula policy for confidentiality) have been proposed for controlling the execution of software [13]. As an example, the attempt to read from a file where the program has insufficient access rights should not be successful. As another example, transferring data from a file with high security classification to a file with low security classification should also not be successful.

The traditional approach to enforcing such security policies is through a *reference monitor* [13] that dynamically tracks the execution of the program; it makes appropriate checks on each basic operation being performed, either blocking the operation or allowing it to proceed. In concrete systems this is implemented as part of the operating system or as part of the interpreter for the language at hand (e.g. the Java byte code interpreter); in both cases as part of the trusted computing base. When modelled using operational semantics, a reference monitor

D. Lea and G. Zavattaro (Eds.): COORDINATION 2008, LNCS 5052, pp. 153–168, 2008.
© Springer-Verlag Berlin Heidelberg 2008

is usually a side condition to an inference rule either preventing or allowing the rule to be applicable. Sometimes it is found to be more cost effective to systematically modify the code so as to explicitly perform the checks that the reference monitor would otherwise have imposed; the term *inlined reference monitors* [9] has been coined for this.

An interesting approach to separation of concerns when programming systems is presented by the notion of *aspect oriented programming* [15,16]. The enforcement of security policies is an obvious candidate for such separation of concerns, e.g. because the security policy can be implemented by more skilled or more trusted programmers, or indeed because security considerations can be retrofitted by (re)defining *advice* to suit the (new) security policy. This requires that a notion of aspects is supported by the programming language. The detailed definition of the advice will then make decisions about how to possibly modify the operation being trapped. In concrete systems this calls for a modified language (like AspectJ [3] for Java) that supports the use of aspects. When modelled using operational semantics a notion of trapping operations and applying advice needs to be incorporated. Usually, it is found to be more cost effective to systematically modify the code so as to explicitly perform the operations that the advice would otherwise have imposed; the term *weaving* (e.g. [3]) has been coined for this.

In many cases the aspect oriented approach provides a more flexible way to deal with modifications in security policies [8,10,11,21,24] than the use of reference monitors [20]. It facilitates to use frameworks for security policies that may be well suited to the task at hand but that are perhaps not of general applicability and therefore not appropriate for incorporating into a reference monitor. We should like to refer to this process as *internalising* the reference monitor into a piece of advice. An example would be the enforcement of policies related to information flow or policies targeting the explicit needs of individuals; in particular this applies to the modelling of discretionary and mandatory access control policies [13] as well as mechanisms for logging actions. Since we do not offer priorities on advice we shall assume that the provision of advices is a priviledged operation.

*Contribution.* Our main contribution is the integration of aspects into a coordination language that facilitates distribution of data, mobility of code, and the ability to work with dynamically evolving, open systems. Rather than invent a completely new language, we define a small kernel language for mobile agents based on KLAIM [5,18,19]. We present this language in Section 2; as in KLAIM, processes and action prefixes (LINDA's **read**, **in**, and **out**) are located.

In our extension action prefixes are the potential joinpoints – the places where execution can be interrupted by a piece of advice. We take the approach that input actions should be trapped *before* a concrete tuple has been selected for input. This is because we find that the alternative approach, to trap after a concrete tuple has been selected for input, would constitute a covert channel [12,13]; indeed, the presence or absence of a tuple in the tuple space might either enable or prevent the advice to trap the action and this would amount to visible behaviour bypassing the security policy.

Trapping an input action *before* a concrete tuple has been selected for input requires our ability to deal with joinpoints that contain constructs for *binding* new variables – we shall call these *open* joinpoints. This is considerably more challenging than the closed joinpoints of traditional aspect oriented language like AspectJ [15]. To be more concrete, when we trap a method call in AspectJ we trap the actual call, i.e. the method name with its actual parameters, rather than the definition of the method, i.e. the method name with its *formal* parameters; in other words AspectJ traps closed joinpoints rather than *open* joinpoints. We show how to solve this challenge in Section 3 and provide a series of examples in Section 4.

The design space for how to introduce advice into coordination languages is quite broad. We have aimed for a modest approach being inspired by the operations of reference monitors; they generally allow to block an action or to let it proceed. A number of extensions can be foreseen – some of these are rather straightforward whereas others pose considerable difficulties; as a case in point it is nontrivial to add advice for ignoring or redirecting a given action. We discuss parts of the design space in Section 5.

## 2    KLAIM

The syntax of our fragment of KLAIM is defined in Table 1. We restrict ourselves to a core language for presentational purposes; it is straightforward to add the actions **newloc** and **eval** but we will not need these for the examples. Despite the rather modest selection of operations in our language it is still useful for quite a variety of applications related to business processes and similar workflow applications.

A net $N$ is a parallel composition of located processes or located tuples. For simplicity, components of tuples can be location constants only. Nets must be closed, meaning that all variables must be in scope of a defining occurrence.

A process $P$ is a parallel composition of processes, a guarded sum of action prefixed processes, or a replication (indicated by the $*$ operator). The guarded sum $\sum_i a_i.P_i$ is written 0 if the index set is empty.

A tuple can be output to a location, input from a location, or read from a location (meaning that it is not removed). Parameters can be location constants $l$, defining occurrences of location variables $!u$, and applied occurrences of a location variable $u$. We use $\ell$ for location expressions (i.e. location variables and constants); and in patterns we use $\ell^\lambda$ which in addition to location expressions also include defining occurrences of locations. The scope of a defining occurrence is the entire process to the right of the occurrence.

*Example 1.* Assume that the location YP, for Yellow Pages, contains pairs of values representing names and phone numbers and that the location DB, for the database of a phone company, contains triples of values representing a particular

**Table 1.** KLAIM Nets and Processes Syntax

---

$$N \in \textbf{Net} \qquad N ::= N_1 \parallel N_2 \mid l :: P \mid l :: \langle \overrightarrow{l} \rangle$$

$$P \in \textbf{Proc} \qquad P ::= P_1 \mid P_2 \mid \sum_i a_i.P_i \mid *P$$

$$a \in \textbf{Act} \qquad a ::= \textbf{out}(\overrightarrow{l})@l \mid \textbf{in}(\overrightarrow{l^\lambda})@l \mid \textbf{read}(\overrightarrow{l^\lambda})@l$$

$$\ell, \ell^\lambda \in \textbf{Loc} \qquad \ell ::= u \mid l \qquad\qquad\qquad \ell^\lambda ::= \ell \mid !u$$

---

phone call, that is, the phone number of the caller, the cost of the call and the name of the recipient. Consider the process:

$$\text{User} :: \textbf{read}(!name, !telno)@\text{YP}.$$
$$\textbf{read}(telno, !val_1, !val_2)@\text{DB}.$$
$$\textbf{out}(val_1)@name$$

Here User will first read a pair from the location YP and assign its two components to the variables $name$ and $telno$. Next the location DB is consulted to read a triple whose first component equals the value of $telno$ and the corresponding second component is assigned to the variable $val_1$ and the corresponding third component is assigned to the variable $val_2$. The final construct will write the first value to the location associated with $name$.

*Well-formedness of Locations and Actions.* To express the well-formedness conditions we shall introduce functions $bv$ and $fv$ for calculating the bound, resp. free, variables of the various kinds of locations that may occur in actions. The definitions are standard, in particular, $bv(l, u, !v) = \{v\}$ whereas $fv(l, u, !v) = \{u\}$.

An input action is well-formed if its sequence $\overrightarrow{\ell^\lambda} = \ell_1, \cdots, \ell_k$ (for $k \geq 0$) of locations is well-formed and this is the case when the following two conditions are fulfilled:

$$\forall i, j \in \{1, \cdots, k\} : i \neq j \Rightarrow bv(\ell_i^\lambda) \cap bv(\ell_j^\lambda) = \emptyset \text{ and}$$
$$bv(\overrightarrow{\ell^\lambda}) \cap fv(\overrightarrow{\ell^\lambda}) = \emptyset$$

The first condition demands that we do not use multiple defining occurrences of the same variable in an action. The second condition requires that bound variables and free variables cannot share any name in a single action. Thus we shall disallow $\textbf{in}(!u, u)@l$ as well as $\textbf{in}(!u, !u)@l$.

*Semantics of KLAIM.* The semantics is given by a one-step reduction relation on nets and is defined in Table 3. We make use of the structural congruence on nets; this is an associative and commutative (with respect to $\parallel$) equivalence relation and the interesting cases are defined in Table 2.

The rule for **out** is rather straightforward; it uses the fact that the action selected may be part of a guarded sum to dispense with any other alternatives.

**Table 2.** KLAIM Structural Congruence

---

$$l :: P_1 \mid P_2 \equiv l :: P_1 \parallel l :: P_2 \qquad\qquad l :: *P \equiv l :: P \mid *P$$

$$\frac{N_1 \equiv N_2}{N \parallel N_1 \equiv N \parallel N_2}$$

---

The rules for **in** and **read** only progress if the formal parameters $\overrightarrow{\ell^\lambda}$ match the candidate tuple $\overrightarrow{l}$. The details of the matching operation are given in Table 4 (explained below); if the matching succeeds and produces a substution then the rule applies; if no substitution is produced (due to a fail in part of the computation) the rule does not apply.

The matching operation of Table 4 returns a substitution $\theta$ being a (potentially empty) list of pairs of the form $[l/u]$; if the list is empty it is denoted by $id$. Notice that the definition does not treat location variables because tuples in the tuple space may only contain location constants and the reaction semantics is restricted to closed nets.

*Example 2.* Continuing Example 1 we may consider the following net and some steps of its execution:

   YP :: ⟨Alice, 55010⟩ || YP :: ⟨Bob, 58266⟩
|| DB :: ⟨55010, 100, Bob⟩ || DB :: ⟨58266, 1000, Alice⟩
|| User :: * **read**($!name, !telno$)@YP. **read**($telno, !val_1, !val_2$)@DB. **out**($val_1$)@$name$
→
   YP :: ⟨Alice, 55010⟩ || YP :: ⟨Bob, 58266⟩
|| DB :: ⟨55010, 100, Bob⟩ || DB :: ⟨58266, 1000, Alice⟩
|| User :: **read**($55010, !val_1, !val_2$)@DB. **out**($val_1$)@Alice
      | * **read**($!name, !telno$)@YP. **read**($telno, !val_1, !val_2$)@DB. **out**($val_1$)@$name$
→
   YP :: ⟨Alice, 55010⟩ || YP :: ⟨Bob, 58266⟩
|| DB :: ⟨55010, 100, Bob⟩ || DB :: ⟨58266, 1000, Alice⟩
|| User :: **out**($100$)@Alice
      | * **read**($!name, !telno$)@YP. **read**($telno, !val_1, !val_2$)@DB. **out**($val_1$)@$name$
→
   YP :: ⟨Alice, 55010⟩ || YP :: ⟨Bob, 58266⟩
|| DB :: ⟨55010, 100, Bob⟩ || DB :: ⟨58266, 1000, Alice⟩
|| Alice :: ⟨100⟩
|| User :: * **read**($!name, !telno$)@YP. **read**($telno, !val_1, !val_2$)@DB. **out**($val_1$)@$name$

In the first step User spawns a thread and reads the pair ⟨Alice, 55010⟩ from YP; the bindings of the variables *name* and *telno* are reflected in the continuation of the thread. In the second step it is only possible to read a triple from DB that has 55010 as its first component; this results in binding $val_1$ and $val_2$ to 100 and Bob, respectively. The last step will then complete the thread by outputting the value 100 to Alice.

**Table 3.** KLAIM Reaction Semantics (on closed nets)

---

$l_s :: \mathbf{out}(\overrightarrow{l})@l_0.P + \cdots \rightarrow l_s :: P \parallel l_0 :: \langle \overrightarrow{l} \rangle$

$l_s :: \mathbf{in}(\overrightarrow{\ell^\lambda})@l_0.P + \cdots \parallel l_0 :: \langle \overrightarrow{l} \rangle \rightarrow l_s :: P\theta$          if $match(\overrightarrow{\ell^\lambda}; \overrightarrow{l}) = \theta$

$l_s :: \mathbf{read}(\overrightarrow{\ell^\lambda})@l_0.P + \cdots \parallel l_0 :: \langle \overrightarrow{l} \rangle \rightarrow l_s :: P\theta \parallel l_0 :: \langle \overrightarrow{l} \rangle$ if $match(\overrightarrow{\ell^\lambda}; \overrightarrow{l}) = \theta$

$$\frac{N_1 \rightarrow N_1'}{N_1 \parallel N_2 \rightarrow N_1' \parallel N_2} \qquad \frac{N \equiv N' \quad N' \rightarrow N'' \quad N'' \equiv N'''}{N \rightarrow N'''}$$

---

**Table 4.** KLAIM Pattern Matching of Templates against Tuples

---

$match(\langle\rangle; \langle\rangle) = id$

$match(\langle \ell_1'^\lambda, \cdots, \ell_k'^\lambda \rangle; \langle l_1, \cdots, l_k \rangle) = $ let $\theta = $ case $\ell_1'^\lambda$ of

                               $l_1' :$ if $l_1' = l_1$ then $id$ else fail

                               $!u :$   $[l_1/u]$

                in $\theta \circ match(\langle \ell_2'^\lambda, \cdots, \ell_k'^\lambda \rangle; \langle l_2, \cdots, l_k \rangle)$

---

*Example 3.* Returning to Example 1 we may want to impose the condition that only some users are allowed to access the location DB containing secret data whereas all users are allowed to read from the location YP containing only public data. This can be expressed with discretionary access control using an *access control matrix* DAC containing triples $(s, o, a)$ identifying which subjects $s$ can perform which operations $a$ on which objects $o$. We may thus equip the semantics of KLAIM with a reference monitor that will consult DAC whenever an action is executed; in particular, whenever User is performing a **read** action on a location $l$ it will check whether (User, $l$, **read**) $\in$ DAC and only proceed if this is the case. Similarly when performing an **out** action on some location $l$ it will check whether (User, $l$, **out**) $\in$ DAC before proceeding.

A comparable policy can be imposed by a reference monitor based on mandatory access control. Here *security levels* are assigned to subjects and object. In the simple case of just two security levels we may give DB the level high and YP the level low. The Bell-LaPadula security policy will then impose that a low user can only perform **read** actions on YP whereas **out** actions can be performed on any location. A high user, on the other hand, will be able to perform **read** actions on both YP and DB. The out action can only be performed on high locations unless a notion of declassification is imposed that will lower the users' security level.

## 3   AspectK

*Syntax.* The syntax of AspectK extends the syntax of KLAIM (Table 1) as shown in Table 5. A system $S$ consists of a net $N$ prefixed by a sequence of

**Table 5.** AspectK Syntax

| $S \in$ **System** | $S ::=$ **let** $\overrightarrow{asp}$ **in** $N$ |
| :--- | :--- |
| $asp \in$ **Asp** | $asp ::= A[cut] \triangleq body$ |
| $body \in$ **Advice** | $body ::=$ **case** $(cond)$ $sbody$ ; $body$ $\mid$ $sbody$ |
| | $sbody ::= as$ **break** $\mid$ $as$ **proceed** $as$ |
| $as \in$ **Act**$^*$ | $as ::= a.as \mid \varepsilon$ |
| $cond \in$ **BExp** | $cond ::=$ **test**$(\overrightarrow{\ell^\lambda})@\ell$ $\mid$ $\ell_1 = \ell_2$ $\mid$ $cond_1 \wedge cond_2$ $\mid$ $\neg\ cond$ |
| $cut \in$ **Cut** | $cut ::= \ell :: a$ |
| $\ell^\lambda \in$ **Loc** | $\ell^\lambda ::= \ell \mid\ !u \mid\ ?u$ |

aspect declarations. An aspect declaration takes the form $A[cut] \triangleq body$, where $A$ is the name of the aspect, $cut$ is the action to be trapped by $A$ and $body$ specifies the way it should be handled.

The keyword **break** indicates that the original action is suppressed and prevents the process from being further executed, whereas the keyword **proceed** allows the original action to execute. In case of multiple aspects that trap an action, all the before actions are executed in declaration order, then the original action (in case of no **break**), and finally the after actions in reverse declaration order. The keyword **break** takes precedence over the keyword **proceed**.

The $cond$ is similar to a standard boolean expression, which will be evaluated to $true$ or $false$. The primitive **test**$(\overrightarrow{\ell^\lambda})@\ell$ will only be evaluated to $true$ in case that there is a tuple that matches $\overrightarrow{\ell^\lambda}$ in the tuple space at location $\ell$.

A cutpoint $cut$ is simply a cut action accompanied by location $\ell$. For the use in cut actions we have extended the definition of $\ell^\lambda$ to incorporate a new location expression $?u$ that is intended to trap both $!u$ and $l$ occurring in actions; this will be made precise in the definition of the $check$ function in Table 9.

*Well-formedness of Cuts.* We define $cl(cut)$ that generates a list of entities involved in a cut. For example:

$$cl(l_s :: \mathbf{in}(!x, y, ?z)@l_0) = \langle l_s, x, y, z, l_0 \rangle$$

In addition to the well-formedness conditions for KLAIM, we require that the variables of $cl(cut)$ are pairwise distinct. When $!u$ or $?u$ is used in a cut pattern, $u$ should only occur in the *after* actions (actions that occur after **proceed**); in particular $u$ should neither be used in any before action nor in any conditionals. No use of $?u$ will be allowed inside tests (use $!u$ instead).

*Semantics of AspectK.* The semantics is given by a one-step reduction relation on well-formed systems and nets. The interesting rules are defined in Table 6 – the rule for reduction on nets and a congruence rule (see Table 3) are omitted – and we also make use of the structural congruence on nets defined in Table 2.

The rules for the three actions come in pairs, as is illustrated in Table 6. One rule takes care of the action when no advice is allowed to interrupt it; this is syntactically denoted by underlining.

The rules for the non-underlined actions all take the same shape and make use of the function $\Phi$ defined in Table 7. The result of $\Phi_f(\Gamma_A; \ell :: a)$ is a sequence of actions trapping $\ell :: a$; $\Gamma_A$ is a global environment of aspects. The index $f$ is

**Table 6.** Reaction Semantics (on closed nets)

---

$$\frac{N \to N' \quad (\text{where globally } \Gamma_A = \overrightarrow{asp})}{\textbf{let } \overrightarrow{asp} \textbf{ in } N \to \textbf{let } \overrightarrow{asp} \textbf{ in } N'}$$

$l_s :: \underline{\textbf{stop}}.P + \cdots \to l_s :: 0$

$l_s :: \underline{\textbf{out}}(\overrightarrow{l})@l_0.P + \cdots \to l_s :: P \parallel l_0 :: \langle \overrightarrow{l} \rangle$

$l_s :: \underline{\textbf{in}}(\overrightarrow{\ell^\lambda})@l_0.P + \cdots \parallel l_0 :: \langle \overrightarrow{l} \rangle \to l_s :: P\theta$      if $match(\overrightarrow{\ell^\lambda}; \overrightarrow{l}) = \theta$

$l_s :: \underline{\textbf{read}}(\overrightarrow{\ell^\lambda})@l_0.P + \cdots \parallel l_0 :: \langle \overrightarrow{l} \rangle \to l_s :: P\theta \parallel l_0 :: \langle \overrightarrow{l} \rangle$   if $match(\overrightarrow{\ell^\lambda}; \overrightarrow{l}) = \theta$

$$\frac{l_s :: \Phi_{\text{proceed}}(\Gamma_A; l_s :: \textbf{out}(\overrightarrow{l})@l_0).P \to N}{l_s :: \textbf{out}(\overrightarrow{l})@l_0.P + \cdots \to N}$$

$$\frac{l_s :: \Phi_{\text{proceed}}(\Gamma_A; l_s :: \textbf{in}(\overrightarrow{\ell^\lambda})@l_0).P \parallel N' \to N}{l_s :: \textbf{in}(\overrightarrow{\ell^\lambda})@l_0.P + \cdots \parallel N' \to N}$$

$$\frac{l_s :: \Phi_{\text{proceed}}(\Gamma_A; l_s :: \textbf{read}(\overrightarrow{\ell^\lambda})@l_0).P \parallel N' \to N}{l_s :: \textbf{read}(\overrightarrow{\ell^\lambda})@l_0.P + \cdots \parallel N' \to N}$$

---

**Table 7.** Trapping Aspects: Step 1

---

$\Phi_f(A[cut] \triangleq body, \Gamma_A; \ell :: a) = \text{case } trap(cut, \ell :: a) \text{ of } \text{fail} : \quad \Phi_f(\Gamma_A; \ell :: a)$
$$\qquad\qquad\qquad\qquad\qquad\qquad\qquad\qquad\qquad\qquad\quad \theta : \quad \kappa_f^{\Gamma_A, \ell :: a}(body\ \theta)$$

$\Phi_f(\varepsilon; \ell :: a) = \text{case } f \text{ of } \textbf{proceed} : \underline{a}$
$$\qquad\qquad\qquad\qquad\qquad\qquad \textbf{break} : \textbf{stop}$$

---

**Table 8.** Trapping Aspects: Step 2

---

$trap(cut, \ell :: a) = \text{case } (cut, \ell :: a) \text{ of}$

$\qquad (\ell_s :: \textbf{out}(\overrightarrow{\ell})@\ell_0, l_s :: \textbf{out}(\overrightarrow{l})@l_0) : \quad check(\langle \ell_s, \overrightarrow{\ell}, \ell_0 \rangle, \langle l_s, \overrightarrow{l}, l_0 \rangle)$

$\qquad (\ell_s :: \textbf{in}(\overrightarrow{\ell^\lambda})@\ell_0, l_s :: \textbf{in}(\overrightarrow{\ell'^\lambda})@l_0) : \quad check(\langle \ell_s, \overrightarrow{\ell^\lambda}, \ell_0 \rangle, \langle l_s, \overrightarrow{\ell'^\lambda}, l_0 \rangle)$

$\qquad (\ell_s :: \textbf{read}(\overrightarrow{\ell^\lambda})@\ell_0, l_s :: \textbf{read}(\overrightarrow{\ell'^\lambda})@l_0) : check(\langle \ell_s, \overrightarrow{\ell^\lambda}, \ell_0 \rangle, \langle l_s, \overrightarrow{\ell'^\lambda}, l_0 \rangle)$

$\qquad \text{otherwise fail}$

---

**Table 9.** Trapping Aspects: Step 3

---

$check(\langle\rangle, \langle\rangle) = id$

$check(\langle\ell_1^\lambda, \ell_2^\lambda, \cdots, \ell_k^\lambda\rangle, \langle\ell_1'^\lambda, \cdots, \ell_k'^\lambda\rangle) = $ let $\theta = $ case $(\ell_1^\lambda, \ell_1'^\lambda)$ of

$$(!u, !u') : [u'/u]$$
$$(?u, !u') : [u'/u]$$
$$(?u, l') : [l'/u]$$
$$(u, l') : [l'/u]$$
$$(l, l') : \text{if } l = l' \text{ then } id \text{ else fail}$$

otherwise fail

in $\theta \circ check(\langle\ell_2^\lambda, \cdots, \ell_k^\lambda\rangle, \langle\ell_2'^\lambda, \cdots, \ell_k'^\lambda\rangle)$

---

**Table 10.** Trapping Aspects: Step 4

---

$\kappa_f^{\Gamma_A, \ell::a}(\textbf{case } cond \; sbody \; ; \; body) = $ case $B(cond)$ of $\textbf{tt} : \quad \kappa_f^{\Gamma_A, \ell::a}(sbody)$

$\qquad\qquad\qquad\qquad\qquad\qquad\qquad\qquad\qquad \textbf{ff} : \quad \kappa_f^{\Gamma_A, \ell::a}(body)$

$\kappa_f^{\Gamma_A, \ell::a}(sbody) = $ case $sbody$ of $as_1 \; \textbf{proceed} \; as_2 : as_1.\Phi_f(\Gamma_A; \ell :: a).as_2$

$\qquad\qquad\qquad\qquad\qquad\qquad as \; \textbf{break} \; : as.\Phi_{\textbf{break}}(\Gamma_A; \ell :: a)$

---

**Table 11.** Trapping Aspects: Step 5

---

$$B(\textbf{test}(\overrightarrow{\ell^\lambda})@l) \quad = \begin{cases} \textbf{tt if } \text{there exists a tuple } \overrightarrow{l} \text{ at location } l \\ \qquad \text{such that } match(\overrightarrow{\ell^\lambda}; \overrightarrow{l}) \neq \textbf{fail} \\ \textbf{ff } \text{otherwise} \end{cases}$$

$$B(l_1 = l_2) \quad = \begin{cases} \textbf{tt if } l_1 = l_2 \\ \textbf{ff } \text{otherwise} \end{cases}$$

$$B(cond_1 \wedge cond_2) = \begin{cases} \textbf{tt if } B(cond_1) = \textbf{tt} \text{ and } B(cond_2) = \textbf{tt} \\ \textbf{ff if } B(cond_1) = \textbf{ff} \text{ or } B(cond_2) = \textbf{ff} \end{cases}$$

$$B(\neg cond) \quad = \begin{cases} \textbf{tt if } B(cond) = \textbf{ff} \\ \textbf{ff if } B(cond) = \textbf{tt} \end{cases}$$

---

either **proceed** or **break**. In general $f$ will be **break** if at least one "break" advice applies, otherwise it will be **proceed**. In case of **proceed** the action $\underline{a}$ is eventually emitted, otherwise it will be dispensed with and be replaced with the **stop** action, killing all the subsequent actions. Recall that advice is searched in the order of declaration and applies in a parenthesis-like fashion.

The function $\Phi$ uses an auxiliary function $trap$ (see Table 8) to step through the aspects in the aspects environment. In each case, $trap$ checks whether the cut matches the action; the check is accomplished by using a further auxiliary function, $check$ (see Table 9), which either fails or produces a substitution for the variables occurring in the cut. The *check* function is essentially an extension of the *match* function (see Table 4) to accommodate the matching of cut patterns. If a cut matches a normal action, we use $\kappa_f^{\Gamma_A,\ell::a}$ (see Table 10) to recursively search for further advices; *body* $\theta$ is computed in the obvious way.

The $\kappa_f^{\Gamma_A,\ell::a}$ function processes the advice associated with a matching cut. The first clause in the definition processes conditional advices using the function $B$, displayed in Table 11, to evaluate the condition. The second clause deals with non-conditional advices which are either **proceed** or **break** advices. In the former case, the before actions and after actions sandwich a recursive call to $\Phi$ to find further applicable aspects. In the latter case, the before actions are performed and $\Phi$ is called recursively to find further applicable aspects taking care to record the fact that a **break** has been encountered. Eventually, when all aspects in the aspect environment have been considered, the second clause of $\Phi$ is invoked (see Table 7). If no **break** has been encountered, the underlined action is emitted, otherwise a **stop** is emitted. In the latter case, the program will terminate after all of the before actions have been executed.

# 4   Example Programs

We now show a series of examples to illustrate how AspectK can be used to encode various security policies.

*Example 4.* The discretionary access control of Example 3 can be imposed by introducing a location DAC containing two kinds of triples

- $\langle user, \mathsf{DB}, \mathbf{read}\rangle$ for selected users, and
- $\langle user, name, \mathbf{out}\rangle$ for the same selected users and all names.

The following aspect declarations will then impose the desired requirements:

$$\mathsf{A}_{\mathsf{DAC}}^{read}[u :: \mathbf{read}(?x, ?y, ?z)@\mathsf{DB}] \triangleq \mathbf{case}(\mathbf{test}(u, \mathsf{DB}, \mathbf{read})@\mathsf{DAC})$$
$$\mathbf{proceed};$$
$$\mathbf{break}$$

$$\mathsf{A}_{\mathsf{DAC}}^{out}[u :: \mathbf{out}(z)@l] \triangleq \mathbf{case}(\mathbf{test}(u, l, \mathbf{out})@\mathsf{DAC})$$
$$\mathbf{proceed};$$
$$\mathbf{break}$$

The first action **read**(!*name*, !*key*)@YP of User in Examples 1 and 2 will not be trapped by any of the aspects so it will simply be performed resulting in binding Alice to *name* and 55010 to *telno* as in Example 2.

The aspect $\mathsf{A}_{\mathsf{DAC}}^{read}$ will trap the second action in Examples 1 and 2 which now is

$$\mathbf{read}(55010, !val_1, !val_2)@\mathsf{DB}$$

The resulting substitution is [User/$u$, 55010/$x$, $val_1/y$, $val_2/z$] and we are evaluating the condition **test**(User, DB, **read**)@DAC. If this test evaluates to *false* then the advice **break** is taken and terminates the execution. Alternatively, we proceed and perform the action **read**(55010, !$val_1$, !$val_2$)@DB thereby giving rise to the binding of 100 to $val_1$ and Bob to $val_2$.

Finally, the aspect $A^{out}_{DAC}$ will trap the last action which is now **out**(100)@Alice; also here the test will succeed and the **proceed** advice will be selected so that the original **out** is executed.

Using aspects it is easy to modify the access control policy so as to allow a user to access his own entries in DB even though he does not have access to the complete database. We simply modify the aspect $A^{read}_{DAC}$ to become

$$A^{read}_{DAC-1}[u :: \mathbf{read}(!x, ?y, ?z)@DB]$$
$$\triangleq \mathbf{break}$$

$$A^{read}_{DAC-2}[u :: \mathbf{read}(x, ?y, ?z)@DB]$$
$$\triangleq \mathbf{case}(\mathbf{test}(u, DB, \mathbf{read})@DAC \vee \mathbf{test}(u, x)@YP)$$
$$\mathbf{proceed};$$
$$\mathbf{break}$$

*Example 5.* To model the mandatory access control policy of Example 3 we introduce a location MAC with the following pairs:

- $\langle$YP, low$\rangle$ reflecting that the phonebook has low security level,
- $\langle$DB, high$\rangle$ reflecting that the customer database has high security level,
- $\langle s, $low$\rangle$ for all users and names $s$ with low security level, and
- $\langle s, $high$\rangle$ for all users and names $s$ with high security level.

We now consider the Bell-LaPadula security policy in a setting where both subjects and objects have fixed security levels. The first part of the policy states that a subject is allowed to read or input data from any object provided that the object's security level dominates that of the object; this is captured by the following aspects (which enforce *no read-up*):

$$A^{read_2}_{MAC}[u :: \mathbf{read}(?x, ?y)@l] \triangleq \mathbf{case}(\neg(\mathbf{test}(u, \mathsf{low})@MAC \wedge \mathbf{test}(l, \mathsf{high})@MAC))$$
$$\mathbf{proceed};$$
$$\mathbf{break}$$
$$A^{read_3}_{MAC}[u :: \mathbf{read}(?x, ?y, ?z)@l] \triangleq \mathbf{case}(\neg(\mathbf{test}(u, \mathsf{low})@MAC \wedge \mathbf{test}(l, \mathsf{high})@MAC))$$
$$\mathbf{proceed};$$
$$\mathbf{break}$$

The second part of the policy, the star property, allows a subject to write to any object provided that the security level of the object dominates that of the subject. This is captured by the following aspect (enforcing *no write-down*):

$$A^{out}_{MAC}[u :: \mathbf{out}(z)@l] \triangleq \mathbf{case}(\neg(\mathbf{test}(u, \mathsf{high})@MAC \wedge \mathbf{test}(l, \mathsf{low})@MAC))$$
$$\mathbf{proceed};$$
$$\mathbf{break}$$

With these aspects in place a user with low security level will only be able to perform the action **read**(!$name$, !$key$)@YP; once he attempts doing the action

**read**$(key, !val_1, !val_2)$@DB the advice **break** will stop the execution. A user with high security level will be able to perform both of these actions but may be stopped at the third action **out**$(val)$@$name$ if the security level of the location bound to *name* turns out to be low.

In order to allow a high user to write to a low name we may introduce *declassification* of security levels. To keep things simple we may do so by introducing a billing location that does not need to adhere to the security policy and replace the process by:

$$
\begin{array}{ll}
\text{User} :: & \textbf{read}(!name, !key)@\text{YP}. \\
& \textbf{read}(key, !val_1, !val_2)@\text{DB}. \\
& \textbf{out}(name, val_1, val_2)@\text{Billing} \\
\| \text{ Billing} :: & \textbf{in}(!n, !v_1, !v_2)@\text{Billing}. \ \textbf{out}(v_1)@n
\end{array}
$$

We add the pair $\langle \text{Billing}, \text{high} \rangle$ to the MAC location thereby allowing all high users to output to Billing; we also modify the aspect for **out** actions to ensure that they are always allowed to **proceed** at the Billing location:

$$
\begin{array}{l}
\text{A}^{out}_{\text{MAC}}[u :: \textbf{out}(z)@l] \triangleq \textbf{case}(\neg(\textbf{test}(u, \text{high})@\text{MAC} \wedge \textbf{test}(l, \text{low})@\text{MAC}) \\
\qquad\qquad\qquad\qquad \vee (u = \text{Billing})) \\
\qquad\qquad\qquad \textbf{proceed}; \\
\qquad\qquad\qquad \textbf{break}
\end{array}
$$

*Example 6.* As a final example, which illustrates the need for actions both before and after **proceed** we define an aspect which maintains a log of **read** action on DB:

$$
\begin{array}{l}
\text{A}_{\text{LOG}}[u :: \textbf{read}(?x, ?y, ?z)@\text{DB}] \triangleq \textbf{in}(sem)@\text{semaphore} \\
\qquad\qquad\qquad\qquad\qquad \textbf{proceed} \\
\qquad\qquad\qquad\qquad\qquad \textbf{out}(u, x, y, z)@\text{logfile}. \\
\qquad\qquad\qquad\qquad\qquad \textbf{out}(sem)@\text{semaphore}
\end{array}
$$

We use a semaphore to ensure that the reads and the updating of the log file are kept in lock step, meaning that at any time at most one **read** action has been performed but still needs to be logged. The before action grabs the semaphore, **proceed** allows the read to be performed and the parameters that are bound in the read are recorded in the log file before the semaphore is released. In a similar way we can log **out** actions.

## 5    Conclusion

*Summary.* We have shown how to extend a coordination language with support for aspect oriented programming. While we have only performed the technical development for a fragment of KLAIM we do believe that our approach and our findings would apply to a larger class of coordination languages.

A distinguishing feature of coordination languages with respect to object oriented languages and web service languages [7] is the need to deal with *open* joinpoints, i.e. joinpoints that contain mechanisms for binding variables. Similar considerations would apply if we were to incorporate aspects into process algebras that, like the $\pi$-calculus, allow a notion of open input (or input from the environment) but would not be necessary for calculi without this feature [1,6,14,22,23]. This calls for considerable care in designing a notion of advice where input actions are trapped *before* a concrete tuple has been selected for input. We argued in the Introduction that the more standard choice of trapping an action after a concrete tuple has been selected would constitute a covert channel in the presence of open joinpoints. Our technical solution to this challenge was presented in Section 3 and we believe it to be applicable to open joinpoints in general.

In our development we focused on just two types of basic advice, **break** and **proceed**, together with actions performed before or after the advice (in order to obtain some of the benefits of **around** advice). We showed by means of examples that our approach is sufficiently flexible for defining aspects for enforcing discretionary and mandatory access control policies as well as mechanisms for logging actions. As argued in the Introduction we find this to be both a more flexible and less error-prone way of accomodating new security policies. Also we only considered the possibility of fixed global advice applicable at all locations.

There are different views as to whether the actions generated by an advice should also be subject to further advice. Throughout the development we have taken the view that this is indeed desirable. But it is straightforward to modify Table 10 to use underlined before and after actions so as to accommodate the alternative view.

Similarly, the use of a global test is often considered hard to implement because of the need to synchronise the whole network [18]. In our examples we have taken the view that we only perform tests on special persistent databases.

We now discuss the possibility of extending our design.

*Types of advice.* We did consider the incorporation of an **ignore** advice, as is commonly expressible in aspect oriented object oriented languages, but somewhat surprisingly found this to be a challenging extension.

To illustrate the problems consider the following advice

$$A_{\text{IGNORE}}[u :: \mathbf{read}(!v)@l_{priv}] \triangleq \mathbf{ignore}$$

for simply ignoring inputs from a private location $l_{priv}$. The problem with this definition is that it might be trapping a **read** action occurring in the following process $l :: \mathbf{read}(!w)@l_{priv}.\mathbf{out}(w)@l_{print}$ which would then become $l : \mathbf{out}(w)@l_{print}$ that contains a free variable; however, our semantics does not ascribe meaning to such processes!

Even a somewhat more useful advice

$$A_{\text{REDIRECT}}[u :: \mathbf{read}(!v)@l_{priv}] \triangleq \mathbf{ignore}\ u :: \mathbf{read}(!v)@l_{sandbox}$$

for redirecting inputs from a private location $l_{priv}$ to a sandbox $l_{sandbox}$ is problematic. Once again consider the program $l :: \mathbf{read}(!w)@l_{priv}.\mathbf{out}(w)@l_{print}$ that is intended to become $l :: \mathbf{read}(!w)@l_{sandbox}.\mathbf{out}(w)@l_{print}$. The problem is that our current notion of substitution does not achieve this effect: while we can bind $v$ to $w$ to obtain the substitution $[w/v]$, we would not normally let the substitution change the defining occurrence $!v$ in $u :: \mathbf{read}(!v)@l_{sandbox}$ to $!w$ so as to yield the desired $u :: \mathbf{read}(!w)@l_{sandbox}$.

This can be solved by suitable extensions of our approach; in particular we can introduce special variables, e.g. $\beta$, that can be substituted also in defining occurrences and write

$$\mathsf{A}_{\mathsf{REDIRECT}}[u :: \mathbf{read}(!\beta)@l_{priv}] \triangleq \mathbf{ignore}\ u :: \mathbf{read}(!\beta)@l_{sandbox}$$

Then the program $l :: \mathbf{read}(!w)@l_{priv}.\mathbf{out}(w)@l_{print}$ would correctly be transformed to $l :: \mathbf{read}(!w)@l_{sandbox}.\mathbf{out}(w)@l_{print}$.

*Local or global advice.* For simplicity we have taken an approach where all advice is given in advance and is global in scope. It would be worthwhile to be able to introduce new pieces of advice and to limit the scope of its applicability. Indeed, it might be natural to consider the aspect environment to be distributed and associated with locations. In that case it would be appropriate to extend the syntax with a $\mathbf{newloc}(u : \Gamma)$ construct with inference rule:

$$l ::^{\Gamma} \mathbf{newloc}(u : \Gamma').P \rightarrow l ::^{\Gamma} P[l'/u] \ || \ l' ::^{\Gamma'} 0 \quad \text{with } l' \text{ fresh}$$

This would constitute a static treatment of scoped advice unlike the dynamic treatment in CaesarJ [2].

This would be useful when dealing with the **eval** action. Here we would extend the syntax of processes with a process identifier $X$ that could match an arbitrary process. Then we might write an advice for executing a process in a sandbox as follows:

$$\mathsf{A}_{\mathsf{SANDBOX}}[u ::^{\gamma} \mathbf{eval}(X)@l_{sensitive}] \triangleq$$
$$\quad \mathbf{newloc}(u_{sandbox} : \gamma[\mathsf{A}_{\mathsf{BOXREAD}}[u ::^{\gamma'} out(v)@w] \triangleq u ::^{\gamma'} \mathbf{out}(v)@u_{sandbox}])$$
$$\quad \mathbf{ignore}$$
$$\quad u ::^{\gamma} \mathbf{eval}(X)@u_{sandbox}$$

When executing a program $l ::^{\Gamma} \mathbf{eval}(P)@l_{sensitive}.P'$ the advice transforms it to a process that evaluates the process in a confined location and redirects all outputs to a confined location.

Clearly a number of additional extensions can be contemplated. For example we might want to have more powerful pointcut languages [4,17] allowing patterns that bind over a number of parameters (in order to avoid having separate advice for each arity of the operations) or giving priorities to advice. However, our goal was to demonstrate both the need to, and the possibility of, dealing with open joinpoints.

*Acknowledgements.* Thanks to Sebastian Nanz for discussions about aspects. This project was partially funded by the Danish Strategic Research Council (project 2106-06-0028) "Aspects of Security for Citizens".

# References

1. Andrews., J.H.: Process-Algebraic Foundations of Aspect-Oriented Programming. Metalevel Architectures and Separation of Crosscutting Concerns: Third International Conference (2001)
2. Aracic, I., Gasiunas, V., Mezini, M., Ostermann, K.: An Overview of CaesarJ. Transactions on Aspect-Oriented Software Development 3880, 135–173 (2006)
3. Avgustinov, P., Christensen, A.S., Hendren, L., Kuzins, S., Lhoták, J., Lhoták, O., de Moor, O., Sereni, D., Sittampalam, G., Tibble, J.: Optimising AspectJ. In: ACM SIGPLAN Conference on Programming Language Design and Implementation, ACM Press, New York (2005)
4. Avgustinov, P., Hajiyev, E., Ongkingco, N., de Moor, O., Sereni, D., Tibble, J., Verbaere, M.: Semantics of static pointcuts in AspectJ. In: Proceedings of the 34th annual ACM SIGPLAN-SIGACT symposium on Principles of programming languages, pp. 11–23 (2007)
5. Bettini, L., Bono, V., De Nicola, R., Ferrari, G., Gorla, D., Loreti, M., Moggi, E., Pugliese, R., Tuosto, E., Venneri, B.: The Klaim Project: Theory and Practice (2003)
6. Bruns, G., Jagadeesan, R., Jeffrey, A., Riely, J.: $\mu$abc: A minimal aspect calculus. In: Proceedings of the 2004 International Conference on Concurrency Theory, pp. 209–224. Springer, Heidelberg (2004)
7. Charfi, A., Mezini, M.: Aspect-oriented web service composition with ao4bpel. In: (LJ) Zhang, L.-J., Jeckle, M. (eds.) ECOWS 2004. LNCS, vol. 3250, pp. 168–182. Springer, Heidelberg (2004)
8. Dantas, D.S.: Analyzing Security Advice in Functional Aspect-oriented Programming Languages. Ph.D Thesis. Princeton University, Computer Science (2007)
9. Erlingsson, Ú., Schneider, F.B.: IRM enforcement of java stack inspection. In: IEEE Symposium on Security and Privacy, pp. 246–255 (2000)
10. Gao, S., Deng, Y., Yu, H., He, X., Beznosov, K., Cooper, K.: Applying Aspect-Orientation in Designing Security Systems: A Case Study. The Sixteenth International Conference on Software Engineering and Knowledge Engineering (2004)
11. Georg, G., Ray, I., France, R.: Using aspects to design a secure system. Engineering of Complex Computer Systems, 117–126 (2002)
12. Gligor, V.D.: A Guide to Understanding Covert Channel Analysis of Trusted Systems. National Computer Security Center (US) (1994)
13. Gollmann, D.: Computer Security. Wiley, Chichester (2006)
14. Jagadeesan, R., Jeffrey, A., Riely, J.: A Calculus of Untyped Aspect-Oriented Programs. In: Cardelli, L. (ed.) ECOOP 2003. LNCS, vol. 2743, pp. 54–73. Springer, Heidelberg (2003)
15. Kiczales, G., Hilsdale, E., Hugunin, J., Kersten, M., Palm, J., Griswold, W.G.: An Overview of AspectJ. In: Knudsen, J.L. (ed.) ECOOP 2001. LNCS, vol. 2072, pp. 327–353. Springer, Heidelberg (2001)
16. Kiczales, G., Lamping, J., Menhdhekar, A., Maeda, C., Lopes, C., Loingtier, J.-M., Irwin, J.: Aspect-oriented programming. In: Aksit, M., Matsuoka, S. (eds.) ECOOP 1997. LNCS, vol. 1241, pp. 220–242. Springer, Heidelberg (1997)
17. Masuhara, H., Kawauchi, K.: Dataflow Pointcut in Aspect-Oriented Programming. In: Ohori, A. (ed.) APLAS 2003. LNCS, vol. 2895, pp. 105–121. Springer, Heidelberg (2003)
18. De Nicola, R., Ferrari, G., Pugliese, R.: Klaim: a kernel language for agents interaction and mobility. Transactions on Software Engineering 24(5), 315–330 (1998)

19. De Nicola, R., Ferrari, G., Pugliese, R.: Programming access control: The KLAIM experience. In: Palamidessi, C. (ed.) CONCUR 2000. LNCS, vol. 1877, pp. 48–65. Springer, Heidelberg (2000)
20. Schneider, F.B.: Enforceable security policies. ACM Trans. Inf. Syst. Secur. 3(1), 30–50 (2000)
21. Verhanneman, T., Piessens, F., De Win, B., Joosen, W.: Uniform Application-level Access Control Enforcement of Organizationwide Policies. In: Proc. 21st Annual Computer Security Applications Conference, pp. 431–440 (2005)
22. Walker, D., Zdancewic, S., Ligatti, J.: A theory of aspects. ACM SIGPLAN Notices 38(9), 127–139 (2003)
23. Wand, M., Kiczales, G., Dutchyn, C.: A semantics for advice and dynamic join points in aspect-oriented programming. ACM Trans. Program. Lang. Syst. 26(5), 890–910 (2004)
24. De Win, B., Joosen, W., Piessens, F.: Developing secure applications through aspect-oriented programming. Aspect-Oriented Software Development, 633–650 (2004)

# Modeling and Analysis of Reo
# Connectors Using Alloy

Ramtin Khosravi[1], Marjan Sirjani[1,2], Nesa Asoudeh[1],
Shaghayegh Sahebi[1], and Hamed Iravanchi[1]

[1] School of Electrical and Computer Engineering,
University of Tehran, Kargar Ave., Tehran, Iran
[2] School of Computer Science,
Institute for Studies in Theoretical Physics and Mathematics,
P.O. Box: 19395-5746, Tehran, Iran
rkhosravi@ece.ut.ac.ir, msirjani@ut.ac.ir,
{n.asoudeh,s.sahebi,h.iravanchi}@ece.ut.ac.ir

**Abstract.** Reo is an exogenous coordination language based on a calculus of channel composition. Different formal models have been developed for this language. In this paper, we present a new approach to modeling and analysis of Reo connectors using Alloy which is a lightweight modeling language based on first-order relational logic. We provide a reusable library of Reo channels in Alloy that can be used to create a model of a Reo connector in Alloy. The model is simple and reflects the original structure of the connector. Furthermore, the model of a connector can be reused as a component for constructing more complex connectors. Using the Alloy Analyzer tool, properties expressed as predicates can be verified by automatically analyzing the execution traces of the Reo connector. We handle the context-sensitive behavior of channels as well as optional constraints on the interactions with environment. Our compositional model can be used as an alternative to other existing approaches, and is supported by a well known tool with a rich set of features such as counterexample generation.

# 1   Introduction

The concept of "coordination" has resulted to a new class of models, formalisms and mechanisms for describing concurrent and distributed computations. A coordination language used to develop a coordination model is able to integrate a set of possibly heterogeneous components together [15]. Reo is a coordination language based on components and connectors [2]. It offers a way for compositional construction of systems out of black-box components. To achieve this, Reo provides a compositional mechanism to construct various connectors (commonly known as Reo *circuits*). This is based on the notion of *channel* as primitive connectors from which more complex ones are constructed. We will review basic concepts of Reo in Sect. 3.1.

D. Lea and G. Zavattaro (Eds.): COORDINATION 2008, LNCS 5052, pp. 169–183, 2008.

As the main use of coordination languages is in modeling reactive and concurrent systems, the problem of verification of models becomes an important issue, because in these systems correctness is much harder to verify manually, or with testing. Our goal is to provide a method to model and analyze Reo connectors using Alloy, which is a lightweight modeling language, based on first-order relational logic [8]. It is supported by an efficient tool called Alloy Analyzer [1] that will serve as the analysis tool in our method. We briefly review the Alloy modeling language in Sect. 3.2.

The basic idea of our method is to model the behavior of a Reo connector by the set of all execution traces of the connector. Each trace is a bounded sequence of states. In our method, the structure of a Reo connector is constructed compositionally, from smaller connectors (which are ultimately basic channels). Each channel imposes a constraint on the states of the trace. Other constraints are the facts that specify the behavior of the environment of the circuit. We will explain our modeling method in more detail in Sect. 4. For the sake of simplicity, our method ignores the values of data passed along Reo channels, and just considers data flow, though it can be extended to handle data values too.

The modular structure of Alloy allows us to separate the definitions of primitive Reo constructs from the description of a circuit. We have provided the definitions of a set of Reo connectors in a module named Relloy [16] that can be used as a reusable library when modeling various circuits. In Sect. 5.1, we will see how to describe a Reo circuit using our method. To analyze a Reo circuit, the modeler provides the properties to be checked in terms of first-order predicate logic formulas, and the Alloy Analyzer automatically checks the properties using a SAT solver. This way of analysis is not "model checking" and is based on checking all execution traces of at most a specified number of states. The traces are generated automatically, satisfying the constraints imposed by the channels and other facts in the model. Analyzing Reo circuits in our model will be more elaborated in Sect. 5.2, with a case study on a round-robin dispatcher [17]. We also address the context-sensitive behavior of connectors, by imposing maximal progress property on the traces (Sect. 6).

The benefits of our method can be summarized in the following items:

**Coverage of Semantics:** As mentioned above, we handle all basic concepts of Reo, as well as the aspects which are normally harder to address, such as context-sensitive behavior and modeling environment. All of these are based on the sound basis of relational logic.

**Compositionality:** The model of Reo connectors are constructed compositionally from smaller ones easily. Issues such as renaming are handled automatically by the block structures of Alloy at language level.

**Clarity:** The description of a Reo connector in our model clearly represents the original structure of the circuit. Since it does not involve complex mathematical notations, it is more familiar to software engineers. As the syntax of the description is textual, it is much easier to work with when modeling large models.

**Tool Support:** Alloy is a well-known language, with an efficient tool support. It offers useful features such as counterexample generation and visualization which can help the modeler to model and debug the connector in small iterations.

As some of the benefits above are inherited from Alloy, our method has got some of its limitations too. The main limitation is that our traces are bounded, so if Alloy cannot find a counterexample, it does not mean there is none. The assumption here is that most flaws can be discovered when considering all possible traces within small bounds exhaustively. Another problem is scalability, as the analysis takes some time when the model becomes large. However, in an ongoing work, we are trying to improve the efficiency by techniques that will be mentioned later. In Sect. 2, we briefly review existing approaches to model Reo semantics.

## 2  Related Work

Different formal semantics have been developed for Reo, including Timed Data Streams (TDS) [3], Constraint Automata (CA) [4], Graph Coloring [5], and Structural Operational Semantics (SOS) [14]. Timed Data Streams model the possible flows of data on connector ports, assigning a time to each interaction (input or output of a data element). The declarative and relational nature of this semantics is one of its strengths; but there is no support for simulation or model checking. Constraint automata is a compositional and operational semantics for Reo. Constraint automata shall be extended with priorities to capture the context sensitive behavior of connectors. Also, the interaction with environment is not modeled and I/O requests are considered always available. A symbolic model checker based on CA semantics is developed [11] and CTL-like properties can be checked.

The idea of graph coloring semantics is marking data flow or its absence by colors. A coloring table for a Reo connector actually describes the possible behavior in a particular configuration of the connector, which includes the states of channels, plus the presence or absence of I/O requests. A coloring corresponds to a possible next step based on that configuration. Here, input and output operations are considered as primitives as well as channels and nodes. A join operation is then defined on coloring tables. To capture the context sensitive behavior of connectors a third color shall be added to the semantics. The goal of graph coloring is more to build a basis for distributed implementation of Reo circuits despite of generating a semantics basis for analysis.

Based on the Structural Operational Semantics (SOS) of Reo a model checker using Maude system [13] is developed.

Our approach is similar to CA in its simple way of modeling the Reo connectors and similar to graph coloring in capturing the behavior by recognizing the blocking nodes and synchronous clusters, to obtain the transitions. Furthermore, our method simply models the behavior of Reo connectors including context sensitive behavior and I/O requests of environment without additional complexity. Also, it provides the support of the already-exist automated analyzer of Alloy.

## 3   Preliminaries

In this section, we briefly review basic concepts of Reo coordination language and Alloy modeling language. Parts of our discussion on Reo are taken from [4] and [2] and the overview of Alloy is mainly based on [9].

### 3.1   Reo

Reo is a coordination language based on components and connectors. As coordination is the main point of concern, the emphasis of Reo is on connectors. A connector is presented as a graph of nodes and edges where edges represent channels and nodes are channel ends. Primitive connectors in Reo are called channels which provide the basic communication mechanisms. A channel always has two ends. There are two types of channel ends: source and sink. The source end is the point where data enters into the channel. The sink end is the point where data leaves the channel. Note that both channel ends may be of the same type (both source or both sink). Channel ends are connected to each other via nodes. If all channel ends adjacent to a node are source ends (resp. sink ends), we call the node a source node (resp. sink node). If there are channel ends of both types, then the node is called a mixed node.

Reo provides operations that enable components to perform I/O on nodes. A component can write data items to a source node that it is connected to. The write operation succeeds only if all (source) channel ends coincident on the node accept the data item, in which case the data item is transparently written to every source end coincident on the node. A component can obtain data items from a sink node that it is connected to through destructive take input operations. A take operation succeeds only if at least one of the (sink) channel ends coincident on the node offers a suitable data item; if there are more, one is selected nondeterministically. A mixed node combines the behavior of a sink node and a source node.

There are several mixed node types in Reo as indicated in Fig. 1. The data items simply flow through a *flow through* node. A *merge node* delivers a value out of one of the incoming channels nondeterministically. A write on a *replication node* succeeds only if all outgoing channels are capable of consuming the written data. We say a node *can be fired*, if it can successfully pass the data according to the mentioned rules.

There are different channel types in Reo. Each channel passes data in a predefined direction. Structurally, each unidirectional channel has a source end that receives data and a sink end that dispenses it. Bidirectional channels have either two source ends, or two sink ends. There are no 'fixed' set of channel types in Reo, and new ones can be defined freely with their own policy for synchronization, buffering, computations, etc.

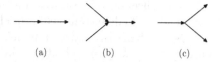

**Fig. 1.** Three types of mixed nodes: (a) flow through, (b) nondeterministic merge, and (c) replication

**Fig. 2.** Channel notations: (a) Sync (b) SyncDrain (c) LossySync (d) FIFO1

Here, we define the channel types that have been used throughout the examples in this paper (Fig. 2). The definition for more channel types can be found in [2]. Note that our reusable library of channels contain more channel types that are presented in this paper and includes most widely used channels types.

The simplest channel is synchronous (Sync) channel that has a source and a sink end, and no buffer. It accepts a data item through its source end if and only if it can simultaneously dispense it through its sink. A synchronous drain (SyncDrain) accepts data items from its both ends simultaneously and the data values will be lost. A lossy synchronous (LossySync) channel is similar to a Sync channel, except that it always accepts all data items through its source end. If it is possible for it to simultaneously dispense the data item through its sink the channel transfers the data item; otherwise the data item is lost. A FIFO1 channel represents an asynchronous channel with a buffer of capacity one. A write operation on the source end succeeds only if the buffer is empty, and a take operation on the sink end succeeds only if the buffer contains data. This buffer may be initially empty or contain some data item.

### 3.2    Alloy

Alloy is a lightweight modeling language based on the first order relational logic [10]. In an Alloy model, there are a number of *signatures* each defining a set of atoms. The definition of a signature may contain a number of *fields* which define *relations* between atoms of signatures. Signatures also serve as types, and subtyping is possible through signature extension. There are also ways to define constraints in the model, using constraint paragraphs. There are four kinds of constraint paragraphs:

*Fact*: A constraint that always holds

*Predicate*: Named and parameterized formulas that can be used elsewhere

*Function*: Named and parameterized expressions that can be used elsewhere

*Assertion*: A constraint that is intended to follow from the facts of a model

Note that facts can be defined in two ways: either following a signature declaration, or elsewhere in the model. In the first case, they are implicitly quantified over all atoms of the signature.

A model in Alloy means a collection of *instances*. Instances are binding of values to variables. Alloy Analyzer finds instances of a model automatically by assigning values to variables satisfying the constraints defined. Model analysis involves constraint solving, and the analyzer embodies a SAT solver. It provides visualization for making sense of solutions and counterexamples it finds [9].

Instructions to Alloy Analyzer to perform its analysis are called *commands*. A *run* command causes the analyzer to search for an instance that witnesses the consistency of a function or a predicate. A *check* command causes it to search for a counterexample to show that an assertion does not hold. Searching for instances is done within finite bounds, specified by the user as *scope*. So, when the search fails, it does not mean that there is no instance satisfying the model (i.e., the model is inconsistent). Alloy analysis is based on *small scope hypothesis*, which says that if we consider all small instances, most flaws will be revealed [10].

In this paper, when writing Alloy definitions and formulas, we sometimes use common mathematical symbols instead of Alloy keywords (e.g. $\forall$ or $\in$ symbols instead of 'all' or 'in' keywords).

## 4  Modeling Basic Reo Constructs in Alloy

In this section, we show how primitive constructs in Reo, nodes, channels and more complex connectors, are modeled in Alloy. We first see how Reo connectors can be constructed from simpler ones structurally, and then study the behavioral modeling of connectors. Note that we defer handling context-sensitive behavior to Sect. 6.

### 4.1  Modeling Connector Structure

The basic goal of Reo is to formalize the concept of connectors which serve as the pathways through which components communicate. A connector in turn, is composed of simpler ones, which are ultimately composed of channels. A component is connected to a connector through a number of externally visible nodes which we call *ports*. The two basic concepts in the model are *nodes* and *connectors* that are represented as two Alloy signatures as follows:

```
sig Node {}
abstract sig Connector {
    conns : set Connector,
    ports : set Node
}
```

According to the above definitions, a node is an atomic concept, but connectors may be constructed recursively from other connectors. The signature *Connector* is marked abstract as concrete connectors will be defined as its subsignatures. For a connector $c$, $c.conns$ represents the set of connectors that are parts of $c$. This model of constructing connectors resembles the *Composite* design pattern [7]. The set $c.ports$ is the set of nodes of $c$ that are accessible from outside (i.e., the nodes of $c$ that are not hidden). These nodes can be attached to the ports of other connectors.

Note that in Alloy, a field of a signature is considered as a relation from that signature to the type of the field. For example, *conns* is a relation that relates each instance of *Connector* to a set of *Connectors* (its parts). So, the notations *c.conns* and *conns[c]* are equivalent.

The simplest form of a connector is a channel, defined by the following signature:

> **abstract sig** *Channel* **extends** *Connector* {
> $e_1, e_2$ : **one** *Node*
> }
> { $(ports = e_1 + e_2) \wedge (conns = \emptyset)$ }

Each *Channel* has two fields $e_1$ and $e_2$, each of them is a reference to a single *Node*. The signature is defined abstract, as it will be refined later into specific channels, but common to all channel are two facts: they have two ports (as the channel ends), and they are atomic connectors, so the *conns* field is the empty set. The expression $e_1 + e_2$ denotes the set $\{e_1, e_2\}$. Each specific channel type has a separate signature extending *Channel*. Normally, the channel types do not add any 'structural' feature to the definition of abstract *Channel*. We will consider the behavior of channels later.

> **sig** *Sync* **extends** *Channel* {}
> **sig** *Drain* **extends** *Channel* {}
> **sig** *Lossy* **extends** *Channel* {}
> **sig** *Fifo* **extends** *Channel* {}

Another simple connector defined is a *Merger* which is used to model merge nodes with two inputs in Reo. A merger has references to two nodes $i_1$ and $i_2$ as its inputs and a third node $o$ as its output node:

> **abstract sig** *Merger* **extends** *Connector* {
> **disj** $i_1, i_2, o$ : **one** *Node*
> }
> { $(ports = i_1 + i_2 + o) \wedge (conns = \emptyset)$ }

To illustrate how a composite connector is constructed, we define a simple connector composed of a FIFO1 channel attached to the end of a synchronous channel (Fig. 3).

> **sig** *SyncFifo* **extends** *Connector* {
> $a, b, d$ : **one** *Node*,
> $s$ : **one** *Sync*, $f$ : **one** *Fifo*
> } {
> $a = s.e_1$
> $d = f.e_2$
> $b = s.e_2 \wedge b = f.e_1$
> $(conns = s + f) \wedge (ports = a + d)$
> }

Note that there are three nodes in an instance of *SyncFifo*, but only two of them (*a* and *d*) comprise the ports of the connector, and the other one (*b*) is 'hidden'. The *SyncFifo* connector defined above can be used in constructing more complex connectors in turn. We will see an example in 5.1.

The above definitions do not constrain the instances to form valid Reo circuits. A few more facts are required to ensure this. The first one states that a node that is hidden in a connector cannot be referenced in the enclosing connectors:

**fact** { $\forall\, c : Connector \mid \nexists\, n : hiddens[c] \mid n \in nodes[^\wedge conns.c]$ }

The expression *hiddens*[*c*] denotes the set of all hidden nodes of *c* and *nodes*[$^\wedge conns.c$] is the set of all nodes in all connectors that are directly or indirectly contain *c* ($^\wedge conns$ is the transitive closure of *conns* relation). We have omitted the definition of the two functions *hiddens* and *nodes* for brevity.

The other facts constrain the composition of the connectors to form a rooted tree. First, we define a singleton signature *Circuit* having a reference to one root connector:

**one sig** *Circuit* {    *root* : **one** *Connector*    }

The first fact below states that the *conns* relation is acyclic, and the two others define *Circuit.root* as the root of the tree:

**fact** {
    $\nexists\, c : Connector \mid c \in c.^\wedge conns$
    $\forall\, c : Connector - Circuit.root \mid c \in Circuit.root.^\wedge conns$
    $\nexists\, c : Connector \mid Circuit.root \in c.conns$
}

## 4.2    Modeling Connector Behavior

To model the behavior of a Reo connector, we use traces of computation which is a common technique in Alloy. For a Reo circuit, we define a *trace* of computation as a sequence of *states*. In each state, we record the state of FIFO1 buffers as well as the set of nodes that are to be fired to go to the next state:

**sig** *State* {
    *fire* : **set** *Node*,
    *full* : **set** *Fifo*
}

The set *fire* is the set of nodes that are to be fired at that state and *full* denotes the set of FIFO1 channels with full buffer.

The notion of state in our method is close to the notion of state in constraint automata. For example, in Fig. 3(a) and 3(b), a simple circuit and its corresponding constraint automaton are shown. Figure 3(c) shows the first five states of an execution trace as used in our method. Assuming the environment is always ready to perform write and take operations on nodes *a* and *d* respectively, in states $T_1, T_3, \ldots$, we have *fire* = $\{a, b\}$, *full* = $\{\}$ and in states $T_2, T_4, \ldots$, we have *fire* = $\{d\}$, *full* = $\{f\}$.

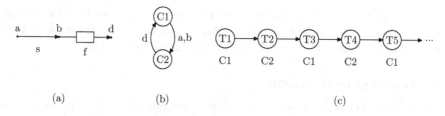

(a)                              (b)                                          (c)

**Fig. 3.** (a) A simple Reo circuit (b) The corresponding constraint automaton with two states $C_1$ (empty buffer) and $C_2$ (full buffer) (c) An execution trace of the circuit – the states $T_{2k+1}$ are corresponding to $C_1$ and the states $T_{2k}$ are corresponding to $C_2$

To model a trace in Alloy, we have reused a standard module *util/ordering* which creates a single linear ordering over the atoms of the signature provided as its input (in our case, *State*). We use the *first* and *last* symbols defined in *util/ordering* to refer to the first and last states of a trace respectively. Note that since Alloy searches for model instances within a bounded scope, the traces are always bounded.

To model the behavior of each channel, we provide a fact that puts a constraint on the behavior of the whole circuit. For example, the behavior of the three simple (stateless) channels is modeled by the following three facts:

> **fact** {
> $\quad \forall\, s : State, c : Sync \mid c.e_1 \in s.fire \Leftrightarrow c.e_2 \in s.fire$
> $\quad \forall\, s : State, c : Drain \mid c.e_1 \in s.fire \Leftrightarrow c.e_2 \in s.fire$
> $\quad \forall\, s : State, c : Lossy \mid c.e_2 \in s.fire \Rightarrow c.e_1 \in s.fire$
> }

Note that since we have ignored the actual data values, the facts for Sync and SyncDrain is the same.

The behavior of a merger connector is defined by the following fact:

> **fact** {
> $\quad \forall\, s : State, m : Merger \mid \{$
> $\qquad \neg\, (m.i_1 \in s.fire \wedge m.i_2 \in s.fire)$
> $\qquad m.o \in s.fire \Leftrightarrow (m.i_1 \in s.fire \vee m.i_2 \in s.fire)$
> $\quad \}$
> }

The behavior of a FIFO1 channel relates two subsequent states of a trace together. In the following fact, *next*[*s*] denotes the next state in the trace, and *last* denotes the last state of the trace:

> **fact** {
> $\quad \forall\, s : State - last, c : Fifo \mid \{$
> $\qquad c.e_2 \in s.fired \Rightarrow (c \in s.full \wedge c \notin next[s].full)$
> $\qquad c.e_1 \in s.fired \Rightarrow (c \notin s.full \wedge c \in next[s].full)$
> $\qquad (c.e_1 \notin s.fired \wedge c.e_2 \notin s.fired) \Rightarrow (c \in s.full \Leftrightarrow c \in next[s].full)$
> $\quad \}$
> }

A primary task of Alloy Analyzer is to assign a value to the *fire* set for each state such that the facts corresponding to the channels are satisfied. This automatically handles nondeterminism in selecting merge inputs.

### 4.3  Modeling Environment

To analyze the behavior of the circuit, we must be able to specify the behavior of the environment (i.e, the components attached to the ports of the root connector). To do this, we add a field *env_ready* to *State* to specify if the environment is ready to perform read/take operations on the ports of the root connector.

```
sig State {
    . . .
    env_ready : set Node
} {
    env_ready ⊆ Circuit.root.ports
    fire ∩ ports ⊆ env_ready
}
```

The first fact constrains the set *env_ready* to contain only ports of the top-most connector, and the second one states that only ready ports can be fired.

The modeler can now provide facts to specify how the environment behaves. Alloy Analyzer automatically assigns values to the set *env_ready* satisfying the given facts when generating all possible traces.

## 5    Modeling and Analyzing Reo Circuits

In this section, we show the modeler's view of our method, that is how a circuit in Reo can be described and analyzed using the primitives explained in Sect. 4. The modular structure of Alloy allows us to define the basic Reo primitives in a separate module (we call it Relloy), and let the modules containing circuit descriptions import those definitions. This way, the circuit module only contains the description of the circuit along with the properties to be analyzed.

### 5.1    Describing a Reo Circuit

A Reo circuit is modeled as a signature extending *Connector*, the same way as defined *SyncFifo* in Sect. 4.1 In this section, we study how a complex circuit can be composed of simpler connectors. Consider the circuit in Fig. 4(a) which dispatches data from node $a$ to nodes $i$, $j$, and $k$ in a round-robin fashion. Instead of directly modeling the circuit, we use three instances of a simpler part connected together (Fig. 4(b)).

The complete description of the above connectors in our method is shown in Fig. 5. The signature *RRPart* models the connector in Fig. 4(b) and *RR* models the whole dispatcher.

The fact paragraph at the end contains two facts. The first fact states that the circuit root to be analyzed is a connector of type *RR*. The second fact determines the set of full FIFO1 channels in the initial state.

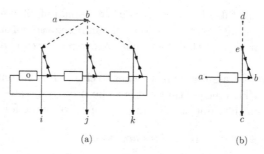

(a)                                   (b)

**Fig. 4.** (a) A round-robin 3-dispatcher circuit (b) A connector used to construct round-robin dispatcher

```
module RoundRobin                          s : one Sync
open Relloy                              } {
                                           c1.a = c3.b
sig RRPart extends Connector {             c2.a = c1.b
  disj a, b, c, d, e : one Node,           c3.a = c2.b
  f : one Fifo,                            c1.c = i
  r : one Drain,                           c2.c = j
  l : one Lossy,                           c3.c = k
  s : one Sync                             c1.d = b
} {                                        c2.d = b
  conns = f + r + s                        c3.d = b
  ports = a + b + c + d                    sync[a, s, b]
  fifo[a, f, b]                            conns = c1 + c2 + c3 + s
  drain[b, r, e]                           ports = a + i + j + k
  lossy[d, l, e]                         }
  sync[e, s, c]
}                                        fact {
sig RR extends Connector {                 Circuit.root in RR
  disj a, b, i, j, k : one Node,           first.full = Circuit.root.c1.f
  disj c1, c2, c3 : one RRPart,          }
```

**Fig. 5.** The description of a round-robin three-dispatcher connector in Alloy

## 5.2   Analyzing Circuits

To check the correctness of a circuit, we can express the desired properties in terms of assertions to be checked by the Alloy Analyzer. To provide an assertion, we can write formulas on the states of nodes and buffers in different states of the execution trace. For example, to express that in every state, only one of the buffers is full, we can write the following assertion (the # operator returns the size of its operand):

```
assert one_full { all s : State | #s.full = 1 }
```

The following command makes Alloy Analyzer search for a counterexample in all possible traces with maximum 10 states:

```
check one_full for 10 State
```

In this case, the response of Alloy Analyzer would be 'No counterexample found. Assertion may be valid.' indicating the property holds for all traces of length at most 10. But if we mistakenly had c3.a = c1.b instead of c3.a = c2.b in the description of $RR$, we would get the response 'Counterexample found. Assertion is invalid.'. By inspecting the given counterexample, we can find out the source of the flaw easily.

As another example, assume that we want to check that the data items written to $a$ are never lost. This means that if $a$ is to be fired in a state, then one of $i$, $j$, or $k$ must be fired in the same state. This is expressed by the following assertion:

$$\forall s : State \mid a \in s.fire \Rightarrow \{i, j, k\} \cap s.fire \neq \emptyset$$

Again, we get a counterexample exposing a case in which the components attached to the ports $i$, $j$, and $k$ are slower than the component writing at $a$. Hence, there is a state in which node $a$ is ready while none of the three other ports are ready. In that case, the data written to $a$ will be lost by all three LossySync channels. To fix this, we must replace the three LossySync channels with a three-way exclusive router[4], connecting $b$ to node $e$ of $RRPart$ connectors. We have made this change, by defining a separate connector for exclusive router (and removing the LossySync channel from $RRPart$) and has successfully checked the above property. Due to lack of space, we do not present the Alloy descriptions here.

## 6   Handling Context-Sensitive Behavior

In this section, we show how to extend our model to handle the behavior exposed by channels like LossySync which is called context-sensitive behavior. An example is shown in figure 6.

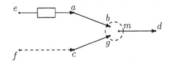

**Fig. 6.** An example of a Reo circuit demonstrating context-sensitive behavior

Consider the situation in which the environment is ready to write to both nodes $e$ and $f$ and is ready to take from $b$. Node $e$ accepts the data item and writes it into the buffer. Considering the LossySync $f$ --→ $c$ in isolation, it may pass the data item to $c$ or lose it. But, the *maximal progress* property of Reo requires it to always pass the data, because nodes $a$ and $b$ cannot be fired, and the merger input $g$ can be fired. Note that the maximal progress is a global property, and cannot be enforced by adding some constraints to the behavioral description of the channel types locally.

To handle these cases, we find which nodes *cannot* be fired in a state, and force every other node to be fired in that state. In each state, some nodes may be locally detected as *blocked*, i.e., they cannot be fired. This may happen in four cases: the first endpoint of a full FIFO1, the second endpoint of an empty FIFO1, the input of a merge that is not selected, and an external port that is not ready.

**pred** *blocked* [$s$ : *State*, $n$ : *Node*] {
    ($\exists$ $c$ : *Fifo* | ($c \in s.full \land n = c.e_1$) $\lor$ ($c \notin s.full \land n = c.e_2$)) $\lor$
    ($\exists$ $m$ : *Merger* | ($n = m.i_1 \lor n = m.i_2$) $\land n \notin s.fire$)
    $n \in$ *Circuit.root.ports* $-$ *s.env_ready*
}

As an example, in Fig. 6, and under the assumption that the environment is ready to write into $e$ and $f$ and read from $b$, $a$ is the only blocked node. When a node is blocked, it may block other nodes from being fired, for example, through channels with synchronous behavior. For each *State* we define a relation *can_block* : *Node* $\rightarrow$ *Node*, such that $(m, n) \in$ *can_block* means that in that state, if $m$ is blocked, then $n$ is blocked too. This may be caused by the existence of a channel with synchronous nature between $m$ and $n$, like Sync, SyncDrain, or LossySync. Another case happens between the output node of merger and its selected input. It is important to not include this relation for the non-selected input, as it may incorrectly block some other nodes in the circuit. This fact is the reason for defining *can_block* as a field of *State*, so that it is computed for each state separately.

**sig** *State* {
    *fire* : **set** *Node*,
    *full* : **set** *Fifo*,
    *can_block* : *Node* $\rightarrow$ *Node*
} {
    $\forall$ $m, n$ : *Node* | $m \rightarrow n \in$ *can_block* $\Leftrightarrow$ {
        ($\exists$ $c$ : *Sync* | ($c.e_1 = m \land c.e_2 = n$) $\lor$ ($c.e_1 = n \land c.e_2 = m$)) $\lor$
        ($\exists$ $c$ : *Drain* | ($c.e_1 = m \land c.e_2 = n$) $\lor$ ($c.e_1 = n \land c.e_2 = m$)) $\lor$
        ($\exists$ $c$ : *Lossy* | ($c.e_1 = m \land c.e_2 = n$)) $\lor$
        ($\exists$ $c$ : *Merger* | ($m \in$ *fire* $\land$ *input*[$c, m$] $\land$ *output*[$c, n$]) $\lor$
           ($n \in$ *fire* $\land$ *input*[$c, n$] $\land$ *output*[$c, m$]))
    }
}

In the above definition, *input* and *output* are two helper predicate to test if node is an input, or is the output of a merger respectively. In our example, the relation *can_block* contains the tuples $\{(a, b), (b, a), (f, c), (c, g), (g, c), (m, g), (g, m), (m, b), (b, m)\}$. Note that the relation is symmetric except for the tuple $(f, c)$ which is introduced by the LossySync $f$ --$\rightarrow$ $c$.

Now we can define when a node is enabled to be fired: if it is not blocked itself, and cannot be blocked by any other blocked node in the circuit. This can be easily checked by getting a transitive closure of *can_block*:

**pred** *enabled* [$s$ : *State*, $n$ : *Node*] {
    $\neg$ *blocked*[$s, n$]
    $\nexists$ $m$ : *Node* | *blocked*[$s, m$] $\land m \rightarrow n \in$ $\hat{}$(*s.can_block*)
}

In the above example, the set of enabled nodes will be $\{e, f, c, g, m, d\}$.

Finally, the following fact imposes the maximal progress constraint on the traces generated:

**fact** $\{ \ \forall \ s : State - last \mid s.fire = \{n : Node \mid enabled[s, n]\} \ \}$

We have implemented the above definitions and facts into the Relloy module, and have successfully analyzed circuits with context-sensitive behavior (like the one in the given example).

## 7   Conclusion and Future Work

We presented a method to model Reo circuits based on relational logic in Alloy. The resulting model preserves the original structure of the Reo circuit, and no complex translation effort is needed. This also makes the circuit description reasonably readable. Also, we have provided a library of different Reo channels as an Alloy module that can be reused when describing circuits. Our method handles basic channel types, compositional construction of more complex connectors, constraints on the environment, and circuits exposing context-sensitive behavior.

We can use Alloy Analyzer to verify properties on circuits. Properties are defined in terms of first-order predicates on the state of nodes and buffers in the execution traces of a circuit. As we can address states in our properties, along with 'next' and 'previous' operators and quantifiers, we can verify temporal properties on the circuit. Because Alloy Analyzer checks the properties on all possible traces, the properties are closely related to Linear Temporal Logic (LTL)[12] formulas [10]. More work is needed to precisely evaluate how expressive is this way to model temporal properties.

One can view our method as an implementation of Reo language in Alloy. But another useful viewpoint is to abstract away Alloy syntax, and view our work as a starting point to provide a formal semantics for Reo based on relational logic. More work is needed to formally define the semantics and compare it to the existing ones.

Our method currently ignores the actual values of data passed through the channels. Although many 'coordination' properties of a circuit can be expressed without explicitly modeling data values, adding this capability improves the expressiveness of the model in general.

Another issue to be addressed is scalability. Using Alloy Analyzer, it takes some time to analyze large connectors. An important observation here is that the description of the connector structure yields in only one instance. On the behavior side, once nondeterministic merge inputs are selected and the ready ports are defined, one can easily compute the *can_block* relation, its transitive closure, and finally the set of enabled nodes easily. In all these cases, we do not require solving SAT models. So, we can do parts of the computation in more efficient languages like Java (like construction of the connector instance from the description). The integration with Alloy can be done using Alloy API for Java. This may lead to a big improvement in the performance of analysis.

Currently, various tools on Reo have been implemented under the Eclipse platform [6]. Integrating our method with the tool set is another direction in which this work can be extended. This includes bi-directional transformation of graphical representation of a circuit to our textual format as both forms are necessary when working with models of different sizes.

## Acknowledgment

We would like to thank Farhad Arbab for his helpful comments on our case study, leading to more detailed modeling of the environment.

## References

1. Alloy Analyzer, http://alloy.mit.edu
2. Arbab, F.: Reo: A channel-based coordination model for component composition. Mathematical Structures in Computer Science 14(3), 1–38 (2004)
3. Arbab, F., Rutten, J.J.: A coinductive calculus of component connectors. In: Wirsing, M., Pattinson, D., Hennicker, R. (eds.) WADT 2003. LNCS, vol. 2755, pp. 34–55. Springer, Heidelberg (2003)
4. Baier, C., Sirjani, M., Arbab, F., Rutten, J.J.: Modeling component connectors in Reo by constraint automata. Science of Computer Programming 61, 75–113 (2006)
5. Clarke, D., Costa, D., Arbab, F.: Connector colouring I: synchronisation and context dependency. In: Proceedings of FOCLASA 2005. ENTCS, vol. 154, pp. 101–119. Elsevier, Amsterdam (2006)
6. Eclipse Coordination Tools homepage, http://homepages.cwi.nl/~koehler/ect
7. Gamma, E., Helm, R., Johnson, R., Vlissides, J.M.: Design Patterns: Elements of Reusable Object-Oriented Software. Addison-Wesley Professional, Reading (1994)
8. Jackson, D., Shlyakhter, I., Sridharan, M.: A micromodularity mechanism. In: Proceedings of Foundations of Software Engineering, pp. 62–73 (2001)
9. Jackson, D.: Alloy3.0 Reference manual (May 10, 2004), http://alloy.mit.edu
10. Jackson, D.: Software abstractions, logic, language, and analysis. MIT Press, Cambridge (2006)
11. Klüppelholz, S., Baier, C.: Symbolic model checking for channel-based component connectors. In: Proceedings of FOCLASA 2006. ENTCS, vol. 175, pp. 19–37. Springer, Heidelberg (2007)
12. Manna, Z., Pnueli, A.: The Temporal Logic of Reactive and Concurrent Systems: Specification. Springer, New York (1992)
13. Maude system, http://maude.cs.uiuc.edu
14. Mousavi, M.R., Sirjani, M., Arbab, F.: Formal semantics and analysis of component connectors in Reo. In: Proceedings of FOCLASA 2005. ENTCS, vol. 154, pp. 83–99. Elsevier, Amsterdam (2005)
15. Papadopoulos, G.A., Arbab, F.: Coordination models and languages. Report SEN-R9834, CWI (December 1998)
16. Relloy Library, http://ece.ut.ac.ir/msirjani/relloy.zip
17. Talcott, C., Sirjani, M., Ren, S.: Comparing Three Coordination Models: Reo, ARC, and RRD. In: Proceedings of FOCLASA 2007 (to appear, 2007)

# Alternating-Time Stream Logic for Multi-agent Systems

Sascha Klüppelholz and Christel Baier*

Technische Universität Dresden, Institut für Theoretische Informatik, Germany
{klueppel,baier}@tcs.inf.tu-dresden.de

**Abstract.** Constraint automata have been introduced to provide a compositional, operational semantics for the exogenous coordination language Reo, but they can also serve interface specification for components and an operational model for other coordination languages. Constraint automata have been used as basis for equivalence checking and model checking temporal logical properties. The main contribution of this paper is to reason about the local view and interaction and cooperation facilities of individual components or coalitions of components by means of a multi-player semantics for constraint automata. We introduce a temporal logic framework that combines classical features of alternating-time logic (*ATL*) for concurrent games with special operators to specify the observable data flow at the I/O-ports of components. Since constraint automata support any kind of synchronous and asynchronous peer-to-peer communication, the resulting game structure is non-standard and requires a series of nontrivial adaptations of the *ATL* model checking algorithm.

## 1   Introduction

In the last decade several models and specification languages for formal reasoning about the middle-ware layer of software have been developed. Such coordination models consist of ad-hoc libraries of functions providing higher-level inter-process communication support in parallel and especially distributed applications. They aim at a clean separation between individual software components and their interactions within their overall software organization. Our approach is inspired by the coordination language Reo [2], which provides the *glue-code* to coordinate components in an exogenous manner. In this paper we use constraint automata, which have been introduced as an operational semantics for Reo [6]. Constraint automata provide a specification formalism for both, the glue-code (e.g. given as a (Reo) network, or another (channel-based) coordination mechanism) and the behavioral interfaces of components, and can serve to formalize the overall behavior of the composite system. Constraint automata capture any kind of synchronous and asynchronous peer-to-peer communication including data-dependencies of I/O-operations. The syntax of constraint automata is similar to ordinary labeled transition systems and related models, such as timed port automata [15], I/O-automata [20], and interface automata [10]. The differences are mainly based on the fact that constraint automata support any kind of channel-based communication. An extensive discussion on the differences and similarities can be found in [6].

---

* The authors are supported by the DFG-NWO project SYANCO and the EU project CREDO.

D. Lea and G. Zavattaro (Eds.): COORDINATION 2008, LNCS 5052, pp. 184–198, 2008.

The purpose of this paper is to provide a multi-agent semantics for constraint automata and an alternating-time temporal logic to specify and verify the components considered as individual players of a multi-agent game. The connected components are the individual players and the network sets up the rules how those players interact with each other. The glue-code might be seen as a complex set of social laws [13,24] the players have to stick to. Constraint automata, interpreted as multi-player game structures, are a special type of concurrent games. The specific challenges of an alternating time approach are caused by the very special mixture of asynchrony and synchrony, mutual dependencies of I/O-operations and data-dependencies. In each state, several concurrent I/O-operations can be enabled, but only some of them might be available once a player refuses some synchronization or declares conditions on the data values accepted on his input ports or on his pending write operations. Furthermore, constraint automata can contain some internal nondeterminism, which yields a rather complex and nonstandard concurrent game structure. We are not aware of any other paper that treats alternating-time aspects for such concurrent games, where the enabledness and also the effect of a concurrent I/O-operation highly depends on the choices of the other players. Our approach allows us to check whether or not some coalition of agents has a strategy to achieve a common goal, no matter how the opponents behave, or which internal nondeterministic choices were made. In contrast to standard concurrent games, see e.g. [1,9], in our approach a coalition's strategy may select sets of I/O-operations or even refuse any I/O-operations.

For specifying and analyzing the local views and interaction possibilities of (coalitions of) agents, we introduce an alternating-time logic, called alternating-time stream logic (*ASL*). The logic *ASL* is a *CTL*-like branching-time logic which combines the features of standard *ATL* [1] with the operators of *BTSL* [18]. The logic *BTSL* has been introduced as a temporal logic for reasoning about (Reo) networks. Beside the standard modalities of *CTL* [8], *BTSL* supports the specification of the observable data flow at the I/O-ports of channels and components by means of regular expressions. The focus of *ATL* is to ask for the existence (and absence) of a coalition's strategy to achieve (avoid respectively) a specific temporal goal once the behavior for each of the components is specified.

For a simple example, we regard a ticket vending machine, which consists of a number of components (e.g. *I/O-device, clock, destination, price, payment, and printer*). The exact behavior of the components might be specified in terms of constraint automata. *ASL* can be used to formalize the property stating that the user (possibly together with some other component like the *clock*) can find a way to trick the other players and get a ticket without paying. A dual *ASL* property would state that no matter what strategy the opponents use, the coalition of opponents will not have a chance to avoid that sending the *cancel* signal always resets all components to their initial configuration.

As a first step we assume *perfect recall* on the systems history and *perfect information* on the global state of the system. This interpretation of constraint automata as a multi-player game is consistent with the standard semantics of *ATL* and adequate if the strategies are viewed as a central control that is aware of all activities in the system.

Our approach differs from other *ATL*-like approaches for concurrent multi-player games in various aspects. First, our nonstandard game structure (see explanations above) requires a revised notion of strategies for (coalitions of) components. Second, since components may refuse any further interaction from some moment on, the concept of finite runs and fairness plays a crucial role in the logic *ASL*. To reason about liveness properties we need an adaption of the standard notion of strong (process) fairness. Our notion of fairness is not a requirement for strategies, but formalizes the ability of certain strategies of a component C to enforce infinite data flow at the I/O-ports of C. Third, *ASL* provides special operators to reason about the observable data flow at the I/O-ports of the components and the nodes of the given network. To the best of our knowledge, such operators have not yet been investigated in the context of alternating-time game models.

***Organization.*** Section 2 gives a brief introduction to constraint automata. In section 3 we provide the multi-player semantics for constraint automata and introduce the notion of a strategy and its runs. Section 4 introduces the temporal logic *ASL* and presents corresponding model checking algorithms. Section 5 introduces fairness assumptions to *ASL* model checking, before section 6 concludes the paper. An extended technical report including the proofs and other technical material is available on the web [19].

## 2    Constraint Automata (CA)

This section summarizes the main concepts of CA. We slightly depart from the syntax of CA as introduced in [6] and deal with transitions $q \xrightarrow{c} p$, where c is a *concurrent I/O-operation*, i.e., c consists of a (possibly empty) node-set $N \subseteq \mathcal{N}$ together with data items for each $A \in N$ that are written or received at node A. In the moment where c is executed there is no data flow at the nodes $A \in \mathcal{N} \setminus N$.

***Concurrent I/O-operations and I/O-streams.*** Let $\mathcal{N}$ be a finite, nonempty set of nodes. We define a concurrent I/O-operation as a function $c : \mathcal{N} \to Data \cup \{\bot\}$, where the symbol $\bot$ means "undefined". We write Nodes(c) for the set of nodes $A \in \mathcal{N}$ such that $c(A) \in Data$, where *Data* is the data domain. For technical reasons, we also allow the *empty* concurrent I/O-operation $c_\emptyset$ with Nodes($c_\emptyset$) $= \emptyset$. It represents any internal step of some component or a non-observable step, where data flow appears at some hidden (invisible) nodes only. We refer to CIO as the set of all concurrent I/O-operations (including $c_\emptyset$). As we suppose $\mathcal{N}$ and *Data* to be finite, the set CIO of concurrent I/O-operations is finite as well. When reasoning about the data flow in a Reo network we will also need a special symbol $\sqrt{}$ that indicates that data flow has stopped. CIO$_{\sqrt{}}$ stands for CIO $\cup \{\sqrt{}\}$.

**Definition 1 (Constraint automata [6]).** A constraint automaton (CA) is a tuple

$$\mathcal{A} = \langle Q, \mathcal{N}, \longrightarrow, Q_0, AP, L \rangle,$$

where Q is a finite and nonempty set of states, $\mathcal{N}$ a finite set of nodes, $\longrightarrow$ is a subset of $Q \times CIO \times Q$ called the transition relation of $\mathcal{A}$, $Q_0 \subseteq Q$ a nonempty set of initial states, *AP* a finite set of atomic propositions, and $L : Q \to 2^{AP}$ a labeling function. We write $q \xrightarrow{c} p$ instead of $(q, c, p) \in \longrightarrow$. Furthermore, we define the set of all I/O-operations enabled in q as CIO(q) $\overset{\text{def}}{=} \{ c \in CIO : q \xrightarrow{c} p \text{ for some } p \in Q \}$.

Intuitively, the nodes correspond to the I/O-ports of the components. For the pictures of CAs we shall use symbolic representations of the transition relation by combining transitions with the same starting and target state. For this purpose, we use I/O-constraints, i.e., propositional formulas in positive normal form that stand for sets of concurrent I/O-operations. The I/O-constraints may impose conditions on the nodes that may or may not be involved and on the data items written on or read from them.

*I/O-constraints (IOC).*  The abstract syntax of I/O-constraints is given by the grammar:

$$ioc ::=\ tt \mid ff \mid A \mid \neg A \mid (d_{A_1},...,d_{A_k}) \in D \mid ioc_1 \wedge ioc_2 \mid ioc_1 \vee ioc_2$$

where $A \in \mathcal{N}, A_1,...,A_k$ are pairwise distinct nodes in $\mathcal{N}$ and $D \subseteq Data^k$. The meaning of an I/O-constraint $ioc$ is a subset $CIO(ioc)$ of $CIO$ defined in the obvious way. We often use simplified notations for the IOCs of the form $(d_{A_1},...,d_{A_k}) \in D$. E.g., the notation $d_A = d_B$ is a shorthand for $(d_A, d_B) \in \{(d_1, d_2) \in Data^2 :\ d_1 = d_2\}$, while $A \wedge (d_B \in P)$ stands for the set $\{c \in CIO :\ \{A, B\} \subseteq Nodes(c) \wedge c(B) \in P\}$.

*Example 1 (CA).*  The following two CAs realize possible implementations for the *destination* component with node set $\mathcal{N}_D = \{E, I, K, O, R\}$ and *price* component with node set $\mathcal{N}_P = \{F, J, M, T, V, W\}$ of the ticket vending machine. Both components are allowed to operate if and only if some data flow occurs on their synchronization ports E and F respectively. In the picture below we use a parameterized representation for states.

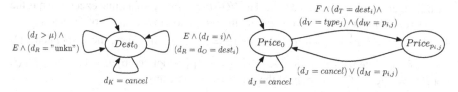

The *destination* component simultaneously reads some destination id (variable $i$) on its input port I and writes the destination string (variable $dest_i$) to the *I/O-device* using port R and its output port O. If the destination number given is too large, i.e., it exceeds a certain maximum $\mu$, the *I/O-device* gets a message that the selected destination is unknown. The *price* component receives two integer values at its input ports T and V for the destination (variable $dest_i$) and ticket type (variable $type_j$) and sends the corresponding price (variable $p_{i,j}$) first to the *I/O-device* using port W and in a second step to the *payment* component using port M. Both automata accept a *cancel* signal at any state and reset to their initial configuration.

*Terminal States.*  A state $q$ is called *terminal* if data flow may stop in state $q$. This is the case if all enabled concurrent I/O-operations require some activity of a component connected to a sink or source node. Formally, state $q$ is said to be terminal if for all concurrent I/O-operations $c$ that are enabled in state $q$, the node-set $Nodes(c)$ is non-empty. Stated differently, state $q$ is terminal iff $c_\emptyset \notin CIO(q)$. Note that data flow does not need to stop in terminal states. Instead data flow continues if there is an enabled concurrent I/O-operation $c$ where the involved components agree on interacting with each other by means of performing the write and read operation specified by $c$. For each non-terminal node q, an invisible transition is enabled, i.e., we have $c_\emptyset \in CIO(q)$. This I/O-operation does not require any interaction with the components that are connected to the sink and source nodes and will fire, unless another transition is taken.

***Executions, Completeness, Paths, I/O-streams.*** An *execution* in $\mathcal{A}$ is a finite or infinite sequence built by instances of consecutive transitions: $\eta = q_0 \xrightarrow{c_1} q_1 \xrightarrow{c_2} \dots$

$$\text{where } q_0, q_1, \dots \in Q, \ c_1, c_2, \dots \in CIO, \text{ and } q_i \xrightarrow{c_{i+1}} q_{i+1} \text{ for all } i \geq 0.$$

To reason about "maximal" behaviors of CAs we introduce the notions of complete executions and paths. An execution is said to be *complete* if it is either infinite or it is finite and ends in a terminal state. A *path* of $\mathcal{A}$ is either an infinite execution or arises from a finite complete execution by adding a special transition symbol $\sqrt{}$ to denote termination. More precisely, the finite paths have the form $\pi = q_0 \xrightarrow{c_1} \dots \xrightarrow{c_n} q_n \xrightarrow{\sqrt{}} q_n$ where $q_n$ is terminal. In the sequel, we shall use the symbol $\eta$ for executions and the symbol $\pi$ to range over paths. We write $Paths(q)$ to denote the set of all paths starting in $q$ and $Exec_{fin}(q)$ for the set of all finite executions starting in $q$. The length $|\pi|$ of a path $\pi$ is the total number of transitions taken in $\pi$ (including the pseudo-transition with label $\sqrt{}$). Thus, the length of an infinite path is $\infty$, while the length of a finite path $\pi$ as above is $n+1$. Let $\pi = q_0 \xrightarrow{c_1} q_1 \xrightarrow{c_2} \dots$ be a path and $0 \leq n < |\pi|$. Then $\pi \downarrow n$ denotes the prefix of path $\pi$ with length $n$, i.e., $\pi \downarrow n \stackrel{\text{def}}{=} q_0 \xrightarrow{c_1} \dots \xrightarrow{c_n} q_n$ is an execution, while for $n = |\pi|$ we have that $\pi \downarrow n = \pi$ is still a path. The *I/O-stream* $ios(\eta)$ of a finite execution $\eta$ is the word over $CIO$ that is obtained by taking the projection to the labels of the transitions. That is, if $\eta = q_0 \xrightarrow{c_1} \dots \xrightarrow{c_n} q_n$ then $ios(\eta) \stackrel{\text{def}}{=} c_1 \dots c_n$. Similarly, the associated I/O-stream for a finite path $\pi = q_0 \xrightarrow{c_1} \dots \xrightarrow{c_n} q_n \xrightarrow{\sqrt{}} q_n$ is defined by $ios(\pi) \stackrel{\text{def}}{=} c_1 \dots c_n \sqrt{}$. Let $IOS = CIO^* \cup CIO^* \sqrt{}$ denote the set of all I/O-streams.

## 3  Constraint Automata as Multi-player Games

In this section we introduce a game-theoretical interpretation for CA. The players are the individual components using (a)synchronous peer-to-peer communication. Each of the players has control over his I/O-behavior at its interface nodes. A player might refuse some or even any synchronization operation with other players. As in ordinary *ATL*, players might build arbitrary coalitions to achieve a certain common goal including a specific temporal behavior. A coalition of players induces a set of controllable nodes $N \subseteq \mathcal{N}$, the union of all controllable coalition nodes, for which the players might try to develop a common strategy to achieve their objective(s). Intuitively, an N-strategy takes the history of the system formalized by a finite execution as input, (i.e., we suppose here perfect recall) and declare the conditions under which the N-agents (members of the coalition) are willing to cooperate with each other and their opponents. For instance, an N-strategy might offer to write data value 0 at a source node $A \in N$, but refuse to write data value 1. The general notion of N-strategies also permits to couple such constraints for the offered I/O-operations at the N-nodes with conditions on the IOCs at the nodes in $\mathcal{N} \setminus N$. Furthermore, an N-strategy might suggest the N-agents to refuse any participation in concurrent I/O-operations. The special symbol *stop* will be used for this purpose.

**Definition 2 (Strategy).** Let $\mathcal{A}$ be a CA as before and let N be a node-set such that $N \subseteq \mathcal{N}$. An N-strategy is a function

$$\mathfrak{S} : Exec_{fin}(\mathcal{A}) \to 2^{CIO \cup \{stop\}},$$

assigning to any finite execution $\eta$ a set $\mathfrak{S}(\eta)$ consisting of I/O-operations $c \in CIO$ or the special symbol *stop* such that if $c \in CIO$ and $Nodes(c) \cap N = \emptyset$ then $c \in \mathfrak{S}(\eta)$.

The intuitive meaning of the condition required for an N-strategy asserts that the N-nodes are not in the position to refuse an I/O-operation $c$ where none of the N-nodes is involved. In particular, invisible I/O-operations (i.e., concurrent I/O-operations with the empty node-set) cannot be ruled out by an N-strategy. A possible refinement for the notion of a strategy would be to allow components to restrict their write operations only and not to cut down any input provided at their boundary nodes. Given an N-strategy $\mathfrak{S}$, the $\mathfrak{S}$-paths are those paths in $\mathcal{A}$, where each of the I/O-operations performed is accepted at any time by the N-nodes and their strategy $\mathfrak{S}$.

**Notation 3 ($\mathfrak{S}$-executions, $\mathfrak{S}$-completeness, $\mathfrak{S}$-paths).** Let $\mathfrak{S}$ be an N-strategy and $\eta = q_0 \xrightarrow{c_1} q_1 \xrightarrow{c_2} \ldots$ a finite or infinite execution in $\mathcal{A}$. Then, $\eta$ is called a $\mathfrak{S}$-*execution* if for any position $i \in \mathbb{N}$ with $i < |\eta|$ we have $c_{i+1} \in \mathfrak{S}(\eta \downarrow i)$. A finite $\mathfrak{S}$-execution $\eta$ of length $n$ is called $\mathfrak{S}$-*complete* if the last state $q_n$ of $\eta$ is terminal and at least one of the following two conditions holds:

(i) $stop \in \mathfrak{S}(\eta)$   or   (ii) there is no $c \in CIO(q_n) \cap \mathfrak{S}(\eta \downarrow n)$ such that $Nodes(c) \subseteq N$.

The first condition indicates that refusing any data flow on the N-nodes is a potential behavior under strategy $\mathfrak{S}$, while the second indicates the possibility for the opponents to do the same on their part (i.e. refusing any synchronization on the $\mathcal{N} \setminus N$ nodes). Furthermore, each infinite $\mathfrak{S}$-execution is said to be $\mathfrak{S}$-complete. A $\mathfrak{S}$-*path* denotes any infinite $\mathfrak{S}$-execution or any finite path $\pi = q_0 \xrightarrow{c_1} \ldots \xrightarrow{c_n} q_n \xrightarrow{\checkmark} q_n$, where $\pi \downarrow n$ is a $\mathfrak{S}$-complete $\mathfrak{S}$-execution. We write $Paths(q, \mathfrak{S})$ to denote all $\mathfrak{S}$-paths starting in q. Similarly, $Exec_{fin}(q, \mathfrak{S})$ denotes the set of all finite $\mathfrak{S}$-executions from q.

**Notation 4 (Memoryless, finite-memory strategies).** An N-strategy $\mathfrak{S}$ is called *memoryless* if $\mathfrak{S}(\eta) = \mathfrak{S}(\eta')$ for all finite executions $\eta$ and $\eta'$ that end in the same state. Memoryless strategies can be seen as functions $\mathfrak{S} : Q \to 2^{CIO \cup \{stop\}}$. Obviously, memoryless strategies are special instances of *finite-memory* strategies, i.e., strategies that make their decisions on the basis of a finite automaton rather than the full history.

## 4   Alternating-Time Stream Logic (ASL)

To reason about the components from a game-theoretic point of view, we introduce *alternating-time stream logic (ASL)* which is inspired by alternating-time temporal logic

(*ATL*) [1]. *ASL* extends *BTSL* [18] to state the possibility for components to cooperate in such way that a certain temporal property or property on the observable data flow holds. *ASL* is a branching time logic with state and path formulas. The state formula fragment is as in *ATL*, but adapted to the CA framework where the alternating-time quantifiers range over the strategies of certain node-sets. Intuitively, these node-sets stand for the interface nodes of one or more components. The existential quantifier $\mathbb{E}_N$ is used to indicate that the components with sink and source nodes in N have a strategy ensuring a certain condition, no matter how the other components connected to the nodes in $\mathcal{N} \setminus N$ behave. The universal quantifier $\mathbb{A}_N$ is dual and serves to state that the components providing the write and read actions at the N-nodes cannot avoid that a certain condition holds. The syntax of the *ASL* path formulas is the same as in *BTSL* and uses the standard until- and release operator, but replaces the standard next modality $\bigcirc$ with special operators $\langle\langle\alpha\rangle\rangle$ and $[\![\alpha]\!]$ to impose conditions on the I/O-streams of finite executions. In path formulas of the type $\langle\langle\alpha\rangle\rangle\Phi$ or $[\![\alpha]\!]\Phi$, the formula $\Phi$ is a state formula while $\alpha$ is a regular expression that stands for a regular language over the alphabet $\mathsf{CIO}_{\sqrt{}}$. This type of formulas is inspired by propositional dynamic logic [12], extended temporal logic [23], and timed scheduled data stream logic [3].

## 4.1  Syntax and Standard Semantics of ASL

In the sequel, we assume a fixed, non-empty and finite node-set $\mathcal{N}$. Furthermore, let *AP* be non-empty and finite set of atomic propositions, which can be viewed as conditions on the states of the automaton. In case of the CA modeling a FIFO-channel an atomic proposition might state that all buffer cells are empty or that the first buffer cell contains a value d in some set $P \subseteq Data$.

***Regular I/O-stream Expressions.***  The abstract syntax of regular I/O-stream expressions, briefly called stream expressions, is given by the following grammar:

$$\alpha ::= ioc \;\Big|\; \sqrt{} \;\Big|\; \alpha^* \;\Big|\; \alpha_1;\alpha_2 \;\Big|\; \alpha_1 \cup \alpha_2$$

where *ioc* ranges over all IOCs. Any stream expression represents a regular set of I/O-streams. The formal definition of the regular languages $IOS(\alpha) \subseteq IOS$ is defined by structural induction. $IOS(ioc)$ is the set consisting of the I/O-streams of length 1 given by *ioc*, i.e., $IOS(ioc) \stackrel{\text{def}}{=} CIO(ioc)$. Similarly, $IOS(\sqrt{})$ is the singleton set consisting of the I/O-stream $\sqrt{}$. Union ($\cup$) has its standard meaning: $IOS(\alpha_1 \cup \alpha_2) \stackrel{\text{def}}{=} IOS(\alpha_1) \cup IOS(\alpha_2)$, while Kleene star ($*$) and concatenation (;) have to ensure that the special termination symbol $\sqrt{}$ can only appear at the end of an I/O-stream:

$$IOS(\alpha^*) \stackrel{\text{def}}{=} \{\varepsilon\} \cup \bigcup_{n \geqslant 1} \{\sigma_1 \ldots \sigma_n : \sigma_i \in IOS(\alpha) \cap \mathsf{CIO}^*, i=1,\ldots,n-1, \sigma_n \in IOS(\alpha)\}$$

$$IOS(\alpha_1;\alpha_2) \stackrel{\text{def}}{=} \{\sigma_1\sqrt{} : \sigma_1\sqrt{} \in IOS(\alpha_1)\} \cup \{\sigma_1\sigma_2 : \sigma_1 \in IOS(\alpha_1) \cap \mathsf{CIO}^*, \sigma_2 \in IOS(\alpha_2)\}$$

**Syntax of ASL.** State-formulas (denoted by capital greek letters $\Phi$, $\Psi$) and path-formulas (denoted by small greek letters $\varphi$, $\psi$) of *ASL* are built by the following grammar:

$$\Phi ::= \text{true} \mid a \mid \Phi_1 \wedge \Phi_2 \mid \neg\Phi \mid \exists\varphi \mid \mathbb{E}_N \varphi$$

$$\varphi ::= \langle\!\langle\alpha\rangle\!\rangle\Phi \mid [\![\alpha]\!]\Phi \mid \Phi_1 \, U \, \Phi_2 \mid \Phi_1 \, R \, \Phi_2$$

where $N \subseteq \mathcal{N}$, $a \in AP$ and $\alpha$ is a regular I/O-stream expression. The quantifier $\exists$ in the syntax of *ASL* state formulas is the standard existential path quantifier of *CTL* and ranges over all paths, while the operator $\mathbb{E}_N$ corresponds an existential quantification over all N-strategies. The dual operator $\mathbb{A}_N \varphi$ stating that no strategy for the nodes in N can avoid $\varphi$ to hold is defined by:

$$\mathbb{A}_N \langle\!\langle\alpha\rangle\!\rangle\Phi \stackrel{\text{def}}{=} \neg\mathbb{E}_N [\![\alpha]\!]\neg\Phi \qquad\qquad \mathbb{A}_N (\Phi_1 \, U \, \Phi_2) \stackrel{\text{def}}{=} \neg\mathbb{E}_N (\neg\Phi_1 \, R \, \neg\Phi_2)$$

$$\mathbb{A}_N [\![\alpha]\!]\Phi \stackrel{\text{def}}{=} \neg\mathbb{E}_N \langle\!\langle\alpha\rangle\!\rangle\neg\Phi \qquad\qquad \mathbb{A}_N (\Phi_1 \, R \, \Phi_2) \stackrel{\text{def}}{=} \neg\mathbb{E}_N (\neg\Phi_1 \, U \, \neg\Phi_2)$$

In an analogous way, the universal *CTL*-path quantifier $\forall$ can be derived by duality from $\exists$. (Alternatively, $\forall\varphi$ can be defined by $\mathbb{E}_\emptyset \varphi$.) Other boolean connectives, like disjunction or implication, are obtained in the obvious way. In the following we shortly write $\mathbb{E}_A \varphi$ for $\mathbb{E}_{\{A\}} \varphi$ and $\mathbb{A}_A \varphi$ for $\mathbb{A}_{\{A\}} \varphi$.

*ASL* path formulas are interpreted over paths in a CA. The modalities $U$ and $R$ denote the ordinary until-operator and release-operator, respectively. The eventually and always operator are obtained in the usual way by $\Diamond\Phi \stackrel{\text{def}}{=} (\text{true} \, U \, \Phi)$ and $\Box\Phi \stackrel{\text{def}}{=} (\text{false} \, R \, \Phi)$.

The intended meaning of $\langle\!\langle\alpha\rangle\!\rangle\Phi$ is that it holds for a path $\pi$ iff $\pi$ has a finite prefix generating an $\alpha$-stream and $\Phi$ holds for the state reached afterwords. $[\![\alpha]\!]\Phi$ is the dual operator of $\langle\!\langle\alpha\rangle\!\rangle\Phi$ and holds for a path $\pi$ iff for all finite prefixes of $\pi$ generating an $\alpha$-stream, formula $\Phi$ holds for the last state of the prefix. The standard *next* operator is derived from the path formula $\bigcirc\Phi \stackrel{\text{def}}{=} \langle\!\langle tt\rangle\!\rangle\Phi$, which asserts the occurrence for some (non-observable) data flow. Recall that $IOS(tt) = CIO(tt) = \text{ClO}$. Thus, $\bigcirc\Phi$ holds for all paths where the underlying execution has at least one transition and $\Phi$ holds afterwords. The presence of some observable data flow can be expressed by $\langle\!\langle A_1 \vee \ldots \vee A_n\rangle\!\rangle\text{true}$, where $\mathcal{N} = \{A_1, \ldots, A_n\}$. The path formula $[\![tt^*; \sqrt{]\!}]\text{false}$ is characteristic for the infinite paths, while $\langle\!\langle tt^*; \sqrt{\rangle\!}\rangle\text{true}$ holds exactly for the finite paths. The terminal states are characterized by the state formula $\exists\langle\!\langle\sqrt{\rangle\!}\rangle\text{true}$, while $\forall\langle\!\langle\sqrt{\rangle\!}\rangle\text{true}$ is satisfied in exactly those states where no concurrent I/O-operation is enabled. *ASL* state formulas are the same as in *BTSL* except for the $\mathbb{E}_N$-operator (and its dual).

For an intuitive example, consider a FIFO-channel with source node A and sink node B. Then the *ASL* state formulas $\mathbb{E}_A \Box\text{empty}$, $\mathbb{E}_A \Box(\text{buffer} \neq 0)$, $\mathbb{A}_B \Diamond\text{empty}$ and $\mathbb{A}_B \Box\text{empty}$ do hold, where $(\text{buffer} \neq 0)$ states that either the buffer is empty or contains a data value different from zero. In case of the ticket vending machine we may ask whether the user (possibly in coalition with other components) controlling three boundary nodes $N = \{C, D, P\}$ (for the *cancel* signal, data items, and payment) has a strategy to get a ticket without paying, i.e. if state formula $\mathbb{E}_{\{C,D,P\}} \langle\!\langle\neg pay^*\rangle\!\rangle ticket\_printed$ holds. A dual *ASL* property states that all components except the user respect the *cancel* signal and reset to their initial configuration. This can be expressed by $\mathbb{A}_{\mathcal{N}\setminus N} [\![tt^*; C]\!]initconf$.

***Standard Semantics of ASL.*** Let $\mathcal{A}$ be a CA and $\pi$ a path in $\mathcal{A}$. The satisfaction relation $\models$ for *ASL* state formulas is defined by structural induction as shown below:

$$q \models \text{true}$$
$$q \models a \qquad \text{iff} \ \ a \in L(q)$$
$$q \models \Phi_1 \wedge \Phi_2 \ \ \text{iff} \ \ q \models \Phi_1 \text{ and } q \models \Phi_2$$
$$q \models \neg \Phi \qquad \text{iff} \ \ q \not\models \Phi$$
$$q \models \exists \varphi \qquad \text{iff} \ \ \text{there exists } \pi \in \text{Paths}(q) \text{ such that } \pi \models \varphi$$
$$q \models \mathbb{E}_N \varphi \qquad \text{iff} \ \ \text{there is an N-strategy } \mathfrak{S} \text{ such that:}$$
$$\text{for all } \pi \in \text{Paths}(q, \mathfrak{S}) : \pi \models \varphi$$

The satisfaction relation $\models$ for *ASL* path-formuls and the path $\pi$ in $\mathcal{A}$ as follows:

$$\pi \models \langle\!\langle \alpha \rangle\!\rangle \Phi \quad \text{iff} \quad \text{there exists } n \in \mathbb{N} \text{ such that } 0 \leqslant n \leqslant |\pi| \text{ and}$$
$$ios(\pi \downarrow n) \in IOS(\alpha) \text{ and } q_n \models \Phi$$
$$\pi \models [\![\alpha]\!] \Phi \quad \text{iff} \quad \text{for all } n \in \mathbb{N} \text{ such that } 0 \leqslant n \leqslant |\pi| \text{ we have:}$$
$$ios(\pi \downarrow n) \in IOS(\alpha) \text{ implies } q_n \models \Phi$$
$$\pi \models \Phi_1 \cup \Phi_2 \quad \text{iff} \quad \text{there exists } n \in \mathbb{N} \text{ such that } 0 \leqslant n < |\pi| \text{ where}$$
$$q_n \models \Phi_2 \text{ and } q_i \models \Phi_1 \text{ for } 0 \leqslant i < n$$
$$\pi \models \Phi_1 R \Phi_2 \quad \text{iff} \quad \text{at least one of the following conditions (i) or (ii) holds:}$$
$$\text{(i) for all } n \in \mathbb{N} \text{ with } 0 \leqslant n < |\pi| \text{ we have: } q_n \models \Phi_2$$
$$\text{(ii) there exists some } n \in \mathbb{N} \text{ with } 0 \leqslant n \leqslant |\pi| \text{ such that:}$$
$$q_n \models \Phi_1 \text{ and } q_i \models \Phi_2 \text{ for } 0 \leqslant i \leqslant n$$

Given a state $q$ and a *ASL* path formula $\varphi$, an N-strategy $\mathfrak{S}$ is called *winning* for the tuple $\langle q, \varphi \rangle$ if $\varphi$ holds for all $\mathfrak{S}$-paths starting in $q$. Thus, $q \models \mathbb{E}_N \varphi$ iff there exists a winning N-strategy for $\langle q, \varphi \rangle$. For the derived operator $\mathbb{A}_N$ we get that $q \models \mathbb{A}_N \varphi$ iff for all N-strategies $\mathfrak{S}$ there exists $\pi \in \text{Paths}(q, \mathfrak{S})$ such that $\pi \models \varphi$, i.e. there is no winning strategy for $\langle q, \varphi \rangle$.

*Example 2 (ASL state formulas).* The CA with node set $\mathcal{N} = \{A, B\}$ depicted below fulfills the following state formula $\mathbb{A}_A \Diamond \neg \exists \bigcirc \text{true}$, stating that an agent controlling A only cannot avoid that a terminal state $q_t$ will eventually be reached.

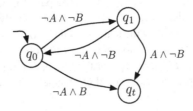

The multi-player game associated with a CA and an *ASL* path formula is *not determined*. In fact, there are path formulas $\varphi$ such that neither the N-agents have a winning strategy for $\varphi$ nor does the opponents (i.e., the $\mathcal{N} \setminus$ N-agents) have a strategy to ensure that $\varphi$ does not hold. The reason for this is that the internal nondeterminism can yield the possibility to generate paths where $\varphi$ holds and paths where $\varphi$ does not hold.

In particular, the *ASL* state formulas $\mathbb{E}_N \varphi$ and $\mathbb{A}_{\mathcal{N} \backslash N} \varphi$ are *not* equivalent[1] and $q \models \mathbb{E}_N \varphi$ implies $q \models \mathbb{A}_{\mathcal{N} \backslash N} \varphi$ holds for all states $q \in Q$, but not vice versa. A simple example illustrating this fact is the following CA with node-set $\mathcal{N} = \{A, B\}$.

*Example 3 (Internal nondeterminism).*

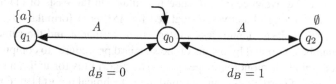

Assume that $a \in AP$ is an atomic proposition which holds in $q_1$ only, i.e. $L(q_1) = \{a\}$ and $L(q_2) = \emptyset$. Since the internal nondeterminism decides whether $q_1$ or $q_2$ will be selected as successor state of $q_0$ when $A$ fires, neither $A$ can enforce nor $B$ can avoid that $q_1$ will be entered in the next step. Thus, we have $q_0 \models \mathbb{A}_B \bigcirc a$ and $q_0 \not\models \mathbb{E}_A \bigcirc a$.

## 4.2 ASL Model Checking

The model checking problem for *ASL* asks whether, for a given CA $\mathcal{A}$ and *ASL* state formula $\Phi$, all initial states $q_0$ of $\mathcal{A}$ satisfy $\Phi$. The main procedure for *ASL* model checking follows the standard approach for *CTL*-like branching-time logics [8] and recursively calculates the satisfaction sets $Sat(\Psi) = \{q \in Q : q \models \Psi\}$ for all sub-formulas $\Psi$ of $\Phi$. The treatment of the *BTSL*-fragment of *ASL* is the same as for *BTSL* (see [18]). The only interesting part is how to calculate $Sat(\mathbb{E}_N \varphi)$ for an *ASL* path formulas $\varphi$ and node-set $N \subseteq \mathcal{N}$. The essential ingredient for this is the predecessor operator $Pre(P, N)$ which is defined as the set of all states $q \in Q$ such that the N-nodes have a strategy which guarantees to move within one step to a state in P.

**Definition 5 (Predecessors).** Let $P \subseteq Q$ and $N \subseteq \mathcal{N}$ a node-set. Then, $Pre(P, N)$ denotes the set of all states $q \in Q$ such that the following two conditions hold:

(i) for all $c \in CIO(q)$ such that $Nodes(c) \cap N = \emptyset$ we have $Post[c](q) \subseteq P$
(ii) there exists a $c \in CIO(q)$ such that $Nodes(c) \subseteq N$ and $Post[c](q) \subseteq P$

where $Post[c](q) \overset{\text{def}}{=} \{p \in Q : q \overset{c}{\rightarrow} p\}$.

Condition (i) is needed to ensure that no uncontrollable transition (from the view of the N-agents) leads to a state outside of P, while condition (ii) asserts the existence of at least one concurrent I/O-operation that can be enforced by the N-agents and certainly leads to a state in P. In fact we have $Pre(P, N) = \{q \in Q : q \models \mathbb{E}_N \bigcirc P\}$.

As for standard *CTL* (and *ATL*), the semantics of the until and release operator have a fixed point characterization. The set $Sat(\mathbb{E}_N (\Phi_1 \cup \Phi_2))$ is the least fixpoint, while the set $Sat(\mathbb{E}_N (\Phi_1 R \Phi_2))$ is the greatest fixpoint of the following operators $2^Q \rightarrow 2^Q$:

$$P \mapsto Sat(\Phi_2) \cup (Pre(P, N) \cap Sat(\Phi_1)) \quad \text{(until)}$$
$$P \mapsto Sat(\Phi_2) \cap (Pre(P, N) \cup Sat(\Phi_1)) \quad \text{(release)}$$

---

[1] The same observation holds for *ATL*\* interpreted over concurrent games, but for other reasons.

Hence, in *ASL* with the standard semantics we have the following *expansion laws*:

$$\mathbb{E}_N(\Phi_1 \cup \Phi_2) \equiv \Phi_2 \vee (\Phi_1 \wedge \mathbb{E}_N \bigcirc \mathbb{E}_N(\Phi_1 \cup \Phi_2)) \tag{1}$$

$$\mathbb{E}_N(\Phi_1 R \Phi_2) \equiv \Phi_2 \wedge (\Phi_1 \vee \mathbb{E}_N \bigcirc \mathbb{E}_N(\Phi_1 R \Phi_2)) \tag{2}$$

where $\equiv$ denotes equivalence of *ASL* state formulas. On the basis of (1) and (2), we obtain that for winning objectives formalized by *ASL* path formulas $\varphi$ of the form $(\Phi_1 \cup \Phi_2)$ or $(\Phi_1 R \Phi_2)$, memoryless strategies are sufficient and the satisfaction set $Sat(\mathbb{E}_N \varphi)$ can be computed by means of the standard procedures to compute least and greatest fixed points of monotonic operators. The algorithms for until and release including the proof of correctness can be found in the technical report [19]. For *ASL* state formulas of the form $\mathbb{E}_N \langle\!\langle \alpha \rangle\!\rangle \Phi$ or $\mathbb{E}_N [\![ \alpha ]\!] \Phi$, we follow an automata-theoretic approach which resembles the standard automata-based *LTL* model checking procedure and relies on a representation of $\alpha$ by means of a finite automaton $\mathcal{Z}$ and a graph analysis of the product $\mathcal{A} \bowtie \mathcal{Z}$. As $\alpha$ is roughly an ordinary regular expression, we can apply standard methods to generate a deterministic finite automata $\mathcal{Z}$ over the alphabet $\text{CIO}_{\sqrt{}}$ such that the accepted language of $\mathcal{Z}$ agrees with $IOS(\alpha)$.

Let $\mathcal{Z} = (Z, \text{CIO}_{\sqrt{}}, \delta, Z_0, Z_F)$, i.e., $Z$ stands for the state space, $z_0$ the initial state, $Z_F$ for the set of final (accept) states and $\delta : Z \times \text{CIO}_{\sqrt{}} \to Z$ for the transition function. In fact, beside the special $\sqrt{}$-transitions, $\mathcal{Z}$ can be viewed as a CA where the set $Z_F$ plays the role of the labeling function which separates the final states from the non-final states. Due to the special role of the symbol $\sqrt{}$ (which can only appear at the end of a word in $IOS(\alpha)$), we can assume that there are special states $z_{accept} \in Z_F$ and $z_{reject} \in Z \setminus Z_F$ such that each $\sqrt{}$-transition leads to one of the states $z_{accept}$ or $z_{reject}$ and that the states $z_{accept}$ or $z_{reject}$ cannot be entered via any other symbol. Given $\mathcal{A}$ and $\mathcal{Z}$, we built the product $\mathcal{A} \bowtie \mathcal{Z}$, similar to the product of finite automata and the join operator for CAs [6], but with a special treatment of the pseudo-transitions with label $\sqrt{}$. In fact, the product construction we use here differs from those used in the *BTSL* model checking procedure [18] since in the context of the $\mathbb{E}_N$-operator we have to incorporate the possibilities of the N-agents to enforce termination. Formally, we define the CA $\mathcal{A} \bowtie_{N,\Phi} \mathcal{Z}$ as follows:

$$\mathcal{A} \bowtie_{N,\Phi} \mathcal{Z} \overset{\text{def}}{=} (S, \mathcal{N} \cup \{A_{stop}\}, \longrightarrow, S_0, AP', L').$$

The state space $S$ is $Q \times Z$ and $A_{stop}$ is a new node-name (not contained in $\mathcal{N}$). This new node is supposed to be controllable. (Thus, for $\mathcal{A} \bowtie_{N,\Phi} \mathcal{Z}$ we will ask for $(N \cup \{A_{stop}\})$-strategies rather than N-strategies.) The initial states are given by

$$S_0 = \{ \langle q, z_0 \rangle : q \in Q_0 \}.$$

The atomic propositions and labeling function in $\mathcal{A} \bowtie_{N,\Phi} \mathcal{Z}$ are given by the set $AP' = \{a_\Phi, accept\}$, where $a_\Phi \in L'(\langle q, z \rangle)$ iff $q \models \Phi$ and $accept \in L'(\langle q, z \rangle)$ iff $z \in Z_F$. The transitions in $\mathcal{A} \bowtie_{N,\Phi} \mathcal{Z}$ are obtained by the following synchronization rule for concurrent I/O-operations $c \in \text{CIO}$ (i.e., $c \neq \sqrt{}$), state $q$ in $\mathcal{A}$, and state $z \in Z \setminus \{z_{accept}, z_{reject}\}$:

$$\frac{q \overset{c}{\to}_\mathcal{A} q' \wedge z \overset{c}{\to}_\mathcal{Z} z'}{\langle q, z \rangle \overset{c}{\to} \langle q', z' \rangle} \tag{3}$$

where we use the subscript $\mathcal{A}$ for the transition relations in $\mathcal{A}$. In addition, we have the following rules for each terminal state q in $\mathcal{A}$ and state $z \in Z \setminus \{z_{accept}, z_{reject}\}$ where $c_{stop}$ is a concurrent I/O-operation with $\mathsf{Nodes}(c_{stop}) = \{A_{stop}\}$ and $c_{stop}(A_{stop})$ is an arbitrary element from the data domain $Data$:

$$\frac{\neg \exists c \in \mathsf{CIO}(q) \text{ s.t. } \mathsf{Nodes}(c) \subseteq N \wedge c_\emptyset \notin \mathsf{CIO}(q)}{\langle q, z \rangle \xrightarrow{c_\emptyset} \langle q, \delta(z, \checkmark) \rangle} \tag{4}$$

$$\frac{\exists c \in \mathsf{CIO}(q) \text{ s.t. } \mathsf{Nodes}(c) \cap N \neq \emptyset \wedge c_\emptyset \notin \mathsf{CIO}(q)}{\langle q, z \rangle \xrightarrow{c_{stop}} \langle q, \delta(z, \checkmark) \rangle} \tag{5}$$

Rule (4) formalizes the fact that if q is terminal (i.e., $c_\emptyset \notin \mathsf{CIO}(q)$) and there is no $c \in \mathsf{CIO}(q)$ such that $\mathsf{Nodes}(c) \subseteq N$ then the opponents of the N-agents may refuse any write or read operation and can therefore enforce data flow to stop. This is modeled in the product by a transition with the label $c_\emptyset$. Rule (5) stands for the fact that whenever q is a terminal node for which some concurrent I/O-operation c is enabled where the N-nodes are involved then the N-agents might decide not to participate in any further I/O-operation. This is modeled in the product by a transition with the label $c_{stop}$ where the new node $A_{stop}$ is supposed to be controllable. We obtain the following two lemmas for *ASL* state formulas of the form $\mathbb{E}_N \langle\!\langle \alpha \rangle\!\rangle \Phi$ and $\mathbb{E}_N [\![\alpha]\!] \Phi$.

**Lemma 1.** Let $\mathcal{A}$ be a CA, $\mathcal{Z} = (Z, \mathsf{CIO}_\checkmark, \delta, Z_0, Z_F)$ a DFA for $\alpha$, q in $\mathcal{A}$, node-sets $N \subseteq \mathcal{N}$ and *ASL* state formulas $\Phi$. Then, the following statements are equivalent:

(a) $q \models \mathbb{E}_N \langle\!\langle \alpha \rangle\!\rangle \Phi$
(b) $\langle q, z_0 \rangle \models \mathbb{E}_{N \cup \{A_{stop}\}} \Diamond (a_\Phi \wedge accept)$
(c) There exists a finite-memory N-strategy $\mathfrak{S}$ for $\mathcal{A}$ that is winning for $\langle q, \langle\!\langle \alpha \rangle\!\rangle \Phi \rangle$

**Lemma 2.** Let $\mathcal{A}$ be a CA, $\mathcal{Z} = (Z, \mathsf{CIO}_\checkmark, \delta, Z_0, Z_F)$ a DFA for $\alpha$, q in $\mathcal{A}$, node-sets $N \subseteq \mathcal{N}$ and *ASL* state formulas $\Phi$. Then, the following statements are equivalent:

(a) $q \models \mathbb{E}_N [\![\alpha]\!] \Phi$
(b) $\langle q, z_0 \rangle \models \mathbb{E}_{N \cup \{A_{stop}\}} \Box (accept \rightarrow a_\Phi)$
(c) there exists a finite memory N-strategy $\mathfrak{S}$ which is winning for $\langle q, [\![\alpha]\!] \Phi \rangle$

Thanks to lemmas 1 and 2 the satisfaction sets $Sat(\mathbb{E}_N \langle\!\langle \alpha \rangle\!\rangle \Phi)$ and $Sat(\mathbb{E}_N [\![\alpha]\!] \Phi)$ can be computed by means of a reduction to the model checking problem for the $\mathbb{E}_N$-operator in combination with the eventually- and always-modalities. More precisely, we first have to construct a DFA $\mathcal{Z}$ for $\alpha$, then built the product $\mathcal{A} \bowtie_{N,\Phi} \mathcal{Z}$ and finally apply the algorithm for until and release respectively, to compute the satisfaction sets for $\mathbb{E}_{N \cup \{A_{stop}\}} \Diamond (a_\Phi \wedge accept)$ and $\mathbb{E}_{N \cup \{A_{stop}\}} \Box (accept \rightarrow a_\Phi)$ in the product. Furthermore the memoryless $(N \cup \{A_{stop}\})$-strategies for the product yield finite-memory winning N-strategies in $\mathcal{A}$ for the objectives $\langle\!\langle \alpha \rangle\!\rangle \Phi$ and $[\![\alpha]\!] \Phi$, respectively.

Assuming that $Sat(\Phi)$ has already been computed the time complexity for computing $Sat(\mathbb{E}_N \langle\!\langle \alpha \rangle\!\rangle \Phi)$ and $Sat(\mathbb{E}_N [\![\alpha]\!] \Phi)$ is linear in the size of CA $\mathcal{A}$ and the DFA $\mathcal{Z}$ for $\alpha$ (which can be exponential in the length of $\alpha$). However, when restricting to the *ATL*-fragment of *ASL* which just uses the standard path modalities U, R and $\bigcirc$, but not $\langle\!\langle\alpha\rangle\!\rangle$ or $[\![\alpha]\!]$, then the worst complexity of the *ASL* model checking algorithm is the same as for standard *ATL*, i.e., linear in the size of $\mathcal{A}$ and the length of the formula.

We conclude this section by a simple observation concerning the case that $\alpha$ is a $\sqrt{}$-free expression (i.e., does not contain a subexpression of the form $\beta;\sqrt{}$). In fact, for $\sqrt{}$-free expressions, the "best" strategy for the N-agents to ensure $[\![\alpha]\!]\Phi$ is to stop the data flow whenever possible. This is formalized in the following lemma.

**Lemma 3 (Winning strategies for $\sqrt{}$-free expressions).** Let $\mathfrak{S}_{stop}$ be the memoryless N-strategy given by $\mathfrak{S}_{stop}(q) = \{stop\} \cup \{c \in \mathsf{CIO} : \mathsf{Nodes}(c) \cap N = \emptyset\}$ for all states q. Then, for each $\sqrt{}$-free stream expression $\alpha$ and state q we have:

$$q \models \mathbb{E}_N\,[\![\alpha]\!]\Phi \text{ iff } \mathfrak{S}_{stop} \text{ is winning for } \langle q, [\![\alpha]\!]\Phi\rangle.$$

Thus, if $\alpha$ is $\sqrt{}$-free then the set $Sat(\mathbb{E}_N\,[\![\alpha]\!]\Phi)$ can be computed by considering the subautomaton $\mathcal{A}'$ of $\mathcal{A}$ that results by the memoryless strategy $\mathfrak{S}_{stop}$ and then computing the satisfaction set for $Sat_{\mathcal{A}'}(\forall[\![\alpha]\!]\Phi)$ in $\mathcal{A}'$. This can be done by means of a *BTSL* model checker [18].

## 5   ASL with Fairness

The concept of fairness serves to rule out pathological behaviors, where certain liveness properties are violated, although they are supposed to hold [14]. The nondeterminism within our multi-player setting demand for some *ASL* fairness assumptions. To illustrate the need for some fairness assumptions, we reuse the deadlock example (2). One would expect that the *ASL* state formula $\mathbb{E}_B \Diamond \neg \exists \bigcirc \mathsf{true}$ would be fulfilled, since the memoryless strategy $\mathfrak{S}$, which tries to write on B whenever $q_0$ is reached during an execution should be winning for $\langle q_0, \Diamond \neg \exists \bigcirc \mathsf{true}\rangle$. But

$$\pi = q_0 \xrightarrow{c_1} q_1 \xrightarrow{c_2} q_0 \xrightarrow{c_1} \dots \in \mathsf{Paths}(q_0, \mathfrak{S}) \text{ and } \pi \not\models \neg \exists \bigcirc \mathsf{true}.$$

The goal of this section is to introduce some fairness assumptions to exclude such undesirable behaviors from our observations.

**Definition 6 ($\langle N, \mathfrak{S}\rangle$-fairness).** Let $\mathcal{A} = \langle Q, \mathcal{N}, \longrightarrow, Q_0, AP, L\rangle$ be a CA, $N \subseteq \mathcal{N}$ a node-set, $\mathfrak{S}$ an N-strategy, and $\pi = q_0 \xrightarrow{c_1} q_1 \xrightarrow{c_2} \dots$ a $\mathfrak{S}$-path in $\mathcal{A}$. Then $\pi$ is called *(strongly)* $\langle N, \mathfrak{S}\rangle$-*fair* if either $\pi$ is finite or for all $c \in \mathsf{CIO}$ we have:

$$\overset{\infty}{\exists} i \geqslant 0. \; c \in \mathsf{CIO}(q_i) \cap \mathfrak{S}(\pi \downarrow i) \text{ and } \mathsf{Nodes}(c) \subseteq N \text{ implies } \overset{\infty}{\exists} i \geqslant 0. \; c_i = c,$$

where $\overset{\infty}{\exists} i$ means "there exists infinitely many i". We write $\mathsf{FairPaths}_{\langle N, \mathfrak{S}\rangle}(q)$ for all $\langle N, \mathfrak{S}\rangle$-fair paths starting in q and $\mathsf{FairPaths}_{\langle N, \mathfrak{S}\rangle}(\mathcal{A})$ for the set of $\langle N, \mathfrak{S}\rangle$-fair paths.

In the above example, $\pi = q_0 \xrightarrow{c_1} q_1 \xrightarrow{c_2} q_0 \xrightarrow{c_1} \dots \notin \mathsf{FairPaths}_{\langle\{B\}, \mathfrak{S}\rangle}(q_0)$ because $\mathfrak{S}$ is willing to write infinitely often on B, but no write operation is ever executed. The semantics of the fair *ASL* path formulas is the same as for *ASL* without fairness (see section 4.1).

The semantics for fair *ASL* state formulas also corresponds to the one without fairness except for:

$$q \models_{\mathsf{fair}} \mathbb{E}_N \varphi \text{ iff there is an N-strategy } \mathfrak{S} \text{ s.t. for all } \pi \in \mathsf{FairPaths}_{\langle N, \mathfrak{S} \rangle}(q) : \pi \models \varphi$$

The underlying model checking algorithms need to be modified and now rely on the bottom up computation of the sets $Sat_{\mathsf{fair}}(\Psi) = \{q \in Q \mid q \models_{\mathsf{fair}} \Psi\}$ for all subformulas $\Psi$. The computation for $Sat_{\mathsf{fair}}(\mathbb{E}_N(\Phi_1 R \Phi_2))$ does not involve any modification at all, as shown in the following lemma.

**Lemma 4 (Release with fairness).** Let $\mathcal{A}$ be a CA, $N \subseteq \mathcal{N}$ a node-set, $q \in Q$ a state in $\mathcal{A}$ and $\Phi_1, \Phi_2$ *ASL* state formulas. Then $q \models_{\mathsf{fair}} \mathbb{E}_N(\Phi_1 R \Phi_2)$ iff $q \models \mathbb{E}_N(\Phi_1 R \Phi_2)$.

The computation of $Sat_{\mathsf{fair}}(\mathbb{E}_N(\Phi_1 U \Phi_2))$ relies on an iterative SCC-calculation in subgraphs of $\mathcal{A}$. The following lemma emerges that the remaining fair computation of $Sat_{\mathsf{fair}}(\mathbb{E}_N \langle\!\langle \alpha \rangle\!\rangle \Phi)$ and $Sat_{\mathsf{fair}}(\mathbb{E}_N [\![\alpha]\!] \Phi)$ can be reduced to eventually and always in the product $\mathcal{A} \bowtie \mathcal{Z}$.

**Lemma 5 (Fairness for ASL I/O-stream expression formulas).** Let $\mathcal{A}$ be a CA, $N \subseteq \mathcal{N}$ a node-set, $\alpha$ a regular I/O-stream expression, $\mathcal{Z}$ a deterministic CA for $\alpha$, and let $\Phi$ be *ASL* state formula. Then, the following observation holds for all states $q \in Q$.

i) $q \models_{\mathsf{fair}} \mathbb{E}_N \langle\!\langle \alpha \rangle\!\rangle \Phi$ in $\mathcal{A}$ iff $\langle q, z_0 \rangle \models_{\mathsf{fair}} \mathbb{E}_{N \cup \{A_{stop}\}} \Diamond (accept \wedge \mathfrak{a}_\Phi)$ in $\mathcal{A} \bowtie \mathcal{Z}$.
ii) $q \models_{\mathsf{fair}} \mathbb{E}_N [\![\alpha]\!] \Phi$ iff $\langle q, z_0 \rangle \models_{\mathsf{fair}} \mathbb{E}_{N \cup \{A_{stop}\}} \Box (accept \rightarrow \mathfrak{a}_\Phi)$ in $\mathcal{A} \bowtie \mathcal{Z}$.

## 6  Conclusion and Future Work

This paper introduces a framework to verify alternating-time properties for a multi-player games derived from CA. The introduced concurrent game semantics captures any complex behavior caused by synchronous and asynchronous peer-to-peer communication, mutual dependencies of I/O-operations and also data-dependencies. Since this game structure is non-standard it takes numerous nontrivial adaptations of the *ATL* model checking algorithm. In future work we will drop our assumption on *perfect information* and *perfect recall* to switch to a more realistic view for exogenous coordination taking the local view [5,7,16,17,21,11,22] into account. In future work we will consider *observation-based strategies* in case of *incomplete information*.

Apart from asking for the existence or absence of a winning strategy for a temporal property the question might raise, if there is a way of connecting the components to make this property hold. This directly leads to the controller synthesis problem where if possible a controlling CA is put in parallel with the other components to ensure the intended behavior. One step further we would like to build the Reo network which glues those components the intended way by using the synthesis approach described in [4].

## References

1. Alur, R., Henzinger, T.A., Kupferman, O.: Alternating-time temporal logic. Journal of the ACM 49, 672–713 (2002)
2. Arbab, F.: Reo: A channel-based coordination model for component composition. Mathematical Structures in Computer Science 14(3), 329–366 (2004)

3. Arbab, F., Baier, C., de Boer, F., Rutten, J.J.M.M.: Models and temporal logics for timed component connectors. In: Proc. of SEFM, pp. 198–207. IEEE CS Press, Los Alamitos (2004)
4. Arbab, F., Baier, C., de Boer, F., Rutten, J.J.M.M., Sirjani, M.: Synthesis of Reo circuits for implementation of component connector automata specifications. In: Jacquet, J.-M., Picco, G.P. (eds.) COORDINATION 2005. LNCS, vol. 3454, Springer, Heidelberg (2005)
5. Azhar, S., Peterson, G.L., Reif, J.H.: On multiplayer non-cooperative games of incomplete information: Part 1&2. Technical report, Durham, NC, USA (1991)
6. Baier, C., Sirjani, M., Arbab, F., Rutten, J.J.M.M.: Modeling component connectors in Reo by constraint automata. In: Science of Computer Programming 61, pp. 75–113 (2006)
7. Chatterjee, K., Doyen, L., Henzinger, T.A., Raskin, J.F.: Algorithms for omega-regular games with imperfect information. CoRR, abs/0706.2619 (2007)
8. Clarke, E.M., Emerson, E.A., Sistla, A.P.: Automatic verification of finite-state concurrent systems using temporal logic specifications. ACM TOPLAS 8(2), 244–263 (1986)
9. de Alfaro, L., Henzinger, T.A.: Concurrent omega-regular games. In: Proc. of LICS, pp. 141–154 (January 2000)
10. de Alfaro, L., Henzinger, T.A.: Interface automata. In: FSE Proc., pp. 109–120. ACM Press, New York (2001)
11. de Wulf, M., Doyen, L., Raskin, J.-F.: A lattice theory for solving games of imperfect information. In: Hespanha, J.P., Tiwari, A. (eds.) HSCC 2006. LNCS, vol. 3927, pp. 153–168. Springer, Heidelberg (2006)
12. Fischer, M.J., Ladner, R.J.: Propositional dynamic logic of regular programs. Journal of Computer and System Science 8, 194–211 (1979)
13. Fitoussi, D., Tennenholtz, M.: Choosing social laws for multi-agent systems: minimality and simplicity. Artif. Intell. 119(1-2), 61–101 (2000)
14. Francez, N.: Fairness. Springer, Heidelberg (1986)
15. Grosu, R., Rumpe, B.: Concurrent timed port automata. Technical Report TUM-I9533, Techn. Univ. München (1995),
    http://www4.informatik.tu-muenchen.de/reports/
16. Hoek, W.v.d., Roberts, M., Wooldridge, M.: Knowledge and social laws. In: AAMAS, pp. 674–681 (2005)
17. Hoek, W.v.d., Wooldridge, M.: Cooperation, knowledge, and time: Alternating-time temporal epistemic logic and its applications. Studia Logica 75(1), 125–157 (2003)
18. Klüppelholz, S., Baier, C.: Symbolic model checking for channel-based component connectors. In: Proc. of FOCLASA 2006. ENTCS, vol. 175(2), pp. 19–37 (2007)
19. Klüppelholz, S., Baier, C.: Alternating-Time Stream Logic for Multi-Agent Systems. Technical report, Technical University Dresden (2008),
    http://wwwtcs.inf.tu-dresden.de/~klueppel/ASLKB2008.pdf
20. Lynch, N., Tuttle, M.R.: An introduction to input/output automata. CWI Quarterly 2(3), 219–246 (1989)
21. Reif, J.H.: The complexity of two-player games of incomplete information. J. Comput. Syst. Sci. 29(2), 274–301 (1984)
22. Schobbens, P.Y.: Alternating-time logic with imperfect recall. In: Proc. of LCMAS. ENTCS, vol. 85(2), pp. 1–12 (2004)
23. Wolper, P.: Specification and synthesis of communicating processes using an extended temporal logic. In: Proc. of POPL, pp. 20–33 (1982)
24. Wooldridge, M.: Social laws in alternating time. In: Lomuscio, A., Nute, D. (eds.) DEON 2004. LNCS (LNAI), vol. 3065, p. 2. Springer, Heidelberg (2004)

# A Formal Account of WS-BPEL[*]

Alessandro Lapadula, Rosario Pugliese, and Francesco Tiezzi

Dipartimento di Sistemi e Informatica Università degli Studi di Firenze

**Abstract.** We introduce B*lite*, a lightweight language for web services orchestration designed around some of WS-BPEL peculiar features like partner links, process termination, message correlation, long-running business transactions and compensation handlers. B*lite* formal presentation helps clarifying some ambiguous aspects of the WS-BPEL specification, which have led to engines implementing different semantics and, thus, have undermined portability of WS-BPEL programs over different platforms. We illustrate the main features of B*lite* by means of many examples, some of which are also exploited to test and compare the behaviour of three of the most known free WS-BPEL engines.

## 1 Introduction

There is an ever increasing acceptance of WS-BPEL (Web Services Business Process Execution Language, [23]) as a standard language for service composition within and across multiple enterprises. The fact that it has become an OASIS standard, however, has not solved all the difficulties of using the language. Indeed, WS-BPEL comes without a formal semantics and its specification document [23], written in 'natural' language, contains a fair number of acknowledged ambiguous aspects that may lead to different interpretations. For example, the relationship between WS-BPEL (multiple) *start activities* and the mechanisms handling race conditions has not been fully explored; moreover, if suitable measures for 'protecting' such critical activities as fault and compensation handlers are not taken into account, then subtle behaviours can arise when implementing activities that cause immediate termination of other activities.

The design of WS-BPEL applications is difficult and error-prone also due to the presence of such intricate features as concurrency and race conditions, forced termination, multiple instances and message correlation, long-running business transactions and compensation handlers. It would thus benefit from the use of *formal methods* because these can provide a framework to precisely describe some aspects of an application, to state and prove its properties, and to direct attention towards issues that might otherwise be overlooked.

As a step in this direction, in this paper we introduce B*lite*, a 'lightweight' variant of WS-BPEL designed around the above mentioned features. B*lite*, being obtained by dropping redundant features from the full-fledged language, permits to focus on those fragments of the design that are more challenging and need more attention. For example, B*lite* clarifies the relationship between compensation activities and the control flow of the originating process, and illustrates the mechanisms for service instance creation and

---

[*] This work has been supported by the EU project Sᴇɴsᴏʀɪᴀ, IST-2005-016004.

D. Lea and G. Zavattaro (Eds.): COORDINATION 2008, LNCS 5052, pp. 199–215, 2008.

identification, and their interplay. Our study can also contribute to the many discussions on compensation and correlation which have been reported by the WS-BPEL technical committee [22] (see, e.g., discussions related to issues 66, 207 and 271).

Moreover, B*lite*'s formal presentation can help clarifying many ambiguous aspects of the WS-BPEL specification and, thus, can be used prescriptively to drive implementations of future WS-BPEL engines. In fact, by means of several examples, we test and compare three of the most known free BPEL engines, namely ActiveBPEL [1], Apache ODE [2] and Oracle BPEL Process Manager [3]. As a matter of fact, the considered engines exhibit quite different behaviours and diverge from the WS-BPEL specification in many important aspects. This is complicating the task of developing WS-BPEL applications and undermining their portability across different platforms.

We also believe that the formalization of WS-BPEL's operational semantics, through the introduction of B*lite*, can also enable tailoring proof techniques and analytical tools typical of process calculi to the needs of WS-BPEL applications. Indeed, on the one hand, alike other standards enabling the web services technology, WS-BPEL does not provide support for guided forms of application development and analysis. On the other hand, it has been shown that type systems, model checking and (bi)simulation analysis provide adequate tools to address topics relevant to the web services technology (see e.g. [21,26]). In the end, this 'proof technology' can pave the way for the development of (semi-)automatic property validation tools.

The rest of the paper is organized as follows. Section 2 presents B*lite*'s syntax and operational semantics. Section 3 illustrates most of the language features at work on modelling a shipping service scenario borrowed from the official WS-BPEL specification. Section 4 presents many peculiar examples and the results of our experimentation with the three WS-BPEL engines mentioned above. Section 5 touches upon more closely related work and directions for future work.

## 2   B*lite*: A 'Lightweight' Variant of WS-BPEL

The language B*lite*[1] is a simplification of WS-BPEL designed around some of its peculiar features like partner links, process termination, message correlation, long-running business transactions and compensation handlers. B*lite* is the result of the usual tension between handiness and expressiveness. Therefore, to keep the design of the language manageable, we intentionally left out other important aspects, including timeouts, event and termination handlers, flow graphs, and sophisticated forms of data handling.

B*lite* provides a formal description of service deployments by only retaining relevant implementation details such as partner links, service definitions and correlation sets. For example, the roles played by service partners in a service interaction are explicitly indicated through *partner links* and *partners*, while such aspects as physical *service binding* described in associated WSDL documents are abstracted away. In request-response interactions, for example, partner links indicate two partners because the requesting partner must provide a callback operation used by the receiving partner to send notifications.

---

[1] We refer the interested reader to [18] for a deeper presentation of which aspects of WS-BPEL are supported by B*lite* and their mapping.

**Table 1.** Syntax of B*lite*

| Basic activities | $b ::= \mathsf{inv}\,\ell^i\,\mathsf{o}\,\bar{x} \mid \mathsf{rcv}\,\ell^r\,\mathsf{o}\,\bar{x} \mid x := e$ | invoke, receive, assign |
| | $\mid \mathsf{empty} \mid \mathsf{throw} \mid \mathsf{exit}$ | empty, throw, exit |
| Structured activities | $a ::= b \mid \mathsf{if}(x)\{a_1\}\{a_2\} \mid \mathsf{while}(x)\,\{a\}$ | basic, conditional, iteration |
| | $\mid a_1\,;a_2 \mid \sum_{j\in J}\mathsf{rcv}\,\ell^r_j\,\mathsf{o}_j\,\bar{x}_j\,;a_j$ | sequence, pick |
| | $\mid a_1\mid a_2 \mid [a\bullet a_f \star a_c]$ | parallel, scope |
| Start activities | $r ::= \mathsf{rcv}\,\ell^r\,\mathsf{o}\,\bar{x} \mid \sum_{j\in J}\mathsf{rcv}\,\ell^r_j\,\mathsf{o}_j\,\bar{x}_j\,;a_j$ | receive, pick |
| | $\mid r\,;a \mid r_1\mid r_2 \mid [r\bullet a_f \star a_c]$ | sequence, parallel, scope |
| Services | $s ::= [r\bullet a_f] \mid \mu \vdash a \mid \mu \vdash a, s$ | definition, instance, multiset |
| Deployments | $d ::= \{s\}_c \mid d_1\|d_2$ | deployment, composition |

Instead, in one-way interactions a partner link indicates a single partner because one of the parties provides all the invoked operations. Besides asynchronous invocation, WS-BPEL also provides a construct for synchronous invocation of remote services. This construct forces the invoker to wait for an answer by the invoked service, that indeed performs a pair of operations *receive-reply*. In B*lite*, this behaviour is rendered in terms of a pair of activities *invoke-receive* executed by the invoker and a pair of activities *receive-invoke* executed by the invoked service.

An important aspect is that, in general, the information provided by partner links is not enough to deliver messages to a service. Indeed, since services are instantiated to serve the received requests, messages need to be delivered not only to the correct partner, but also to the correct instance of the service that the partner provides. To achieve this, WS-BPEL relies on the business data exchanged rather than on specific mechanisms, such as *WS-Addressing* [9] or low-level correlation methods based on SOAP headers. Specifically, B*lite* exploits *correlation variables* that permit to declare the parts of a message that are instance dependent, e.g. *order number* or *client id*, so that a message can be routed to the correct service instance on the basis of the values of the correlation variables it provides, independently of any routing mechanism.

**Syntax.** The syntax of B*lite* is given in Table 1. Services are *structured activities* built from *basic activities* by exploiting operators for conditional choice $\mathsf{if}(\cdot)\{\cdot\}\{\cdot\}$, iteration $\mathsf{while}(\cdot)\{\cdot\}$, sequential composition $\cdot\,;\cdot$, pick $\sum_{j\in J}\mathsf{rcv}\cdots;\cdot$ (i.e., external choice with the constraint that $\mid J\mid > 1$), parallel composition $\cdot\mid\cdot$ and scope $[\cdot \bullet \star \cdot]$. A scope activity $[a \bullet a_f \star a_c]$ groups a primary activity $a$ together with a fault handling activity $a_f$ and a compensation activity $a_c$. *Start activities* $r$ are structured activities that initially can only execute receive activities.

In the sequel, we shall use $\cdot + \cdot$ to abbreviate binary external choice. We let sequence have higher priority (i.e. bind more tightly) than parallel composition and external choice, i.e. $a_1\,;a_2\mid a_3\,;a_4$ stands for $(a_1\,;a_2)\mid(a_3\,;a_4)$ and $a_1\,;a_2 + a_3$ stands for $(a_1\,;a_2) + a_3$. Moreover, we adopt the convention that fault and compensation activities may be omitted from a scope construct, in which case they are intended to be throw and empty, respectively.

Data can be shared among different activities through *shared variables* (ranged over by $x, x', \dots$). The set of manipulable *values* (ranged over by $v, v', \dots$) is left unspecified; however, we assume that it includes the set of *partner names* (ranged over by $p, q, \dots$) and the set of *operation names* (ranged over by $o, o', \dots$). We use $u$ to range over partners and variables and $w$ to range over values and variables. *Expressions* (ranged over by $e, e', \dots$) are left unspecified but contain, at least, values and variables.

Notation $\bar{\cdot}$ stands for tuples of objects, e.g. $\bar{x}$ is a compact notation for denoting the tuple of variables $\langle x_1, \dots, x_h \rangle$ (with $h \geq 0$). We assume that variables in the same tuple are pairwise distinct. The special notation $\tilde{\cdot}$ stands for tuples of one or two objects, e.g. $\tilde{p}$ denotes either $\langle p_1, p_2 \rangle$ or $\langle p_1 \rangle$. Tuples can be constructed using a concatenation operator $\cdot : \cdot$, i.e. $\langle p, u \rangle : \langle x_1, \dots, x_h \rangle$ returns $\langle p, u, x_1, \dots, x_h \rangle$. We will write $Z \triangleq W$ to assign a symbolic name $Z$ to the term $W$.

Partner links $\ell^r$ of receive activities can be either $\langle p, u \rangle$ or $\langle p \rangle$, where $p$ is the partner providing the operation and $u$ is a partner or variable used to send messages in reply. Indeed, service partners used for receiving messages must be known at design-time, while the partners used to send messages in reply may be dynamically determined. Partner links $\ell^i$ within invoke activities can be either $\langle u, p \rangle$ or $\langle u \rangle$, where $u$ is the partner providing the operation and, possibly, $p$ is a partner used to receive messages in reply. Like before, this latter partner must be statically known, thus it cannot be a variable.

*Deployments* are finite compositions of multisets of service *instances* $\mu \vdash a$, containing at most one service *definition* $[r \bullet a_f]$ and associated to a *correlation set* $c$, namely a (possibly empty) set of *correlation variables*. A service definition provides a 'top-level' scope (i.e. a scope that cannot be compensated) and offers a choice of alternative receives among multiple start activities. Each service instance $\mu \vdash a$ has its own (private) state $\mu$. States are (partial) functions mapping variables to values and are written as collections of pairs of the form $\{x \mapsto v\}$. The state obtained by updating $\mu$ with $\mu'$, written as $\mu \circ \mu'$, is inductively defined by: $\mu \circ \mu'(x) = \mu'(x)$ if $x \in dom(\mu')$ (where $dom(\mu)$ denotes the domain of $\mu$) and $\mu(x)$ otherwise. The empty state is denoted by $\emptyset$. In the sequel, we will only consider *well-formed* deployments, i.e. compositions where the sets of partners used for handling requests within different deployments are pairwise disjoint. The rationale is that each service definition has its own partner names and all its instances run within the same deployment where the definition resides.

**Operational Semantics.** The semantics is defined over an enriched syntax that also includes *protected activities* $(\!|a|\!)$, *unsuccessful termination* stop, *messages* $\ll \tilde{p} : o : \bar{v} \gg$ and *scopes* of the form $[a \bullet a_f \star a_c \triangle a_d]$. The first three 'auxiliary' activities are used to replace, respectively, unsuccessfully completed scopes (with their protected default compensation), compulsorily or faultily terminated services (with stop), and invoke activities (with the message they produced). Instead, such scopes as $[a \bullet a_f \star a_c \triangle a_d]$ are dynamically generated to store in $a_d$ the compensation activities of the immediately enclosed scopes that have successfully completed, together with the order in which they must be executed. In the sequel, empty, exit, throw, stop and messages will be called *short-lived* activities and will be generically indicated by sh.

The operational semantics of Blite deployments is defined in terms of a structural congruence and a reduction relation. The *structural congruence*, written $\equiv$, identifies syntactically different terms which intuitively represent the same term. It is defined as

**Table 2.** Structural congruence for B*lite* activities and deployments

| | | | |
|---|---|---|---|
| $a \mid empty \equiv a$ | $empty ; a \equiv a ; empty \equiv a$ | $stop \mid stop \equiv stop$ | $stop ; a \equiv stop$ |

$$(\!(\!(a)\!)\!) \equiv (\!(a)\!) \qquad (\!(sh)\!) \equiv sh \qquad (\!\ll\tilde{p}:o:\bar{v}\gg \mid a)\!) \equiv \ \ll\tilde{p}:o:\bar{v}\gg \mid (\!(a)\!)$$

$$[a \bullet a_f \star a_c] \equiv [a \bullet a_f \star a_c \triangle empty] \qquad (\ll\tilde{p}:o:\bar{v}\gg \mid a_1);a_2 \equiv \ \ll\tilde{p}:o:\bar{v}\gg \mid (a_1 ; a_2)$$

$$[\ll\tilde{p}:o:\bar{v}\gg \mid a \bullet a_f \star a_c \triangle a_d] \equiv \ \ll\tilde{p}:o:\bar{v}\gg \mid [a \bullet a_f \star a_c \triangle a_d] \quad if \ \neg a \Downarrow_{throw}$$

$$\frac{a \equiv a' \quad a_f \equiv a_f' \quad a_c \equiv a_c' \quad a_d \equiv a_d'}{[a \bullet a_f \star a_c \triangle a_d] \equiv [a' \bullet a_f' \star a_c' \triangle a_d']}$$

---

$$\frac{r \equiv r' \quad a_f \equiv a_f'}{\{[r \bullet a_f] , s\}_c \equiv \{s, [r' \bullet a_f']\}_c} \qquad \frac{a \equiv a'}{\{\mu \vdash a, s\}_c \equiv \{s, \mu \vdash a'\}_c}$$

$$d_1 \| d_2 \equiv d_2 \| d_1 \qquad (d_1 \| d_2) \| d_3 \equiv d_1 \| (d_2 \| d_3) \qquad \{\mu \vdash empty , s\}_c \equiv \{s\}_c$$

$$\{\mu \vdash stop , s\}_c \equiv \{s\}_c \qquad \{\mu \vdash empty\}_c \| d \equiv d \qquad \{\mu \vdash stop\}_c \| d \equiv d$$

the least congruence relation induced by a given set of equational laws. In Table 2, we explicitly show, in the upper part, the laws for empty, stop, protected activities, messages and scopes, and, in the lower part, the laws for services and deployments. Standard laws stating, e.g., that sequence is associative, parallel composition is commutative and associative, are omitted. A few observations on the structural laws are in order. Activity empty acts as the identity element both for sequence and parallel composition. Multiple stop in parallel are equivalent to just one stop, moreover stop disables subsequent activities. The protection operator is idempotent, and short-lived activities are implicitly protected, thus messages can go in/out of the scope of a protection operator. Default compensation is initially empty. Messages do not block subsequent activities and scope completion, except when throw is active in the scope (this is checked by predicate $\cdot \Downarrow_{throw}$ that will be explained later on). Structural congruence is extended to scopes, instances and deployments in the obvious way. Moreover, the order in which definition and instances occur within a deployment does not matter, and deployment composition is commutative and associative. Instances like $\mu \vdash$ empty and $\mu \vdash$ stop are terminated and, thus, can be removed. Similarly, deployments only containing terminated instances are terminated too and can be removed.

The *reduction relation* over deployments, written $\rightarrowtail$, exploits a labelled transition relation over structured activities, written $\xrightarrow{\alpha}$, where $\alpha$ is generated by the grammar:

$$\alpha \ ::= \ \tau \ \mid \ x \leftarrow v \ \mid \ !\tilde{p}:o:\bar{v} \ \mid \ ?\ell^r:o:\bar{x} \ \mid \ \boxminus \ \mid \ r \ \mid \ (a)$$

The meaning of labels is as follows: $\tau$ indicates message productions, guard evaluations for conditional and iteration or installation/activation of compensations; $x \leftarrow v$ indicates assignment of value $v$ to variable $x$; $!\tilde{p}:o:\bar{v}$ and $?\ell^r:o:\bar{x}$ indicate execution of invoke and receive activities for operation $o$, where $\tilde{p}$ and $\bar{v}$ match with $\ell^r$ and $\bar{x}$, respectively; $\boxminus$ indicates forced termination of a service instance; $r$ indicates production of a fault

**Table 3.** Basic, auxiliary and structured activities

$$\mu \vdash \mathsf{inv}\, \ell^i \circ \bar{\mathsf{x}} \xrightarrow{\tau} \ll\mu(\ell^i):\mathsf{o}:\mu(\bar{\mathsf{x}})\gg \quad (\text{inv}) \qquad\qquad \mathsf{rcv}\, \ell^r \circ \bar{\mathsf{x}} \xrightarrow{?\,\ell^r:\mathsf{o}:\bar{\mathsf{x}}} \mathsf{empty} \quad (\text{rec})$$

$$\mu \vdash \mathsf{x} := \mathsf{e} \xrightarrow{\mathsf{x}\leftarrow\mu(\mathsf{e})} \mathsf{empty} \quad (\text{asg}) \qquad\qquad\qquad\qquad \mathsf{throw} \xrightarrow{\iota^r} \mathsf{stop} \quad (\text{thr})$$

$$\mathsf{exit} \xrightarrow{\boxplus} \mathsf{stop} \quad (\text{term}) \qquad \ll\tilde{\mathsf{p}}:\mathsf{o}:\bar{\mathsf{v}}\gg \xrightarrow{!\tilde{\mathsf{p}}:\mathsf{o}:\bar{\mathsf{v}}} \mathsf{empty} \quad (\text{msg}) \qquad \dfrac{\mu \vdash \mathsf{a} \xrightarrow{\alpha} \mathsf{a}'}{\mu \vdash (\!|\mathsf{a}|\!) \xrightarrow{\alpha} (\!|\mathsf{a}'|\!)} \ (\text{prot})$$

$$\dfrac{\mu \vdash \mathsf{a}_1 \xrightarrow{\alpha} \mathsf{a}_1'}{\mu \vdash \mathsf{a}_1\,;\mathsf{a}_2 \xrightarrow{\alpha} \mathsf{a}_1'\,;\mathsf{a}_2} \ (\text{seq}) \qquad \sum_{j\in J} \mathsf{rcv}\, \ell_j^r \circ_j \bar{\mathsf{x}}_j\,;\mathsf{a}_j \xrightarrow{?\,\ell_h^r:\mathsf{o}_h:\bar{\mathsf{x}}_h} \mathsf{a}_h\ ,\ h \in J \ (\text{pick})$$

$$\dfrac{\mathsf{a} = \begin{cases} \mathsf{a}_1 & \text{if } \mu(\mathsf{x}) = \mathsf{tt} \\ \mathsf{a}_2 & \text{if } \mu(\mathsf{x}) = \mathsf{ff} \end{cases}}{\mu \vdash \mathsf{if}(\mathsf{x})\{\mathsf{a}_1\}\{\mathsf{a}_2\} \xrightarrow{\tau} \mathsf{a}} \ (\text{if}) \qquad \dfrac{\mathsf{a}' = \begin{cases} \mathsf{a}\,;\mathsf{while}(\mathsf{x})\,\{\mathsf{a}\} & \text{if } \mu(\mathsf{x}) = \mathsf{tt} \\ \mathsf{empty} & \text{if } \mu(\mathsf{x}) = \mathsf{ff} \end{cases}}{\mu \vdash \mathsf{while}(\mathsf{x})\,\{\mathsf{a}\} \xrightarrow{\tau} \mathsf{a}'} \ (\text{while})$$

$$\dfrac{\mu \vdash \mathsf{a}_1 \xrightarrow{\alpha} \mathsf{a}_1' \quad \alpha \notin \{\boxplus, \iota^r\} \quad \neg(\mathsf{a}_2 \Downarrow_{\mathsf{throw}} \vee\, \mathsf{a}_2 \Downarrow_{\mathsf{exit}})}{\mu \vdash \mathsf{a}_1\,|\,\mathsf{a}_2 \xrightarrow{\alpha} \mathsf{a}_1'\,|\,\mathsf{a}_2} \ (\text{par}_1) \qquad \dfrac{\mathsf{a}_1 \xrightarrow{\alpha} \mathsf{a}_1' \quad \alpha \in \{\boxplus, \iota^r\}}{\mathsf{a}_1\,|\,\mathsf{a}_2 \xrightarrow{\alpha} \mathsf{a}_1'\,|\,\mathsf{end}(\mathsf{a}_2)} \ (\text{par}_2)$$

$$[\mathsf{empty} \bullet \mathsf{a}_f \star \mathsf{a}_c \vartriangle \mathsf{a}_d] \xrightarrow{(\mathsf{a}_c)} \mathsf{empty} \ (\text{done}_1) \qquad [\mathsf{stop} \bullet \mathsf{a}_f \star \mathsf{a}_c \vartriangle \mathsf{a}_d] \xrightarrow{\tau} (\!|\mathsf{a}_d\,;\mathsf{a}_f|\!) \ (\text{done}_2)$$

$$\dfrac{\mu \vdash \mathsf{a} \xrightarrow{\alpha} \mathsf{a}' \quad \alpha \notin \{\iota^r, (\mathsf{a}'')\}}{\mu \vdash [\mathsf{a} \bullet \mathsf{a}_f \star \mathsf{a}_c \vartriangle \mathsf{a}_d] \xrightarrow{\alpha} [\mathsf{a}' \bullet \mathsf{a}_f \star \mathsf{a}_c \vartriangle \mathsf{a}_d]} \ (\text{exec})$$

$$\dfrac{\mathsf{a} \xrightarrow{(\mathsf{a}'')} \mathsf{a}'}{[\mathsf{a} \bullet \mathsf{a}_f \star \mathsf{a}_c \vartriangle \mathsf{a}_d] \xrightarrow{\tau} [\mathsf{a}' \bullet \mathsf{a}_f \star \mathsf{a}_c \vartriangle \mathsf{a}''\,;\mathsf{a}_d]} \ (\text{done}_3)$$

$$\dfrac{\mathsf{a} \xrightarrow{\iota^r} \mathsf{a}'}{[\mathsf{a} \bullet \mathsf{a}_f \star \mathsf{a}_c \vartriangle \mathsf{a}_d] \xrightarrow{\tau} [\mathsf{a}' \bullet \mathsf{a}_f \star \mathsf{a}_c \vartriangle \mathsf{a}_d]} \ (\text{fault})$$

signal from inside a scope; (a) indicates successful completion of a scope that can be compensated by the structured activity a.

The relation $\xrightarrow{\alpha}$ is defined by the rules in Table 3 with respect to a state $\mu$, that is omitted when unnecessary (writing a $\xrightarrow{\alpha}$ a' instead of $\mu \vdash$ a $\xrightarrow{\alpha}$ a'). Before commenting the rules, we introduce the auxiliary functions and predicates they exploit. Specifically, the predicates a $\Downarrow_{\mathsf{exit}}$ and a $\Downarrow_{\mathsf{throw}}$ check the ability of a of performing exit or throw, respectively. They are defined inductively on the syntax of activities and act as an homomorphism in all cases, but for conditional choice and iteration for which they hold false, and for the following cases

$$\mathsf{exit} \Downarrow_{\mathsf{exit}} \qquad \mathsf{throw} \Downarrow_{\mathsf{throw}} \qquad \dfrac{\mathsf{a}_1 \Downarrow_{\mathsf{exit}}}{\mathsf{a}_1\,;\mathsf{a}_2 \Downarrow_{\mathsf{exit}}} \qquad \dfrac{\mathsf{a}_1 \Downarrow_{\mathsf{throw}}}{\mathsf{a}_1\,;\mathsf{a}_2 \Downarrow_{\mathsf{throw}}} \qquad \dfrac{\mathsf{a} \Downarrow_{\mathsf{exit}}}{[\mathsf{a} \bullet \mathsf{a}_f \star \mathsf{a}_c \vartriangle \mathsf{a}_d] \Downarrow_{\mathsf{exit}}}$$

The function $\mathsf{end}(\cdot)$, given an activity a, returns the activity obtained by only retaining short-lived and protected activities inside a. It is defined inductively on the syntax of activities, the most significant cases being

**Table 4.** Matching rules / Is there an active receive along $\tilde{p}$ and $o$ matching $\bar{v}$?

$$\text{match}(c, \mu, x, v) = \begin{cases} \{x \mapsto v\} & \text{if } x \notin c \lor (x \in c \land x \notin dom(\mu)) \\ \emptyset & \text{if } x \in c \land \{x \mapsto v\} \in \mu \end{cases}$$

$$\text{match}(c, \mu, v, v) = \emptyset \qquad \frac{\text{match}(c, \mu, w_1, v_1) = \mu' \quad \text{match}(c, \mu, \bar{w}_2, \bar{v}_2) = \mu''}{\text{match}(c, \mu, (w_1, \bar{w}_2), (v_1, \bar{v}_2)) = \mu' \circ \mu''}$$

$$\frac{|\text{match}(c, \mu, \ell^r : o : \bar{x}, \tilde{p} : o : \bar{v})| < n}{\mu \vdash \text{rcv}\, \ell^r\, o\, \bar{x}\,;\, a \Downarrow_{\tilde{p}:o:\bar{v}}^{c,n}} \qquad \frac{\exists h \in J. \; |\text{match}(c, \mu, \ell_h^r : o_h : \bar{x}_h, \tilde{p} : o : \bar{v})| < n}{\mu \vdash \sum_{j \in J} \text{rcv}\, \ell_j^r\, o_j\, \bar{x}_j\,;\, a_j \Downarrow_{\tilde{p}:o:\bar{v}}^{c,n}}$$

$$\frac{\mu \vdash a_1 \Downarrow_{\tilde{p}:o:\bar{v}}^{c,n}}{\mu \vdash a_1\,;\, a_2 \Downarrow_{\tilde{p}:o:\bar{v}}^{c,n}} \qquad \frac{\mu \vdash a_1 \Downarrow_{\tilde{p}:o:\bar{v}}^{c,n} \;\lor\; \mu \vdash a_2 \Downarrow_{\tilde{p}:o:\bar{v}}^{c,n}}{\mu \vdash a_1 \mid a_2 \Downarrow_{\tilde{p}:o:\bar{v}}^{c,n}}$$

$$\frac{\mu \vdash a \Downarrow_{\tilde{p}:o:\bar{v}}^{c,n}}{\mu \vdash (\!|a|\!) \Downarrow_{\tilde{p}:o:\bar{v}}^{c,n}} \qquad \frac{\mu \vdash a \Downarrow_{\tilde{p}:o:\bar{v}}^{c,n}}{\mu \vdash [a \bullet a_f \star a_c \triangle a_d] \Downarrow_{\tilde{p}:o:\bar{v}}^{c,n}} \qquad \frac{\mu \vdash a \Downarrow_{\tilde{p}:o:\bar{v}}^{c,n} \;\lor\; s \Downarrow_{\tilde{p}:o:\bar{v}}^{c,n}}{\mu \vdash a, s \Downarrow_{\tilde{p}:o:\bar{v}}^{c,n}}$$

$$\text{end}(sh) = sh \qquad \text{end}((\!|a|\!)) = (\!|a|\!) \qquad \text{end}(a_1\,;\, a_2) = \text{end}(a_1)$$

$$\text{end}([a \bullet a_f \star a_c \triangle a_d]) = [\text{end}(a) \bullet a_f \star a_c \triangle a_d]$$

where $a_1$ may not be congruent to empty or to $\ll \tilde{p} : o : \bar{v} \gg$, or to parallel compositions of them. In the remaining cases, $\text{end}(\cdot)$ returns stop, except for parallel composition for which it acts as an homomorphism.

We now briefly comment on the rules in Table 3. Rules (inv) and (asg) state that invoke and assign activities can proceed only if their arguments are *closed* expressions (i.e. expressions without uninitialized variables) and can be evaluated (i.e. $\mu(\cdot)$ returns a value). By rule (rec), a receive activity offers an invocable operation along a given partner link. Rules (thr) and (term) report production of fault and forced termination signals, respectively. Auxiliary activities behave as expected: a message can always be delivered (rule (msg)) and the protected activity $(\!|a|\!)$ behaves like a (rule (prot)). Rule (seq) takes care of activities executed sequentially, while rule (pick) permits to choose among alternative receive activities. Rules for conditional choice and iteration ((if) and (while), resp.) are standard. Execution of parallel activities is interleaved (rules (par$_1$) and (par$_2$)), except when a terminate/fault activity can be executed (rule (par$_2$)), in which case all parallel activities must immediately terminate except for short-lived activities and protected fault/compensation handlers. In other words, termination activities throw and exit are executed eagerly.

By rules (done$_1$) and (done$_3$), scope completions can be compensated according to the WS-BPEL *default* compensation behaviour (i.e. in the reverse order of completion) by the immediately enclosing scope. Notably, scopes like $[\text{empty} \bullet a_f \star a_c \triangle a_d]$ have not completed yet and when a scope completes, the default compensation $a_d$ of inner scopes is not passed to the enclosing scope (rule (done$_1$)). Rule (exec) permits to

**Table 5.** Reduction rules for B*lite* deployments (where $t_1 = \ell^r : o : \bar{x}$ and $t_2 = \bar{p} : o : \bar{v}$)

$$
\frac{a_1 \xrightarrow{?t_1} a_1' \quad a_2 \xrightarrow{!t_2} a_2' \quad \mathsf{match}(c_1, \mu_1, t_1, t_2) = \mu_1' \quad \neg(\mu_1 \vdash a_1, s_1 \Downarrow_{t_2}^{c_1, |\mu_1'|})}{\{\mu_1 \vdash a_1, s_1\}_{c_1} \,\|\, \{\mu_2 \vdash a_2, s_2\}_{c_2} \ \succ\!\!\!\rightarrow\ \{\mu_1 \circ \mu_1' \vdash a_1', s_1\}_{c_1} \,\|\, \{\mu_2 \vdash a_2', s_2\}_{c_2}} \ \text{(com)}
$$

$$
\frac{[r \bullet a_f \star \mathsf{empty}] \xrightarrow{?t_1} a_1 \quad a_2 \xrightarrow{!t_2} a_2' \quad \mathsf{match}(c_1, \emptyset, t_1, t_2) = \mu_1 \quad \neg(s_1 \Downarrow_{t_2}^{c_1, |\mu_1|})}{\{[r \bullet a_f], s_1\}_{c_1} \,\|\, \{\mu_2 \vdash a_2, s_2\}_{c_2} \ \succ\!\!\!\rightarrow\ \{\mu_1 \vdash a_1, [r \bullet a_f], s_1\}_{c_1} \,\|\, \{\mu_2 \vdash a_2', s_2\}_{c_2}} \ \text{(new)}
$$

$$
\frac{\mu \vdash a \xrightarrow{x \leftarrow v} a' \quad \mathsf{match}(c, \mu, x, v) = \mu'}{\{\mu \vdash a, s\}_c \ \succ\!\!\!\rightarrow\ \{\mu \circ \mu' \vdash a', s\}_c} \ \text{(var)}
\qquad
\frac{d_1 \ \succ\!\!\!\rightarrow\ d_1'}{d_1 \,\|\, d_2 \ \succ\!\!\!\rightarrow\ d_1' \,\|\, d_2} \ \text{(part)}
$$

$$
\frac{\mu \vdash a \xrightarrow{\alpha} a' \quad \alpha \notin \{?t_1, !t_2, x \leftarrow v\}}{\{\mu \vdash a, s\}_c \ \succ\!\!\!\rightarrow\ \{\mu \vdash a', s\}_c} \ \text{(pass)}
\qquad
\frac{d \equiv d_1 \quad d_1 \ \succ\!\!\!\rightarrow\ d_2 \quad d_2 \equiv d'}{d \ \succ\!\!\!\rightarrow\ d'} \ \text{(cong)}
$$

perform any action of the primary activity a except for fault emission and scope completion. In particular, inner forced terminations are propagated externally outside the scope. Differently from forced termination, faults arising within a scope are managed internally (rule (fault)), and the corresponding handler is installed when the main activity completes (rule (done$_2$)). By rule (done$_2$), default compensation is performed *after* termination of the primary activity and before fault handling. Note that compensation activities do not store any state with them: hence, if the state changes between the compensation being stored and executed, the current state is used.

A few auxiliary functions are also used in the semantics of deployments defined in Table 5. The rules for communication and updating of variables ((com), (new) and (var)) need a mechanism for checking if an assignment of some values $\bar{v}$ to $\bar{w}$ complies with the constraints imposed by the given correlation set $c$ and state $\mu$ and, in case of success, returns a state $\mu'$ for the variables in $\bar{w}$ that records the effect of the assignment. This mechanism is implemented by the function $\mathsf{match}(\cdot, \cdot, \cdot, \cdot)$ defined through the rules in the upper part of Table 4. Notice that $\mathsf{match}(\cdot, \cdot, \cdot, \cdot)$ is undefined when $\bar{w}$ and $\bar{v}$ have different length or when $x \in c$ and $\{x \mapsto v'\} \in \mu$ for some $v' \neq v$ (since the state $\{x \mapsto v\}$ does not comply with $c$ and $\mu$). Rules (com) and (new) also use the auxiliary predicate $s \Downarrow_{\bar{p}:o:\bar{v}}^{c,n}$, defined inductively on the syntax of $s$ in the lower part of Table 4, that checks the ability of $s$ of performing a receive on the operation $o$ exploiting the partner link $\bar{p}$, matching the tuple of values $\bar{v}$ and generating a state with fewer pairs than $n$ that complies with $c$ and the current state of the activity performing the receive.

Finally, we linger on the rules in Table 5. By rule (com), communication can take place when two service instances perform matching receive and invoke activities complying with the correlation set of the receiving instance. Notice that matching covers both partner link $\bar{p}$ and business data $\bar{v}$. Communication generates a state that updates the state of the receiving instance. If more than one matching receive activity is able to process a given invoke, then only the more defined one (i.e. the receive that generates the 'smaller' state) progresses (predicate $\cdot \Downarrow_{\cdot}^{\cdot}$ serves this purpose). This mechanism permits to correlate messages to different service instances and to model the precedence of an existing service instance over a new service instantiation (rule (new), see also the *Multiple start and conflicting receive activities* example in Section 4). In rules (com) and (new), the assumption about *well-formedness* of deployments finds full employment, because it avoids to check every single deployment for possible conflicting receive activities. By rule (new), service instantiation can take place when a service definition and a service instance perform matching receive and invoke activities, respectively. By rule (var), correlation variables cannot be reassigned if the new value does not match with the old one. Moreover, if an assignment takes place, its effect is global to the instance, i.e. the state is updated. By rule (pass), execution of activities different from communications or assignments can always proceed. If part of a larger deployment evolves, the whole composition evolves accordingly (rule (part)) and, as usual, structural congruent deployments have the same reductions (rule (cong)).

## 3 A Shipping Service Scenario

We consider an extended version of the shipping service described in the official specification of WS-BPEL [23] (Section 15.1). This example will allow us to illustrate most of the language features, including correlation sets, shared variables, flow control structures, fault and compensation handling. We will see that, in particular, scope activities are especially useful for modelling fault handling and compensation behaviours, while exit activities are useful to exit from while loops and terminate the customer instance.

The shipping service handles the shipment of orders. From the service point of view, orders are composed of a number of items. The service offers two types of shipment: shipments where the items are held and shipped together and shipments where the items are shipped piecemeal until the order is fulfilled. The service specification in B*lite* is

$$s_{ship} \triangleq [\; \mathsf{rcv} \langle p_{ship}, x_{cust} \rangle o_{req} \langle x_{id}, x_c, x_{items} \rangle \; ;$$
$$\mathsf{if}\,(x_c)\,\{\, \mathsf{inv} \langle x_{cust} \rangle o_{notice} \langle x_{id}, x_{items} \rangle \,\}\{[\, a_{ship} \bullet \mathsf{inv} \langle x_{cust} \rangle o_{err} \langle x_{id}, \text{``sorry''} \rangle \,]\}\,]$$

$$a_{ship} \triangleq [\, a_{priceCalc} \star a_{comp} \,] \; ; x_{shipped} := 0 \; ;$$
$$\mathsf{while}\,(x_{shipped} < x_{items})\,\{$$
$$\quad x_{count} := rand() \; ;$$
$$\quad \mathsf{if}\,(x_{count} \leqslant 0)\,\{\, x_{ratio} := x_{shipped} \,/\, x_{items} \; ; \mathsf{throw}\,\}$$
$$\qquad\qquad \{\, \mathsf{inv} \langle x_{cust} \rangle o_{notice} \langle x_{id}, x_{count} \rangle \; ; x_{shipped} := x_{shipped} + x_{count} \,\}\,\}$$

$p_{ship}$ is the partner associated to the shipping service, $o_{req}$ is the operation used to receive the shipping request, and $\langle x_{id}, x_c, x_{items} \rangle$ is the tuple of variables used for the request shipping message: $x_{id}$ stores the order identifier, that is used to correlate the ship notice(s) with the ship order, $x_c$ stores a boolean indicating whether the order is to be shipped complete or not, and $x_{items}$ stores the number of items in the order. Shipping notices and error messages to customers are sent using the partner stored in $x_{cust}$ and the operations $o_{notice}$ and $o_{err}$, respectively. A notice message is a tuple composed of the order identifier and the number of items in the shipping notice. When partial shipment is acceptable, $x_{shipped}$ is used to record the number of items already shipped.

Our example extends that in [23] by allowing the service to generate a fault in case the shipping company has ended the stock of items (this is modelled by function $rand()$

returning an integer less than or equal to 0). The fault is handled by sending an error message to the customer and by compensating the inner scope, that has already completed successfully. Function $rand()$ returns a random integer number and represents an internal interaction with a back-end system. For the sake of simplicity, we do not further describe this interaction. Moreover, we do not show services $a_{priceCalc}$ and $a_{comp}$. Basically, the former calculates the shipping price according to the value assigned to $x_{items}$ and sends the result to the accounts department. The latter is the corresponding compensation activity, that sends information about the non-shipped items to the accounts department and sends a refund to the customer according to the ratio (stored in $x_{ratio}$) between the shipped items (stored in $x_{shipped}$) and the required ones (stored in $x_{items}$). Now, consider the following composition of a deployment containing the shipping service definition and a deployment containing a customer's invocation of the service

$$\{ s_{ship} \}_{\{x_{id}\}} \| \{\mu_{cust} \vdash \text{inv} \langle p_{ship}, p_{cust} \rangle o_{req} \langle y_{id}, y_c, y_{items} \rangle ; a_{cust}\}_{\{y_{id}\}}$$

where $\mu_{cust} = \{y_{id} \mapsto 123, y_c \mapsto \text{ff}, y_{items} \mapsto 50\}$ and $a_{cust}$ is the following term

$$y_{shipped} := 0 ; \text{while} (y_{shipped} < y_{items}) \{$$
$$\text{rcv} \langle p_{cust} \rangle o_{notice} \langle y_{id}, y_{count} \rangle ; y_{shipped} := y_{shipped} + y_{count}$$
$$+ \text{rcv} \langle p_{cust} \rangle o_{err} \langle y_{id}, y_{err} \rangle ; \text{exit} \}$$

In the first computational step, the customer's invocation is consumed and an instance of the shipping service is created. Thus the overall computation becomes

$$\{ s_{ship}, \mu_{ship} \vdash [ a_{ship} \bullet \text{inv} \langle x_{cust} \rangle o_{err} \langle x_{id}, \text{"}sorry\text{"} \rangle ] \}_{\{x_{id}\}} \| \{\mu_{cust} \vdash a_{cust}\}_{\{y_{id}\}}$$

where $\mu_{ship}$ is $\{x_{id} \mapsto 123, x_c \mapsto \text{ff}, x_{items} \mapsto 50, x_{cust} \mapsto p_{cust}\}$. The computation can now go on, e.g., with the inner scope $[a_{priceCalc} \star a_{comp}]$ that successfully completes while its continuation fails, e.g., $rand()$ returns an integer less than or equal to 0.

## 4   Evaluations of BPEL Engines

We now present some illustrative examples and use them to test and compare the behaviour of three well-known free WS-BPEL engines, namely Oracle BPEL Process Manager [3], ActiveBPEL Engine [1], and Apache ODE [2] (the latter two are open source projects, whereas Oracle BPEL is distributed under the Oracle Technology Network Developer License). For our evaluation, we have taken into account fundamental features of WS-BPEL that remained unchanged since its initial version. Due to lack of space, we refer the interested reader to [18] for further details and examples.

*Example 1 (Message correlation).* For our simplification purposes, tuples can be used to represent XML messages by adopting the convention that the first field of each tuple acts as a 'tag' (like originally proposed in the coordination language Linda [12]). Tuples plus correlation variables can be exploited to correlate, by means of their same contents, different service interactions logically forming a same 'session'. For example, consider the two uncorrelated receive activities of the following service definition:

$$\{\,[\,\text{rcv}\,\langle p\rangle\,o\,\langle x\rangle\,;\,\text{rcv}\,\langle p\rangle\,o'\,\langle y\rangle\,;\,a\,]\,\}_{\{x,y\}}$$

The fact that the messages for operations $o$ and $o'$ are uncorrelated implies that, e.g., if there are concurrent instances then successive invocations for the same instance can be mixed up and be delivered to different instances. If one thinks it right, this behavior can be prevented simply by correlating consecutive messages by means of some correlation data, e.g. the first received value as in the following modified service definition:

$$\{\,[\,\text{rcv}\,\langle p\rangle\,o\,\langle x\rangle\,;\,\text{rcv}\,\langle p\rangle\,o'\,\langle x,y\rangle\,;\,a\,]\,\}_{\{x,y\}}$$

A particular case is when the two previous receives are identical, i.e. when we have:

$$\{\,[\,\text{rcv}\,\langle p\rangle\,o\,\langle x\rangle\,;\,\text{rcv}\,\langle p\rangle\,o\,\langle x\rangle\,;\,a\,]\,\}_{\{x\}}$$

Note that the WS-BPEL specification permits to consecutively receive a same request on a specific partner and operation ([23], Section 10.4), and does not mention that possible conflicting receives could arise. To illustrate, include a client process as follows:

$$\{\,[\,\text{rcv}\,\langle p\rangle\,o\,\langle x\rangle\,;\,\text{rcv}\,\langle p\rangle\,o\,\langle x\rangle\,;\,a\,]\,\}_{\{x\}}\|\{\,\{y\mapsto v\}\vdash\text{inv}\,\langle p\rangle\,o\,\langle y\rangle\,;\,\text{inv}\,\langle p\rangle\,o\,\langle y\rangle\,\}_\emptyset$$

The client process performs two requests that, according to the semantics of B*lite*, trigger only one instantiation of the service. Thus, the only possible evolution leads to

$$\{\,[\,\text{rcv}\,\langle p\rangle\,o\,\langle x\rangle\,;\,\text{rcv}\,\langle p\rangle\,o\,\langle x\rangle\,;\,a\,]\,,\,\{x\mapsto v\}\vdash[a]\,\}_{\{x\}}$$

Differently from B*lite*, when executing this example, Oracle BPEL creates two instances, one for each received request. An important consequence, and an unexpected side effect, is that the created instances are in conflict and, then, will never be executed. Instead, ActiveBPEL and Apache ODE, just like B*lite*, exploit the received data to correlate two consecutive receives and, thus, prevent creation of a new instance. However, if the client performs a third invocation $\text{inv}\,\langle p\rangle\,o\,\langle y\rangle$, Apache ODE is not able to serve this last request, while ActiveBPEL behaves properly.

*Example 2 (Persistent messages).* In service-oriented systems communication paradigms are usually asynchronous (mainly for scalability reasons [5]), in the sense that there may be an arbitrary delay between the sending and the receiving of a message, the ordering in which messages are received may differ from that in which they were produced, and a sender cannot determine if and when a sent message will be received. We can guess from [23], Section 10.4, that this is also the case of WS-BPEL. To illustrate, consider the following B*lite* term:

$$\{\,[\,\text{rcv}\,\langle p\rangle\,o_1\,\langle x\rangle\,;\,\text{rcv}\,\langle p\rangle\,o_2\,\langle x,z\rangle\,;\,a\,]\,\}_{\{x\}}$$
$$\|\{\,\{y_1\mapsto v,y_2\mapsto v'\}\vdash\text{inv}\,\langle p\rangle\,o_2\,\langle y_1,y_2\rangle\,;\,\text{inv}\,\langle p\rangle\,o_1\,\langle y_1\rangle\,\}_\emptyset$$

After the message $\ll\langle p\rangle:o_2:\langle v,v'\rangle\gg$ is produced by the first invoke activity, a service instance is created as a result of consumption of the message produced by the second invoke activity.

$$\{ [\operatorname{rcv} \langle p \rangle \, o_1 \, \langle x \rangle ; \operatorname{rcv} \langle p \rangle \, o_2 \, \langle x, z \rangle ; a] \}_{\{x\}}$$
$$\| \{ \{y_1 \mapsto v, y_2 \mapsto v'\} \vdash \ll \langle p \rangle : o_2 : \langle v, v' \rangle \gg \, | \operatorname{inv} \langle p \rangle \, o_1 \, \langle y_1 \rangle \}_\emptyset \rightarrowtail$$
$$\{ [\operatorname{rcv} \langle p \rangle \, o_1 \, \langle x \rangle ; \operatorname{rcv} \langle p \rangle \, o_2 \, \langle x, z \rangle ; a], \{x \mapsto v\} \vdash [\operatorname{rcv} \langle p \rangle \, o_2 \, \langle x, z \rangle ; a] \}_{\{x\}}$$
$$\| \{ \{y_1 \mapsto v, y_2 \mapsto v'\} \vdash \ll \langle p \rangle : o_2 : \langle v, v' \rangle \gg \}_\emptyset$$

Now, the first produced message is not considered expired and, thus, can be consumed by the newly created service instance.

$$\{ [\operatorname{rcv} \langle p \rangle \, o_1 \, \langle x \rangle ; \operatorname{rcv} \langle p \rangle \, o_2 \, \langle x, z \rangle ; a], \{x \mapsto v, z \mapsto v'\} \vdash [a] \}_{\{x\}}$$
$$\| \{ \{y_1 \mapsto v, y_2 \mapsto v'\} \vdash \operatorname{empty} \}_\emptyset$$

All the examined BPEL engines 'tacitly' agree with this communication paradigm, although no explicit requirement is reported in the WS-BPEL specification.

*Example 3 (Multiple start and conflicting receive activities).* The WS-BPEL specification permits to use multiple start activities ([23], Section 10.4), however it is not clear how conflicting receive activities must be handled. The following example shows that conflicting receive activities can be enabled when a service definition with multiple start activities is instantiated. Consider the three composed deployments

$$\{ [ (\operatorname{rcv} \langle p_1 \rangle \, o \, \langle x \rangle \, | \operatorname{rcv} \langle p_2 \rangle \, o \, \langle x, z \rangle ) ; a] \}_{\{x\}} \| \{ \{y \mapsto v\} \vdash \operatorname{inv} \langle p_1 \rangle \, o \, \langle y \rangle \}_\emptyset$$
$$\| \{ \{y_1 \mapsto v, y_2 \mapsto v'\} \vdash \operatorname{inv} \langle p_2 \rangle \, o \, \langle y_1, y_2 \rangle \}_\emptyset$$

After message $\ll \langle p_1 \rangle : o : \langle v \rangle \gg$, produced by invocation $\operatorname{inv} \langle p_1 \rangle \, o \, \langle y \rangle$, has been processed by $\operatorname{rcv} \langle p_1 \rangle \, o \, \langle x \rangle$, the overall composition becomes

$$\{ [ (\operatorname{rcv} \langle p_1 \rangle \, o \, \langle x \rangle \, | \operatorname{rcv} \langle p_2 \rangle \, o \, \langle x, z \rangle ) ; a], \{x \mapsto v\} \vdash [\operatorname{rcv} \langle p_2 \rangle \, o \, \langle x, z \rangle ; a] \}_{\{x\}}$$
$$\| \{ \{y_1 \mapsto v, y_2 \mapsto v'\} \vdash \operatorname{inv} \langle p_2 \rangle \, o \, \langle y_1, y_2 \rangle \}_\emptyset$$

Now, the definition and the instance of the service compete for receiving the same message sent by the invoke activity $\operatorname{inv} \langle p_2 \rangle \, o \, \langle y_1, y_2 \rangle$. In cases like this, the WS-BPEL specification requires that the invocation is only delivered to the existing instance, which prevents creation of a new instance. In fact, in B*lite* the above term can only reduce to

$$\{ [ (\operatorname{rcv} \langle p_1 \rangle \, o \, \langle x \rangle \, | \operatorname{rcv} \langle p_2 \rangle \, o \, \langle x, z \rangle ) ; a], \{x \mapsto v, z \mapsto v'\} \vdash [a] \}_{\{x\}}$$

In case of conflicting receives, the WS-BPEL specification document prescribes to raise the standard fault bpel:conflictingReceive. For example, this situation readily occurs when a service exploits multiple start activities, because of race conditions on incoming messages among the service definition and the created instances. However, in such cases, it does not seem fair to raise a fault because the correlation data contained within each incoming message should be sufficient to decide if the message has to be routed to a specific instance or to the service definition. This is indeed a tricky question. For example, Oracle BPEL raises the fault bpel:conflictingReceive also in these situations. ActiveBPEL behaves differently and, just like B*lite*, exploits correlation to restrict instantiation to one service instance, whereas multiple start activities are not currently supported by Apache ODE.

*Example 4 (Scheduling for parallel execution).* While using the BPEL engines, we have also experimented that they implement the parallel operator in a different manner. For example, in WS-BPEL, the expected behaviour of the following term:

$$x_1 := v_1 \mid x_2 := v_2 \mid x_3 := v_3$$

is that the three assignments are executed in an unpredictable order that may change in different executions. In fact, only Apache ODE implements this semantics, while the other two engines execute the assignments in an order fixed in advance (that is from left to right in case of ActiveBPEL and from right to left in case of Oracle BPEL).

*Example 5 (Forced termination).* The WS-BPEL specification ([23], Section 12.6) says: "The <sequence> and <flow> constructs *must* be terminated by terminating their behavior and applying termination to all nested activities currently active within them". This definition is ambiguous because it is not clear what "nested activities currently active" means in case of termination due to <exit> or <throw> activities. For example, Oracle BPEL interprets the behaviour end($a_1$ ; $a_2$) as it were $a_1$ ; $a_2$ if it is prompted by activity <exit>, and as end($a_1$), if it is prompted by activity <throw>. ActiveBPEL is more faithful to WS-BPEL and B*lite* for which all currently running activities are terminated as soon as possible without any fault handling or compensation ([23], Section 10.10). But, differently from B*lite*, ActiveBPEL does not distinguish short-lived from basic activities and makes them terminate in the same way. Finally, Apache ODE is compliant with B*lite*, because function end($\cdot$) retains short-lived activities.

*Example 6 (Eager execution of termination activities).* As previously stated, in order to be compliant with the WS-BPEL requirement stating that termination activities must end immediately all currently running activities ([23], Section 10.10), in the semantics of B*lite* activities throw and exit have higher priority than the remaining ones. E.g., consider the following structured activity:

$$a \triangleq \mathsf{throw} \mid \mathsf{sh}_1 \ ; \ \mathsf{sh}_2 \mid \mathsf{rcv}\,\langle p \rangle \, o \, \langle x \rangle \ ; \ a'$$

In B*lite*, by executing the activity throw, this term can only reduce to:

$$\mathsf{stop} \mid \mathsf{end}(\mathsf{sh}_1 \ ; \ \mathsf{sh}_2) \mid \mathsf{end}(\mathsf{rcv}\,\langle p \rangle \, o \, \langle x \rangle \ ; \ a') \equiv \mathsf{stop} \mid \mathsf{sh}_1$$

While ActiveBPEL agrees with this requirement, Oracle BPEL and Apache ODE do not implement any prioritized behavior for termination activities. Thus, for example, the above term a can evolve by firstly performing the activity $\mathsf{sh}_1$ and then the activity throw; this way, the activity $\mathsf{sh}_2$ is not terminated.

*Example 7 (Protected handlers).* The following structured activity consists of a top-level scope with two inner parallel scopes, one of which being a sequence of two scopes.

$$a \triangleq [ \, ( \, [ \, [ \, a_1 \bullet \mathsf{throw} \star a_c ] ; [ \, a_2 \bullet \mathsf{throw} \star \mathsf{empty} \, ] \bullet \mathsf{throw} \star \mathsf{empty} \, ]$$
$$\mid [ \, a_3 \bullet \mathsf{throw} \star \mathsf{empty} \, ] ) \bullet \mathsf{empty} \, ]$$

For the sake of presentation, suppose that $a_1$ performs an assignment and completes, say $a_1 \triangleq x_1 := v_1$, while both activities $a_2$ and $a_3$ perform an assignment and reduce to the throw activity, say $a_i \triangleq x_i := v_i$ ; throw for $i = 2, 3$. Now, consider a deployment containing a service instance $\mu \vdash a$ such that variables $x_1$, $x_2$ and $x_3$ are not in $dom(\mu)$. A possible computation is the following one

$$\{\mu \vdash a\}_c \xrightarrow{\;(1)\;} \{\mu_1 \vdash [\,(\,[\,[\text{empty} \bullet \text{throw} \star a_c\,]\,;$$
$$[\,a_2 \bullet \text{throw} \star \text{empty}\,] \bullet \text{throw} \star \text{empty} \,\triangle\, \text{empty}\,]$$
$$|\,[\,a_3 \bullet \text{throw} \star \text{empty}\,]\,) \bullet \text{empty} \star \text{empty}\,]\}_c$$

$$\xrightarrow{\;(2)\;} \{\mu_1 \vdash [\,(\,[\,[\,a_2 \bullet \text{throw} \star \text{empty}\,] \bullet \text{throw} \star \text{empty} \,\triangle\, (a_c\,;\text{empty})\,]$$
$$|\,[\,a_3 \bullet \text{throw} \star \text{empty}\,]\,) \bullet \text{empty} \star \text{empty}\,]\}_c$$

$$\xrightarrow{\;(3)\;} \{\mu_2 \vdash [\,(\,[\,[\text{throw} \bullet \text{throw} \star \text{empty}\,] \bullet \text{throw} \star \text{empty} \,\triangle\, a_c\,]$$
$$|\,[\,a_3 \bullet \text{throw} \star \text{empty}\,]\,) \bullet \text{empty} \star \text{empty}\,]\}_c$$

$$\xrightarrow{\;(4)\;} \{\mu_2 \vdash [\,(\,[\,[\text{stop} \bullet \text{throw} \star \text{empty}\,] \bullet \text{throw} \star \text{empty} \,\triangle\, a_c\,]$$
$$|\,[\,a_3 \bullet \text{throw} \star \text{empty}\,]\,) \bullet \text{empty} \star \text{empty}\,]\}_c$$

$$\xrightarrow{\;(5)\;} \{\mu_2 \vdash [\,(\,[\,[\,\llparenthesis\text{throw}\rrparenthesis \bullet \text{throw} \star \text{empty} \,\triangle\, a_c\,]$$
$$|\,[\,a_3 \bullet \text{throw} \star \text{empty}\,]\,) \bullet \text{empty} \star \text{empty}\,]\}_c$$

$$\xrightarrow{\;(6)\;} \{\mu_2 \vdash [\,(\,[\,[\,\llparenthesis\text{stop}\rrparenthesis \bullet \text{throw} \star \text{empty} \,\triangle\, a_c\,]$$
$$|\,[\,a_3 \bullet \text{throw} \star \text{empty}\,]\,) \bullet \text{empty} \star \text{empty}\,]\}_c$$

$$\xrightarrow{\;(7)\;} \{\mu_2 \vdash [\,(\,(\llparenthesis a_c\,;\text{throw}\rrparenthesis \,|\, [\,a_3 \bullet \text{throw} \star \text{empty}\,]\,) \bullet \text{empty} \star \text{empty}\,]\}_c$$

$$\xrightarrow{\;(8)\;} \{\mu_3 \vdash [\,(\,(\llparenthesis a_c\,;\text{throw}\rrparenthesis \,|\, [\,\text{throw} \bullet \text{throw} \star \text{empty}\,]\,) \bullet \text{empty} \star \text{empty}\,]\}_c$$

$$\xrightarrow{\;(9)\;} \{\mu_3 \vdash [\,(\,(\llparenthesis a_c\,;\text{throw}\rrparenthesis \,|\, [\,\text{stop} \bullet \text{throw} \star \text{empty}\,]\,) \bullet \text{empty} \star \text{empty}\,]\}_c$$

$$\xrightarrow{\;(10)\;} \{\mu_3 \vdash [\,(\,(\llparenthesis a_c\,;\text{throw}\rrparenthesis \,|\, \llparenthesis\text{throw}\rrparenthesis\,) \bullet \text{empty} \star \text{empty}\,]\}_c$$

$$\xrightarrow{\;(11)\;} \{\mu_3 \vdash [\,(\,(\,\text{end}(\llparenthesis a_c\,;\text{throw}\rrparenthesis) \,|\, \llparenthesis\text{stop}\rrparenthesis\,) \bullet \text{empty} \star \text{empty}\,]\}_c$$
$$\equiv \{\mu_3 \vdash [\,(\,(\llparenthesis a_c\,;\text{throw}\rrparenthesis \,|\, \text{stop}\,) \bullet \text{empty} \star \text{empty}\,]\}_c$$

where the reductions are labelled by numbers indicating the corresponding steps. When $a_1$ completes, the compensation handler $a_c$ is inserted into the default compensation activities of its enclosing scope (1-2). When execution of $a_2$ rises a fault, then the fault is caught by the corresponding fault handler (3-7) that activates the default compensation $a_c$ ; throw. This activity is protected, by using the auxiliary operator $\llparenthesis \cdot \rrparenthesis$, from the effect of the forced termination triggered by the parallel scope [ $a_3$ • throw ★ empty ] (7-11).

We end by remarking two aspects of the compensation mechanism prescribed by the WS-BPEL specification ([23], Sections 12.5 and 10.10). First, compensation handlers of faultily terminated scopes should not be installed. Second, fault and compensation handlers should not be affected by the activities causing the forced termination. However, both aspects are not faithfully implemented in Oracle BPEL, while ActiveBPEL and Apache ODE meet these specific requirements and adhere to B*lite* semantics.

*Evaluation Results.* The results of our experiments, summarized in Table 6, point out that the engines we have experimented with are not fully compliant with B*lite*, that, in our opinion, faithfully represents the intended semantics of WS-BPEL. This is also a consequence of the lack of a formal semantics for WS-BPEL, that would have disambiguated the intricate and complex features of the language. We believe that B*lite*, and

**Table 6.** B*lite* compliance

| | Oracle BPEL | ActiveBPEL | Apache ODE |
|---|:---:|:---:|:---:|
| Message correlation (Ex. 1) | + | + | + |
| Consecutive conflicting receives (Ex. 1) | − | + | +/− |
| Persistent messages (Ex. 2) | + | + | + |
| Multiple start (Ex. 3) | − | + | − |
| Parallel execution (Ex. 4) | − | − | + |
| Short-lived activities (Ex. 5) | + | − | + |
| Function end(·) (Ex. 5) | − | + | + |
| Eager execution (Ex. 6) | − | + | − |
| Protected handlers (Ex. 7) | − | + | + |
| Compensation handler installation (Ex. 7) | − | + | + |

works with similar goals, other than as a guide for the development of faithful implementations since the early stages, can be also used to make future versions of existing implementations more compatible.

## 5   Concluding Remarks

We have introduced B*lite*, a significative and non-redundant fragment of WS-BPEL, designed around some of its peculiar features like partner links, process termination, message correlation, long-running business transactions and compensation handlers. Our formal presentation of B*lite* helps clarifying some undefined/ambiguous aspects of the WS-BPEL specification. For example, we have formalized the close relationship between multiple start activities and race conditions. By means of several examples, we have also pointed out that the behaviour of three of the most used free BPEL engines (namely, ActiveBPEL, Apache ODE and Oracle BPEL Process Manager) differs from each other and from the WS-BPEL specification in many important aspects.

Several formal semantics of WS-BPEL were proposed in the literature (for an overview see [24]). Many of these efforts aim at formalizing a *complete* semantics for WS-BPEL using Petri nets [24,19], but do not cover such dynamical aspects as service instantiation and message correlation. Other works [11,14] using process calculi focus instead on small and relatively simple subsets of WS-BPEL. Another bunch of related works [15,20] formalize the semantics of WS-BPEL by encoding parts of the language into more foundational orchestration languages. Our work differs for the number of features that are simultaneously modelled and for the fact that dynamical aspects are fully taken into account. Recently, a very general and flexible framework for error recovery has been introduced in [13]; this framework extends [14] with dynamic compensation, modelling in particular the dependency between fault handling and the request-response communication pattern.

Some other relevant related works are [7,6,4]. In the first two, the authors propose a formal approach to model compensation in transactional calculi and present a detailed comparison with [8]. The third is an extension of the asynchronous $\pi$-calculus with long-running (scoped) transactions. The language has a scope construct which plays a role similar to the scope activity presented in our semantics, but it is not aimed at capturing the order in which compensations should be activated. On the contrary, the semantics we propose faithfully captures the intended semantics of WS-BPEL, thus for example compensations are activated in the reverse order w.r.t. the order of completion of the original scopes.

Our programme is to provide a framework for the design and the verification of WS-BPEL applications that supports analysis of service orchestration. As a further step in this direction, in [18] we have also defined an encoding from B*lite* to COWS [16], a calculus for orchestration of web services that we recently proposed, and we have formalized the properties enjoyed by the encoding. By relying on these results, we plan to devise methods to analyze B*lite* specifications (and the WS-BPEL applications they model) by exploiting the analytical tools already developed for COWS, such as the stochastic extension defined in [25] that enables quantitative reasoning on service behaviours, the type system introduced in [17] that permits to check confidentiality properties, and the logic and model checker presented in [10] that permits expressing and checking functional properties of services.

**Acknowledgements.** We thank the anonymous referees for their useful comments.

# References

1. ActiveBPEL 4.1 (September 2007), `http://www.active-endpoints.com`
2. Apache ODE 1.1.1 (August 2007), `http://ode.apache.org`
3. Oracle BPEL Process Manager 10.1.3 (December 2007), `http://www.oracle.com/technology/bpel`
4. Bocchi, L., Laneve, C., Zavattaro, G.: A calculus for long-running transactions. In: Najm, E., Nestmann, U., Stevens, P. (eds.) FMOODS 2003. LNCS, vol. 2884, pp. 124–138. Springer, Heidelberg (2003)
5. Brown, A., Johnston, S., Kelly, K.: Using service-oriented architecture and component-based development to build web service applications, TR, Rational Software Corp. (2002)
6. Bruni, R., Butler, M.J., Ferreira, C., Hoare, C.A.R., Melgratti, H.C., Montanari, U.: Comparing two approaches to compensable flow composition. In: Abadi, M., de Alfaro, L. (eds.) CONCUR 2005. LNCS, vol. 3653, pp. 383–397. Springer, Heidelberg (2005)
7. Bruni, R., Melgratti, H.C., Montanari, U.: Theoretical foundations for compensations in flow composition languages. In: POPL, pp. 209–220. ACM, New York (2005)
8. Butler, M.J., Ferreira, C.: An operational semantics for StAC, a language for modelling long-running business transactions. In: De Nicola, R., Ferrari, G.L., Meredith, G. (eds.) COORDINATION 2004. LNCS, vol. 2949, pp. 87–104. Springer, Heidelberg (2004)
9. Box, D.: et al. Web services addressing. W3C member submission, August 10 (2004)
10. Fantechi, A., Gnesi, S., Lapadula, A., Mazzanti, F., Pugliese, R., Tiezzi, F.: A model checking approach for verifying COWS specifications. In: FASE 2008. LNCS, vol. 4961. Springer, Heidelberg (2008)
11. Geguang, P., Xiangpeng, Z., Shuling, W., Zongyan, Q.: Semantics of BPEL4WS-like fault and compensation handling. In: Fitzgerald, J.S., Hayes, I.J., Tarlecki, A. (eds.) FM 2005. LNCS, vol. 3582, pp. 350–365. Springer, Heidelberg (2005)
12. Gelernter, D.: Generative communication in Linda. ACM TOPLAS 7(1), 80–112 (1985)

13. Guidi, C., Lanese, I., Montesi, F., Zavattaro, G.: On the interplay between fault handling and request-response service invocations. In: ACSD, IEEE CS Press, Los Alamitos (to appear, 2008)
14. Guidi, C., Lucchi, R., Gorrieri, R., Busi, N., Zavattaro, G.: SOCK: a calculus for service oriented computing. In: Dan, A., Lamersdorf, W. (eds.) ICSOC 2006. LNCS, vol. 4294, pp. 327–338. Springer, Heidelberg (2006)
15. Laneve, C., Zavattaro, G.: Foundations of web transactions. In: Sassone, V. (ed.) FOSSACS 2005. LNCS, vol. 3441, pp. 282–298. Springer, Heidelberg (2005)
16. Lapadula, A., Pugliese, R., Tiezzi, F.: A Calculus for Orchestration of Web Services. In: De Nicola, R. (ed.) ESOP 2007. LNCS, vol. 4421, pp. 33–47. Springer, Heidelberg (2007)
17. Lapadula, A., Pugliese, R., Tiezzi, F.: Regulating data exchange in service oriented applications. In: Arbab, F., Sirjani, M. (eds.) FSEN 2007. LNCS, vol. 4767, pp. 223–239. Springer, Heidelberg (2007)
18. Lapadula, A., Pugliese, R., Tiezzi, F.: A formal account of WS-BPEL (full version), Technical report, Univ. Firenze (2008), http://rap.dsi.unifi.it/cows
19. Lohmann, N.: A feature-complete Petri net semantics for WS-BPEL 2.0. In: Web Services and Formal Methods. LNCS, vol. 4937, pp. 77–91. Springer, Heidelberg (2008)
20. Mazzara, M., Lucchi, R.: A pi-calculus based semantics for WS-BPEL. Journal of Logic and Algebraic Programming 70(1), 96–118 (2006)
21. Meredith, L.G., Bjorg, S.: Contracts and types. Commun. ACM 46(10), 41–47 (2003)
22. OASIS WSBPEL TC. WS-BPEL issues list, http://www.oasis-open.org/committees/download.php/20228/WS_BPEL_issues_list.html
23. OASIS WSBPEL TC. Web Services Business Process Execution Language Version 2.0 (April 2007), http://docs.oasis-open.org/wsbpel/2.0/OS/wsbpel-v2.0-OS.html
24. Ouyang, C., van der Aalst, W.M.P., Breutel, S., Dumas, M., ter Hofstede, A.H.M., Verbeek, H.M.W.: Formal semantics and analysis of control flow in WS-BPEL (revised version). Technical report, BPM Center Report (2005), http://www.BPMcenter.org
25. Prandi, D., Quaglia, P.: Stochastic COWS. In: Krämer, B.J., Lin, K.-J., Narasimhan, P. (eds.) ICSOC 2007. LNCS, vol. 4749, pp. 245–256. Springer, Heidelberg (2007)
26. van Breugel, F., Koshkina, M.: Models and verification of BPEL. Technical report (2006), http://www.cse.yorku.ca/~franck/research/drafts/tutorial.pdf

# How to Infer Finite Session Types in a Calculus of Services and Sessions

Leonardo Gaetano Mezzina

IMT Lucca, Institute for Advanced Studies, Italy
leonardo.mezzina@imtlucca.it

**Abstract.** The notion of session is fundamental in service oriented applications, as it separates interactions between different instances of the same service, and it groups together basic units of work. Together with sessions, session types were introduced to track the type of the values exchanged in each session. In this paper we propose an algorithm to infer a restricted form of session types and we show that the problem is not directly related to the unification since we are in a context with duality in interactions. The discussion is based on a SCC-like [3] calculus adapted to fit session types. The calculus simplifies the discussion imposing strong syntactic constraints, but the ideas and the proposed algorithm can be adopted to study the type inference for other session oriented calculi. Also an OCaml prototype of the algorithm has been developed to show its feasibility.

## 1 Introduction

Sessions are used to structure interactions among parties resulting in a clearer and bug free way to write communicating programs. Session oriented calculi [13,14,20,12] were proposed to reason formally about communication patterns that encompass the simple *one-way* remote procedure call [7,8,9,2] but also allow for more sophisticated message exchanges.

Since the $\pi$-calculus is the *lingua franca* for expressing concurrent processes, we can translate sessions in $\pi$-calculus, representing them like a freshly created channel (a session channel) used by both the client and the particular service instance (created to serve the client) as an exchanging context.

However, from the type system point of view no (interesting) session channel is well typed under the simply typed $\pi$-calculus [17] which allows to transmit only a single type of message over each channel. Thus, session types were introduced to type session channels so as to describe both sequences (of input/output) and choices (internal/external) taking place on a session side.

The duality of session types also changes the way to consider the type inference problem which is no longer directly related to the unification as for the simply typed $\pi$-calculus. In fact, in the simply typed $\pi$-calculus we consider both input and output actions (which are dual) to reconstruct the channel sort, that is, sorting says what kind of values each channel can input and output. For example, the process $xc \mid \overline{x}5$ uses the channel $x$ to input values of an unknown type (the

D. Lea and G. Zavattaro (Eds.): COORDINATION 2008, LNCS 5052, pp. 216–231, 2008.

same as $c$), say $\alpha_1$, and to output an integer value. Here we can safely substitute $\alpha_1$ with $int$ and judge this channel of type $chan(int)$; i.e. a channel used to exchange integer values. However, in a dual interaction we independently need the type of each side of the communication and, for example, the type of $x$ become $?(int)$ (input of an integer) for the first side of the parallel and $!(int)$ (output of an integer) for the second side. This separation easily allows to judge that the interaction is safe, since each side performs the dual action with respect to the other side. It is worth noticing that the substitution $\{\alpha_1 \mapsto int\}$ still holds. The reasoning can be iterated if we want to capture types expressing sequence of inputs and outputs; e.g., $xc.\overline{x}c \mid \overline{x}5.xy$ then we have both types $?(int).!(int)$ and $!(int).?(int)$ in which we unified the type of the first value exchanged in the sequence and the type of the second value exchanged in the sequence. Similar considerations are made for the type inference algorithm described in [10].

Furthermore, session types extend basic sequences of actions adding both external and internal choices which can be considered as a set of offered options exposed by means of labels and as a selection among a set of options respectively. Unfortunately, the expressivity introduced by choices makes the type inference problem not directly related to the unification. First of all, the labels of each choice are unordered and also we would accept the comparison between an internal choice that offers more options and its external choice counterpart; that is, the "unification" could be possible if a part chooses only some of the options offered by the dual part. Given this, one may argue that the problem is similar to what is described in [19,18] for an object calculus and successfully solved by means of kinds. However, we think that the use of kinds for session types is not trivial since each session may offer multiple choices at different levels of nesting.

Instead, we tackle the problem by introducing another kind of constraints, indicated by $\bowtie$, between two dual session types. Moreover, an algorithm is proposed to solve this kind of constraints together with the simple equality (unifiable) equations.

To have a practical result, we apply the algorithm in the service oriented architecture scenario for reconstructing the type of each service. Thus, we model a system in which each service invocation creates a new session permitting both the exchanging of correlated messages and the isolation from different instances of the same service. As the possibility of different clients for a service, we assume persistent services always available for client requests.

The algorithm is built on top of a language with SCC-like [3] syntax since its syntactic constraints permits to focus our attention on at most two sessions usages each time (the current session and the parent session) whilst it maintains the expressivity to write interesting programs (such as factorial service) to test our results. Notwithstanding, the results can be adapted to any language, for example, our language is a particular instance of the system studied in [20], constraining the typing $\Delta$ to contain at most two session channels at the same time.

*Outline of the paper.* Section 2 fixes the syntax and the operational semantics of our session calculus. Section 3 shows the classic nondeterministic typing rules. Section 4 presents the type inference algorithm subdivided in two parts:

$$
\begin{array}{lll}
P, Q ::= & \mathbf{0} & \text{(nil)} \\
& |\quad s.P & \text{(service definition)} \\
& |\quad \overline{v}.Q & \text{(invocation)} \\
& |\quad \textbf{if } v = v_1 \textbf{ then } P \textbf{ else } Q & \text{(if-then-else)} \\
& |\quad (\tilde{x}).P & \text{(tuple input)} \\
& |\quad \langle \tilde{v} \rangle.P & \text{(value output)} \\
& |\quad \Sigma_{i=1}^{n}(l_i).P_i & \text{(label guarded sum)} \\
& |\quad \langle l \rangle.P & \text{(label choice)} \\
& |\quad \textbf{return } \tilde{v}.P & \text{(value return)} \\
& |\quad P|Q & \text{(parallel)} \\
& |\quad (\nu s)P & \text{(service restriction)} \\
\\
v \quad ::= & \mathsf{f}(\tilde{v}) & \text{(external function call)} \\
& |\quad x & \text{(variable)} \\
& |\quad s & \text{(service)} \\
& |\quad \ldots, -1, 0, 1, \ldots & \text{(integer)}
\end{array}
$$

**Fig. 1.** Syntax of our service calculus

---

a constraints extractor and a solving algorithm. We have also implemented all the algorithms described [15] and Section 5 shows some examples of usage of our tool.

## 2    A Session Oriented Calculus

Our processes are generated by the abstract syntax in Figure 1, where the meta-variable $x$ ranges over variables, $s$ over service names and $l$ over labels. Values can be either a variable, a service, an integer or the result of an *external function* call f.

As usual $\mathbf{0}$ identifies the inaction process (omitted in tail position), $|$ is the parallel composition of two processes and $(\nu s)$ is the restriction of $s$. Service definition $s.P$ and service invocation $\overline{v}.Q$ are used to instantiate a new session, i.e., a way to put in direct connection a service instance $P$ with the body $Q$ of the invocation client. For each service invocation a fresh instance of the body is generated to serve the client, in this manner the service is ready for another client invocation. Once the service side and the client side are connected by means of a session, both parties can communicate via dual operators. This means that if one side performs an input $(\tilde{x}).P$, the other side can send a value tuple with $\langle \tilde{v} \rangle.P$ and if one side offers a choice $\Sigma_{i=1}^{n}(l_i).P_i$, the other side can select a label with $\langle l \rangle.P$.

To logically connect client and service instance, we use a special session construct $r \triangleright P$ and $r \triangleright Q$ which says that both, the service instance $P$ and the client invocation body $Q$ agree on the private name $r$ and they will use it as communication context. Sessions can be arbitrarily nested and the operator $\textbf{return } \tilde{v}.P$ is used to output a value upward the parent session.

Binders are $(\nu s)P$ for $s$ in $P$ and $(\tilde{x}).P$ for $\tilde{x}$ in $P$; the former is the binder for service names and the latter is the binder for variables. As usual processes are considered up to alpha equivalence and the set of free names is defined in the standard way. Moreover, the operation of substitution $P[\tilde{v}/\tilde{x}]$ is the standard capture avoiding substitution of variables with values.

Differently from [4], we formalize the operational semantics of the calculus by a one-step reduction relation $\rightarrow$ up to the standard structural congruence $\equiv$ plus the rule $r \triangleright (\nu m)P \equiv (\nu m)(r \triangleright P)$ if $r \neq m$, for sessions handling, where $m$ range over both session and service names.

$$
\begin{array}{lll}
(Inv) & \mathbb{D}[\![\mathbb{C}[\![\overline{s}.P]\!] \mid \mathbb{C}_1[\![s.Q]\!]]\!] \rightarrow \mathbb{D}[\![(\nu r)\mathbb{C}[\![r \triangleright P \mid r \triangleright Q]\!] \mid \mathbb{C}_1[\![s.Q]\!]]\!] & r \notin \mathsf{fn}(\mathbb{C}[\![\overline{s}.P]\!] \| Q) \\
(Com) & \mathbb{C}[\![r \triangleright (\tilde{x}).P \mid r \triangleright \langle \tilde{v} \rangle.Q]\!] \rightarrow \mathbb{C}[\![r \triangleright P[\tilde{v}/\tilde{x}] \mid r \triangleright Q]\!] & \\
(Lcom) & \mathbb{C}[\![r \triangleright \Sigma_{i=1}^{n}(l_i).P_i \mid r \triangleright \langle l_k \rangle.Q]\!] \rightarrow \mathbb{C}[\![r \triangleright P_k \mid r \triangleright Q]\!] & (1 \leq k \leq n) \\
(Ret) & \mathbb{C}[\![r \triangleright (\tilde{x}).P \mid r \triangleright (r_1 \triangleright \mathtt{return}\ \tilde{v}.Q \mid Q')]\!] \rightarrow \mathbb{C}[\![r \triangleright P[\tilde{v}/\tilde{x}] \mid r \triangleright (r_1 \triangleright Q \mid Q')]\!] & \\
(IfT) & \mathbb{C}[\![\mathtt{if}\ v = v_1\ \mathtt{then}\ P\ \mathtt{else}\ Q]\!] \rightarrow \mathbb{C}[\![P]\!] & (v = v_1) \downarrow \mathtt{true} \\
(IfF) & \mathbb{C}[\![\mathtt{if}\ v = v_1\ \mathtt{then}\ P\ \mathtt{else}\ Q]\!] \rightarrow \mathbb{C}[\![Q]\!] & (v = v_1) \downarrow \mathtt{false} \\
(Scop) & P \rightarrow P' \Rightarrow (\nu m)P \rightarrow (\nu m)P' & \\
(Str) & P \equiv P'\ P' \rightarrow Q'\ Q' \equiv Q \Rightarrow P \rightarrow Q & \\
& \text{where}\ \mathbb{C}, \mathbb{D} ::= [\cdot] \mid \mathbb{C}|P \mid r \triangleright \mathbb{C} &
\end{array}
$$

Priority of the operators in order of increasing relevance is: $|$ , $\triangleright$ and $\nu$ so, for example $r \triangleright P|Q$ means $(r \triangleright P)|Q$ and $(\nu r)P|Q$ means $((\nu r)P)|Q$.

Rule (Inv) shows how the invocation of a service creates a new session that puts in direct communication an instance of the service with the client body; now the two processes are able to communicate.

The rules (Com), (Lcom) show respectively how a tuple is transmitted between the two sides of a session and how the process $Q$ can choose one of the options offered by $P$. Rule (Ret) illustrates how a nested session $r_1$ can output a value, upward the parent session, which is read by $P$ in the dual side of $r$. Both the rules (Com) and (Ret) manage similar communication patterns to what is defined in [5] which describes a variant of *Mobile Ambients* calculus [6].

As an example consider the following `calc` service

`calc.(sum).(x, y).⟨add(x, y)⟩ + (inc).(x).⟨add(x, 1)⟩`

which offers two options. Option **sum** reads $(x, y)$ from the client and replies with the result of the external function call add. The add function is only available on one session side, directly implemented in some programming language (i.e., add $= \lambda(x, y).x{+}y$). Option **inc** only inputs a value and then emits the result. One client that successful interacts with the service is:

$\overline{\mathtt{calc}}.\langle \mathbf{sum} \rangle.(1, 1).(res).\mathtt{return}\ res$

After rules (Inv) and (Lcom) are applied, the parallel of the two processes above become:

$r \triangleright (\mathtt{x,y}).\langle \mathsf{add}(\mathtt{x,y}) \rangle \mid r \triangleright (1, 1).(res).\mathtt{return}\ res \rightarrow$
$r \triangleright \langle \mathsf{add}(1, 1) \rangle \mid r \triangleright (res).\mathtt{return}\ res \rightarrow r \triangleright \mathbf{0} \mid r \triangleright \mathtt{return}\ 2$

At the end of interaction, the client has the result in the $res$ variable which is returned to the parent session.

$$
\begin{aligned}
\mathsf{wf}(\mathbf{0}, X) &= X \\
\mathsf{wf}(s.P, X) &= \mathsf{wf}(P, X \setminus s) \\
\mathsf{wf}(\overline{v}.P, X) &= \mathsf{wf}(P, X) \\
\mathsf{wf}(\text{if } v = v_1 \text{ then } P \text{ else } Q, X) &= \mathsf{wf}(Q, \mathsf{wf}(P, X)) \\
\mathsf{wf}((\tilde{x}).P, X) \wedge \mathsf{wf}(\langle \tilde{v} \rangle.P, X) &= \mathsf{wf}(P, X) \\
\mathsf{wf}(\Sigma_{i=1}^{n}(l_i).P_i, X) &= \mathsf{wf}(P_n, \mathsf{wf}(P_{n-1}, \dots \mathsf{wf}(P_1, X)) \; \forall i, j.l_i \neq l_j \text{ if } i \neq j \\
\mathsf{wf}(\langle l \rangle.P, X) \wedge \mathsf{wf}(\text{return } \tilde{v}.P, X) &= \mathsf{wf}(P, X) \\
\mathsf{wf}(P|Q, X) &= \mathsf{wf}(Q, \mathsf{wf}(P, X)) \\
\mathsf{wf}((\nu s)P, X) &= \mathsf{wf}(P, X \cup \{s\})
\end{aligned}
$$

**Fig. 2.** Definition of wf

## 3   Typing

### 3.1   Well Formedness

In this sub-section we discuss the notion of well-formed process. Since we are in a context with duality each service restriction $(\nu s)$ authorizes to use in its scope both $s$ as service declaration and $\overline{s}$ as service invocation. However, syntax does not constrain programmers to insert a service declaration in the scope of a restriction, and it can happen that a process has a service invocation without the corresponding declaration. Thus, we require our processes to have at least the service declaration for each service restriction. This requirement, besides to be reasonable, is also crux to successfully solve the constraints generated with the type inference algorithm (see Proposition 1).

The formal definition of well formedness is built from the function wf (Figure 2) which takes a process with all bound and free names different, the set of service names that should be declared and returns the set of names not still declared.

**Definition 1 (Well formedness).** *A process $P$ is well formed if* $\mathsf{wf}(P, \emptyset) = \emptyset$

The definition ensures the process $P$ declares every service annunciated by means of restrictions (no matters where!). Moreover, all the labels of a choice must be different.

From now on, all the processes we are going to handle are implicitly assumed to satisfy Definition 1.

### 3.2   Typing Rules

The set of types is defined by the abstract syntax in Figure 3. Session types (ranged over by $T$,$U$) express sequences of typed tuples of input and output. Intuitively, types capture the actions performed in a side of a session; $?(S_1, \dots, S_n).T$ expresses the fact that a process performs an input within a session and then behaves like $T$. Similar holds for $!(S_1, \dots, S_n).T$ in which an output action is

$$
\begin{array}{lll}
T, U ::= & \textbf{end} & \text{(no action)} \\
| & ?(S_1, \ldots, S_n).T & \text{(input of a tuple)} \\
| & !(S_1, \ldots, S_n).T & \text{(output of a tuple)} \\
| & \&\{l_1 : T_1, \ldots, l_n : T_n\} & \text{(external choice)} \\
| & \oplus\{l_1 : T_1, \ldots, l_n : T_n\} & \text{(internal choice)} \\
S \quad ::= & int & \text{(basic integers type)} \\
| & [T] & \text{(session type)}
\end{array}
$$

**Fig. 3.** Syntax of types

performed, instead. The type of an external choice is a list of (offered) labels with the corresponding subprocess usage. Also, the type of an internal choice contains a list, because multiple choices may be performed at the same time.

Sorts $S$ can be either the type of a service $[T]$ or an integer.

Our set of type judgments is in Figure 4. Type judgments for values take the form $\Gamma \vdash v : S$ where the *type environment* $\Gamma$ is a finite partial mapping from variables, services and external function names to sorts and function types. When $x \notin dom(\Gamma)$ (same holds for $s \notin dom(\Gamma)$) we write $\Gamma, x : S$ for the type environment obtained by extending $\Gamma$ with the binding of $x$ to $S$. First four rules for values are standard and the signature of each used external function must be inserted in the environment as functional type (rule (FuncV)) because they are not bound by the process.

Type judgments for processes take the form $\Gamma \vdash P : T; U$ where $T$ is the type of the current session, while the type $U$ represents outputs of $P$ towards the parent session. The type of $\mathbf{0}$ in (Tzero) is $\textbf{end}; \textbf{end}$ since no action is performed neither in the current nor towards the parent session. The typing rule (Tnew) infers the right type of a service inserting it in the environment. Rule (Tdef) constraints the protocol of the service to be the same as the body type of the process $P$ and no return is allowed toward the parent session. This condition is necessary, because we want that the service body does not interfere within the client's context. (Tinv) checks the service behaves in the dual manner with respect to the current client. Here, the dual of $T$, written $\overline{T}$ is inductively defined as:

$$
\overline{?(\tilde{S}).T} = !(\tilde{S}).\overline{T} \qquad \overline{!(\tilde{S}).T'} = ?(\tilde{S}).\overline{T'} \qquad \overline{\textbf{end}} = \textbf{end}
$$
$$
\overline{\&\{l_1 : T_1, \ldots, l_n : T_n\}} = \oplus\{l_1 : \overline{T_1}, \ldots, l_n : \overline{T_n}\}
$$
$$
\overline{\oplus\{l_1 : T_1, \ldots, l_n : T_n\}} = \&\{l_1 : \overline{T_1}, \ldots, l_n : \overline{T_n}\}
$$

Rules (Tin), (Tout) and (Tret) insert the usage type in the correct place. Rule (Tbranch) considers any subset of the branches while rule (Tchoice) can arbitrarily add some branches. The shape of the rule (Tchoice) is necessary since, the if-then-else construct allows choosing between many branches at the same time and also different clients can invoke the same service making their own choices. When we have multiple paths, returns to the parent session must have the same type $U$. The nondeterminism in the rules (Tbranch) and (Tchoice) is typical for

$$\text{(SER)} \quad \Gamma, s : S \vdash s : S \qquad \text{(VAR)} \quad \Gamma, x : S \vdash x : S \qquad \text{(INTV)} \quad \Gamma \vdash n : int$$

$$\text{(FUNCV)} \quad \frac{\Gamma \vdash v_1 : S_1 \dots \Gamma \vdash v_n : S_n}{\Gamma, \mathsf{f} : S_1 \times \dots \times S_n \to S' \vdash \mathsf{f}(v_1, \dots, v_n) : S'}$$

$$\text{(TZERO)} \quad \Gamma \vdash \mathbf{0} : end; end$$

$$\text{(TNEW)} \quad \frac{\Gamma, s : S \vdash P : T; U}{\Gamma \vdash (\nu s)P : T; U}$$

$$\text{(TIF)} \quad \frac{\Gamma \vdash P : T; U \quad \Gamma \vdash Q : T; U}{\Gamma \vdash \text{if } v = v_1 \text{ then } P \text{ else } Q : T; U}$$

$$\text{(TDEF)} \quad \frac{\Gamma \vdash P : T; end \quad \Gamma \vdash s : [T]}{\Gamma \vdash s.P : end; end}$$

$$\text{(TINV)} \quad \frac{\Gamma \vdash P : T; U \quad \Gamma \vdash v : [T'] \quad \overline{T} = T'}{\Gamma \vdash \overline{v}.P : U; end}$$

$$\text{(TIN)} \quad \frac{\Gamma, \tilde{x} : \tilde{S} \vdash P : T; U}{\Gamma \vdash (\tilde{x}).P : ?(\tilde{S}).T; U}$$

$$\text{(TOUT)} \quad \frac{\Gamma \vdash P : T; U \quad \Gamma \vdash \tilde{v} : \tilde{S}}{\Gamma \vdash \langle \tilde{v} \rangle.P : !(\tilde{S}).T; U}$$

$$\text{(TRET)} \quad \frac{\Gamma \vdash P : T; U \quad \Gamma \vdash \tilde{v} : \tilde{S}}{\Gamma \vdash \text{return } \tilde{v}.P : T; !(\tilde{S}).U}$$

$$\text{(TBRANCH)} \quad \frac{I \subseteq \{1, \dots, n\} \quad \forall i \in \{1, \dots, n\} \quad \Gamma \vdash P_i : T_i; U}{\Gamma \vdash \Sigma_{i=0}^{n}(l_i).P_i : \&\{l_j : T_j\}_{j \in I}; U}$$

$$\text{(TCHOICE)} \quad \frac{l = l_i \in \{l_1, \dots, l_n\} \quad \Gamma \vdash P : T_i; U}{\Gamma \vdash \langle l \rangle.P : \oplus\{l_1 : T_1, \dots, l_n : T_n\}; U}$$

$$\text{(TPARL)} \quad \frac{\Gamma \vdash P : T; end \quad \Gamma \vdash Q : end; end}{\Gamma \vdash P|Q : T; end}$$

$$\text{(TPARR)} \quad \frac{\Gamma \vdash P : end; end \quad \Gamma \vdash Q : T; end}{\Gamma \vdash P|Q : T; end}$$

**Fig. 4.** Typing rules

$$\text{(TBRANCHSD)} \quad \frac{\forall i \in \{1, \dots, n\} \quad \Gamma \vdash_{\mathsf{SD}} P_i : T_i; U}{\Gamma \vdash_{\mathsf{SD}} \Sigma_{i=0}^{n}(l_i).P_i : \&\{l_i : T_i\}_{i \in \{1, \dots, n\}}; U}$$

$$\text{(TCHOICESD)} \quad \frac{\Gamma \vdash_{\mathsf{SD}} P : T; U}{\Gamma \vdash_{\mathsf{SD}} \langle l \rangle.P : \oplus\{l : T\}; U}$$

$$\text{(TINVSD)} \quad \frac{\Gamma \vdash_{\mathsf{SD}} P : T; U \quad \Gamma \vdash_{\mathsf{SD}} v : [T'] \quad T \bowtie T'}{\Gamma \vdash_{\mathsf{SD}} \overline{v}.P : U; end}$$

$$\text{(TIFSD)} \quad \frac{\Gamma \vdash_{\mathsf{SD}} P : T; U \quad \Gamma \vdash_{\mathsf{SD}} Q : T'; U \quad T'' = \mathsf{merge}(T, T')}{\Gamma \vdash_{\mathsf{SD}} \text{if } v = v_1 \text{ then } P \text{ else } Q : T''; U}$$

**Fig. 5.** Syntax directed typing rules

session type systems, and it is actually useful in subject reduction proofs (see [4] for the subject reduction proof of the current framework).

The two rules for parallel composition (TparL) and (TparR) allow parallel composition of two processes only if at least one does not make any action in both the current session and the parent session, i.e., it has type end; end.

Now we show an example of typing,

*Example 1.* Take the calculator example. The type $!(int, int).?(int); !(int)$ expresses the client usage after the sum choice: the output of two integers is followed by the reading of the result and an integer is returned outside the session (the type after semicolon always stands for a return action, that is, an output out of the current session). Previous in-session usage is compared with the dual session usage $?(int, int).!(int)$ to ensure the soundness of the invocation. Below we report the typing proof, where we let $\Gamma = calc : [\&\{\mathsf{sum} :?(int, int).!(int)\}]$

$$
\cfrac{
  \cfrac{
    \cfrac{
      \cfrac{
        \Gamma \vdash \mathtt{return}\ x : \mathsf{end}; !(int)
      }{\Gamma \vdash (x).\mathtt{return}\ x : ?(int); !(int)}\ \text{(Tin)}
    }{\Gamma \vdash \langle 1, 1 \rangle.(x).\mathtt{return}\ x : !(int, int).?(int); !(int)}\ \text{(Tout)}
  }{\Gamma \vdash \langle \mathsf{sum} \rangle.\langle 1, 1 \rangle.(x).\mathtt{return}\ x : \oplus\{\mathsf{sum} :!(int, int).?(int)\}; !(int)}\ \text{(Tchoice)}
}{\Gamma \vdash \overline{\mathtt{calc}}.\langle \mathsf{sum} \rangle.\langle 1, 1 \rangle.(x).\mathtt{return}\ x : !(int); \mathsf{end}}\ \text{(Tinv)}
$$

It is worth noticing that we are authorized to apply the rule (Tinv) because $\Gamma(\mathtt{calc}) = [\oplus : \{\mathsf{sum} :!(int, int).?(int)\}]$. Thus, the assumption about calc ignores the option labeled with inc since it is useless for this particular client.

The main problem we are going to face in the algorithmic type inference is due to the nondeterministic nature of the typing rules for choices. Relatively to the previous example, it is not strictly necessary to discard the inc branch when inserting the type of the calc service in the environment (rule (Tbranch)). In fact, rule (Tchoice) would allow to correctly typecheck the client even if the inc branch were not specified. Consequently, a client can arbitrarily discard unused branches allowing to correctly typecheck other clients with different choices.

## 4 Type Inference

### 4.1 Syntax Directed Rules

Before introducing an algorithm for the type inference we need to solve the nondeterminism of the type system (due to both rules (Tchoice) and (Tbranch)) replacing it with another set of syntax directed rules, shown in Figure 5 (only different rules are reported). Next, we are able to show that the two set of rules coincide so that we can use the syntax directed rules to formulate our algorithm.

The previous type system permits to arbitrarily add or remove the branches of a choice until the rule (Tinv) holds. We factorize out the nondeterminism building the type with all the currently available information, which is equivalent to take all the branches in rule (TbranchSD) and only one branch in rule (TchoiceSD). Also, the new rule (TifSD) needs a way to deterministically get the correct type, and it uses the support function merge defined in Figure 6. In other words, merge works as follow: if both $P$ and $Q$ are internal choices we create a new type with those branches that are not within the intersection of the two sets of labels plus the merge of those branches that are within the intersection. In fact, a compliant external choice should account for all the possible

$$\text{merge}(\textbf{end}, \textbf{end}) \qquad\qquad\qquad\qquad\qquad = \textbf{end}$$
$$\text{merge}(!(\tilde{S}).T, !(\tilde{S}).T') \qquad\qquad\qquad\qquad = !(\tilde{S}).\text{merge}(T, T')$$
$$\text{merge}(?(\tilde{S}).T, ?(\tilde{S}).T') \qquad\qquad\qquad\qquad = ?(\tilde{S}).\text{merge}(T, T')$$
$$\text{merge}(\oplus\{l_1 : T_1, \ldots, l_n : T_n\}, \oplus\{l'_1 : T'_1, \ldots, l'_m : T'_m\}) = \oplus\{_{\forall i\, \exists j\, l_i = l'_j} l_i : \text{merge}(T_i, T'_j)\, ,$$
$$_{\forall i, j\, l_i \neq l'_j} l_i : T_i\, ,\ _{\forall j, i\, l'_j \neq l_i} l'_j : T'_j\}$$
$$\text{merge}(\&\{l_1 : T_1, \ldots, l_n : T_n\}, \&\{l'_1 : T'_1, \ldots, l'_m : T'_m\}) = \&\{_{\forall i\, \exists j\, l_i = l'_j} l_i : \text{merge}(T_i, T'_j)\}$$

**Fig. 6.** Merge for the if branches

$$\textbf{end} \bowtie \textbf{end}$$
$$\oplus\{l_1 : T_1, \ldots, l_n : T_n\} \bowtie \&\{l'_1 : T'_1, \ldots, l'_m : T'_m\} = \forall i, j\, l_i = l'_j\ \to\ T_i \bowtie T'_j\ \wedge$$
$$\{l_1, \ldots, l_n\} \subseteq \{l'_1, \ldots, l'_m\}$$
$$?(\tilde{S}).T \bowtie !(\tilde{S}).T' \qquad\qquad\qquad\qquad\qquad = T \bowtie T'$$

**Fig. 7.** Services Join

options the process could select during its evaluation. Instead, if we are merging two branches of an external choice we are able only to guarantee options that are within the intersection of the set of labels and additionally these branches must be mergeable.

The problem is that, at this point, the standard syntactic equivalence is not useful for the comparison of two types since the branches in internal choices are a subset of the corresponding branches in external choices. The $\bowtie$ relation reported in Figure 7, combined with the symmetric cases, solves the above problem and is used by (InvSD) to validate the client protocol (it is just a restricted form of subtyping, written as a symmetric operator).

The next lemma shows that a typable process in $\vdash$ is also typable in $\vdash_{\textsf{SD}}$ and vice versa. In this manner, we can build our type inference algorithm on top of the syntax directed rules throwing out nondeterminism.

**Lemma 1.** *If* $\Gamma \vdash P : T; U$ *then there exist* $\Gamma'$ *and* $T'$ *s.t.* $\Gamma' \vdash_{\textsf{SD}} P : T'; U$. *Conversely, if* $\Gamma \vdash_{\textsf{SD}} P : T; U$ *is derivable, so is,* $\Gamma \vdash P : T; U$.

*Proof.* Straightforward induction on derivations of $\Gamma \vdash P : T; U$ and $\Gamma \vdash_{\textsf{SD}} P : T; U$. □

### 4.2 Tree Unification

The inference algorithm relies on a unification algorithm unify among trees as the one described in [16]. Nevertheless, in order to use this algorithm we need to clarify how to build trees starting from our types. We first introduce the standard set of type variables $V$, and a set of constants $K = \{\textbf{end}, int\}$. The meta variable $\alpha$ ranges over the elements of $V$. A production for type variables is also added to the syntax of sorts in Figure 3. A tree type is a partial function $\mathcal{T}$ from the set of finite strings over the alphabet of positive integers (describing paths in the

tree), to a ranked alphabet $L = \{[\ \ ], \ .\ \} \cup V \cup K \cup \{?^i, !^i, \&^i, \oplus^i | i > 0\}$ where
the rank of $V \cup K$ is 0, the rank of $[\ \ ]$ is 1 and the rank of $\{?^i, !^i, \&^i, \oplus^i | i > 0\}$
is $i$. For example, if $\mathcal{T}(\pi) = [\ \ ]$ then $\mathcal{T}(\pi \cdot 1)$ is defined, which means, if in the
tree following the path as specified by the string $\pi$ we find a $[\ \ ]$ then we can
use the string $\pi \cdot 1$ to retrieve the service type.

**Definition 2 (treeof).** *The function* treeof *translates types into trees and is
inductively defined as:*

$$
\begin{aligned}
\mathsf{treeof}(?(S_1, \ldots, S_n).T) &= ?^n(\mathsf{treeof}(S_1), \ldots, \mathsf{treeof}(S_n)).\mathsf{treeof}(T) \\
\mathsf{treeof}(!(S_1, \ldots, S_n).T) &= !^n(\mathsf{treeof}(S_1), \ldots, \mathsf{treeof}(S_n)).\mathsf{treeof}(T) \\
\mathsf{treeof}(\&\{l_1 : T_1, \ldots, l_n : T_n\}) &= \&^n\{l'_1 : \mathsf{treeof}(T_1), \ldots, l'_n : \mathsf{treeof}(T_n)\} \\
\mathsf{treeof}(\oplus\{l_1 : T_1, \ldots, l_n : T_n\}) &= \oplus^n\{l'_1 : \mathsf{treeof}(T_1), \ldots, l'_n : \mathsf{treeof}(T_n)\} \\
\mathsf{treeof}(K) &= K \\
\mathsf{treeof}(\alpha) &= \alpha
\end{aligned}
$$

*where $(l'_1, \ldots, l'_n)$ is an ordering of $(l_1, \ldots, l_n)$*

Trees follow the same structure as types but we need arity annotations and a
fixed ordering among the labels of each choice.

The substitution returned by unify is a mapping $p : V \to \mathcal{T}$. Given a substitution $p$ and a tree $\mathcal{T}$, we obtain the tree $p\mathcal{T}$ as the result of the simultaneous
substitution of the tree $p\alpha$ for each occurrence of variable $\alpha$ in $\mathcal{T}$. Standard
substitution composition is written as $p \cdot p'$ if $p$ and $p'$ are two substitutions.
Another subtle aspect is that valid substitutions returned by the unify must be
acyclic (this can be verified e.g., by using the so-called *occur-check*), because
(for simplicity) the current type system does not handle regular recursive types.
Recursive types would permit to typecheck process like $(\nu a)(a.(x).\overline{x}.\langle x \rangle | \overline{a}.\langle a \rangle)$
and could be handled by allowing a solution for cyclic substitutions. Hereafter,
we will use types and trees interchangeably, since they are isomorphic.

## 4.3   An Algorithm to Extract Constraints

The type inference is subdivided in two parts: the constraints extraction part
and the solving part. For the first part, the algorithm INF, depicted in Figure 8,
takes a process $P$ and an environment $\Gamma$. $\Gamma$ contains an entry for each service
and variable in $P$ corresponding to either a type variable (meaning that we
rely on the algorithm to find out the type of a name) or a sort (if we simply
want typecheck). Moreover, $\Gamma$ must contain the functional type of each external
function used as a value; environment $\Gamma$ *restricted with the set of free names of*
$P$ is denoted $\Gamma_{\downarrow fn(P)}$. The algorithm returns a triple: a set $\mathcal{C}$ of constraints, the
type $T$ of actions in the current session and the type $U$ of outputs upwards the
parent session. The set $\mathcal{C}$ of constraints contains equations of the form $T = T'$
and $T \bowtie T'$.

Basically, INF is extracted by reading the syntax directed rules (Figure 5) in a
bottom-up manner and generating an equality constraint when the rule requires
two types to be equal: e.g., in the if case of the algorithm we add an equation
that requires equality for the returned type of both $P$ and $Q$ since the rule

(TifSD) requires two $U$'s. It is worth noticing that, with an abuse of notation, we use merge for indicating a slightly different function from that defined in Figure 6, the new one behaves like the original function but also returns an equality constraint in each case the previous function requires syntactical equality. It is not expressively annotated when the algorithm fails but it should be clear that an error is generated each time the code does not match the algorithm expectation. E.g., a subtle case is in the invocation when we directly read from $\Gamma$ the type of the value; we implicitly expect the value to be either a variable or a service (neither a function nor an integer) bound in the environment.

Next theorem is fundamental for the soundness of our results and it shows that if we have a substitution that solves the constraints set generated with $\mathtt{INF}(P, \Gamma)$ then such a substitution applied to $\Gamma$ yields a correct typing for each service and variable in $P$.

**Theorem 1.** *Let* $\mathtt{INF}(Q, \Gamma) = (\mathcal{C}_1, T_1, U_1)$, $Q \equiv (\nu\tilde{s})P$ *and $p$ a substitution for each type variable in $\mathcal{C}_1$ to a concrete type (a type without type variables). Then, $\vDash p\mathcal{C}_1$ holds if and only if* $(p\Gamma)_{\downarrow\mathsf{fn}(P)} \vdash_{\mathsf{SD}} P : pT_1; pU_1$.

*Proof.* The assumption on $p$ is required for throwing out some valid solutions and recover the soundness with respect to the syntax directed typing rules; we reserve the problem of *principal typing* for further investigations. $\Rightarrow$ By induction on the first applied rule in the algorithm, we sketch some cases. If $\mathtt{INF}(s'.P', \Gamma)$ the respective case is applied. By inductive hypothesis $\vDash p\mathcal{C}$ holds and $(p\Gamma)_{\downarrow\mathsf{fn}(P')} \vdash_{\mathsf{SD}} P' : pT;\mathsf{end}$. Also if $\vDash p(\mathcal{C} \cup \{\Gamma(s) = [T]\})$ holds we can instantiate the premises of the rule (TdefSD) to obtain the typing for $(p\Gamma)_{\downarrow\mathsf{fn}(P')}, s : pT \vdash_{\mathsf{SD}} s.P' : \mathsf{end};\mathsf{end}$. In the case of rules that introduce binders $p\Gamma$ is used to get the correct type. For example, if $\mathtt{INF}((\nu s)P', \Gamma)$ then $(p\Gamma)_{\downarrow\mathsf{fn}(P')\backslash s}, s : p\Gamma(s) \vdash_{\mathsf{SD}} P' : pT; pU$ and consequently $(p\Gamma)_{\downarrow\mathsf{fn}((\nu s)P')} \vdash_{\mathsf{SD}} (\nu s)P' : pT; pU$. $\Leftarrow$ By induction on the last applied rule in the type system. For example if the last applied rule was (TinvSD) we have that $p(\Gamma_{\downarrow\mathsf{fn}(P')})(v) = [T']$ and that $T' \bowtie pT''$ holds in the premises, where $pT''$ is the typing of $P'$ in $\overline{v}.P'$. Since by inductive hypothesis $\vDash p\mathcal{C}$ holds then $\vDash p(\mathcal{C} \cup \{T' \bowtie T''\})$ holds too. $\qquad\square$

## 4.4    How to Solve the Constraints Set

At the end of the previous sub-section we show the fundamental role played by the substitution $p$, solution of the constraints set; next we show how to algorithmically get such a solution.

The algorithm in Figure 9, in OCaml like syntax, is used to find the solution of the constraints set $\mathcal{C}$ (which is treated like an ordered list of constraints). If the equation is a simple equality, it can be directly solved by unify, which returns a substitution applied to both the environment and the tail of the constraints list. If the constraint is a $\bowtie$ equation we are comparing two dual sides of a session and we cannot directly unify. In fact, as discussed in the introduction, the information which can be unified is only that information on the types of the trasmitted/received tuples since they should be the same for both sides.

$\text{VALUEINF}(x, \Gamma) = (\emptyset, \Gamma(x))$

$\text{VALUEINF}(s, \Gamma) = (\emptyset, \Gamma(s))$

$\text{VALUEINF}(n, \Gamma) = (\emptyset, int)$

$\text{VALUEINF}(f(v_1, \ldots, v_n), \Gamma) =$
$$\begin{aligned}
&\text{let } (\mathcal{C}_1, S_1) = \text{VALUEINF}(v_1, \Gamma) \ldots \ldots (\mathcal{C}_n, S_n) = \text{VALUEINF}(v_n, \Gamma) \\
&\qquad \Gamma(f) = S_1 \times \ldots \times S_n \to S \\
&\text{in } (\mathcal{C}_1 \cup \ldots \cup \mathcal{C}_n, S)
\end{aligned}$$

$\text{INF}(s.P, \Gamma) =$
$$\begin{aligned}
&\text{let } (\mathcal{C}, T, U) = \text{INF}(P, \Gamma) \\
&\qquad U = \text{end} \\
&\qquad \mathcal{C}_1 = \mathcal{C} \cup \{\Gamma(s) = [T]\} \\
&\text{in } (\mathcal{C}_1, \text{end}, \text{end})
\end{aligned}$$

$\text{INF}(\overline{v}.P, \Gamma) =$
$$\begin{aligned}
&\text{let } (\mathcal{C}, T, U) = \text{INF}(P, \Gamma) \\
&\qquad \mathcal{C}_1 = \mathcal{C} \cup \{\Gamma(v) \bowtie [T]\} \\
&\text{in } (\mathcal{C}_1, U, \text{end})
\end{aligned}$$

$\text{INF}((x_1, \ldots, x_n).P, \Gamma) =$
$$\begin{aligned}
&\text{let } (\mathcal{C}, T, U) = \text{INF}(P, \Gamma) \\
&\text{in } (\mathcal{C}, ?(\Gamma(x_1), \ldots, \Gamma(x_n)).T, U)
\end{aligned}$$

$\text{INF}(\langle v_1, \ldots, v_n \rangle.P, \Gamma) =$
$$\begin{aligned}
&\text{let } (\mathcal{C}, T, U) = \text{INF}(P, \Gamma) \\
&\qquad (\mathcal{C}_1, S_1) = \text{VALUEINF}(v_1, \Gamma) \ldots \ldots (\mathcal{C}_n, S_n) = \text{VALUEINF}(v_n, \Gamma) \\
&\text{in } (\mathcal{C} \cup \mathcal{C}_1 \cup \ldots \cup \mathcal{C}_n, !(S_1, \ldots, S_n).T, U)
\end{aligned}$$

$\text{INF}(\text{return } v_1, \ldots, v_n.P, \Gamma) =$
$$\begin{aligned}
&\text{let } (\mathcal{C}, T, U) = \text{INF}(P, \Gamma) \\
&\qquad (\mathcal{C}_1, S_1) = \text{VALUEINF}(v_1, \Gamma) \ldots \ldots (\mathcal{C}_n, S_n) = \text{VALUEINF}(v_n, \Gamma) \\
&\text{in } (\mathcal{C} \cup \mathcal{C}_1 \cup \ldots \cup \mathcal{C}_n, T, !(S_1, \ldots, S_n).U)
\end{aligned}$$

$\text{INF}(\text{if } v = v_1 \text{ then } P \text{ else } Q, \Gamma) =$
$$\begin{aligned}
&\text{let } (\mathcal{C}, T, U) = \text{INF}(P, \Gamma) \\
&\qquad (\mathcal{C}_1, T_1, U_1) = \text{INF}(Q, \Gamma) \\
&\qquad (\mathcal{C}_2, T_2) = \text{merge}(T, T_1) \\
&\qquad \mathcal{C}_2 = \mathcal{C}_2 \cup \{U = U_1\} \\
&\text{in } (\mathcal{C} \cup \mathcal{C}_1 \cup \mathcal{C}_2, T_2, U)
\end{aligned}$$

$\text{INF}((\nu s)P, \Gamma) =$
$$\begin{aligned}
&\text{let } (\mathcal{C}, T, U) = \text{INF}(P, \Gamma) \\
&\text{in } (\mathcal{C}, T, U)
\end{aligned}$$

$\text{INF}(P|Q, \Gamma) =$
$$\begin{aligned}
&\text{let } (\mathcal{C}, T, \text{end}) = \text{INF}(P, \Gamma) \\
&\qquad (\mathcal{C}_1, T_1, \text{end}) = \text{INF}(Q, \Gamma) \\
&\qquad T = \text{end} \lor T_1 = \text{end} \\
&\qquad \text{if } T{==}\text{end then } T_2{=}T_1 \\
&\qquad \text{else if } T1{==}\text{end then } T_2{=}T \\
&\text{in } (\mathcal{C} \cup \mathcal{C}_1, T_2, \text{end})
\end{aligned}$$

$\text{INF}(\Sigma_{i=1}^n (l_i).P_i, \Gamma) =$
$$\begin{aligned}
&\text{let } (\mathcal{C}_1, T_1, U_1) = \text{INF}(P_i, \Gamma) \ldots \ldots (\mathcal{C}_n, T_n, U_n) = \text{INF}(P_n, \Gamma) \\
&\qquad \mathcal{C}' = \bigcup_i \{U_i = U_{i+1}\} \quad \forall i \in 1 \ldots n-1 \\
&\text{in } (\mathcal{C}' \cup \mathcal{C}_1 \cup \ldots \cup \mathcal{C}_n, \&\{l_1 : T_1, \ldots, l_n : T_n\}, U_1)
\end{aligned}$$

$\text{INF}(\langle l \rangle.P, \Gamma) =$
$$\begin{aligned}
&\text{let } (\mathcal{C}, T, U) = \text{INF}(P, \Gamma) \\
&\text{in} (\mathcal{C}, \oplus\{l : T\}, U)
\end{aligned}$$

**Fig. 8.** The algorithm to extract constraints

```
let solve C Γ=
match C with
   []->Γ
   |T = T1::C' -> let p=unify(T,T1) in solve(pC',pΓ)
   |α ⋈ T  ::C' -> solve(C'@[α ⋈ T], Γ)
   |T ⋈ T1::C' -> let p=compunify(T,T1) in solve(pC',pΓ)
```

**Fig. 9.** An algorithm to solve the constraints set

$$\text{compunify}(\text{end}, \text{end}) = \epsilon \qquad \text{compunify}([T], [T']) = \text{compunify}(T, T')$$
$$\text{compunify}(?(\tilde{S}).T, !(\tilde{S}').T') \qquad\qquad = \text{unify}(\tilde{S}, \tilde{S}') \cdot \text{compunify}(T, T')$$
$$\text{compunify}(\&\{l_1 : T_1, \ldots, l_n : T_n\}, \oplus\{l'_1 : T'_1, \ldots, l_m : T'_m\}) = \bigcup_{l_i = l'_j} \text{compunify}(T_i, T'_j)$$
$$\{l'_1, \ldots, l'_m\} \subseteq \{l_1, \ldots, l_n\}$$

**Fig. 10.** compunify

The compunify defined in Figure 10 (with symmetric cases) solves a $\bowtie$ equation by unifying the type of the tuples received and transmitted ($\cdot$ indicates the composition of substitutions and $\epsilon$ the empty substitution); the other cases follow the same pattern as their syntactic counterparts defined in Figure 7.

It is worth noticing that we cannot solve an equation of form $\alpha \bowtie T$ because this kind of equation does not contain any information. In these cases, the algorithm chooses to append the equation to the rest $C'$ since another iteration could substitute the type variable with a more concrete type. The following proposition shows that this is always the case since sooner or later all service definitions become available, thanks to the well-formedness of $P$.

**Proposition 1.** *Let $(C, \_, \_) = \text{INF}(P, \Gamma)$ and $P$ a closed process with respect to services and variables. For each constraint $\alpha \bowtie [T] \in C$, it is possible to find in $C$ a series of constraints that yields a substitution $\{\alpha \mapsto T'\}$ and $T'$ is not a type variable.*

*Proof.* Note that constraints $\alpha \bowtie [T]$ are generated by the service invocation $\overline{v}.P$ and $\alpha$ is the type of the value $v$ used for invocation. Suppose we first solve from $C$ all the unification constraints. Consequently, we produce the new constraints set $C'$. The remaining constraints $\alpha \bowtie [T]$ in $C'$ are because $\alpha$ is introduced by an input binder. In this case we have an usage of the form $?(\alpha)$ to be compared with an usage of the form $!(T_1)$ otherwise compunify fails. If $T_1$ is not a type variable compunify returns the substitution $\{\alpha \mapsto T_1\}$. Otherwise, if $T_1 = \alpha_1$ is a type variable then it must exists (since $P$ is closed and well formed) an equation $\alpha_1 \bowtie T_2$ and we can reiterate the reasoning to find out the desiderated substitution. The reasoning terminates and it is bounded by the number of service invocations in $P$.

Thanks to the previous Proposition we can show that even if there are unguarded appends, solve terminates.

**Theorem 2.** solve *terminates.*

*Proof.* The set of constraints decreases at each iteration except in the third case. By Proposition 1 there must exist a substitution that returns the concrete form of $\alpha$ in a finite number of steps. Let $|\mathcal{C}|$ be the total number of constraints in the set and $d$ the number of the $\bowtie$ equations. The measure we are going to define is $|\mathcal{C}| + d!$, where $d!$ denotes the factorial of $d$. In fact, we need at most $|\mathcal{C}|$ steps to solve all the equality equations and at most all the permutations of $d$ to find the correct resolution order of the $\bowtie$ equations.                          □

# 5   Running Examples Extracted from the Tool

We developed the described algorithm in OCaml [15] and in this section we show some examples of executions with the generated constraints set and the relative solution. Consider that the algorithm makes some initial work to alpha renaming the process in such a way that all bound and free names are different as implicitly expected by the INF function.

*Example 2.* We start with a classical functional flavor, factorial service. Even if this function is recursive, its typing does not require recursive types, as each session is isolated from each other. A client invokes the service and returns the result upwards. Furthermore, the example shows how nested services work.

```
(νfatt)
    fatt.(n).
    if n=1 then ⟨1⟩ else
        (νutil)
        util.f̅a̅t̅t̅.⟨sub(n,1)⟩.(x).return x  |  u̅t̅i̅l̅.(x₁).return mul(x₁,n)
  |  f̅a̅t̅t̅.⟨5⟩.(res).return res
```

First of all we need to instruct the tool, linking in the environment $\Gamma$ only the types of the external functions; $\Gamma = \{\text{sub} : int \times int \to int, \text{mul} : int \times int \to int\}$. Now running INF with the previous process and $\Gamma' = \Gamma \cup \{\text{fatt} : \alpha_1, \text{n} : \alpha_6, \text{util} : \alpha_3, \text{x} : \alpha_5, \text{x}_1 : \alpha_4, \text{res} : \alpha_2\}$ yields the following constraints:

$$
\begin{array}{lll}
\alpha_1 = [?(\alpha_6).!(int).\mathsf{end}] & \alpha_3 = [!(\alpha_5).\mathsf{end}] & \alpha_6 = int \\
\alpha_3 \bowtie [?(\alpha_4).\mathsf{end}] & \alpha_1 \bowtie [!(int).?(\alpha_5).\mathsf{end}] & \alpha_4 = int \\
\alpha_1 \bowtie [!(int).?(\alpha_2).\mathsf{end}] & int = int &
\end{array}
$$

The solving algorithm computes the right solution, $\text{fatt} : [?(int).!(int).\mathsf{end}]$, $\text{n} : int$, $\text{x} : int$, $\text{x}_1 : int$, $\text{res} : int$, $\text{util} : [!(int).\mathsf{end}]$.

*Example 3.* The second program shows how the type inference works for an invocation of a dynamically received service name.

```
(νb)((νa)(a.(sum).(x,y).⟨add(x,y)⟩ + (inc).(x₁).⟨add(x₁,1)⟩  |  b.⟨a⟩)|
    b̅.(z).z̅.⟨sum⟩.⟨2,3⟩.(res))
```

This time $\Gamma$ contains only the definition of add and $\Gamma' = \Gamma \cup \{b : \alpha_1, a : \alpha_4, x : \alpha_5, y : \alpha_6, x_1 : \alpha_7, z : \alpha_3, res : \alpha_2\}$. INF returns

$$\alpha_4 = [\&\{\textbf{sum} :?(\alpha_6, \alpha_5).!(int).\textbf{end}, \textbf{inc} :?(\alpha_7).!(int).\textbf{end}\}] \quad \alpha_6 = int \quad \alpha_5 = int$$
$$\alpha_1 = [!(\alpha_4).\textbf{end}] \quad \alpha_1 \bowtie [?(\alpha_3).\textbf{end}] \quad \alpha_3 \bowtie [\oplus\{\textbf{sum} : \{!(int, int).?(\alpha_2).\textbf{end}\}]$$

and solve produces the solution

b : $[!([\&\{\textbf{sum} :?(int, int).!(int).\textbf{end}, \textbf{inc} :?(int).!(int).\textbf{end}\}]).\textbf{end}], x : int,$
a : $[\&\{\textbf{sum} :?(int, int).!(int).\textbf{end}, \textbf{inc} :?(int).!(int).\textbf{end}\}], y : int, x_1 : int,$
z : $[\&\{\textbf{sum} :?(int, int).!(int).\textbf{end}, \textbf{inc} :?(int).!(int).\textbf{end}\}], res : int$

*Example 4.* This example shows how an external function can input services and return services as well. In particular, the function lb has type $[!(int)] \times [!(int)] \rightarrow [!(int)]$; it inputs a couple of services and returns a service.

$(\nu \text{loadbalance})(\nu a)(\nu b)(\text{loadbalance}.\langle \text{lb}(a,b)\rangle | b.4 | a.4)$
$\qquad\qquad | \overline{\text{loadbalance}}.(x).\overline{x}.(res))$

The inferred types are loadbalance : $[!([!(int)].\textbf{end}]).\textbf{end}], a : [!(int).\textbf{end}], b : [!(int).\textbf{end}], x : [!(int).\textbf{end}], res : int$

## 6   Conclusions and Future Work

In this paper we studied an algorithm to infer session types. This is a preliminary study and we studied only a restricted form of session types in a syntactically constrained language which does not give to the programmer the freedom to directly use session channels. In spite of these limitations, we shown that with respect to the simply typed $\pi$-calculus a context with dual interactions and choices needs a new type of equations allowing for duality.

Moreover, typical typing systems for session types are nondeterministic due to the choices, both internal and external, embedded in the types. In fact, standard rules leave the entire freedom; one can add and remove branches until both the invocation protocol and the service specification are not syntactically equivalent (modulo duality). Thus, we have proposed a set of syntax directed rules which uses the if-then-else to deterministically expand choice branches and a corresponding relation to be used in place of the syntactical equivalence. Successively, we have developed an algorithm to infer types, subdivided in two parts: constraints extractor and solver.

As a consequence, the present ideas can be adopted as a base to the enhancement of the algorithm, adding $\mu$-types [11], extending the model with multi-parti session types [1] and studying the inference for [20].

## References

1. Bonelli, E., Compagnoni, A.: Multipoint. session types for a distributed calculus. In: Proceedings of 3rd Trustworthy Global Computing, Sophia-Antipolis, France (2007)

2. Booth, D., Liu, C.: Web Services Description Language (WSDL) Version 2.0 Part 0: Primer (2006), http://www.w3.org/TR/2006/CR-wsdl20-primer-20060327.
3. Boreale, M., Bruni, R., Caires, L., De Nicola, R., Lanese, I., Loreti, M., Martins, F., Montanari, U., Ravara, A., Sangiorgi, D., Vasconcelos, V., Zavattaro, G.: SCC: A service centered calculus. In: Bravetti, M., Núñez, M., Zavattaro, G. (eds.) WS-FM 2006. LNCS, vol. 4184, pp. 38–57. Springer, Heidelberg (2006)
4. Bruni, R., Mezzina, L.G.: A deadlock free type system for a calculus of services and sessions (submitted 2007),
   http://www.di.unipi.it/~bruni/publications/scctype.ps.gz
5. Bugliesi, M., Castagna, G., Crafa, S.: Access control for mobile agents: The calculus of boxed ambients. ACM Trans. Program. Lang. Syst. 26(1), 57–124 (2004)
6. Cardelli, L., Gordon, A.D.: Mobile ambients. Theor. Comput. Sci. 240(1), 177–213 (2000)
7. Chinnici, R., Haas, H., Lewis, A., Moreau, J.-J., et al.: Web Services Description Language (WSDL) Version 2.0 Part 2: Adjuncts (2006),
   http://www.w3.org/TR/2006/CR-wsdl20-adjuncts-20060327
8. Chinnici, R., Moreau, J.-J., Ryman, A., Weerawarana, S.: Web Services Description Language (WSDL) Version 2.0 Part 1: Core Language (2006),
   http://www.w3.org/TR/2006/CR-wsdl20-20060327
9. Christensen, E., Curbera, F., Meredith, G., Weerawarana, S.: Web Services Description Language (WSDL) 1.1 (2001),
   http://www.w3.org/TR/2001/NOTE-wsdl-20010315
10. Dezani-Ciancaglini, M., Mostrous, D., Yoshida, N., Drossopoulou, S.: Session types for object-oriented languages. In: Thomas, D. (ed.) ECOOP 2006. LNCS, vol. 4067, pp. 328–352. Springer, Heidelberg (2006)
11. Gapeyev, V., Levin, M., Pierce, B.: Recursive subtyping revealed. J. Funct. Program. 12(6), 511–548 (2002)
12. Garralda, P., Compagnoni, A., Dezani-Ciancaglini, M.: Bass: boxed ambients with safe sessions. In: PPDP 2006: Proceedings of the 8th ACM SIGPLAN symposium on Principles and practice of declarative programming, pp. 61–72. ACM Press, New York (2006)
13. Gay, S., Hole, M.: Subtyping for session types in the pi calculus. Acta Inform. 42(2), 191–225 (2005)
14. Honda, K., Vasconcelos, V., Kubo, M.: Language primitives and type discipline for structured communication-based programming. In: Hankin, C. (ed.) ESOP 1998. LNCS, vol. 1381, pp. 122–138. Springer, Heidelberg (1998)
15. Mezzina, L.G.: OCaml prototype of the type inference algorithm, http://www.lmezzina.com/sesstypes.zip
16. Robinson, J.A.: Logic and logic programming. Commun. ACM 35(3), 40–65 (1992)
17. Vasconcelos, V., Honda, K.: Principal typing-schemes in a polyadic -calculus (1992)
18. Vasconcelos, V.T.: Recursive types in a calculus of objects. Transactions of Information Processing Society of Japan 35(9), 1828–1836 (1994)
19. Vasconcelos, V.T., Tokoro, M.: A typing system for a calculus of objects. In: Nishio, S., Yonezawa, A. (eds.) ISOTAS 1993. LNCS, vol. 742, pp. 460–474. Springer, Heidelberg (1993)
20. Yoshida, N., Vasconcelos, V.: Language primitives and type discipline for structured communication-based programming revisited: Two systems for higher-order session communication. Electron. Notes Theor. Comput. Sci. 171(4), 73–93 (2007)

# An Event-Based Coordination Model for Context-Aware Applications

Angel Núñez and Jacques Noyé

OBASCO project, École des Mines de Nantes – INRIA, LINA
4, rue Alfred Kastler. B.P. 20722, 44307 Nantes cedex 3, France
{Angel.Nunez,Jacques.Noye}@emn.fr
http://www.emn.fr/x-info/obasco

**Abstract.** Context-aware applications adapt their behavior depending on changes in their environment context. Programming such applications in a modular way requires to modularize the global context into more specific contexts and attach specific behavior to these contexts. This is reminiscent of aspects and has led to the notion of context-aware aspects. This paper revisits this notion of context-aware aspects in the light of previous work on concurrent event-based aspect-oriented programming (CEAOP). It shows how CEAOP can be extended in a seamless way in order to define a model for the coordination of concurrent adaptation rules with explicit contexts. This makes it possible to reason about the compositions of such rules. The model is concretized into a prototypical modeling language.

## 1  Introduction

A *context-aware application* is an application that is able to adapt its behavior in order to best meet its users' need. It does so by taking into account *context* information, *i.e.*, any piece of information *relevant to the interaction between a user and an application* [1]. This typically includes information on the physical environment (*e.g.*, noise level, time of day, location, computer resources) as well as the social environment of the user (*e.g.*, nearby people, previous interactions, objectives, mood). The versatility of this notion of context has lead to a focus on context modelling and structuring [2,3] against the dynamic aspects of context change.

Some (reactive) context-aware applications [4,5,6,7,8] adapt their behavior using Event-Condition-Action (ECA) rules (first used in the field of reactive databases [9]), also referred to as *adaptation rules*. An ECA rule defines an action to be performed as a reaction to some event under a certain condition. In context-aware applications, the event part refers to context changes, the condition part to the current context and the action part to an adaptive behavior. In spite of the fact that the necessity of coordinating adaptation rules was early proposed (coordinated adaptation [5]), not much work has been done in this regard. As this paper shows, uncoordinated adaptation rules may lead to an inconsistent application state.

D. Lea and G. Zavattaro (Eds.): COORDINATION 2008, LNCS 5052, pp. 232–248, 2008.
© Springer-Verlag Berlin Heidelberg 2008

Let us illustrate this point with an example (inspired by an example used in the presentation of Fact Spaces [10]). Suppose Bob has a laptop that is able to control the house devices in terms of his location in the house. In the living room there is a video projector and speakers. Both devices support wireless connection to the laptop. Bob has programmed his laptop such that, when he is in the living room, the laptop connects to the video projector and the speakers, and opens a video player to play his favorite music clips in the living room.

Bob has however noted an undesirable behavior. Sometimes he can watch the clips in the video projector but the corresponding sound is not played in the speakers. Instead, he hears the music of his roommate Alice, who has a similar laptop. This is because Alice has programmed her laptop to listen to music in the living room, which only requires an audio connection. So, when Bob arrives after her, she has already a connection to the speakers. To solve this, Bob has reprogrammed his laptop. The context in which the clips have to be played is when he is in the living room and he has access to both the projector and the speakers. Now, when Alice and Bob are in the living room one can listen to music if Alice has arrived first, otherwise one can watch and listen to music clips.

Last week Alice has changed her preferences. Now she has reprogrammed her laptop to also play music clips in the living room (in the same way as Bob). Since then, a problem sometimes arises when Alice and Bob arrive at the same time in the room: nobody can see their clips. The reason is that sometimes Alice's laptop gains access to the speakers, whereas Bob's laptop gains access to the video projector. Since each laptop requires access to both resources in order to play the clips, no clip is played. We can see this situation as a kind of (context-aware) deadlock.

The behaviors programmed by Bob and Alice can be seen as adaptation rules that adapt the video player and the resources to the context of a presence of Bob and Alice in the living room. This is an example of uncoordinated adaptation leading to an inconsistent state in the application. We propose a model for the coordination of concurrent adaptation rules. The model is based on a model of concurrent aspects, CEAOP [11], and is provided in the form of a language for modeling the adaptation of applications to context changes. The language extends Finite State Processes (FSP) [12] proposed by Kramer *et al.*, which is a simple algebraic notation to describe process models. In our language, an application written in plain FSP syntax is enhanced with explicit contexts and adaptation rules. The enhanced application is translated into pure FSP and checked against the LTSA tool [12] to detect concurrency problems.

This paper is structured as follows. Section 2 briefly describes FSP and shows how our running example is modeled in FSP. Section 3 presents our language and at the same time describes how the running example can be enhanced with explicit contexts and adaptation rules. Section 4 describes the model of concurrent adaptation rules. Section 5 discusses related work. Finally, Sect. 6 concludes.

## 2  Overview of FSP

### 2.1  Syntax and Informal Semantics

A Labeled Transition System (LTS) is a form of state machine description, such that its transitions are labeled with action names. The left of Fig. 1 models, for instance, the behavior of a person that **enters** and **leaves** a room. The action **enter** causes a transition from *state(0)* to *state(1)*, and the action **leave** causes a transition from *state(1)* to *state(0)*.

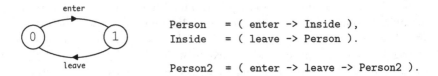

```
Person   = ( enter -> Inside ),
Inside   = ( leave -> Person ).

Person2  = ( enter -> leave -> Person2 ).
```

**Fig. 1.** Light switch state machine

Finite State Processes (FSP) is a simple algebraic notation to describe process models. Each FSP description has a corresponding state machine (LTS) description. Figure 2 shows a simplified version of the FSP syntax (the full syntax can be found in [12]). This syntax definition, as well as the other definitions shown in this paper, are based on the syntax definition formalism SDF [13] (close to EBNF) and its implementation with scannerless generalized-LR parsing (SGLR) [14,15]. An SDF production $s_1...s_n$ -> $s_0$ defines that an instance of non-terminal $s_0$ can be produced by concatenating elements from symbols $s_1...s_n$, in that order. SDF provides notation for optional ( *?* ) and iterated ( *\**,*+* ) non-terminals. The notation $\{s\ lit\}^+$ represents a list of *s* separated by *lit*.

| | |
|---|---|
| *ProcId* = *ProcBody* . | -> *ProcDef* |
| *Proc* | -> *ProcBody* |
| *Proc* , { *LocalProcDef* , }+ | -> *ProcBody* |
| *ProcId* = *LocalProc* | -> *LocalProcDef* |
| ( { *Branch* \| }+ ) | -> *Proc* |
| { *ActLabel* -> }+ -> *ProcId* | -> *Branch* |
| *Label* | -> *ActLabel* |

**Fig. 2.** FSP syntax definition

The definition of a finite state process (*ProcDef*) associates an identifier (*ProcId*) to a body (*ProcBody*). The body consists of a process expression (*Proc*) and an optional list of local process definitions (*LocalProcDef*). A process expression is a choice between one or more branches separated by the choice operator |. A branch (*Branch*) is a sequence of action labels separated by the sequence operator ->, and terminated by a process identifier. Processes defined in the body are referenced by their identifiers, whose scope is the definition of the finite state process. The non-terminal *ActLabel* is intentionally introduced for further use.

An FSP starts behaving as its process expression. It performs a sequence of actions until a reference to another process (or the same process) is found. Then, the FSP continues behaving as the referenced process. As an example, the code on the right of Fig. 1 illustrates two equivalent FSPs for the person's behavior. `Person` performs the action `enter` and continues behaving as the process `Inside`. Then, it performs the action `leave` and comes back to the initial state. `Person2` is a more compact notation for the same behavior.

*Parallel* processes can be built by composing sequential or parallel processes using the operator ||. Parallel composition corresponds to the synchronized product of the corresponding automata. *Shared actions* constrain parallel composition so that an action shared by a set of processes is performed at the same time by all the processes of the set. Relabeling and hiding operations can be used to define which actions are actually shared at composition time. FSP is used to model applications as a set of processes together with their interactions through shared actions.

### 2.2    Modeling the Motivation Example Using FSP

Let us illustrate FSP by modeling the behavior of our running example, without adaptation rules. Bob and Alice enter and leave the living room and both an audio and a video resources are ready to accept connections. Figure 3 shows this model. The basic behavior of a user is modeled by the process `Person` of the previous section. The activity of Alice is modeled by the process `alice:Person`, an "instance" of the process `Person`, whose actions are prefixed by `alice`. Analogously, the activity of Bob is modeled by the process `bob:Person`. The process `Resource` models a resource, which can be `acquired` by a user and afterward `released`. The video resource is modeled by the process `{alice.video,bob.video}::Resource`, an instance of the process `Resource`, whose transitions are duplicated and each duplicate is prefixed by `alice.video` and `bob.video`, respectively. This means that there are two distinct actions (`alice.video.acquire` and `bob.video.acquire`) to obtain the video resource and similarly two actions to free it (`alice.video.release` and `bob.video.release`). Analogously the process `{alice.audio,bob.audio}::Resource` models the audio resource. The access to each resource is mutually exclusive. Finally, the process `Application` models the application by composing all the processes using the composition operator ||.

## 3    The Language

This section presents our language for modeling the adaptation of applications to context changes. The language extends FSP with *adaptation rules*, *contexts*, and *context rules*. An adaptation rule is used to adapt a base application by triggering *reactions* to the occurrence of particular base actions. In our example,

```
Resource      = ( acquire -> release -> Resource ).

||Application = (  alice:Person || bob:Person
                || {alice.video, bob.video}::Resource
                || {alice.audio, bob.audio}::Resource ).
```

**Fig. 3.** Model of the application in FSP

an adaptation rule can trigger playing clips as a reaction to the entrance of a user in the living room and can stop playing clips as a reaction to the user's exit. A context is used to abstract a situation, e.g. the presence of a user in the living room. A context rule improves adaptation rules by attaching behavior to abstract contexts rather than to concrete actions. Once defined, context rules can be instantiated with respect to concrete contexts. In our example, a context rule can attach the behavior of playing clips to an abstract context denoting a situation when clips should be played. By instantiating the context rule, it is possible to associate this situation to the presence of a user in the living room. Decomposing adaptation rules into contexts and context rules makes it easier to capture context-awareness by making the notion of context explicit. It also improves modularity and reuse.

The overall language is built as a combination of languages, namely FSP, adaptation rules, contexts, and context rules. Thanks to the use of SDF, we can easily combine the FSP syntax definition presented in Sect. 2 with the other languages. We use *grammar mixins*, i.e. syntax definitions parameterized with the context in which they are used. We explain this notion in the remainder of this section as we present the different parts of the language.

### 3.1   Adaptation Rules

An adaptation rule is used to adapt an application. The application that is the subject of this adaptation is denoted as the *base* application. Furthermore, we use the term "base" as an adjective to denote an entity that belongs to the base application, *e.g.* base action.

Let us call *events* the base actions. An adaptation rule in our language can be seen as a process that observes events and can optionally react by introducing actions, called *reactions*, where observing an event means synchronizing on it. The definition of an adaptation rule only talks about the events of interest in each state. A complete process model of the rule, which defines what happens for each event in each state, is generated by a compiler, which translates our language to FSP. In particular, new transitions, that we call *waiting loops*, are created in each state for each (shared) label not explicitly taken care of. These transitions simply loop back to their source state.

Figure 4 shows the syntax of an adaptation rule, which is very similar to the FSP syntax. We use grammar mixins in order to reuse the FSP syntax. An adaptation rule is defined as an identifier and a body. The body has the same syntax as an FSP body (mixin *ProcBody[[RuleCtx]]*), but the mixin parameter is propagated within *ProcBody* and makes it possible to define new productions, here for *ActLabel*, which may now, in the context of an adaptation rule, include a reaction, distinguished through the operator =>. The prefix + is used to easily recognize adaptation rules.

```
+ ProcId = ProcBody[[RuleCtx]]   .  -> RuleDef
Label => Reaction                   -> ActLabel[[RuleCtx]]
{ Label ; }+                        -> Reaction
```

```
+PlayRule    = ( enter -> Inside),
  Inside     = ( video.acquire -> Video | audio.acquire -> Audio
               | leave -> PlayRule ),
  Video      = ( audio.acquire => play -> Played | leave -> PlayRule ),
  Audio      = ( video.acquire => play -> Played | leave -> PlayRule ),
  Played     = ( leave => stop -> PlayRule ).
```

**Fig. 4.** Syntax of an adaptation rule (at the top) and example of an adaptation rule that triggers the actions that **plays** and **stops** clips (at the bottom)

As an example, the process **PlayRule** at the bottom of Fig. 4 illustrates an adaptation rule that plays the clips in the living room. Note the use of the operator => to indicate the reactions **play** and **stop**. This rule can be afterward instantiated for each user using prefixing, *e.g.* **alice:PlayRule** corresponds to the adaptation rule that plays the clips for Alice.

Adaptation rules are expressive enough to observe context changes and react. However, without an independent notion of context, contexts are implicitly embedded in the adaptation rules to the detriment of modularity and easy reasoning.

### 3.2  Context

**Context Modeling.** A fundamental part of a context-aware application is context modeling. Due to its versatility, the notion of context can be represented in different ways like *key-value* models, *logic-based* models and *ontology-based* models [16]. The choice of a specific model depends on the required level of abstraction. *The exact GPS position of a person might not be of value for an application but the name of the room the person is in, may be* [3]. We aim to abstract the notion of context as much as possible in order to facilitate the definition of adaptation rules and the verification of the adapted systems.

A context represents an environmental state. Adaptation rules adapt an application with respect to such a state. Usually, this adaptation is required as soon as the context changes, which means that adaptation rules are triggered as soon as the change is detected. The application detects context changes through computations such as the evaluation of a value in a key-value model, or the detection of a new fact in a logic-based model. We consider these computations as *context-switch events* and we model a context using them. In addition, we assume that these events can be extracted from the application model. For example, this is when `alice.enter` occurs that the system can detect that Alice is in the living room. In this setting, we model a context as the tuple *(context, in, out, context provider)*, where *context* is the name given to the context, *in* and *out* are context-switch events, *in* refers to the event making the system detect that it is in *context*, *out* refers to the event making the system detect that it is not in *context* anymore, and *context provider* is a process that defines these events. In the remainder, it will be said that a context is *active* in all the states following the *in* action and preceding the *out* action, otherwise it will be said to be *inactive*.

**Context Providers.** A context is defined in a *context provider*, which has the same name as the context. A context provider is a process that observes events and indicates what are the context-switch ones. A context provider can be either *primitive* or *composite*. A primitive context provider observes events and annotates, with the suffixes `:in` and `:out`, the *in* and *out* actions, respectively.

Figure 5 shows the syntax of a primitive context provider. A primitive context provider is defined as an identifier and a body with the same syntax as an FSP. Furthermore, an action label in the context of a primitive context provider, can be a label followed by the suffix `:in` or `:out`. Figure 5 also illustrates a primitive context provider, namely `LivingRoom`, which defines the context of being in the living room. This context observes the base action `enter` and the sequence `enter -> leave`. As the annotations indicate, the context is activated at `enter` and deactivated at `leave`. In a similar way, we define the context `Connected`, which models a resource connection context. A context provider can be instantiated using prefixing, *e.g.* `video:Connected` represents the context of a connection to the video resource.

```
@ ProcId = ProcBody[[CpCtx]] .    -> PrimCxtDef
Label Suffix                       -> ActLabel[[CpCtx]]
:in | :out                         -> Suffix

@LivingRoom = ( enter:in -> leave:out -> LivingRoom ).
@Connected  = ( acquire:in -> release:out -> Connected ).
```

**Fig. 5.** Syntax of a primitive context provider (at the top) and example (at the bottom)

More complex contexts can be defined by composing simple context providers using operators. We provide the three basic logical operators: the conjunction operator `&`, the disjunction operator `|`, and the negation operator `!`. For example, the context `LivingRoom & Connected` is active when both `LivingRoom` and `Connected` are active, i.e. when in the context `LivingRoom`, `Connected` becomes active, or vice-versa. In an analogous way, the context `LivingRoom | Connected` is active when either `LivingRoom` or `Connected` is active. Finally, `!LivingRoom`

```
@ ProcId = ! ProcId .              -> CompCxtDef
@ ProcId = ProcId BinOp ProcId .   -> CompCxtDef
& | |                              -> BinOp

@Ready = ( LivingRoom & video:Connected & audio:Connected ).
```

**Fig. 6.** Syntax of a composite context provider (at the top) and example (at the bottom)

is active when LivingRoom is inactive, *i.e.* it is a context that is initially active and becomes inactive as soon as LivingRoom becomes active.

Figure 6 shows the syntax of a composite context provider. This figure also defines the context Ready as the conjunction of the context LivingRoom and the context Connected, instantiated for each resource. Because of the conjunction, Ready models the context in which a user is in the living room and a resource has been connected for him/her.

## 3.3 Context Rules

We define *context rules* as a means to define adaptation rules that abstract the context away. A context rule can be seen as a parameterized adaptation rule that receives a context as a parameter, and can observe the context-switch events *in* and *out* associated to this context (through actions denoted by the keywords in and out, respectively). Once defined, a context rule can be instantiated for a concrete context. Figure 7 shows the syntax of a context rule (*CtxRuleDef*) and its instantiation (*CtxRuleInst*).

The rule that plays the clips of our running example can be written in a modular way using a context rule, as shown at the bottom of Fig. 7. PlayDef defines such a rule in terms of a generic context. In the same way, we can model a rule, namely ConnDef, that attempts to acquire a resource. It observes the beginning of the context and can either react by performing acquire, if the resource is free, or observe the deactivation of the context. Afterwards, it releases the resource if it was previously acquired. These rules can be instantiated for the concrete contexts LivingRoom and Ready. A context rule can be prefixed, *e.g.* alice:PlayDef would correspond to the rule that plays clips for Alice. The prefixing of a context rule is such that all the actions of the rule are prefixed, except the context-switch events.

## 3.4 Composition

Adaptation rules adapt a base application. In terms of FSP, this adaptation means a composition. We provide the operators + and * for denoting the sequential composition of the FSP that represents a base application with one or more (context) adaptation rules, whose syntax is shown in Fig. 8.

```
+ ProcId ( ProcId ) = ProcBody[[CrCtx]] .          -> CtxRuleDef
{ ActLabel[[CrCtx]] -> }+ -> ProcId ( ProcId )     -> Branch
Label => Reaction                                  -> ActLabel[[CrCtx]]
( in | out ) => Reaction                           -> ActLabel[[CrCtx]]
in | out                                           -> ActLabel[[CrCtx]]
+ ProcId = ProcId( ProcId ) .                      -> CtxRuleInst
```

```
+PlayDef(Cxt)   = ( in => play -> out => stop -> PlayDef(Cxt) ).
+ConnDef(Cxt)   = ( in => acquire -> out => release -> ConnDef(Cxt),
                  | in => out -> ConnDef(Cxt) ).
+ConnRule       = ConnDef(LivingRoom).
+PlayRule       = PlayDef(Ready).
```

**Fig. 7.** Syntax of a context rule (at the top) and examples (at the bottom)

```
|| ProcId = BaseExpr SeqOp ProcId .      -> Adaptation
ProcId                                   -> BaseExpr
BaseExpr SeqOp ProcId                     -> BaseExpr
+ | *                                    -> SeqOp
```

**Fig. 8.** Syntax of the composition of an application and adaptation rules

The composition of the base application with a single rule gives as a result a new FSP denoting an adapted base application. This composition is such that a reaction defined for an event takes place after the event is performed by all the base processes synchronizing on such an event. Furthermore, these processes cannot continue until the reaction has been performed.

When applying several rules, these operators are left-associative, i.e. if $B$ is a standard FSP, and $R1$ and $R2$ are rules, then $B + R1 + R2$ is the same as ( $B + R1$ ) + $R2$. $B$ is first composed with $R1$ giving as a result a new adapted application that is afterward composed with $R2$. As a result, if two rules apply to the same event, some form of precedence takes place. Let us consider the example above when considering individual events. The general scheme is that the reaction of $R2$ precedes the reaction of $R1$. In other words, the last adaptation has priority. When considering context rules, this general scheme is applied to all the events when using the operator +. The operator * behaves slightly differently with respect to "out" reactions, which are in reverse order: the "in" reaction of $R2$ precedes the "in" reaction of $R1$, but the "out" reaction of $R2$ comes after the "out" reaction of $R2$ in order to obtain a form of nesting.

## 3.5  Adaptation Rules and Aspects

Aspect-Oriented Programming [17] makes it possible to localize concerns that cannot be encapsulated in standard modularization systems. In our language, an adaptation rule can be seen as a kind of aspect. It observes actions that are scattered in the definition of other processes and introduces behavior. However, a specific property of aspects is that they may prevent the base program from executing some actions, and this is clearly not supported by our adaptation rules.

We include support for aspects in our language by extending the syntax of adaptation rules with *aspect expressions*. The extension allows adaptation rules to observe when a base action is about to happen. Then, it can introduce actions before and/or after the occurrence of the action. In addition, it can prevent the base program from performing such an action. An adaptation rule is equipped with aspect expressions of the form *action > before; ps; after*, where *action* is a base action, *before* a sequence of actions performed before *action*, *after* a sequence of actions performed after *action*, and *ps* either skip or proceed. The action skip means that the base action must be skipped and the action proceed means that this base action must take place. With this extension, expressions of the form *event => reaction* are syntactic sugar for the expression *event > proceed; reaction*. For the sake of simplicity, this paper just deals with the case *ps* is proceed and only after actions are defined. Figure 9 shows the way the syntax of (context) adaptation rules is extended.

| | |
|---|---|
| *Label > Advice* | *-> ActLabel[[RuleCtx]]* |
| *Label > Advice* | *-> ActLabel[[CrCtx]]* |
| ( in \| out ) *> Advice* | *-> ActLabel[[CrCtx]]* |
| ( *Label* ; )* *PS* ( ; *Label* )* | *-> Advice* |
| proceed \| skip | *-> PS* |

**Fig. 9.** Extension of (context) adaptation rules with aspect expressions

Including support for aspects in the language allows us to reuse previous work on concurrent event-based aspect-oriented programming (CEAOP) [11,18,19]. In this way, we add support for concurrent rules using the model of concurrent aspects as the next section shows.

This section has presented a language to model context-aware applications. Our running example can be modeled in a modular way using explicit context and context rules. The next section is about coordinating rules in order to avoid inconsistent states in an application.

## 4   Concurrent Adaptation Rules

We denote as concurrent adaptation rules all the rules that are triggered by the same event. In our running example, the rule that attempts to open a video connection is concurrent with the one for an audio connection. Both rules are triggered by the same event: the entry to the living room. The uncoordinated behaviors of these rules may lead to an inconsistent state in the base application, as mentioned in the introduction of this paper. The necessity of coordinating concurrent rules has already been presented as the necessity of coordinated adaptation [5]. We contribute to this by presenting a model for the coordination of adaptation rules.

Adaptation rules are translated into aspects, as shown in the previous section. Thus, the schemes for aspect coordination introduced by CEAOP can be used for adaptation rules, based on a combination of event renaming and hiding, and the use of specific operators. In the following we present the main points behind the coordination of aspects restricted to adaptation rules, *i.e.* aspects that always proceed and that only define after advices. More details about coordinating full-blown aspects are available in [11]. In our model, a base application is considered as a combination of several processes, and an adaptation rule as an independent process that is coordinated with the base application and the other adaptation rules. Adaptation rules are translated into FSPs, which are composed with the FSPs that model the base application. Some variability is allowed for the coordination, which determines the way the translation is done, as described in the remainder of this section.

## 4.1   Coordinating the Base Application with Adaptation Rules

An adaptation rule can be composed with the base application following several coordination schemes: (1) the reactions to an event can be performed in the background as soon as the event occurs, while the base application may continue its normal computation, (2) the base application may wait until the reaction has been performed, or (3) the reactions can be performed in parallel with the event. We embody these schemes in the operator sync(*base, rule, parallel, yield*), where *base* is the FSP that models the base application, *rule* is an adaptation rule, *parallel* is a boolean value denoting whether reactions are triggered in parallel with events, and *yield* is a boolean value denoting whether the base application has to wait for the end of the reactions. In this setting, an expression $B + R$ using the operator + of Sect. 3.4 is equivalent to sync($B, R,$ false, true), i.e. the reactions occur after the event and the base application waits for the end of them.

The coordination, using the operator sync, of an adaptation rule declaring an expression *event* => *reaction* -> $Q$ is implemented as follows. The reaction is translated into the sequence at the bottom of Fig. 10. The base application is instrumented such that all the occurrences of *event* -> $P$ are translated into the sequence at the top of Fig. 10. The following *synchronization events* are included in the translations: pb_*event* (the event is about to be performed), pe_*event* (the event has been just performed), and e_*event* (the end of the event scope). Figure 10 illustrates a coordination sync($B, R,$ false, true). The labels surrounded with squares correspond to the synchronization events and the vertical lines represent the different rendezvous. After a first rendezvous at pb_*event*, the base application performs *event*. A second rendezvous is at pe_*event*. Then, the actions denoted by *reaction* are performed until a last rendezvous at e_*event*. The different options of sync can be achieved by hiding events. For example, if pe_*event* is hidden the reaction is parallel to the event, or if e_*event* is hidden the application does not wait for the reaction.

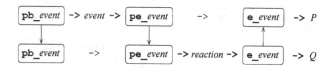

**Fig. 10.** Coordination of an application and an adaptation rule

## 4.2 Coordinating Adaptation Rules

Let us come back to our running example and consider the rules for triggering the video and audio connections. These rules are not coordinated, leading to an inconsistent state in the application. Ordering the way resources are acquired is a known manner to solve this problem. This means coordinating adaptation rules.

Adaptation rules can be composed together using operators. The result of applying an operator is a composite rule that can be afterward composed with the base application. Two concurrent adaptation rules can be coordinated using two different schemes: (1) reactions to a shared event can be performed sequentially, or (2) they can be performed in parallel. We reuse the CEAOP operators to implement these schemes: the operator Fun implements sequential reactions, and the operator ParAnd parallel reactions.

The implementation is as follows. Let us consider two adaptation rules declaring expressions of the form *event* => *reaction1* -> *Q*, and *event* => *reaction2* -> *R*, respectively. Analogously to the previous section, the expressions are translated into the sequences on the middle and at the bottom of Fig. 11, respectively. The base application is instrumented such that all the occurrences of *event* -> *P* are translated into the sequence at the top of Fig. 11. This figure illustrates the operator Fun. This operator uses relabeling to impose a rendezvous (indicated by a vertical line) between pe_*event* of the first rule and e_*event* of the third one by giving a common name pe1_*event*. As a result, the reactions are performed sequentially in the order *reaction2* -> *reaction1*. Without this renaming, *reaction1* would run in parallel with *reaction2*, which is the behavior determined by ParAnd. (see Fig. 12). The operator Fun is used to implement the composition of a base application with two rules using the operator + as defined in Sect. 3.4.

## 4.3 Coordinating Contexts and Adaptation Rules

A context provider is a process that observes events and indicates which are the context-switch ones. A context rule uses these context-switch events in order to define reactions that depends on the context. Therefore, the coordination of the base application, context providers and context rules is done through these events.

At the implementation level, some instrumentation is required. Let us consider that a context is activated at the second occurrence of an event foo. In this case, it is not possible to say that foo is the context-switch event, because the first occurrence of foo does not activate the context. It is necessary to define

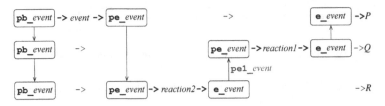

**Fig. 11.** Coordination of adaptation rules using the operator **Fun**

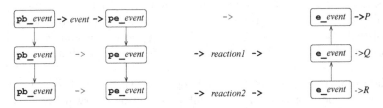

**Fig. 12.** Coordination of adaptation rules using the operator **ParAnd**

other events "representing" each context-switch event, generated at the same time as the original context-switch event. If the name of the context is *context*, then **in_***context* and **out_***context* represent the context-switch events *in* and *out*, respectively.

Finally, a context provider is implemented as an adaptation rule throwing as a reaction to the occurrence of a context-switch event the corresponding pseudo context-switch event. Context rules are translated into adaptation rules by replacing the **in** and **out** events by the corresponding pseudo context-switch events.

This section has shown a model for the coordinated adaptation of an application using explicit contexts and adaptation rules. Coordinating schemes such as ordering reactions make it possible to keep a consistent application state while adapting the application.

## 5   Related Work

Fact Spaces [10] is a logic-based approach to context-awareness implemented in a concrete language called CRIME. One of the main ideas behind the model of Fact Spaces, inherited from Linda, is the existence of a distributed data base of knowledge populated with shared facts. Each time a fact is added or removed from the data base, subscribed applications are notified. New facts can be added or actions in applications can be triggered as soon as their required facts are matched. These rules correspond to a list of facts, which have to be satisfied in order to trigger actions or publish other facts. Our language provides support for defining similar rules but using events instead of facts. This allows us to easily model concurrent rules and analyze concurrency properties using pre-existing frameworks, which in a logic-based system is harder.

ContextL [20] is an object-oriented programming language that allows for Context-oriented Programming. It provides means to associate partial classes and method definitions with *layers* and to activate and deactivate such layers in the control flow of a running program depending on the current context. Thus, the behavior of objects is extended with the activated layers. Although our approach is at the modeling level, we can find similarities. The behavior of an object modeled in an FSP can be extended with context rules, which can be seen as a kind of layers. Reactions are triggered depending on whether a given context is active or not. A unique feature of our approach is that we specifically deal with *concurrent* adaptation rules, whereas ContextL has no specific support for concurrent layers.

Shankar *et. al* introduced the ECPAP framework for policy-based management of a pervasive system [21]. The framework manages policies based on the Event-Condition-Action pattern: a policy defines an action to be performed when an event occurs under a given condition. In addition, the action is triggered only if a precondition holds, and it is considered successful if a postcondition is satisfied after its execution. The approach deals with concurrent policies, *i.e.* policies that define actions for a common event. When this event occurs a Petri net (built at compile time) defines an optimal order of execution of the involved actions. The adaptation rules of our approach are comparable with the policies of the ECPAP framework. Indeed, when considering individual events, our adaptation rules are based on a form of ECA pattern. However, our approach is more abstract. We consider events not only as environmental events but also as any kind of action (join point) in the computation of a system. In this way, an action triggered by an adaptation rule can be seen as an event by another rule, thus permitting the detection of possible conflicts between adaptation rules. Furthermore, linking related events using explicit events makes it possible to detect other kinds of conflicts between rules. Finally, we include an explicit notion of context and introduce context rules. The management of pre- and postcondition together with the automatic ordering of reactions is an interesting feature of the ECPAP framework that would be worth including in our approach.

In the area of Aspect-Oriented Programming, Tanter *et al.* introduced *context-aware aspects* [22], as aspects that match base-program joint points depending on whether a given context is active. They stated the necessity of context as a first-class entity in aspect-oriented languages that has to be stateful, composable and parameterized. Our approach augments the proposal of Tanter *et al.* by providing support to concurrent context-aware aspects.

Finally, our approach is based on CEAOP [11] and therefore includes stateful aspects [23]. In our approach, part of a stateful aspect can be factorized out in the notion of context. The instantiation of a context rule with a concrete context can be seen as the completion of the initial state machine of a stateful aspect with the states and transitions defined in the concrete context.

# 6   Conclusion

This paper has presented an approach to model coordinated adaptation of context-aware applications by enhancing a simple process calculus, FSP, with adaptation rules, context, context rules, and aspects. We have built an extension of the LTSA tool that supports processes written using our language.[1] The extension translates (context) adaptation rules and context providers into FSPs. Then, these FSPs are manipulated with the standard LTSA tool in order to check concurrency properties.

Note that our main contribution is not in expressiveness (everything is translated into FSP), but rather in clarity of the specification and modular reasoning. In this regard, we provide a model that simplifies the analysis of concurrency properties in context-aware applications. Furthermore, our approach can be used as a model for context-aware applications that takes concurrency into account.

We are now interested in the use of this modeling language in two complementary directions: the analysis of existing programs, e.g. programs written using CRIME rules, with respect to their concurrency properties, as well as the synthesis of actual implementations by refining part of the model (e.g. adding parameters to actions) and combining the refined language to a general-purpose programming language (e.g. Java) that could be used to implement the atomic actions. Some work has already been done in this direction as we have previously explored the possibility of using CEAOP as the basis of combining Java components and aspects using behavioral interfaces [19]. When considering aspects, these interfaces have much in common with adaptation rules.

**Acknowledgments.** We would like to thank the anonymous reviewers for their helpful comments and mention that this work has been partly supported by the project AMPLE: Aspect- Oriented, Model-Driven, Product Line Engineering (STREP IST-033710).

# References

1. Dey, A.K., Abowd, G.D.: Towards a better understanding of context and context-awareness. In: Proceedings of the CHI 2000 Workshop on the What, Who, Where, When and How of Context-Awareness, Georgia Tech. (April 2000)
2. Gu, T., Pung, H.K., Zhang, D.Q.: Toward an OSGi-based infrastructure for context-aware applications. IEEE Pervasive Computing 3(4), 66–74 (2004)
3. Baldauf, M., Dustdar, S., Rosenberg, F.: A survey on context-aware systems. International Journal of Ad Hoc and Ubiquitous Computing 2(4), 263–277 (2007)
4. Rakotonirainy, A., Indulska, J., Loke, S.W., Zaslavsky, A.B.: Middleware for reactive components: An integrated use of context, roles, and event based coordination. In: Guerraoui, R. (ed.) Middleware 2001. LNCS, vol. 2218, pp. 77–98. Springer, Heidelberg (2001)

---

[1] Implementation available at http://www.emn.fr/x-info/anunezlo/ltsa-modeling/.

5. Efstratiou, C., Cheverst, K., Davies, N., Friday, A.: An architecture for the effective support of adaptive context-aware applications. In: Tan, K.-L., Franklin, M.J., Lui, J.C.-S. (eds.) MDM 2001. LNCS, vol. 1987, pp. 15–26. Springer, Heidelberg (2000)
6. Ahn, J., Chang, B.M., Doh, K.G.: A Policy Description Language for Context-Based Access Control and Adaptation in Ubiquitous Environment. In: Zhou, X., Sokolsky, O., Yan, L., Jung, E.-S., Shao, Z., Mu, Y., Lee, D.C., Kim, D.Y., Jeong, Y.-S., Xu, C.-Z. (eds.) EUC Workshops 2006. LNCS, vol. 4097, pp. 650–659. Springer, Heidelberg (2006)
7. Daniele, L., Costa, P.D., Pires, L.F.: Towards a Rule-Based Approach for Context-Aware Applications. In: Pras, A., van Sinderen, M. (eds.) EUNICE 2007. LNCS, vol. 4606, pp. 33–43. Springer, Heidelberg (2007)
8. de Ipiña, D.L., Katsiri, E.: An ECA Rule-Matching Service for Simpler Development of Reactive Applications. IEEE DSOnline 2(7) (2001)
9. Paton, N.W., Díaz, O.: Active Database Systems. ACM Computing Surveys 31(1), 63–103 (1999)
10. Mostinckx, S., Scholliers, C., Philips, E., Herzeel, C., Meuter, W.D.: Fact Spaces: Coordination in the face of disconnection. In: Murphy, A.L., Vitek, J. (eds.) CO-ORDINATION 2007. LNCS, vol. 4467, pp. 268–285. Springer, Heidelberg (2007)
11. Douence, R., Le Botlan, D., Noyé, J., Südholt, M.: Concurrent aspects. In: Proceedings of the 4th International Conference on Generative Programming and Component Engineering (GPCE 2006), pp. 79–88. ACM Press, New York (2006)
12. Magee, J., Kramer, J.: Concurrency: State Models and Java, 2nd edn. Wiley, Chichester (2006)
13. Visser, E.: Syntax Definition for Language Prototyping. PhD thesis, University of Amsterdam (September 1997)
14. Visser, E.: Scannerless Generalized-LR Parsing. Technical Report P9707, Programming Research Group, University of Amsterdam (July 1997)
15. van den Brand, M.G.J., Scheerder, J., Vinju, J.J., Visser, E.: Disambiguation Filters for Scannerless Generalized LR Parsers. In: Horspool, R.N. (ed.) CC 2002. LNCS, vol. 2304, pp. 143–158. Springer, Heidelberg (2002)
16. Strang, T., Popien, C.L.: A Context Modeling Survey. In: Workshop on Advanced Context Modelling, Reasoning and Management, UbiComp 2004 - The Sixth International Conference on Ubiquitous Computing (September 2004)
17. Kiczales, G., Lamping, J., Mendhekar, A., Maeda, C., Lopes, C.V., Loingtier, J.-M., Irwin, J.: Aspect-oriented programming. In: Aksit, M., Matsuoka, S. (eds.) ECOOP 1997. LNCS, vol. 1241, pp. 220–242. Springer, Heidelberg (1997)
18. Núñez, A., Noyé, J.: A domain-specific language for coordinating concurrent aspects in Java. In: Douence, R., Fradet, P. (eds.) 3ème Journée Francophone sur le Développement de Logiciels Par Aspects (JFDLPA 2007) (March 2007)
19. Núñez, A., Noyé, J.: A seamless extension of components with aspects using protocols. In: Reussner, R., Szyperski, C., Weck, W. (eds.) WCOP 2007 - Components beyond Reuse - 12th International ECOOP Workshop on Component-Oriented Programming (July 2007)
20. Costanza, P., Hirschfeld, R.: Language constructs for context-oriented programming: An overview of ContextL. In: DLS 2005: Proceedings of the 2005 Symposium on Dynamic Languages, pp. 1–10. ACM, New York (2005)
21. Shankar, C.S., Campbell, R.H.: Ordering management actions in pervasive systems using specification-enhanced policies. In: 4th IEEE International Conference on Pervasive Computing and Communications (PerCom 2006), Pisa, Italy, March 13-17, 2006, pp. 234–238. IEEE Computer Society, Los Alamitos (2006)

22. Tanter, É., Gybels, K., Denker, M., Bergel, A.: Context-Aware Aspects. In: Löwe, W., Südholt, M. (eds.) SC 2006. LNCS, vol. 4089, pp. 227–242. Springer, Heidelberg (2006)
23. Douence, R., Fradet, P., Südholt, M.: Composition, reuse and interaction analysis of stateful aspects. In: Murphy, G.C., Lieberherr, K.J. (eds.) Proceedings of the 3rd International Conference on Aspect-Oriented Software Development, AOSD 2004, Lancaster, UK, March 22-24, 2004, pp. 141–150. ACM, New York (2004)

# Formal Analysis of BPMN Via a Translation into COWS*

Davide Prandi[1], Paola Quaglia[2], and Nicola Zannone[3]

[1] Dip. di Medicina Sperimentale e Clinica,
Univ. Magna Graecia di Catanzaro, Italy
[2] Dip. di Ing. e Scienza dell'Informazione, Univ. di Trento, Italy
[3] Dep. of Computer Science, Univ. of Toronto, Canada

**Abstract.** A translation of the Business Process Modeling Notation into the process calculus COWS is presented. The stochastic extension of COWS is then exploited to address quantitative reasoning about the behaviour of business processes. An example of such reasoning is shown by running the PRISM probabilistic model checker on a case study.

## 1 Introduction

A challenging question for organisations is how to create strong, yet flexible, business processes. Business Process Management is emerging as a means for understanding the activities that organisations can perform to optimise their business processes or to adapt them to new organisational needs. Specifically, it defines the activities to be performed by organisations to manage and, if necessary, to improve their business processes. Business Process Management activities concern the design and capture of existing business processes as well as the analysis of new ones. In this setting, the definition of languages for modelling business processes is a key step in Business Process Management due to the need of describing their structure and behaviour.

Different languages have been proposed in literature to model business processes (e.g., [6,25,27]). Among them, the Business Process Modeling Notation (BPMN) [19] is emerging as the de-facto standard modelling notation in industry. BPMN was designed to provide a graphical notation for XML-based business process languages, such as WS-BPEL [18]. Therefore, business analysts can take advantage from the use of BPMN since they can exploit facilities for generating executable WS-BPEL code from BPMN graphical models [20]. Unfortunately, BPMN is informal and leaves room for ambiguity about its semantics [5]. Moreover, it does not allow for formal analysis. These issues are challenging and call for formal frameworks encoding graphical elements into formal specifications.

Process calculi have been proved powerful enough to formalise the activities performed within a business process, to render in a natural way the parallelism and concurrency of interactions among participants as well as to analyse the

* This work has been partially sponsored by the project SENSORIA, IST-2005-016004.

overall process behaviour. In particular, in this paper we present a translation of BPMN into the Calculus of Orchestration of Web Services (COWS) [13]. A stochastic extension of COWS [22] is then exploited to obtain semantic models that are quantitatively verified using the PRISM [10] model checker. Such a quantitative reasoning aims to assist system designers in the evaluation and comparison of design alternatives with the intent of driving them in the selection of an appropriate infrastructure supporting the business process.

The choice of COWS is motivated, on one hand, by the fact that, being a foundational calculus, it is based on a very small set of primitives associated with a formal operational semantics that can be exploited for the automated derivation of the behaviour of the specified services. On the other hand, the language is strongly inspired by WS-BPEL, providing, among the rest, macros for fault and compensation handlers. Not least, an on-the-fly model checker for the qualitative verification of COWS specifications is already available [7]. So the proposed translation of BPMN into COWS allows testing business processes against, e.g., responsiveness properties like "after a request, a response is eventually sent to the requesting customer".

The paper is organised as follows. Sec. 2 and Sec. 3 present a brief overview of BPMN and of COWS, respectively. A small business process used as a case study is also illustrated. The translation from BPMN to COWS is then reported in Sec. 4. The following section (Sec. 5) provides some reasoning on the quantitative analysis carried on the case study via PRISM. Sec. 6 discusses related works and presents some final remarks.

## 2   BPMN

BPMN [19] provides a standard graphical notation for business process modelling. A business process is represented as a Business Process Diagram (BPD), which is composed of a set of partially ordered activities executed by the participants of the process. A BPD is essentially a collection of *pools*, *objects*, *sequence flows*, and *message flows*. Pools represent the participants to the business process. Objects can be *events*, *activities*, or *gateways*. Sequence flows determine the execution order between two objects in the same pool. The behaviour of a process is described by tracking the path(s) of a *token* through a process. A token is an abstract object that traverses the sequence flow passing through the objects of the process. Finally, message flows represent message exchange between two objects in different pools. Fig. 1 presents the core subset of BPMN elements which populate the domain of our translation into COWS.

Events may represent the start of a process (*start event*), the end of a process (*end event*), or something that might happen during the process (*intermediate event*). Intermediate events can also be attached to task. Different types of events are available. Here we consider *none event*, *message event*, and *error event*. None events are used when the modeller does not specify the type and can be start or end events. The meaning of a message event depends on its "position" in the BPD. A start message event represents the fact that a message arrives

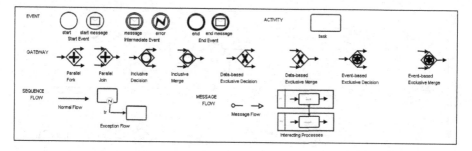

**Fig. 1.** A core subset of BPMN elements

from a participant and triggers the start of the process; an end message event indicates that a message is sent to a participant at the end of the process; and an intermediate message event indicates that a message arrives from or is sent to a participant during the process execution. An error message is for error handling. If the error is part of a normal flow, it throws an error; if it is attached to the boundary of an activity, it catches the error.

An activity is either a *task* or a *subprocess* (For the sake of simplicity, subprocesses are not dealt with in this paper). A task is an atomic activity. BPMN defines different task types. Here we consider *service tasks*, which provide some service, *receive tasks*, which wait for a message from another participant, *send tasks*, which send a message to another participant, and *none tasks*, which do nothing.

A gateway is a connector used to control sequence flows. Different types of gateways have been defined in BPMN. A *parallel fork gateway* is used to create parallel flows and a *parallel join gateway* is used to synchronise incoming parallel flows. An *exclusive decision gateway* defines a set of alternative paths, each of them is associated with a conditional expression. Only one path can be taken during the execution of the process on the basis of conditions. Conditions may be based either on *data-base entries* or on *external events*. An *exclusive merge gateway* is used as a merge for alternative sequence flows. An *inclusive decision gateway* is a branching point where each alternative is associated with a condition. Differently from exclusive decision, all sequence flows with a true evaluation of the corresponding condition will be traversed. Finally, an *inclusive merge gateway* synchronises all tokens produced upstream.

To illustrate what BPDs are, Fig. 2 shows the diagram for a credit request scenario. This example is an excerpt of a case study analysed in the course of the SENSORIA project. The goal of the scenario is twofold: ensuring the due support to the customer during his credit request application, and reducing the effort of bank employees in preparing an offer. The customer invokes the credit portal. If the authentication process succeeds, he is required to insert his data, the desired credit amount, and security values; otherwise, the process terminates and an error message is produced. The information inserted by the customer is checked against consistency and for validation purposes. In particular, a validation service is invoked. If such a service returns a positive answer, the data are uploaded to the bank and the process goes on. Otherwise, the customer has to update his data.

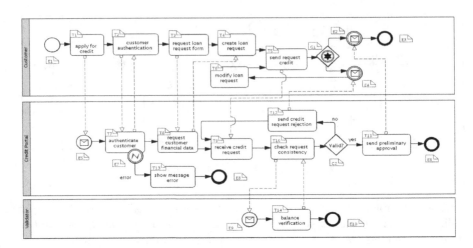

**Fig. 2.** Credit Request Process in BPMN

# 3   COWS: A Short Overview

In this section we present COWS [13], a foundational language for SOC that combines elements of well-known process calculi (e.g., the $\pi$-calculus [17]) with constructs inspired by WS-BPEL [18]. The computational units of COWS are *services*. They are expressed as structured activities built by combining basic activities by means of a small number of primitive operators. As it is typical for many process calculi, COWS services are given a formal operational semantics in terms of a set of syntax-driven axioms and rules which can be used to describe the dynamics of the system at hand. Specifically, those rules define a *transition relation* $\rightarrow$, with $s \rightarrow s'$ meaning that service $s$ can execute a computation step and transform into service $s'$. Interested readers are referred to [13] for a detailed description of COWS semantics. Here we just provide an overview of the language and of the interpretation of its constructs.

The syntax of COWS is based on three countable and pairwise disjoint sets: the set of *names*, the set of *variables*, and the set of *killer labels*. The very basic activities in COWS are request and invoke operations which occur at *endpoints*. In [13], endpoints are identified by both a *partner* and an *operation* name. Here, for simplifying the notation, we let endpoints be denoted by single identifiers, and consider a monadic version of the calculus, that is, we suppose that request/invoke interactions can carry one single (vs. many) parameter at a time.

The terms of the COWS language are generated by the following grammar:

$$s ::= u!\,w \mid [d]s \mid g \mid s \mid s \mid \{|s|\} \mid \mathbf{kill}(k) \mid *\,s$$
$$g ::= \mathbf{0} \mid p?\,w.\,s \mid g+g$$

Intuitively, service $u!\,w$ performs an *invoke* (sending) activity over endpoint $u$ with parameter $w$, where $w$ can be either a name or a variable. The actual scope of parameters has to be explicitly defined using the delimitation operator $[\_]\_$. Basically, $[d]s$ denotes that the scope of $d$ is exactly $s$, where $d$ can be either a name or a variable or a killer label. Terms of the language can also be generated by guarded commands $g$. In this case services can either be the empty activity $\mathbf{0}$, or a choice between two guarded commands $(g+g)$, or a request-guarded service $p?\,w.\,s$ that waits for a matching communication over the endpoint $p$ and then proceeds as $s$ after the (possible) instantiation of the input parameter $w$. In what follows, whenever the parameter of an invoke or request activity is irrelevant, we simply write $u!$ and $p?$ for $u!\,x$ or $[x]p?\,x$, respectively. Also, we usually omit the trailing '. $\mathbf{0}$' from $p?\,w.\,\mathbf{0}$.

Furthermore, services can be described as parallel composition of other services, as, e.g., in $s_1 \mid s_2$. The intended behaviour of service $s_1 \mid s_2$ is given by all the possible communications given rise by matching the invoke (request) actions of $s_1$ over any endpoint $p$ with the request (invoke) actions of $s_2$ over $p$. Interactions can take place only if either the involved parameters coincide or the request parameter is a variable. For instance,

$$p!\,n \mid [x](p?\,x.\,s) \rightarrow \mathbf{0} \mid s\{^n\!/\!x\}$$

where $x$ is used for variables and $s\{^n\!/\!x\}$ represents for the substitution of $n$ for $x$ in service $s$.

The choice operator $\_+\_$ models non-determinism. Either of its two arguments can be chosen, and this causes the other be discharged. For instance, service

$$p!\,n \mid ([x_1](p?\,x_1.\,s_1) + [x_2](p?\,x_2.\,s_2))$$

can evolve into either $\mathbf{0} \mid s_1\{^n\!/\!x_1\}$ or $\mathbf{0} \mid s_2\{^n\!/\!x_2\}$.

The protection primitive, written $\{\!|\_|\!\}$, saves from killer signals sent out by means of the $\mathbf{kill}(\_)$ primitive. The intended behaviour of $\mathbf{kill}(k)$ is to block the activities of all unprotected parallel services in the scope of the killer label $k$. For example, a kill activity inhibits unprotected communication

$$[k][w](p!\,n \mid p?\,w.\,s \mid \mathbf{kill}(k)) \rightarrow [k][w](\mathbf{0} \mid \mathbf{0} \mid \mathbf{0})$$

while, if the communication is protected,

$$[k][w](\{\!|p!\,n \mid p?\,w.\,s|\!\} \mid \mathbf{kill}(k)) \rightarrow [k][w](\{\!|p!\,n \mid p?\,w.\,s|\!\} \mid \mathbf{0})$$

The replication operator $*\_$ is used to model recursion. Intuitively, $*\,s$ behaves as the parallel composition $*\,s \mid s$, namely applying replication to $s$ means that as many copies of $s$ are spawned as necessary. For instance, the following evolution is possible:

$$\begin{aligned} &*\,[w]p?\,w.\,s \mid p!\,n \mid p!\,m &\rightarrow\\ &*\,[w]p?\,w.\,s \mid s\{^n\!/\!w\} \mid \mathbf{0} \mid p!\,m &\rightarrow\\ &*\,[w]p?\,w.\,s \mid s\{^m\!/\!w\} \mid s\{^n\!/\!w\} \mid \mathbf{0} \mid \mathbf{0} \end{aligned}$$

The example shows the case when, at the first step, a copy of $[w]p?\,w.\,s$ communicates with $p!\,n$, and at the second step another copy interacts with $p!\,m$.

COWS allows some higher level imperative and orchestration constructs to be encoded as combinations of the small set of primitives described so far. The encoding of those constructs, written $\langle\!\langle \_ \rangle\!\rangle$, is defined in full detail in [13]. Below we provide the intuition underpinning the constructors used in this work: imperative conditional statements, sequential compositions of services, and fault handlers. The encoding of these constructs is obtained as a combination of communications over reserved endpoints.

Conditional statements can be rendered as follows

$$\langle\!\langle \mathbf{if}\ c\ \mathbf{then}\ s_1\ \mathbf{else}\ s_2 \rangle\!\rangle \triangleq [\,p\,](p!\,\widehat{c} \mid (p?\ \mathbf{true}.\ \langle\!\langle s_1 \rangle\!\rangle + p?\ \mathbf{false}.\ \langle\!\langle s_2 \rangle\!\rangle))$$

where $\widehat{c}$ stays for the evaluation of the condition $c$ and can either assume the value $\mathbf{true}$ or the value $\mathbf{false}$. If $c$ is evaluated $\mathbf{true}$, a communication between $p!\,\widehat{c}$ and $p?\ \mathbf{true}$ takes place enabling service $s_1$; otherwise, service $s_2$ is triggered. The scope of endpoint $p$ is delimited to avoid interference with other services.

COWS does not natively support sequential composition of services, here written $s_1;\ s_2$. As in CCS [16], however, this can be encoded by resorting to invoke activities over a special endpoint for termination, say $p_{s_1\_done}$ for service $s_1$. Intuitively, if the encoding of $s_1$ is such that each possible execution path has $p_{s_1\_done}!$ as latest action, then a possible encoding for $s_1;\ s_2$ is the following:

$$\langle\!\langle s_1;\ s_2 \rangle\!\rangle \triangleq [\,p_{s_1\_done}\,](\langle\!\langle s_1 \rangle\!\rangle \mid p_{s_1\_done}?\,.\ \langle\!\langle s_2 \rangle\!\rangle)$$

Here notice that, because of killer activities, termination in COWS slightly differs from termination in CCS. A service $s$ is actually terminating if no kill action is enabled when the unprotected $p_{s\_done}!$ can be performed.

Fault handlers can also be expressed in terms of COWS primitives. Here we present an encoding that departs from that proposed in [13] to meet the BPMN informal semantics. The fault generator activity $\mathbf{throw}(\phi)$ is used to rise a fault signal $\phi$ via the invoke $p_{fault\_\phi}!$ that triggers the execution of the appropriate handler. The scope activity $[s_1 : \mathbf{catch}(\phi)\{s_2\}]$ executes its normal behaviour $s_1$, until either $s_1$ terminates or a fault signal $\phi$ triggers the execution of the handler $s_2$:

$$\langle\!\langle [s_1 : \mathbf{catch}(\phi)\{s_2\}] \rangle\!\rangle \triangleq$$
$$[\,k\,][\,k'\,][\,p_{s_1\_done}\,](\langle\!\langle s_1 \rangle\!\rangle;\ p_{s_1\_done}! \mid p_{s_1\_done}?\,.\ \mathbf{kill}(k') \mid \langle\!\langle \mathbf{catch}(\phi)\{s_2\} \rangle\!\rangle_k)$$

If $s_1$ signals its termination through $p_{s_1\_done}!$, the catch activity is killed; otherwise $s_2$ is enabled and $s_1$ is killed by the catch:

$$\langle\!\langle \mathbf{catch}(\phi)\{s_2\} \rangle\!\rangle_k \triangleq p_{fault\_\phi}?\,.\ (\mathbf{kill}(k) \mid \{\!|\langle\!\langle s_2 \rangle\!\rangle|\!\})$$

## 4   From BPMN to COWS

This section provides the intuition underlying the translation of core BPDs into COWS services. Each BPMN object has an interface that is used to connect it to other objects. This interface is made of request processing waiting for a token from the previous objects (if any), and invoke activities sending the token to the next objects (if any).

The basic idea of the translation is to interpret each object as a distinct COWS service. Services are then assembled using parallel compositions in such a way that COWS terms corresponding to connected objects can communicate to each other. Specifically, request activities correspond to incoming edges of the graph, and invoke activities to outgoing edges. Besides the interface, each object has a kernel, which defines the behaviour of the object itself in terms of the actions that are executed when the object is triggered. Our translation describes the message flow along the objects of the business process at hand. In this way, the transition system of the translating COWS service gives a compact representation of the possible paths of tokens within the business process.

The compositional translation of BPMN objects into COWS services is compactly presented in Tab. 1. As a pre-processing phase, we assume that each object of the diagram is firstly labelled by a name, so that no homonym between nodes and no homonym between edges is given raise. In particular, we adopt both in Tab. 1 and in the forthcoming examples the following easy labelling technique. First we associate distinct names with all the objects in the BPD, then we preliminarily give each edge the same name as the node it points to. If a node, say $N$, has more than one incoming edge, then the preliminary names of these edges are converted into $N1, N2, \ldots$ after an arbitrary ordering. Preliminary objects are otherwise confirmed.

A *none start event* starts a business process by generating a token, and it is modelled as a service performing the invoke activity $p_X!$, where $X$ is the object pointed by the start event. (Here notice that the name $p_X$ used as endpoint is automatically determined by the labels in the diagram). Symmetrically, a *none end event* $E$ determines the end of the process and it is encoded as a service that consumes all the tokens generated upstream, that is, as a replicated request processing $p_E?$. The replication operator ensures that every incoming token is consumed by a none end event. Indeed, due for instance to the presence of cycles in the diagram, the number of produced tokens is not known a priori. A *message start event* is triggered when receiving a message by means of $p_E? w$ and then it activates the process by performing the invoke activity $p_Y!$.

Every time a *none task* $T$ receives a token from the incoming flow (denoted by $p_T?$), a token for the outgoing sequence flow is generated (denoted by $p_Y!$ if the outgoing edge points to $Y$). A *receive task* $T$ gets a token by means of a $p_{T1}?$ action, then it receives a message $w$ when executing the activity $p_{T2}? w$, and it finally produces a token for next object $Y$. A *send task* $T$ gets a token by means of $p_T?$, and later on it sends a message $msg$ by performing $p_Z!$. When $msg$ is sent, the task is completed [19, p. 65]. The token is thus passed to the next object $Y$. We do not provide an encoding of service tasks since their kernel depends on the particular service they are supposed to provide. Designers can define them in terms of existing constructs using, for instance, predefined patterns.

**Table 1.** Translation of core BPMN into COWS

| | | |
|---|---|---|
| None start event | (s) ⟶ x | $p_X!$ |
| None end event | ⟶ (E) | $* p_E? . \mathbf{0}$ |
| Message start event | (E ✉) ⟶ Y | $* [w] p_E? w . p_Y!$ |
| None task | ⟶ [T] ⟶ Y | $* p_T? . p_Y!$ |
| Receive task | T1 [T] Y, T2 | $* [w] p_{T1}? . p_{T2}? w . p_Y!$ |
| Send task | ⟶ [T] ⟶ Y, Z | $* ((p_T? . p_Z! msg); p_Y!)$ |
| Error event (normal flow) | E ⟶ (N) ⟶ x, tr1 | $* (p_E? . \mathbf{throw}(tr1); p_X!)$ |
| Error event (exception flow) | T1 (N) T2, tr1 | $[\langle\!\langle T1 \rangle\!\rangle : \mathbf{catch}(tr1)\{\langle\!\langle T2 \rangle\!\rangle\}]$ |
| Parallel fork gateway | ⟶ (+) Y, Z, G | $* p_G? . (p_Y! \mid p_Z!)$ |
| Parallel join gateway | G1 (+) Z, G2 | $* ((p_{G1}? \mid p_{G2}?); p_Z!)$ |
| Inclusive decision gateway | G (◯) Y c1, Z c2 | $* p_G? . (\mathbf{if}\ \hat{c1}\ \mathbf{then}\ p_Y! \mid \mathbf{if}\ \hat{c2}\ \mathbf{then}\ p_Z!)$ |
| Inclusive merge gateway | G1 (◯) Z, G2 | $* ((p_{G1}? + p_{G2}? + (p_{G1}? \mid p_{G2}?)); p_Z!)$ |
| Exclusive decision gateway | G (✕) Y c1, Z c2 | $* p_G? . (\mathbf{if}\ \hat{c1}\ \mathbf{then}\ p_Y!\ \mathbf{else\ if}\ \hat{c2}\ \mathbf{then}\ p_Z!)$ |
| Exclusive merge gateway | G1 (✕) Z, G2 | $(* p_{G1}? . p_Z!) \mid (* p_{G2}? . p_Z!)$ |

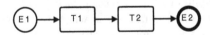

**Fig. 3.** BPD Example 1

As an easy example, consider the BPMN process in Fig. 3. Its complete translation into COWS is given as:

$$E1 \mid T1 \mid T2 \mid E2 = p_{T1}! \mid * p_{T1}? . p_{T2}! \mid * p_{T2}? . p_{E2}! \mid * p_{E2}?$$

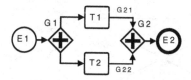

**Fig. 4.** BPD Example 2

The operational semantics of the calculus prescribes how sequence flows proceed within the service. Specifically:

$$p_{T1}! \mid * p_{T1}? . p_{T2}! \mid * p_{T2}? . p_{E2}! \mid * p_{E2}? . \mathbf{0} \rightarrow \qquad (1)$$

$$\mathbf{0} \mid * p_{T1}? . p_{T2}! \mid p_{T2}! \mid * p_{T2}? . p_{E2}! \mid * p_{E2}? . \mathbf{0} \rightarrow \qquad (2)$$

$$\mathbf{0} \mid * p_{T1}? . p_{T2}! \mid \mathbf{0} \mid * p_{T2}? . p_{E2}! \mid p_{E2}! \mid * p_{E2}? . \mathbf{0} \rightarrow \qquad (3)$$

$$\mathbf{0} \mid * p_{T1}? . p_{T2}! \mid \mathbf{0} \mid * p_{T2}? . p_{E2}! \mid \mathbf{0} \mid * p_{E2}? . \mathbf{0} \mid \mathbf{0} \qquad (4)$$

First, a token flows from $E1$ to $T1$ via a communication along the endpoint $p_{T1}$. Then the token is passed to $T2$, and finally it gets consumed by $E2$. The service highlighted in (4) is stuck as no matching invoke/request activities are enabled.

*Error events* are used for error handling. An error event in normal flow $E$ receives the token, throws an error *tr1*, and releases the token. When an error event $E$ is attached to the boundary of a task $T1$, $T1$ is executed until either it completes or a trigger *tr1* is caught. In this case, it generates an exception flow by stopping $T1$ and activating $T2$.

A *parallel fork gateway* $G$ repeatedly performs a request processing at $p_G$, that is, it waits for a token, and then it proceeds as the parallel composition of two invoke activities $p_Y$ and $p_Z$. Namely, it produces a token for each of the following objects Y and Z. A *parallel join gateway* first synchronises with its incoming sequence flows. This is represented as the parallel composition of the requests $p_{G1}?$ and $p_{G2}?$. A token is then released to the next object $Z$ via the execution of the invoke activity $p_Z!$. As an example, service $S$ below is the translation of the diagram in Fig. 4.

$$S = E1 \mid G1 \mid T1 \mid T2 \mid G2 \mid E2$$

where:

$$E1 = p_{G1}! \qquad\qquad G1 = * p_{G1}? . (p_{T1}! \mid p_{T2}!)$$
$$T1 = * p_{T1}? . p_{G21}! \qquad G2 = * ((p_{G21}? \mid p_{G22}?); p_{E2}!)$$
$$T2 = * p_{T2}? . p_{G22}! \qquad E2 = * p_{E2}? . \mathbf{0}$$

Fig. 5 describes the behaviour of service $S$ by tracking how the tokens flow along the diagram. Initially, only the communication over the endpoint $p_{G1}$ is enabled. This represents the fact that the token can only pass from the start event $E1$ to the parallel fork gateway $G1$, written $\xrightarrow{E1 \to G1}$ in Fig. 5. Then, the service $G1$ generates a parallel flow and two invoke activities are simultaneously enabled: one over the endpoint $p_{T1}$, and the other over the endpoint $p_{T2}$. The

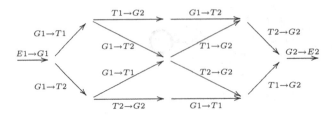

**Fig. 5.** Behaviour of the process of Fig. 4

interleaving semantics of the parallel composition of COWS services allows the derivation of non-trivial paths of the token flow. Consider, for instance, the top level path along the graph in Fig. 5, namely:

$$(E1{\to}G1)(G1{\to}T1)(T1{\to}G2)(G1{\to}T2)(T2{\to}G2)(G2{\to}E2)$$

This path is relative to the case when task $T1$ completes before task $T2$ gets its token. Also, Fig. 5 shows that a token cannot possibly reach the end event $E2$ before both $T1$ and $T2$ terminate their execution.

*Inclusive decision gateways* are translated as services that can transmit the token to the following objects, under the proviso that the corresponding condition is satisfied. One should notice that "if none of inclusive decision gate condition expressions are evaluated as true, then the process is considered to have an invalid model" [19, p. 78]. However, it is up to the modeller (rather than to the encoding) to ensure that at least one condition is evaluated true during the execution of the business process. To avoid possible problems, BPMN allows modellers to set a *default* gate that is selected if none of the other gates is chosen. In our approach the *default* gate is modelled as a gate whose condition is the negation of the disjunction of the other conditions. For instance, if gates have conditions $c_1$ and $c_2$, the *default* condition is $\neg(c_1 \vee c_2)$. *Inclusive merge gateways* synchronise all the tokens produced upstream. This makes the semantics non-local because it requires one to know how many tokens have been produced upstream before deciding whether to immediately release the token or wait. It is a matter of debate how to manage the non-local semantics of this sort of gateways (see for instance [24,26]). Existing solutions, however, either impose some restrictions on the syntax of BPMN (e.g., avoiding cycles), or define a formal semantics that deviate from the informal one. For pragmatic reasons, we provide a semantics that "includes" the informal one. Since tokens can arrive at either $p_{G1}$, or $p_{G2}$, or both, inclusive merge gateways are translated using the choice operator and considering all possible alternatives. During the analysis, when global information are available, the transition system can be refined by cutting out those portions that do not correspond to possible behaviours of the business process. The motivations for our choice are twofold. First, to get compositionality we cannot consider global information at translation time. Second, any reasonable implementation of an inclusive merge gateway uses time-outs to stop waiting for tokens. In this way, the gateway might not synchronise even when both tokens arrive. This would introduce unexpected paths in the transition system which could be analysed in our quantitative framework.

*Exclusive decision gateways* are translated in such a way that the token passes to object $Y$ only if condition $c1$ is true. If this is not the case, and if $c2$ is verified, then the token is sent to $Z$. Also, *default* gates may be used analogously to the case of inclusive decision gateways. *Exclusive merge gateways* are treated as simple by-passes: each incoming token, no matter where it is coming from, is passed to the next object $Z$. *Event-based exclusive gateways* (not reported in Tab. 1) are encoded in a similar way. The difference is that the selection of the gate depends on the caught event rather than on the satisfiability of conditions.

## 5   Quantitative Analysis of Business Processes

Testing and visualising the behaviour of business processes in a timed context before implementing them allows one to correct or optimise the design of the system [4]. For instance, the designer of a new process may have different alternatives to implement the same task. The decision on which alternative should be adopted is usually driven by its cost and performance. System designers thus need tools to compare and evaluate possible design alternatives. In this section, we illustrate a quantitative reasoning on BPDs, relying on the encoding presented in Sec. 4.

The operational semantics of COWS provides a full qualitative description of the behaviour of business processes. Recently, a stochastic extension of COWS was presented [22], where the syntax and semantics of the calculus have been enriched along the lines of Markovian extensions of process calculi [9,23]. In this way the semantic models associated with BPDs result to be Continuous Time Markov Chains, a popular model for automated verification. In the above mentioned extension, basic actions are associated with a random duration governed by a negative exponential distribution that is characterized by a unique parameter, called *rate*. In this way activities become pairs of the shape $(\mu, r)$, where $\mu$ represents the basic action, and $r$ is the rate of $\mu$. Once enabled, the probability that a certain activity $(\mu, r)$ is performed within a period of time of length $t$ is $1 - e^{-rt}$. Also, the mean value of an exponentially distributed variable with parameter $r$ is $1/r$, and rates to be associated with basic actions can be determined by estimating mean values for the various objects of BPDs. For instance, in our experiments we assumed that, depending on whether encryption is used or not, task $T_7$ of Fig. 2 (the authenticate costumer task ) may require from 30 to 150 units of time. This corresponds to adopting rates varying from $0.0\overline{3}$ to $0.00\overline{6}$. More generally, running the same formula on chains obtained for different rate values of a certain action allows to analyze the sensitivity of the global behaviour to the duration of that particular action.

For testing our approach, we have implemented the semantics of COWS in PRISM [10], a stochastic model checker for the formal modelling and analysis of systems. PRISM supports the automated analysis of a wide range of quantitative

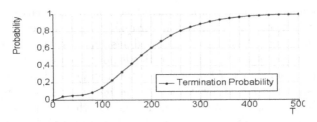

**Fig. 6.** Termination probability

properties. The property specification language is based on the Continuous Stochastic Logic [1], a probabilistic extension of the classical temporal logic CTL.

In the remainder of this section, we report an excerpt of the analysis of the credit request process of Sec. 2 against a few properties. The symbol `terminate` is a short-end for any state representing that (*i*) either the costumer receives a preliminary approval for the credit loan request; (*ii*) or the customer fails the authentication procedure. Below we comment on the results obtained by checking our COWS service of the credit request process against the three logic formulae F1, F2, and F3.

- F1 = P $\geq$ 1 [true U$\leq$ 240 `terminate`]. This formula expresses that *with probability 1 the system terminates in at most 240 units of time*, namely F1 is *true* if the system reaches one of the relevant states with probability 1 before 240 units of time. F1 is *false* for our model.
- F2 = P=? [true U$\leq$ 240 `terminate`]. This formula refines the former one by asking *which is the probability that the system terminates in at most 240 units of time*. Here the result is *0.75*.
- F3 = P=? [true U[T,T] `terminate`]. This formula further refines the previous ones by asking *which is the probability that the system terminates at time T*. Fig. 6 shows the PRISM plot resulting with F3 for our COWS model.

Finally, we briefly mention how to use PRISM to evaluate possible implementations of a business process. In a business process some phases can be critical. For instance, authenticating the customer (task $T_7$ in Fig. 2) is a critical operation in the credit request process. Different authentication software can be used to implement $T_7$. Each of them provides a different level of encryption, more secure it is more time it requires. Fig. 7 plots the probability that the system terminates at time $T$ when using different authentication software. With the faster software, 30 units of time, the probability of completing the procedure is higher than 0.85. As the authentication software employs more sophisticated encryption algorithms, the time duration increases, e.g., 60, 150, 300, and 600 units of time. It emerges that sophisticated authentication software can drastically affect the performance of the system. Therefore, system designers should make a trade off between the security and performance of the system when choosing the authentication software to be adopted. The framework proposed in this paper aims at assisting them in the decision making process.

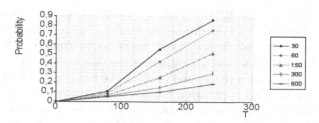

**Fig. 7.** Cost evaluation

# 6   Related Works and Concluding Remarks

Few proposals have already addressed the problem of defining a formal semantics for BPMN. To the best of our knowledge, the first work in this setting is
due to Wong et al. [28], who encoded BPMN in CSP. In particular, they used
the language and behavioural semantics of CSP as denotational model. Based
on it, they provided methods for specifying behavioural properties of business
processes as well as for comparing BPMN diagrams. Differently from our work,
the encoding is not compositional and so may not scale well to large business
processes. Another definition of formal semantics for a subset of BPMN was
made by Dijkman et al. [5]. They proposed a formal semantics of BPMN using
Petri Nets. Our translation is defined over a super-set of the BPMN fragment
considered in [5] where inclusive gateways are not dealt with, and tasks have one
incoming sequence flow only, and can either send messages or receive messages,
but cannot send and receive simultaneously. The translation presented in this
paper relates well to [21], where an encoding of sequence and state diagrams into
the $\pi$-calculus [17] is proposed. Similarly to our approach, objects of sequence
and state diagrams are represented as $\pi$-calculus processes and then all such processes are composed by synchronising their interface via parallel composition.

Many interpretations of web services and business process specifications in
terms of process calculi have been proposed over the last few years. For instance, Cámara et al. [3] provided an encoding of business process specifications
in CCS [16]. Many efforts were also addressed to the enhancement of well-known
process calculi with constructs inspired by those of WS-BPEL to better capture specific features of web service systems. Their common goal is to provide
a sound mathematical ground to web services definitions as well as to improve
their reliability using the analysis tools developed for process calculi. For instance, Meredith et al. [15] used process calculi with type systems [11] to check
compatibility between web services. Other works [2,8] extended the $\pi$-calculus
with process mobility and with operations for data interaction, so getting a quite
rich and flexible model. Other proposals deal with issues of web transactions such
as interruptible processes, failure handlers, and time. This is the case of [12,14]
that respectively present timed and untimed extensions of the $\pi$-calculus.

The aim of the present work is to set the basis for the development of a platform for the formal analysis of business processes. To this end, we have presented

a semantic foundation for BPMN based on COWS, a calculus equipped with qualitative and quantitative operational semantics. The compositionality of the approach allows us to easily derive COWS specifications from the XML files generated by existing BPMN modelling applications. We have applied the PRISM probabilistic model checker to test and visualise the behaviour of a BPMN model in a timed context. This application intends to assist system designers in the decision making when implementing business processes. Currently, we are extending the platform with analysis facilities tailored to test if, with probability close to 1, the actual implementation of a business process is consistent with its specification.

# References

1. Aziz, A., Sanwal, K., Singhal, V., Brayton, R.K.: Model-checking continous-time Markov chains. ACM TOCL 1(1), 162–170 (2000)
2. Brown Jr., A.L., Laneve, C., Meredith, L.G.: PiDuce: A Process Calculus with Native XML Datatypes. In: Bravetti, M., Kloul, L., Zavattaro, G. (eds.) EPEW/WS-EM 2005. LNCS, vol. 3670, pp. 18–34. Springer, Heidelberg (2005)
3. Cámara, J., Canal, C., Cubo, J., Vallecillo, A.: Formalizing WSBPEL Business Processes Using Process Algebra. Electr. Notes Theor. Comput. Sci. 154(1), 159–173 (2006)
4. Desel, J., Erwin, T.: Modeling, Simulation and Analysis of Business Processes. In: Business Process Management, Models, Techniques, and Empirical Studies, pp. 129–141. Springer, Heidelberg (2000)
5. Dijkman, R., Dumas, M., Ouyang, C.: Formal Semantics and Automated Analysis of BPMN Process Models. Preprint 7115, Queensland University of Technology (2007)
6. Eshuis, R., Wieringa, R.: Verification support for workflow design with UML activity graphs. In: Proc. of ICSE 2002, pp. 166–176. ACM Press, New York (2002)
7. Fantechi, A., Gnesi, S., Lapadula, A., Mazzanti, F., Pugliese, R., Tiezzi, F.: A model checking approach for verifying COWS specifications. In: FASE 2008. LNCS, vol. 4961. Springer, Heidelberg (2008)
8. Gardner, P., Maffeis, S.: Modelling dynamic web data. Theor. Comput. Sci. 342(1), 104–131 (2005)
9. Hillston, J.: A Compositional Approach to Performance Modelling. Cambridge University Press, Cambridge (1996)
10. Hinton, A., Kwiatkowska, M., Norman, G., Parker, D.: PRISM: A Tool for Automatic Verification of Probabilistic Systems. In: Hermanns, H., Palsberg, J. (eds.) TACAS 2006. LNCS, vol. 3920, pp. 441–444. Springer, Heidelberg (2006)
11. Igarashi, A., Kobayashi, N.: A generic type system for the pi-calculus. Theor. Comput. Sci. 311(1-3), 121–163 (2004)
12. Laneve, C., Zavattaro, G.: Foundations of Web Transactions. In: Sassone, V. (ed.) FOSSACS 2005. LNCS, vol. 3441, pp. 282–298. Springer, Heidelberg (2005)
13. Lapadula, A., Pugliese, R., Tiezzi, F.: Calculus for Orchestration of Web Services. In: De Nicola, R. (ed.) ESOP 2007. LNCS, vol. 4421, pp. 33–47. Springer, Heidelberg (2007), http://rap.dsi.unifi.it/cows/
14. Mazzara, M., Lanese, I.: Towards a unifying theory for web services composition. In: Bravetti, M., Núñez, M., Zavattaro, G. (eds.) WS-FM 2006. LNCS, vol. 4184, pp. 257–272. Springer, Heidelberg (2006)

15. Meredith, L.G., Bjorg, S.: Contracts and types. Commun. ACM 46(10), 41–47 (2003)
16. Milner, R.: Communication and Concurrency. International Series in Computer Science. Prentice hall, Englewood Cliffs (1989)
17. Milner, R.: Communicating and mobile systems: the $\pi$-calculus. Cambridge University Press, Cambridge (1999)
18. OASIS. Web Services Business Process Execution Language – Version 2.0. Public Review Draft (2006)
19. Object Management Group. Business Process Modeling Notation (BPMN) Specification. Final adopted specification (February 2006)
20. Ouyang, C., van der Aalst, W.M.P., Dumas, M., Breutel, S., ter Hofstede, A.H.M.: Translating BPMN to BPEL, BPM Report BPM-06-02. BPMcenter.org (2006)
21. Pokozy-Korenblat, K., Priami, C.: Toward Extracting $\pi$-calculus from UML Sequence and State Diagrams. Electr. Notes Theor. Comput. Sci. 101, 51–72 (2004)
22. Prandi, D., Quaglia, P.: Stochastic COWS. In: Krämer, B.J., Lin, K.-J., Narasimhan, P. (eds.) ICSOC 2007. LNCS, vol. 4749, pp. 245–256. Springer, Heidelberg (2007)
23. Priami, C.: Stochastic $\pi$-calculus. The Computer Journal 38(7), 578–589 (1995)
24. Russell, N., Arthur, H.M., van der Aalst, W.M.P., Mulyar, N.: Workflow control-flow patterns: A revised view. Technical report, BPMcenter.org (2006)
25. Van der Aalst, W.M.P., Pesic, M.: A declarative approach for flexible business processes management. In: Eder, J., Dustdar, S. (eds.) BPM Workshops 2006. LNCS, vol. 4103, pp. 169–180. Springer, Heidelberg (2006)
26. van der Aalst, W.M.P., Desel, J., Kindler, E.: On the semantics of EPCs: A vicious circle. In: Business Process Management with Event driven Process Chains, pp. 71–79 (2002)
27. Vivas, J., Montenegro, J.A., Lopez, J.: A Formal Business Modelling Approach to Security Engineering with the UML. In: Boyd, C., Mao, W. (eds.) ISC 2003. LNCS, vol. 2851, pp. 381–395. Springer, Heidelberg (2003)
28. Wong, P.Y.H., Gibbons, J.: A Process Semantics for BPMN, Oxford. University Computing Laboratory (Preprint, 2007), http://web.comlab.ox.ac.uk/

# Encrypted Shared Data Spaces

Giovanni Russello[1], Changyu Dong[1], Naranker Dulay[1],
Michel Chaudron[2], and Maarten van Steen[3]

[1] Imperial College London
[2] Eindhoven University of Technology
[3] Vrije Universiteit Amsterdam

**Abstract.** The deployment of Share Data Spaces in open, possibly hostile, environments arises the need of protecting the confidentiality of the data space content. Existing approaches focus on access control mechanisms that protect the data space from untrusted agents. The basic assumption is that the hosts (and their administrators) where the data space is deployed have to be trusted. Encryption schemes can be used to protect the data space content from malicious hosts. However, these schemes do not allow searching on encrypted data. In this paper we present a novel encryption scheme that allows tuple matching on completely encrypted tuples. Since the data space does not need to decrypt tuples to perform the search, tuple confidentiality can be guaranteed even when the data space is deployed on malicious hosts (or an adversary gains access to the host). Our scheme does not require authorised agents to share keys for inserting and retrieving tuples. Each authorised agent can encrypt, decrypt, and search encrypted tuples without having to know other agents' keys. This is beneficial inasmuch as it simplifies the task of key management. An implementation of an encrypted data space based on this scheme is described and some preliminary performance results are given.

## 1 Introduction

Coordination through Shared Data Spaces (SDS) also called generative communication, forms an attractive model for developing distributed and component-oriented systems as it supports referential and temporal decoupling of processes [9]. Referential decoupling means that components exchange data without the need to know each other. Temporal decoupling means that those components do not even have to be online at the same time. This way, components can be connected to or disconnected from the data space at any time, making it easier to combine or replace. The SDS model was introduced by the coordination language Linda [8]. Storage in Linda takes place in a so-called *tuple space*. In a tuple space, data is stored as persistent objects, called *tuples.*

The early implementations of SDSes were *closed* systems, in the sense that they were realised by compiling application and SDS code altogether. Once the system was deployed and executed, it was not possible to add or remove application components. In such systems, security was not a issue and the original Linda model was conceived without addressing security concerns.

D. Lea and G. Zavattaro (Eds.): COORDINATION 2008, LNCS 5052, pp. 264–279, 2008.

In contrast, *open* systems were introduced where the SDS is not bound to an application but is an autonomous process with its own resources. The main advantage of open SDS systems is that persistent data storage can be offered to applications. In this way, applications could dynamically join and leave the computational environment. This is clearly a feature suited to distributed applications. With its small API and the decoupling of communication in space and time, the SDS model provides an effective coordination layer for distributed applications.

Distributed applications are deployed in environments that range from small ad-hoc networks of portable devices (such as Body Area Networks) up to wide area networks (such as the Internet). In such scenarios applications are faced with many security threats that the original Linda model does not address. For instance, denial of service attacks could be performed by malicious agents inserting a large number of tuples into the data space. Still, a malicious agent can remove any tuples from the space interfering with the other agents that are using the space. This can be even more serious when the tuples contain sensitive information.

Such security deficiencies pose a limitation on the usability of the SDS model for real-world applications. Early work presented by Wood in [20] discusses the introduction of access control mechanisms, such as ACLs and capabilities, that could be used for controlling access to the SDS content. Several other approaches have proposed access control mechanisms that employ secret information associated with SDSes and their content. In [12], an agent must know the password associated with the space in order to get access to it. In [11,19] the secret information is represented by locks that are associated with tuple instances. To get access to a tuple, an agent must provide the specific lock associated with the tuple.

Although access control mechanisms are necessary for allowing authorised operations on the data space, they are not always adequate to protect data confidentiality. The common assumption of these approaches is that the host where the data space is deployed is managed by a trustworthy entity that (1) correctly enforces access control mechanisms and (2) is *oblivious* of the data that is stored in the data space. However, such an assumption does not always hold when sharing data over a wide area network such the Internet.

A solution to enforce the confidentiality of tuples against malicious hosts is to encrypt the tuple content as proposed in [2]. However, because the ciphertexts are not meaningful, it is not possible to perform search operations. A trusted data space can temporarily decrypt the data, perform the search and return the results to the agent. Alternatively, if the data space doesn't have access to the decryption keys, the encrypted data can be returned to the agent that decrypts the data locally. The first solution cannot protect data confidentiality from malicious hosts, while the second one is potentially very inefficient in communications. Moreover, issues related to key management (i.e., key distribution, key revocation, etc.) are not addressed.

In this paper we propose an efficient approach for guaranteeing that tuple confidentiality is protected against malicious hosts. We developed a novel encryption scheme that allows the execution of search operations on encrypted tuples, without having the data space decrypt the data. Another important property of our encryption scheme is that it does not require agents to share secret keys. Each authorised agent can encrypt, decrypt, and search encrypted tuples without having to know other agents' keys. This greatly simplifies the task of key management. In particular, it avoids re-encrypting the tuple content when a key needs to be revoked. To the best of our knowledge, this is the first approach that proposes such features for the shared data space model. Finally, we integrate the encryption scheme in a SDS implementation and carry out some preliminary performance analysis.

The paper is organized as follows. Section 2 introduces the original SDS model. Section 3 surveys recent developments aiming at providing security in the SDS model. In Section 4, we describe on our encryption scheme. In Section 5, we discuss and evaluate our encrypted SDS implementation. In this paper our main focus to guarantee data confidentiality in case a host is compromised. However, the SDS and its content can face other security threats when its host is compromised. In Section 6, we discuss some of those security threats. We conclude in Section 7 with some final thoughts and future research directions.

## 2    The Shared Data Space Model

The shared data space model was introduced by the coordination language Linda [8]. Linda provides three basic operations: out, in and rd. The out operation inserts a tuple into the tuple space. The in and rd operations respectively take (destructive) and read (non-destructive) a tuple from the tuple space, using a template for matching. The tuple returned must exactly match every value of the template. Templates may contain wildcards, which match any value. Whereas putting a tuple inside the tuple space is non-blocking (i.e. the process that puts the tuple returns immediately from the call to out), reading and taking from the tuple space is blocking: the call returns only when a matching tuple is found. In the original model two more operations were introduced: the inp and rdp. These operations are predicate versions of in and rd: they too try to return a matching tuple. However, if there is no such tuple they do not block but return a value indicating failure.

In Linda it is also possible to fork a process inside a tuple space through so-called *live tuples*. To insert a live tuple inside a tuple space the eval operation is used. eval is similar to an out and it is specific for live tuples. Once a live tuple is inserted in a tuple space it carries out the specified computation. Afterwards, a live tuple turns into an ordinary data tuple, and it can be used as such. In the implementation of a SDS presented later on in this paper the inp, rdp, and eval operations are not supported.

## 3    Related Work

This section provides a critical overview of exiting approaches providing security for shared data space.

Secure Lime, described in [12], introduces several security extension to Lime [14]. Since Lime's primary environment is a network of mobile low-resource hosts, the main concern of the developers was to introduce security enhancements with low overhead of the original Lime's model. Security extensions are implemented as two levels of access control: at tuple space level and single tuple level. At the tuple space level, it is possible to protect access to a tuple space by means of a password. An agent will be considered authorized to access a tuple space if it knows the password for the given tuple space. At the tuple level, agents can specify for each tuple that they insert passwords for granting both read and take accesses. Inter-host communication uses unsecured links. For avoiding eavesdropping of messages, each serialized tuple is encrypted using the respective password for accessing the tuple space. It should be noted that it is not a good practice to use a password as an encryption key.

SecOS [19] introduces the notion of *lock* for controlling access to a tuple. A lock is a labeled value that specifies the key that should be used to grant access to a given tuple. The simplest lock is represented by a symmetric key where the same label can be used for locking and unlocking a tuple. Also, asymmetric locks can be used. In this case, two different keys are necessary for locking and unlocking a tuple. A public key is used for locking a tuple and a private one is used for unlocking it. SecOS also provides finer grained access control at the level of single fields in a tuple. Each field in a tuple can be protected by a separate lock.

SecSpaces [11] provides a similar approach to that of SecOS. In SecSpaces labels are used as an access control mechanism to protect tuples and tuple fields. SecSpace provides two more extensions. The first extension concerns partitioning the tuple space. The partitioning of a tuple space avoids all agents having the same view on the data contained in a tuple space. Instead of a physical separation in different tuple spaces, in SecSpaces the tuple space partitioning is achieved through the introduction of a partition field in the tuples. A template can match a tuple in a given partition only if the correct actual value is given in the partition field. A template with a wildcard value in the partition field is considered not valid. This means that a process has to know the name of the partition for accessing the content. The second extension regards the distinction between consumers that can only execute read operations and consumers that can only execute take operations. This extension is provided via specified fields in the tuples, called *control fields*. To be an authorized read consumer, the process has to provide in the template issued by the read operation the exact value on the read control field of a tuple.

Linda with multicapabilities [18] is an approach where the capability concept is applied to the Linda model. Capabilities are the means by which agents can access to tuples and SDS. In particular, a multicapability is a special capability that refers to a group of tuples. A multicapability consists of three parts: $u$, a unique identifier which is the reference to a collection of tuples; $t$, a template that matches the tuples that the multicapability refers to; $p$, a set of permitted operations on the matching tuples. To be able to exchange tuples, tow or more agents have to share the same multicapability that refers to the same set of tuples. In case a multicapability has to be revoked, the authors adopt the common solution of introducing *indirect multicapability objects*. A multicapability now refers to the indirection object, which in turn refers to the intended tuple set. The deletion of the indirection object has the effect of removing the multicapability.

In all the approaches presented above, tuples are stored in the data space as plaintext. Indeed, then basic assumption of these approaches is that the data space host is trusted. However, if an adversary gets access to the host where the data space is deployed, tuples could still be retrieved and accessed. The only exception to this is KLAIM [2]. KLAIM provides privacy by means of encryption. In the framework proposed, a key can be used for encrypting the data value contained in a field. The model does not provide any access restrictions to the tuple space. This means that encrypted tuples can be retrieved by agents that do not have the right key for decrypting the content. If a tuple is withdrawn from the tuple space by an agent that cannot access it, it is up to that agent to reintroduce the tuple back to the space. The tuple space API is extended with two operations that execute the decryption process before returning the tuple to the application: ink and readk. If the decryption fails, then the ink operation inserts the tuple back into the space. It should be made clear that the key used for encrypting the data is not shared between the entities and the data space. The ink and readk operations perform the decryption locally to the node where the entity is deployed. This has a negative impact on the communication utilisation.

Although KLAIM is the only approach that encrypts the data when it is stored in the space, it does not support encrypted search. Therefore it is necessary to have in the tuples cleartext fields. Assuming that there is a secure channel between the agent and the data space, an attacker can still gain some information on the matched tuple if it has access to the data space host. However, if the data space supports encrypted search then an attacker can not gather any information about the tuple content by just looking at the ciphertext. Another common drawback of the above approaches is that agents are required to share a secret (either a key or a password). The revocation of the secret in the event that it gets compromised requires the re-distribution of a new secret and the creation and/or modification of the data space to be protected by the new secret. The same needs to be done in case that access privileges have to be removed to an agent.

To protect the confidentiality of shared data spaces from both unauthorised clients and from the SDS host(s) we introduce a novel encryption scheme that supports encrypted searches over encrypted shared data spaces. Furthermore, the scheme does not require agents to share secret keys.

## 4   Multi-agent Searchable Encryption Scheme

This section presents our encryption scheme for a multi-agent searchable encrypted data space. The aim of this section is to describe the required cryptographic details of the scheme and its properties. For a more detailed description refer to [4].

## 4.1   Cryptographic Preliminaries

Our multi-user searchable encryption scheme employs *RSA public-key encryption* [15] and *Discrete Logarithms*. RSA involves two asymmetric keys. The key pair is generated as follows: First choose two random large prime $p$ and $q$ such that $|p| \approx |q|$. Then compute $n = pq$ and $\phi(n) = (p-1)(q-1)$. Find a random integer $e < \phi(n)$ and $gcd(e, \phi(n)) = 1$. Compute $d$ such that $ed \equiv 1 \ mod \ \phi(n)$. $(n, e)$ is the public key and $d$ is the private key. To encrypt, compute $c = m^e \ mod \ n$. To decrypt, compute $m = c^d \ mod \ n$. In the rest of the paper, we assume all arithmetic to be $mod \ n$ unless stated otherwise. Discrete Logarithms in finite fields are one-way functions. Namely, given a prime $p$, a generator $g$ of the multiplicative group $Z_p^*$ and $g^x \ mod \ p$, it is hard to find $x$. Discrete Logarithms have been used in constructing public-key encryption schemes [5], digital signature schemes and zero-knowledge proof protocols.

Both RSA and Discrete Logarithms use *Modular exponentiation* as basic operations and the exponents can be split multiplicatively. In RSA, for example we can find $e_1, e_2$ such that $e_1 e_2 \equiv e \ mod \ \phi(n)$. The two shares of $e$ can be given to two parties, then the two parties can collaboratively encrypt a message. Given a message $m$, one party encrypts it as $m^{e_1} \ mod \ n$ and the other party re-encrypts it as $(m^{e_1})^{e_2} \equiv m^{e_1 e_2} \equiv m^e \ mod \ n$. The decryption key can also be split in the same way.

This idea is used in *proxy cryptography* and was first introduced in [3]. In a proxy encryption scheme, a ciphertext encrypted by one key can be transformed by a proxy function into the corresponding ciphertext for another key without revealing any information about the keys and the plaintext. There are many applications of proxy encryption, e.g. secure email lists [17], access control systems [18] and attribute based publishing of data [19]. A comprehensive study on proxy cryptography can be found in [13].

The encryption schema that we use in our system combines the property of proxy cryptography where each authorised agent has a unique key with the capability of performing tuple matching on encrypted data.

## 4.2   Architecture

The system has the following components:

- Client: a client is any agent interacting with the data space.
- Encrypted Shared Data Space(eSDS): is used for storing and retrieving tuples, performing encrypted searching operations, authenticating valid clients, and safely storing encryption and decryption keys. The eSDS is also capable of storing and retrieving tuples in plaintext or partially encrypted. The basic assumption is that we trust the eSDS to perform these operations correctly. Although conceptually we refer to the eSDS as a single component, it could be physically distributed across several hosts.

– Key Management Server (KMS): The KMS is a fully trusted server which is responsible for all the key-related operations, e.g. key generation, distribution, and revocation. Although requiring a trusted KMS seems at odds with using a less trusted node where the data space is running, we will show that the KMS is lightweight, it requires less resources and management. Securing the KMS is also much easier. Because of this, the KMS can be offline most of the time.

## 4.3   System Setup

To initialise the encryption system, the KMS runs the setup algorithm to generate public and secret parameters which will be used for the whole lifetime of the system. The algorithm is described as follows:

The algorithm first takes a security parameter $k$ and runs the key generation algorithm using standard RSA which generates $(p, q, n, \phi(n), e, d)$. It then generates $\{p', q', g, x, h, a, g^a h^a\}$ satisfying the following constraints: $p'$ and $q'$ are two large prime numbers such that $q'$ divides $p' - 1$; $g$ is a generator of $G_{q'}$, the unique order-$q'$ subgroup of $Z_{p'}^*$; and $h \equiv g^x \bmod p'$ where $x$ is chosen uniformly randomly from $Z_{q'}$. $a$ is also a random number from $Z_{q'}$.

The parameters needed for encryption/decryption are $n, p', q', g, h, g^a h^a$ and need to be published system-wide. The key material is represented by the parameters $p, q, \phi(n), e, d, x, a$ and must be kept secretly. In particular, the $(e, d, a)$ are called "Master Keys" for the system.

## 4.4   Client Key Generation and Revocation

When a new client is enrolled into the system, the KMS must generate a unique key set for the client. The key set is derived from the key material using the following algorithm:

For a client $i$, the KMS generates $e_{i1}, e_{i2}, d_{i1}, d_{i2}, a_{i1}, a_{i2}$ such that $e_{i1}e_{i2} \equiv e \bmod \phi(n)$, $d_{i1}d_{i2} \equiv d \bmod \phi(n)$ and $a_{i1}a_{i2} \equiv a \bmod q'$. Key generation can be efficiently done in the following way. Let us consider the generation of the $e_{i1}, e_{i2}$ pair. The KMS randomly chooses $e_{i1} < \phi(n)$, where $gcd(e_{i1}, \phi(n)) = 1$. Since $e_{i1}x \equiv 1 \bmod \phi(n)$ has always a solution, then $e_{i2} \equiv ex \bmod \phi(n)$ always satisfies $e_{i1}e_{i2} \equiv e \bmod \phi(n)$. The KMS then sends $(e_{i1}, d_{i1}, a_{i1})$ to client $i$ and $(e_{i2}, d_{i2}, a_{i2})$ to the eSDS through secure channels.

In our system it is possible to authenticate a client and establish a secure channel between the client and the eSDS using the corresponding key pairs. Because $e_{i1}d_{i1}e_{i2}d_{i2} \equiv ed \equiv 1 \bmod \phi(n)$, $k_1 = e_{i1}d_{i1}$ and $k_2 = e_{i2}d_{i2}$ form another RSA key pair. This key pair can be used for public key mutual authentication and for establishing a secure channel, e.g. SSL.

When a client's access privilege is revoked, the KMS sends an instruction to the eSDS to request the removal of the client's corresponding keys. After the keys have been removed, the client cannot access the data unless the KMS generates new keys for it.

## 4.5   Tuple Encryption

In our system, tuple encryption is performed in two steps. A tuple is first encrypted by the client using its own private key. The encrypted tuple is then sent to the eSDS, where the tuple is re-encrypted using the node's key that correspond to that client. Client side encryption prevents the eSDS (and its hosting site) from knowing the data in the tuple whereas the eSDS side encryption makes it possible for other authorised clients in the system to retrieve the tuple in clear text. The encryption process for client $i$ is shown in Fig. 1. For a tuple $t = \langle d_1; ...; d_n \rangle$, we denote the value of a field at position $x$ by $d_x$.

On the client side, a tuple is first encrypted using a semantically secure symmetric encryption algorithm $E$ [10]. For each tuple, client $i$ randomly picks a key $K$ from the key space of $E$. Each value of the tuple's fields $d_x$ is encrypted under the key $K$ which generates a ciphertext $c_{x1} = E_K(d_x)$. The symmetric key $K$ is then encrypted by algorithm $CEnc$ which is identical to the RSA-OAEP (Optimal Asymmetric Encryption Padding) encryption algorithm [1] and uses

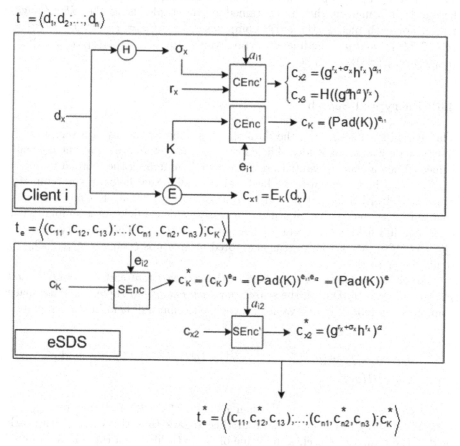

**Fig. 1.** Encryption of a tuple on client $i$ and data space

$e_{i1}$ as the encryption key. RSA-OAEP enhances RSA by using a probabilistic padding scheme and has been proved to be IND-CCA2 (Indistinguishable Adaptive Chosen Ciphertext Attack) secure [7]. The ciphertexts of the symmetric keys is $c_K = (Pad(K))^{e_{i1}}$.

During the search for a matching tuple, the data space content is kept encrypted. The matching is done using an opportunely modified values of the tuple field, called *keywords*. Keywords are computed as follows by the client using the algorithm $CEnc'$ and sent together with the tuple to the eSDS. For each value $d_x$ of a tuple field , the client $i$ computes $\sigma_x = H(d_x)$ using a hash function $H$. The client also picks a random number $r_x \in Z_{q'}$ and computes $c_{x2} = (g^{r_x + \sigma_x} h^{r_x})^{a_{i1}} \bmod p', c_{x3} = H((g^a h^a)^{r_x})$, where $g, h, g^a h^a, p'$ are public parameters in the system and $a_{i1}$ is the client's keyword encryption key. The client then sends the encrypted tuple $t_e = \langle (c_{11}, c_{12}, c_{13}); ...; (c_{n1}, c_{n2}, c_{n3}); c_K \rangle$ to the eSDS.

After receiving the encrypted tuple, the eSDS retrieves $e_{i2}$ and $a_{i2}$, the corresponding encryption keys for the client $i$. It re-encrypts the symmetric key by computing $c_K^* = c_K^{e_{i2}}$ using the $SEnc$ algorithm. The eSDS processes the keywords information that is contained in the tuple using the $SEnc'$ algorithm. For each filed $x$, the eSDS computes $c_{x2}^* = c_{x2}^{a_{i2}} = (g^{r_x + \sigma_x} h^{r_x})^{a_{i1} a_{i2}} = (g^{r_x + \sigma_x} h^{r_x})^a \bmod p'$. The final encrypted tuple stored is $t_e^* = \langle (c_{11}, c_{12}^*, c_{13}); ...; (c_{n1}, c_{n2}^*, c_{n3}); c_K^* \rangle$.

## 4.6    Encrypted Search

The searching of a tuple in the data space is done by means of a template. A template may contains wildcard fields, that in our system are represented as null values. When a client $j$ wants to retrieve a tuple matching the template $temp = \langle z_1, ..., z_n \rangle$, $j$ first computes the hash value of all actual fields in the template. Since a wildcard field matches any actual values in a tuple, it is not necessary that our encrypted search algorithm processes wildcard fields of a template. For each non-null field $x$ the client $j$ generates $\sigma_x^* = H(z_x)$. Then $j$ encrypts $\sigma_x^*$ as $Q_x = g^{-\sigma_x^* a_{j1}}$. At this point, the encrypted template is $temp_e = \langle Q_1; ...; Q_n \rangle$. $j$ sends $temp_e$ to the eSDS.

The eSDS computes for each field of the received template $Q_x' = Q_x^{a_{j2}} \bmod p' = g^{-\sigma_x^* a} \bmod p'$. During the search, for each encrypted tuple, the data space computes the following two values for each $x$-th non-null field in the template:

$$y_{x1} = c_{x2}^* Q_x' = (g^{r_x + \sigma_x} h^{r_x})^a g^{-\sigma_x^* a} = (g^{ar_x + a\sigma_x} h^{ar_x}) g^{-a\sigma_x^*} \bmod p'$$
$$y_{x2} = H(y_1)$$

We can see that if $d_x = z_x$ then $a\sigma_x - a\sigma_x^* = 0$, and therefore $y_{x1} = (g^{ar_x} h^{ar_x}) = (g^a h^a)^{r_x} \bmod p'$. From this follows that the value in the $x$-th field of the template matches the value of the $x$-th filed in a tuple if and only if $y_{x2} = c_{x3}$ (because $y_{x2} = H((g^a h^a)^{r_x}) = c_{x3}$).

## 4.7    Tuple Decryption

When a matching tuple is found, the eSDS computes the following before sending the tuple to the client $j$. For each field $x$ in the matching tuple $t_e^* = \langle (c_{11}, c_{12}^*, c_{13}) ; ...; (c_{n1}, c_{n2}^*, c_{n3}); c_K^*) \rangle$ the eSDS computes $c_K' = (c_K^*)^{d_{j2}}$ and sends to $j$ the following tuple $t_e' = \langle (c_{11}; ...; c_{n1}; c_K') \rangle$. The client $j$ retrieves the key for encrypting the data items by computing $(c_K')^{d_{j1}} = (c_K^*)^d = (K)^{ed} = K$. The client $j$ can decrypt the value of each field by computing $d_x = E_K^{-1}(c_{x1})$.

## 5    Implementation and Performance

In this section, we discuss the implementation and performance of the eSDS based on the encryption scheme. The prototype is an extension of our implementation of a distributed SDS, called GSpace [16].

Figure 2 provides an overview of the modules that are part of our architecture. Clients and the eSDS are different processes that reside in different hosts. A client $C_i$ communicates with the eSDS by means of a proxy, called **eSD-SProxy**. The eSDSProxy takes care of hiding from the client all the details for the communication with the eSDS and deals with the cryptographic operations. To connect to an eSDS, a client creates a new **eSDSProxy** as follows:

```
eSDSProxy p = new eSDSProxy ("SpaceName");
```

The argument is used by the proxy to load in its **KeyStore** (KS) the appropriate key pair for tuple encryption and decryption and for establishing a secure connection with the eSDS. The proxy performs tuple encryption and decryption using the **Proxy Encryption Module (PEM)**.

Tuples and templates are subclasses of the `Tuple` class. A tuple can be defined in such a way that when it is stored in the eSDS it can contain both cleartext and encrypted fields. A field in a tuple will be stored encrypted only when its type is one of the following: `eInt`, `eChar`, `eDouble`, and `eString`. These are classes that we define to represent the encrypted form of the corresponding Java classes. Therefore, if a tuple is defined as follows:

```
MyTuple(eString name, eInt age, Integer weight)
```

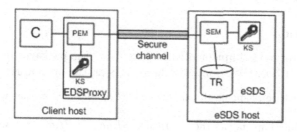

**Fig. 2.** Overview of the architecture of the our eSDS prototype

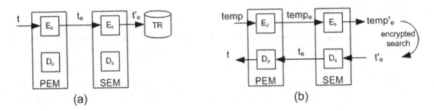

**Fig. 3.** Encryption steps executed for storing and retrieving a tuple using our scheme

when such a tuple is stored in the eSDS, only the first two fields will be encrypted. Field `weight` will be stored in cleartext.

A client (by means of its proxy) establishes a secure communication with the eSDS. The eSDS authenticates the client and the corresponding key is loaded into the KS of the eSDS. The eSDS performs tuple encryption, decryption and encrypted search by means of its **Space Encryption Module (SEM)**. Tuples are stored in the **Tuple Repository (TR)**.

In the implementation, a put operation is used to insert a tuple in the space. read and take operations are used for retrieving tuples; the former returns a copy of a matching tuple whether the latter destructively removes the matching tuple. When these operations are executed, tuples and templates are transformed according to our encryption scheme. Figure 3 shows the cryptographic operations executed in the PEM and SEM on tuples and templates for a put and a read (or take) operation.

Let us assume that a tuple t has to be stored encrypted (i.e., all of its fields must be encrypted). Figure 3-(a) shows the steps executed for a put operation. The fields of tuple $t$ are encrypted in the PEM using the submodule $E_p$ [1]. The encrypted tuple $t_e$ is sent to the eSDS where it is re-encrypted by SEM's submodule $E_s$[2]. The tuple $t'_e$ is stored in the TR.

Figure 3-(b) shows the case of a read operation. For a read operation a template $temp$ is used for finding a matching tuple. The non-null fields in the template are encrypted by the submodule $E_p$ that produces the encrypted template $temp_e$. $temp_e$ is sent to the eSDS where it is re-encrypted in $temp'_e$. This is used for performing the encrypted search. When an encrypted tuple $t_e$ matches the template $temp'_e$, the tuple must be decrypted before it is returned to the client. First, $t'_e$ is decrypted in the SEM using the $D_s$ submodule and it is transformed in $t_e$. $t_e$ is returned to the client's proxy that decrypts it using $D_p$, returning the tuple in cleartext t to the client.

## 5.1   Evaluation

The eSDS prototype is implemented in Java using the packages provided in the standard Java 1.5 distribution. We chose AES as the symmetric cipher which

---

[1] This submodule implements the algorithms $CEnc$ and $CEnc'$ that we described in Section 4.

[2] This submodule implements the algorithms $SEnc$ and $SEnc'$ that we described in Section 4.

encrypts the actual data and SHA-1 as the hash function. For the RSA-based proxy encryption scheme, we used 1024-bit keys. For the keyword encryption scheme, $q'$ was 160-bit and $p'$ was 1024-bit. The tests were executed on a Intel Pentium IV 3.2 GHz (dual core) with 1 GB of RAM.

The first evaluation consisted of measuring the execution time for the encryption and decryption submodules. In particular, we measured the execution time for:

- Client Encryption: consists in the execution of $E_p$, that is encrypting tuple fields using the symmetric cipher, encrypting the symmetric key and encrypting the keywords.
- eSDS Encryption: consists in the execution of $E_s$, that is the re-encryption of the symmetric key and the keywords using the eSDS keys.
- eSDS Decryption: pre-decryption of the symmetric key by executing $D_s$.
- Client Decryption: decryption of the symmetric key and the tuple fields by executing $D_p$.

Table 1 provides the results of our test for the execution of the encryption and decryption operations. The time is given in milliseconds for a single execution of each operation calculated on the average time for 10,000 executions. The tuple and template used for the experiments consisted in a single field of type eString with 4 chars.

We also measured the time for finding a matching tuple using our encrypted search. In the data space, 10000 encrypted tuple were stored and only one was a match for the template used in the search. We ensured that the matching tuple was the last tuple to be evaluated (worst case scenario). Tuples and template consisted of a single eString filed with 4 chars. Under these conditions, the time required for finding the matching tuple is around 600 milliseconds. Basically, each matching test takes around 0.06 milliseconds.

Given the results of this performance analysis, we can say that the use of our scheme is well suited for cases where a large number of tuples need to be searched. The search is performed entirely within the data space and the result that is returned is a tuple matching the given template. In contrast, when executing the same experiment using an approach as in KLAIM, executing cycles and bandwidth would be wasted. In fact, the result that is given back to a client is a partial match to the given template (only the fields not encrypted are used for the matching). The client has to decrypt the tuple and if the values of the encrypted fields are not the intended ones then the client has to re-encrypt the tuple and send it back to the space.

**Table 1.** Performance of Encryption and Decryption Operations

| Execution Step | Execution Time (ms) |
|---|---|
| Client Encryption | 53 |
| eSDS Encryption | 37 |
| eSDS Decryption | 37 |
| Client Decryption | 37 |

# 6  Host Attack

In this section, we discuss some of the attacks that can be performed by malicious hosts.

Existing research focused on protecting the data space from attacks performed by malicious clients. The assumption is that hosts where the data space is deployed are fully trusted while clients are not to be trusted. As discussed in [6], existing approaches protect the data space against malicious clients that:

1. remove and/or forge tuples from a data space to disrupt the collaboration between genuine clients, and
2. insert into a data space a large number of tuples to consume all resources.

Because hosts are fully trusted, there are no mechanisms in place that can guarantee the confidentiality of data stored in the data space against the hosts other than encrypting non-searchable data.

In our attack model, we assume that a host is *honest-but-curious*. We trust the host to correctly authenticate the clients and to perform the operations as requested by the clients. The confidentiality of the data is protected from the host while supporting search on the protected data. However, in deploying the data space on untrusted hosts other concerns need to be addressed. In the following, we list some of these concerns and the threats to which the data space is exposed to. Our aim is not to provide a concrete solution to each of them, but to highlight possible future research directions that aim to protect the data space from untrusted hosts.

*Integrity.* An attacker that has access to the data space hosts could threaten the integrity of the data space in several ways. For one, the attacker could alter the authorisation process allowing unauthorised clients to access the tuples (even if the clients are not able to decrypt them) or it could deny access to authorised clients. An attacker can alter the semantics of the data space operations. For instance, a client can be blocked in executing a retrieving operation while the matching tuple is in the space; the attacker can re-send back to a client a tuple that was the result of a previous operation (replay attack); additionally, the attacker can discard tuples inserted by legitimate clients modifying in this way the results of retrieval operations. Although no mechanisms could prevent the attacker form performing such attacks, methods developed for database systems could help in detecting and mitigating some of those attacks. For example, methods based on cryptographic techniques and hash functions would allow a client to determine whether the returned result corresponds to the real content of the database. These methods could be extended to include the notion of time with the encrypted representation of the actual content of the data space. In this way, a client would be able to detect whether the blocking for a removal operation was caused maliciously by a host or just because the tuple was not present at the time the request was made. To make sure that tuples inserted by genuine clients are not discarded by malicious hosts some global encrypted indexing could be used. Finally, the integrity of tuples can also be compromised. For instance, an attacker can change or reorder tuple fields (reordering attack).

*Availability.* Clients that try to connect to the SDS hosts may experience some disruptions. For instance, the data space host is not reachable or it requires a long time for replying. These disruptions may be caused maliciously by the attacker. In order to mitigate such attacks, mechanisms that ensure accountability are required. Accountability is the property that allows the participants of a system to determine and expose misbehavior. In this way, clients can determine whether hosts are behaving correctly. Accountable mechanisms have been proposed for network storage as in [21].

*Traffic Analysis.* By monitoring the timing and frequency of the communication between hosts and clients, an attacker can gather useful information. By monitoring the execution time of encryption and decryption operations on tuples an attacker can gather enough information to efficiently recover the client key. For instance, in [17] Song shows that it is possible to use such an attack to recover a password exchanged in the SSH protocol 50 times faster than using a brute force attack. The attacker can also built a statistical attack by comparing the templates with the matching tuples.

*Collusion.* One of the major concerns in proxy encryption schemes comes from a collusion attack. If a client colludes with an attacker that has access to all the EDS side keys, then it is possible to recover the master keys by combining their keys. Collusion-resistant proxy encryption schemes is an open problem. However, we can lower the risk of collusion to an acceptable level by implementing other mechanisms. For example, we can limit the access to the keys by using tamper-proof devices. We can also split the master keys into multiple shares and introduce additional servers, making collusion more difficult. Monitoring and auditing to detect collusion can also help to mitigate the risk.

# 7   Conclusions and Future Work

In this paper, we presented a novel encryption scheme that ensure tuples confidentiality even in the case that the data space is deployed on untrusted hosts.

The scheme supports encrypted search for a matching tuple over the encrypted data space. In this way, the data space never has access to tuples in cleartext protecting the confidentiality of the its content from nosey hosts. Moreover, the scheme does not require the clients to share secret keys. Each client has its own key that can be used for retrieving tuples encrypted by other clients' keys. This greatly reduces the burden of key management. for instance, when a key of a client is revoked it is not necessary to invalidate all the other clients' keys and re-encrypt the entire data space content.

We provided an implementation of an encrypted SDS using the presented scheme and performed some preliminary performance analysis.

Finally, we discussed a wider class of security threats that arise when data spaces are deployed in untrusted hosts. This threat analysis can be seen as a starting point for some future work. We are currently looking at Private

Information Retrieval (PIR) schemes that would allow a user to retrieve tuples from a data space without revealing to its host which items were searched.

As concluding thought, we would like to point out that although this scheme has been presented in the context of the SDS model, it could be applicable to any other systems where the confidentiality of data shared among several entities must be protected, i.e. databases, publish subscribe systems, email servers, etc.

# References

1. Bellare, M., Rogaway, P.: Optimal Asymmetric Encryption. In: De Santis, A. (ed.) EUROCRYPT 1994. LNCS, vol. 950, pp. 92–111. Springer, Heidelberg (1995)
2. Bettini, L., De Nicola, R.: A Java Middleware for Guaranteeing Privacy of Distributed Tuple Spaces. In: Guelfi, N., Astesiano, E., Reggio, G. (eds.) FIDJI 2002. LNCS, vol. 2604, pp. 175–184. Springer, Heidelberg (2003)
3. Blaze, M., Bleumer, G., Strauss, M.: Divertible protocols and atomic proxy cryptography. In: Nyberg, K. (ed.) EUROCRYPT 1998. LNCS, vol. 1403, pp. 127–144. Springer, Heidelberg (1998)
4. http://www.doc.ic.ac.uk/~cd04/papers/noshare.pdf
5. Elgamal, T.: A public key cryptosystem and a signature scheme based on discrete logarithms. IEEE Transactions on Information Theory 31(4), 469–472 (1985)
6. Focardi, R., Lucchi, R., Zavattaro, G.: Secure shared data-space Coordination Languages: a Process Algebraic survey. Science of Computer Programming 63(1), 3–15 (2006)
7. Fujisaki, E., Okamoto, T., Pointcheval, D., Stern, J.: Rsa-oaep is secure under the rsa assumption. In: Kilian, J. (ed.) CRYPTO 2001. LNCS, vol. 2139, pp. 260–274. Springer, Heidelberg (2001)
8. Gelernter, D.: Generative Communication in Linda. ACM Trans. Prog. Lang. Syst. 7(1), 80–112 (1985)
9. Gelernter, D., Carriero, N.: Coordination Languages and their Significance. Commun. ACM 35(2), 96–107 (1992)
10. Goldreich, O.: Foundations of Cryptography. Basic Applications, vol. II. Cambridge University Press, Cambridge (2004)
11. Gorrieri, R., Lucchi, R., Zavattaro, G.: Supporting Secure Coordination in Sec-Spaces. In: Fundamenta Informaticae, IOS Press, Amsterdam (2005)
12. Handorean, R., Roman, G.C.: Secure Sharing of Tuple Space in Ad Hoc Settings. In: Focardi, R., Zavattaro, G. (eds.) Electronic Notes in Theoretical Computer Science, Elsevier, Amsterdam (2003)
13. Ivan, A.A., Dodis, Y.: Proxy cryptography revisited. In: NDSS, The Internet Society (2003)
14. Picco, G.P., Murphy, A.L., Roman, G.-C.: Lime: Linda Meets Mobility. In: Garlan, D., Kramer, J. (eds.) Proc. 21st Int'l Conf. on Software Engineering (ICSE 1999), Los Angeles (USA), pp. 368–377. ACM Press, New York (1999)
15. Rivest, R.L., Shamir, A., Adleman, L.M.: A method for obtaining digital signatures and public-key cryptosystems. Commun. ACM 21(2), 120–126 (1978)
16. Russello, G.: Separation and Adaptation of Concerns in a Shared Data Space. Ph.D. Thesis, Department of Computer Science, Eindhoven University of Technology (June 2006)
17. Song, D.X., Wagner, D., Tian, X.: Timing Analysis of Keystrokes and Timing Attacks on SSH. In: Proc. of 10th USENIX Security Symposium (2001)

18. Udizir, N., Wood, A., Jacob, J.: "Coordination with Multicapabilities. In: Jacquet, J.-M., Picco, G.P. (eds.) COORDINATION 2005. LNCS, vol. 3454, pp. 79–93. Springer, Heidelberg (2005)

19. Vitek, J., Bryce, C., Oriol, M.: Coordinating Processes with Secure Spaces. In: Proc. of Conf. on Coordination Models and Languages, Science of Computer Programming, vol. 46, pp. 163–193 (2003)

20. Wood, A.: Coordination with attributes. In: Ciancarini, P., Wolf, A.L. (eds.) CO-ORDINATION 1999. LNCS, vol. 1594, p. 21. Springer, Heidelberg (1999)

21. Yumerefendi, A.R., Chase, J.S.: Strong accountability for network storage. ACM Trans. on Storage 3(3) (October 2007)

# CiAN: A Workflow Engine for MANETs

Rohan Sen, Gruia-Catalin Roman, and Christopher Gill

Department of Computer Science and Engineering
Washington University in St. Louis
Campus Box 1045, One Brookings Drive, St. Louis, MO 63130, U.S.A.
{rohan.sen,roman,cdgill}@wustl.edu

**Abstract.** The practice of using workflows to model complex activities
in stable networks is commonplace and is supported by many commer-
cially available workflow management systems (WfMSs). However, the
use of workflows to model collaborative activities in mobile environments,
while possible at the model level, has not gained traction due to the lack
of a suitable WfMS for mobile networks and devices. This paper seeks
to address this need. We present CiAN, a choreography-based workflow
engine that is designed with MANETs in mind. We describe the design, architecture, and communication protocols used by CiAN as well
as its implementation using Java. An evaluation of the communication
protocol used to coordinate among various workflow participants across
MANETs is also presented.

## 1 Introduction

Workflows can be conceptualized as a set of related tasks that are arranged according to a specific order and structure to accomplish a higher level goal in
a collaborative manner. Workflows are commonly represented and specified in
terms of graphs or petri-nets [23]. Software systems that execute these workflow
specifications are called Workflow Management Systems (WfMSs). In the current
state of the art, WfMSs such as ActiveBPEL [9], Oracle Workflow Engine [18],
Biztalk [7], etc. operate across wired networks and execute workflows that encode complex business processes such as insurance claims processing, inventory
control, loan approvals, among others.

A WfMS has two main functions: assigning tasks in the workflow to suitable
hosts and subsequently invoking them in the correct order, passing any data or
notifications between them as necessary. The performance of all the tasks by
multiple participants collectively accomplishes the collaborative activity specified by the workflow. Current designs for WfMSs reflect the stable and reliable
environment in which they operate. The architecture of these systems are centralized and interactions with the various distributed components are typically
synchronous calls made "just-in-time".

In this paper, we describe the design of a WfMS targeted to mobile settings.
Our work is motivated by the fact that while the workflow model is robust
enough to describe more expansive forms of collaborations (including collaborations involving both humans and software in the physical world), it is not in

D. Lea and G. Zavattaro (Eds.): COORDINATION 2008, LNCS 5052, pp. 280–295, 2008.

widespread use due to the lack of a suitable WfMS to execute such workflows. A mobile WfMS that can operate over a mobile ad hoc network (MANET) can be used as a general purpose coordination mechanism for the activities of workers at a remote outdoor construction site, management of emergency responders in the event of a toxic chemical spill, or directing the activities of a geological survey team where setting up a traditional WfMS over a temporary LAN, even if possible, is not desirable.

However, developing a WfMS for MANETs has several implications, the most significant of which is the paradigm shift from centralized management to a distributed management scheme. In addition, appropriate communication and coordination protocols need to be developed so that participants can interact over a dynamic and fragmented network. CiAN, which stands for Collaboration in Ad hoc Networks, is a clean sheet approach to building a WfMS that is flexible enough to operate across a MANET. CiAN is designed from the ground up to function in a choreographed manner, i.e., in a manner that does not require a central coordinating entity. Novel features of CiAN include a distributed management system that functions at the level of granularity of a single task, a communication protocol that combines publish-subscribe, store-and-forward, and content-based routing to foster communication across the MANET between various hosts performing the workflow, and an ability to adapt the workflow execution according to changes in the context in which the execution takes place.

## 2 Background

Before we present the features of our system in detail, we describe precisely our target environment and the differences between operating in a choreographed manner as opposed to the more commonplace orchestrated manner.

For CiAN, we assume that there exists a group of human users, each of whom is equipped with a relatively powerful mobile computing device (in the remainder of the paper we refer to the device and user collectively as a *host*). We assume that all hosts are co-located initially but may separate once the workflow execution has begun. Since the devices are carried on the person of the users, we assume that the devices are physically mobile and that their motion pattern is the same as their associated user. The devices are capable of communicating with each other using 802.11b/g/n radios when they are within communication range of each other. However, such *windows of communication* (the intervals of time during which a pair of hosts are within range) may be transient due to the mobility of the associated human user.

Each host that participates in the execution of a workflow provides: (1) A name, assumed to be unique in the network, (2) A schedule with entries that indicate when it is not available. Each entry consists of a start time, location at the start time, end time, and location at the end time. When hosts are assigned tasks, they add them to their schedule so that they are not assigned additional tasks that conflict, and (3) A list of services offered. This list includes software services on the mobile devices and the associated user's capabilities, e.g., a metal

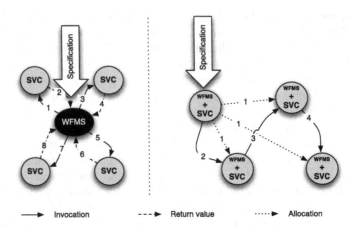

**Fig. 1.** Orchestration vs. Choreography (SVC = Service & WFMS = Workflow Mgmt. System.

worker may have welding capabilities. We assume that each host maintains a local knowledge base [12] in which it keeps information about other hosts in the network. Initially the knowledge base contains information only about the local host. However, over time, the knowledge base is populated with information about other hosts when pairs of hosts are within communication range of each other via a gossiping protocol. The contents of the knowledge base can be queried by other components of the middleware. It should be noted that due to all hosts being co-located initially, each host has knowledge of all others in the network. However, future updates to host knowledge are dispersed via gossiping which may lead to asymmetric information in the network.

Since there is no central coordinating entity in this environment, all management functions must be handled in a distributed manner. This requires the execution model to be *choreographed*. In choreography, the responsibility for executing the workflow is divided up a priori by an allocation algorithm (not covered in this paper. Please refer to [25]). The various participants then interact with each other directly via a peer-to-peer model using pre-established standardized protocols. This is in sharp contrast to the more common *orchestrated* architecture where a centralized entity is responsible for executing the entire workflow and synchronously invokes services (in workflow order) to complete tasks. The differences between these approaches are shown pictorially in Figure 1.

The following section describes our design for a choreography-based WfMS along with the communication protocols for communicating with various components across the MANET.

## 3   System Design

According to the W3C definition, choreography "defines re-usable common rules that govern the ordering of exchanged messages, and the provisioning patterns of collaborative behavior, as agreed upon between two or more interacting participants.". In the context of our WfMS, this translates to the allocation of tasks to hosts (which in combination with the workflow structure describes the agreed upon collaboration patterns among participating hosts) while the execution engine is responsible for implementing the rules and protocols governing the exchange of messages. To keep these two concerns separate, CiAN operates in two modes: (1) *planning* - which is used to allocate tasks in the workflow and (2) *standard* - which is used by the hosts whose responsibility is to perform the tasks that have been allocated to it. This paper focusses on the standard mode. We include a brief presentation of the planning mode for completeness.

## 3.1   CiAN in Planning Mode

The Planning Mode of CiAN is responsible for implementing a scheme to inform each participating host of its role in the overall workflow. If the allocation of tasks is being done centrally, a single host operates in planning mode (hereinafter referred to simply as the *planning host*) and runs a centralized allocation algorithm [13] which allocates individual tasks to hosts. If the allocation of tasks is being done in a distributed manner [25], then several hosts run in planning mode. The host that initiates the workflow is responsible for fragmenting the workflow and passing it to the other hosts running in planning mode along with a set of rules for task allocation. For the purposes of our discussion, we will assume that the allocation process is centralized followed by a distributed, choreographed execution. It should also be noted that a host can run the planning and standard modes of CiAN simultaneously, if it so desires.

The planning host allocates each task in the workflow to a *suitable* host, where a suitable host is defined as a host whose capabilities are a superset of the capability requirements of the task, and whose motion pattern allows it to be at the location at which the task needs to be performed at the time it needs to be performed. Figure 2 shows the system architecture on the planning host. An external application injects the workflow specification into the planning system by way of the Planner. The Planner passes this specification to the Allocator, which runs an appropriate *allocation algorithm* (e.g., [13] or [25]) to determine the hosts that are assigned to each task in the workflow. It then annotates the specification with these allocations and returns it to the Planner. The Planner then feeds the specification to the Route Information unit, which augments the specification with metadata (used for data routing - described later in this section). This augmented specification is then returned to the Planner which now forwards it to the Specification Disbursement Policy module, which breaks the workflow into its constituent tasks and sends each task specification to the host that has been allocated to perform it using the Communication Middleware. Each task specification sent out includes (1) the input edges to the task, their merging and synchronization pattern [27], and the tasks at the source of the edges, (2) the service that must be invoked for that task, and (3) the output edges to the task, their splitting and synchronization pattern [27], and the tasks at the sinks of the edges.

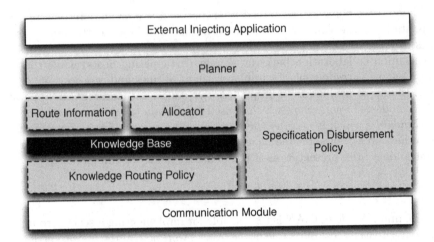

**Fig. 2.** CiAN planning architecture

There are a few points to note in the figure. The components with dotted borders are interfaces, i.e., they can be realized by alternate policies as long as they meet the interface requirements. One simple example of this is the replacement of the Allocator which implements a centralized algorithm in our description this far with one that sets up a distributed allocation policy. The Allocator uses the schedule and service list provided by each host (stored in the Knowledge Base as described in Section 2) to determine the allocation of the tasks to hosts based on their capabilities and motion constraints. Recall that since hosts are co-located initially, the planning host has access to information about all participating hosts.

### 3.2   CiAN in Standard Mode

The Standard Mode of CiAN is responsible for managing the choreographed execution of the workflow on individual hosts and then disbursing results to the hosts that are responsible for executing subsequent tasks. At a high level, the Standard Mode on a given host works as follows: (1) It waits for a task to be allocated to the host on which it is executing. (2) When a task is allocated, it receives the specification for that task and installs it within the system and goes back to waiting (either on inputs to the task it has installed or additional task allocations). (3) If an input to an installed task is received, it runs the input synchronization logic for that task (see Figure 4). If the logic is satisfied, the values received are passed to the task for execution. If not, then additional inputs may be required and the system waits for these. (4) When the task execution has been completed, it runs the output synchronization logic for that task and transmits the values to the tasks at the sinks of the outgoing edges. We now describe this process in detail.

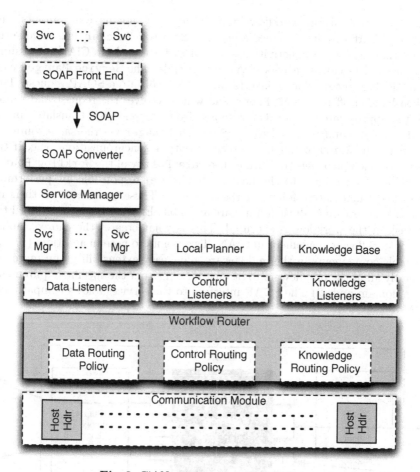

**Fig. 3.** CiAN runtime system architecture

The architecture of CiAN in standard mode is shown in Figure 3. When the task specification arrives, the `Communication Module` passes it to the `Workflow Router`. The arrival of the specification is regarded as a *control message*, so it is given to the `Control Routing Policy` module of the `Workflow Router`, which in turn notifies any `Control Listeners` that may be listening for these messages. The default `Control Listener` parses the task specification and creates a `Service Manager` for the task. The `Service Manager` contains the input synchronization and output synchronization logic mentioned above, which are parametrized according to the information in the task specification received. For example, if a task has three incoming edges with AND join semantics, the input synchronization logic would not be satisfied until it had received values from all three edges. The `Service Manager` creates *subscriptions* for each of its inputs, which is a request for data generated by its preceding tasks (we will cover subscriptions later in this section). At this point a task is waiting on its inputs before it can start executing.

The first task in any workflow by definition does not have any inputs, and hence can start executing immediately. The `Service Manager` must invoke the service that performs the activity associated with the task. In CiAN, we assume that all services can be accessed via SOAP calls. The `Service Manager` calls the `SOAP Converter` which converts the service call into a SOAP request. This is then handed off to a `SOAP Front End` which receives the request and routes it to the appropriate service. The response from the service is translated into a SOAP response and returned to the `Service Manager` via the same route. At this stage, the `Service Manager` executes output synchronization logic. If the logic is satisfied, it passes the data to the `Data Policy` of the `Workflow Router` which then transmits it to the host(s) that is(are) responsible for performing the task(s) immediately following the first task. These tasks wait on their inputs and execute once all the inputs are available. Execution continues until the last task in the workflow is executed. This is what creates the choreographed form of workflow management in CiAN. Two points to note in addition: (1) The pluggable components in the middleware allow easy extensibility and more importantly allow the middleware to be customized as per the specific requirements of the domain and (2) The SOAP interface to the services allows compatibility with Web services.

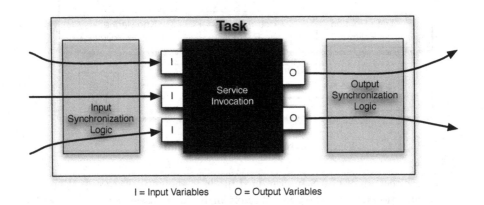

I = Input Variables    O = Output Variables

**Fig. 4.** Task and synchronization logic

## 3.3   Communication in MANETs

Thus far, we have described how individual tasks get executed but have not covered how the coordination of the hosts performing the tasks is handled. At the coordination and communication layer, there are two key issues: (1) The hosts are connected by a MANET, whose topology evolves rapidly over time and where unpredictable disconnections are commonplace, making it difficult to maintain long lasting routes between host pairs. (2) The workflow specification indicates which *task* a result must be delivered to or obtained from but not the *host* that is executing those tasks. We addressed these issues via a publish-subscribe-like protocol that opportunistically gossips data and subscriptions among hosts when they are directly connected with each other. The scheme is described in detail below.

The Communication Module on each host transmits a beacon periodically. When the Communication Module on another host receives such a beacon, it creates a Host Handler for that host. The Host Handler tries to establish a direct connection between the hosts using TCP/IP streams. Thus, as long as the hosts are in communication range, the Host Handler acts as the local proxy of the remote host and handles communication between them. Since direct communication is the most reliable and inexpensive form of communication in a MANET, all information in CiAN is transmitted when two hosts are directly connected. Thus, when the Host Handler establishes a connection, it synchronizes the knowledge base of the two hosts using the time of acquisition of any knowledge as a tie breaker. It also sends to and receives data or subscription messages from the other host as appropriate. All data and subscription messages received are passed to the Data Routing Policy in the Workflow Router. If a data message is intended for a task on the local host, the Data Routing Policy passes it to the Service Manager of the target task. The Service Manager then runs the synchronization logic to see if a valid set of inputs have been received.

While this form of communication is acceptable for gossiping, it does not meet all our requirements, specifically, it provides no means for a message exchange to take place between two hosts that are never directly connected to each other. This restriction can result in critical data from one task not reaching the next. A simple solution to this problem is to simply address each message to its destination host and use a MANET routing protocol to deliver the message. However, this has two drawbacks: (1) MANET routes do not last often and are expensive to maintain, and (2) it strongly associates a task with a host, which while not desirable is preferably avoided. Our approach is instead a store and forward approach based on a routing policy we have developed. At the planning stage, we augment each task with a unique number (the metadata mentioned earlier) such that it is greater than all its parents' numbers but lesser than all its childrens' (tasks that are siblings may have numbers lesser or greater depending on the graph traversal method used). When each host receives a task spec, it assigns a number to itself that is the same as the number of the task. If multiple tasks are assigned, then it initially chooses the lowest numbered task. Once the task associated with that number has been completed, it examines the remaining set of tasks allocated to it and chooses the lowest number available. Subscriptions (generated by tasks to solicit inputs) have the number of the subscribing task, and the number of the task whose input is desired. Similarly, when a task finishes execution, the data is labeled with the generating task number and the number of the task(s) that should receive the data. The messages are routed using one of the following three schemes: *Scheme 1* - Data is routed to any host that has a number between the generating task number and the target task number or has no number in a strictly increasing fashion. Subscriptions are routed similarly but in a strictly decreasing function. Routing to a host with no number is neither a decrease nor an increase. *Scheme 2* - Data can be routed to any host that has a number between the starting task number and the target task number in a strictly increasing order. Subscriptions are routed to hosts between the target task number and the ending task number. Routing to hosts without a number is also permitted. *Scheme 3* - This scheme is identical to Scheme 1 with one exception. Any message can be routed outside the permissible range but this triggers a counter. If the message moves to a host in range (as defined by Scheme 1) before the counter expires, the counter is reset, otherwise the message is destroyed.

Scheme 1 generates the lowest number of messages in the network but is restrictive in the sense that the number of hosts that a message can be routed to is much smaller than the total number of hosts collaborating. Scheme 2 increases the permissible range but generates additional messages. Scheme 3 maintains the low range of Scheme 1 but allows limited transgressions, which represents the most favorable tradeoff between number of messages and number of hosts to which the message can be routed. The use of task numbers for routing instead of host names or IP addresses achieves the decoupling between tasks and hosts.

Thus, communication of data between a pair of hosts proceeds as follows: The `Service Manager` on the receiving host issues a subscription for the data. When the source host has finished executing the source task, the `Service Manager` on that host creates a data message which it then passes to the `Data Routing Policy`. At this stage, our publish-subscribe-like protocol takes over and gossips it using one of the schemes described above. When a subscription and its corresponding data "meet" on a host, a match is generated and the data forwarded to the subscriber using AODV [22]. When the data is received on the receiving host, it is passed to the `Service Manager` who then runs the synchronization logic and invokes the next task.

### 3.4    Exploiting Mobility

Mobile systems work in a physical environment and it is desirable that these systems adapt their behavior to their environment. For WfMSs, this can be achieved by the use of *selection conditions*. Each edge to a task may have one or more selection conditions with one or more associated sub-conditions. If an edge has at least one selection condition for which all its sub-conditions evaluate as true, then the edge is marked *active*, otherwise the edge is marked as *inactive*. The sub-conditions that make up the selection condition are of the form `paramname, comparator, value` where `paramname` can be the name of an edge, a parameter in the local knowledge base, or the name of a sensor. For example `sensor:velocity, >, 10m/s` tests if the velocity of the host is greater than 10m/s.

This type of support can be built through extensions to existing languages, or a new language like the XML-based CiAN Workflow Specification which we are developing (see `mobilab.cse.wustl.edu/Projects/CiAN` for more information). Due to space constraints, it is not possible to describe all the tags in the CiAN specification. A detailed explanation of all the specification features and examples is available online at `http://mobilab.cse.wustl.edu/Projects/CiAN`.

# 4    Evaluation

We implemented a prototype of the CiAN WfMS in Java. The calls to external services are SOAP calls. To translate between the textual representation of the input values and SOAP requests, we use kSOAP [17], a third party library. The task of invoking the service and obtaining the return value is handled by Sliver [10], a middleware developed in our lab. Sliver currently supports the invocation of Java services only. However, since the request and response are in the form of a SOAP message, CiAN can invoke services in another language by simply adding a third party SOAP front end that is capable of invoking services written in another language. In other words, CiAN can invoke any service that can be invoked via SOAP calls if an appropriate front end is provided. Hosts participating in the workflow can register their own front end with CiAN, resulting in a situation where one host runs Java services while another runs C++ services while a third might run both. Thus, CiAN is not restricted to services written in any programming language. With the addition of language specific parsers, CiAN can also support any workflow specification language.

In addition to our implementation, we measured the performance of our publish-subscribe-like protocol to exchange data among hosts across a MANET. This is the most crucial piece of the CiAN WfMS and its primary potential bottleneck. Invocations of services to perform tasks do not take much time or resources as they are local service calls. Rather, transmitting results and receiving inputs takes significantly more time due to the communication delays. We refer to the time when tasks are being invoked and performed as *relevant time* and the time spent getting the results of one task to another as *overhead time*. Note that the system may be idle during relevant time periods (especially if the task involves a human user doing some physical chore), but it is not considered wasted time as a task is actually being performed. In our experiments, we focused on the overhead of our system since relevant time cannot be reduced due to the task duration limits set in the workflow specification.

We simulated the performance of the communication module (which influences the overhead values) using the NS2 network simulator. The transmission range was set to 25m using the 2-ray ground propagation model and the 802.11b MAC layer was used. Though the range of 802.11b can be higher than 25m, higher ranges require more power, which is not desirable on power constrained mobile devices. Host movement was modeled using the random waypoint mobility model with hosts moving at a uniform speed of 1.7 m/s, which is close to human walking speed.

With mobile hosts, it is not appropriate to compare performance as a function of the number of hosts solely as additional factors are involved such as the speed of the hosts and the total area that a group of hosts are responsible for. Hence, we use a concept called *upper bound coverage* to determine the fraction of the total area that is within communication range of at least one host in a single second. The formula for coverage is $(h/a)(\pi.r^2 + 2.s.r)$ where $h$ is the number of hosts, $a$ the total area, $r$ the communication radius of hosts, and $s$ the speed of the hosts. The second term gives the instantaneous area that falls within the communication radius of a single host plus the differential area covered in the second under consideration. This is multiplied by the number of hosts to give the upper bound covered by all hosts and then divided by the area to give a fraction in the range $0 \leq$ coverage $\leq 1$ with 1 indicating full coverage and 0 indicating no coverage. The coverage upper bound is reached only if every point in the area is covered exclusively by one host. In practice, the coverage is lower than the upper bound due to certain points falling within the range of more than one host. Holding area a constant, increasing the number of hosts, speed or the communication radius influences coverage positively while increasing area holding the other quantities constant influences the coverage negatively. Intuitively, more coverage means that it is more likely for a host to be at a particular location whereas less coverage indicates that a host is less likely to be at a specific location. We used this environment to simulate the execution of randomly generated workflows, the results of which appear below. Each data point is an average of 30 runs.

**Expt. 1 - Completing Workflows.**In this experiment, we examined the influence of our protocols on workflow completion. As a baseline, we used a protocol that delivers data and subscriptions directly without using intermediate hosts, i.e., in a peer to peer manner during opportunistic encounters. We measured (1) the number of tasks completed and (2) the number of tasks that failed due to a communication error when using the baseline protocol as well as each of our three schemes. The remaining tasks failed due to a dependency on the tasks that failed due to communication errors. The results are shown in Figure 5. Each of our schemes outperformed the baseline with Scheme 3 showing the best performance. All schemes showed close to 100% completions when the coverage was greater than 0.25. This illustrates that workflows are more likely to complete when one of our schemes is used. In the case of the workflows that failed to complete using our scheme, the reason was almost always due to aberrant mobility patterns where a host isolated itself from the rest of the network. It should be noted that we set an upper bound of 25000 seconds for each trial. This upper bound is 200% of the worst case time in which a workflow was actually completed.

**Expt. 2 - Influence of Coverage on Overhead.** Figure 6 shows the relation between coverage and overhead. Each data point is an average of executing 50 workflows. As can be seen, an increased coverage of the area in which the workflow is executing leads to lower overhead, primarily due to the availability of more routing options. An interesting observation is that there was a lot of variance in the data points for lower values of coverage. This can be explained as follows: the coverage captures the area that a host "touches" over the interval of a second averaged over all hosts participating in the workflow. When low coverage is prevalent, hosts may cover a the "correct" subset of the total area in which a large fraction of the workflow tasks must take place. This can result in low overhead. However, if the hosts cover a different subset of the area that does not include many tasks in the workflow, the overhead increases due to non-availability of hosts to perform tasks or route results. The notion of "correct coverage" is inherently tied to the

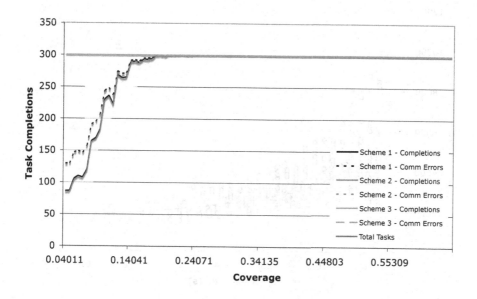

**Fig. 5.** Completions w.r.t. coverage

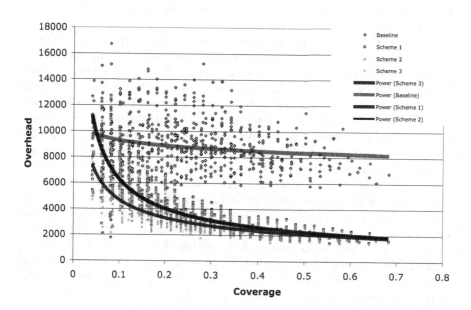

**Fig. 6.** Overhead w.r.t. of coverage

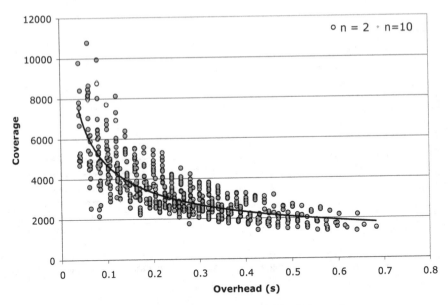

**Fig. 7.** Varying the value of 'n' in Scheme 3

workflow being executed (different workflows need different subsets of the area covered). Hence, coverage gives a sense of the performance but may be subject to high variances at the bottom of the scale.

**Expt. 3 - Influence of 'n' on Scheme 3.** Our final experiment involves a deeper study of Scheme 3 of our routing protocol. In Scheme 3, data and subscriptions are allowed to be routed outside their permitted range for a limited number of hops, i.e., the value of 'n'. In this experiment, we show the overhead of Scheme 3 with two values of 'n' - low and high. As can be seen in Figure 7, the value of 'n' did not significantly improve performance. The higher value of 'n' completed on average only a few seconds faster. We attribute this small difference to the fact that we chose environments where host density was not excessively sparse, and the fact that hosts encountered each other sufficiently often to pass on messages. We do expect to see a bigger difference for extremely low values of coverage.

Our results indicate that our routing protocol based on the task numbers improves upon the performance of naive approaches in terms of workflow completions as well as the overhead associated with communication. In addition, due to only a limited flooding of packets (within the range of task numbers), the packets in the network are significantly lower, leading to reduced bandwidth and power usage. These results are encouraging. However, we do intend to refine our approach to achieve more efficiency in future work.

## 5   Related Work

A WfMS is the piece of software that executes a compatible workflow specification. Today, innumerable WfMSs are available as both commercial and open source software such as FLOWer [3], AgentWork [20], Caramba [8], Groove [6], and I-Flow [15]. ActiveBPEL [9], JBoss [19], Oracle Workflow Engine [18] are just a few of the engines available today that run BPEL workflows while BizTalk [7] supports XLANG. Each of these engines is designed for orchestrated operation in wired settings.

In [5], message passing is used to distribute data in a wired setting while MoCA [14] uses proxies for distributed control. MoCA has some design features that support mobile environments while Exotica/FDMC [2] describes a scheme to handle disconnected mobile hosts. In AWA/PDA [26], the authors adopt a mobile agent based approach based on the GRASSHOPPER agent system. WORKPAD [11] is designed to meet the challenges of collaboration in a peer-to-peer MANET involving multiple human users. WORKPAD's shortcoming is that it requires at least one member of a MANET to be connected with a central entity that coordinates the mobile devices. Our work is targeted to an environment similar to that of WORKPAD. However, our approach is different in that we use choreography rather than a central coordinator.

With a choreography-based system, a leading concern is the process by which a workflow is distributed across various participants and then executed. In [21], the authors describe the process by which a monolithic workflow specification can be fragmented and eventually distributed across multiple hosts while in [5], the authors parse a BPEL specification, discard all the structural constructs and use the *link* construct to build a more graph-like specification. Several systems exist that achieve partial choreography, a survey of which appears in [16]. OSIRIS [24] is one such system where individual nodes maintain a hyperdatabase (HDB) to which is pushed service execution requests by a set of global process repositories. The choice of who to push the request to is handled by established load balancing techniques. ADEPT$_{Distribution}$ [4] describes a scheme for distributed execution of workflows such that the number of network messages is minimized. Additional efforts are ongoing to define protocols and standards for choreography such as in WS-CDL [1].

In summary, there are large bodies of work in orchestrated systems and languages supporting orchestrated systems in wired settings or environments with limited mobility. Our work advanced the state of the art by bringing workflows to the most dynamic type of mobile networks - MANETs - via the design of a lightweight, decentralized, and choreographed WfMS.

## 6   Conclusion

WfMSs that provide orchestrated workflow management across stable wired networks are a proven technology today. However, when a WfMS is developed with a mobile environment in mind, the centralized nature of orchestrated systems must give way to distributed and choreographed systems. In this paper, we described CiAN, a WfMS designed for MANETs that uses choreography of services to complete workflow tasks. CiAN uses a publish-subscribe-like protocol that takes results from a task and delivers them to the host responsible for executing the immediately succeeding tasks without going through a central coordinating entity. This protocol was developed with MANETs in mind where routes between hosts are transient and can break in an unpredictable manner. In our evaluations, we found that the calls to the services that occur locally on individual hosts took significantly less time than the process of communicating data and results between hosts. We evaluated three variants of our communication protocol all of which showed 100% completion when coverage upper bound was greater than a quarter of the total area and with reasonable amounts of overhead relative to the total specified duration of the workflow. We plan to build on this work and add new features like workflow cycles and error management in future work.

# References

1. WS-CDL v1.0 (November 2005), http://www.w3.org/TR/ws-cdl-10/
2. Alonso, G., Gunthor, R., Kamath, M., Agrawal, D., El Abbadi, A., Mohan, C.: Exotica/FDMC: A Workflow Management System for Mobile and Disconnected Clients. Parallel and Distributed Databases 4(3) (1996)
3. Athena, P.: Flower User Manual (2001)
4. Bauer, T., Dadam, P.: A Distributed Execution Environment for Large-Scale Workflow Management Systems with Subnets and Server Migration. In: Proc. of CoopIS, pp. 99–108 (1997)
5. Chafle, G., Chandra, S., Mann, V., Nanda, M.G.: Decentralized Orchestration of Composite Web Services. In: Proc. of the 13th Intl. WWW Conference, pp. 134–143 (2004)
6. Microsoft Corp. Groove Virtual Office, http://www.groove.net/home/index.cfm
7. Microsoft Corp. The BizTalk Server, http://www.microsoft.com/biztalk/
8. Dustdar, S.: Caramba - A Process-Aware Collaboration System Supporting Ad hoc and Collaborative Processes in Virtual Teams. Distributed and Parallel Databases 15, 45–66 (2004)
9. Active Endpoints. ActiveBPEL engine,
   http://www.active-endpoints.com/active-bpel-engine-overview.htm
10. Hackmann, G., et al.: Sliver: A BPEL Workflow Process Execution Engine for Mobile Devices. In: Dan, A., Lamersdorf, W. (eds.) ICSOC 2006. LNCS, vol. 4294, pp. 503–508. Springer, Heidelberg (2006)
11. Mecella, M., et al.: WORKPAD: an Adaptive Peer-to-Peer Software Infrastructure for Supporting Collaborative Work of Human Operators in Emergency/Disaster Scenarios. In: Proc. of CTS (May 2006)
12. Sen., R., et al.: Knowledge Driven Interactions with Services Across Ad Hoc Networks. In: Proc. of ICSOC, pp. 222–231 (2004)
13. Sen, R., et al.: Coordinating Workflow Allocation & Execution in Mobile Environments. In: Murphy, A.L., Vitek, J. (eds.) COORDINATION 2007. LNCS, vol. 4467, pp. 249–267. Springer, Heidelberg (2007)
14. Sacramento, V., et al.: An Architecture supporting the development of Collaborative Applications for Mobile Users. In: Proc. of WETICE 2004, pp. 109–114 (2004)
15. Fujitsu. i-Flow Developers Guide (1999)
16. Hahn, C.: A Comprehensive Investigation of Distribution in the Context of Workflow Management. In: Proceedings of ICPADS, pp. 187–192 (2001)

17. Haustein, J., Siegel, J.: ksoap (2006), http://www.ksoap.org
18. Oracle Inc. Oracle Workflow, http://www.oracle.com/technology/products/integration/workflow/workflow_fov.html
19. JBoss Labs. JBoss Application Server, http://www.jboss.com/docs/index
20. Muller, R., Greiner, U., Rahm, E.: AgentWork: A Workflow System Supporting Rule-based Workflow Adaptation. Data and Knowledge Engineering (2004)
21. Muth, P., Wodtke, D., Weissenfels, J., Dittrich, A.K., Weikum, G.: From Centralized Workflow Specification to Distributed Workflow Execution. Journal of Intelligent Information Systems 19(2), 159–184 (1998)
22. Perkins, C.E., Royer, E.M.: Ad hoc On-Demand Distance Vector Routing. In: Proc. of WMCSA, pp. 90–100 (1999)
23. Peterson, J.L.: Petri Net Theory and the Modeling of Systems. Prentice-Hall, Englewood Cliffs (1981)
24. Schuler, C., Weber, R., Schuldt, H., Schek, H.-J.: Scalable Peer-to-Peer Process Management The OSIRIS Approach. In: Proc. of ICWS, pp. 26–34 (2004)
25. Sen, R., Roman, G.-C., Gill, C.: Distributed Allocation of Workflow Tasks in MANETs. Technical report, Washington University in St. Louis (2007)
26. Stormer, H., Knorr, K.: PDA- and Agent-based Execution of Workflow Tasks. In: Proceedings of Informatik 2001, pp. 968–973 (2001)
27. van der Aalst, W.M.P.: Workflow Patterns. Distributed and Parallel Databases 14, 5–51 (2003)

# A Process Calculus for Mobile Ad Hoc Networks

Anu Singh, C.R. Ramakrishnan, and Scott A. Smolka

Department of Computer Science, Stony Brook University,
Stony Brook, NY 11794-4400, USA
{anusingh,cram,sas}@cs.sunysb.edu

**Abstract.** We present the $\omega$-calculus, a process calculus for formally modeling and reasoning about *Mobile Ad Hoc Wireless Networks* (MANETs) and their protocols. The $\omega$-calculus naturally captures essential characteristics of MANETs, including the ability of a MANET node to broadcast a message to any other node within its physical transmission range (and no others), and to move in and out of the transmission range of other nodes in the network. A key feature of the $\omega$-calculus is the separation of a node's communication and computational behavior, described by an $\omega$-process, from the description of its physical transmission range, referred to as an $\omega$-process *interface*.

Our main technical results are as follows. We give a formal operational semantics of the $\omega$-calculus in terms of labeled transition systems and show that the state reachability problem is decidable for finite-control $\omega$-processes. We also prove that the $\omega$-calculus is a conservative extension of the $\pi$-calculus, and that late bisimulation (appropriately lifted from the $\pi$-calculus to the $\omega$-calculus) is a congruence. Congruence results are also established for a weak version of late bisimulation, which abstracts away from two types of internal actions: $\tau$-actions, as in the $\pi$-calculus, and $\mu$-actions, signaling node movement. Finally, we illustrate the practical utility of the calculus by developing and analyzing a formal model of a leader-election protocol for MANETs.

## 1 Introduction

A Mobile Ad Hoc Network (MANET) is a network of autonomous mobile nodes connected by wireless links. Each node $N$ has a physical transmission range within which it can directly transmit data to other nodes. Any node that falls within $N$'s transmission range is considered a *neighbor* of $N$. Nodes can move freely in a MANET, leading to rapid change in the network's communication topology.

Two aspects of MANETs make them especially difficult to model using existing formal specification languages such as process algebras. First, MANETs use wireless links for local broadcast communication: a MANET node can transmit a message simultaneously to all nodes within its transmission range, but the message cannot be received by any node outside that range. Secondly, the neighborhood of nodes that lie within the transmission range of a node can change unpredictably due to node movement, thereby altering the set of nodes that can receive a transmitted message.

D. Lea and G. Zavattaro (Eds.): COORDINATION 2008, LNCS 5052, pp. 296–314, 2008.
© Springer-Verlag Berlin Heidelberg 2008

Ideally, the specification of a MANET node's control behavior should be independent of its neighborhood information. Since, however, the eventual recipients of a local broadcast message depend on this information, a model of a MANET-based protocol given in a traditional process calculus must intermix the computation of neighborhood information with the protocol's control behavior. This tends to render such models unnatural and unnecessarily complex.

In this paper, we present the $\omega$-calculus, a conservative extension of the $\pi$-calculus that has been designed expressly to address the MANET modeling problems outlined above. A key feature of the $\omega$-calculus is the separation of a node's communication and computational behavior, described by an $\omega$-process, from the description of its physical transmission range, referred to as an $\omega$-process *interface*. This separation allows one to model the control behavior of a MANET protocol, using $\omega$-processes, independently from the protocol's underlying communication topology, using process interfaces. (A similar separation of concerns has been achieved in several recently introduced process calculi for wireless and mobile networks [12,9,8,5], but not, as we argue in Section 6, as simply and naturally as in the $\omega$-calculus.)

As discussed further in Section 2, $\omega$-process interfaces are comprised of *groups*, which operationally function as local broadcast ports. Mobility is captured in the $\omega$-calculus via the dynamic creation of new groups and dynamically changing process interfaces. The group-based abstraction for local broadcast in a wireless network is a natural one; it appears also in [6], where it is shown how to model MANETs in the UPPAAL model checker for timed automata.

**Main Contributions.**    The rest of the paper is organized around our main technical results, which include the following:

- Section 2 provides an informal introduction to the basic features of the $\omega$-calculus.
- Section 3 presents the formal operational semantics of the $\omega$-calculus in terms of labeled transition systems and structural-congruence rules. The calculus is presented in three stages: $\omega_0$, the core version of the calculus, focuses on local broadcast and mobility; $\omega_1$ extends $\omega_0$ with unicast communication and scope extrusion; $\omega_2$ extends $\omega_1$ by allowing multi-threaded behavior at the process level. Unless otherwise noted, the expression "the $\omega$-calculus" refers to $\omega_2$, the most general version of the calculus. We in fact show in Section 4 that $\omega_2$ is a conservative extension of the $\pi$-calculus.
- Section 4 defines bisimulation for the $\omega$-calculus and proves that it is a congruence. We obtain similar results for a weak version of bisimulation, which treats as unobservable two types of internal actions: $\tau$-actions, as in the $\pi$-calculus, and $\mu$-actions, signaling node movement. Full proofs of these results appear in [16].
- Section 5 illustrates the practical utility of the calculus by developing and analyzing a formal $\omega$-calculus model of a leader-election algorithm for MANETs [17].

Section 6 considers related work and Section 7 offers our concluding remarks.

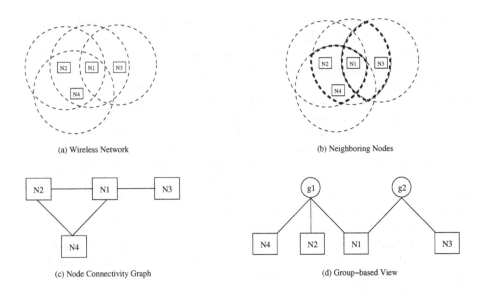

(a) Wireless Network                    (b) Neighboring Nodes

(c) Node Connectivity Graph             (d) Group–based View

**Fig. 1.** Multiple views of a MANET network

## 2   The $\omega$-Calculus: An Informal Introduction

As an illustrative example of the $\omega$-calculus, consider the MANET of Fig. 1(a) comprising the four nodes $N_1$, $N_2$, $N_3$, $N_4$. The dotted circle centered around a node indicates the node's transmission range, and all nodes are assumed to have the same transmission range. Thus, $N_1$ is within the transmission range of $N_2$, $N_3$, and $N_4$ and vice versa, and $N_2$ and $N_4$ are in each other's transmission range. Fig. 1(b) highlights the *maximal sets of neighboring nodes* in the network, one covering $N_1$, $N_2$, and $N_4$, and the other covering $N_1$ and $N_3$. A maximal set of neighboring nodes corresponds to a *maximal clique* in the network's node connectivity graph (Fig. 1(c)), and, equivalently, to an $\omega$-calculus *group* (local broadcast port), as illustrated in Fig. 1(d). The set of groups to which a node is connected is specified by the *interface* of the underlying process; i.e. the process executing at the node. Thus, the $\omega$-calculus expression for the network is the parallel composition $N_1|N_2|N_3|N_4$, where $N_1 = P_1 : \{g_1, g_2\}$, $N_2 = P_2 : \{g_1\}$, $N_3 = P_3 : \{g_2\}$, $N_4 = P_4 : \{g_1\}$, for process expressions $P_1$, $P_2$, $P_3$ and $P_4$.

Note that process interfaces may contain groups that do not correspond to maximal cliques. Such groups are redundant in the sense that do not represent any additional connectivity information. Group $g_2$ of Fig. 2 is an example of a redundant group. A *canonical* form for $\omega$-calculus expressions can be defined in which redundant groups are elided.

Fig. 1 provides multiple views of the topology of the MANET at a particular moment in time. As discussed below, the network topology may change over time due to node movement, a feature of MANETs captured operationally in the $\omega$-calculus via dynamic updates of process interfaces.

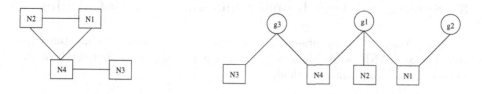

**Fig. 2.** (a) Node Connectivity Graph after $N_3$'s movement  and  (b) View in $\omega$-calculus

**Local Broadcast in the $\omega$-calculus.**  The $\omega$-calculus action to locally broadcast a value $x$ is $\overline{b}x$, while $\mathbf{r}(y)$ is the action for receiving a value $y$. Thus, when a process transmits a message, only the message $x$ to be sent is included in the specification. The set of possible recipients depends on the process's current interface: only those processes that share a common group with the sender can receive the message and this information is not part of the syntax of local broadcast actions. In the example of Fig. 1, if $P_2$ can broadcast a message and $P_1$, $P_3$, $P_4$ are willing to receive it, then the expression

$$N = \mathbf{r}(x).P_1':\{g_1, g_2\} \mid \overline{b}u.P_2':\{g_1\} \mid \mathbf{r}(y).P_3':\{g_2\} \mid \mathbf{r}(z).P_4':\{g_1\}$$

may evolve to

$$N = P_1'\{u/x\}:\{g_1, g_2\} \mid P_2':\{g_1\} \mid \mathbf{r}(y).P_3':\{g_2\} \mid P_4'\{u/z\}:\{g_1\}$$

Observe that $P_3$ does not receive the message since $N_3$ is not in $N_2$'s neighborhood.

**Node Mobility in the $\omega$-calculus.**    Node mobility is captured through the dynamic creation of new groups and dynamically changing process interfaces. Fig. 2 shows the topology of the network of Fig. 1 after $N_3$ moves away from $N_1$'s transmission range and into $N_4$'s transmission range. $N_3$'s movement means that the $\omega$-calculus expression

$$(\nu g_1)(\nu g_2)(P_1:\{g_1, g_2\} \mid P_2:\{g_1\} \mid P_3:\{g_2\} \mid P_4:\{g_1\})$$

evolves to

$$(\nu g_1)(\nu g_2)(P_1:\{g_1, g_2\} \mid P_2:\{g_1\} \mid (\nu g_3)(P_3:\{g_3\} \mid P_4:\{g_1, g_3\}))$$

The new group $g_3$ in the above expression represents the new maximal set of neighboring nodes $N_3$ and $N_4$ that arises post-movement. We use the familiar $\nu g$ notation for group-name scoping.

**Nodes vs. Processes.**  In an $\omega$-calculus specification, nodes typically represent physical devices; as such, the calculus does not provide a primitive for node creation. Process creation, however, is supported, as processes model programs and other executables that execute within the confines of a device.

# 3   Syntax and Transitional Semantics of the $\omega$-Calculus

We begin this section by presenting the syntax and semantics of $\omega_0$, our core calculus for MANETs. We then introduce the extensions to $\omega_0$ that result in the more expressive $\omega_1$- and $\omega_2$-calculi.

## 3.1   Syntax of $\omega_0$

A system description in the $\omega_0$-calculus comprises a set of *nodes*, each of which runs a sequential *process* annotated by its *interface*. We use **N** and **P** to denote the sets of all nodes and all processes, respectively, with $M, N$ ranging over nodes and $P, Q$ ranging over processes. We also use names drawn from two disjoint sets: **Pn** and **Gn**. The names in **Pn**, called *pnames* for *process names*, are used for data values. The names in **Gn**, called *gnames* for *group names*, are used for process interfaces. We use $x, y, z$ to range over **Pn** and $g$ (possibly subscripted) to range over **Gn**. The $\omega_0$-calculus has a two-level syntax describing nodes and processes, respectively.

The syntax of $\omega_0$-calculus processes is defined by the following grammar:

$$P ::= nil \mid Act.P \mid P + P \mid [x = y]P \mid A(\vec{x})$$
$$Act ::= \overline{b}x \mid r(x) \mid \tau$$

Action $\overline{b}x$ represents the local broadcast of a value $x$, while the reception of a locally broadcasted value is denoted by $r(x)$. Internal (silent) actions are denoted by $\tau$. Process *nil* is the deadlocked process; $Act.P$ is the process that can perform action $Act$ and then behave as $P$; and $+$ is the operator for nondeterministic choice. Process $[x = y]P$ (where $x$ and $y$ are pnames) behaves as $P$ if names $x$ and $y$ match, and as *nil* otherwise. $A(\vec{x})$ denotes *process invocation*, where $A$ is a process name (having a corresponding definition) and $\vec{x}$ is a comma-separated list of actual parameters (pnames) of the invocation. A process definition is of the form $A(\vec{x}) \overset{\text{def}}{=} P$, and associates a process name $A$ and a list of formal parameters $\vec{x}$ (i.e. distinct pnames) with process expression $P$. Process definitions may be recursive.

The following grammar defines the syntax of $\omega_0$-calculus node expressions:

$$M ::= \mathbf{0} \mid P{:}G \mid (\nu g)M \mid M|M$$

$\mathbf{0}$ is the inactive node, while $P{:}G$ is a node with process $P$ having interface (set of gnames) $G$. The operator $(\nu g)$ is used to restrict the scopes of gnames. $M|N$ represents the parallel composition of node expressions $M$ and $N$. Node expressions of the form $P{:}G$ are called *basic node expressions*, while those containing the restriction or parallel operator are called *structured node expressions*. Note that gnames occur only at the node level, capturing the intuition that, in an ad hoc network, the behavioral specification of a (basic) node (represented by its process) is independent of its underlying interface.

**Table 1.** Structural congruence relation

| | |
|---|---|
| N1. $M \equiv M \mid 0$ | N8. $P\!:\!G \equiv Q\!:\!G$, if $P \equiv Q$ |
| N2. $M_1 \mid M_2 \equiv M_2 \mid M_1$ | N9. $P\!:\!G \equiv (\nu g)(P\!:\!G \cup \{g\})$, if $g \notin G$ |
| N3. $(M_1 \mid M_2) \mid M_3 \equiv M_1 \mid (M_2 \mid M_3)$ | |
| N4. $(\nu g)M \equiv M$, if $g \notin fgn(M)$ | |
| N5. $(\nu g)M \mid N \equiv (\nu g)(M \mid N)$, if $g \notin fgn(N)$ | P1. $P + Q \equiv Q + P$ |
| N6. $(\nu g_1)(\nu g_2)M \equiv (\nu g_2)(\nu g_1)M$ | P2. $(P + Q) + R \equiv P + (Q + R)$ |
| N7. $M \equiv N$, if $M \equiv_\alpha N$ | P3. $P \equiv Q$, if $P \equiv_\alpha Q$ |

*Free and Bound Names.* Pname $x$ is free in $\overline{b}x.P$ and bound in $\mathbf{r}(x).P$. Gname $g$ is bound in $(\nu g)M$, and all gnames in $G$ are free in $P\!:\!G$. In a process definition of the form $A(\overrightarrow{x}) \stackrel{\text{def}}{=} P$, $\overrightarrow{x}$ are the only names that may occur free in $P$. The set of all names, free names and bound names in a process expression $P$ are denoted by $n(P)$, $fn(P)$ and $bn(P)$, respectively. Similarly, the set of all pnames and gnames in a node expression $M$ are denoted by $pn(M)$ and $gn(M)$, and those that occur free are denoted by $fpn(M)$ and $fgn(M)$, respectively. The set of all free names in a node expression $M$ is given by $fn(M) = fpn(M) \cup fgn(M)$. An expression without free names is called *closed*. An expression that is not *closed* is said to be *open*. The theory developed in the following sections is applicable to both *open* and *closed* systems (expressions).

## 3.2   Transitional Semantics of $\omega_0$

The transitional semantics of the $\omega_0$-calculus is defined in terms of a structural congruence relation $\equiv$ (Table 1) and a labeled transition relation $\stackrel{\alpha}{\longrightarrow} \subseteq \mathbf{N} \times \mathbf{N}$, where $\alpha$ is the *transition label*. As such, only node expressions have transitions, and these are of the form $M \stackrel{\alpha}{\longrightarrow} M'$. There are several varieties of transition labels. When a node of the form $P\!:\!G$ broadcasts a value $x$, it generates a transition labeled by $\overline{G}x$. When $P\!:\!G$ receives a broadcast value $x$, the corresponding transition label is $G(x)$. Actions $\mu$ and $\tau$ also serve as transition labels, with $\mu$, as explained below, indicating node movement, and $\tau$ representing internal (silent) actions.

For transition label $\alpha$, the sets of bound names and gnames of $\alpha$ are denoted $bn(\alpha)$ and $gn(\alpha)$, respectively, and defined as follows:
$bn(\overline{G}x) = \emptyset$, $bn(G(x)) = \{x\}$, $bn(\mu) = \emptyset$, $bn(\tau) = \emptyset$.
$gn(\overline{G}x) = G$, $gn(G(x)) = G$, $gn(\mu) = \emptyset$, $gn(\tau) = \emptyset$.

The transitional semantics of the $\omega_0$-calculus is given by the inference rules of Tables 2 and 3, with the former supplying the inference rules for basic node expressions and the latter for structured node expressions. Rules CHOICE, MATCH, and DEF of Table 2 are standard. Rules MCAST and RECV of Table 2, together with COM of Table 3, define a notion of *local broadcast* communication. RECV states that a basic node with process interface $G$ can receive a local broadcast on any gname in $G$. This, together with COM, means that a local-broadcast sender can synchronize with any local-broadcast receiver with whom it shares a gname (i.e. the receiver is in the transmission range of the sender).

**Table 2.** Transition rules for basic node expressions

| Rule Name | Rule | Side Condition |
|---|---|---|
| MCAST | $$\dfrac{}{(\overline{\mathbf{b}}x.P){:}G \xrightarrow{\overline{G}x} P{:}G}$$ | |
| RECV | $$\dfrac{}{(\mathbf{r}(x).P){:}G \xrightarrow{G(x)} P{:}G}$$ | |
| CHOICE | $$\dfrac{P{:}G \xrightarrow{\alpha} P'{:}G}{(P+Q){:}G \xrightarrow{\alpha} P'{:}G}$$ | |
| MATCH | $$\dfrac{P{:}G \xrightarrow{\alpha} P'{:}G}{([x{=}x]P){:}G \xrightarrow{\alpha} P'{:}G}$$ | |
| DEF | $$\dfrac{P\{\vec{y}/\vec{x}\}{:}G \xrightarrow{\alpha} P'{:}G}{A(\vec{y}){:}G \xrightarrow{\alpha} P'{:}G}$$ | $A(\vec{x}) \stackrel{def}{=} P$ |

**Table 3.** Transition rules for structured node expressions

| Rule Name | Rule | Side Condition |
|---|---|---|
| STRUCT | $$\dfrac{N \equiv M \quad M \xrightarrow{\alpha} M' \quad M' \equiv N'}{N \xrightarrow{\alpha} N'}$$ | |
| MOBILITY $(I)$ | $$\dfrac{}{M \mid P{:}G \xrightarrow{\mu} M \mid P{:}G'}$$ | $G' \neq G,$ $G' \subseteq G \cup fgn(M),$ $\chi(M \mid P{:}G) \models I \implies$ $\chi(M \mid P{:}G') \models I$ |
| PAR | $$\dfrac{M \xrightarrow{\alpha} M'}{M \mid N \xrightarrow{\alpha} M' \mid N}$$ | $bn(\alpha) \cap fn(N) = \emptyset$ |
| COM | $$\dfrac{M \xrightarrow{\overline{G}x} M' \quad N \xrightarrow{G'(y)} N'}{M \mid N \xrightarrow{\overline{G}x} M' \mid N'\{x/y\}}$$ | $G \cap G' \neq \emptyset$ |
| GNAME-RES1 | $$\dfrac{M \xrightarrow{\alpha} M'}{(\nu\, g)M \xrightarrow{\alpha \backslash \{g\}} (\nu\, g)M'}$$ | |
| GNAME-RES2 | $$\dfrac{M \xrightarrow{\overline{G}x} M'}{(\nu\, g)M \xrightarrow{\tau} (\nu\, g)M'}$$ | $G = \{g\}$ |

Local-broadcast synchronization results in a local-broadcast transition label of the form $\overline{G}x$, thereby enabling other receivers to synchronize with the original send action. In contrast to the broadcast calculi of [4,12], a node that is capable of receiving a local broadcast is not forced to synchronize with the sender. The semantics of local broadcast in the $\omega$-calculus allows a receiver to ignore a local-broadcast event even if this node is in the transmission range of the broadcasting node. A semantics of this nature captures the lossy transmission inherent in MANETs. The semantics of local broadcast can easily be modified to force all potential receivers to receive a local broadcast.

GNAME-RES1 and GNAME-RES2 define the effect of closing the scope of a gname. GNAME-RES1 states that a restricted gname cannot occur in a transition label. In GNAME-RES1, let $G$ be the set of gnames in $\alpha$; i.e., $G = gn(\alpha)$. Then the transition label $\alpha \setminus \{g\}$ in the consequent of this rule denotes $\alpha$ with the occurrence of gnames in $\alpha$ replaced by $G \setminus \{g\}$, given that $G \setminus \{g\} \neq \emptyset$ and $\alpha \notin \{\tau, \mu\}$. Note that if $\alpha = \tau$ ($\alpha = \mu$), then $\alpha \setminus \{g\} = \tau$ ($\alpha \setminus \{g\} = \mu$). GNAME-RES2 states that when all gnames of a local-broadcast-send action are restricted, it becomes a $\tau$-action. MCAST, GNAME-RES1 and GNAME-RES2 together mean that a local-broadcast send is non-blocking; i.e., it can be performed on a set of restricted groups even when there are no corresponding receive actions. In contrast, other actions containing gnames, such as local-broadcast receive, are not covered by GNAME-RES2, and hence have blocking semantics: a system cannot perform actions involving restricted gnames unless there is a corresponding synchronizing action.

The notion of structural congruence (Table 1) considered in rule STRUCT is defined for processes (rules P1-P3) in the standard way—$P$ and $Q$ are structurally congruent if they are alpha-equivalent or congruent under the associativity and commutativity of the choice ('+') operator—and then lifted to nodes (rules N1-N9). Two basic node expressions are structurally congruent if they have identical process interfaces and run structurally congruent processes (rule N8). Rules N4-N6 are for restriction on gnames. Rule N9 allows basic nodes to create and acquire a new group name or drop a local group name. Structural congruence of nodes includes alpha-equivalence (rule N7) and the associativity and commutativity of the parallel ('|') operator (rules N2 and N3).

**Semantics of Mobility.** The semantics of node movement is defined by the MOBILITY rule, which states that the process interface of node $P : G$ can change from $G$ to $G'$ whenever the node is in parallel with another node $M$. In particular, the side condition $G' \subseteq G \cup fgn(M)$ stipulates that $P$ may drop gnames from its interface or acquire free gnames from $M$.

The MOBILITY rule reflects the fact that $P$'s interface may change when node $P{:}G$, or the nodes around it, are in motion. A change in $P$'s interface may further result in a corresponding change in the overall network topology. Note that the rule does not specify which nodes moved, only that the topology has been updated as the result of movement of one or more nodes.

Process interfaces provide an abstract specification of network topology in terms of node connectivity graphs. Formally, the *node connectivity graph* of a node expression $M$, denoted by $\chi(M)$, is an undirected graph $(V, E)$ such that $V$, the set of vertices, are the basic nodes of $M$ (i.e. subexpressions of $M$ of the form $P : G$) and $E$, the set of edges, is defined as follows. There is an edge between two vertices $P_1 : G_1$ and $P_2 : G_2$ of $\chi(M)$ only if $P_1$ and $P_2$'s interfaces overlap; i.e. $G_1 \cap G_2 \neq \emptyset$ (assuming bound names of $M$ are unique and distinct from its free names). The node connectivity graph for the $\omega_0$ node expression of Fig. 1(d) is given in Fig. 1(c).

The third side condition to the MOBILITY rule, expressed in terms of node connectivity graphs, allows one to impose different models of node movement on the calculus. Specifically, the side condition decrees that, whenever $M \xrightarrow{\mu} M'$ is derived using the MOBILITY rule, the resulting transition must preserve a *mobility invariant* expressed as a property over the node connectivity graph. A mobility invariant is a decidable property over undirected graphs. For example, $k$-connectedness, for a given $k$, is a candidate mobility invariant, as is true, indicating no constraints on node movement. We write $G \models I$ to indicate that undirected graph $G$ possesses property $I$. We thus have that the MOBILITY rule in particular, and the calculus's semantics in general, are parameterized by the mobility invariant, thus taking into account the constraints on node movement.

### 3.3   The $\omega_1$- and $\omega_2$-Calculi

The $\omega_1$- and $\omega_2$-calculi are defined in a modular fashion by adding new syntactic constructs, and associated inference rules for their semantics, to the $\omega_0$-calculus.

*Extending $\omega_0$ to $\omega_1$.* Syntactically, we obtain $\omega_1$ from $\omega_0$ as follows:

- We add restriction operators for *pnames* for both process-level and node-level expressions. We use the standard notation of $(\nu x)P$ for a pname $x$ restricted to a process expression $P$, and $(\nu x)N$ for a pname $x$ restricted to a node expression $N$. As usual, $x$ is bound in $(\nu x)P$ and $(\nu x)N$.
- We introduce unicast communication as a prefix operator for process expressions. Although unicast in principle can be implemented on top of broadcast, we prefer to give it first-class status, as it is a frequent action in MANET protocols. Doing so also facilitates concise modeling and deterministic reasoning (only the intended recipient can receive a unicast message). We use the standard notation of $\overline{x}y$ to denote the sending of name $y$ along $x$, and $x(y)$ to denote the reception of a name along $x$ that will bind to $y$. As usual, $x$ and $y$ are free in the expression $\overline{x}y.P$, and $x$ is free and $y$ is bound in $x(y).P$.

Semantically, the introduction of scoped pnames needs new inference rules to handle scope extrusion. We add OPEN and CLOSE rules (as in the $\pi$-calculus [11]) and, in addition to the broadcast communication rule (COM) of $\omega_0$, a rule for communication of bound names. We also add RES rules at the process and node levels to disallow communication over a restricted name. These additional rules follow closely the standard rules for handling scopes and scope extrusion in the

**Table 4.** Transition rules for unicast communication in $\omega_1$-calculus

| Rule Name | Rule | Side Condition |
|---|---|---|
| UNI-SEND | $$(\overline{z}x.P){:}G \xrightarrow{\overline{z{:}G}x} P{:}G$$ | |
| UNI-RECV | $$(z(x).P){:}G \xrightarrow{z{:}G(x)} P{:}G$$ | |
| UNI-COM | $$\dfrac{M \xrightarrow{\overline{z{:}G}x} M' \quad N \xrightarrow{z{:}G'(y)} N'}{M\,|\,N \xrightarrow{\tau} M'\,|\,N'\{x/y\}}$$ | $G \cap G' \neq \emptyset$ |

$\pi$-calculus; details are omitted. New structural congruence rules are added to take the restriction of pnames into account. For instance, restriction of pnames and gnames commute (i.e. $(\nu x)(\nu g)N \equiv (\nu g)(\nu x)N$), and the restriction operator can be pushed into or pulled out of node and process expressions as long as free names are not captured. At first glance, it may appear that the structural congruence rules for scope extension of pnames are redundant in the presence of the scope-extrusion rules (OPEN/CLOSE). However, the OPEN/CLOSE rules are essential for reasoning about open systems, and the scope extension rules are essential for defining normal forms; see [16].

The addition of unicast communication raises certain interesting issues with respect to mobility. Recall that *groups* encapsulate the locality of a process. When two processes share a private name, they can use that name as a channel of communication. However, after establishing that link, if the processes move away from each other, they may no longer be able to use that name as a channel. In summary, unicast channels should also respect the locality of communication. We enforce this in the $\omega_1$-calculus by annotating unicast action labels with the interfaces of the participating processes, and allowing synchronization between actions only when their interfaces overlap (meaning that the processes are in each other's transmission range). Hence, the execution of a unicast send action of value $x$ on channel $z$ by a basic node with process interface $G$ is represented by action label $\overline{z{:}G}x$; the corresponding receive action is labeled $z{:}G(x)$.

The semantic rules for unicast send (UNI-SEND), receive (UNI-RECV), and synchronization (UNI-COM) are given in Table 4. Scope extrusion via unicast communication is accomplished by naturally extending their $\pi$-calculus counterparts (OPEN/CLOSE) rules as follows. Bound-output actions (due to OPEN) are annotated with the interface of the participating process, and the CLOSE rule applies only when the interfaces overlap. These extensions are straightforward, and the details are omitted.

Note that the scope of a name may encompass different processes regardless of their interfaces, and hence two processes may share a secret even when they are outside each others transmission ranges. The restriction we impose is that shared names can be used as unicast channels only when the processes are within each others transmission ranges.

*Extending $\omega_1$ to $\omega_2$.* We obtain the $\omega_2$-calculus by adding the parallel compo-
sition ('|') operator at the process level, thereby allowing concurrent processes
within a node. This addition facilitates e.g. the modeling of communication between layers of a protocol stack running at a single node; it also renders the
$\pi$-calculus a subcalculus of the $\omega_2$-calculus. In $\omega_2$, the actions of two processes
within a node may be interleaved. Moreover, two processes within a node can synchronize using unicast (binary) communication. We add PAR, COM and CLOSE
rules corresponding to intra-node interleaving, synchronization and scope extrusion, respectively; these rules are straightforward extensions of the corresponding
rules in the $\pi$-calculus.

## 4   Bisimulation, Congruence Results and Other Properties of the $\omega$-Calculus

In this section, we prove some fundamental properties of the $\omega$-calculus, including
congruence results for strong bisimulation and a weak version of bisimulation
that treats $\tau$- and $\mu$-actions as unobservable.

*Embedding of the $\pi$-Calculus.* The $\omega$-calculus is a conservative extension of the
$\pi$-calculus [11]. That is, every process expression $P$ in the $\pi$-calculus can be
syntactically translated to an $\omega$-node expression $M$ such that the transition
system generated by $M$ directly corresponds to the one generated by $P$. This
property is formally stated by the following theorem, which is readily proved by
induction on the length of derivations.

**Theorem 1.** *Let $P$ be a process expression in the $\pi$-calculus. Then $P : \{g\}$ is
a node expression in the $\omega$-calculus, where $g$ is a fresh group name not in $P$.
Moreover, $P \xrightarrow{\alpha} P'$ is a transition derivable from the operational semantics
of the $\pi$-calculus if and only if $P : \{g\} \xrightarrow{\alpha'} P' : \{g\}$ is derivable from the
operational semantics of the $\omega$-calculus, and one of the following conditions hold:
(i) $\alpha = \alpha' = \tau$; (ii) $\alpha = x(y)$ and $\alpha' = x : \{g\}(y)$; (iii) $\alpha = \overline{x}y$ and $\alpha' = \overline{x : \{g\}}y$ ;
or (iv) $\alpha = (\nu y)\overline{x}y$ and $\alpha' = (\nu y)\overline{x : \{g\}}y$, for some names $x, y$.*

*Decidability of the Finite-Control Fragment.* In the *finite-control* fragment of the
$\pi$-calculus, recursive definitions are not allowed to contain the parallel operator
('|') nor unguarded occurrences of process identifiers. Reachability properties are
decidable for closed process expressions (i.e. those without free names) specified
in the finite-control fragment [3]. We can extend the notion of finite control to
the $\omega$-calculus, and show that reachability remains decidable for closed node
expressions. Formally, we say that an $\omega$-calculus expression $N$ is *reachable* from
$M$ (denoted by $M \longrightarrow^* N$) if there is a finite sequence of transitions $M \xrightarrow{\alpha_1} M_1 \xrightarrow{\alpha_2}
M_2 \cdots \xrightarrow{\alpha_n} N$. We then have the following result.

**Theorem 2.** *Let $M$ be a finite-control $\omega$-calculus expression such that $M$ is
closed w.r.t. names. Then, the set of node expressions reachable from $M$ modulo
the structural congruence relation, i.e., $\{N \mid M \longrightarrow^* N\}_\equiv$, is finite.*

Theorem 2 is of practical importance in verifying MANET system specifications. Its proof is based on the observation that, in the $\omega$-calculus, the physical notion of neighborhood is represented abstractly by group-based connectivity information. This ensures that only a finite number of equivalent configurations need be analyzed.

*Bisimulation for the $\omega$-calculus.* The definition of strong (late) bisimulation for the $\pi$-calculus [11] can be extended to the $\omega$-calculus.

**Definition 1.** *A relation $S \subseteq \mathbf{N} \times \mathbf{N}$ on nodes is a strong simulation if $M \, S \, N$ implies:*

- *$fgn(M) = fgn(N)$, and*
- *whenever $M \xrightarrow{\alpha} M'$ where $bn(\alpha)$ is fresh then:*
  - *if $\alpha \in \{G(x), z : G(x)\}$, there exists an $N'$ s.t. $N \xrightarrow{\alpha} N'$ and for each pname $y$, $M'\{y/x\} \, S \, N'\{y/x\}$,*
  - *if $\alpha \notin \{G(x), z : G(x)\}$, there exists an $N'$ s.t. $N \xrightarrow{\alpha} N'$ and $M' \, S \, N'$.*

$S$ *is a* strong bisimulation *if both $S$ and $S^{-1}$ are strong simulations. Nodes $M$ and $N$ are* strong bisimilar, *written $M \sim N$, if $M \, S \, N$, for some strong bisimulation $S$.*

**Proposition 3.** *(i) $\sim$ is an equivalence; and (ii) $\sim$ is the largest strong bisimulation.*

Strong bisimulation is a congruence for the $\omega$-calculus, as formally stated in Theorem 4.

**Theorem 4 (Congruence).** *$\sim$ is a congruence relation; i.e., for all nodes $M_1$, $M_2 \in \mathbf{N}$, the following hold:*
*(i) $M_1 \sim M_2$ implies $\forall x \in \mathbf{Pn} : (\nu x)M_1 \sim (\nu x)M_2$;*
*(ii) $M_1 \sim M_2$ implies $\forall g \in \mathbf{Gn} : (\nu g)M_1 \sim (\nu g)M_2$; and*
*(iii) $M_1 \sim M_2$ implies $\forall N \in \mathbf{N} : M_1|N \sim M_2|N$.*

We have also defined a notion of *weak bisimulation* for the $\omega$-calculus, in which $\tau$- and $\mu$-actions are treated as unobservable. Its definition is similar to that for strong bisimulation (Definition 1) and is given in [16]. There, we also establish that weak bisimulation, like its strong counterpart, is a congruence for the $\omega$-calculus.

## 5    Case Study: Modeling and Verifying a Leader Election Protocol for MANETs

**Syntactic Extensions to the $\omega$-calculus.**    The $\omega$-calculus provides the basic mechanisms needed to model MANETs. In order to make specifications more concise, we extend the calculus to a polyadic version (along the same lines as the polyadic pi-calculus [10]) and also add support for data types such as bounded

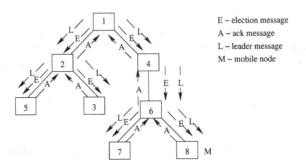

**Fig. 3.** Message flow in leader election protocol

integers and structured terms. The matching prefix is extended to include equality over these types. Terms composed of these types can be used as values in a unicast or local broadcast transmission, or as actual parameters for a process invocation. The modifications to the theory developed in the preceding sections (Sections 3-4) to account for these syntactic extensions to the calculus are straightforward.

**A Leader Election Protocol for MANETs.** The algorithm of [17] elects the node with the maximum id among a set of connected nodes as the leader of the connected component. A node that initiates the leader election sends an *election* message to its neighboring nodes. The recipients of the *election* message mark the node from which they received the message as their parent and send the *election* message to their neighbors, thereby building a spanning tree with the initiator as the root. After sending an *election* message, a node awaits acknowledgements from its children in the spanning tree. A child node $n$ sends its parent an acknowledgement *ack* with the maximum id in the spanning tree rooted at $n$. The maximum id in the spanning tree is propagated up the tree to the root. The root node then announces the leader to all the nodes in its spanning tree by sending a *leader* message. To keep track of the neighbors of a node, *probe* and *reply* messages are used periodically. When a node discovers that it is disconnected from its *leader*, it initiates an election process. The flow of *election*, *ack*, and *leader* messages is depicted in Fig. 3, where the node with id 1 is the initiator.

**Description of the Protocol in the $\omega$-calculus.** We model a network as the parallel composition of basic $\omega$-nodes, whose process interfaces reflect the initial topology of the network. Each node runs an instance of process *node*(*id, chan, init, elec, lid, pChan*) defined in Fig. 4. The meaning of this process's parameters is the following: *id* is the node identifier; *chan* is an input channel; *init* indicates whether the node initiates the election process; *elec* indicates whether the node is part of the election process; *lid* represents the node's knowledge of the leader id; and *pChan* is the parent's input channel. These parameters are represented by pnames and integers.

/* A node may receive an *election* or a *leader* message. */

$node(id, chan, init, elec, lid, pChan) \overset{def}{=}$
   $r(election(sndrChan)). processElection(id, chan, init, 1, lid, pChan, sndrChan)$
   $+ r(leader(maxid)). processLeader(id, chan, init, elec, lid, pChan, maxid)$

/* Node that initiates election process broadcasts *election* msg and awaits *ack* in state *awaitAck*. */

$initElection(id, chan, init, elec, lid, pChan) \overset{def}{=}$
   $\overline{b}\, election(chan). awaitAck(id, chan, init, 1, id, none)$

/* When a node receives an *election* message it reaches the *processElection* state where it broadcasts the *election* message and goes to state *awaitAck*. */

$processElection(id, chan, init, elec, lid, pChan, sndrChan) \overset{def}{=}$
   $\overline{b}\, election(chan). awaitAck(id, chan, init, elec, lid, sndrChan)$

/* A node in *awaitAck* state may receive an *ack* and reach *processAck* state or it may nondeterministically conclude that it has received *ack* from all its children in the spanning tree. In the latter case, it declares the leader by broadcasting a *leader* message if it is the initiator. Otherwise, it sends (unicast) an *ack* to its parent node (*pChan*) with the maximum id in the spanning tree rooted at this node. */

$awaitAck(id, chan, init, elec, lid, pChan) \overset{def}{=}$
   $chan(ack(maxid)). processAck(id, chan, init, elec, lid, pChan, maxid)$
   $+ [init = 1]\, \overline{b}\, leader(lid). node(id, chan, init, 0, lid, pChan)$
   $+ [init = 0]\, \overline{pChan}\, ack(id, lid). node(id, chan, init, elec, lid, pChan)$

/* On receiving an *ack*, a node stores the maximum of the ids received in *ack* messages. */

$processAck(id, chan, init, elec, lid, pChan, maxid) \overset{def}{=}$
   $[maxid >= lid]\, awaitAck(id, chan, init, elec, maxid, pChan)$
   $+ [maxid < lid]\, awaitAck(id, chan, init, elec, lid, pChan)$

/* On receiving a *leader* message, a node sets its *lid* parameter to the *maxid* in the *leader* message. If *maxid* is less than *lid*, then either the node was not part of the election process or did not report *ack* to its parent node (probably because it moved away from its parent). In either case, it broadcasts its *lid* as the maximum id. */

$processLeader(id, chan, init, elec, lid, pChan, sndrChan, maxid) \overset{def}{=}$
   $[maxid = lid]\,($
      $[elec = 1]\, \overline{b}\, leader(maxid). node(id, chan, init, 0, lid, pChan)$
      $+ [elec = 0]\, node(id, chan, init, 0, lid, pChan)$
   $)$
   $+ [maxid > lid]\, \overline{b}\, leader(maxid). node(id, chan, init, 0, maxid, pChan)$
   $+ [maxid < lid]\, \overline{b}\, leader(lid). node(id, chan, init, 0, lid, pChan)$

**Fig. 4.** $\omega$-calculus encoding of the leader election protocol for MANETs

$$M = (\nu a)(\nu b)(\nu c)(\nu d)(\nu e)(\nu h)(\nu i)(\nu j)(\nu g_1)(\nu g_2)(\nu g_3)(\nu g_4)(\nu g_5)(\nu g_6)(\nu g_7)$$
$$(initElection(1, a, 1, 0, 1, none) : \{g_1, g_2\}$$
$$|\, node(2, b, 0, 0, 2, none) : \{g_1, g_3, g_4\}$$
$$|\, node(3, c, 0, 0, 3, none) : \{g_4\}$$
$$|\, node(4, d, 0, 0, 4, none) : \{g_2, g_5\}$$
$$|\, node(5, e, 0, 0, 5, none) : \{g_3\}$$
$$|\, node(6, h, 0, 0, 6, none) : \{g_5, g_6, g_7\}$$
$$|\, node(7, i, 0, 0, 7, none) : \{g_6\}$$
$$|\, node(8, j, 0, 0, 8, none) : \{g_7\})$$

**Fig. 5.** $\omega$-calculus specification of leader election protocol for an 8-node tree-structured network

A node may receive *election*, *ack*, and *leader* messages, representing an election message, an acknowledgement to the election process, and a leader message, respectively. We need not consider *probe* and *reply* messages in our model because a node can broadcast to its neighbors without knowing its neighbors, and the effect of disconnection between nodes can be modeled using the choice operator. The $\omega$-calculus model of the protocol is given in Fig. 4. The messages, their parameters, and the parameters used in the definitions appearing in Fig. 4 are explained below:

**Messages:** *election(sndrChan)*; *ack(maxid)*; *leader(maxid)*.

**Message parameters:** *sndrChan*: input channel of the sender of the message; *maxid*: maximum id seen so far by the sender of the message.

**Definition parameters:** *id*: id of the node, *chan*: input channel of the node; *init*: 1 if node initiated the election process, 0 otherwise; *elec*: 1 if node is participating in the election process, 0 otherwise; *lid*: node's knowledge of the leader id; *pChan*: input channel of the node's parent in the spanning tree; *sndrChan*: input channel of the sender node of the message; *maxid*: maximum id seen so far by the node.

An example specification of an eight-node network running the leader election protocol of Fig. 4 is given in Fig. 5. The initial network topology is the same as that of the network of Fig. 3. The node with id 1 (*initElection*) is designated to be the initiator of the leader-election process. The last parameter *none* in the process invocations indicates that the parent channel is initially not known to the processes.

**Verifying the Leader Election Protocol Model.** Following our earlier encoding of the semantics of value-passing CCS and the $\pi$-calculus [15,21] using the XSB tabled logic-programming system [18], we encoded the transitional semantics of the $\omega$-calculus using Prolog rules. Each inference rule of the semantics is encoded as a rule for a predicate **trans**, which evaluates the transition relation of a given $\omega$-calculus model. We also encoded a weak bisimulation checker for the $\omega$-calculus in Prolog. The weak version of the transition relation, abstracting $\tau$- and $\mu$-transitions, is encoded as the **dtrans** predicate. The predicate **nb(S1, S2)** checks if two $\omega$-specifications $S1$ and $S2$ are weak bisimilar. Using this implementation, we verified the following correctness property for the leader election

**Table 5.** Verification statistics for $\omega$-calculus model of leader election protocol

| Nodes | Tree | | | Ring | | |
|---|---|---|---|---|---|---|
| | States | Transitions | Time(sec) | States | Transitions | Time(sec) |
| 5 | 77 | 96 | 0.97 | 98 | 118 | 1.22 |
| 6 | 168 | 223 | 3.35 | 212 | 281 | 4.45 |
| 7 | 300 | 455 | 11.55 | 453 | 664 | 17.58 |
| 8 | 663 | 1073 | 45.85 | 952 | 1560 | 71.22 |

protocol for MANETs: *Eventually a node with the maximum id in a connected component is elected as the leader of the component, and every node connected to it (via one or more hops) learns about it.*

The verification was performed on models having *tree-* and *ring*-structured initial topologies. A distinguished node (with maximum id, for example, node 8 marked 'M' for "mobile" in Fig. 3) was free to move as long as the network remained connected. A mobility invariant was used to constrain the other nodes to remain connected to their neighbors. For verification purposes, we added a node *final* to the model that remains connected to all other nodes. A node, upon learning its leader, forwards this information to node *final*. After *final* receives messages from every other node with their leader ids equal to the maximum id in the network, it performs the observable action $action(leader(MaxId))$. The closed $\omega$-specification of the protocol was checked for weak bisimilarity with an $\omega$-specification that emits $action(leader(MaxId))$ as the only observable action. Weak bisimilarity between these two specifications indicates that the correctness property is true of the system.

We verified the correctness property for networks containing 5 through 8 nodes. Table 5 lists the states, transitions and time (in seconds) it took our Prolog implementation of the calculus and weak bisimulation checker to verify the property for networks with initial tree and ring topologies. We consider this implementation to be a prototype. Its main purpose is to demonstrate the feasibility and straightforwardness of implementing the calculus in a tabled logic-programming system. As future work, we plan to develop an optimizing compiler for the $\omega$-calculus, along the lines of one for the $\pi$-calculus implemented in the MMC model checker [20]. As these prior results demonstrate, this should significantly improve the performance of our implementation.

We observed a number of benefits in using the $\omega$-calculus to model the leader election protocol for MANETs. (1) The concise and modular nature of our specification is a direction consequence of the calculus's basic features, including separation of control behavior (processes) from neighborhood information (interfaces), and modeling support for unicast, local broadcast, and mobility. (2) The mobility constraints imposed on the model are specified independently of the control logic using a mobility invariant. For the case at hand, the invariant dictates that all nodes other than a distinguished node (node 8 in Fig. 3) remain connected to their initial neighbors. Thus, during protocol execution, process interfaces may change at will as long as the mobility invariant is maintained.

(3) Our specification of the protocol is given in the finite-control sub-calculus of the $\omega$-calculus, thereby rendering it amenable to automatic verification (bisimulation checking); see also Theorem 2.

# 6   Related Work

Several process calculi have recently been developed for wireless and mobile ad hoc networks. The closest to our work are CBS# [12], CWS [9], CMN [8], and CMAN [5]. These calculi provide local broadcast and separate control behavior from neighborhood information. However, there are significant differences between these calculi and ours, which we now discuss. CBS# [12], based on the CBS process algebra of [14], supports a notion of located processes. Node connectivity information is given independently of a system specification in terms of node connectivity graphs. The effect of mobility is achieved by nondeterministically choosing a node connectivity graph from a family of such graphs when a transition is derived. In contrast, the $\omega$-calculus offers a single, integrated language for specifying control behavior and connectivity information, and permits reasoning about changes to connectivity information within the calculus itself.

In CWS [9], node location and transmission range are a part of the node syntax. Node movement is not supported, although the authors suggest the addition of primitives for this feature. CWS is well-suited for modeling device-level behaviors (e.g., interference due to simultaneous transmissions) in wireless systems.

In CMN [8], a MANET node is a named, located sequential process that can broadcast within a specific transmission radius. Both the location and transmission radius are values in a physical coordinate system. Nodes are designated as mobile or stationary, and those of the former kind can move to an arbitrary location (resulting in a tau-transition). Bisimulation as defined for CMN is based on a notion of physically located observers. A calculus based on physical locations may pose problems for model checking as a model's state space would be infinite if locations are drawn from a real coordinate system.

In CMAN [5], each node is associated with a specific *location*. Furthermore, each node $n$ is annotated by a *connection set*: the set of locations of nodes to which $n$ is connected. Connections sets thus determine the network topology. Synchronous local broadcast is the sole communication primitive. The connection set of a node explicitly identifies the node's neighbors. Consequently, when a node moves, its neighbors actively participate by removing from (or adding to) their connection sets the location of the moving node. This explicit handling of connection information affects the modularity of the calculus's semantics (the definition of bisimulation, in particular), and may preclude reasoning about open systems. In contrast, in the $\omega$-calculus, neighborhood information is implicitly maintained using groups, thereby permitting us to define bisimulation relations in a natural way.

Other calculi for mobile processes that have been proposed in the literature include the $\pi$-calculus [11], $b\pi$-calculus [4], HOBS [13], distributed process calculus $D\pi$ [7], and the ambient calculus [2]. These calculi could be used to model MANETs but not as in a concise and natural fashion as with the $\omega$-calculus.

# 7  Conclusions and Future Work

The $\omega$-calculus, introduced in this paper, is a conservative extension of the $\pi$-calculus that permits succinct and high-level encodings of MANET systems and protocols. The salient aspect of the calculus is its group-based support for local broadcast communication over dynamically changing network topologies. We have shown that reachability of system states is decidable for the finite-control fragment of the calculus, and late bisimulation and its weak counterpart is a congruence. We illustrated the practical utility of the new formalism by using it to develop a model of a leader-election algorithm for MANETS [17]. We also showed how the calculus's operational semantics can be readily encoded in the XSB tabled logic-programming system, thereby allowing us to generate transition systems from $\omega$-calculus specifications. We used this feature to implement a weak bisimulation checker for the $\omega$-calculus, which we then used to verify certain key properties of our encoding of the leader election algorithm of [17].

We have also considered the problem of adding a $\pi$-calculus-like *mismatch* operator to the $\omega$-calculus [16], the introduction of which necessitates a lifting of the calculus's transitional semantics to a symbolic one. This is to ensure that terms identified as unequal do not violate substitution of free names in expressions. As desired, the congruence results of Section 4 can be established for this extension as well [16].

As mentioned in Section 5, future work involves the development of an optimizing compiler for the $\omega$-calculus, along the lines of one for the $\pi$-calculus implemented in the MMC model checker [20]. MMC exploits the use of binary synchronization in the $\pi$-calculus, generating specialized rules from which the transition system can be derived efficiently at model-checking time. The MMC compiler enables MMC to match the efficiency of model checkers for non-mobile systems. Extending such compilation techniques to broadcast and multicast communication is an open problem. Another avenue of future work is the development of a compositional model checker for the $\omega$-calculus, such as of those for CCS and the $\pi$-calculus [1,19]. A model checker of this nature would permit verification of infinite families of MANETs. Finally, the $\omega$-calculus models bidirectional connectivity between nodes. Since certain MANET protocols rely on unidirectional node connections, it would be fruitful to extend the calculus with such a modeling capability.

**Acknowledgements.**  We thank Massimo Merro for his valuable comments on an earlier version of this paper. Research supported in part by NSF grants CCR-0205376, CNS-0509230, CNS-0627447, and ONR grant N000140710928.

# References

1. Basu, S., Ramakrishnan, C.R.: Compositional analysis for verification of parameterized systems. In: Garavel, H., Hatcliff, J. (eds.) TACAS 2003. LNCS, vol. 2619, pp. 315–330. Springer, Heidelberg (2003)

2. Cardelli, L., Gordon, A.D.: Mobile ambients. In: Nivat, M. (ed.) FOSSACS 1998. LNCS, vol. 1378. Springer, Heidelberg (1998)
3. Dam, M.: On the decidability of process equivalences for the $\pi$-calculus. Theoretical Computer Science 183, 215–228 (1997)
4. Ene, C., Muntean, T.: A broadcast-based calculus for communicating systems. In: Intl. Workshop on Formal Methods for Parallel Programming: Theory and Applications (2001)
5. Godskesen, J.C.: A calculus for mobile ad hoc networks. In: Murphy, A.L., Vitek, J. (eds.) COORDINATION 2007. LNCS, vol. 4467, pp. 132–150. Springer, Heidelberg (2007)
6. Godskesen, J.C., Gryn, O.: Modelling and verification of security protocols for ad hoc networks using UPPAAL. In: Proc. 18th Nordic Workshop on Programming Theory (October 2006)
7. Hennessy, M., Riely, J.: Resource access control in systems of mobile agents. In: High-Level Concurrent Languages. Electr. Notes Theor. Comput. Sci., vol. 16.3, pp. 3–17 (1998)
8. Merro, M.: An observational theory for mobile ad hoc networks. In: Proc. MFPS 2007. Electr. Notes Theor. Comput. Sci., vol. 173, pp. 275–293. Elsevier, Amsterdam (2007)
9. Mezzetti, N., Sangiorgi, D.: Towards a calculus for wireless systems. In: Proc. MFPS 2006. Electr. Notes Theor. Comput. Sci., vol. 158, pp. 331–354. Elsevier, Amsterdam (2006)
10. Milner, R.: The polyadic pi-calculus: a tutorial. In: Logic and Algebra of Specification, pp. 203–246. Springer, Heidelberg (1993)
11. Milner, R., Parrow, J., Walker, D.: A calculus of mobile processes, Parts I and II. Information and Computation 100(1), 1–77 (1992)
12. Nanz, S., Hankin, C.: A framework for security analysis of mobile wireless networks. Theoretical Computer Science 367(1-2), 203–227 (2006)
13. Ostrovsky, K., Prasad, K.V.S., Taha, W.: Towards a primitive higher order calculus of broadcasting systems. In: PPDP, pp. 2–13. ACM, New York (2002)
14. Prasad, K.V.S.: A calculus of broadcasting systems. Sci. Comput. Program. 25(2-3), 285–327 (1995)
15. Ramakrishna, Y.S., Ramakrishnan, C.R., Ramakrishnan, I.V., Smolka, S.A., Swift, T., Warren, D.S.: Efficient model checking using tabled resolution. In: Grumberg, O. (ed.) CAV 1997. LNCS, vol. 1254, pp. 143–154. Springer, Heidelberg (1997)
16. Singh, A., Ramakrishnan, C.R., Smolka, S.A.: A process calculus for mobile ad hoc networks (2008), http://www.lmc.cs.sunysb.edu/~anusingh/omega/
17. Vasudevan, S., Kurose, J.F., Towsley, D.F.: Design and analysis of a leader election algorithm for mobile ad hoc networks. In: ICNP, pp. 350–360. IEEE Computer Society, Los Alamitos (2004)
18. XSB. The XSB logic programming system, http://xsb.sourceforge.net
19. Yang, P., Basu, S., Ramakrishnan, C.R.: Parameterized verification of pi-calculus systems. In: Hermanns, H., Palsberg, J. (eds.) TACAS 2006. LNCS, vol. 3920, pp. 42–57. Springer, Heidelberg (2006)
20. Yang, P., Dong, Y., Ramakrishnan, C.R., Smolka, S.A.: A provably correct compiler for efficient model checking of mobile processes. In: Hermenegildo, M.V., Cabeza, D. (eds.) PADL 2004. LNCS, vol. 3350, pp. 113–127. Springer, Heidelberg (2005)
21. Yang, P., Ramakrishnan, C.R., Smolka, S.A.: A logical encoding of the pi-calculus: Model checking mobile processes using tabled resolution. International Journal on Software Tools for Technology Transfer (STTT) 6(1), 38–66 (2004)

# Actors with Multi-headed Message Receive Patterns

Martin Sulzmann[1], Edmund S.L. Lam[2], and Peter Van Weert[3,*]

[1] Programming, Logics and Semantics Group, IT University of Copenhagen
Rued Langgaards Vej 7, 2300 Copenhagen S Denmark
sulzmann@itu.dk
[2] School of Computing, National University of Singapore
S16 Level 5, 3 Science Drive 2, Singapore 117543
lamsoonl@comp.nus.edu.sg
[3] Department of Computer Science, Katholieke Universiteit Leuven
Celestijnenlaan 200A, B-3001 Heverlee, Belgium
Peter.VanWeert@cs.kuleuven.be

**Abstract.** The actor model provides high-level concurrency abstractions to coordinate simultaneous computations by message passing. Languages implementing the actor model such as Erlang commonly only support single-headed pattern matching over received messages. We propose and design an extension of Erlang style actors with receive clauses containing multi-headed message patterns. Patterns may be non-linear and constrained by guards. We provide a number of examples to show the usefulness of the extension. We also explore the design space for multi-headed message matching semantics, for example first-match and rule priority-match semantics. The various semantics are inspired by the multi-set constraint matching semantics found in Constraint Handling Rules. This provides us with a formal model to study actors with multi-headed message receive patterns. The system can be implemented efficiently and we have built a prototype as a library-extension to Haskell.

## 1 Introduction

We all know the free lunch is over. We must write concurrent programs to take advantage of the next generation of multi-core architectures. But writing correct concurrent programs using the traditional model of threads and locks is inherently difficult and error-prone. Message-based concurrency provides the programmer the ability to exchange messages without relying on low-level locking and blocking mechanisms. A particular popular form of message-based concurrency is actor style concurrency [1] as implemented by the Erlang language [2].

In Erlang, an actor comes with an asynchronous message queue also known as mailbox. Erlang actors communicate by sending and receiving messages. Sending is a non-blocking (asynchronous) operation. Each sent message is placed in the actors mailbox and immediately returns to the sender. Messages are processed via receive clauses which resemble pattern matching clauses found in

---

* Research Assistant of the Research Foundation – Flanders (FWO-Vlaanderen).

D. Lea and G. Zavattaro (Eds.): COORDINATION 2008, LNCS 5052, pp. 315–330, 2008.
© Springer-Verlag Berlin Heidelberg 2008

functional/logic languages. Receive clauses are tried in sequential order. The receive operation is blocking. If none of the receive clauses applies we suspend until a matching message is delivered.

Receive clauses in Erlang are restricted to a *single-headed* message pattern. That is, each receive pattern matches at most one message, possible constrained by a guard. There are situations where we wish to match against multiple messages. Via *multi-headed* message patterns we can give a direct encoding of such problems. But such patterns are not commonly supported in Erlang style languages. The programmer herself must therefore either explicitly keep track of the set of partial matches or resort to nested received clauses. This leads to clumsy and error-prone code as we will see later in Section 2.

In this paper, we make the following contributions:

- We propose and design an extension of Erlang style actors with receive clauses containing multi-headed message patterns. Patterns may be non-linear (i.e. have multiple occurrences of the same pattern variable) and be constrained by guards. There are several possibly ways how to define multi-head message matching, for example either first-match or rule priority-match. We explore both alternatives in detail (Section 4).
- We have implemented a library-based prototype in Haskell (Section 5).

We draw our inspiration from prior work in the concurrent constraint logic programming community. Specifically, we adopt the various multi-set constraint matching semantics found in Constraint Handling Rules [6]. Section 3 provides the necessary background information. We discuss related work in Section 6. Section 7 concludes and discusses some possible future work.

We assume that the reader has some basic familiarity with Erlang and functional languages such as Haskell. We will write example programs in Haskell syntax [15] extended with actors. The Haskell extension uses some minor syntactic sugar compared to our library-based extension described in Section 5. Throughout the paper whenever we refer to actors we mean Erlang style actors.

## 2   Motivating Example

We motivate multi-headed message receive patterns via a classic concurrency challenge, the Santa Claus problem [18].

*Santa Claus First Match (Variant).* Santa repeatedly sleeps until wakened by either all of his nine reindeer, back from their holidays, or by a group of three of his ten elves. If awakened by the reindeer, he harnesses each of them to his sleigh, delivers toys with them and finally unharnesses them (allowing them to go off on holiday). If awakened by a group of elves, he shows each of the group into his study, consults with them on toy R&D and finally shows them each out (allowing them to go back to work). Santa chooses the *first matching* group of either elves or reindeer waiting.

*Single-Headed Solution.* We give a solution in Haskell extended with Erlang style actors. We omit some unimportant tasks such as "deliver toys" and "show study" and assume that initially ten elves and nine deer are sent to the Santa actor which appear in random order in Santa's mailbox.

```
data SantaMsg = Deer Int | Elf Int

santa sanActor DeerAcc ElvesAcc =
  receive sanActor of
    Deer x -> if length (Deer x:DeerAcc) == 9
                 then ''Deliver toys etc''
                 else santa sanActor (Deer x:DeerAcc) ElvesAcc
    Elf x -> if length (Elf x:ElvesAcc) == 3
                 then ''Show study etc''
                 else santa sanActor DeerAcc (Elf x:ElvesAcc)
```

The critical task for Santa is to check for nine reindeer and three elves. Santa will pick the group whichever arrives first. In Erlang, receive patterns are single-headed. Therefore, the Santa actor accumulates the set of deer and elves received so far. We are slightly more explicit compared to Erlang in that the `receive` primitive takes the actor as the first argument and the receive clauses as second argument (similar to case statements). The actual behavior is like in Erlang. Receive clauses are tried from top to bottom, for one message at a time. If a message does not match any of the clauses we try the next message. In our case, we first match the current message against the deer pattern. If the match fails, we check for an elf. If this match fails as well, we move on to the next message and the process repeats itself. If none of the messages match we block and wait for new messages to arrive. This case does not apply here because there are only deer or elf messages. The receive clauses are exhaustive. The point to note is that Erlang actors apply a *first-match semantics* which selects the first clause (starting from the top) that matches the messages as they come in (the actors mailbox).

*Multi-Headed Solution.* Via multi-headed message patterns we can omit the accumulation of partial matches entirely. Here is a solution using our proposed multi-head extension:

```
santa2 sanActor =
  receive sanActor of
    Deer x1, Deer x2, Deer x3, Deer x4, Deer x5,
    Deer x6, Deer x7, Deer x8, Deer x9 -> ''Deliver toys etc''
    Elf x1, Elf x2, Elf x3 -> ''Show study etc''
```

We explain the semantics for such an extension in terms of multi-set constraint matching semantics studied in the context of Constraint Handling Rules (CHR) [6]. CHR is a concurrent committed-choice constraint logic programming language to transform (rewrite) multi-sets of constraints into simpler ones. Constraints correspond to messages, and the left-hand side of a CHR rule corresponds to the pattern of a receive clause. Concretely, we adopt the refined CHR

semantics [3] which finds a match for the left-hand side of a CHR rule by processing constraints in sequential order and testing CHR rules from top to bottom.
For single-headed CHR rules, this is essentially the first-match actor semantics.
The refined CHR semantics provides for a formal basis to extend the first-match
actor semantics with multi-headed message receive patterns involving guards.

*Guarded Multi-Heads.* Suppose not every group of three elves is compatible. For
example, either only odd or even numbered elves are willing to work together.
Via guards we can easily impose this condition:

```
santa3 sanActor =
  receive sanActor of
    Deer x1, Deer x2, Deer x3, Deer x4, Deer x5,
    Deer x6, Deer x7, Deer x8, Deer x9 -> ''Deliver toys etc''
    Elf x1, Elf x2, Elf x3 when allOddorEven [x1,x2,x3] -> ''Show study etc''
  where
    allOddorEven xs = (and (map xs odd)) || (and (map xs even))
```

*Multi-Heads are Unordered.* The message order in patterns is irrelevant. For
example, the multi-headed receive clauses `Deer x, Elf y -> body` and `Elf y,
Deer x -> body` are equivalent. The rationale behind this design choice is as
follows. We treat the multiple messages in a pattern as an un-ordered multi-set
because, for the user, the order in which messages arrive is not observable. A
specific order among messages can be imposed using nested receive clauses. For
instance, the following program text gives priority to the elf:

```
receive someActor of
 Elf y -> receive someActor of
             Deer x ->
```

Nested receive clauses in combination with `otherwise` statements (introduced
shortly) can be essential to express priorities as we demonstrate next.

*Santa Claus Priority-Match (Original).* In the original specification of the Santa
Claus problem [18], instead of choosing the *first* matching group of three elves
or nine reindeer waiting, Santa needs to give *priority* to the reindeer if there
are *matching* groups of both elves and reindeer waiting. Under a first-match
semantics, our previous solutions `santa` and `santa2` do not obey the priority
given to a group of deer. Suppose for example that at the moment the `receive`
statement is executed, three elves and nine deer are waiting in Santa's mailbox,
with the elves appearing first in the mailbox. The first-match semantics of receive
patterns then selects the three elves (hence execute "show study"), even though
nine deer are waiting. The priority given to the deer has to be encoded explicitly:

```
santa4 sanActor =
  receive sanActor of
    Deer x1, Deer x2, Deer x3, Deer x4, Deer x5,
    Deer x6, Deer x7, Deer x8, Deer x9 -> ''Deliver toys etc''
    otherwise -> receive sanActor of
                    Elf x1, Elf x2, Elf x3 -> ''Show study etc''
                    otherwise -> santa4 sanActor
```

First, we check if there are nine deer (waiting) in Santa's mailbox. Otherwise, we call a nested receive statement to check for three elves. Otherwise, the process repeats itself. The `otherwise` statement corresponds to 'after 0' in Erlang. This branch applies if none of the other branches could find a match. The outer `otherwise` for instance applies if there are fewer than nine deer in Santa's mailbox. Enforcing priorities manually via `otherwise` and nested receive statements leads to clumsy code. For concurrency problems with priorities a different semantics is warranted in which receive clauses are executed in (textual) order. Incidentally, in the CHR literature a semantics has been recently suggested [12] in which rewrite rules can be executed in textual order. If we adopt such a semantics to the actor setting, solution `santa2` immediately solves the Santa Claus Priority-Match problem.

*Summary.* Thanks to multi-headed message receive patterns the programmer is relieved from the tedious and non-trivial task if building the set of partial matches herself. In combination with guards this leads to more concise and maintainable code. Erlang style actors follow the first-match semantics. The refined CHR semantics [3] is a conservative extension of this semantics to the setting of multi-set matching involving guards. Certain concurrency problems, however, are more naturally solved using a rule priority-match semantics which has also been explored in the CHR context.

In the up-coming section, we provide background information on the first-match and rule priority-match semantics. In Section 4, we formalize an extension of actors with multi-headed message patterns which can be constrained by guards. The extension is parametric in terms of the underlying message match semantics for receive clauses. In case we adopt a first-match CHR style semantics for message patterns, we obtain a conservative extension of Erlang style actors.

# 3   Constraint Handling Rules Matching

We review the essentials of the multi-set constraint matching semantics of Constraint Handling Rules (CHR). The actual CHR framework is much richer than presented here. CHR also supports constraint propagation and built-in constraints such as unification constraints. We ignore these additional features.

Figure 1 introduces some basic syntactic categories. Constraints are terms built via constructors $K$. Constraints carry a distinct number to distinguish multiple appearances of a constraint $c$. Rule patterns consist of a head and guard component. A CHR rule also consists of a rule body which we ignore here. We are only interested in the multi-set constraint match semantics of CHR and not in CHR execution. In the actor context, a rule pattern corresponds to a receive pattern and a rule body corresponds to the body of a receive clause. The guard must evaluate to a Boolean value. Constraints in rule heads have distinct, increasing occurrences with respect to their textual order in a program.

**Constraints**

|   |   | $K$ | Constructor name |
|---|---|---|---|
|   | $c$ | $::= K\ c...c$ | Constraint |
|   |   | $\mid x$ | Constraint variable |
|   | $cn$ | $::= c\#n$ | Numbered constraint |
|   | $co$ | $::= c : j$ | Occurrence constraint |
|   | $cno$ | $::= c\#n : j$ | Active constraint |

**Substitution**

$$\theta ::= [c_1/x_1, ..., c_n/x_n]$$

**Rule patterns**

| $H$ | $::= co \mid H \wedge H$ | Head |
|---|---|---|
| $G$ | $::= e$ | Guard |
| $RP$ | $::= H$ when $G$ | Rule pattern |
|   | $\mid H$ |   |
| $\mathcal{RP}$ | $::= \{RP_1, ..., RP_n\}$ | Set of rule patterns |

**Executables**

$$M ::= N \mid [cno|N]$$
$$N ::= [] \mid [cn|N]$$

**Store**

$$St ::= [] \mid [cn|St]$$

**Matching States**

| $\langle M, St \rangle$ | Intermediate |
|---|---|
| $\langle M, St, \theta, RP \rangle$ | Successful |
| $\langle [], St \rangle$ | Failure |

**Fig. 1.** Constraint Handling Rules Essential Syntax

---

For example, the rule heads derived from the `santa3` function in the previous section are

$$Deer\ x_1 : 1 \wedge ... \wedge Deer\ x_9 : 9$$

and

$$Elf\ x_1 : 10 \wedge Elf\ x_2 : 11 \wedge Elf\ x_3 : 12$$

Thus, we can perform a systematic search for a match.

The idea is that all (numbered) constraints are initially stored in a list $M$. We use Prolog syntax to denote a list $[x|xs]$ with first element $x$ and tail $xs$. The symbol $[]$ denotes the empty list and $++$ denotes list concatenation. In the CHR context, $M$ is referred to as the execution stack. Here, it is more appropriate to view $M$ as a list corresponding to the actors mailbox. Constraints in $M$ are executed in sequential order to find a match with a rule pattern. We execute constraints by activating them with the initial occurrence number 1. We will increase the occurrence until a match is found. Otherwise, we deactivate the current active constraint by putting it into the store and start with a new active constraint. In case of the first-match semantics, this strategy guarantees that constraints are processed in sequential order and rules are tried from top to bottom. Below are the formal details.

**Matching reduction:** $\langle M, St \rangle \longrightarrow_{First-\mathcal{RP}} \langle M, St \rangle$ and $\langle M, St \rangle \longrightarrow_{First-\mathcal{RP}}$
$\langle M, St, \theta, RP \rangle$

(Activate) $\qquad\qquad \langle [c\#n|M], St \rangle \longrightarrow_{First-\mathcal{RP}} \langle [c\#n : 1|M], St \rangle$

(Match) $\qquad$
$$\frac{\begin{array}{c} H_1, c' : j, H_2 \text{ when } G \in \mathcal{RP} \\ \theta(G) \text{ evaluates to } True \quad St_1 \mathbin{+\!\!+} St_2 \mathbin{+\!\!+} St' =_{set} St \\ \theta(c') = c \quad \theta(H_1) = St_1 \quad \theta(H_2) = St_2 \quad \text{for some } \theta \end{array}}{\langle [c\#n : j, M], St \rangle \longrightarrow_{First-\mathcal{RP}} \langle M, St', \theta, H_1 \wedge c' : j \wedge H_2 \text{ when } G \rangle}$$

(Continue) $\qquad$
$$\frac{j < maxOccur(\mathcal{RP})}{\langle [c\#n : j|M], St \rangle \longrightarrow_{First-\mathcal{RP}} \langle [c\#n : j + 1|M], St \rangle}$$

(Deactivate) $\qquad$
$$\frac{j \geq maxOccur(\mathcal{RP})}{\langle [c\#n : j|M], St \rangle \longrightarrow_{First-\mathcal{RP}} \langle M, St \mathbin{+\!\!+} [c\#n] \rangle}$$

(Step1) $\qquad$
$$\frac{\langle M, St \rangle \longrightarrow_{First-\mathcal{RP}} \langle M', St' \rangle}{\langle M, St \rangle \longrightarrow^*_{First-\mathcal{RP}} \langle M', St' \rangle}$$

(Step2) $\qquad$
$$\frac{\langle M, St \rangle \longrightarrow_{First-\mathcal{RP}} \langle M', St', \theta, RP \rangle}{\langle M, St \rangle \longrightarrow^*_{First-\mathcal{RP}} \langle M', St', \theta, RP \rangle}$$

(Trans) $\dfrac{\langle M_1, St_1 \rangle \longrightarrow^*_{First-\mathcal{RP}} \langle M_2, St_2 \rangle \quad \langle M_2, St_2 \rangle \longrightarrow^*_{First-\mathcal{RP}} \langle M_3, St_3 \rangle}{\langle M_1, St_1 \rangle \longrightarrow^*_{First-\mathcal{RP}} \langle M_3, St_3 \rangle}$

**Fig. 2.** CHR Multi-Set First Match Semantics

## 3.1   First-Match Semantics

Our presentation largely follows the CHR description [3], which we adapt to our specialized setting. Figure 2 describes the CHR multi-set first-match semantics as a transition system $\longrightarrow^*_{First-\mathcal{RP}}$ among states $\langle M, St \rangle$ where $M$ represents the constraints to be executed and $St$ holds the already processed constraints. The set $\mathcal{RP}$ holds the rule patterns. Initially, we start in the state $\langle M, [] \rangle$. The goal is to reach a successful state $\langle M', St, \theta, RP \rangle$ where $RP$ is the (first) rule pattern matched by a (sequentially processed) sequence of constraints in $M$, $\theta$ is the matching substitution, $St$ holds the already processed constraints that did not contribute to the match, and $M'$ are the remaining constraints. State $\langle [], St \rangle$ indicates failure: none of the constraints in the initial $M$ trigger a rule pattern.

The search for a match is performed by activating the leading constraint in $M$ by assigning it the occurrence number 1. See rule (Activate). Rule (Match) checks whether the active constraint matches a constraint in the head of a rule pattern at the respective position. We consult the store to find constraints $St_1$ and $St_2$ which match the remaining constraints $H_1$ and $H_2$ in the head. The symbol $=_{set}$

**Matching reduction:** $\langle M, St \rangle \longrightarrow^*_{Priority-\mathcal{RP}} \langle M, St \rangle$ and $\langle M, St \rangle \longrightarrow^*_{Priority-\mathcal{RP}} \langle M, St, \theta, RP \rangle$

$$\mathcal{RP} = \{RP_1, ..., RP_n\}$$

$$\text{(Succ)} \quad \frac{\forall 1 \leq j < i \; \langle M, St \rangle \longrightarrow^*_{First-\{RP_j\}} \langle [], St'_j \rangle \quad \langle M, St \rangle \longrightarrow^*_{First-\{RP_i\}} \langle M', St', \theta, RP_i \rangle}{\langle M, St \rangle \longrightarrow^*_{Priority-\mathcal{RP}} \langle M', St', \theta, RP_i \rangle}$$

$$\mathcal{RP} = \{RP_1, ..., RP_n\}$$

$$\text{(Fail)} \quad \frac{\forall 1 \leq j \leq n \; \langle M, St \rangle \longrightarrow^*_{First-\{RP_j\}} \langle [], St'_j \rangle}{\langle M, St \rangle \longrightarrow^*_{Priority-\mathcal{RP}} \langle [], St_n \rangle}$$

**Fig. 3.** CHR Multi-Set Rule Priority Match Semantics

denotes set equality among lists. The statement $St_1 +\!\!+ St_2 +\!\!+ St' =_{set} St$ holds if each element in $St_1 +\!\!+ St_2 +\!\!+ St'$ appears in $St$ and vice versa. This implies that the order of constraints in patterns does not matter which is a sensible choice for our (actor) setting as argued in Section 2. The equality test among constraints ignores numbering of constraints and occurrences. If the guard can be satisfied as well, we report the successfully found match. Otherwise, we continue our search by incrementing the occurrence number of the active constraint. See rule (Continue). This is only sensible if the maximum occurrence in any constraint in $\mathcal{RP}$, computed via function $maxOccur(\cdot)$, is smaller than the current occurrence number. Otherwise, we deactivate the constraint by putting it into the store. See rule (Deactivate). The order among messages is retained. That is, for any initial state $\langle M, [] \rangle$ and intermediate state $\langle M', St \rangle$ we have that $M = St +\!\!+ M'$. We keep repeatedly applying rules (Activate), (Match), (Continue) and (Deactivate), in that order, until we either reach a successful or failure state.

To summarize, the first-match semantics finds a match by processing constraints in sequential order and checking for a matching rule pattern from top to bottom (in the textual order).

### 3.2   Rule Priority-Match Semantics

We consider a rule priority-match semantics which guarantees that rule patterns are executed in (textual) order. Figure 3 contains the details. We apply the first-match semantics on each rule pattern and select the first successful match in textual order. We assume that $RP_j$ appears before $RP_{j+1}$ in the program which can be specified via occurrences associated to head constraints.

Next, we consider some examples to illustrate the differences between both semantics.

### 3.3   Examples

The first example is given in Figure 4. We assume that $A$ and $B$ are constant messages. Therefore, each (Match) reductions make use of the identity

**Receive clause:**

```
receive act of
    A,A -> "RP₁"      -- RP₁ = A : 1 ∧ A : 2
    B   -> "RP₂"      -- RP₂ = B : 3
```

$$\mathcal{RP} = \{RP_1, RP_2\}$$

**First-Match reduction:**

|  |  | $\langle [A\#1, B\#2, A\#3], [] \rangle$ |
|---|---|---|
| (Act-Cont-Deact) | $\longrightarrow_{First-\mathcal{RP}}$ | $\langle [B\#2, A\#3], [A\#1] \rangle$ |
| (Activate) | $\longrightarrow_{First-\mathcal{RP}}$ | $\langle [B\#2 : 1, A\#3], [A\#1] \rangle$ |
| (Continue ×2) | $\longrightarrow_{First-\mathcal{RP}}$ | $\langle [B\#2 : 3, A\#3], [A\#1] \rangle$ |
| (Match) | $\longrightarrow_{First-\mathcal{RP}}$ | $\langle [A\#3], [A\#1], identSubst, RP_2 \rangle$ |

**Rule Priority-Match reduction:**

|  |  | $\langle [A\#1, B\#2, A\#3], [] \rangle$ |
|---|---|---|
| (Act-Cont-Deact) | $\longrightarrow_{First-\{RP_1\}}$ | $\langle [B\#2, A\#3], [A\#1] \rangle$ |
| (Act-Cont-Deact) | $\longrightarrow_{First-\{RP_1\}}$ | $\langle [A\#3], [A\#1, B\#2] \rangle$ |
| (Activate) | $\longrightarrow_{First-\{RP_1\}}$ | $\langle [A\#3 : 1], [A\#1, B\#2] \rangle$ |
| (Match) | $\longrightarrow_{First-\{RP_1\}}$ | $\langle [], [B\#2], identSubst, RP_1 \rangle$ |

**Fig. 4.** Example 1

---

(matching) substitutions *identSubst*. Each reduction step is annotated with the corresponding reduction rule. For brevity, we shorten reduction steps. For example, we write

|  |  | $\langle [A\#1, B\#2, A\#3], [] \rangle$ |
|---|---|---|
| (Act-Cont-Deact) | $\longrightarrow_{First-\mathcal{RP}}$ | $\langle [B\#2, A\#3], [A\#1] \rangle$ |

as a short-hand for

|  |  | $\langle [A\#1, B\#2, A\#3], [] \rangle$ |
|---|---|---|
| (Activate) | $\longrightarrow_{First-\mathcal{RP}}$ | $\langle [A\#1 : 1, B\#2, A\#3], [] \rangle$ |
| (Continue ×3) | $\longrightarrow_{First-\mathcal{RP}}$ | $\langle [A\#1 : 4, B\#2, A\#3], [] \rangle$ |
| (Deactivate) | $\longrightarrow_{First-\mathcal{RP}}$ | $\langle [B\#2, A\#3], [A\#1] \rangle$ |

The first-match reduction applies $RP_2$. We sequentially process constraints, searching for the first match for a rule pattern from top to bottom. Starting with the initial list of executables $[A\#1, B\#2, A\#3]$, we find that $B\#2$ form the first match for rule pattern $RP_2$. On the other hand the rule priority-match reduction applies $RP_1$. We strictly apply rule patterns in (textual) order. Based on the priority of rules, $A\#1, A\#3$ form a match for the first rule pattern $RP_1$.

In the second example in Figure 5, we apply the first-match and rule priority-match on the initial list of executables $[A\#1, B\#2]$. In both cases only rule pattern $RP_2$ applies. The first-match reduction is almost identical to Example 1 where we additionally find constraint $A\#3$ in the initial $M$. But this constraint does not contribute to the first match. In case of the rule priority-match reduction we first try $RP_1$ which fails and then we try $RP_2$ which leads to success.

**Receive clause:**

```
receive act of
    A,A -> "RP₁"      -- RP₁ = A : 1 ∧ A : 2
    B   -> "RP₂"      -- RP₂ = B : 3
```

$$\mathcal{RP} = \{RP_1, RP_2\}$$

**First-Match reduction:**

$$\langle [A\#1, B\#2], [] \rangle$$

(Act-Cont-Deact)     $\longrightarrow_{First-\{RP_1, RP_2\}} \langle [B\#2], [A\#1] \rangle$

(Activate)     $\longrightarrow_{First-\{RP_1, RP_2\}} \langle [B\#2 : 1], [A\#1] \rangle$

(Continue ×2)     $\longrightarrow_{First-\{RP_1, RP_2\}} \langle [B\#2 : 3], [A\#1] \rangle$

(Match)     $\longrightarrow_{First-\{RP_1, RP_2\}} \langle [], [A\#1], identSubst, RP_2 \rangle$

**Rule Priority-Match reductions:**

$$\langle [A\#1, B\#2], [] \rangle$$

(Act-Cont-Deact)     $\longrightarrow_{First-\{RP_1\}} \langle [B\#2], [A\#1] \rangle$

(Act-Cont-Deact)     $\longrightarrow_{First-\{RP_1\}} \langle [], [A\#1, B\#2] \rangle$

$$\langle [A\#1, B\#2], [] \rangle$$

(Act-Cont-Deact)     $\longrightarrow_{First-\{RP_2\}} \langle [B\#2], [A\#1] \rangle$

(Activate)     $\longrightarrow_{First-\{RP_2\}} \langle [B\#2 : 1], [A\#1] \rangle$

(Continue ×2)     $\longrightarrow_{First-\{RP_2\}} \langle [B\#2 : 3], [A\#1] \rangle$

(Match)     $\longrightarrow_{First-\{RP_2\}} \langle [], [A\#1], identSubst, RP_2 \rangle$

**Fig. 5.** Example 2

## 4    Actors with Multi-headed Message Patterns

Figure 6 introduces the syntax and Figures 7 and 8 introduce the semantics of an elementary actor language which supports multi-headed message patterns. In example programs, we use "," (comma) to separate multi-headed message patterns whereas in our (internal) syntax we use ∧. We assume a distinct pattern variable otherwise to support otherwise statements. The otherwise pattern (if present) does not appear anywhere else in the program but in the last pattern of a receive statement. We assume that the variables in a guard statement $e_i'$ appear in the associated pattern $p_i$.

We define the semantics in terms of a small-step Wright/Felleisen style semantics [20]. We assume a fixed set of actors, each identified by a unique actor identification number, $aid$ for short. Each actor has a mailbox $M$ and the actor's behavior is specified by an expression $e$. We execute actors in random order. See rule (Schedule) in Figure 8. We simply evaluate the actor expression $k$ number of steps. Evaluation affects the actors mailbox and has as a side effect the sending of messages. We append sent messages to the appropriate mailboxes via the operations $S@a$ and $S@AP$. See rules (AS1-4). In rule (AS3), we attach a unique number to the message to distinguish multiple occurrences of the same message.

**Expressions**

$$
\begin{array}{lll}
e &::= x & \text{Variable} \\
&\mid K\ e...e & \text{Message} \\
&\mid \lambda x.e \mid e\ e & \text{Function and application} \\
&\mid \textsf{receive}\ [p_i\ \textsf{when}\ e'_i \rightarrow e_i]_{i \in I} & \text{Message receive} \\
&\mid \textsf{send}\ aid\ e & \text{Message send} \\
&\mid () & \text{Don't care} \\
p &::= p' \mid p \wedge p & \text{Single-head and multi-head pattern} \\
p' &::= x & \text{Variable pattern} \\
&\mid \textsf{otherwise} & \text{Otherwise pattern} \\
&\mid K\ p'...p' & \text{Message pattern}
\end{array}
$$

**Actor**

$$
\begin{array}{ll}
a ::= (aid, M, e) & \\
\quad aid & \text{Actor identification} \\
\quad M & \text{Mailbox} \\
\quad e & \text{Behavior}
\end{array}
$$

**Fig. 6.** MiniActor Language

Evaluation of expressions is described in Figure 7. Rule (Send) yields a don't care expression but has the side effect of sending a message. Side effects are collected in a multi-set of constraints. We may send the same message twice to the same actor. The symbol $\uplus$ denotes multi-set union. We do not care much about the order of sent messages which may be random. Evaluation of receiving of messages is parametric in terms of the match semantics described earlier. We first describe the general receive rules in terms of a generic-match reduction $\longrightarrow^*_{X-\mathcal{RP}}$ before we consider the impact of a specific matching policy.

Matching starts in the initial state $\langle M, [] \rangle$ where $M$ is the actor's current mailbox. In rule (Receive) we have found a successful match. From the successful state $\langle M', St, \theta, p_j\ \textsf{when}\ e'_j \rightarrow e_j \rangle$ we collect the list $St$ of already processed messages which have not been involved in the matching. We put these messages back into the actor's mailbox in their original order (see also rule (Deactivate) in Figure 2). We then continue executing the successful receive body $\theta(e_j)$. In the (Otherwise) case, we leave the mailbox unchanged. There is no rule for covering failure which means that evaluation of a receive clause will block until a successful match is found.

In case we instantiate $\longrightarrow^*_{X-\mathcal{RP}}$ with the first-match reduction relation from Section 3, we obtain a conservative extension of Erlang-style actors with multi-headed message receive patterns. The first-match semantics guarantees the following **Monotonicity Property:**

$$
\begin{array}{ll}
\textbf{If} & \langle M, [] \rangle \longrightarrow^*_{First-\mathcal{RP}} \langle M', St, \theta, p_j\ \textsf{when}\ e'_j \rightarrow e_j \rangle \\
\textbf{then} & \langle M \mathbin{+\!\!+} M'', [] \rangle \longrightarrow^*_{First-\mathcal{RP}} \langle M' \mathbin{+\!\!+} M'', St, \theta, p_j\ \textsf{when}\ e'_j \rightarrow e_j \rangle
\end{array}
$$

This property says that any successful match remains valid if further messages arrive in the actor's mailbox. This is a fairly important property and shows that

**Values**
$$v ::= \lambda x.e \mid K\ v_1...v_n \mid ()$$

**Send effects**
$$S ::= \emptyset \mid \{\text{send } aid\ K\ v_1...v_n\} \mid S \uplus S$$

**Evaluation contexts:**
$$E ::= [\,] \mid E\ v \mid K\ E...E \mid \text{receive } [p_i \text{ when } E \to e_i]_{i \in I} \mid \text{send } aid\ E$$

**Expression reduction:** $\langle M, e \rangle \xrightarrow{S} \langle M, e \rangle$

(Beta)     $\langle M, (\lambda x.e)\ v \rangle \xrightarrow{\emptyset} \langle M, [v/x]e \rangle$

(Send)
$$\frac{S = \{\text{send } aid\ K\ v_1...v_n\}}{\langle M, \text{send } aid\ K\ v_1...v_n \rangle \xrightarrow{S} \langle M, () \rangle}$$

(Receive)
$$\frac{\begin{array}{c}\mathcal{RP} = \{p_1 \text{ when } e_1' \to e_1, ..., p_n \text{ when } e_n' \to e_n\} \\ \langle M, [\,] \rangle \longrightarrow^*_{X-\mathcal{RP}} \langle M', St, \theta, p_j \text{ when } e_j' \to e_j \rangle \\ p_j \neq \text{otherwise} \quad \text{for some } j \in \{1,...,n\} \\ M'' = St \mathbin{+\!\!+} M'\end{array}}{\langle M, \text{receive } [p_i \text{ when } e_i' \to e_i]_{i \in \{1,...,n\}} \rangle \xrightarrow{\emptyset} \langle M'', \theta(e_j) \rangle}$$

(Otherwise)
$$\frac{\begin{array}{c}\mathcal{RP} = \{p_1 \text{ when } e_1' \to e_1, ..., p_n \text{ when } e_n' \to e_n\} \\ \langle M, [\,] \rangle \longrightarrow^*_{X-\mathcal{RP}} \langle M', St, \theta, p_n \text{ when } e_n' \to e_n \rangle \\ p_n = \text{otherwise}\end{array}}{\langle M, \text{receive } [p_i \text{ when } e_i' \to e_i]_{i \in \{1,...,n\}} \rangle \xrightarrow{\emptyset} \langle M, e_n) \rangle}$$

(Context) $\dfrac{\langle M, e \rangle \xrightarrow{S} \langle M', e' \rangle}{\langle M, E[e] \rangle \xrightarrow{S} \langle M', E[e'] \rangle}$     (Step) $\dfrac{\langle M, e \rangle \xrightarrow{S} \langle M', e' \rangle}{\langle M, e \rangle \xrightarrow{S}{}^* \langle M', e' \rangle}$

($k$-Step)
$$\frac{\begin{array}{c}\langle M_1, e_1 \rangle \xrightarrow{S_1} \langle M_2, e_2 \rangle ....\langle M_{k-1}, e_{k-1} \rangle \xrightarrow{S_{k-1}} \langle M_k, e_k \rangle \\ S_k = S_1 \uplus ... \uplus S_{k-1}\end{array}}{\langle M_1, e_1 \rangle \xrightarrow{S_k}{}^k \langle M_k, e_k \rangle}$$

(Trans)
$$\frac{\langle M_1, e_1 \rangle \xrightarrow{S_1}{}^* \langle M_2, e_2 \rangle \quad \langle M_2, e_2 \rangle \xrightarrow{S_2}{}^* \langle M_3, e_3 \rangle}{\langle M_1, e_1 \rangle \xrightarrow{S_1 \uplus S_2}{}^* \langle M_3, e_3 \rangle}$$

**Fig. 7.** Expression Semantics

we can treat the actor's mailbox as a "lazy" structure. That is, the mailbox represents a stream of incoming messages.

If we employ the rule priority-match semantics from Section 3, however, newly arrived messages can invalidate earlier (match) choices. For instance, consider the rule priority-match reduction in Figure 5. Suppose that at some later stage

**Actor pool**
$$AP ::= \emptyset \mid \{a\} \mid AP \cup AP$$

**Actor send:** $S@a$ and $S@AP$

(AS1) $$\emptyset @ (aid, M, e) = (aid, M, e)$$

(AS2) $$\frac{aid \neq aid'}{\{\text{send } aid \ K \ v_1...v_n\} \uplus S@(aid', M, e) = S@(aid', M, e)}$$

(AS3) $$\frac{aid = aid' \quad \text{unique number } m}{\{\text{send } aid \ K \ v_1...v_n\} \uplus S@(aid', M, e) = S@(aid', M \!+\!\!+\! [K \ v_1...v_n \# m], e)}$$

(AS4) $$S@\{a_1, ..., a_n\} = \{S@a_1, ..., S@a_n\}$$

**Actor reduction:** $AP \longrightarrow AP$

(Schedule) $$\frac{\begin{array}{c} AP = \{(aid, M, e)\} \cup AP' \\ \langle M, e \rangle \xrightarrow{s}{}^k \langle M', e' \rangle \\ AP'' = \{S@(aid, M', e')\} \cup S@AP' \end{array}}{AP \longrightarrow AP''}$$

(Step) $$\frac{AP \longrightarrow AP'}{AP \longrightarrow^* AP'}$$   (Trans) $$\frac{AP_1 \longrightarrow^* AP_2 \quad AP_2 \longrightarrow^* AP_3}{AP_1 \longrightarrow^* AP_3}$$

**Fig. 8.** MiniActor Semantics

the message $A\#5$ arrives (already attached with a unique number). The rule priority-match reduction in Figure 4 shows that in this case, a different rule pattern may be applied.

On the other hand, under a rule priority-match semantics we can read off the priorities directly from the receive clauses. Under a first-match semantics, we need to explicitly program priorities via otherwise and nested receive statements. This often leads to clumsy and hard to maintain code. See the discussion in Section 2. In summary, we believe that both semantics represent interesting, alternative design choices for an actor language, and it will depend on the application which semantics is the better choice.

## 5   Implementation

We have implemented a prototype as a library extension in Haskell using the Glasgow Haskell Compiler [7]. GHC supports light-weight threads. Therefore, our implementation scales well to many actors. The latest version including examples can be downloaded via [9].

We briefly highlight the main features of our implementation. We support strongly typed actors in the sense that an actor's mailbox can only holds messages of a certain (data) type. The actual mailbox consists of two parts. A buffer for recently sent messages is represented as a transacted channel to manage conflicts among multiple writers. A transacted channel is a linked list in shared memory where access is protected by Software Transactional Memory. In the future we plan to support distributed channels to support sending of messages across the network. The second part of the mailbox is a linked list to process $\langle M, St \rangle$ by a single reader. We use pointers to indicate the start of $M$ and $St$.

Our implementation applies the first-match scheme outlined in Section 3. We process messages in $M$ in sequential order. If $M$ is empty, we check the buffer and transfer any recently sent messages to $M$. If the buffer is empty, we wait for new messages to arrive. Our current prototype [9] performs a sequential search for matching messages. To improve the performance, one possible optimization is message indexing. For example, consider rule pattern Sell x,Buy x. Suppose the active message Sell SomeObject in $M$ matches part of the rule head. We then need to find a matching partner Buy SomeObject in $St$. We can achieve a faster lookup of candidate partners by using (hash)-indexing. Another optimization is the early scheduling of guards. For example, consider the rule pattern Foo x,Bar y,Erk z when x > y. Suppose that Foo 1 is our active message and what remains is to find matching partners Bar y and Erk z for some y and z such that x>y. As soon as we have found a possible candidate Bar y we should schedule (i.e. test) the guard 1>y to reduce the search space. We plan to integrate the above and other common CHR optimizations [10,16]. into later versions of our system.

## 6   Related Work

In their foundational work, Kahn and Saraswat [11] establish connections between the actor programming model and concurrent constraint logic programming. Our work follows their footstep by providing a formal model for multi-headed message receive patterns with guards based on CHR style multi-set constraint matching semantics.

The basic motivation and idea of multi-headed message receive patterns can already be found in the earlier work [5]. The concepts of receptionists and activators introduced in [5] correspond to what we called heads and rules respectively. However, there are noticeable differences. In [5], receptionists and activators are first class entities that can be communicated. Also, activators may be combined using both conjunction and disjunction. Whilst in [5], non-determinism issues are resolved by introducing fairness conditions, we consider a conservative extension of Erlang style actors, and propose a (in the context of actors) novel rule-priority match semantics. Our prototype also shows that the language extension can be implemented efficiently.

The main advantage of multi-headed message receive patterns is the ability to expression complex synchronization patterns. In [5] two types of synchronization are considered: input and reply synchronization; [19] only considers the latter. For reply synchronization, we will consider some syntactic sugar, as in [5,19], that allows actors to reply on messages. We believe that in our system we can express all synchronization patterns found in these works. Reply delegation (cf. [5, 19]) for instance is already possible by communicating the requesting actor's address. Further work is needed to support this claim.

Closest to our work is some recent work by Haller and Van Cutsem [8]. Like us they use the abstractions in the language (they use Scala we use Haskell) to avoid non-sensical pattern specifications. They focus on the implementation of join patterns [4] by means of extensible pattern matching. There are close connections between the join and actor model, and their system has support for join-style actors (what we call multi-headed message receive patterns). However, their approach appears to be more limiting. They can only support a limited form of guards, it is unclear whether they can support our non-linear patterns at all. Furthermore, they do not specify the semantics of their system.

## 7 Conclusion

We have studied an extension of Erlang style multi-headed message receive patterns with guards. Such an extension is useful as supported by a number of examples. We have explored two possible semantics by adapting previously studied CHR multi-set matching semantics. The first-match semantics gives us a conservative extension of Erlang style actors to the setting of multi-headed message receive patterns with guards. We have also explored a rule priority-match semantics which guarantees that rule patterns are executed in (textual) order. For certain applications this semantics is the better choice. The original CHR semantics proposed in [12] is more general and can express more complicated, even dynamic, user-defined priorities. How to exploit more complex priority-based execution control in the actor setting is subject of future work.

Both semantics can be implemented efficiently as shown by previous work [3,13, 16]. Our library-based prototype exploits some of these methods. We plan to integrate further optimizations, and conduct more experimentations in future work.

In another line of work, we will enrich join patterns with CHR style guards and non-linear patterns. In the join context, patterns can be be executed concurrently. We wish to parallelize the concurrent execution of join patterns. Contrast this to actor receive patterns which are executed sequentially (either following the first-match or rule priority-match semantics). We have already started work on the parallelization of CHR [14], and explored a CHR style enriched join pattern language [17]. We plan to report more detailed results in the future.

**Acknowledgments.** We thank the reviewers for their helpful comments.

## References

1. Agha, G.: ACTORS: A Model of Concurrent Computation in Distributed Systems. MIT Press, Cambridge (1986)
2. Armstrong, J., Virding, R., Wikström, C., Williams, M.: Concurrent Programming in Erlang, 2nd edn. Prentice-Hall, Englewood Cliffs (1996)

3. Duck, G.J., Stuckey, P.J., García de la Banda, M.J., Holzbaur, C.: The refined operational semantics of Constraint Handling Rules. In: Demoen, B., Lifschitz, V. (eds.) ICLP 2004. LNCS, vol. 3132, pp. 90–104. Springer, Heidelberg (2004)
4. Fournet, C., Gonthier, G.: The join calculus: A language for distributed mobile programming. In: Barthe, G., Dybjer, P., Pinto, L., Saraiva, J. (eds.) APPSEM 2000. LNCS, vol. 2395, pp. 268–332. Springer, Heidelberg (2002)
5. Frølund, S., Agha, G.: Abstracting interactions based on message sets. In: Ciancarini, P., Nierstrasz, O., Yonezawa, A. (eds.) ECOOP-WS 1994. LNCS, vol. 924, pp. 107–124. Springer, Heidelberg (1995)
6. Frühwirth, T.: Theory and practice of Constraint Handling Rules. J. Logic Programming, Special Issue on Constraint Logic Programming 37(1–3), 95–138 (1998)
7. Glasgow haskell compiler home page, http://www.haskell.org/ghc/
8. Haller, P., Van Cutsem, T.: Implementing Joins using extensible pattern matching. LNCS, vol. 5052. Springer, Heidelberg
9. HaskellActor, http://code.google.com/p/haskellactor/
10. Holzbaur, C., García de la Banda, M.J., Stuckey, P.J., Duck, G.J.: Optimizing compilation of Constraint Handling Rules in HAL. TPLP 5(4-5), 503–531 (2005)
11. Kahn, K., Saraswat, V.A.: Actors as a special case of concurrent constraint (logic) programming. In: Proc. of OOPSLA/ECOOP, pp. 57–66. ACM, New York (1990)
12. De Koninck, L., Schrijvers, T., Demoen, B.: User-definable rule priorities for CHR. In: Proc. of PPDP 2007, pp. 25–36. ACM, New York (2007)
13. De Koninck, L., Stuckey, P.J., Duck, G.J.: Optimizing compilation of CHR with rule priorities. In: FLOPS 2008. LNCS, vol. 4989. Springer, Heidelberg (2008)
14. Lam, E.S.L., Sulzmann, M.: A concurrent Constraint Handling Rules implementation in Haskell with software transactional memory. In: Proc. of DAMP 2007, pp. 19–24. ACM Press, New York (2007)
15. Peyton Jones, S. (ed.): Haskell 98 Language and Libraries: The Revised Report. Cambridge University Press, Cambridge (2003)
16. Schrijvers, T.: Analyses, Optimizations and Extensions of Constraint Handling Rules. PhD thesis, K.U.Leuven, Leuven, Belgium (June 2005)
17. Sulzmann, M., Lam, E.S.L.: Haskell – Join – Rules. In: Draft Proc. of IFL 2007 (September 2007)
18. Trono, J.A.: A new exercise in concurrency. SIGCSE Bull. 26(3), 8–10 (1994)
19. Varela, C., Agha, G.: Programming dynamically reconfigurable open systems with SALSA. SIGPLAN Not 36(12), 20–34 (2001)
20. Wright, A.K., Felleisen, M.: A syntactic approach to type soundness. A syntactic approach to type soundness 115(1), 38–94 (1994)

# A Compositional Trace Semantics for Orc

Dimitrios Vardoulakis and Mitchell Wand

Northeastern University
dimvar@ccs.neu.edu, wand@ccs.neu.edu

**Abstract.** Orc [9] is a language for task orchestration. It has a small set of primitives, but sufficient to express many useful programs succinctly. We identify an ambiguity in the trace semantics of Kitchin et al. [9]. We give possible interpretations of the ambiguous definition and show that the semantics is not adequate regardless of the interpretation. We remedy this situation by providing new operational and denotational semantics with a better treatment of variable binding, and proving an adequacy theorem to relate them. Also, we investigate strong bisimulation in Orc and show that bisimulation implies trace equivalence but not vice versa.

## 1 Introduction

Orc [9] is a concurrent programming language for web-service orchestration. It is small yet usefully programmable, making it a good vehicle for the study of distributed processes in the presence of timeouts and communication failures. Orc uses autonomous computing units called *sites* to perform sequential computation and other basic services. It then provides operators to coordinate the execution of sites and build larger processes.

The question of the practical applicability of Orc is outside the scope of this paper. Popular concurrent programming patterns like fork-join parallelism can be coded in Orc, and also the workflow patterns of van der Aalst et al. [12]. The practical aspects of the language are discussed in [11, 9, 6]. Here, we will discuss the formal properties of Orc.

- The existing trace semantics for Orc [9] is ambiguous when there is a naming conflict between free and bound variables. We resolve the ambiguity and show that the semantics is not adequate.
- We suggest that dynamic binding of variables be prohibited because it invalidates an equivalence between Orc processes proved in [9].
- We provide new operational and denotational semantics which fix the aforementioned problems and prove an adequacy theorem to relate them.
- We investigate strong bisimulation in Orc and show that it is a congruence. We use it to prove useful equivalences between Orc processes. Last, we show that strong bisimulation implies trace equivalence but not vice versa.

This paper is organized as follows. We give a quick overview of Orc in the next section. Then we present the existing semantics [9] and its deficiencies in section 3. In section 4, we give our semantics for Orc. We study strong bisimulation in Orc in section 5. We discuss related work in section 6 and conclude in section 7.

D. Lea and G. Zavattaro (Eds.): COORDINATION 2008, LNCS 5052, pp. 331–346, 2008.

## 2    Overview of Orc

The simplest Orc program is a *site call*. For example, the site call *IsPrime(N)* sends the number $N$ to a site named *IsPrime*. We imagine that this site will return *true* if $N$ is prime and *false* otherwise. Similarly, we imagine that the result of the site call *RedditFeed(today)* will be a page of today's technical news. In Orc terminology, we use the word *publication* to refer to the result of a site call. A site may respond to a call at most once and it can also ignore the request. Note that the same site call at different times may publish different values.

In *symmetric composition* $(f \mid g)$ the two processes are evaluated in parallel and there is no interaction between them. The composite process publishes all the values published by $f$ and $g$. For instance, the process *(IsPrime(N) | RedditFeed(today))* can publish at most two values.

The *sequencing* operator $(f > x > g)$ is used to spawn threads. Process $f$ starts running, and whenever $f$ publishes some value $v$, an instance of $g$ with $v$ bound to $x$ is launched in parallel. For example, $((IsPrime(N) \mid RedditFeed(today)) > x > Print(x))$ may print twice, if both *IsPrime(N)* and *RedditFeed(today)* publish. If $f$ does not publish, $g$ is not run.

Last, we can use the **where** operator to terminate a process after it publishes. The expression $(f$ **where** $x :\in g)$ starts evaluating $f$ and $g$ in parallel. However, the parts of $f$ that depend on $x$ block until $x$ acquires a value. If $g$ publishes, the value published is bound to $x$ in $f$ and $g$ is terminated. Therefore, the expression $(Print(x)$ **where** $x :\in (IsPrime(N) \mid RedditFeed(today)))$ will either print a boolean or today's technical news, maybe none, but not both.

The operators we saw up to now do not allow us to write recursive processes. To do that, we can define expressions like the following:

$$DOS(x) \triangleq Ping(x) \mid DOS(x)$$

This is a simple denial-of-service attack; the process $DOS(ip)$ pings $ip$ an unbounded number of times.

At this point we have explained the features of Orc informally and we can proceed to discuss its formal syntax and semantics.

## 3    The Existing Semantics of Orc and Its Deficiencies

### 3.1    Syntax - Operational Semantics

The syntax of Orc is shown in Fig. 1. An Orc program consists of a finite set of mutually recursive declarations and an expression that is evaluated with these declarations in scope. We use $\Delta$ to refer to the set of declarations. The terms "expression" and "process" will be used interchangeably.

The process **0** is the inert process. The actual parameter of a site call or a call to a defined expression is either a variable or a value. Values do not have types; they all belong to some generic set *Val*. Orc is not higher-order: a process is not a value. In what follows, we assume that processes are *well-formed*, i.e. do not contain $E_i(p)$ when there are fewer than $i$ declarations in the program.

$$\begin{array}{ll}
\text{Program} & P ::= D_1, \ldots, D_k \text{ in } e \\
\text{Expression} & e ::= \mathbf{0} \mid M(p) \mid let(p) \mid E_i(p) \mid (e_1 \mid e_2) \mid e_1 >x> e_2 \mid e_1 \textbf{ where } x :\in e_2 \\
\text{Parameter} & p ::= x \mid v \\
\text{Declaration} & D_i ::= E_i(x) \triangleq e
\end{array}$$

**Fig. 1.** Syntax of Orc

$$\text{(SITECALL)} \quad \frac{k \text{ fresh}}{M(v) \xrightarrow{M_k(v)} ?k}$$

$$\text{(SEQ1N)} \quad \frac{f \xrightarrow{a} f' \quad a \neq !v}{f >x> g \xrightarrow{a} f' >x> g}$$

$$\text{(SITERET)} \quad ?k \xrightarrow{k?v} let(v)$$

$$\text{(SEQ1V)} \quad \frac{f \xrightarrow{!v} f'}{f >x> g \xrightarrow{\tau} (f' >x> g) \mid [v/x]g}$$

$$\text{(LET)} \quad let(v) \xrightarrow{!v} \mathbf{0}$$

$$\text{(DEF)} \quad \frac{(E_i(x) \triangleq f_i) \in \Delta}{E_i(p) \xrightarrow{\tau} [p/x]f_i}$$

$$\text{(ASYM1N)} \quad \frac{f \xrightarrow{a} f'}{f \textbf{ where } x :\in g \xrightarrow{a} f' \textbf{ where } x :\in g}$$

$$\text{(SYM1)} \quad \frac{f \xrightarrow{a} f'}{f \mid g \xrightarrow{a} f' \mid g}$$

$$\text{(ASYM1V)} \quad \frac{g \xrightarrow{!v} g'}{f \textbf{ where } x :\in g \xrightarrow{\tau} [v/x]f}$$

$$\text{(SYM2)} \quad \frac{g \xrightarrow{a} g'}{f \mid g \xrightarrow{a} f \mid g'}$$

$$\text{(ASYM2)} \quad \frac{g \xrightarrow{a} g' \quad a \neq !v}{f \textbf{ where } x :\in g \xrightarrow{a} f \textbf{ where } x :\in g'}$$

**Fig. 2.** Existing operational semantics for Orc [9]

The operational semantics uses labeled transitions (Fig. 2). The metavariables $f, g$ range over processes. Every transition is of the form $f \xrightarrow{a} f'$, meaning that process $f$ takes a step to $f'$ with event $a$. The events that occur during transitions are publications, internal events, site calls and site responses:

$$BaseEvent ::= !v \mid \tau \mid M_k(v) \mid k?v$$

Let's take a closer look at the rules. When process $M(v)$ calls site $M$ with value $v$, a site call event occurs and a fresh handle $k$ is allocated to identify the call (rule SITECALL). The resulting process $?k$ is just an idle thread waiting for an answer to the call with handle $k$. It is a necessary addition to the syntax to represent intermediate state.

If the site replies with some value $w$, $?k$ performs a site response event $k?w$ and becomes $let(w)$, as shown in rule SITERET. By rule LET, $let(w)$ publishes $w$ and becomes $\mathbf{0}$, which has no further transitions.

None of the above steps is guaranteed to happen; $M(v)$ may delay the site call to $M$ indefinitely, if the call happens $M$ may never respond, and if it responds the value may not be published.

$$(let(y) \mid let(2)) >\!x\!> M(x) \overset{\tau}{\to} \qquad \text{by LET, SEQ1V}$$
$$((let(y) \mid \mathbf{0}) >\!x\!> M(x)) \mid M(2) \overset{M_k(2)}{\to} \quad \text{by SITECALL, SYM2}$$
$$((let(y) \mid \mathbf{0}) >\!x\!> M(x)) \mid ?k \overset{k?11}{\to} \quad \text{by SITERET, SYM2}$$
$$((let(y) \mid \mathbf{0}) >\!x\!> M(x)) \mid let(11) \overset{!11}{\to} \quad \text{by LET, SYM2}$$
$$((let(y) \mid \mathbf{0}) >\!x\!> M(x)) \mid \mathbf{0}$$

**Fig. 3.** Possible evaluation of $(let(y) \mid let(2)) >\!x\!> M(x)$

Defined expressions $E_i(p)$ are called by name (rule DEF). The actual parameter $p$ is substituted for $x$ in the body of $E_i$ and the process continues as $[p/x]f_i$. This substitution is marked by an internal event $\tau$.

The rules for symmetric composition are simple; $f \mid g$ takes a step if either $f$ or $g$ takes a step. The steps of the sub-processes can be interleaved arbitrarily.

Process $f >\!x\!> g$ takes a step if $f$ takes a step (rule SEQ1N). If $f$ publishes $v$ the process performs an internal event and launches a new instance of $g$ in parallel (rule SEQ1V). We can think of $x$ as an implicit communication channel between $f$ and $g$.[1]

In asymmetric composition $f$ **where** $x :\in g$, $f$ and $g$ execute in parallel unless $g$ publishes. Then, $g$ is terminated and the published value $v$ is communicated via $x$ to $f$ (rule ASYM1V). Rule ASYM2 shows the non-publication steps of $g$, and ASYM1N shows the steps of $f$. Note that a $let(x)$ or a site call $M(x)$ in $f$ will block waiting for a publication from $g$.

The example in Fig. 3 illustrates the use of some of the rules. Observe that processes can evaluate even when they have free variables.

Using the rules of Fig. 2, $M(x)$ has no transitions. It behaves like $\mathbf{0}$. However, in a context that can provide a value for $x$ (see Fig. 3) $M(x)$ can publish and $\mathbf{0}$ cannot. To model this behavior, Kitchin et al. add one more rule:

$$(\text{SUBST}) \quad f \overset{[v/x]}{\to} [v/x]f$$

We call this new event a *receive* event.[2] Any process $f$ can perform any receive step, even for variables not free in $f$ (of course then $[v/x]f = f$). The constraint is that the SUBST rule cannot be applied to parts of an expression, in other words the event '$a$' in the previous rules cannot be a receive event for any variable.

The reflexive and transitive closure of the transition relation is called *execution*:

**Definition 1 (Execution).** $t$ *is an execution of* $f$ *i.e.* $f \overset{t}{\to}^* f'$ *iff*

- $t = \varepsilon$ *and* $f \equiv f'$, *or*
- $t = a\,t'$ *and for some* $f''$, $f \overset{a}{\to} f''$ *and* $f'' \overset{t'}{\to}^* f'$

For instance, some executions of $let(x)$ are: $[2/x]\,[1/x]\,!2$, $\quad [3/y]\,[2/x]\,!2$

If $t$ is a sequence of events then $t \backslash a$ is the sequence of events obtained from $t$ when all instances of event $a$ are removed.

---

[1] versus the explicit prefix form $x(y).P$ of the $\pi$-calculus.

[2] This was called *substitution* event in [9].

**Definition 2.** *The trace set* $\langle f \rangle$ *of a process* $f$ *is* $\{t \backslash \tau \mid t$ *is an execution of* $f\}$

For example, every trace of $M(v)$ is a prefix of $\sigma_1 \, M_k(v) \, \sigma_2 \, k?w \, \sigma_3 \, !w \, \sigma_4$ where $\sigma_1, \ldots, \sigma_4$ are arbitrary sequences of receives and $w$ is an arbitrary value.

## 3.2  Trace Semantics

Kitchin et al. attempt to provide a denotational semantics for processes by overloading the Orc combinators to work on trace sets. They define $T_1 \mid T_2$, $T_1 >x> T_2$, and $T_1$ **where** $x :\in T_2$ as follows.

### Symmetric Composition

**Definition 3 (Merge).** *For traces* $t_1$ *and* $t_2$, $t_1 \mid t_2$ *is the set of all* $t$ *such that*
- $t_1$ *and* $t_2$ *are subsequences of* $t$ *and every event of* $t$ *belongs to at least one of* $t_1$ *and* $t_2$
- *every common event of* $t$ *(i.e. an event that belongs to both* $t_1$ *and* $t_2$*) is a receive event*
- *if* $t_1$ *and* $t_2$ *contain receives for the same variable* $x$, *the first receive for* $x$ *in both* $t_1$ *and* $t_2$ *is a common event of* $t$

For example, if $t_1 = [1/x] \, !1$, $t_2 = [1/x] \, [4/x] \, M_k(4)$, $t_3 = [2/x] \, [11/y]$ then $(t_1 \mid t_2)$ contains three elements, including $[1/x] \, [4/x] \, !1 \, M_k(4)$, and $(t_2 \mid t_3)$ is empty.

For trace sets, define $T_1 \mid T_2 = \bigcup_{t_1 \in T_1, t_2 \in T_2} t_1 \mid t_2$.

### Sequencing

Define the operator: $T \upharpoonright [v/x] = \{t \mid [v/x] \, t \in T\}$. This selects the traces in $T$ that start with $[v/x]$ and removes the leading receive event from these traces. For sequences of receives, define inductively:

$$T \upharpoonright \varepsilon = T$$
$$T \upharpoonright ([v/x] \, \sigma) = (T \upharpoonright [v/x]) \upharpoonright \sigma$$

Also, when a trace $t$ has no publications we write $\bar{P}(t)$ and when $t$ has no receives for $x$ we write $\bar{R}(x,t)$.

**Definition 4.** *For trace* $s$ *and trace set* $T$, *define the set* $s >x> T$ *by:*

$$\begin{cases} \{s\} & \bar{P}(s) \\ s_1((s_2 >x> T') \mid (T' \upharpoonright [u/x])) & s = s_1!u\,s_2, \ \bar{P}(s_1), \\ & D \text{ is the sequence of receives in } s_1, \ T' = T \upharpoonright D \end{cases}$$

*Note: Any receive event* $[v/x]$ *in* $s$ *is unrelated to* $x$ *in* $(s >x> T)$

For trace sets, define $T_1 >x> T_2 = \bigcup_{s \in T_1} s >x> T_2$.

Every trace $s$ of $f$ that does not publish is also a trace of $\langle f \rangle >x> \langle g \rangle$. Moreover, if $s$ contains a publication, an instance of $g$ is launched in parallel and the remaining transitions of $f$ may spawn more instances of $g$. For example, consider

$\langle let(y) \rangle >x> \langle let(y) \mid let(x) \rangle$. The trace $([2/y]\,!2)$ is in $\langle let(y) \rangle$ and $D$ is $[2/y]$. Also, $([2/y]\,[2/x]\,!2\,!2) \in \langle let(y) \mid let(x) \rangle$. Therefore, $([2/x]\,!2\,!2) \in \langle let(y) \mid let(x) \rangle \upharpoonright D$ which gives $(!2\,!2) \in T' \upharpoonright [2/x]$. Hence, $([2/y]\,!2\,!2) \in \langle let(y) \rangle >x> \langle let(y) \mid let(x) \rangle$.

The note in the definition of $s >x> T$ which we copy directly from [9] is ambiguous; what happens if $s$ contains an event $[v/x]$ ? We discuss possible interpretations of the note in the following section.

## Asymmetric Composition

**Definition 5.** *For traces $t_1$ and $t_2$, define the set $t_1$ **where** $x :\in t_2$ by:*

$$\begin{cases} t_1 \mid t_2 & \bar{P}(t_2) \\ (t_{11} \mid t_{21})t_{12} & t_1 \equiv t_{11}[v/x]t_{12}, \ \bar{R}(x, t_{11}) \\ & t_2 \equiv t_{21}!v\,t_{22}, \ \bar{P}(t_{21}) \\ \emptyset & otherwise \end{cases}$$

*Note: Any receive event $[v/x]$ in $t_2$ is unrelated to $x$ in $(t_1$ **where** $x :\in t_2)$*

For trace sets, define $\langle f \rangle$ **where** $x :\in \langle g \rangle = \bigcup_{t_1 \in \langle f \rangle, \, t_2 \in \langle g \rangle} t_1$ **where** $x :\in t_2$.

If $t_2$ does not publish, asymmetric composition is like symmetric composition. If it publishes $v$ and $t_1$ receives $v$, the part of $t_2$ prior to the publication is merged with the part of $t_1$ prior to the receive; followed by the rest of $t_1$. The rest of $t_2$ is discarded. The third branch disallows the creation of nonsensical traces that combine a $t_1$ that receives $v_1$ for $x$ with a $t_2$ that publishes $v_2$.

Like sequencing, the definition of $t_1$ **where** $x :\in t_2$ is ambiguous about the treatment of receives for $x$ in $t_2$.

## 3.3   Problems of Compositionality

To show that these definitions give a compositional semantics, Kitchin et al. make the following claims:

*Claim.* 1. $\langle f \mid g \rangle = \langle f \rangle \mid \langle g \rangle$
2. $\langle f >x> g \rangle = \langle f \rangle >x> \langle g \rangle$
3. $\langle f$ **where** $x :\in g \rangle = \langle f \rangle$ **where** $x :\in \langle g \rangle$

We believe Claim 1 is true, but Claims 2 and 3 are problematic.

### Sequencing
The truth of Claim 2 depends on the interpretation of the ambiguous note.

1. Rename the bound variable $x$ to avoid naming conflicts:
   Let $h = let(1) >x> \mathbf{0}$. The trace $[3/x]$ is in $\langle let(1) \rangle$. Therefore, we pick a fresh variable $y$ and alpha-rename every event $[v/x]$ in $\langle \mathbf{0} \rangle$ to $[v/y]$. Let $Z$ be the set we obtain after the alpha-renaming. Then, the set $[3/x] >x> \langle \mathbf{0} \rangle$ is defined to be equal to $[3/x] >y> Z$. By rule SUBST however, $\langle \mathbf{0} \rangle$ contains every finite sequence of receives, so there is no fresh variable to pick for the alpha-renaming; by this interpretation the set $[3/x] >x> \langle \mathbf{0} \rangle$ is undefined.

2. Receive events for $x$ in $s$ are not allowed in $s >x> T$:
   By this interpretation, the definition of $s >x> T$ becomes

$$\begin{cases} \{s\} & \bar{P}(s), \bar{R}(x, s) \\ s_1((s_2 >x> T') \mid (T' \upharpoonright [u/x])) & s = s_1!u\, s_2,\ \bar{R}(x,s),\ \bar{P}(s_1),\ D \text{ is the} \\ & \text{sequence of receives in } s_1,\ T' = T \upharpoonright D \\ \emptyset & \text{otherwise} \end{cases}$$

Let $h = M(1) > x > let(x)$. By rules SUBST, SITECALL and SEQ1N, $[3/x]\, M_k(1) \in \langle h \rangle$. Let $t = [3/x]\, M_k(1)$. We prove by contradiction that $t \notin (\langle M(1) \rangle > x > \langle let(x) \rangle)$, hence $\langle f > x > g \rangle \neq \langle f \rangle > x > \langle g \rangle$. Assume that $t \in (\langle M(1) \rangle > x > \langle let(x) \rangle)$. Then, there exists $s \in \langle M(1) \rangle$ such that $t \in (s > x > \langle let(x) \rangle)$.

   a) If the first branch of the definition was used to produce $t$ then $t = s$ which gives $\bar{R}(x, t)$, a contradiction.
   b) If the second branch of the definition was used, then $s$ is of the form $(\sigma_1\, M_k(1)\, \sigma_2\, k?w\, \sigma_3\, !w\, \sigma_4)$ where $\sigma_1, \ldots, \sigma_4$ are arbitrary sequences of receive events for variables different from $x$. But then, $\sigma_1$ must be $[3/x]$ which is a contradiction because $\bar{R}(x, s)$. We conclude that there is no $s \in \langle M(1) \rangle$ such that $t \in (s > x > \langle let(x) \rangle)$.

3. The note is simply a reminder that receives for $x$ in $s$ and receives for $x$ in the traces of $T$ refer to different variables, and has no other impact:
   In this interpretation, the definition of $s >x> T$ is not influenced by the note; receives for $x$ in $s$ are treated like receives for other variables. Let $h = let(2) >x> let(x)$, $s = [1/x]\,!2$, $t = [1/x][2/x]\,!1$. Clearly, $s \in \langle let(2) \rangle$ and the sequence of receives in $s$ is $[1/x]$.
   Also, $t \in \langle let(x) \rangle$ and $\{t\} \upharpoonright [1/x] = \{[2/x]\,!1\} \Rightarrow ([2/x]\,!1) \in T' \Rightarrow \{[2/x]\,!1\} \upharpoonright [2/x] = \{!1\}$. Then, $([1/x]\,!1) \in \langle let(2) \rangle > x > \langle let(x) \rangle$. But this trace cannot be produced by the operational semantics of $h$; every operational trace of $h$ is of the form $(\sigma_1\,!2\,\sigma_2)$ where $\sigma_1$ and $\sigma_2$ are arbitrary sequences of receives. Thus, $\langle f >x> g \rangle \neq \langle f \rangle >x> \langle g \rangle$

## Asymmetric Composition

Claim 3 is false independent of the note, as the following simple counterexample shows. Let $h = let(x)$ **where** $x :\in \mathbf{0}$. The only operational rule that applies to $h$ is SUBST, which takes $h$ to itself. This means that a trace of $h$ can consist only of receive events. By SUBST and LET, $t = ([2/x]\,!2) \in \langle let(x) \rangle$ and also $\varepsilon \in \langle \mathbf{0} \rangle$. Then, $(([2/x]\,!2)$ **where** $x :\in \varepsilon) = (([2/x]\,!2) \mid \varepsilon) = \{[2/x]\,!2\}$ which yields $([2/x]\,!2) \in (\langle let(x) \rangle$ **where** $x :\in \langle \mathbf{0} \rangle)$. Clearly, $t \notin \langle h \rangle$. Therefore, $\langle f$ **where** $x :\in g \rangle \neq \langle f \rangle$ **where** $x :\in \langle g \rangle$

## Dynamic Binding

Consider the defined expression $E(x) \triangleq e$. Kitchin et al. [9] do not impose any constraint on $e$, so it may contain variables other than $x$. In this case, dynamic binding can take place during the execution of a process. This invalidates a bisimulation result in [9], namely that when $x \notin \mathrm{fv}(g)$

$$(f \mid g) \text{ where } x :\in h \sim (f \text{ where } x :\in h) \mid g$$

$$\text{(SITEC)} \quad \frac{k \text{ fresh}}{\Delta, \Gamma \vdash M(v) \xrightarrow{M_k(v)} ?k}$$

$$\text{(DEF)} \quad \frac{(E_i(x) \triangleq f_i) \in \Delta}{\Delta, \Gamma \vdash E_i(v) \xrightarrow{\tau} [v/x]f_i}$$

$$\text{(SITECV)} \quad \frac{\Gamma(x) = v}{\Delta, \Gamma \vdash M(x) \xrightarrow{[v/x]} M(v)}$$

$$\text{(DEFV)} \quad \frac{(E_i(x) \triangleq f_i) \in \Delta \quad \Gamma(x) = v}{\Delta, \Gamma \vdash E_i(x) \xrightarrow{[v/x]} E_i(v)}$$

$$\text{(SITER)} \quad \frac{}{\Delta, \Gamma \vdash ?k \xrightarrow{k?v} let(v)}$$

$$\text{(SEQ)} \quad \frac{\Delta, \Gamma \vdash f \xrightarrow{a} f' \quad \bar{P}(a)}{\Delta, \Gamma \vdash f >x> g \xrightarrow{a} f' >x> g}$$

$$\text{(LET)} \quad \frac{}{\Delta, \Gamma \vdash let(v) \xrightarrow{!v} 0}$$

$$\text{(SEQ-P)} \quad \frac{\Delta, \Gamma \vdash f \xrightarrow{!v} f'}{\Delta, \Gamma \vdash f >x> g \xrightarrow{\tau} (f' >x> g) \mid [v/x]g}$$

$$\text{(LETV)} \quad \frac{\Gamma(x) = v}{\Delta, \Gamma \vdash let(x) \xrightarrow{[v/x]} let(v)}$$

$$\text{(ASYM-L)} \quad \frac{\Delta, \Gamma \vdash f \xrightarrow{a} f' \quad \bar{R}(x, a)}{\Delta, \Gamma \vdash f \text{ where } x :\in g \xrightarrow{a} f' \text{ where } x :\in g}$$

$$\text{(SYM-L)} \quad \frac{\Delta, \Gamma \vdash f \xrightarrow{a} f'}{\Delta, \Gamma \vdash f \mid g \xrightarrow{a} f' \mid g}$$

$$\text{(ASYM-R)} \quad \frac{\Delta, \Gamma \vdash g \xrightarrow{a} g' \quad \bar{P}(a)}{\Delta, \Gamma \vdash f \text{ where } x :\in g \xrightarrow{a} f \text{ where } x :\in g'}$$

$$\text{(SYM-R)} \quad \frac{\Delta, \Gamma \vdash g \xrightarrow{a} g'}{\Delta, \Gamma \vdash f \mid g \xrightarrow{a} f \mid g'}$$

$$\text{(ASYM-P)} \quad \frac{\Delta, \Gamma \vdash g \xrightarrow{!v} g'}{\Delta, \Gamma \vdash f \text{ where } x :\in g \xrightarrow{\tau} [v/x]f}$$

**Fig. 4.** Our operational semantics for Orc

Let $E(x) \triangleq let(y)$, $f_1 = (0 \mid E(2))$ **where** $y :\in let(1)$, $f_2 = (0$ **where** $y :\in let(1)) \mid E(2)$. Then $\tau\tau!1$ is an execution of $f_1$ but not of $f_2$ because in any execution of $f_2$ a receive for $y$ must precede the publication. The details of this are left to the reader.

**Note:** After the completion of this work, we contacted the authors of [9], who suggested corrections to their definitions. In $s >x> T$, $D$ is the sequence of receive events in $s_1$ for variables other than $x$. In $t_1$ **where** $x :\in t_2$, add the side-condition $\bar{R}(x, t_1)$ to the first branch; the notes are no longer needed. Our counterexamples do not apply to the changed definitions; however we did not try to verify the adequacy of the fixed semantics.

Note that our counterexamples use processes where free and bound variables have distinct names, but since any process can take any receive step the naming conflict cannot be avoided in the traces.

## 4  New Operational and Trace Semantics for Orc

### 4.1  Operational Semantics

Our operational semantics for Orc is shown in Fig. 4. Here is a summary of the changes.

$\Delta, \Gamma \vdash let(x) \text{ where } x :\in (M(x) \mid let(x)) \xrightarrow{[\text{"hi"}/x]}$    by LET-VAR, SYM-R, ASYM-R

$let(x) \text{ where } x :\in (M(x) \mid let(\text{"hi"})) \xrightarrow{\tau}$    by LET, SYM-R, ASYM-P

$let(\text{"hi"})$

**Fig. 5.** Possible evaluation when $(x, \text{"hi"}) \in \Gamma$

**No Dynamic Binding.** The syntax of the language is unchanged. However, in a declaration $E_i(x) \triangleq f_i$ we demand that $fv(f_i) \subseteq \{x\}$. Hence, no dynamic binding can take place during process evaluation. This approach is also taken by Wehrman et al. [15].

**Defined Expressions are Called by Value.** Since we do not know of any Orc program where call-by-name functionality is absolutely necessary, we made this change because it simplifies the technical treatment.

**A Process $f$ Can Take a $[v/x]$ Step Only When $x$ is Free in $f$.** By thinking of variables as channels, we say that $f$ can receive only on a channel it knows i.e. when $x$ is free in $f$.

When $x$ is not free in $f$ a receive $[v/x]$ would leave $f$ unchanged, therefore such receives can be harmlessly forbidden. Consequently, closed processes do not take any receive steps throughout their execution.

The condition $x \in fv(f)$ is necessary but not sufficient for a receive step, for example the process $\mathbf{0} >y> let(x)$ is inert.

**Addition of an Environment $\Gamma$.** Let $f$ take a $[v/x]$ step to $f'$. This means that if $f$ is plugged in a process-context that can provide $v$ for $x$, $f$ can receive $v$ and behave like $f'$ (as in Fig. 3 for $M(x)$).

We use environments to model process contexts. An environment is a partial function from variables to values. The metavariable $\Gamma$ ranges over environments. With this formulation, $M(x)$ can go to $M(v)$ only when $(x, v)$ is in $\Gamma$, and is inert otherwise. Note that, unlike traditional environments in operational semantics, $\Gamma$ can be non-empty at the beginning of the evaluation of a process and it remains unchanged throughout the evaluation. This is because $\Gamma$ keeps track of the free variables in a process, but local binding is handled by substitution (e.g. rule SEQ-P).

By using $\Gamma$ instead of a SUBST-like rule which can be applied to whole processes only, we do not need to differentiate between receives and base events.

$$Event ::= BaseEvent \mid [v/x]$$

So, the event '$a$' in our rules refers to any event, not just to a base event. Also, observe that in ASYM-L $f$ cannot proceed with a receive for $x$. Its parts that depend on $x$ are blocked waiting for a publication from $g$. See Fig. 5 for a sample evaluation using the new operational semantics.

$$[\![0]\!] = \lambda\varphi.\lambda\rho.\{\varepsilon\}$$
$$[\![let(v)]\!] = \lambda\varphi.\lambda\rho.\{!v\}_{\mathrm{p}}$$
$$[\![let(x)]\!] = \lambda\varphi.\lambda\rho.\mathbf{case}\ \rho(x)\ \mathbf{of}\ \mathrm{Absent} \Rightarrow \{\varepsilon\}$$
$$v \quad \Rightarrow \{[v/x]\ !v\}_{\mathrm{p}}$$
$$[\![M(v)]\!] = \lambda\varphi.\lambda\rho.\{\ M_k(v)\ k?w\ !w \mid k\ \mathrm{fresh}\,,\ w \in \mathit{Val}\}_{\mathrm{p}}$$
$$[\![M(x)]\!] = \lambda\varphi.\lambda\rho.\mathbf{case}\ \rho(x)\ \mathbf{of}\ \mathrm{Absent} \Rightarrow \{\varepsilon\}$$
$$v \quad \Rightarrow \{\ [v/x]\ M_k(v)\ k?w\ !w \mid k\ \mathrm{fresh}\,,\ w \in \mathit{Val}\}_{\mathrm{p}}$$
$$[\![?k]\!] = \lambda\varphi.\lambda\rho.\{\ k?w\ !w \mid w \in \mathit{Val}\}_{\mathrm{p}}$$
$$[\![E_i(v)]\!] = \lambda\varphi.\lambda\rho.\{\ \tau\ t \mid t \in \varphi_i(v)\}_{\mathrm{p}}$$
$$[\![E_i(x)]\!] = \lambda\varphi.\lambda\rho.\mathbf{case}\ \rho(x)\ \mathbf{of}\ \mathrm{Absent} \Rightarrow \{\varepsilon\}$$
$$v \quad \Rightarrow \{\ [v/x]\ \tau\ t \mid t \in \varphi_i(v)\}_{\mathrm{p}}$$
$$[\![h \mid g]\!] = \lambda\varphi.\lambda\rho.\ [\![h]\!]\varphi\rho \ \|\ [\![g]\!]\varphi\rho$$
$$[\![h >x> g]\!] = \lambda\varphi.\lambda\rho.\bigcup\nolimits_{s \in [\![h]\!]\varphi\rho}\ s \gg \lambda v.([\![g]\!]\varphi\rho[x = v])\backslash[v/x]$$
$$[\![h\ \mathbf{where}\ x :\in g]\!] = \lambda\varphi.\lambda\rho.\ \left(\bigcup\nolimits_{v \in \mathit{Val}}\ [\![h]\!]\varphi\rho[x = v]\right) <_x [\![g]\!]\varphi\rho$$

**Fig. 6.** Trace Semantics of Orc

## 4.2   Denotational Semantics

We now present our denotational semantics for Orc, which is based on complete partial orders. The meaning of a process is a set of traces in the presence of environments for the declarations $\mathit{Fenv}$ and variables $\mathit{Env}$:

$$[\![f]\!] : [\mathit{Fenv} \to [\mathit{Env} \to P]\!]$$

A trace is a (possibly empty) sequence of events. Unlike the previous trace semantics, internal events appear in traces. Trace sets are prefix-closed and ordered by inclusion. They are also non-empty because the empty trace $\varepsilon$ is a trace of any process. Last, we consider traces of finite length only; an infinite trace is represented by the set of all its finite prefixes.

$$\mathit{Traces} = \mathit{Event}^*,\ \text{a discrete CPO.}$$
$$P = \{\ S \mid S \subseteq \mathit{Traces} \wedge S \neq \emptyset \wedge S\ \text{is prefix-closed}\}$$
$$\mathit{Val} = \text{the set of all values, a discrete CPO.}$$
$$\mathit{Var} = \text{the set of all variable names, a discrete CPO.}$$
$$\mathit{Env} = [\mathit{Var} \to (\mathit{Val} \cup \{\mathrm{Absent}\})]$$
$$\mathit{NoRecv} = \{\ S \mid S \in P \wedge \forall t \in S, x \in \mathit{Var}.\ \bar{R}(x, t)\}$$
$$\mathit{Fenv} = ([\mathit{Val} \to \mathit{NoRecv}])^k$$

Consider a declaration $(E_i(x) \triangleq f_i)$. Since only $x$ can be free in $f_i$, the traces of $E_i(v)$ do not contain any receives. $\mathit{NoRecv}$ is a CPO with bottom element $\{\varepsilon\}$ and $\mathit{Fenv}$ inherits its order from $\mathit{NoRecv}$ in the usual way. We do not need names to refer to the declared processes, we can index them by the order of declaration.

The definitions of the meaning functions can be found in Fig. 6. Juxtaposition of traces means concatenation. Various auxiliary operators are defined in Fig. 7. The operations $t\backslash a$, $t_1 \| t_2$, $t_\mathrm{p}$ and $(t_1 <_x t_2)$ are lifted to trace sets in the obvious way.

Remove event '$a$' from a trace:
$$t \backslash a \triangleq \begin{cases} \varepsilon & t = \varepsilon \\ t' \backslash a & t = at' \\ a'\,(t' \backslash a) & t = a't' \text{ and } a \neq a' \end{cases}$$

Merge:
$$t_1 \parallel t_2 \triangleq \begin{cases} \{t_1\} & t_2 = \varepsilon \\ \{t_2\} & t_1 = \varepsilon \\ a(t_1' \parallel t_2) \cup b(t_1 \parallel t_2') & t_1 = at_1' \text{ and } t_2 = bt_2' \end{cases}$$

Prefix-closure:
$$t_{\mathrm{p}} \triangleq \begin{cases} \{\varepsilon\} & t = \varepsilon \\ \{\varepsilon, a\} \cup a\,t_{\mathrm{p}}' & t = at' \end{cases}$$

Sequencing combinator:
$$s \gg F = \begin{cases} \{s\} & \bar{P}(s) \\ s_1\,\tau\,((s_2 \gg F) \parallel F(v)) & s \equiv s_1!vs_2\,, \bar{P}(s_1) \end{cases}$$

Asymmetric combinator:
$$t_1 <_x t_2 = \begin{cases} t_1 \parallel t_2 & \bar{R}(x, t_1)\,, \bar{P}(t_2) \\ t_1 \parallel t_{21}\tau & \bar{R}(x, t_1)\,, t_2 \equiv t_{21}!v\,t_{22}\,, \bar{P}(t_{21}) \\ (t_{11} \parallel t_{21}\tau)(t_{12} \backslash [v/x]) & t_1 \equiv t_{11}[v/x]t_{12}\,, \bar{R}(x, t_{11})\,, \\ & t_2 \equiv t_{21}!v\,t_{22}\,, \bar{P}(t_{21}) \\ \{\varepsilon\} & \text{otherwise} \end{cases}$$

Empty environment $\rho_0$:
$$\rho_0(x) = \text{Absent} \qquad \text{for all } x$$

**Fig. 7.** Various Definitions

We can easily establish the following properties of the meaning functions:

**Theorem 1 (Prefix Closure of Trace Sets).** *For all $f, \varphi, \rho$, $[\![f]\!]\varphi\rho \in P$*

**Theorem 2 (Continuity of Denotations).** *For all $f$, $[\![f]\!]$ is continuous.*

**Lemma 1 (Substitution).** $[\![[v/x]f]\!]\varphi\rho = ([\![f]\!]\varphi\rho[x = v])\backslash[v/x]$

One might expect $[\![[v/x]f]\!]\varphi\rho$ to be equal to $[\![f]\!]\varphi\rho[x = v]$. However, since in the latter $v$ is provided by the environment we have to remove $[v/x]$ from $f$'s traces in order to equate it with $[v/x]f$.

The proofs of these and all subsequent theorems can be found in [13]. Finally, we apply the usual fixed-point technique [16] to give the denotation of a set of declarations $\Delta$: we define an *Fenv* transformer $\hat{\Delta}$ by

$$\hat{\Delta} = \lambda\varphi.(\lambda v.([\![f_1]\!]\varphi\rho_0[x = v])\backslash[v/x] \times \cdots \times \lambda v.([\![f_k]\!]\varphi\rho_0[x = v])\backslash[v/x])$$

$\hat{\Delta}$ is continuous, so we define $[\![\Delta]\!]$ as its least fixed point

$$[\![\Delta]\!] = \mathrm{fix}(\hat{\Delta})$$

To prove the correctness of our semantics we need to show that the executions of a process match its traces.

**Theorem 3 (Adequacy)**
*If* $\rho = \rho_0[x_1 = v_1]\dots[x_m = v_m]$, $\Gamma = \{(x_1, v_1), \dots, (x_m, v_m)\}$ *then*

$$t \in [\![f]\!][\![\Delta]\!]\rho \quad \textit{iff} \quad \exists f'. \, \Delta, \Gamma \vdash f \xrightarrow{t}{}^* f'$$

The theorem is proved by induction on the length of $t$. It relies on the following lemma, which is proved by structural induction on $f$.

**Lemma 2.** *If* $\rho = \rho_0[x_1 = v_1]\dots[x_m = v_m]$, $\Gamma = \{(x_1, v_1), \dots, (x_m, v_m)\}$ *then*

$$at \in [\![f]\!][\![\Delta]\!]\rho \quad \textit{iff} \quad \exists f'. \, \Delta, \Gamma \vdash f \xrightarrow{a} f' \textit{ and } t \in [\![f']\!][\![\Delta]\!]\rho$$

Let's look at an interesting property concerning the publications of a process $f$. When a sub-process of $f$ publishes, the publication is either masked as a $\tau$ and sent to another sub-process (SEQ-P, ASYM-P), or it is observed by $f$'s context. Observable publications do not trigger other events of $f$. The next lemma shows that there is no causality between a publication and the events that follow it in a trace.

**Lemma 3.** *If* $s_1 \, !v \, s_2 \in [\![f]\!][\![\Delta]\!]\rho$ *then* $s_1(!v \parallel s_2) \subseteq [\![f]\!][\![\Delta]\!]\rho$

### 4.3   Semantics Insensitive to Internal Events

Any Orc process can be a building block of a larger process, e.g. *IsPrime(N)* in $(Print(x)$ **where** $x :\in (IsPrime(N) \mid RedditFeed(today)))$. In such situations, the internal events of a process are not observable by its context, in the sense that they do not entail communication between the process and the rest of the system. Instead, $\tau$ events represent communication that takes place *within* the process. Therefore, we would like to have a semantics insensitive to internal events:

**Definition 6.** $\{\!| f |\!\} \triangleq \lambda \varphi . \lambda \rho . [\![f]\!]\varphi \rho \backslash \tau$

One could also define $\{\!| f |\!\}$ compositionally and independent of $[\![f]\!]$ and then prove definition 6 as a theorem.

Obviously, $[\![f]\!] = [\![g]\!]$ implies $\{\!| f |\!\} = \{\!| g |\!\}$. Therefore, this semantics is less discriminating than the semantics in section 4.2. We can now prove the following equivalence, which is false in our original trace semantics:

**Lemma 4.** *For all* $f, \rho$   $\{\!| f |\!\}\{\!|\Delta|\!\}\rho = \{\!| f >x> let(x) |\!\}\{\!|\Delta|\!\}\rho$

For any $\Delta$ such that $f, g, h$ are well-formed,

1. $f \mid 0 \sim_\Delta f$
2. $f \mid g \sim_\Delta g \mid f$
3. $f \mid (g \mid h) \sim_\Delta (f \mid g) \mid h$
4. $(f \mid g) >x> h \sim_\Delta (f >x> h) \mid (g >x> h)$
5. $f >x> (g >y> h) \sim_\Delta (f >x> g) >y> h$     if $x \notin \text{fv}(h)$
6. $(f \mid g) \text{ where } x :\in h \sim_\Delta (f \text{ where } x :\in h) \mid g$     if $x \notin \text{fv}(g)$
7. $(f >y> g) \text{ where } x :\in h \sim_\Delta (f \text{ where } x :\in h) >y> g$     if $x \notin \text{fv}(g)$
8. $(f \text{ where } x :\in g) \text{ where } y :\in h \sim_\Delta (f \text{ where } y :\in h) \text{ where } x :\in g$
   if $y \notin \text{fv}(g)$ and $x \notin \text{fv}(h)$

**Fig. 8.** Strongly Bisimilar Processes

# 5 Strong Bisimulation Congruences

In [9], Kitchin et al. state some useful equivalences between processes using strong bisimulation [10]. However, some of these equivalences are invalid because of dynamic binding in the declarations. Also, they do not show bisimulation to be a congruence and do not investigate the relation between bisimulation and trace equivalence. For our semantics, we define a family of strong bisimulation relations indexed by $\Delta$:

**Definition 7 ($\Delta$-bisimulation).** *Let $\Delta$ be a set of declarations. Then, a binary relation $\mathfrak{R}$ on processes is a $\Delta$-bisimulation iff*

1. *$\mathfrak{R}$ is symmetric*
2. *for any $(f, g) \in \mathfrak{R}$ and for any $\Gamma$ if $\Delta, \Gamma \vdash f \xrightarrow{a} f'$ then $\exists g'. \Delta, \Gamma \vdash g \xrightarrow{a} g'$ and $(f', g') \in \mathfrak{R}$*

**Definition 8 (Largest Strong Bisimulation).** $\sim_\Delta \triangleq \bigcup \{ \mathfrak{R} \mid \mathfrak{R} \text{ is a } \Delta\text{-bisim.} \}$

For different declaration sets we get different bisimulations. For example,

$$E_1(v) \sim_{\Delta_1} (let(v) >x> M(x)) \quad \text{for} \quad \Delta_1 = \{E_1(x) \triangleq M(x)\}$$

but

$$E_1(v) \not\sim_{\Delta_2} (let(v) >x> M(x)) \quad \text{for} \quad \Delta_2 = \{E_1(x) \triangleq 0\}$$

We can prove the equivalences in [9] using our new operational semantics (see Fig 8). Naturally, symmetric composition is commutative and associative (equiv. 2, 3). Symmetric composition can be distributed over sequencing because symmetrically composed processes do not communicate with each other (equiv. 4). Equivalence 6 verifies our intuition that a (**where** $x$)-context does not influence a process $g$ if $x$ is not free in $g$.

**Lemma 5.** *For any $\Delta$, $\sim_\Delta$ is a congruence relation*

The proof proceeds by induction on contexts. By lemma 5, the equivalences of Fig. 8 become congruences automatically. Congruence is important in a concurrent setting, because we can replace a process in a system with a congruent process without affecting the behavior of the system. The following example illustrates congruences 1, 2 and 6 when $x \notin \text{fv}(g)$

$$g \text{ where } x :\in h \sim_\Delta (\mathbf{0} \mid g) \text{ where } x :\in h \sim_\Delta (\mathbf{0} \text{ where } x :\in h) \mid g$$

Definition 7 is universally quantified over $\Gamma$. This helps establish a connection between strong bisimulation and trace equivalence:

**Theorem 4.** *If $f \sim_\Delta g$ then for any $\rho$,* $\quad [\![f]\!][\![\Delta]\!]\rho = [\![g]\!][\![\Delta]\!]\rho$

As one might expect, trace equivalence does not imply bisimilarity:
Let $f = let(y) \text{ where } y :\in (let(1) >x> (let(2) \mid let(3)))$
and $g = (let(y) \text{ where } y :\in let(x)) \text{ where } x :\in (let(2) \mid let(3))$.
For any $\Delta, \rho$ we get $[\![f]\!][\![\Delta]\!]\rho = [\![g]\!][\![\Delta]\!]\rho = \{\tau\tau!2, \tau\tau!3\}_\text{p}$.
Let $\mathfrak{R}$ be a $\Delta$-bisimulation and $(f, g) \in \mathfrak{R}$. Then, $g$ must be able to match the steps of $f$.
$\Delta, \Gamma \vdash f \xrightarrow{\tau} let(y) \text{ where } y :\in ((\mathbf{0} >x> (let(2) \mid let(3))) \mid (let(2) \mid let(3))) \equiv f'$
The possible $\tau$ transitions of $g$ are
$\Delta, \Gamma \vdash g \xrightarrow{\tau} let(y) \text{ where } y :\in let(2) \equiv g'$
$\Delta, \Gamma \vdash g \xrightarrow{\tau} let(y) \text{ where } y :\in let(3) \equiv g''$
It should be obvious that $(f', g') \notin \mathfrak{R}$ and $(f', g'') \notin \mathfrak{R}$ because $g', g''$ have lost one publishing option while $f'$ maintains both. Formally, by the contrapositive of theorem 4 we get $f' \not\sim_\Delta g'$ and $f' \not\sim_\Delta g''$ because their trace sets differ. Assuming that $\mathfrak{R}$ exists leads to a contradiction, therefore $f \not\sim_\Delta g$.

We now discuss a limitation of our semantics. Let $f_1 = let(y) >x> let(x)$, $f_2 = let(y) >x> let(y)$, $\Gamma = \{(y, 42)\}$. These processes exhibit similar behaviors in $\Gamma$, they can receive 42 and publish it. However, they are not bisimilar. The reason is that the right-hand-side of $f_1$ will receive 42 from the left-hand-side, whereas the right-hand-side of $f_2$ will receive 42 from the context. We know that this difference is unimportant because the value published by both will always be the same, but we cannot equate such processes using our operational semantics. A possible solution would be to propagate the receives with rules like:

$$(\text{SYM-L}') \frac{\Delta \vdash f \xrightarrow{[v/x]} f'}{\Delta \vdash f \mid g \xrightarrow{[v/x]} f' \mid [v/x]g}$$

We have not verified the correctness of this semantics. We opted for the simpler semantics and as a trade-off lost the ability to equate a small class of Orc processes.

## 6   Related Work

Task orchestration is related to various industrial standards for business transactions (e.g. WSBPEL [1], WSCDL [8]). Academics have also looked at other aspects of business transactions, such as compensations (see [2,3,4,5]). A formal specification for a subset of WSBPEL has been proposed as well [14].

The semantics in [9] and this paper are asynchronous. Misra et al. [11] augment the operational semantics of [9] with a synchronous semantics. This is an operational semantics that gives priority to internal events, thus allowing the possibility for processes to synchronize on external interactions. However, they do not give a denotational semantics, nor do they state any theorems. Hoare et al. [7] present a tree-based denotational semantics for Orc, and sketch an operational semantics based on the same trees. They prove a number of interesting denotational equivalences, but do not state any theorem relating the operational and denotational semantics. Wehrman et al. [15] have developed a timed semantics for Orc, but in their semantics the observable events are quite different; except publications, all other events are internal.

## 7  Conclusions

In this paper we presented operational and denotational semantics for Orc, a language for task orchestration. We proved an adequacy theorem, showing that the operational transitions of a process coincide with its denotational traces. This is not the case in [9], as demonstrated in section 3. We also discussed strong bisimulation in Orc and showed it to be a congruence. Finally, we showed that in Orc strong bisimulation is more discriminating than trace equivalence, which is also the case in other process calculi like CCS and the $\pi$-calculus.

## References

1. Alves, A., Arkin, A., et al.: Web Services Business Process Execution Language version 2.0. Technical report (April 2007),
   http://docs.oasis-open.org/wsbpel/2.0/wsbpel-v2.0.pdf
2. Bruni, R., Melgratti, H.C., Montanari, U.: Theoretical Foundations for Compensations in Flow Composition Languages. In: Palsberg, J., Abadi, M. (eds.) Proceedings of the 32nd ACM SIGPLAN-SIGACT Symposium on Principles of Programming Languages, pp. 209–220. ACM, New York (2005)
3. Butler, M.J., Ferreira, C.: A Process Compensation Language. In: Grieskamp, W., Santen, T., Stoddart, B. (eds.) IFM 2000. LNCS, vol. 1945, pp. 61–76. Springer, Heidelberg (2000)
4. Butler, M.J., Ferreira, C.: An Operational Semantics for StAC, a Language for Modelling Long-Running Business Transactions. In: De Nicola, R., Ferrari, G.L., Meredith, G. (eds.) COORDINATION 2004. LNCS, vol. 2949, pp. 87–104. Springer, Heidelberg (2004)
5. Butler, M.J., Hoare, C.A.R., Ferreira, C.: A Trace Semantics for Long-Running Transactions. In: Abdallah, A.E., Jones, C.B., Sanders, J.W. (eds.) Communicating Sequential Processes. LNCS, vol. 3525, pp. 133–150. Springer, Heidelberg (2005)
6. Cook, W.R., Patwardhan, S., Misra, J.: Workflow Patterns in Orc. In: Ciancarini, P., Wiklicky, H. (eds.) COORDINATION 2006. LNCS, vol. 4038, pp. 82–96. Springer, Heidelberg (2006)

7. Hoare, C.A.R., Menzel, G., Misra, J.: A Tree Semantics for an Orchestration Language, Lecture Notes for NATO summer school, Marktoberdorf (August 2004)
8. Kavantzas, N., Burdett, D., et al.: Web Services Choreography Description Language version 1.0. Technical report (November 2005), http://www.w3.org/TR/ws-cdl-10/
9. Kitchin, D., Cook, W.R., Misra, J.: A Language for Task Orchestration and its Semantic Properties. In: Baier, C., Hermanns, H. (eds.) CONCUR 2006. LNCS, vol. 4137, pp. 477–491. Springer, Heidelberg (2006)
10. Milner, R.: Operational and Algebraic Semantics of Concurrent Processes. In: van Leeuwen, J. (ed.) Handbook of Theoretical Computer Science. Formal Models and Semantics (B), vol. B, pp. 1201–1242. MIT Press, Elsevier (1990)
11. Misra, J., Cook, W.R.: Computation Orchestration: A Basis for Wide-Area Computing. Software and Systems Modeling 6(1), 83–110 (2007)
12. van der Aalst, W.M.P., ter Hofstede, A.H.M., Kiepuszewski, B., Barros, A.P.: Workflow Patterns. Distributed and Parallel Databases 14(1), 5–51 (2003)
13. Vardoulakis, D., Wand, M.: A Compositional Trace Semantics for Orc. Technical report, Northeastern University, College of Computer and Information Science (March 2008), http://www.ccs.neu.edu/~dimvar/papers/orc-coord.pdf
14. Viroli, M.: Towards a Formal Foundation to Orchestration Languages. Electr. Notes Theor. Comput. Sci. 105, 51–71 (2004)
15. Wehrman, I., Kitchin, D., Cook, W.R., Misra, J.: A Timed Semantics of Orc (unpublished)
16. Winskel, G.: The Formal Semantics of Programming Languages. MIT Press, Cambridge (1993)

# Author Index

Abreu, João   1
Asoudeh, Nesa   169

Baier, Christel   184
Bettini, Lorenzo   17
Bhargavan, Karthikeyan   33
Bistarelli, Stefano   50
Bruni, Roberto   67
Bundgaard, Mikkel   83

Chaudron, Michel   264

De Nicola, Rocco   17, 100
Dong, Changyu   264
Dulay, Naranker   264

Fantechi, Alessandro   117
Fiadeiro, José Luiz   1

Gabbrielli, Maurizio   50
Gill, Christopher   280
Glenstrup, Arne John   83
Gordon, Andrew D.   33
Gorla, Daniele   100

Haller, Philipp   135
Hankin, Chris   153
Hansen, René Rydhof   100
Hildebrandt, Thomas   83
Højsgaard, Espen   83

Iravanchi, Hamed   169

Khosravi, Ramtin   169
Klüppelholz, Sascha   184

Lam, Edmund S.L.   315
Lanese, Ivan   67
Lapadula, Alessandro   199
Loreti, Michele   17

Melgratti, Hernán   67
Meo, Maria Chiara   50
Mezzina, Leonardo Gaetano   216

Najm, Elie   117
Narasamdya, Iman   33
Nielson, Flemming   100, 153
Niss, Henning   83
Noyé, Jacques   232
Núñez, Angel   232

Prandi, Davide   249
Probst, Christian W.   100
Pugliese, Rosario   100, 199

Quaglia, Paola   249

Ramakrishnan, C.R.   296
Riis Nielson, Hanne   100, 153
Roman, Gruia-Catalin   280
Russello, Giovanni   264

Sahebi, Shaghayegh   169
Santini, Francesco   50
Sen, Rohan   280
Singh, Anu   296
Sirjani, Marjan   169
Smolka, Scott A.   296
Sulzmann, Martin   315

Tiezzi, Francesco   199
Tuosto, Emilio   67

Van Cutsem, Tom   135
Van Steen, Maarten   264
Van Weert, Peter   315
Vardoulakis, Dimitrios   331

Wand, Mitchell   331

Yang, Fan   153

Zannone, Nicola   249

# Lecture Notes in Computer Science

Sublibrary 2: Programming and Software Engineering

For information about Vols. 1– 4346
please contact your bookseller or Springer

Vol. 5052: D. Lea, G. Zavattaro (Eds.), Coordination Models and Languages. X, 347 pages. 2008.

Vol. 5030: H. Mei (Ed.), High Confidence Software Reuse in Large Systems. XII, 388 pages. 2008.

Vol. 5020: J. Barnes, Ada 2005 Rationale. IX, 267 pages. 2008.

Vol. 5014: J. Cuellar, T.S.E. Maibaum (Eds.), FM 2008: Formal Methods. XIII, 436 pages. 2008.

Vol. 5007: Q. Wang, D. Pfahl, D.M. Raffo (Eds.), Making Globally Distributed Software Development a Success Story. XIV, 422 pages. 2008.

Vol. 4989: J. Garrigue, M.V. Hermenegildo (Eds.), Functional and Logic Programming. XI, 337 pages. 2008.

Vol. 4966: B. Beckert, R. Hähnle (Eds.), Tests and Proofs. X, 193 pages. 2008.

Vol. 4954: C. Pautasso, É. Tanter (Eds.), Software Composition. X, 263 pages. 2008.

Vol. 4951: M. Luck, L. Padgham (Eds.), Agent-Oriented Software Engineering VIII. XIV, 225 pages. 2008.

Vol. 4949: R.M. Hierons, J.P. Bowen, M. Harman (Eds.), Formal Methods and Testing. XIII, 367 pages. 2008.

Vol. 4937: M. Dumas, R. Heckel (Eds.), Web Services and Formal Methods. IX, 169 pages. 2008.

Vol. 4916: P. Merino, S. Leue (Eds.), Formal Methods: Applications and Technology. X, 251 pages. 2008.

Vol. 4906: M. Cebulla (Ed.), Object-Oriented Technology. VIII, 204 pages. 2008.

Vol. 4902: P. Hudak, D.S. Warren (Eds.), Practical Aspects of Declarative Languages. X, 333 pages. 2007.

Vol. 4899: K. Yorav (Ed.), Hardware and Software: Verification and Testing. XII, 267 pages. 2008.

Vol. 4888: F. Kordon, O. Sokolsky (Eds.), Composition of Embedded Systems. XII, 221 pages. 2007.

Vol. 4880: S. Overhage, C.A. Szyperski, R. Reussner, J.A. Stafford (Eds.), Software Architectures, Components, and Applications. X, 249 pages. 2008.

Vol. 4849: M. Winckler, H. Johnson, P. Palanque (Eds.), Task Models and Diagrams for User Interface Design. XIII, 299 pages. 2007.

Vol. 4839: O. Sokolsky, S. Taşıran (Eds.), Runtime Verification. VI, 215 pages. 2007.

Vol. 4834: R. Cerqueira, R.H. Campbell (Eds.), Middleware 2007. XIII, 451 pages. 2007.

Vol. 4829: M. Lumpe, W. Vanderperren (Eds.), Software Composition. VIII, 281 pages. 2007.

Vol. 4824: A. Paschke, Y. Biletskiy (Eds.), Advances in Rule Interchange and Applications. XIII, 243 pages. 2007.

Vol. 4821: J. Bennedsen, M.E. Caspersen, M. Kölling (Eds.), Reflections on the Teaching of Programming. X, 261 pages. 2008.

Vol. 4807: Z. Shao (Ed.), Programming Languages and Systems. XI, 431 pages. 2007.

Vol. 4799: A. Holzinger (Ed.), HCI and Usability for Medicine and Health Care. XVI, 458 pages. 2007.

Vol. 4789: M. Butler, M.G. Hinchey, M.M. Larrondo-Petrie (Eds.), Formal Methods and Software Engineering. VIII, 387 pages. 2007.

Vol. 4767: F. Arbab, M. Sirjani (Eds.), International Symposium on Fundamentals of Software Engineering. XIII, 450 pages. 2007.

Vol. 4765: A. Moreira, J. Grundy (Eds.), Early Aspects: Current Challenges and Future Directions. X, 199 pages. 2007.

Vol. 4764: P. Abrahamsson, N. Baddoo, T. Margaria, R. Messnarz (Eds.), Software Process Improvement. XI, 225 pages. 2007.

Vol. 4762: K.S. Namjoshi, T. Yoneda, T. Higashino, Y. Okamura (Eds.), Automated Technology for Verification and Analysis. XIV, 566 pages. 2007.

Vol. 4758: F. Oquendo (Ed.), Software Architecture. XVI, 340 pages. 2007.

Vol. 4757: F. Cappello, T. Herault, J. Dongarra (Eds.), Recent Advances in Parallel Virtual Machine and Message Passing Interface. XVI, 396 pages. 2007.

Vol. 4753: E. Duval, R. Klamma, M. Wolpers (Eds.), Creating New Learning Experiences on a Global Scale. XII, 518 pages. 2007.

Vol. 4749: B.J. Krämer, K.-J. Lin, P. Narasimhan (Eds.), Service-Oriented Computing – ICSOC 2007. XIX, 629 pages. 2007.

Vol. 4748: K. Wolter (Ed.), Formal Methods and Stochastic Models for Performance Evaluation. X, 301 pages. 2007.

Vol. 4741: C. Bessière (Ed.), Principles and Practice of Constraint Programming – CP 2007. XV, 890 pages. 2007.

Vol. 4735: G. Engels, B. Opdyke, D.C. Schmidt, F. Weil (Eds.), Model Driven Engineering Languages and Systems. XV, 698 pages. 2007.

Vol. 4716: B. Meyer, M. Joseph (Eds.), Software Engineering Approaches for Offshore and Outsourced Development. X, 201 pages. 2007.

Vol. 4709: F.S. de Boer, M.M. Bonsangue, S. Graf, W.-P. de Roever (Eds.), Formal Methods for Components and Objects. VIII, 297 pages. 2007.

Vol. 4680: F. Saglietti, N. Oster (Eds.), Computer Safety, Reliability, and Security. XV, 548 pages. 2007.

Vol. 4670: V. Dahl, I. Niemelä (Eds.), Logic Programming. XII, 470 pages. 2007.

Vol. 4652: D. Georgakopoulos, N. Ritter, B. Benatallah, C. Zirpins, G. Feuerlicht, M. Schoenherr, H.R. Motahari-Nezhad (Eds.), Service-Oriented Computing ICSOC 2006. XVI, 201 pages. 2007.

Vol. 4640: A. Rashid, M. Aksit (Eds.), Transactions on Aspect-Oriented Software Development IV. IX, 191 pages. 2007.

Vol. 4634: H. Riis Nielson, G. Filé (Eds.), Static Analysis. XI, 469 pages. 2007.

Vol. 4620: A. Rashid, M. Aksit (Eds.), Transactions on Aspect-Oriented Software Development III. IX, 201 pages. 2007.

Vol. 4615: R. de Lemos, C. Gacek, A. Romanovsky (Eds.), Architecting Dependable Systems IV. XIV, 435 pages. 2007.

Vol. 4610: B. Xiao, L.T. Yang, J. Ma, C. Muller-Schloer, Y. Hua (Eds.), Autonomic and Trusted Computing. XVIII, 571 pages. 2007.

Vol. 4609: E. Ernst (Ed.), ECOOP 2007 – Object-Oriented Programming. XIII, 625 pages. 2007.

Vol. 4608: H.W. Schmidt, I. Crnković, G.T. Heineman, J.A. Stafford (Eds.), Component-Based Software Engineering. XII, 283 pages. 2007.

Vol. 4591: J. Davies, J. Gibbons (Eds.), Integrated Formal Methods. IX, 660 pages. 2007.

Vol. 4589: J. Münch, P. Abrahamsson (Eds.), Product-Focused Software Process Improvement. XII, 414 pages. 2007.

Vol. 4574: J. Derrick, J. Vain (Eds.), Formal Techniques for Networked and Distributed Systems – FORTE 2007. XI, 375 pages. 2007.

Vol. 4556: C. Stephanidis (Ed.), Universal Access in Human-Computer Interaction, Part III. XXII, 1020 pages. 2007.

Vol. 4555: C. Stephanidis (Ed.), Universal Access in Human-Computer Interaction, Part II. XXII, 1066 pages. 2007.

Vol. 4554: C. Stephanidis (Ed.), Universal Acess in Human Computer Interaction, Part I. XXII, 1054 pages. 2007.

Vol. 4553: J.A. Jacko (Ed.), Human-Computer Interaction, Part IV. XXIV, 1225 pages. 2007.

Vol. 4552: J.A. Jacko (Ed.), Human-Computer Interaction, Part III. XXI, 1038 pages. 2007.

Vol. 4551: J.A. Jacko (Ed.), Human-Computer Interaction, Part II. XXIII, 1253 pages. 2007.

Vol. 4550: J.A. Jacko (Ed.), Human-Computer Interaction, Part I. XXIII, 1240 pages. 2007.

Vol. 4542: P. Sawyer, B. Paech, P. Heymans (Eds.), Requirements Engineering: Foundation for Software Quality. IX, 384 pages. 2007.

Vol. 4536: G. Concas, E. Damiani, M. Scotto, G. Succi (Eds.), Agile Processes in Software Engineering and Extreme Programming. XV, 276 pages. 2007.

Vol. 4530: D.H. Akehurst, R. Vogel, R.F. Paige (Eds.), Model Driven Architecture - Foundations and Applications. X, 219 pages. 2007.

Vol. 4523: Y.-H. Lee, H.-N. Kim, J. Kim, Y.W. Park, L.T. Yang, S.W. Kim (Eds.), Embedded Software and Systems. XIX, 829 pages. 2007.

Vol. 4498: N. Abdennahder, F. Kordon (Eds.), Reliable Software Technologies - Ada-Europe 2007. XII, 247 pages. 2007.

Vol. 4486: M. Bernardo, J. Hillston (Eds.), Formal Methods for Performance Evaluation. VII, 469 pages. 2007.

Vol. 4470: Q. Wang, D. Pfahl, D.M. Raffo (Eds.), Software Process Dynamics and Agility. XI, 346 pages. 2007.

Vol. 4468: M.M. Bonsangue, E.B. Johnsen (Eds.), Formal Methods for Open Object-Based Distributed Systems. X, 317 pages. 2007.

Vol. 4467: A.L. Murphy, J. Vitek (Eds.), Coordination Models and Languages. X, 325 pages. 2007.

Vol. 4454: Y. Gurevich, B. Meyer (Eds.), Tests and Proofs. IX, 217 pages. 2007.

Vol. 4444: T. Reps, M. Sagiv, J. Bauer (Eds.), Program Analysis and Compilation, Theory and Practice. X, 361 pages. 2007.

Vol. 4440: B. Liblit, Cooperative Bug Isolation. XV, 101 pages. 2007.

Vol. 4408: R. Choren, A. Garcia, H. Giese, H.-f. Leung, C. Lucena, A. Romanovsky (Eds.), Software Engineering for Multi-Agent Systems V. XII, 233 pages. 2007.

Vol. 4406: W. De Meuter (Ed.), Advances in Smalltalk. VII, 157 pages. 2007.

Vol. 4405: L. Padgham, F. Zambonelli (Eds.), Agent-Oriented Software Engineering VII. XII, 225 pages. 2007.

Vol. 4401: N. Guelfi, D. Buchs (Eds.), Rapid Integration of Software Engineering Techniques. IX, 177 pages. 2007.

Vol. 4385: K. Coninx, K. Luyten, K.A. Schneider (Eds.), Task Models and Diagrams for Users Interface Design. XI, 355 pages. 2007.

Vol. 4383: E. Bin, A. Ziv, S. Ur (Eds.), Hardware and Software, Verification and Testing. XII, 235 pages. 2007.

Vol. 4379: M. Südholt, C. Consel (Eds.), Object-Oriented Technology. VIII, 157 pages. 2007.

Vol. 4364: T. Kühne (Ed.), Models in Software Engineering. XI, 332 pages. 2007.

Vol. 4355: J. Julliand, O. Kouchnarenko (Eds.), B 2007: Formal Specification and Development in B. XIII, 293 pages. 2006.

Vol. 4354: M. Hanus (Ed.), Practical Aspects of Declarative Languages. X, 335 pages. 2006.

Vol. 4350: M. Clavel, F. Durán, S. Eker, P. Lincoln, N. Martí-Oliet, J. Meseguer, C. Talcott, All About Maude - A High-Performance Logical Framework. XXII, 797 pages. 2007.

Vol. 4348: S. Tucker Taft, R.A. Duff, R.L. Brukardt, E. Plödereder, P. Leroy, Ada 2005 Reference Manual. XXII, 765 pages. 2006.